Health, Safety, and Nutrition

for the Young Child

Health, Safety, and Nutrition

for the Young Child

4th Edition

Lynn R. Marotz

Marie Z. Cross

Jeanettia M. Rush

Delmar Publishers®

I(T)P® An International Thomson Publishing Company

Albany • Bonn • Boston • Cincinnati • Detroit • London • Madrid
Melbourne • Mexico City • New York • Pacific Grove • Paris • San Francisco
Singapore • Tokyo • Toronto • Washington

NOTICE TO THE READER

Publisher does not warrant or guarantee any of the products described herein or perform any independent analysis in connection with any of the product information contained herein. Publisher does not assume, and expressly disclaims, any obligation to obtain and include information other than that provided to it by the manufacturer.

The reader is expressly warned to consider and adopt all safety precautions that might be indicated by the activities herein and to avoid all potential hazards. By following the instructions contained herein, the reader willingly assumes all risks in connection with such instructions.

The Publisher makes no representation or warranties of any kind, including but not limited to, the warranties of fitness for particular purpose or merchantability, nor are any such representations implied with respect to the material set forth herein, and the publisher takes no responsibility with respect to such material. The publisher shall not be liable for any special, consequential, or exemplary damages resulting, in whole or part, from the readers' use of, or reliance upon, this material.

Cover Illustration: Alexander Piejko

Cover Design: TDB Publishing Services

Delmar Staff
Publisher: William Brottmiller
Senior Editor: Jay Whitney
Associate Editor: Erin O'Connor Traylor
Developmental Editor: Judith Boyd Nelson

Project Editor: Marah Bellegarde
Production Coordinator: James Zayicek
Art and Design Coordinator: Timothy J. Conners
Senior Editorial Assistant Glenna Stanfield

Printed in the United States of America
5 6 7 8 9 10 XXX 02 01 00 99

For more information, contact Delmar, 3 Columbia Circle, PO Box 15015, Albany, NY 12212-0515; or find us on the World Wide Web at http://www.delmar.com

International Division List

Japan:
Thomson Learning
Palaceside Building 5F
1-1-1 Hitotsubashi, Chiyoda-ku
Tokyo 100 0003 Japan
Tel: 813 5218 6544
Fax: 813 5218 6551

Australia/New Zealand
Nelson/Thomson Learning
102 Dodds Street
South Melbourne, Victoria 3205
Australia
Tel: 61 39 685 4111
Fax: 61 39 685 4199

UK/Europe/Middle East:
Thomson Learning
Berkshire House
168-173 High Holborn
London
WC1V 7AA United Kingdom
Tel: 44 171 497 1422
Fax: 44 171 497 1426

Latin America:
Thomson Learning
Seneca, 53
Colonia Polanco
11560 Mexico D.F. Mexico
Tel: 525-281-2906
Fax: 525-281-2656

Canada:
Nelson/Thomson Learning
1120 Birchmount Road
Scarborough, Ontario
Canada M1K 5G4
Tel: 416-752-9100
Fax: 416-752-8102

Asia:
Thomson Learning
60 Albert Street, #15-01
Albert Complex
Singapore 189969
Tel: 65 336 6411
Fax: 65 336 7411

Library of Congress Cataloging-in-Publication Data
Marotz, Lynn R.
Health, safety & nutrition for the young child / Lynn R. Marotz, Marie Z. Cross, Jeanettia M. Rush. — 4th ed.
p. cm.
Includes bibliographical references and index.
ISBN 0-8273-7273-6 (without electronic study guide)
ISBN 0-8273-8353-3 (with electronic study guide)
1. Children—Health and hygiene. 2. Children—Nutrition. 3. Children's accidents—Prevention. I. Cross, Marie Z. II. Rush, Jeanettia M. III. Title.
[DNLM: 1. Child Care. 2. Child Nutrition. 3. Accident Prevention—in infancy & childhood. 4. Safety. WS 113 M355h 1997]
RJ101.M347 1997
649'.1—dc20
DNLM/DLC
for Library of Congress

96-28773
CIP

Brief Contents

Contents

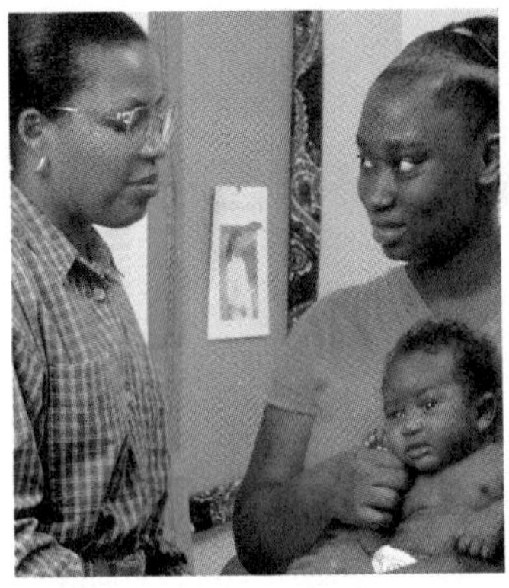

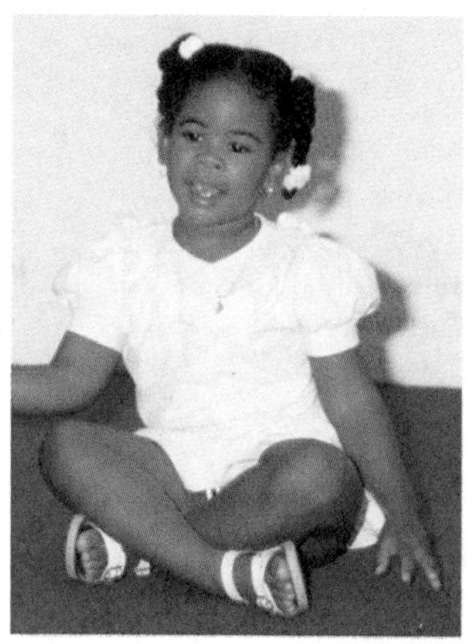

Unit 4
Foods and Nutrients: Basic Concepts............... 287

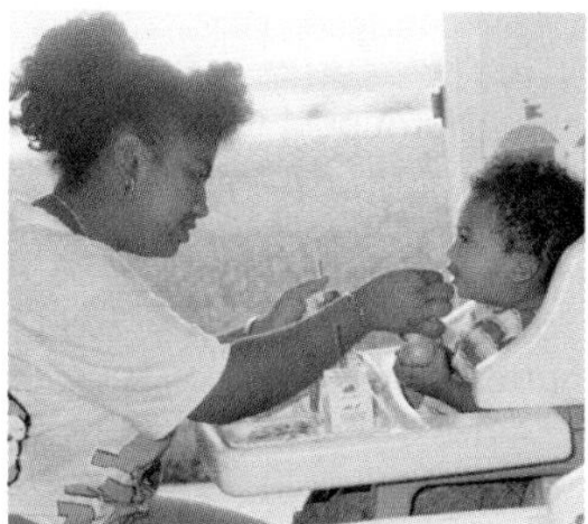

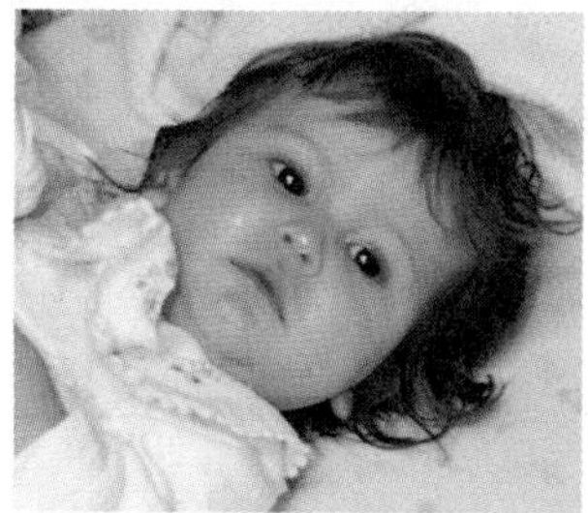

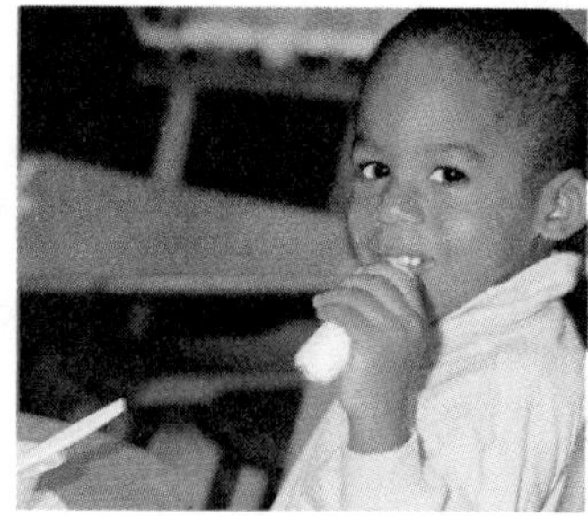

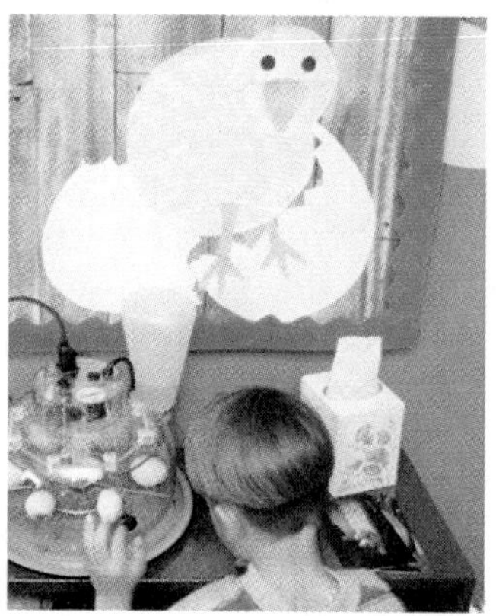

List of Select Figures

List of Tables

Preface

THE ORIGINAL IN A FOURTH EDITION

We are pleased to present the fourth edition of *Health, Safety, and Nutrition for the Young Child*. This best-selling, full color early education book was the first text to address the three most crucial areas of child development:

- Children's health status;
- A safe, yet challenging learning environment; and
- Proper nutrition.

THE INTENDED AUDIENCE

Health, Safety, and Nutrition for the Young Child is intended for students working in an educational setting, for child caregivers, and for adults and parents who desire additional information about current concepts in the fields of health, safety, and nutrition and their relationship to the young child. The text is also intended to help adults assist young children in developing good habits and attitudes, and to assume lifelong responsibility for their own well-being.

CURRENT COVERAGE

The fourth edition of this text includes updated information on the most current issues in child care. Emphasis is given to the topic of quality child care and organizing quality care environments for children. In addition, the fourth edition includes increased coverage of AIDS and children, ADD, ADHD, Sudden Infant Death Syndrome (SIDS), lead poisoning, diabetes, seizures, allergies, asthma, eczema, sickle cell anemia, immunization, emergency care, and common illnesses, as well as life-threatening conditions.

OTHER SPECIAL COVERAGE

- The new "Food Guide Pyramid"
- Infant feeding concerns
- Toddler feeding
- Sample activity plans

ORGANIZATION

The 21 chapters of the book comprehensively cover all the areas caregivers, teachers, and paraprofessionals need to understand to improve social conditions affecting the health of young children.

Pedagogy assists the student in mastering each chapter:

1. "Terms to Know" are listed at the beginning of each chapter, in color where they appear within the chapter, and again in the glossary at the back of the book. Reinforcement and cross-referencing enhance comprehension.
2. Objectives appear at the beginning of each chapter to focus the reader on key areas of learning.
3. Bulleted lists alert the reader to specific examples.
4. Real life, colorful photographs taken on location at centers and schools, show children as they work and play in appropriate settings.
5. The summary, briefly restating each main point, concludes the chapter and is followed by:
   - Suggested Activities;
   - Chapter Review Questions;
   - References; and
   - Additional Reading (for those who need more).

Appendices, designed to be used in conjunction with all 21 chapters include:

- Nutrition analysis of various fast foods
- Growth charts
- Sources for additional information
- Federal Food Program listings

A comprehensive glossary and index conclude the text with reader-friendly cross-references.

DESIGN

We were proud to present the first full-color early childhood textbook and we continue that tradition with a beautiful contemporary design in this edition.

All new colors and attractive new unit and chapter openers invite the reader into the book. Multicultural photographs, all taken on location at child care centers and schools, plus art contribute to the visual appeal of the text.

ANCILLARIES

The Instructor's Manual includes answers to review questions, test items, multimedia resources, discussion topics, and from the United States Department of Agriculture, *The Nutritive Value of Foods.*

Flash! electronic study guide for Windows is an optional student aid.

THE ULTIMATE GOAL

A child's health status, a safe but challenging learning environment, and proper nutrition affect the care, nurturance, and optimal physical and cognitive development of the young child. Over a decade ago, each of these subject areas was viewed a separate entity, but research has shown that the correlation among them is so intertwined that they cannot be completely separated. Philosophies concerning health care have also undergone notable change. Today, there is a great deal of attention being focused on the concept of health promotion and preventive health care—approaches that recognize that direct relationships exist between health status, safety, nutrition, and numerous social and environmental factors including poverty; inequality of medical care and pollution; and informed individuals who accept responsibility for their own well-being and who work to improve social conditions affecting health.

ABOUT THE AUTHORS

Lynn R. Marotz received her Ph.D. from the University of Kansas, M. Ed. from the University of Illinois, and a B. S. in Nursing from the University of Wisconsin. She has served as the Health and Safety Coordinator and Associate Director of the Edna A. Hill Child Development Center for twenty years. In addition, she teaches several courses in the Early Childhood program (Department of Human Development and Family Life, University of Kansas) including health/safety/nutrition, and administration, and provides comprehensive training related to these topics for students in the undergraduate and graduate Early Childhood Teacher Education programs. Her contributions include numerous conference presentations, writings, professional appointments, and involvement in state and community organizations that advocate for children and families.

Jeanettia M. Rush, R. D., L. D., received her M. A. in human development from the University of Kansas. A graduate of the dietetics and institutional management program at Kansas State University and the Dietetics Internship program of the University of California, she has worked as a hospital dietitian for 12 years and as a nutrition consultant for Meals On Wheels and Educare Laboratory Child Care Center. Other experience includes nutritionist with Johnson County, Kansas Health Department Prenatal/WIC Programs. She is currently employed as a clinical dietitian serving rehabilitation, critical care, and neurology units. Other duties include serving as adjunct faculty for the AP-4 dietetics internship program.

Marie Cross received her B. S., M. S., and Ph.D. degrees from the University of Wisconsin and is currently an emeritus associate professor in the Department of Human Development at the University of Kansas. Her teaching experience includes undergraduate courses in basic and applied nutrition and graduate courses related to nutrition and child development. Research involves the development of appropriate materials for nutrition education programs at levels ranging from preschool to college. She is a member of the nutrition advisory committee for Head Start in eastern Kansas.

AN ACKNOWLEDGMENT TO THOSE WHO HELPED

The authors wish to express their appreciation to a number of special people whose encouragement and technical assistance helped to bring this book to fruition. They would like to extend their appreciation to Jim Murray, RN, M. I. C. T.

and training officer with the Douglas County Ambulance Service for reviewing the materials on emergency first aid. They also wish to thank the various photographers for their unique abilities to capture the delight of young children and the editorial and production staff at Delmar Publishers for their encouragement and guidance in preparing this book.

The authors would like to extend a special thank you to the following reviewers for their comments and recommendations:

Sheila Abamowitz
Orange County Community College
Middletown, New York

Diane Altman
City College of Chicago
Chicago, Illinois

Marsha Bickford
Faulkner State Community College
Mobile, Alabama

Teresa Frazier
Thomas Nelson Community College
Hampton, Virginia

Diane Harper
Macon Technical Institute
Macon, Georgia

Clarissa Leister
Director of SECA
Little Rock, Arkansas

Marion Leithead
Gardner Bible College
Alberta, Canada

Julie Love
Flint River Technical Institute
Thomaston, Georgia

Chris Schweitzer
International Correspondence School
Scranton, Pennsylvania

Ingrid Vail
Harrisburg Area Community College
Harrisburg, Pennsylvania

UNIT 1

Health, Safety, and Nutrition: An Introduction

Chapter 1

Interrelationship of Health, Safety, and Nutrition

Terms to Know

health
preventive
health promotion
habit
heredity
sedentary
nutrient
obese
resistance
malnutrition
undernutrition
overnutrition

Objectives

After studying this chapter, you should be able to:

- Describe the interrelationship of health, safety, and nutrition.
- List five environmental factors that have a negative effect on health.
- List five environmental factors that have a positive effect on health.
- State how nutrition affects children.
- Differentiate between overnutrition and undernutrition.
- Describe health promotion.
- Identify three factors that affect children's safety.
- State three ways through which early childhood caregivers can protect the health, safety, and nutrition of their young children.

Many positive changes have taken place over the last several years in attitudes and practices relative to personal *health*. The concept of *preventive* health care has emerged in response to costly medical care and realization that the medical profession is not always able to cure every health problem. Immunization programs, fluoridation of water supplies, and regulation of chemical dumping are examples of preventive practices that are conducted on a national scale. Avoidance of smoking and substance abuse (drugs and alcohol), a low dietary intake of animal fat, and toothbrushing are examples of personal practices that are preventive in nature.

Preventive health care also encompasses ***health promotion***, which is based on the changing philosophic principle that individuals can exercise control over many factors that affect personal health. Research data have provided conclusive evidence that changes in individual lifestyles and behaviors can lead to improved health status (Canadian Nurses Association, 1992; Poest, 1990). Children and adults can learn to accept greater responsibility for developing and maintaining attitudes, ***habits***, practices, and choices that will promote good health (Novello, 1991). This includes establishing good dietary habits, such as eating balanced meals, practicing safety behaviors such as wearing seat belts, exercising regularly, and seeking early treatment for occasional illness and injury.

The concept of health promotion also assumes that individuals will take responsibility for social and environmental issues that affect the short- and long-term quality of everyone's health, safety, and nutritional status, such as:

- poverty
- unequal access to medical care
- adverse effects of television advertising
- substance abuse
- pesticides and chemical additives in food
- child abuse and neglect
- air and water pollution

Parents and caregivers can help children begin to recognize the importance of such complex issues and to develop an understanding for the impact they have on everyone's well-being. In addition, adults can demonstrate their initiative by supporting actions and policies that contribute to healthier environments and lifestyles for society as a whole.

HEALTH

Definitions of health are as numerous as the factors that affect it. In the past, the term referred only to an individual's physical status and emphasis was placed on the treatment of apparent disorders. Today, the concept of health is much broader and encompasses more than the absence of illness and disease. International professional groups such as the World Health Organization describe health as a state or quality of total physical, mental, and social well-being. Each element is assumed to make an equally important contribution to health. Furthermore, factors affecting the quality of one element are known to have an effect on the others. For example, a stressful home environment may lead to frequent illness, such as stomachaches or headaches in children. Also, the presence of a child with a chronic illness or a disability in the home can have profound effects on the state of the parents' mental health.

This broader concept of health also recognizes that children and adults do not exist in isolated settings. Rather, they are important members of a variety of social groups, including families, peers, community, and society. The quality of one's social interactions and contributions to these groups often affects, and is affected by, the state of an individual's health.

Factors Influencing Health

Health status is determined, in part, by specific biological materials that are inherited at conception and influenced by numerous factors in the environment. Thus, health status is a dynamic quality that can change from setting to setting, moment to moment, day to day, and year to year.

Heredity. Characteristics transmitted from parents to their children at the time of conception determine all of the genetic traits of a new, unique individual. **Heredity** sets the limits for growth, development, and health potential, Figure 1–1. It partly explains why children in one family are short while those from another family are tall. Heredity helps to explain why some individuals have allergies or need glasses while others do not.

The heredity factor can be useful for predicting those children who are likely to inherit tendencies for certain health problems such as heart disease, cancer, diabetes, or certain mental health conditions. Early detection of these conditions is very important for minimizing their long-term effect on a child's health.

Figure 1–1 Heredity sets the limits for growth, development, and health potential.

Figure 1–2 Physical, social, and cultural factors affect the nature of our responses.

Environment. While heredity provides the basic building materials that determine one's health, the environment plays an equally important role. In a simplified way, environment is made up of physical, social, economic, and cultural factors. These factors influence the way people perceive and respond to their surroundings, Figure 1–2. In turn, they affect one's physical, mental, and behavioral patterns, and ultimately influence the way in which an individual's inherited potentials will be realized (Charlesworth, 1996). Some environmental factors are positive and promote good health:

- good dietary habits
- physical exercise and adequate rest
- quality medical and dental care
- a safe and sanitary environment
- limited stress
- good interpersonal relationships

On the other hand, exposure to chemicals and pollution, abuse, illness, obesity, *sedentary* lifestyles, poverty, stress, poor diet, and inadequate medical and dental care are negative influences and interfere with the achievement of optimal growth and development.

SAFETY

Safety refers to the behaviors and practices that protect children and adults from risk or injury. Safety is of special concern with young children because their well-being is directly affected by a safe environment. Accidents account for the greatest single cause of death among children 1 to 14 years of age. Consequently, effective prevention of accidental injury and death must be a primary task of the adult caregiver (Mickalide, 1993).

Accidents resulting in even minor injuries have an immediate effect on a child's health. Learning and participation in activities are temporarily interrupted, and if an injury is serious, it may cause a child to be absent from the classroom for a prolonged period of time. Serious injuries also result in added medical expenses, discomfort, and increased stress for both the child and family.

Factors Affecting Children's Safety

An awareness of children's developmental abilities at various stages is a critical factor that affects their safety (Allen, 1994; Santrock, 1995). Adults can use this information to identify sources of potential danger in the child's environment. Knowing that an infant enjoys hand-to-mouth activities should alert adult caregivers to continuously check the environment for small objects or poisonous substances that could be accidentally ingested. Recognizing the toddler's curiosity and desire to explore the unknown should make adults concerned about such things as children wandering away, pedestrian safety, unsupervised pools, and availability of unsafe materials.

Limits or rules set by concerned adults are another important factor affecting children's safety, Figure 1–3. Rules must be expressed in simple terms that children can understand, yet not be so overly restrictive that they create fear. Rules should be taught and consistently enforced. However, caregivers must be cautious not to become overly trusting of a child who has supposedly "learned the rules" because spontaneity frequently takes precedence over learned behaviors. Adults are always responsible for children's safety. Caregivers must also be aware of circumstances in their own lives and environments that may reduce effectiveness and contribute to accidents that involve children.

Figure 1–3 Children can be encouraged to explore in safe environments.

NUTRITION

Nutrition can be defined as "all the processes used by the adult or child to take in food and to digest, absorb, transport, utilize, and excrete food substances" (Endres, 1990). The components or substances found in foods are called *nutrients*.

Food is essential for life; what children and adults eat affects their nutritional status as well as their health. Food supplies essential nutrients that the body requires for:

- energy
- growth and development
- normal behavior
- resistance to illness and infection
- tissue repair

A daily intake of essential nutrients depends on eating a variety of foods in adequate amounts. However, the availability of food is often determined by one's environment—the availability of money, geographic location, cultural preferences, and consumer knowledge of good nutrition. The majority of children in the United States live in a time and place where food is abundant. Yet, there is growing concern for the number of children who may not be getting enough or the right types of foods to eat.

Effects of Nutrition on Children

Nutritional status affects children's behavior. Well-nourished children are more alert and attentive and are better able to benefit from physical activity and learning experiences. Poorly nourished children may be quiet and withdrawn, or hyperactive and disruptive during class activities (Underwood, 1990). *Obese* children also face many problems. They are often slow and less able to participate in physical activity. They may suffer from added ridicule and emotional stress by being excluded from peer groups (Kennedy, 1995).

Children's *resistance* to infection and illness is also definitely influenced by their nutritional status (Guthrie, 1989). Children who are well nourished are less likely to become ill; they also recover more quickly when they are sick. Poorly nourished children are more susceptible to infections and illness. Illness also increases the need for some nutrients. Thus, poor nutrition creates a cycle of illness, poorer nutritional status, and lowered resistance to illness.

Malnutrition. *Malnutrition* is a serious problem for many infants and young children but it is not always associated with poverty or a deprived environment. Children of middle and upper income families may also be malnourished because of unwise food selections. Frequent fast food meals, snacking habits, concern over weight control, and skipped meals can seriously limit the variety of food choices, which in turn, limit the nutrients ingested (Hurley, 1992).

Malnutrition occurs when there is a prolonged imbalance between the nutrients required and the nutrients that are actually eaten. Malnutrition may be the result of:

- *undernutrition* — an inadequate intake of one or more nutrients
- *overnutrition* — overconsumption of one or more nutrients

It is important that both of these conditions be avoided in the infant and young child. An adequate intake of all required nutrients is most critical during early periods of active growth and development. Also, the effects of nutritional deficiency on physical development during certain stages of infancy and early childhood cannot always be reversed with improved dietary intake (Super, 1990).

HEALTH, SAFETY, AND NUTRITION: AN INTERDEPENDENT RELATIONSHIP

Health, safety, and nutrition are closely related because the quality of one affects the quality of the others. For example, dietary habits have a definite effect on one's long-term health and well-being. A healthy child is more likely to accept and eat a nutritious meal than a child who is ill. Pain, injury, and infection often decrease a child's appetite. At the same time, they place additional stress on the child's body and increase the need for certain nutrients, e.g., protein, carbohydrates, vitamins, and minerals. Recovery from illness and injuries occurs more rapidly if these nutrients are supplied in adequate amounts. In other words, health affects nutritional requirements, while at the same time essential nutrients are necessary to restore and maintain health.

Good nutrition also plays an important role in safety and accident prevention. The child or adult who arrives at school having eaten little or no breakfast may experience low blood sugar. This results in decreased alertness and slowed reaction time, which causes the individual to be more accident-prone and less able to avoid serious injury. Children and adults who are overweight are also more likely to have accidents; excess weight impedes physical activity. Children who are overweight tire more quickly and may be slower to react in accident situations.

IMPLICATIONS FOR EARLY CHILDHOOD CAREGIVERS

The mothers of more than 50 percent of all preschool children currently work outside of the home (Children's Defense Fund, 1992). As a result, child care centers and day-care homes serve more children now than at any other time in history. Because these children spend many hours away from their families, it is important that caregivers be alert to children's health, safety, and nutritional needs. Activities, environments, meal planning, and supervision should reflect a commitment to promoting the optimal growth and development of each infant and child served. Programs can fulfill this commitment by providing:

- protection
- services
- education

Protection

Early childhood programs have a moral and legal obligation to protect the children they serve. The physical arrangement of all spaces occupied by children should receive special attention. Both indoor and outdoor areas must be planned carefully to provide environments that are safe and designed to meet the developmental needs of young children. Daily inspections and prompt removal of hazardous materials, and careful selection of developmentally appropriate equipment and activities help to prevent accidents. Careful teacher supervision and the establishment of rules also reduce the chance for accidental injury.

Policies that address the health, safety, and nutritional needs of children are important for early childhood programs to establish. These policies should reflect the goals and philosophy of an individual program. Examples of some general policy areas might include:

- Who is responsible for providing first aid?
- What types of emergency information should be obtained from parents?
- When and how are emergency procedures, e.g., fire drills and earthquake preparedness, practiced with children and staff?

Licensing requirements make it necessary for child care facilities to adopt additional health policies, such as:

- How are sanitary conditions in the classrooms and food preparation areas to be monitored?
- What types of children will be accepted into the program?

For legal protection, centers may also need to establish policies, such as:

- What types of activities require special parental permission?
- When can information concerning a child be released? To whom?
- What pick-up procedures must be followed before releasing a child? Special identification? Permission forms?

To be most useful, policies must be written in clear, concise terms that can be easily understood. Policies should describe the expectations and actions the program considers important and the penalty for noncompliance. New policies should be fully explained and copies of the policies made available to parents and/or staff who may be directly affected.

Measures taken to protect infants and young children from unnecessary illness and disease are also an important responsibility of teachers and caregivers. Adherence to good sanitary standards and personal health practices such as disinfecting tables after each diaper change and careful handwashing help to control the spread of infectious disease in group settings. Education of both children and adult caregivers also helps to ensure success.

Services

As a result of changes in society and family structure, responsibility for children's total health care is often shared by parents and caregivers. However, primary responsibility for a child's health care still belongs to the parents. Parental consent must always be obtained before arrangements are made for any special testing, screening procedures, or treatment. To function effectively in this new role, teachers and caregivers must have up-to-date information, a sound understanding of health, safety, and nutrition issues that affect young children, and a cooperative partnership with parents.

Early identification of health impairments is critical to optimal realization of a child's growth and development (Allen, 1994). Caregivers occupy an ideal position for observing children's health and identifying children who require additional evaluation by health professionals. Various screening tests, such as vision, hearing, and speech should be made available to children. Families can also be referred to appropriate resources in the community that provide these screenings.

Education

Early childhood is a prime time to promote good health, safety, and nutrition education. It is also a time when caregivers can help young children begin to develop an awareness of social and environmental issues that affect their well-being. Early childhood programs have an obligation to provide children with accurate information and help them establish good habits and attitudes. Often these behaviors become well established during the early years and are carried over into adulthood (Hendricks, 1988; Green, 1986). For these reasons, it is important that parents and caregivers capitalize on children's developmental readiness to learn. Learning positive behaviors from the very beginning is much easier than having to reverse poor habits later in life, Figure 1–4.

Educational experiences related to health, safety, and nutrition should interest and excite children to participate in their own care. Learning can become more meaningful when woven into children's daily experiences, Figure 1–5. For example, exercise can accompany musical activities, good nutrition can be stressed during snack time or science activities, and the importance of handwashing can be combined with cooking or art activities. Teaching in this manner helps children begin to understand the value of concepts and how to integrate them into their daily lives.

Figure 1–4 Good health habits, such as handwashing, are learned through early and repeated experiences.

Figure 1–5 Daily experiences provide ideal opportunities for learning about health, safety, and nutrition.

Educational experiences, however, must gradually go beyond teaching children only simple facts and rules. Caregivers must also help children develop problem-solving skills and learn to be adaptable in a variety of settings and situations.

The fact that children often learn more from what they see than what they are told cannot be overlooked. Setting good examples of positive health, safety, and nutrition practices is one of the most important responsibilities that caregivers and parents share. Some of these positive practices include buckling seat belts, eating a variety of foods, frequent handwashing, and getting adequate exercise. Such role modeling helps to create environments where young children begin to learn, understand, and assume responsibility for their own well-being.

Summary

Preventive health care is a relatively new concept. It recognizes that health attitudes and practices are learned behaviors. It encourages individuals to take an active role in developing and maintaining practices that promote good health. Early childhood is perhaps the most critical time for establishing these habits.

Health is a dynamic state of physical, mental, and social well-being. It allows children to realize their inherited potentials. It also permits children to function effectively as members of peer groups, families, and society, Figure 1–6.

Genetic characteristics and environmental factors together shape the quality of an individual's health. Environments that are clean and safe, quality medical and dental care, and good nutrition all contribute to children's optimal growth and development.

A strong commitment to health, safety, and nutrition is essential for early childhood programs. It encourages children's maximum growth and development by providing protection, services, and educational experiences to the children.

Figure 1–6 Good health allows children to function effectively with their peers.

Suggested Activities

1. Contact local law enforcement, fire and public school authorities. Find out what types of safety programs are available for young children. Invite several representatives to present their information to your class. Discuss how appropriate and effective their programs are for children.
2. Observe a child eating lunch or dinner. What foods does the child eat? What foods are refused? Based on your observation, do you think the child is developing healthy eating habits? If there is an adult present, observe the adult's eating practices. Do you think the adult exhibits healthy eating habits? Do the adult's food likes and dislikes have any influence on what the children eat?
3. Review a menu from a child care center. Are a variety of foods served to children? Are meals and snacks offered at times when children are likely to be hungry? Are foods nutritious and appealing to children? Are they likely to eat the food?
4. Contact your local public health department. Make arrangements to observe a routine well-child visit.
5. Compile a list of child care services available in your community. Note the variety of programs and services offered. Select five programs at random; check to see if they have waiting lists. If there is a waiting list, how long can

parents expect to wait for placement of their child? How many of these programs accept children with special needs, e.g., physical disabilities, behavior problems, giftedness, learning disabilities? What adaptations are made for these children in their programs?

Chapter Review

A. Define the following terms:

1. preventive health care
2. nutrient
3. heredity
4. undernutrition
5. overnutrition

B. Multiple Choice. Select the best answer.

1. Current definitions of health include
   a. physical status
   b. emotional status
   c. social interactions
   d. all of these
2. Health care is *primarily* the responsibility of
   a. teachers
   b. parents
   c. the extended family
   d. each child
3. Environmental factors that may influence health include
   a. physical activity
   b. difficulty making friendships
   c. adequate nutrition
   d. all of these
4. All essential nutrients can be obtained daily by
   a. eating the same foods every day
   b. eating fruits and vegetables in season
   c. eating a wide variety of foods daily
   d. none of these
5. Factors that affect children's safety include
   a. careful supervision
   b. awareness of developmental skills
   c. setting limits and rules
   d. all of these

6. Undernourished children may exhibit the following behavior(s)
   a. withdrawal
   b. disruptive behavior
   c. hyperactivity
   d. all of these
7. The limits of growth and development are set by
   a. heredity
   b. good nutrition
   c. adequate medical supervision
   d. all of these
8. Health, safety, and nutrition education should be
   a. taught as a separate subject
   b. woven into daily experiences
   c. the responsibility of parents only
   d. treated lightly in the preschool environment

C. Briefly answer each of the following:

1. List five environmental factors that have a negative effect on health.
2. List five environmental factors that have a positive effect on health.
3. Explain how heredity contributes to health.
4. Explain why an abundant food supply does not ensure good nutrition for everyone.
5. List three bodily processes that are sustained through the consumption of food.
6. Explain how illness affects a child's nutritional needs.
7. Name three ways that a child care program can promote and protect the health, safety, and nutrition of young children enrolled.

References

Allen, K. E., and Marotz, L. 1994. *Developmental Profiles: Pre-birth Through Eight.* Albany, NY: Delmar Publishers Inc.

Canadian Nurses Association. 1992. *Position Statement: Health Promotion.* Ottawa, Ontario: Canadian Nurses Association.

Charlesworth, R. 1996. *Understanding Child Development.* Albany, NY: Delmar Publishers Inc.

Children's Defense Fund. 1992. *The State of America's Children, 1992.* Washington, DC: Children's Defense Fund.

Endres, J. B., and Rockwell, R. E. 1990. *Food, Nutrition, and the Young Child.* Columbus, OH: Merrill.

Green, K., and Bird, J. 1986. The Structure of Children's Beliefs About Health and Illness. *Journal of School Health*, 56(8): 325–328.

Guthrie, H. 1989. *Introductory Nutrition.* St. Louis: Times Mirror/Mosby.

Hendricks, C., Peterson, F., Windsor, R., Poehler, D., and Young, M. 1988. Reliability of Health Knowledge Measurement in Very Young Children. *Young Children*, 58(1): 21–25.

Hurley, J. S. 1992. *Wellness.* Guilford, CT: Dushkin Publishing Group.

Kennedy, E., and Goldberg, J. 1995. What Are American Children Eating? Implications for Public Policy. *Nutrition Reviews*, 53(5): 111–125.

Mickalide, A. 1993. Parent's Perceptions and Practices Concerning Childhood Injury: 1987–1992. *Childhood Injury Prevention Quarterly*, 4(4): 29–32.

Novello, A.C. 1991. Healthy Children Ready to Learn: The Surgeon General's Initiative for Children. *Journal of School Health*, 61(8): 359–360.

Poest, C. A., Williams, J. R., Witt, D. D., and Atwood, M. E. 1990. Challenge Me to Move: Large Muscle Development in Young Children. *Young Children*, 45(5): 4–10.

Santrock, J. 1995. *Children.* Madison, WI: WCB Brown & Benchmark.

Super, C., Herrera, M. and Mora, J. 1990. Long-Term Effects of Food Supplementation and Psychological Intervention on the Physical Growth of Columbian Infants At Risk of Malnutrition. *Child Development*, 61: 29–49.

Underwood, N., Wolff, D., Howse, J., Brosnahan, M., and Burke, D. 1990. The Children's Struggle. *Maclean's*, 103: 63–64.

Additional Reading

Committee on Diet and Health, Food and Nutrition Board, Commission on Life Sciences, National Research Council. 1989. Dietary Intake and Nutritional Status: Trends and Assessment. *Diet and Health: Implications for Reducing Chronic Disease.* Washington, DC: National Academy Press.

Healthy People 2000: National Health Promotion and Disease Prevention Objectives. 1990. Washington, DC: U. S. Government Printing Office, Publication No. 017-001-00473.

NAEYC. Reaffirming a National Commitment to Children. 1995. *Young Children*, 50(3): 61–63.

Schlicker, S., Borra, S., and Regan, C. 1994. The Weight and Fitness Status of United States Children. *Nutrition Reviews*, 52(1): 11–16.

UNIT 2

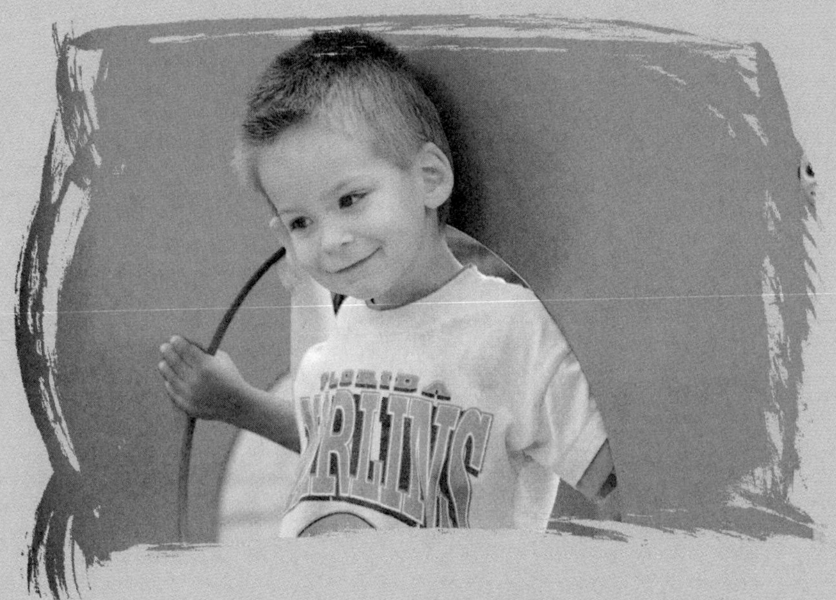

Health of the Young Child: Maximizing the Child's Potential

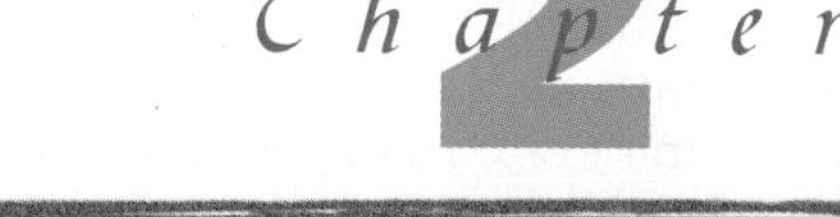

Chapter 2

Promoting Good Health

Terms to Know

autonomy
norms
normal
growth
head circumference
bonding
deciduous teeth
development
well child
characteristics

Objectives

After studying this chapter, you should be able to:

- Identify growth and developmental characteristics of the infant and preschool child.
- List three areas of special concern regarding children's health.
- Describe how teachers can provide for the safety of infants and of preschool children.
- Explain how caregivers influence children's mental health.
- Describe at least four practices that contribute to a child's improved dental health.

The period of infancy is truly a marvel when one considers the dramatic changes in growth and development that occur in a relatively short span of time. The infant progresses from a stage of dependency and relative passiveness to one that enables the child to explore the environment and communicate with others. The spectacular changes in growth and development that occur during this first year will never again be repeated throughout the entire lifespan.

The toddler years are characterized by an explosive combination of improved locomotion, seemingly unending energy, delightful curiosity, and an eagerness to become independent. Driven by the desire for *autonomy* or personal identity, toddlers display an intense determination to do things for themselves. As a result, special attention to safety and accident prevention must be a prime concern for caregivers.

The preschool years are a time of great excitement and tremendous accomplishments. As children pass through this stage of life they continue to explore the world around them, but with an added dimension of understanding. The preschool child's efforts and skills become increasingly sophisticated, while concentration on basic needs such as eating, sleeping, mobility, and communicating grows less intense. Moving toward a sense of independence becomes a major task. Unlimited amounts of energy are united with a spirit of curiosity, imagination, and adventurous instincts. This creates a dynamic child who continues to need careful adult supervision and guidance.

GROWTH AND DEVELOPMENT

Early childhood programs encompass education and care for children from infancy through eight years of age, including before- and after-school services. For this reason, it is important that teachers and caregivers be familiar with the normal changes in growth and development taking place during each of these ages. A basic understanding of typical growth and development allows adults to work more effectively with young children (Charlesworth, 1996). They are better prepared to help children master the critical skills and behaviors that are necessary during each stage by providing activities that are both appropriate and interesting and by setting realistic performance standards. This is also important information to have when setting up educational programs and environments that will protect and promote the health, safety, and nutrition of young children. Knowledge of growth and development aids in the recognition of health impairments and deviations in children's skill levels and behaviors. Through such an understanding, adults can maximize the child's good health and zest for life.

Discussions of growth and development often make reference to the "average" or "normal" child; such a child probably does not exist. Every child is a unique individual—a product of different experiences, environments, interactions, and heredity, Figure 2–1. These factors lead to considerable variation in the rate at which children grow and acquire various skills and behavior (Allen, 1994). As a result, each child differs in some way from all other children.

Norms have been established for children's growth and development to serve as useful frames of reference. These norms represent the average or approximate age when the majority of children demonstrate a particular behavior or skill. Therefore, the term *normal* implies that while many children can perform a particular skill, some will be more advanced, and others may be somewhat slower, yet they are still considered to be within the normal range.

Figure 2–1 Each child is a unique individual—a product of different experiences, environments, interactions, and heredity.

Growth

The term *growth* refers to the many physical changes that occur as a child matures. Although the process of growth takes place without much conscious control, there are many factors that affect both the quality and quantity of growth:

- genetic potential
- cultural influences
- adequate nutrition
- health status
- level of emotional stimulation
- socioeconomic factors
- parent responsiveness

Infants (0–12 months). The average newborn weighs approximately 7–8 pounds (3.2–3.6 kg) at birth and is approximately 20 inches (50 cm) in length. Growth is rapid during the first year; an infant's birth weight nearly doubles by the fifth month and triples by the end of the first year (Santrock, 1994). An infant weighing 8 pounds (3.6 kg) at birth should weigh 16 pounds (7.3 kg) at 5 months and approximately 24 pounds (10.9 kg) at 12 months.

Increases in length during the first year represent approximately 50 percent of the infant's original birth length. An infant measuring 21 inches (52.5 cm) at birth should reach a length of approximately 31.5 inches (78.7 cm) at 12 months of age. A larger percentage of this gain takes place during the first six months when an infant may grow as much as one inch (2.5 cm) per month.

Rapid growth of the brain causes the infant's head to appear large in proportion to the rest of the body. Measurements of *head circumference* are important indicators of normal growth. Measurements should increase steadily and equal the chest circumference by the end of the first year.

Other physical changes that occur during the first year include the growth of hair and the eruption of teeth (four upper and four lower). The eyes begin to focus and move together by the third month and hearing becomes more acute. Areas of special concern with regard to infant health include:

- nutritional requirements
- adequate provisions for sleep
- *bonding* or maternal attachment
- early stimulation—emotional, sensory, motor, cognitive
- safety and accident prevention
- identification of birth defects and health impairments

Toddlers (12–30 months). The toddler continues to make steady gains in height and weight, but at a much slower rate than during infancy. A weight increase of 6–7 pounds (2.7–3.2 kg) per year is considered normal and reflects a total gain of nearly four times the child's birth weight by the age of two. The toddler grows approximately 3–5 inches (7.5–12.5 cm) in height per year. Body proportions change and result in a more erect and adultlike appearance.

Eruption of "baby" or *deciduous teeth* is completed by the end of the toddler period (Deciduous teeth consist of a set of 20 temporary teeth.) Toddlers can learn to brush their new teeth as an important aspect of preventive health care, although some adult supervision is still needed. Special attention should also be paid to providing foods that include all of the essential nutrients and promote good dental health, since appetite typically decreases during the toddler years. These foods include fruits and vegetables, dairy products, meats, and whole-grain products.

High activity levels require that the toddler get at least 10–12 hours of uninterrupted sleep daily. In addition, most toddlers continue to nap one to two hours each day. Safety awareness and accident prevention continue to be a top priority for caregivers of toddlers, Figure 2–2.

Preschoolers/Early School-age (2 1/2–8 years). During the preschool years a child's appearance becomes more streamlined and adultlike in form. Head size remains approximately the same, while the child's trunk (body) and extremities (arms and legs) continue to grow. Gradually, the head appears to separate from the trunk as the neck lengthens. Legs grow longer and at a faster rate than the arms, adding extra inches to the child's height. The characteristic chubby shape of the toddler is gradually lost as muscle tone and strength increase. These changes are also responsible for the flattening of the abdomen, or stomach, and straighter posture.

Gains in weight and height are relatively slow but steady throughout this period. At 3 years of age, children weigh approximately five times their weight at birth.

Figure 2–2 Safety is a major concern in toddler care.

An ideal weight gain for a preschool child is approximately 4–5 pounds (1.8–2.3 kg) per year. However, a greater proportion of the preschool child's growth is the result of increases in height rather than weight. The typical preschool child grows an average of 2 to 2 1/2 inches (5.0–6.3 cm) per year. By the time children reach 6 years of age, they have nearly doubled their original birth length (from approximately 20 inches to 40 inches (50–100 cm)). This combination of growth and muscle development causes the young child to take on a longer, thinner appearance.

Adequate nutrition continues to be a prime consideration (Satter, 1987). High activity levels replace the rapid growth of earlier years as the primary demand for calories. A general rule for estimating the number of calories a child needs is to begin with a base of 1,000 calories and add an additional 100 calories per birthday. (A 7-year-old would need approximately 1,700 calories.) However, this period is often marked by lessened appetite and poor eating habits. As a result, parents and caregivers must carefully note children's actual food intake as well as their development of good nutritional habits.

Sleep is also an important requirement for optimum growth. When days are long and tiring or unusually stressful, the young child's need for sleep may be even greater. Most preschool and early school-aged children require eight to twelve hours of uninterrupted sleep at night in addition to daytime periods of rest. However, bedtime and afternoon naps often become a source of conflict between children and parents or caregivers. Preschool children tend to be so intensely busy and involved in play activities that they are reluctant to take time out for sleep. Nevertheless, young children benefit from a rest or break in their normal daytime activities. Planned quiet times with books, puzzles, quiet music, or a small toy may be sufficient for many children.

After age five or six, children tend to experience fewer illnesses, especially colds and other respiratory tract infections. Previous exposures to many of these illnesses and increased maturity improve their overall resistance. Vision also continues to improve, resulting in a decreased incidence of farsightedness.

Development

In the span of one year, remarkable changes take place in the infant's *development*. The child progresses from a stage of complete dependency on adults to one marked by the acquisition of language and the formation of rather complex thought patterns. Infants also become more social and outgoing near the end of the first year and seemingly enjoy and imitate the adults around them (Allen, 1994).

The toddler and preschool periods see a continued refinement of language, perceptual, motor, cognitive, and social achievements. Improved motor and verbal skills enable the toddler to explore, test, and interact with the environment for the purpose of determining personal identity or autonomy.

Developmental gains enable the preschool-aged child to perform self-care and fine motor tasks with improved strength, speed, accuracy, control, and ease. The beginning of a conscience slowly emerges. This is an important step in the process of socialization as it allows children to exercise control over some of their own emotions. Friendships with peers become increasingly important as preschool children begin to extend their sphere of acquaintances beyond the limit of family members.

Six-, seven-, and eight-year-olds are motivated by a strong desire to achieve. Participation in sports and other vigorous activities help children improve their motor skills. Rewards and adult approval continue to be important and help children build self-esteem. During this stage, children also begin to sort out gender identity through increased social contacts.

A summary of major developmental achievements is presented in Table 2–1. It should be remembered that such a list represents the accomplishments that the majority of children can perform at a given age. It should also be noted that not every child achieves all of these tasks. Many factors, some of which are beyond the control of the individual child, influence the acquisition of such skills.

PROMOTION OF GOOD HEALTH

Today, concern for children's health and welfare is shared by a variety of people. Changes in current lifestyles, trends, and expectations have resulted in a shifting of some of the responsibilities for children's health to the cooperative efforts of parents, teachers, child caregivers, and health professionals.

How are parents, caregivers, and teachers to determine whether or not children are healthy? What are the qualities of a *well child*? *Characteristics* of normal growth and development can be helpful in evaluating children's overall health status and developmental progress. However, they must be used cautiously, as there

TABLE 2–1 Major Developmental Achievements

AGE	ACHIEVEMENTS
2 months	Lifts head up when placed on stomach. Follows moving person or object with eyes. Imitates or responds to smiling person with occasional smiles. Turns toward source of sound. Begins to make simple sounds and noises. Grasps objects with entire hand; not strong enough to hold on. Enjoys being held and cuddled.
4 months	Has good control of head. Reaches for and grasps objects with both hands. Laughs out loud; vocalizes with coos and giggles. Waves arms about. Holds head erect when supported in a sitting position. Rolls over from side to back to stomach. Recognizes familiar objects, e.g., bottle, toy.
6 months	Grasps objects with entire hand; transfers objects from one hand to the other and from hand to mouth. Sits alone with minimal support. Deliberately reaches for, grasps and holds objects. Plays games and imitates, e.g., peek-a-boo. Teeth begin to erupt. Prefers primary caregiver to strangers. Babbles using different sounds. Raises up and supports weight of upper body on arms.
9 months	Sits alone; able to maintain balance while changing positions. Picks up objects with pincer grasp (first finger and thumb). Begins to crawl. Attempts words such as "mama" and "dada". Hesitant toward strangers. Explores new objects by chewing or placing them in mouth.
12 months	Pulls up to a standing position. May "walk" by holding on to objects. Stacks several objects one on top of the other. Responds to simple commands and own name. Babbles using jargon in sentence-like form. Uses hands, eyes and mouth to investigate new objects. Can hold own eating utensils.
18 months	Crawls up and down stairs one at a time. Walks unassisted; has difficulty avoiding obstacles in pathway. Less fearful of strangers. Enjoys being read to; likes toys for pushing and pulling. Vocabulary consists of approximately 5–50 words, can name familiar objects. Helps feed self, manages spoon and cup.

(Continued)

TABLE 2–1 Major Developmental Achievements (Continued)

AGE	ACHIEVEMENTS
2 years	Runs, walks with ease; can kick and throw a ball; jumps in place. Speaks in two- to three-word sentences; asks simple questions; knows about 200 words. Displays parallel play. Daytime toilet trained. Voices displeasure.
3 years	Climbs stairs using alternating feet. Can hop and balance on one foot. Feeds self. Can help dress and undress; washes own hands and brushes teeth with help. Is usually toilet trained. Curious; asks and answers questions. Enjoys drawing, cutting with scissors, painting, clay, and make-believe. Can throw and bounce a ball. States name; recognizes self in pictures.
4 years	Dresses and undresses self; helps with bathing; manages own toothbrushing. Enjoys creative activities: paints, draws with detail, models with clay, builds imaginative structures with blocks. Rides a bike with confidence, turns corners, maintains balance. Climbs, runs and hops with skill and vigor. Enjoys friendships and playing with small groups of children. Enjoys and seeks adult approval. Understands simple concepts, e.g., shortest, longest, same.
5 years	Expresses ideas and questions clearly and with fluency. Vocabulary consists of approximately 2500–3000 words. Substitutes verbal for physical expressions of displeasure. Dresses without supervision. Seeks reassurance and recognition for achievements. Play is active and energetic, especially outdoors. Throws and catches a ball with relative accuracy. Cuts with scissors along a straight line; draws in detail.
6 years	Plays with enthusiasm and vigor. Develops increasing interest in books and reading. Displays greater independence from adults; fewer requests for help. Forms close friendships with several peers. Improved motor skills; can jump rope, hop and skip, ride a bicycle. Enjoys conversation. Sorts objects by color and shape.
7 and 8 years	Enjoys friends; seeks their approval. Increased curiosity and interest in exploration. Develops greater clarity of gender identity. Motivated by a sense of achievement. Begins to reveal a moral consciousness.

is much variation within the so-called normal range. Table 2–2 identifies some of the physical and behavioral qualities based on these norms, which can be observed in the healthy preschool child. Similar lists can be generated for infants and toddlers based on characteristics of growth and development.

TABLE 2–2 Characteristics of the Healthy Preschool Child

	YES	NO
A. Physical Characteristics		
1. alert and enthusiastic	X	
2. enjoys vigorous, active play	X	
3. appears rested		
4. firm musculature		
5. growth—slow, steady increases in height and weight		
6. not easily fatigued		
7. inoffensive breath		
8. legs and back straight		
9. teeth well formed—even, clean, free from cavities		
10. lips and gums pink and firm		
11. skin clear (color is important) and eyes bright		
12. assumes straight posture		
13. large motor control well developed		
14. beginning to develop fine motor control		
15. good hand–eye coordination		
B. Social Behaviors		
1. enthusiastic		
2. curious—interested in surroundings		
3. enters willingly into a wide range of activities		
4. happy and friendly; cheerful most of the time		
5. developing self-confidence; anticipates success, copes with failure		
6. shares in group responsibilities		
7. works and plays cooperatively with peers		
8. respects other's property		
9. appreciates and understands other's feelings		
10. adapts to new situations		
11. enjoys friends and friendships		
12. participates in cooperative play		
13. understands language; can express thoughts and feelings to adults and peers		
14. demonstrates courage in meeting difficulties; recovers quickly from upsets		
15. begins to exercise self-control		

(Continued)

TABLE 2–2 Characteristics of the Healthy Preschool Child (Continued)

	YES	NO
C. Characteristic Work Behaviors		
1. attentive		
2. begins to carry tasks through to completion		
3. increasing attention span		
4. is persistent in activities; is not easily frustrated		
5. can work independently at times		
6. demonstrates an interest in learning; curiosity		
7. shows originality, creativity, imagination		
8. accepts responsibility		
9. responds quickly and appropriately to directions and instructions		
10. works and shares responsibilities with others		
11. accepts new challenges		
12. adaptable		

SPECIAL CONSIDERATIONS

Child care providers can have considerable influence on children's well-being. Many opportunities exist for promoting good health and strengthening the concepts of preventive care.

Teachers, parents, and caregivers should give special consideration to important aspects of health, safety, and nutrition based on a child's age and stage of development. Three of these areas will be discussed: accident prevention, dental health, and mental health.

Accident Prevention

Accidental injuries, especially those involving motor vehicles, pose the greatest threat to the lives of children. They are responsible for more than one-half of all deaths among children under five years of age. Each year an additional one million children sustain injuries that require medical attention. Many children are left permanently disabled (Mickalide, 1993).

An understanding of normal growth and development is particularly useful when planning for the safety of young children. Many of the characteristics that make children exciting and a joy to work with are the same characteristics that make them likely victims of accidents. Children's skills are seldom as well developed as their determination, and in their zealous approach to life they often fail to recognize inherent dangers. Limited experience makes it difficult for them to always anticipate the consequences of their actions. Special precautions are needed whenever infants or children with disabilities are present. For these reasons, safety

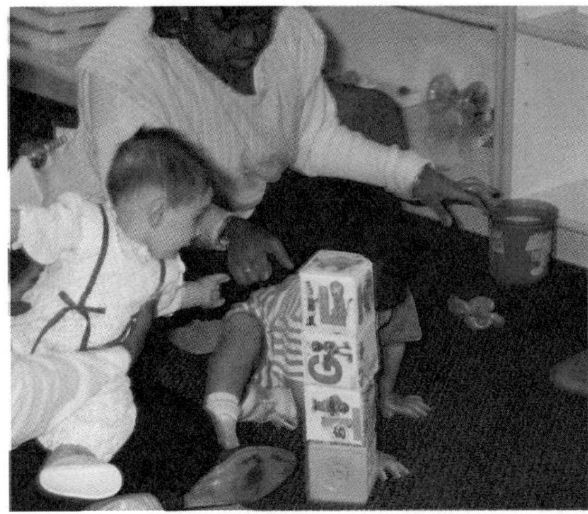

Figure 2–3 Adults must be continuously aware of hazards in children's environments.

awareness and accident prevention must be given prime consideration in group care settings and in a child's home, Figure 2–3. Approaches to safety management will be discussed in Chapter 9.

Dental Health

The past decade has witnessed significant improvements in the condition of children's teeth. Decreases in the incidence of dental caries and gum disease have resulted from widespread education programs. The addition of fluoride to water supplies and toothpaste, and advancements in dentistry have also helped (Berkeley Wellness Letter, 1990). However, dental care continues to be an area of concern. Some children have never been treated by a dentist because preventive dental care can be expensive. Often it is one of the first types of health care to be eliminated by families facing economic difficulties. Also, many parents hold the mistaken belief that "baby" or deciduous teeth are relatively unimportant because they eventually fall out. This belief is incorrect because temporary teeth are necessary for:

- chewing
- the spacing of permanent teeth
- shaping of the jaw bone
- development of speech

The condition of children's teeth can also have a direct effect on their behavior and ability to learn. Neglected dental care can result in painful cavities and infected teeth making it difficult for children to concentrate and maintain interest in tasks and activities. Proper dental care must be practiced from birth, with special attention given to:

- diet
- hygienic practices—e.g., toothbrushing, flossing
- regular dental examinations
- prompt treatment of dental problems

A child's first visit to the dentist should be scheduled when the child is between 2 and 2 1/2 years of age. Initial visits should be a pleasant experience and allow the child to become acquainted with the dentist, routine examinations, and cleanings without the discomfort of painful dental work. Hopefully, such positive experiences will foster a healthy attitude toward dental care and discourage children from anticipating future dental examinations with fear and anxiety. Routine checkups at six- to twelve-month intervals are generally recommended as part of a preventive dentistry program.

Diet has an unquestionable effect on children's dental health (Satter, 1987). Proper tooth formation depends on an adequate intake of protein and minerals, particularly calcium and fluoride. One of the most devastating influences on diet, however, is the consumption of large amounts of highly refined and sticky carbohydrates. This includes those found in cakes, cookies, candies, gum, soft drinks, sweetened cereals, and dried fruits, e.g., raisins, dates, prunes. Caregivers can help young children begin to adopt good dietary habits by limiting the frequency and amounts of sweets they are served and by substituting nutritious foods for those that are highly sweetened.

A daily routine of good oral hygiene is also essential for the promotion of good dental health. An infant's teeth should be wiped with a small, wet washcloth to remove pieces of food. Around 15 months of age, children can begin learning how to brush their teeth. Several steps caregivers and parents can take to increase children's interest in learning to brush their own teeth include:

- purchasing a small, soft toothbrush in the child's favorite color
- storing the toothbrush where the child can reach it
- providing a footstool or chair so the child can reach the sink. **Caution:** Supervise the child closely to prevent slipping or falling.
- demonstrate the toothbrushing procedure so the child knows what to expect
- encourage the child to brush teeth at least twice daily—once in the morning and again before going to bed
- construct a simple chart where children can place a check each time they brush their teeth; this provides a good method for reinforcing regular toothbrushing habits.

Toddlers can be taught to brush their teeth with an adult's help. When a child is first learning toothbrushing skills, it is a good idea for an adult to brush over the teeth at least after one of the brushings each day to be sure all areas are clean. Children can also be taught alternative methods for cleaning teeth between brushings. These methods include rinsing out the mouth with water after eating, and eating raw foods such as apples, pears, carrots, and celery that provide a natural cleansing action on the teeth.

Preschool children are usually able to brush with minimal adult supervision. Although their technique may not always be perfect, children are establishing a lifelong habit of good toothbrushing. In addition to proper technique, the use of a toothbrush containing fluoride has proven to be very beneficial in reducing dental cavities. However, caution children not to swallow the toothpaste: too much fluoride can be harmful.

The question of whether or not young children should learn to floss their teeth is best answered by the individual child's dentist. Although the practice is regarded as beneficial, much depends on the child's maturity and fine motor skills. Parents can floss the teeth of children who are too young to floss their own teeth.

Regular dental supervision also contributes to good dental health. However, it cannot replace daily attention to good nutrition and hygiene. During routine examinations, dentists look for signs of any dental problems and also review the child's toothbrushing technique, diet, and personal habits that may have an effect on their teeth such as thumbsucking or grinding the teeth. Cleaning and an application of fluoride are generally included with routine examinations. Fluoride added to city water supplies has also proven to significantly reduce tooth decay (Berkeley Wellness Letter, 1990). New preventive treatments, such as sealants (a plasticlike material applied over the grooves of teeth to protect them from decay), also help reduce children's dental problems (Berkeley Wellness Letter, 1991; McCormack-Brown, 1989).

Mental Health

The promotion of children's well-being recognizes the close relationship that exists between mental and physical health. Early childhood educators have long taught many positive mental health concepts. They help young children learn to communicate with others, control their impulsive and aggressive behaviors, express their emotions, develop independence, handle success and failure, respond with ease to new situations, and feel good about themselves. Children who develop these skills improve their chances for enjoying a lifetime of good mental health.

The quality of children's mental health is determined by their ability to cope with their environment and adjust to change. The way children feel about themselves and others is also important (Kuebli, 1994). However, to be emotionally healthy, children must first experience satisfaction of their need for food, water, sleep, shelter, safety, love, security, and achievement. These basic needs must be met before children can move on to develop a sense of autonomy, form good relationships with others, and function effectively in group settings.

Teachers and caregivers play a major role in fostering positive mental health among young children (Cadiz, 1994). They can best achieve this goal by:

- promoting good mental health practices
- preventing emotional problems
- identifying children with possible emotional disturbances
- assisting parents to arrange treatment for children with emotional problems

The teacher's and caregiver's own emotional state is very important if they are to be successful in helping young children achieve good mental health. Teachers and caregivers must have a sense of self-worth; they should feel confident that what they are doing is worthwhile. At the same time, they should be aware of their capabilities as well as their limitations. Teachers must also be able to exercise control over their emotions if they expect children to do the same. Teachers and caregivers must be honest and understanding. They should be able to accept success and failure, set realistic goals for themselves and the children they work with, and communicate effectively with others.

The emotional climate of a classroom or child care setting also has a significant impact on children's mental health. Consider the following situations and decide which classroom is most inviting:

> *Kate enters the classroom excited and eager to tell her teacher about the tooth she lost last night and the quarter she found under her pillow from the "tooth fairy." Without any greeting, the teacher hurries to check Kate in and informs her that she is too busy to talk right now, "but maybe later." When they are finished, the teacher instructs Kate to find something to do without getting into trouble. Kate quietly walks away to her locker.*
>
> *Ted arrives at the child care center and is reluctant to leave his mother. The care provider greets Ted and his mother. "Ted, I am so glad that you came to school today. We are going to build with the wooden blocks, and I know that is one of your favorite activities. Perhaps you would like to build something for your mother before it is time for her to go home." Ted eagerly builds a barn with several "animals" in the yard around it and proudly looks to his mother for approval. When Ted's mother is ready to leave, he waves good-bye.*

Clearly, the classroom atmosphere or mood is influenced by the teacher's actions and responses, which in turn have a direct effect on children's behavior, Figure 2–4. Young children are more receptive and likely to respond enthusiastically to caregivers who are warm, loving, and sensitive to their special needs. Using

Figure 2–4 The teacher influences the classroom atmosphere, which in turn, affects children's behavior.

ridicule, sarcasm, threats, or discipline that is inconsistent or harsh is inappropriate and will have a negative impact on children's emotional development. When children are forced to cope with unpleasant situations of this type, they often develop and respond with undesirable behaviors. However, an emotional climate that encourages and supports mutual cooperation, respect, trust, acceptance, and independence allows children to build a strong foundation of positive mental health attitudes.

Understanding the developmental characteristics of young children facilitates the caregiver's efforts to promote good mental health. Respect must be shown for a child's individuality, for each child has qualities that are worthy of recognition. All children like to be praised for their efforts. However, they should also be accepted for who they are and not only for what they can do. Teachers and caregivers should be impartial; favoritism cannot be tolerated.

Teachers and caregivers can promote children's mental health in other, more subtle ways. For example, activity or curriculum planning should take into account the developmental level and ability of each child. Providing tasks and activities that are appropriate for their skill levels makes it possible for children to attain success more often than failure and frustration (Marshall, 1989). Children need to experience the rewards of achievement for continued motivation and interest in learning. Schedules should also be planned carefully to allow for alternating periods of activity and rest, work and play, and indoor and outdoor times.

Stress in children's lives has a definite effect on the state of their mental and physical health. Stressful situations, such as abusive treatment, poverty, unrealistic parental demands, chronic illness, physical impairments, or being left alone for long periods, can have a serious impact on children's emotional state. However, many everyday experiences that adults take in stride can also provoke feelings of undue anxiety, tension, and stress in the young child:

- separation from parents
- new experiences—e.g., moving, placement in a day care center, mother going to work, birth of a sibling, a new teacher, being left with a sitter
- illness and hospitalization
- divorce of parents
- death of a pet, family member, or close friend
- conflict of ideas; confrontations with parents, friends, or teachers
- overstimulation due to hectic schedules, participation in numerous extracurricular activities

Inexperience and the immature development of children's coping mechanisms make it more difficult for them to handle stressful experiences in a healthy fashion (Jaffe, 1991). Teachers should always be alert to sudden changes in children's behavior that may be a reflection of stress, anxiety, or inner turmoil (Furman, 1995; Honig, 1986). Signs of behavior disturbances can range from those that are less serious: nailbiting, hair twisting, body rocking, or shyness; to more serious problems: repeated aggressiveness, destructiveness, withdrawal, depression, nightmares, psychosomatic illnesses, or poor performance in school. Symptoms of physical illness may also develop, including ulcers, headaches, vomiting, diarrhea, or difficulty breathing.

Understandably, all children undergo occasional periods of emotional instability or undesirable behavior. Short-term or one-time incidences are usually no cause for concern. However, when a child consistently demonstrates abnormal behaviors, an intervention program or therapy may be necessary.

It may be difficult for parents to always recognize abnormal behaviors in their own children. Some emotional problems develop slowly, over a long period of time and, therefore, may be difficult to distinguish from normal behaviors. Some parents may find it difficult to talk about or admit that their child has an emotional disturbance. Others, unknowingly, may be the cause of their children's problems.

For whatever reasons, it may be the teacher or caregiver who first recognizes abnormal behavior. They occupy an ideal position for identifying children's mental health status and documenting inappropriate behaviors. They can also use their expertise to help parents become aware of these problems, counsel them in appropriate behavior management techniques, or refer them to seek professional therapy for their child.

Teachers and caregivers can also be instrumental in helping children deal with stress by recognizing early changes in behavior, by providing a stable environment, and by encouraging children to talk about their feelings (Honig, 1986). They can also help children develop good self-esteem and learn ways to cope with stressful events (Wittmer, 1994). Some of these methods include:

- the use of music for relaxation
- progressive relaxation techniques—the process of contracting and relaxing various body parts, beginning at one end of the body and moving toward the other
- relaxation activities—the use of imagery and visualization, make-believe, let's pretend, books and stories, movement activities
- short periods of vigorous physical activity followed by rest
- art activities—water play, clay and playdough, painting
- dramatic play—using dolls and puppets to act out feelings of fear, anger or frustration

There are also many books that can be read and discussed with children:

Adoff, A. 1973. *Black Is Brown Is Tan.* NY: Harper & Row.

Berenstain, S. and Berenstain J. 1988. *The Berenstain Bears and the Trouble with Adults.* NY: Random House.

Berenstain, S. and Berenstain, J. 1986. *The Berenstain Bears and the Bad Habit.* NY: Random House.

Berenstain, S. and Berenstain, J. 1982. *The Berenstain Bears in a Fight.* NY: Random House.

Carlson, N. 1990. *I Like Me.* NY: Puffin Books.

Eisenberg, P. 1992. *You're My Nikki.* NY: Dial Books for Young Children.

Gantos, J. 1978. *Worse Than Rotten.* Boston, MA: Houghton Mifflin.

Lewis, J. 1993. *Claire and Friends.* Brookline, MA: Creative License Press.

Little, L. and Greenfield, E. 1978. *I Can Do It Myself.* NY: Thomas Y. Crowell Co.

Magorian, M. 1990. *Who's Going to Take Care of Me?* NY: HarpC Child Books.

Petty, K. and Firmin, C. 1991. *Feeling Left Out.* Hauppage, NY: Aladdin Books.
Riddell, C. 1987. *Bird's New Shoes.* NY: Henry Holt & Company.
Stanton, E. and Stanton, H. 1978. *Sometimes I like to Cry.* Chicago, IL: Whitman & Co.
Stevenson, J. 1978. *The Worst Person in the World.* NY: Mulberry Books.
Thurman, C. 1989. *A Time for Remembering.* NY: Simon & Schuster.
Velthuijus, M. 1994. *Frog Is Frightened.* NY: Tambourine Books.
Viorst, J. 1993. *Sad Underwear.* NY: Antheneum Books.
Viorst, J. 1992. The Good-Bye Book. NY: Aladdin Books
Viorst, J. 1972. *Alexander and the Terrible, Horrible, No Good, Very Bad Day.* NY: Antheneum Books.
Waber, B. 1976. *But Names Will Never Hurt Me.* Boston, MA: Houghton Mifflin.
Watson, J. and Switzer, R., MD. 1987. *Sometimes I Get Angry.* NY: Crown Publishers.
Watson, J. and Switzer, R., MD. 1987. *Sometimes I'm Afraid.* NY: Crown Publishers.
Watson, J. and Switzer, R., MD. 1987. *Sometimes I'm Jealous.* NY: Crown Publishers.
Wayne von Konigslow, A. 1990. *That's My Baby.* Toronto, Canada: Annick Press.
Weninger, B. and Marks, A. 1995. *Good-bye Daddy.* NY: North-South Books.

The topic of stress is receiving increased attention in current literature and research. As mental health problems and deaths from suicide continue to escalate among children, stress management must continue to be of utmost concern to parents and caregivers.

Summary

Growth is rapid during infancy, while the rate becomes markedly slower during the preschool and school-age years. Children become taller and more adultlike in the process. As their gross motor skills improve, more time and effort are spent acquiring fine motor skills. Although children are able to manage much of their own personal care by the end of this period, adults should continue to make certain that children's need for nutrition, sleep, love, security, and protection are adequately met.

Perhaps one of the most dramatic transformations that occurs from infancy through the early school-aged period relates to socialization. Whereas the infant's social relationships are initially limited in scope, friendships and group interaction become more important to the older child. However, the process of separation from parents may continue to be difficult for some children.

Today, many persons are concerned with children's health. Growth and development norms are one effective means for evaluating children's health status and developmental progress. An evaluation of children's physical and social characteristics, as well as their work habits, can also provide additional clues. Teachers and caregivers must remember that there are many differences in the so-called "normal" range.

Because of the influential position early childhood teachers and caregivers occupy, they must demonstrate a commitment to the health and safety of young children. This obligation can be met by providing adequate health services, health education programs and healthy, safe settings. Three areas of special concern for the young child are accident prevention, dental health, and mental health.

Suggested Activities

1. Observe a group of preschool-aged children during free-choice or outdoor times for two 15-minute intervals. For each observation, select a different child and record the number of times that child engages in cooperative play. Repeat this observation procedure with a group of toddlers. Note any differences.
2. Read the book *Think of Something Quiet* by Clare Cherry. Discuss your reactions to the book. Do you see this information as having any value in your own life? In small groups, practice some of the techniques suggested.
3. Write to the American/Canadian Dental Association or contact a local dentist and request information on children's dental care. Decide how you could implement this knowledge in a child care program.
4. Invite a child mental health specialist to speak to your class. Find out what types of problems are treated most often and how caregivers can help prevent these problems in young children.
5. Develop a checklist, similar to the one in Table 2–2, identifying appropriate characteristics for infants and for toddlers.
6. Visit your Public Health Department. Ask about educational materials.

Chapter Review

A. Multiple Choice. Select the best answer.

1. The leading cause of death among preschool children is
   a. birth defects
   b. accidents
   c. communicable illnesses
   d. hereditary diseases
2. Dental care of deciduous or "baby" teeth is
   a. controversial
   b. unnecessary
   c. very important
   d. only needed in extreme cases

3. Good dental hygiene for preschool children should include all of the following *except*
   a. regular dental examinations
   b. use of toothpaste containing fluoride
   c. proper brushing technique
   d. elimination of all sweets and carbohydrates from the diet
4. Growth during the preschool years
   a. is slow but steady
   b. occurs only in height, not weight
   c. increases rapidly
   d. is insignificant
5. Norms for growth and development
   a. state definite ages when children should be able to perform specific skills
   b. give an average age when most children are able to perform a behavior or skill
   c. have little relevance for most children
   d. list characteristics of the "well" child
6. At one year of age, a boy who weighed 7 pounds 9 ounces at birth can be expected to weigh
   a. 22 pounds 11 ounces
   b. 18 pounds
   c. 30 pounds 4 ounces
   d. 15 pounds 2 ounces

B. Answer the following questions by filling in the blanks. Then, take the first letter of each answer and place it in the appropriate square that follows Question 6 to form an important word.

1. Major gains in the preschool child's growth are due to increases in ________________.
2. A comprehensive health program should include services, ________________ ________________ and provisions for a healthy environment.
3. ________________ are the leading cause of death among children under the age of fourteen.
4. Teachers can promote children's mental health by planning activities that are appropriate for their ________________ of skill.
5. ____________________ and caregivers have a tremendous responsibility to protect the safety of young children they care for.
6. Good dental care depends on a nutritious diet, good oral ________________ ________________ and routine dental examinations.

C. Briefly answer each of the following questions.

1. How many hours of sleep are recommended for the toddler each day?
2. What are some ways that a child, who refuses to sleep, can be encouraged to rest quietly?
3. An infant is expected to grow what percent in length during the first year?
4. What is another term used to describe "baby" teeth?
5. How does environment affect children's mental health?
6. Explain the relationship between good dental health and learning.
7. Would it be realistic to expect an 11-month-old infant to be toilet trained? Explain. Should parents be concerned if their 9-month-old infant cannot sit up without support?
8. List the purposes served by deciduous teeth.

References

Allen, K. E., and Marotz, L. R. 1994. *Developmental Profiles: Birth to Six.* Albany, NY: Delmar Publishers Inc.

Cadiz, S. 1994. Striving for Mental Health in the Early Childhood Center Setting. *Young Children*, 49(3): 84–86.

Charlesworth, R. 1996. *Understanding Child Development.* Albany, NY: Delmar Publishers Inc.

Flurry Over Fluoride. 1990, December. *University of California, Berkeley Wellness Letter*, p. 2.

Furman, R. A. 1995. Helping Children Cope with Stress and Deal with Feelings. *Young Children*, 50(2): 33–41.

Honig, A. 1986. Stress and Coping in Children (Part I). *Young Children*, 41(4): 50–63.

Honig, A. 1986. Stress and Coping in Children (Part II). *Young Children*, 41(5): 47–59.

Jaffe, M. 1991. *Understanding Parenting.* Dubuque, IA: Wm. C. Brown Publishers.

Kuebli, J. 1994. Young Children's Understanding of Everyday Emotions. *Young Children*, 49(3): 36–47.

Marshall, H. H. 1989. The Development of Self-Concept. *Young Children*, 44(5): 44–51.

McCormack-Brown, K. R., Clark, B. J., and McDermott, R. J. 1989. Dental Pit and Fissure Sealants: Implications for School Health Personnel. *Journal of School Health*, 59(2): 69–73.

Mickalide, A. 1993. Parent's Perceptions and Practices Concerning Childhood Injury: 1987 vs. 1992. *Childhood Injury Prevention Quarterly*, 4(4): 29–32.

Santrock, J. W. 1994. *Child Development.* Madison, WI: Brown & Benchmark.

Satter, E. 1987. *How to Get Your Kid to Eat. . . . But Not Too Much.* Palo Alto, CA: Bull Publishing Company.

Sealants. May 1991. *University of California, Berkeley Wellness Letter*, p. 7.

Wittmer, D. and Honig, A. 1994. Encouraging Positive Social Development in Young Children. *Young Children*, 49(5): 4–12.

Additional Reading

Bullock, J. 1993. Lonely Children. *Young Children*, 48(6): 53–57.

Carlsson-Paige, N., and Levine, D. 1992. Making Peace in Violent Times: A Constructivist Approach to Conflict Resolution. *Young Children*, 48(1): 4–13.

Cohen, L., and Spenciner, L. 1994. *Assessment of Young Children.* White Plains, NY: Longman Publishing.

Dinwiddie, S. 1994. The Saga of Sally, Sammy, and the Red Pen: Facilitating Children's Social Problem Solving. *Young Children*, 49(5): 13–17.

Essa, E. 1990. *A Practical Guide to Solving Preschool Behavior Problems.* Albany, NY: Delmar Publishers Inc.

Greenberg, P. 1991. *Character Development: Encouraging Self-Esteem & Self-Discipline in Infants, Toddlers, and 2 Year Olds.* Washington, DC: NAEYC.

Kump, T. 1995. The Facts About Baby Teeth. *Parents*, 70(6): 65–66.

McCracken, J. B. 1986. *Reducing Stress in Young Children's Lives.* Washington, DC: NAEYC.

Oken-Wright, P. 1992. From Tug of War to "Let's Make a Deal": The Teacher's Role. *Young Children*, 48(1): 15–20.

Pica, R. 1995. *Experiences in Movement with Music, Activities, and Theory.* Albany, NY: Delmar Publishers Inc.

Solter, N. 1992. Understanding Tears and Tantrums. *Young Children*, 47(4): 64–68.

What Would Linus Do With His Blanket If His Thumbsucking Were Treated? December 1990. *Child Health Alert*, p. 5.

Woolery, J., and Wellman, H. 1993. Origin and Truth: Young Children's Understanding of Imaginary Mental Representations. *Child Development*, 64: 1–17.

Chapter 3

Health Appraisals

Terms to Know

impairment
appraisal
chronic
atypical
observations
symptom
anecdotal
diagnosis

Objectives

After studying this chapter, you should be able to:

- State why it is important for teachers and caregivers to observe children's health.
- Explain the relationship between health and learning.
- List four sources for gathering information about a child's health.
- Identify five health specialists who may be called upon to evaluate children's health.
- Describe how to conduct a health inspection.
- Discuss the value of parent contacts.

A major goal of early childhood programs is to encourage and enhance the growth and development potential of each child. However, in order to achieve these goals, a child must enjoy good health. Even the most sophisticated teaching methods and learning theories are likely to fail if a child is troubled by illness, health *impairments*, or emotional problems. A hearing defect, for example, can distort what the child actually hears, the child's perception of letter and word sounds, pronunciation, and voice tone. Consider the long-term effects such misperceptions can have on a child's future learning skills.

Health problems do not necessarily have to be obvious or complex to have a negative effect on a child's ability to learn. Even a simple cold, toothache, temporary hearing loss, or chronic tonsillitis will interfere with a child's energy level, cooperation, attention span, interest, and enjoyment of learning. It is imperative that early childhood educators and caregivers be continuously aware of the health status of young children. They play an important role in recognizing the early signs of many health problems before learning is seriously affected.

CONCERN FOR CHILDREN'S HEALTH

Child care programs and schools make a significant contribution to the well-being of young children through health services, educational programs, and provisions for a healthy learning environment. A successful health program depends on health *appraisals* to identify, supply information about, and adequately meet the needs of children with health impairments. The term health appraisal refers to an evaluation or assessment of an individual's state of health. Because health is not a static quality, the process of appraising health must be carried on continuously. A child's state of health can change dramatically in a relatively short time span as illustrated in the following example.

> *Erin appeared to be feeling well and was eager to play when he arrived at the center that morning. By 10:00 AM, however, he became restless and was not interested in any of the classroom activities offered to him. The teacher noticed that Erin was constantly rubbing his right ear. By 11:30 AM Erin was crying and complaining of an earache.*

Thus, it is important for teachers and caregivers to be observant and alert to changes in a child's appearance and behavior at all times, Figure 3–1. Such changes can be the first indication of an illness or *chronic* health impairment.

Information Gathering

Information necessary for evaluating children's health can be gathered from a variety of sources, including:

- dietary assessment
- health histories
- results of medical examinations
- teacher health inspections
- dental examinations

Figure 3–1 Caregivers should be alert to changes in children's appearance and behavior.

- vision and hearing screenings
- speech evaluations
- psychological testing
- developmental evaluations
- parent interviews

Several of these procedures can be administered by early childhood educators, while others require the services of specially trained health professionals. Often, the process of identifying a specific health impairment requires the cooperative efforts of specialists from several different fields:

- pediatric medicine
- nursing
- speech
- dietetics
- dentistry
- psychology
- education
- ophthalmology
- social work
- audiology

Health information should be collected from a variety of appropriate sources before any final conclusions are reached about a child's condition. The results of one health appraisal method alone are often too limited and may present a biased picture of the problem. A child faced with strange surroundings or an unfamiliar adult examiner may behave in *atypical* ways, thereby making screening evaluation difficult. The anxiety of new experiences may also cause the young child to behave abnormally. Gathering pertinent information about a child from several sources helps to eliminate these problems. Such an approach also presents the most accurate picture of an illness or impairment and its effect on the child's daily life. For example, combining caregiver and parent observations with the results of a hearing screening may confirm the need to refer a child to a hearing specialist.

OBSERVATION AS A SCREENING TOOL

Teachers and caregivers are important members of the health team who watch over the orderly growth and development of young children. It is not necessary for them to have extensive training in health and medicine. Rather, they make their most valuable contributions through skilled *observations*. Watching children work and play provides the teacher with many clues about potential health problems.

Health observations are one of the simplest, least costly, and most effective screening techniques available to child caregivers. Many of the tools necessary for making objective health observations are already at their disposal. Sight is perhaps the most important; much can be learned about children's health by merely watching them in action. A simple touch can detect a fever or enlarged lymph glands. Odors may indicate lack of cleanliness or an infection. Careful listening may reveal breathing difficulties or changes in voice quality. Conversations may reveal poor peer relationships, frequent health complaints, or problems in the child's home. Utilizing one's senses to the fullest—seeing children as they really are, hearing what they really have to say, and responding to their true needs—requires time, patience, and practice to perfect.

Teachers and child caregivers occupy an excellent position for observing the health of young children (Leavitt, 1991). They see children functioning in a variety of settings and activities for extended periods of time, Figure 3–2. Observation skills, combined with a knowledge of normal growth and development, permit careful assessment of a child's skills and abilities. A baseline that documents the usual

Figure 3–2 Teachers and caregivers see children functioning in various settings. This gives them an excellent opportunity to observe the children for potential health problems.

behavior and appearance for each child can be established through continuous observation; changes or deviations can then be quickly noted.

Assessment of children's growth and development must be done cautiously. Teachers and caregivers must remember that a wide range of normal behaviors and skill attainment exists within each developmental stage. Norms merely represent the average age at which most children are able to perform certain skills. For example, many three year olds can reproduce the shape of a circle, name and match primary colors, and walk across a balance beam. There will be some three year olds, however, who will not be able to perform these tasks. This does not imply that these children are not "normal." Some children simply take longer than others to master certain skills. Teachers can use developmental norms to alert themselves to the child with potential health impairments, as well as those who may require extra help acquiring certain skills.

HEALTH INSPECTIONS

The daily inspection or checking of each child requires only a minute or two of the caregiver's time, and should be carried out in addition to continuous observations. Checking children in this manner enhances the caregiver's ability to detect early signs and symptoms of illness and health impairments.

Parents should be encouraged to remain with their child during the inspection process. Their presence may be comforting to the child and serve to answer any questions that may arise. Also, by observing the health check firsthand, a parent's concern about the procedure can be lessened. If a parent is unavailable, a second caregiver can witness the check as a precaution.

Method

A quiet area set aside in the classroom is ideal for conducting health inspections. The observer may choose simply to sit on the floor with the children or provide a more structured setting with a table and chairs. By designating the same area each day for health inspections, young children will know where they are expected to check in.

A systematic approach is the surest and most efficient method for conducting health inspections. By establishing a routine, the caregiver can be assured that health inspections will be consistent and thorough each time. Table 3–1 provides a sample checklist that can serve as a guideline for observations. It is organized so that inspections are made from top to bottom of the child and then front to back. This list is by no means exhaustive or the only method available. Caregivers may wish to adapt the procedure to their own setting and particular needs of children with whom they work.

A teacher should begin health inspections by observing children as they enter the room and approach the teacher. Many clues about their well-being, e.g., personal cleanliness, weight changes, signs of illness, facial expressions, posture, skin color, and coordination can be noted quite easily. A teacher or caregiver can also utilize this opportunity to gain important insight into the quality of relationship

TABLE 3–1 Health Observation Checklist

1. *General appearance*—weight change (gain or loss), fatigue, excitability, skin color, size for age group
2. *Scalp*—observe for itching, sores, cleanliness
3. *Face*—general appearance, expression (e.g., fear, anxious, happy), color
4. *Eyes*—look for redness, tearing, puffiness, coordinated eye movements, sensitivity to light, squinting, frequent rubbing, styes, or sores
5. *Ears*—check for drainage, frequent earaches, bewildered looks or inappropriate responses
6. *Nose*—runny, sneezing, deformity, frequent rubbing, congestion
7. *Mouth*—inspection of teeth for cavities or malformations; inside of mouth for redness, spots or sores, or malformations; mouth breathing
8. *Throat*—look for enlarged, red or infected tonsils or red throat with or without white spots
9. *Neck*—check for enlarged glands if you question any of the other findings
10. *Chest*—watch child's breathing for wheezing, rattles, labored breathing (shortness of breath), frequent coughing with or without other symptoms
11. *Skin*—observe the child's front and back for color, rashes, scratches, bumps, bruises, unusual scars, or injuries
12. *Speech*—clarity, substitution of letter sounds, stuttering, monotone voice, nasality, appropriateness for age
13. *Extremities*—equal length, straight, check posture, coordination, pigeon-toed, bowed legs
14. *Behavior*—observe level of activity, alertness, degree of cooperativeness appropriate for age, appetite, sleep habits, irritable or excitable, motor skills

between parent and child by observing as they arrive and interact together. These observations can help to explain why some children exhibit certain behaviors. For example, does the parent have a tendency to do everything for the child—take off boots, hang up coats, pick up items the child has dropped—or does the parent encourage the child to try to do these things? Is the child allowed to answer questions or does the parent provide all of the answers?

Following these initial observations, the teacher can begin checking individual children. First, a flashlight is used to inspect the mouth and throat, Figure 3–3. A quick look inside the mouth can alert the caregiver to the child with an unusually red throat, swollen or infected tonsils, dental caries, or other disorders. Additional observations of the hair and face, including the eyes, ears, and nose, can also be made at this time.

Next, the front of the body, including the chest, abdomen, and arms, is inspected for signs of rashes, skin color, or unusual scratches, bumps, or bruises. Because many of the rashes associated with communicable disease begin on the warmer areas of the body, e.g., chest, back, neck, and forearms, these parts should be looked at carefully, Figure 3–4. When these steps are completed, the child is asked to turn around and similar inspections are made of the head, hair, and back.

Figure 3–3 By observing a child, a teacher will find many clues about the child's well-being.

Figure 3–4 Checklists are useful for systematically observing and recording children's health status.

When the more formal aspects of the health inspection process are completed, the teacher should continue making observations. Qualities of balance, coordination, posture, and size can be easily noted as an infant crawls away or an older child walks over to join friends. Information gathered from both formal health inspections and teacher observations contribute to an awareness of a child's total state of health—physical, mental, emotional, and social well-being.

With time, observers become more skillful in conducting health inspections and making significant observations. Experience enables the teacher or caregiver to gain the sensitivity and skills necessary to distinguish between signs and *symptoms* that are normal and those that are abnormal. Gradually, it becomes easier for the observer to recognize not only very obvious changes, but also the more subtle differences that may be cause for concern.

Recording

Caregivers are indispensable as observers and recorders of children's health information. Their frequent and close contact with children permits them to play an important role in the promotion of health. Written notes should be made following the inspection of each child. Space provided on daily attendance records is one very good method for recording important *anecdotal* information. Simple checklists are also useful for systematically observing and recording children's health status.

Recorded observations must be precise and specific. To say that a child "looks sick" is much too vague and can be interpreted differently by everyone reading it. To state that a child is flushed, has a fever of 101°F (38.3°C), and is covered with a fine red rash is more meaningful.

Carefully recorded observations can be useful for the early detection of illness and health impairments. Such information is often very beneficial to health professionals when making a *diagnosis*. Recorded observations can be useful for determining whether a child is too ill to remain in group care. Patterns of illness or behavior changes can also be traced from the daily health records. Children known to have had close contact with an identified case of head lice or chicken pox, for example, can be watched closely for the next several weeks.

Whatever recording method is used, the important thing to remember is that the information should be available and meaningful to other personnel working with the child. Notes scribbled on scratch paper tucked in the back of a notebook are often lost and useless to others. Also, it must be remembered that information about a child's health status is confidential and should only be shared with caregivers or teachers who are working directly with the child.

Interpretations

Observations are an essential component of the overall health appraisal process. Teachers and caregivers, however, must be careful not to attempt diagnosing the specific nature of children's health problems. However, skillful questioning, careful listening, watching, and keen interest in the problems of children make the observer's contribution invaluable. Teachers and caregivers can collect much of the information necessary for evaluating a child's health status and reaching a final diagnosis. Once findings are accurately recorded, meaningful information can be shared with other allied professionals. Responsibility for interpreting the signs and symptoms of children's health problems and confirming a diagnosis always belongs to trained health professionals.

Managing Health Risks

In addition to assessing the progress and needs of individual children, the teacher or caregiver also has an obligation to protect the health of other children in the classroom; observations provide an effective means for accomplishing this task. Communicable illnesses, and the risks associated with each, pose one of the most frequent threats to the well-being of young children in group settings (Kendricks, 1995). The task of identifying sick children is made easier because their appearance and behavior are often different from the day-to-day norm. Changes in their appearance and behavior are often the first sign of an impending illness. It is during the early stages of an illness that a child is most contagious and most likely to infect other children. Therefore, removing a sick child from the classroom can help reduce the chances of exposing other children.

Other Benefits

Health observations can yield important information that can be useful for the early detection of health problems. The earlier health impairments are recognized and treatment is begun, the less damaging they may be to a child's ability to learn.

While early identification is probably the most important consideration, there are other benefits that can be gained from the opportunity. Time can be spent talking with children on an individual basis, which busy schedules too often discourage. Young children especially enjoy these private conversations. They often are more spontaneous in their expressions, sharing the joy of a new pet, the pain of a scraped knee, the fear of harsh discipline at home, or the excitement of having captured a fuzzy caterpillar.

INVOLVING PARENTS

Daily health inspections provide an excellent opportunity for actively involving parents in children's preventive health care. Frequent parent contacts help to build a relationship of understanding and trust between staff and parents, Figure 3–5. Some parents may be hesitant, at first, to initiate contacts with the teacher or caregiver regarding their child's health needs. However, through repeated encouragement, interest and assistance, effective lines of communication can quickly be established (Essa, 1996).

During the health check-in procedure, parents should be encouraged to ask questions and voice concerns about their child's behavior, physical condition, habits, or adjustment to care. In addition, parents can often provide simple explanations for problems that the teacher or caregiver observe. For example, a child's fatigue or aggressiveness may be the result of a new puppy, a grandmother's visit, a new baby in the home, or a seizure the night before. Allergies or a red vitamin taken at breakfast may be the cause of a questionable red throat. Without this direct sharing of information, such symptoms might otherwise be cause for concern.

Contacts with parents during health inspections are also a good time to alert them to outbreaks of communicable illnesses. They can be informed of specific signs and symptoms to watch for and are thus more likely to keep sick children at home.

Figure 3–5 Talking with parents helps the staff build a relationship of understanding and confidence.

Parents' Responsibility

Primary responsibility for a child's health care always belongs to the parents. Parents are ultimately responsible for maintaining their child's health, following through with recommendations, and obtaining any necessary evaluations and treatments.

Often parents are the first to sense that something is wrong with their child. However, some parents delay seeking professional advice, either denying that the problem is real or hoping the child will eventually outgrow it. They may not realize the serious consequences health problems can have on a child's ability to learn successfully. Also, it is often difficult for parents to determine the exact nature or cause of a child's health impairment and where to turn for appropriate health care or treatment.

Occasionally, parents fail to take the initiative to provide for any type of routine health care. Some parents find it difficult to understand the need for medical care when a child does not appear to be sick, while others cannot afford preventive health care. With today's rising medical care costs, it is fairly easy to see why this might occur. Cost, however, should not discourage parents from obtaining necessary medical attention because most communities offer a variety of free or low-cost health services for young children, including:

- Head Start Programs
- Child Find Screening Programs
- Medicaid Assistance
- Well Child Clinics
- Crippled Children's Services
- University-Affiliated Training Centers and Clinics
- Public Health Immunization Centers

These agencies and services can usually be located in the telephone directory or by contacting the local Public Health Department.

Teachers and caregivers can be very instrumental in helping parents understand the importance of and need for regularly scheduled health care for their child. Familiarity with community health resources facilitates knowledgeable referrals and helps parents secure the type of health care needed for each child (Peterson, 1987).

HEALTH EDUCATION

Daily health inspections also provide an opportunity for informal health education. Caregivers can help young children begin to develop an awareness of their own health. Simple questions about many topics, such as hygiene, nutrition, exercise, and sleep, can be discussed with even very young children. For example:

- "Sandy, did you brush your teeth this morning? Brushing helps to keep teeth healthy and prevents cavities."
- "Alexander, what did you eat for breakfast this morning before coming to school? Food gives us energy to work and play."
- "Marion, have you had a drink of water yet today? Our bodies need water in order to grow and stay healthy."

Spontaneous conversations such as these help children assume some interest in their own health care. Even the young child can begin to recognize and establish preventive health practices which promote good health. Also, the cooperation and trust that is gained through daily health inspections is important for future contacts that a child may have with health professionals.

Parent Education

Health inspections provide an effective means for educating parents. Many aspects of children's care and health education lend themselves to informal discussions with both parents and children during the health inspection process:

- toy safety
- the importance of eating breakfast
- nutritious snack ideas
- the benefits of exercise
- cleanliness
- children dressing appropriately for the weather
- dental hygiene

Including parents in health education programs brings about an improved understanding of the health principles and goals stressed with the children. It also helps to encourage a greater degree of consistency in the health practices and attitudes between school and the child's home.

Summary

Teachers and child caregivers play a valuable role in the promotion of children's health. Good health is essential for effective learning. Illness and health impairments interfere with this process. Because a child's health status can change very quickly, it is necessary to make continuous health observations.

Health observations are a valuable tool for evaluating all aspects of a child's state of health—physical, mental, social, and emotional. It is one of the simplest and most inexpensive screening techniques available. The information gathered from health observations may be useful to health specialists for diagnosing or ruling out many health problems. Caution should be exercised, however, when using developmental norms to determine whether a child is "normal."

There are many benefits to be gained from health observations and inspections. For example, conditions that threaten the well-being of an individual child or others in a classroom can be quickly identified and referred for treatment. Health inspections also provide an excellent opportunity for personal or one-on-one conversations with young children. They also provide an opportunity for involving parents in children's health care and health education.

The responsibility of the parents must not be overlooked as caregivers become more involved in children's health care. Rather, the efforts of the caregiver should complement those of the parents. They can help parents accept the need to provide care for their child and assist them in locating appropriate health services in the community.

Suggested Activities

1. With another student, role play health inspections. Record your findings.
2. Invite a public health nurse from a well-child clinic or a local pediatrician to speak to the class about routine health care for children under 6 years of age.
3. Visit several preschools and child care centers in your community. Note whether any type of health inspection is performed as children arrive. Describe the method used at each center.
4. Develop a list of resources available in your community and state for children with vision impairments, speech impairments, cerebral palsy, and mental disabilities. Be creative in your search; consider child care options, special equipment needs, auxiliary services, family financial assistance, etc.

Chapter Review

A. Match the term in column II with the correct definition in column I.

Column I	Column II
1. the process of writing down health data	a. health
2. a problem that interferes with one's ability to function	b. impairment
3. evaluation or assessment of an individual's health	c. observations
4. to gather information by looking and listening	d. symptom
5. physical maturation	e. appraisal
6. a bodily change noticed by the affected individual	f. recording
7. to examine or look at carefully	g. diagnosis
8. formal or informal meetings	h. parent contacts
9. a state of complete physical, mental, and social well-being	i. development
10. development toward maturity	j. inspection
11. the act of determining an illness or disorder from signs and symptoms	k. growth

B. Read the following case study and answer the questions that follow.

Lynette's teacher has recently become concerned about her ability to see. He has noticed that when stories are read to the children, Lynette often loses interest, frequently leaves her place in the circle, and crawls closer to him in order to see the pictures he holds up. The teacher has also observed that Lynette looks very closely at puzzles and pictures she is coloring. Lynette's parents have expressed some concern about her clumsiness at home. An initial vision screening test, administered by the school nurse, reveals that Lynette's vision is not within normal limits. She was referred to an eye specialist for further evaluation.

1. What behaviors did Lynette exhibit that made her teacher suspect some type of vision disorder?
2. Identify the various sources from which information concerning Lynette's vision problem was obtained before she was referred to an eye specialist.
3. If the teacher suspected a vision problem, why didn't he just go ahead and recommend that Lynette get glasses?
4. What responsibilities do teachers and caregivers have when they believe that a child has a health impairment?

C. Briefly answer the following questions.

1. List four sources for gathering information that can be useful in evaluating children's health.
2. Name five professionals who are trained to identify specific health impairments of children.
3. Describe the relationship between health and learning?
4. Name six areas to observe during a health inspection.
5. How can teacher observations benefit the health of a child?
6. How can daily health inspections involve parents in the preventive health care of their children?

References

Essa, E. 1996. *Introduction to Early Childhood Education.* Albany, NY: Delmar Publishers Inc.

Kendrick, A., Kaufman, R., and Messenger, K. 1995. *Healthy Young Children: A Manual for Programs.* Washington, DC: National Association for the Education of Young Children.

Leavitt, R. L., and Eheart, B. K. 1991. Assessment in Early Childhood Programs. *Young Children.* 46(5): 4–9.

Morgan, E. L. 1989. Talking with Parents When Concerns Come Up. *Young Children.* 44(2): 52–56.

Peterson, N. L. 1987. *Early Intervention for Handicapped and At-Risk Children.* Denver, CO: Love Publishing Company.

Additional Reading

Brink, S., and Nader, P. R. February 1984. "Comprehensive Health Screening in Elementary Schools: An Outcome Evaluation." *Journal of School Health,* 54(2): 75–78.

Hills, T. 1993. Assessment in Context—Teachers and Children at Work. *Young Children,* 48(5): 20–28.

Maddox, M., and Edgar, E. November 1983. "Implementing EPSDT Screening in the Public School: Resolving Some Issues." *Journal of School Health,* 53(9): 536.

Mennie, J., and Klinger, M. J. April 1984. "Health Department Services for Preschools and Day Care Centers." *Journal of School Health,* 54(4): 160–61.

Chapter 4

Health Assessment Tools

Terms to Know

intervention
skeletal
neurological
amblyopia
strabismus
myopia
hyperopia
conductive
receptive
sensorineural
speech
misarticulations
lethargy
pallor
mottling
nutrient intake
skinfold

Objectives

After studying this chapter, you should be able to:

- List five screening procedures that can be used to assess a child's health status.
- Name three vision defects that can be detected through vision screening.
- Match the recommended screening test to the condition or behavior that indicates its need.
- Identify the physical signs of common nutritional deficiencies.
- Describe two methods used for dietary assessment.

It is essential that teachers and caregivers familiarize themselves with the variety of methods and screening tools available for evaluating children's health. Several commonly used procedures are described in this unit. The ultimate purpose of all such methods is the protection and improvement of children's health. Objective data collected from a combination of screening procedures provide (1) the most reliable information for health promotion, (2) the early detection of potentially disabling or handicapping conditions that may affect children's growth and intellectual development, and (3) the opportunity to adjust programs so that the needs of individual children are met.

HEALTH RECORDS

Information contained in children's permanent health records can help promote well-being, if the data are current and sufficiently detailed. Unfortunately, the types of records maintained by early childhood programs vary considerably in quality and quantity from one center to another. State licensing regulations often specify the kinds of records a center must keep on file. Because licensing requirements generally reflect only minimal standards, child care centers may want to consider additional forms of documentation. Selection of appropriate health-related records and forms should be consistent with the program's goals and philosophy. Records should provide comprehensive information about individual children and afford adequate legal protection for the children, staff, and center.

A permanent health record should be kept on file for each child enrolled in a program. It should contain the following essential information:

- child/family health history
- copy of a recent medical assessment (physical examination)
- immunization records
- emergency contact information
- record of dental examinations
- attendance data
- school-related accidents or injuries
- parent conferences related to the child's health
- results of special testing, e.g., vision, hearing, speech
- medications administered while the child is at school

Information found in children's health records can be used for many purposes:

- determining health status
- identifying possible problem areas
- developing *intervention* programs
- evaluating the success of treatments
- coordinating services
- making *referrals*
- following a child's progress
- research

Health records contain much private information about children and their families. Teachers and caregivers must respect the confidential nature of these records. Only information that will improve effectiveness and interaction should be shared with those who are working directly with a child. Personal facts concerning a child or family must be kept strictly confidential. They should not serve as topics for casual conversation among teachers, staff, or with other parents. No portion of a child's health record should ever be released to another agency, school, health professional, or clinician until written permission is obtained from the child's parent or guardian. A special release form such as the one shown in Figure 4–1 can be used for this purpose. The form should clearly designate the nature of information that is to be released and the agency or person to whom it is to be sent. It must be dated and signed by the parent or guardian; a copy is retained in the child's folder.

INFORMATION RELEASE FORM

I understand the confidentiality of any personally identifiable information on my child shall be maintained in accordance with PL 93-380, federal and state regulations and used only for the educational benefit of my child. Personally identifiable information about my child will be released only with my consent. With this information, I hereby grant the

____
(Name of program, agency, or person)

permission to release the following types of information:

Medical information ________________
Assessment reports ________________
Child histories ________________
Progress reports ________________
Clinical reports ________________
(Other) ________________

to:____
(Name of agency or person to whom information is to be sent)

regarding ____________________ ____________ ____
Child's Name Birthdate Sex

____
Signature of Parent or Guardian

____
Relationship of Representative

____
Date

Figure 4–1 A sample information release form.

Recordkeeping is most efficient when one person is responsible for the maintenance of all health records. However, meaningful contributions regarding concerns, findings, or conversations related to a child's health should be added by any teacher or staff member working with the child. This makes records more complete and useful. Health records can serve as legal documentation and should be kept on file by the center for approximately five years.

Child Health Histories

Health histories contain important background and current information about a child. Questions about family members are usually included in order to provide a more comprehensive picture of the child. Parents should be asked to complete a child health history form when their child is accepted into a preschool or child care program.

Much variation can be found in the type of background information that is requested. Unless a center is required to use a standard form, it can adapt or develop a format that best suits its own specific needs. Sample forms can be obtained from other centers and reviewed to determine the types of questions a program wants to include. A child health history form should request certain basic information:

- facts related to the child's birth
- family circumstances, e.g., numbers and ages of family members, predominant languages spoken
- major developmental milestones
- previous injuries, illnesses, surgery, or hospitalizations
- personal habits, e.g., toileting, food problems, napping
- parent concerns, e.g., behavior problems, social development, language skills
- special health conditions, e.g., allergies, asthma, epilepsy, diabetes, blindness, hearing loss

Information contained in health histories can contribute to a better understanding of each child's uniqueness, including past health events and potential risks for future health problems. This knowledge is also extremely useful for assessing a child's general state of health and enables caregivers to set reasonable goals and expectations for individual children. Programs can be adjusted to meet children's special needs, such as a hearing loss, the use of a wheelchair for locomotion, or a mild language delay. However, caution must be exercised not to set expectation levels unnecessarily low for children based on this information alone (Peterson, 1987). A child's ability to learn must never be discounted unless an impairment is definitely known to restrict the educational process or performance. Lowering goals and expectations may limit what a child is willing to try, for often children will achieve only what is expected and may not be encouraged to progress or strive to develop their true potential.

Child health histories also provide the teacher with insight into the kind of routine medical supervision a child has received in the past. This knowledge may be very useful when making referrals, because it often reflects the value parents place on preventive health care.

Medical and Dental Examinations

Most states require children to have a complete health examination before entering a child care program. Some states require this examination to be updated yearly. It is generally recommended that well children who are less than one year of age have a routine medical checkup every 2–3 months. Children two to three years of age should be examined every 6 months and children four and older should be seen by their doctor annually. More frequent medical supervision may be necessary when health problems exist.

Current health information is obtained from the parent and child during the course of the examination. Questions related to physical, mental, and social development are asked to help the examiner assess the child's total state of health. The child's immunization record is reviewed and additional immunizations are given as indicated. Body parts and systems, such as the heart, lungs, eyes, ears, ***skeletal*** and ***neurological*** development, and gastrointestinal function (stomach and intestines) are carefully examined. Head circumference is routinely measured on all infants and children until 36 months of age to be certain that the head size is increasing at an acceptable rate. Height, weight, and blood pressure readings (after age 3) are also taken and compared to past records to determine if a child's growth is progressing satisfactorily. Lack of growth may be an indication of other health problems. Specialized tests may be needed, such as blood tests for anemia, sickle cell disease, or lead poisoning. Urinalysis or tuberculin testing may also be ordered to provide more complete information about a child's health.

While dental examinations are seldom required for enrollment in child care programs, their benefits are unquestionable. Preventive checkups for young children are generally recommended at six or twelve month intervals and include a visual inspection of the teeth, cleaning, and an application of fluoride.

SCREENING PROCEDURES

Screening tests are an essential part of the comprehensive health assessment of young children. Some procedures can be administered by caregivers, while others require the services of professional clinicians. Their purpose complements the preventive health concept by ensuring that a particular system is functioning as it should. Screening tests are also used to identify children with possible impairments that may require professional evaluation. These tests are generally quick, inexpensive, and efficient to administer to groups of children. Routine screening also helps children become accustomed to evaluation procedures as a part of a health maintenance routine.

Many screening procedures are available for evaluating various aspects of children's health; however, they are not designed to diagnose specific conditions. Rather, the results obtained from these tests simply provide additional information and should be used to complement the observations of teachers and parents.

Measurements of Height and Weight

The first five years of life are an important period of growth. Changes in height and weight are dramatic during infancy, while the growth continues steadily, but at a much slower rate in the preschool years. Measurements of height are particularly important because they provide a reliable means for evaluating a child's long-term health and nutritional status (see Appendix B for growth curves that show norms by age and gender of the child). Fluctuations in weight, on the other hand, usually reflect short-term variables, such as a recent illness, infection, or temporary emotional stress. However, it must be remembered that a child's growth potential is ultimately governed by inherited characteristics. This is especially important to remember when working with children from different ethnic backgrounds.

The practice of measuring height and weight is one method caregivers and teachers can easily use to assess children's health, Figure 4–2. It does not require any special skills or training and can be completed in a relatively short period of time. Children are fascinated to see how much they have grown or how big they are in comparison to their friends. Caregivers can use this opportunity as a valuable learning experience to encourage the interests of young children in their own growth and health. Simple individual or group growth charts can be constructed with crayon and paper. By plotting measurements of height and weight each time, children can visualize their growth from one measurement to the next.

Ideally, height and weight should be measured at 4–6 month intervals and recorded in the child's permanent health file. However, a child's growth cannot be accurately evaluated from one measurement. A single measurement is unlikely to

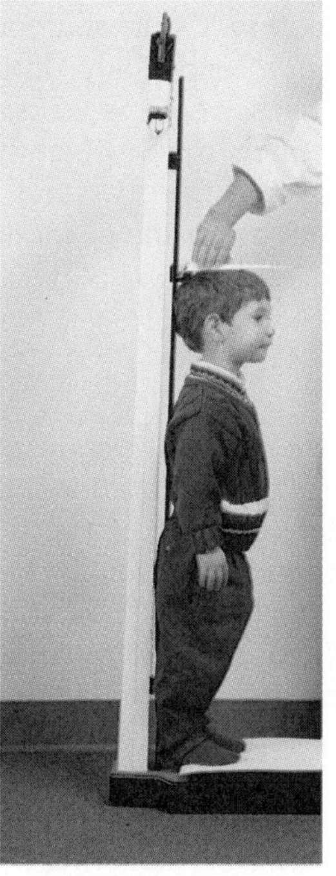

Figure 4–2 Measurements of height and weight provide a good index of children's health.

identify the child who is experiencing a growth disturbance related to physical illness or emotional difficulties. Rather, what is most important is the pattern of changes that occur over a period of time. Height and weight data should also be recorded in the child's permanent health file. Comparisons can then be made with previous measurements and standardized growth charts to determine if the child's growth is progressing normally. Growth charts are available from:

Mead Johnson Nutrition Division
2404 Pennsylvania Avenue
Evansville, IN 47721

Ross Laboratories
625 Cleveland Avenue
Columbus, OH 43216

Wyeth Laboratories
P.O. Box 8099
Philadelphia, PA 19101

Examples of growth charts are also included in Appendix B.

SENSORY DEVELOPMENT

The sensory system affects all parameters of a child's growth and development. Five special senses comprise the sensory system: vision, hearing, smell, touch, and taste. The young child utilizes these senses to receive, interpret, process, and respond to external environmental cues and stimulation. Optimal functioning of the sensory system is, therefore, of critical importance, especially during the early stages of growth and development. Of the five senses, perhaps vision and hearing are two of the most critical to young children, since much of early learning is dependent on what the child hears and sees. The Eye Care Council (1994) estimates that 20 percent of children entering Kindergarten have undetected vision problems that will interfere with learning.

VISION SCREENING

Parents, teachers, and caregivers too often assume that because children are young and healthy they naturally have good vision. This assumption may not always be correct. Vision impairments affect approximately one out of every four children of school age (*Vision Screening in Schools*). The impairment may be present at birth or develop as a child matures or experiences certain illnesses, infections, or injuries. For this reason, an infant's eyes should be examined for abnormalities and muscle imbalance at 3, 6, and 12 months and yearly thereafter to avoid the risk of permanent loss of vision (Wasserman, 1992). Early detection of vision impairments also improves a child's chances for rapid and successful treatment.

Often, it is the teacher or caregiver who first notices clues in the young child's behavior that indicate a vision disorder, Figure 4–3. One reason is that as greater

Figure 4–3 The teacher or caregiver is often the first to notice signs of a child's vision problem.

demands are placed on a child to perform tasks accurately, vision problems often become more apparent. Also, it is unlikely that young children will know when their vision is not normal, especially if they have never experienced good vision before. A careful comparison of screening results and observations provide the most accurate assessment of children with potential impairments of vision.

Special attention should be paid to children who have other known physical handicaps and to those who are repeatedly unsuccessful in achieving tasks that depend on visual cues. Delays in identifying vision problems can seriously affect the learning process and chances for successfully treating the condition. Children with vision impairments may also be inappropriately labelled. Many times visually impaired children are considered to be slow learners or mentally retarded when they simply cannot see well enough to learn (Allen, 1994). The following case study illustrates the point:

> *The teachers were concerned about Tina. She was easily frustrated and unable to complete many preacademic tasks, such as puzzles, color identification, and simple object labelling. She appeared clumsy and often avoided participation in large motor activities during outdoor time. These problems were not typical of most children Tina's age (three years, eight months). Her teachers considered placing Tina in a special classroom for children with learning disabilities. However, during routine vision screening, Tina's vision was discovered to be 20/200. With corrective glasses and slight modifications in teaching techniques, immediate improvement was observed in Tina's performance.*

TABLE 4–1 Detection of Visual Abnormalities in the Infant

Observe the infant closely for:

- roving eye movements that are suggestive of blindness
- one or both eyes continuously crossed
- eyes that wander in opposite directions
- inability to focus or follow a moving object (after three months of age)
- pupil of one eye larger than the other
- absence of a blink reflex
- eyelids not completely raised
- cloudiness on the eyeball

Methods of Assessment

Early detection of visual defects requires observing young children carefully for signs of potential problems, Table 4–1. Some observable signs of visual impairments may include:

- rubs eyes frequently
- attempts to brush away blurs
- is irritable with close work
- is inattentive to distant tasks, e.g., a movie, catching a ball
- strains to see distant objects, squints, or screws up face
- blinks often when reading; holds books too close or far away
- is inattentive with close work; quits after a short time
- closes or covers one eye to see better
- tilts head to one side
- appears cross-eyed at times
- reverses letters, words
- stumbles over objects; runs into things
- complains of repeated headaches or double vision
- poor eye-hand coordination

It is important that children have their eyes tested by a vision specialist at least once before age five. Vision problems are not outgrown, nor do they improve. Routine screenings are useful for making sure vision is developing properly and to locate children with possible visual defects, Figure 4–4. Teachers, caregivers, and parent volunteers can be trained by health professionals to administer most vision screening tests. An infant's vision can be tested by holding an object, such as a rattle, ten to twelve inches away and observing the infant's ability to focus on (fixation) and track, or follow, the object as it is moved in a 180° arc around the infant.

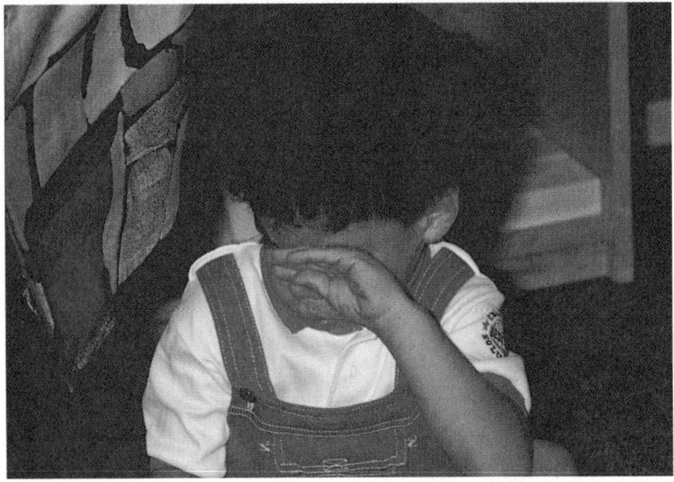

Figure 4–4 Frequent eye rubbing could indicate potential vision problems.

The infant's eyes should also be observed carefully for uncoordinated movements as the object is moved closer (convergence) and farther away from the face. In addition, the blink reflex (sweep hand quickly in front of the eyes; observe for blinking), and pupil response (shine a penlight, held 4–6 inches away, into the eye; pupil should become smaller) should also be checked. Abnormal responses should be evaluated by a health care professional.

Children 3 years and older can be screened using one of several standardized tests. The Snellen E (or Illiterate E) and HOTV Symbols are two methods used to test distance acuity (Bishop, 1988). They are reliable and do not require that a child know letters of the alphabet. A child's eyes are first tested together, then separately. Standards for passing the Snellen E are age related: 20/40 (3 yr.), 20/30 (4 yr.), 20/20 (5 yr.). Standards for passing the HOTV are similarly age related: 10/20 (3 yr.), 10/15 (4 and 5 yr.).

It is always important that children understand the procedure or type of response that is expected, or test results may not be reliable. Any child who fails the initial screening should be rescreened within two weeks. If the child fails a second screening, referral should be made to an eye care professional.

Children with more than one line difference between eyes would be referred to an eye specialist for additional evaluation. A home version of the Illiterate E test entitled, "Home Test for Preschoolers," is available to parents from:

National Society to Prevent Blindness
500 E. Remington Road
Schaumberg, IL 60173

Additional testing should be conducted to evaluate 3–5-year-olds for convergence, depth perception (Titmus Fly), binocular fusion (Worth 4-Dot; Random Dot E), and deviations in pupil position (holding penlight 12 inches from child's face, direct light at bridge of the nose; position of light reflection should be equal on both pupils; deviations require professional evaluation).

Information concerning symptoms of visual impairments, various testing procedures, and supplies can be obtained by writing to the National Society to Prevent Blindness or to the:

American Academy of Ophthalmology
655 Beach Street
San Francisco, CA 94109

Common Disorders

Three vision defects that screening programs attempt to identify in young children include:

- amblyopia
- strabismus
- myopia

Amblyopia, or "lazy eye," is a condition that develops because of a distortion of the child's vision. This distortion is commonly thought to result from an imbalance of the eye muscles, although other causes have been suggested. A child with amblyopia often shows no outward signs or symptoms of this visual impairment; it cannot be detected by merely looking at the child. Children with amblyopia often experience double vision because the images received from either eye cannot be focused together. In an effort to make sense out of the images it receives, the brain begins to ignore the vision from the weaker eye. Gradually, the vision in the weaker eye diminishes.

Prompt medical treatment can prevent this type of vision loss from becoming permanent. A significant amount of sight can often be restored if amblyopia is discovered and treated before the child reaches the age of five or six. The results are even more favorable if therapy can be started earlier. The most common method of treatment consists of wearing a patch over the stronger eye, thus forcing the weaker eye to work harder, Figure 4–5. When the muscles of the weaker eye have been sufficiently strengthened and vision has improved, the patching process is discontinued. Corrective glasses and special eye exercises are other methods sometimes prescribed to treat amblyopia.

Strabismus, or cross-eye, also results from an imbalance of the eye muscles. Strabismus can often be recognized by uncoordinated eye movements as the infant or child attempts to focus on objects. Generally, only one of the child's eyes is affected, causing it to turn either inward or outward. As in amblyopia, double vision occurs because the eyes are unable to focus together. Images from the weaker eye are blocked out by the brain to avoid confusion, and vision gradually deteriorates. Early recognition and treatment of strabismus is essential to restore normal vision. Today, even infants are being treated aggressively for this condition. Several methods are used to treat strabismus, including surgical correction, patching of the unaffected eye, and eye exercises.

Figure 4–5 Common vision defects affecting young children can include amblyopia, strabismus, and myopia.

Myopia, or nearsightedness, is sometimes a problem for young children but is more common among school-aged children. A child who is nearsighted can see near objects, but has poor distant vision. Children with myopia may appear clumsy and stumble or run into objects. Squinting is also typical behavior of these children as they attempt to bring distant objects into focus.

Farsightedness, or *hyperopia*, is considered by some authorities to occur naturally in very young children because of immature development of eye structures. However, as children grow older, this condition is thought often to correct itself. Children who are farsighted can see objects clearly in the distance, but have difficulty focusing on near objects. They may complain of headaches, tired eyes, and blurred vision following periods of close work. Hyperopia cannot be detected with most routine screening procedures. Teacher and parent observations may provide the best clues to this disorder. Referral to a professional eye specialist is necessary.

Color blindness affects only a small percentage of children and is generally limited to males. Females may be carriers of this hereditary defect, but are rarely affected themselves. The most common form of color blindness involves the inability to discriminate between red and green. Testing very young children for color blindness is difficult and often omitted, since learning is not seriously affected and no treatment is available.

Management

When a child is suspected of having vision problems, parents should be counselled to arrange for an additional evaluation. Vision testing is available through a number of sources, including pediatricians, "well-child" clinics, public health departments, professional eye doctors, and public schools. Some local organizations also provide financial assistance for professional examinations and glasses.

Children who do not pass an initial vision screening should be retested. Failure to pass a second screening necessitates referral to a professional eye specialist for more extensive evaluation and diagnosis. However, results obtained from routine vision testing should be viewed with some caution because they are not necessarily a guarantee that a child does or does not have a problem. Most routine screening procedures are not designed to test for all types of vision impairments. Consequently, there will always be some over-referral of children who do not have any problems, while other children with defects will be missed. It is for this reason that the observations of teachers and parents are so extremely important.

HEARING SCREENING

The development of speech patterns, ***language***, and learning depends upon a child's ability to hear. Undetected hearing impairments may also affect a child's social interactions, emotional development, and performance in school. The early diagnosis of any hearing loss is extremely critical. Unfortunately, children with hearing losses are sometimes inappropriately labelled as slow learners, retarded, or "behavior problems." Failure to hear properly often causes children to respond and behave in seemingly inappropriate ways.

Methods of Assessment

Inappropriate responses and behaviors may be the first indication that a child is not hearing properly (Watt, 1993). Signs of hearing loss range from very obvious problems to those that are subtle and more difficult to identify. An observant parent or caregiver may notice behaviors that could indicate a hearing loss:

- frequent mouth breathing
- turns toward the direction of sound
- slowness in acquiring language; development of poor speech patterns
- difficulty understanding and following directions
- asks to have statements repeated
- rubs or pulls at ears
- mumbles, shouts, or talks loudly
- appears quiet, withdrawn; rarely interacts with others
- uses gestures rather than words
- does well in activities that do not depend on hearing
- imitates others at play
- responds to questions inappropriately
- mispronounces many word sounds
- unusual voice quality—extremely high, low, hoarse, or monotone
- failure to respond to normal sounds and voices

Hearing tests are most often conducted by either trained paraprofessionals or audiologists, Figure 4–6. An audiologist is a specially prepared clinician who uses nonmedical techniques to diagnose hearing impairments. Routine hearing screening procedures test for the normal range of tones used in everyday conversation.

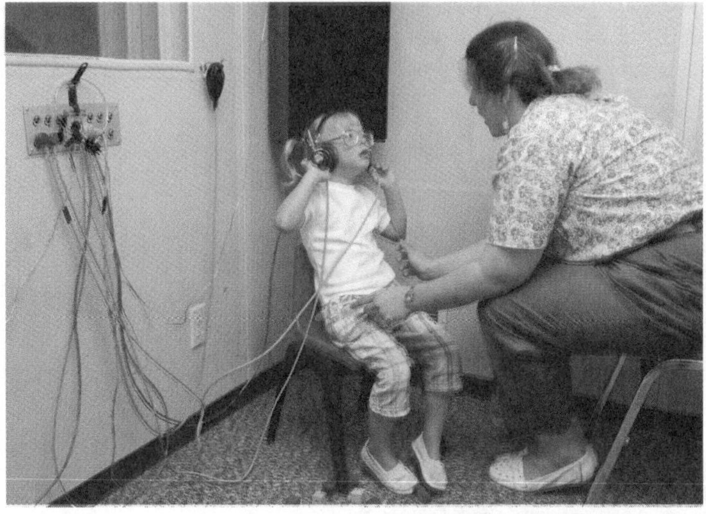

Figure 4–6 Hearing tests are conducted by audiologists or trained professionals.

Children should have their hearing tested at least once during the preschool years and more often if a hearing problem is suspected.

An infant's hearing can be evaluated from the time of birth by checking responses to various intensities of sound, e.g., eye blinking, turning head to locate sound, or stopping to suck, Table 4–2. Older infants and toddlers can be tested by observing as they turn to locate sounds (often emitted through speakers in formal testing procedures), Figure 4–7.

Most preschool children are able to complete routine hearing screening with little trouble. However, sometimes an unfamiliar situation involving new people, instruments and equipment, a novel task, or a lack of understanding or cooperation may interfere with the child's performance and cause unreliable results to be obtained from the test. These factors must be given special consideration when test results are analyzed.

TABLE 4–2 Early Signs of Hearing Abnormalities in the Infant

Observe an infant carefully for:

- absence of a startle response to a loud noise
- failure to stop crying briefly when adult speaks to baby (3 months)
- failure to turn head in direction of sound, such as a doorbell or a dog barking (4 months)
- absence of babbling or interest in imitating simple speech sounds (6–8 months)
- no response to adult commands, such as "no"

Figure 4–7 An infant's response to sound can be used to test hearing.

Teachers and parents can be extremely helpful by preparing and training young children in advance for hearing screening (Brown, 1982). In the classroom and at home, children can practice concentrated listening for short periods of time. Also, activities that involve the use of headphones, e.g., telephone operators, airplane pilots, radio announcers, will help children feel more comfortable when they are asked to put on headphones for screening purposes. Teachers should try to find out what response method, e.g., raising one hand, pressing a button, pointing to pictures, or dropping a wooden block into an empty can, the children will be expected to use. This activity can also be practiced in the classroom. If a special room will be used for testing purposes, teachers should try to arrange for children to visit the facilities and look at the equipment beforehand. These special preparations will make hearing screening less frightening for young children and increase the reliability of test results.

Common Disorders

Many hearing impairments are present at birth (Batshaw, 1992). Infectious illnesses experienced by a mother during pregnancy and premature birth are two factors known to increase the risk of hearing loss in children. Hearing impairments are frequently present in children who have other physical disabilities. Permanent and temporary hearing impairments can also be associated with other health conditions, including:

- allergies
- frequent colds
- repeated ear infections
- birth defects
- head injuries or trauma

Hearing defects should also be considered in children whose relatives have hearing losses. Parents who express concern about their children's hearing should be listened to carefully and encouraged to seek a professional evaluation.

The most common forms of hearing loss are classified as conductive, receptive, and sensorineural.

- *conductive* affects the volume of word tones. (For example, a child usually hears loud, but not soft sounds. This type of hearing loss occurs because sound waves are transmitted improperly from the external ear to structures of the inner ear, as when fluid accumulates in the child's middle ear.)
- *receptive* affects the range of tones heard. (For example, a child may hear high, but not low tones. This type of hearing loss occurs when the sensory structures of the inner ear have been damaged.)
- *sensorineural*, a less common form of hearing loss, results when sound impulses cannot reach the brain because of damage to the auditory nerve or brain itself. (These children can actually hear sounds, but they are not able to understand what they hear.) These children are considered to have a learning disability that requires special educational management.

Management

Many types of hearing impairments can be successfully treated if they are recognized in the early stages. Treatment of hearing impairments is based on the underlying cause and may range from drug therapy to surgery. In some cases, a hearing aid may be helpful or, in extreme cases, the child may need to learn sign language.

A child suspected of having a sudden or gradual hearing loss should be referred to a family physician for medical diagnosis or to an audiologist for a hearing evaluation. Parents can make arrangements for testing through the child's doctor, a speech and hearing clinic, public health department, public schools, or an audiologist.

A teacher or caregiver who understands how different impairments affect children's ability to hear can take appropriate steps to improve learning conditions. Such measures might include:

- giving individualized instructions
- facing or standing near the child when speaking
- bending down to the child's level to make it easier for the child to hear and understand what is being said
- speaking slowly and clearly

- using gestures to illustrate what is being said, e.g., pointing to the door when it is time to go outside
- demonstrating what the child is expected to do, e.g., picking up a bead and threading it on a shoestring

Additional information about hearing impairments and testing procedures can be obtained from:

American Association of Speech-Language-Hearing
10801 Rockville Pike
Rockville, MD 20852

SPEECH AND LANGUAGE EVALUATION

Throughout the early years, impressive gains are evident in both the number of words children understand (receptive vocabulary) and use to express themselves (expressive vocabulary). Generally, children's receptive vocabulary is more extensive than their expressive vocabulary. For example, most young children can follow instructions and understand simple directions long before they can clearly express themselves.

Children's language becomes increasingly fluent and complex with time and experience. The infant gradually acquires several words by one year of age, but understands many more. Vocabulary expands rapidly during the toddler years to include approximately 50–300 different words (Allen, 1994). Most two-year-olds speak in simple 2–3 word phrases:

- Go bye bye?
- Me do it!
- My ball!

The preschool child's vocabulary continues to increase significantly to include approximately 1500 words. By the age of four, a child speaks in adultlike sentences to communicate ideas in both past and present tenses. The child also asks and answers questions and provides vivid descriptions of everyday events:

- When is Mommy coming home?
- I don't want to eat my green beans!
- Where did the firetruck go?

Six-, seven-, and eight-year-olds demonstrate added skill in expressing themselves and understanding complex statements.

Many factors influence the development of *speech* and language. Young children acquire many of their early language skills by imitating speech heard in their homes (Jaffe, 1991). If parents speak with a particular accent or have an unusual voice tone, their children are likely to exhibit similar qualities. Cultural variations also have a strong influence on language usage and speech patterns. It would be easy to consider a child, for whom English is a second language, as having delayed language skills if a teacher were not aware of the child's background. For this reason, it is important that teachers become familiar with children and their families when evaluating speech and language development.

Methods of Assessment

Parents often realize that their child has a speech problem, but may not know what to do about it. Many people believe that children eventually outgrow such impairments. Indeed, some children have developmentally appropriate ***misarticulations*** that will improve as they grow older. For example, a 3-year-old may pronounce "r" as "w" as in "wabbit" (rabbit) or "s" as "th" as in "thong" (song). Nevertheless, children who demonstrate speech or speech patterns that are not developmentally appropriate should be referred to a speech therapist for a thorough evaluation. A hearing test should also be included in this evaluation to rule out the possibility of a hearing loss that may be affecting the child's speech. Speech and hearing clinics are frequently associated with colleges and universities, medical centers, child development centers, and public school systems. A listing of certified speech and hearing specialists can be obtained by writing to the American Speech, Language, and Hearing Association (see Appendix C).

Common Disorders

The term speech impairment has many different meanings to persons working with children. For some, the term refers only to more obvious problems, such as stuttering, lisping, or unintelligent speech patterns. For others, a wide range of conditions are cause for concern, e.g., a monotone voice, nasality, improper pitch of the voice, a voice tone that is too high or too low, omissions of certain letter sounds, or misarticulations of word sounds.

The range of speech and language disorders is as great as the variations in normal speech and language development (Cohen, 1994). Some deviant speech patterns include:

- no speech by two years of age
- stuttering
- substitution of word sounds
- rate of speech that is too fast or unusually slow
- monotone voice
- no improvement in speech development
- unintelligent speech by three years of age

Management

Parents, teachers, and caregivers must not overlook their importance as role models in a child's speech and language development. Early language experiences and stimulation encourage the child's effective use of language. However, teachers and caregivers should not hesitate to refer children for professional evaluation if their speech and language patterns interfere with or make communication difficult. Early recognition and treatment is critical for helping young children successfully overcome many speech impairments.

NUTRITIONAL ASSESSMENT

There is no question that the quality of children's diets has a direct effect on their behavior and state of health. Problems related to over- and under-consumption of food and nutrients are of growing concern. Rising food costs and difficult economic conditions are forcing many families to sacrifice the quality and quantity of food they purchase and serve. Television advertising also has a negative influence on children's food selections. Increased consumption of "fast foods" and the extensive use of prepackaged foods in meal preparation add to a further decline in the quality of many children's diets.

Direct observations of children's behavior and physical appearance can provide some preliminary information about their nutritional and general health status. Many signs can be easily noted during daily health checks. For example, facial *pallor*, dry skin, or *lethargy* may be indications of poor food habits. Healthy, well-nourished children usually exhibit the following physical signs:

- height appropriate for age
- weight appropriate for height
- bright, clear eyes—no puffiness, crusting or paleness of inner lids
- clear skin—good color; no pallor or scaliness
- teeth—appropriate number for age; no caries or *mottling*
- gums—pink and firm; not puffy, dark red or bleeding
- lips—soft, moist; no cracking at corner of mouth
- tongue—pink; no cracking, smooth spots or deep red color

Assessment Methods

Selecting an appropriate method for assessing children's nutritional status depends upon the child's age, reason for evaluation, type of information desired, and available resources. The methods most commonly used include:

- dietary assessment—is used to determine adequacy of nutrient intake and other nutritional deficiencies. The child's eating patterns are monitored for various lengths of time (24 hours, 1–7 days) and actual food intake is recorded, Figure 4–8. Dietary information is then analyzed for nutritional content according to one of several methods, e.g., Food Guide Pyramid, nutrient analysis, RDAs (see Chapter 13) to determine if *nutrient intake* is adequate.

- anthropometric assessment—is based on simple measurements of height, weight, and head circumference. Comparisons are made with standardized norms (see Appendix B). Additional measurements of *skinfold* thickness and mid-arm circumference are sometimes also taken (Pipes, 1993). These measurements yield specific information about a child's growth.

NUTRITIONAL ASSESSMENT

Dear Parent:

Nutrition is a very important part of our program. In order for us to plan appropriate nutrition-education activities and menus to meet your child's needs, we need to know your child's eating patterns. This information will also help us obtain an overview of the eating habits of young children as a group. Please take the time to fill out this questionnaire carefully.

NAME ______________________________ AGE ________ DATE __________

1. How many days a week does your child eat the following meals or snacks?
   a morning meal __________
   a lunch or midday meal __________
   an evening meal __________
   a midmorning snack __________
   a midafternoon snack __________
   an evening snack __________
   snack during the night __________
2. When is your child most hungry?
   morning __________
   noon __________
   evening __________
3. What foods does your child dislike?
   ____
4. Is your child on a special diet? Yes __________ No __________
   If yes, why? ____
   Describe diet ____
   Diet prescribed by whom? ____
5. Does your child eat things not usually considered food e.g., paste, dirt, paper? __________
   If yes, how often? ____
   What is eaten?____
6. Is your child taking a vitamin or mineral supplement?
   Yes __________ No __________ If yes, what kind? __________
7. Does your child have any dental problems that might create a problem when eating certain foods?____________________
8. Has your child ever been treated by a dentist?__________
9. Does your child have any diet-related health problems?
   Diabetes__________ Allergies____________________
   Other______________________________
10. Is your child taking any medication for a diet-related health problem?
    ____
11. How much water does your child normally drink throughout the day?
    ____
12. Please list as accurately as possible what your child eats and drinks on a typical day. If yesterday was a typical day, you may use those foods and drinks.

TIME	PLACE	FOOD	AMOUNT

Figure 4–8 Sample questionnaire for obtaining information about a child's eating habits.

- clinical assessment—involves observing a child for signs of nutritional deficiency, Table 4–3. It is not a reliable method because of its subjective nature and the fact that physical symptoms often do not appear until a deficiency is severe.
- biochemical assessment—involves laboratory testing of various body tissues and fluids, such as urinalysis or hemoglobin (testing for iron level) to validate concerns related to over- or under-consumption of nutrients. These tests are usually ordered by a health care provider and performed by trained laboratory technicians.

Common Disorders

Teachers and caregivers need to be alert to several nutritional problems that may affect children's health. Poor dietary habits, resulting in inadequate intake of essential nutrients, can lead to malnutrition over a period of time. Vitamins A and C,

TABLE 4–3 Physical Signs of Malnutrition

TISSUE	SIGN	CAUSE
Face	Pallor	Niacin, iron deficiency
	Scaling of skin around nostrils	Riboflavin, B_6 deficiency
Eyes	Hardening of cornea and lining: pale lining	Iron deficiency
	Foamy spots in cornea	Vitamin A deficiency
Lips	Redness: swelling of mouth and lips; cracking at corners of mouth	Riboflavin deficiency
Teeth	Decayed or missing	Excess sugar (or poor dental hygiene)
	Mottled enamel	Excess fluoride
Tongue	Red, raw, cracked, swollen	Niacin deficiency
	Magenta color	Riboflavin deficiency
	Pale	Iron deficiency
Gums	Spongy, red, bleeding	Vitamin C deficiency
Skin	Dry, flaking	Vitamin A deficiency
	Small underskin hemorrhages	Vitamin C deficiency
Nails	Brittle, ridged	Iron deficiency

iron, and calcium are the nutrients most commonly missing from children's diets today. Long-term use of certain medications can also interfere with the absorption of some nutrients. Many children are undernourished simply because they do not get enough to eat. These children are often below average in height and weight, irritable, anemic, and listless (see Appendix B). Their poor state of nutrition also limits their ability to learn.

Not all malnourished children are thin and emaciated. Children who are overweight can also be malnourished. Because the bulk of their diet often consists of sugars and starches, they appear to be well fed, yet lack many of the nutrients essential for good health. Inactivity also contributes significantly to their weight problems.

Another serious nutritional health problem is that of obesity (Schlicker, 1994). Approximately 12 to 30 percent of all children in the United States are considered overweight for their age. Suggested causes include metabolic disorders, emotional stress, heredity, lack of physical activity and, perhaps most significant, poor eating habits.

Children who are overweight or obese often face additional health problems. Excess weight limits their participation in much needed physical activity. Children who are obese tend to be less coordinated, experience shortness of breath with exertion, and tire more quickly. Teasing, ridicule, and rejection by others can also lead to maladjustment problems. Children who are overweight also have a tendency to remain overweight as adults and, therefore, face an increased risk of medical complications, including heart disease, stroke, and diabetes.

Management

Obesity in young children cannot be ignored. Prevention is always the most effective method. However, promising results can also be obtained by taking action while a child is young and still in the process of establishing lifelong eating habits (Kennedy, 1995). For maximum success, a treatment program for weight control must include the cooperation of the child, parents, teachers, and health personnel.

The goal of any weight control program is to help young children and their parents develop a new awareness about:

- meal planning and nutritious eating habits
- methods for increasing children's daily activity level, Figure 4–9 (For example, children can be asked to run errands, walk a pet, or help with daily household chores.)
- acquainting children with new outside interests, hobbies, or activities, such as swimming, dance, neighborhood baseball, or learning to ride a bike (Involvement in fun activities can divert children's attention away from food.)
- finding ways to help children experience success and develop a positive self-image. (For example, praise received for simple achievements can make children feel good about themselves—"Lonnie, you did a nice job of sweeping all the sand off the sidewalk." For many children, praise replaces food as an important source of satisfaction.)

Figure 4–9 Increasing children's activity level can help to control their weight.

Long-term weight control is enhanced by attending to all aspects of a child's well-being, e.g., physical, emotional, and social. Children should not be placed on weight reduction programs unless they are under a doctor's supervision. Weight reduction programs must be designed to meet all the nutritional needs of children to ensure normal growth and development. Education and role modeling are also important factors in the management of nutrition and promotion of healthier lifestyles.

REFERRALS

The initial step in making successful referrals involves gaining the parent's trust and cooperation. Referrals are of little use unless parents follow through with recommendations. Knowing something about the beliefs, customs, habits, and people of the community can influence the way in which referrals are conducted. For example, mistrust of the medical profession, poverty, job conflicts, religious beliefs, a lack of transportation, or education will certainly affect a parent's response.

Meeting with the child's parents, or calling them on the telephone, are usually the most effective methods for making referrals:

Caregiver: "I am concerned about Ryan's vision. On several occasions, I have noticed that his right eye turns inward more than the left eye and that he holds his head close to materials when he is working. Have you observed any of these behaviors at home?

Parent: "Yes, but we didn't know if it was anything to worry about."

Caregiver: "I cannot be sure if Ryan has anything wrong with his eyes, but the behaviors I have observed can sometimes be an indication of vision problems and should be checked carefully by an eye specialist. If you need help locating a doctor or making an appointment, I will be glad to help you. I will also give you a written copy of my observations to take with you. Please let me know the date of Ryan's appointment after you have made it."

If such personal contacts with parents are not possible, a well-written letter is also appropriate. Parents should be given copies of any screening test results or anecdotal notes, which they can forward to the specialist who will be evaluating the child. This gesture will improve the efficiency of the referral process. Also, a teacher who is familiar with local services, such as hospitals, clinics, health departments, medical specialists, private and public service agencies, and various sources of funding can be very helpful to parents in obtaining the comprehensive medical care and assistance that the child requires.

Follow-up contacts with parents should be made in a week to determine if arrangements have been made for further diagnostic testing or treatments and again after the appointment has been completed. Any results or recommendations that might affect the child's experiences in school can be shared at this time. Knowledge of this information enables child caregivers to make any necessary adjustments in the instructional program or learning environment. Follow-up contacts can also be used to reinforce the positive influences of preventive health care on children's performance and convey to parents a genuine interest in their child's well-being.

Summary

Teachers and caregivers play an important role in the health assessment of young children. In addition to their skillful observations, teachers have access to a variety of health information concerning each child. Permanent health records provide a rich source of background and current information that can be useful in promoting good health and for identifying potentially handicapping conditions. Results obtained from routine screening procedures, e.g., measures of height and weight, vision, hearing, dental, nutritional, developmental, can also help to shed light on children's disabilities. Caregivers must remember that most routine screening tests have certain limitations and, as a result, a child's performance on such tests must be interpreted carefully.

The process of assessing children's health involves gathering information from a variety of sources. Teachers can initiate the referral process with reasonable assurance when it is based on documented information. Ideally, the reasons for making a referral should be discussed with the child's parents. A follow-up contact is necessary to determine if the recommendations have been carried out.

Suggested Activities

1. Locate and read instructions for administering the Snellen E and HOTV eye screening tests. With another student, practice testing one another.
2. Devise a monitoring system whereby daily food intakes are recorded for each child in a group setting. This information is primarily intended to provide information about daily food consumption to parents. Factors to consider are:
   a. What nutritional information is needed? In what form?
   b. Who is responsible for collecting this data?
   c. How can this information be obtained efficiently?
   d. How can food intake records increase opportunities for communication with parents?
   e. What other uses can food intake records serve for the caregiver?
3. Collect samples of child history forms from several centers or day care facilities in your town. Review the types of information that are requested most often. Design your own form.
4. Attend a signing class. Learn to say "hello" and "good-bye" in sign language.
5. Measure and record the heights and weights of fifteen children, ages 3–5, in a day care center. Use the Growth Charts (Appendix B) to evaluate your data. Are most children's height/weight "normal" based on their age? Overweight? Underweight? What conclusions can you draw?
6. Obtain an audiometer. Have someone demonstrate the technique for testing hearing. Encourage students to practice on one another.
7. Research or develop several activities to improve children's cardiovascular fitness.

Chapter Review

A. Define the following terms:

1. audiologist
2. conductive hearing loss
3. sensorineural hearing loss
4. receptive vocabulary
5. expressive vocabulary
6. anthropometric assessment
7. nutrient deficiency

B. Multiple Choice. Select the best answer.

1. Amblyopia is the result of
   a. imbalance of the eye muscle
   b. infection
   c. trauma or injury
   d. an unknown cause
2. Children's health records are useful for
   a. identifying possible problem areas
   b. evaluating the success of treatments
   c. following a child's progress
   d. all of these
3. A recognizable imbalance of the eye muscle is called
   a. hyperopia
   b. myopia
   c. strabismus
   d. none of these
4. Biochemical assessment involves
   a. measurements of height and weight
   b. observable signs of nutrient deficiency
   c. laboratory tests
   d. food intake records
5. Referrals should be based on
   a. screening test results
   b. teacher observations
   c. parent concerns
   d. all of these
6. Hearing losses are often found in children who
   a. are from low income families
   b. have allergies and frequent ear infections
   c. are small for their age
   d. live in colder climates
7. A healthy approach to the management of obesity in children can include all of the following except
   a. providing well-balanced meals and snacks
   b. involving the child in a new sport
   c. drastically limiting the child's caloric intake
   d. reducing the amount of time spent watching television
8. Lettitia, age 3 1/2, refuses to drink milk or eat any vegetables except corn and peas. What methods are available to caregivers for evaluating the nutritional adequacy of her diet?
   a. biochemical assessment
   b. dietary assessment
   c. anthropometric assessment

9. Nutrients that are commonly lacking in children's diets include:
   a. calcium, iron, vitamins A and C
   b. fat and protein
   c. protein and calcium
   d. carbohydrates and iron

C. Select the screening test that would be recommended for children with the following behaviors, signs, or symptoms. Place the appropriate code letter in each space.

H Hearing screening
V Vision screening
D Developmental screening
HW Height and weight
Dt Dental screening
S Speech evaluation
N Nutrition evaluation

_____ 1. frequent blinking; often closes one eye to see
_____ 2. stutters whenever he is tense and in a hurry to speak
_____ 3. usually listless; appears very small for her chronological age
_____ 4. stumbles over objects in the classroom; frequently walks into play equipment in the play yard
_____ 5. very crooked teeth that make his speech difficult to understand
_____ 6. seems to ignore the teacher's requests; shouts at the other children to get their attention
_____ 7. awkward; has great difficulty running and climbing; tires easily because of obesity
_____ 8. a five-year-old who has trouble catching a ball, pedaling a bicycle and cutting with scissors
_____ 9. appears to focus on objects with one eye while the other eye looks off in another direction
_____ 10. multiple cavities; in recent weeks has not been able to concentrate on any task
_____ 11. is extremely shy and withdrawn; spends the majority of her time playing alone, imitating the actions of other children
_____ 12. seems extremely hungry at snack time; always asks for extra servings and takes food left on other children's plates when the teacher isn't looking
_____ 13. becomes hoarse after shouting and yelling during outdoor time
_____ 14. arrives at school each morning with potato chips, candy, or a cupcake
_____ 15. a 4 1/2-year-old who whines and has tantrums to get his own way

References

Allen, K. E., and Marotz, L. 1994. *Developmental Profiles.* Albany, NY: Delmar Publishers Inc.

Batshaw, M. L., and Perret, Y. 1992. *Children With Disabilities.* Baltimore, MD: Paul H. Brooks

Bishop, V. 1988. Making Choices in Functional Vision Evaluation: Noodles, Needles, and Haystacks. *Journal of Visual Impairment and Blindness,* 82(3): 94–99.

Brown, M., and Collar, M. 1982, September/October. "Research—Effects of Prior Preparation on the Preschooler's Vision and Hearing Screening." *Journal of Maternal/Child Nursing,* 7(5): 323–28.

Cohen, L., and Spenciner, L. 1994. *Assessment of Young Children.* New York: Longman.

Jaffe, M. 1991. *Understanding Parenting.* Dubuque, IA: Wm. C. Brown.

Kennedy, E., and Goldberg, J. 1995. What Are American Children Eating? *Nutrition Reviews,* 53(5): 111–126.

Peterson, N. L. 1987. *Early Intervention for Handicapped and At-Risk Children.* Denver, CO: Love Publishing Company.

Pipes, P. L. 1993. *Nutrition in Infancy and Childhood.* St. Louis, MO: C. V. Mosby Co.

Schlicker, S., Borra, S., and Regan, C. 1994. The Weight and Fitness Status of United States Children. *Nutrition Reviews,* 52(1): 11–17.

Vision Screening In Schools. New York: National Society to Prevent Blindness.

Wasserman, R., Croft, C., and Brotherton, S. 1992. Preschool Vision Screening in Pediatric Practice: A Study from the Pediatric Research in Office Settings (PROS) Network. *Pediatrics,* May 1992: 834–838.

Watt, M., Roberts, J., and Zeisel, S. 1993. Ear Infections in Young Children: The Role of the Early Childhood Educator. *Young Children,* 49(1): 65–72.

Additional Reading

Allen, K. E., and Schwartz, I. S. 1996. *The Exceptional Child: Inclusion in Early Childhood Education.* Albany, NY: Delmar Publishers Inc.

Bowe, F. G. 1995. *Birth to Five: Early Childhood Special Education.* Albany, NY: Delmar Publishers Inc.

First, L., and Palfrey, J. 1994. The Infant or Young Child with Developmental Delay. *The New England Journal of Medicine,* 330: 478–483.

Hills, T. 1993. Assessment in Context—Teachers and Children at Work. *Young Children,* 48(5): 20–28.

Lyon, M., and Lyon, D. 1986. Early Detection of Hearing Loss: A Follow-up Study. *Canadian Journal of Public Health,* 77: 221–224.

Miller, R., 1996. *The Developmentally Appropriate Inclusive Classroom in Early Education.* Albany, NY: Delmar Publishers Inc.

National Health Statistics: NCHS Growth Curves for Children. 1976. Series II, No. 165, U. S. Department of Health, Education, and Welfare, Monthly Vital Statistics Report, U. S. Government Printing Office.

National Institutes of Health. 1993. *NIH Consensus Statement (Early Identification of Hearing Impairment in Infants and Young Children,* 11(1): 1–25.

Spiegel, D., Fitzgerald, J., and Cunningham, J. 1993. Parent Perceptions of Preschooler's Literacy Development: Implications for Home-School Partnerships. *Young Children,* 48(5): 74–79.

Waldron, K. A. 1996. *Introduction to a Special Education: The Inclusive Classroom.* Albany, NY: Delmar Publishers Inc.

Yoshinaga-Itano, C. 1995. Universal Hearing Screening for Infants: Simple, Risk-Free, Beneficial, and Justified. *Audiology Today,* 7(1): 13.

Chapter 5

Conditions Affecting Children's Health

Terms to Know

anemia
endocrine
alignment
hormone
hyperglycemia
dehydration
seizures
hyperactivity
syndrome

Objectives

After studying this chapter, you should be able to:

- Describe seven chronic conditions that affect children's health.
- List the symptoms of seven chronic health conditions.
- State the factors that make chronic health problems difficult to identify in young children.
- Describe good body mechanics for sitting, standing, and lifting.
- Identify the caregiver's role in dealing with chronic health problems.

More important than the occasional illnesses young children experience are chronic or long-term health problems. For many children, major social factors contribute significantly to the development of chronic illnesses and serve as barriers to improvement of their health. When evaluating conditions affecting a child's health, one must consider:

- financial limitations that may affect the family's access to medical care and good nutrition
- exposure to chemical pollution of water, air, and food supplies
- increased stress
- disruption of the traditional family unit
- exposure to persuasive television advertising

Often, chronic conditions go unrecognized because their signs and symptoms are less obvious than those of most acute illnesses. Some chronic health problems, such as sickle cell anemia and diabetes, may be present from the time of birth. Other chronic conditions, such as seizures and lead poisoning, may develop slowly so their appearance is difficult to detect; the child may not even realize that something is wrong. The closeness of parents may also make it more difficult for them to recognize and accept chronic health problems in their child.

Undiagnosed and untreated health conditions can interfere with the development of early learning skills. Teachers and caregivers should work closely with parents to identify and refer children with existing health problems to appropriate professionals for evaluation and treatment. The earlier chronic health problems are identified and treatment is begun, the less negative their effect will be on children's ability to learn.

FATIGUE

Most children experience periods of fatigue and listlessness from time to time. Growth spurts, late bedtimes, a morning of strenuous outdoor play, or recovery from a recent illness may account for these occasional incidences. However, when a child shows repeated or continuous signs of fatigue, parents and teachers should be concerned.

Typically, young children have remarkable vigor, enthusiasm, and interest in daily activities. Chronic fatigue is not a normal condition for young children, and may be a sign of some other health problem, including:

- poor nutrition
- chronic infection
- periods of rapid growth
- insufficient hours of rest and sleep
- medications
- *anemia*
- *endocrine* (hormonal) disorders
- allergies
- lead poisoning

Careful evaluation of the child's personal habits and lifestyle may reveal a reason for chronic fatigue. A complete medical examination can detect any existing health problems. If no specific cause can be identified, there are several steps parents and caregivers can take to improve the child's general well-being:

- better dietary habits
- moderate exercise and activity
- increased rest, e.g., naps, earlier bedtimes, brief periods of rest during the day
- alternating periods of activity and rest
- coping with stress

Teachers and caregivers can also incorporate many of these remedies into daily classroom routines.

POSTURE

Good posture and correct body *alignment* are necessary for many of the physical activities children engage in, such as walking, jumping, running, skipping, standing, sitting, and balancing. Many problems related to poor posture can be avoided by helping young children develop good postural habits from the beginning.

Orthopedic problems (those relating to skeletal and muscular systems) are not common among young children. However, there are several conditions that warrant early diagnosis and treatment:

- birth injuries, e.g., hip dislocation, fractured collarbone
- abnormal or unusual walking patterns, e.g., limping, pigeon-toed
- bowed legs
- knock-knees
- flat feet
- unusual curvature of the spine
- difference in length of the extremities (arms and legs)

Some irregularities of posture disappear spontaneously as young children mature. For example, it is not uncommon for infants and toddlers to have bowed legs or to later walk slightly pigeon-toed. By age three or four, these problems often correct themselves. If these conditions persist beyond the age of four, they should be evaluated by health professionals. Early detection and treatment can prevent many long-term or permanent deformities.

Good posture is an excellent topic for classroom discussion, demonstrations, rhythm and movement activities, games, and art projects, Figure 5–1. Concepts and techniques that children learn can be shared with parents so they are reinforced at home (Pica, 1995). Parent newsletters can include suggestions for good posture, children can illustrate basic posture concepts in pictures, and parents can be invited to attend a class demonstration of good body alignment.

Although the acts of sitting and standing seem quite natural, it is important that children learn the following good body mechanics:

- Sit squarely in a chair with the back against the back of the chair and both feet flat on the floor.

Figure 5–1 Good posture is an excellent topic for rhythm and movement activities.

- Sit on the floor with legs crossed in front or with both legs extended out in front. Children should be discouraged from sitting in a "W" position.
- Stand with the shoulders square, the chin up, and the chest out. Distribute body weight evenly over both feet to avoid placing added stress on one or the other hip joints.
- Lift and carry heavy objects using the stronger muscles of the arms and legs rather than the weaker muscles of the back. Get close to the object to be lifted. Stand with the feet slightly apart to give a wider base of support, and stoop down to lift rather than just bend over.

DIABETES

The incidence of diabetes among young children is relatively low. However, teachers and caregivers should be familiar with the signs, symptoms, and treatment of diabetes. When diabetes appears in young children, it is more difficult to control. Growth, unpredictable changes in activity levels, irregular eating habits, and frequent exposure to respiratory infections challenge the successful management of the juvenile diabetic (Balik, 1986).

Diabetes is a chronic health problem that occurs when the pancreas does not produce enough insulin. Insulin is a *hormone*. Its major function is to aid in the storage of sugars and starches ingested in the diet and later to release this as energy to the body cells. Absence or inadequate amounts of insulin allow sugar to circulate freely in the blood stream rather than be stored and released when needed. A high level of sugar in the blood is called *hyperglycemia* or diabetic coma. Without medical treatment, this condition gradually worsens and can eventually lead to convulsions and death. Early signs of diabetes include:

- weight loss
- fatigue
- frequent urination
- *dehydration*
- excessive thirst and hunger
- frequent infections
- slow healing
- itching and dry skin

It is important that teachers and caregivers be aware of any diabetic children in their programs. In addition to the potential dangers of undiagnosed diabetes, there are also complications associated with its treatment. Most diabetic children must take daily injections of insulin. A dose that is too small or too large requires different emergency treatment (see Chapter 10).

Valuable information about the child's condition can be gathered by meeting with parents before the diabetic child begins to attend a school or child care center. Parents can alert caregivers to changes in their child's behavior and appearance that may signal impending complications. Caregivers also need to ask about dietary restrictions and management so these can be followed carefully while the child is in care, Figure 5–2. Plans for handling emergencies can also be worked out

Figure 5–2 It is important to follow all special dietary restrictions.

with parents at this time. Telephone numbers and names of contact persons should be reviewed with parents periodically.

Equipped with this knowledge, a teacher is in a better position to recognize and cope with emergencies. This can be a source of comfort to the parents of a diabetic child for often they feel uneasy about leaving their child in the care of others. Teachers are also in a unique position to help diabetic children learn to accept their condition and lead well-adjusted lives.

SEIZURES

It is not uncommon to have children who experience *seizures* in a child care setting. Unlike many other chronic health problems, mention of terms such as seizures, convulsions, or epilepsy arouse feelings of fear and anxiety in many persons. Prior knowledge and planning enable teachers and caregivers to respond with skill and confidence when caring for children who experience this disorder, Table 5–1.

TABLE 5–1 How Caregivers Can Help a Child Who Experiences Seizures

1. Be aware of any children with seizure disorders in the classroom. Find out what the child's seizures are like, if medication is taken to control the seizures, and whether the child is limited in any way by the disorder.
2. Know emergency first aid measures. Develop guidelines for staff members to follow whenever a child has a seizure; review the guidelines periodically.
3. Use the presence of an epileptic child in the classroom as a learning experience for other children. Provide simple explanations about what epilepsy is; encourage children to ask questions and express their feelings. Help children learn to accept those who have special problems.
4. Gain a better understanding of epilepsy and seizure disorders. Read books and articles, view films, and talk with health professionals and parents.
5. Obtain and read the following books and pamphlets that are written for children. Share them with children in the classroom.
   - *All About Epilepsy,* Epilepsy Foundation of America, 4351 Garden City Drive, Landover, MD 20785.
   - Bookbinder, S. R. *Mainstreaming: What Every Child Needs to Know About Disabilities*. Exceptional Parent Press, 296 Boylston Street, Third Floor, Boston, MA 02116.
   - Silverstein, A. *Epilepsy*. Philadelphia: J. B. Lippincott Co., 1975.
   - Young, M. *What Difference Does it Make, Danny?* London: Andre Deutsch Limited, 1980.

Figure 5–3 Teachers need to know what to do in the event of a seizure.

The term seizure describes a cluster of symptoms rather than a particular disease, Figure 5–3. Seizures are caused by abnormal electrical impulses within the brain. This abnormal activity leads to involuntary or uncontrollable movements of various body parts. Their intensity varies, depending on the type of seizure. Some seizures involve only a momentary lapse of attention or interruption of thought while others may last several minutes and cause vigorous, spasmodic contractions of the entire body. Temporary loss of consciousness, frothing, and loss of bowel and bladder control may also accompany some types of seizures.

The exact cause of a seizure is often difficult to determine. However, several conditions are known to initiate seizure activity in young children:

- fevers that are high or rise rapidly (especially in infants)
- brain damage
- infections that affect the central nervous system, such as meningitis or encephalitis
- tumors
- head injuries
- lead, mercury, and carbon monoxide poisoning
- hypoglycemia (low blood sugar)
- drug reactions

Heredity has also been suggested as a possible cause of seizures. In many cases, the exact cause may never be known.

Seizures are generally classified according to the pattern of symptoms the child presents (Whaley, 1995). The most common types of seizures are:

- febrile
- petit mal
- grand mal
- focal
- temporal lobe

Approximately 5–10 percent of all infants and children under three years of age experience febrile seizures (Camfield, 1993). These seizures are triggered by high fever and may cause a child to lose consciousness and have involuntary jerking movements involving the entire body. Febrile seizures usually disappear when the fever subsides, and are, therefore, not thought to be serious or to result in any permanent damage.

Caregivers may be the first to notice the subtle, abnormal behaviors exhibited by children with petit mal seizures. This type of seizure is characterized by momentary losses of attention, including:

- repeated incidences of daydreaming
- staring off into space
- a blank appearance
- brief fluttering of the eyes
- temporary interruption of speech or activity
- twitching or dropping of objects

Petit mal seizures generally occur in children 4–10 years of age and are characterized by a brief loss of consciousness, usually lasting ten to thirty seconds. Children will suddenly stop the activity in which they are engaged and resume it after the seizure subsides. Parents should be informed of the teacher's or caregiver's observations and encouraged to contact the child's physician.

Grand mal seizures are the most common form of seizure disorder. Convulsive movements usually involve the entire body, often making them frightening to the observer. Some children experience an aura or warning immediately before a seizure begins. This warning may be in the form of a certain sound, smell, taste, sensation, or visual cue. Sudden rigidity or stiffness (tonic phase) is followed by a loss of consciousness and generalized muscular contractions (clonic phase). When the seizure ends, children will usually awaken briefly. They may complain of headache or dizziness before falling asleep for a period of several hours.

The involuntary convulsive movements of a focal seizure begin at the tip of an extremity and may spread toward the body trunk. The child does not always lose consciousness with this type of seizure. Spontaneous episodes of unusual behavior are a feature of temporal lobe seizures; the behavior is considered unusual because it is inappropriate for the circumstances. For example, a child may burst out in sudden hysterical laughter, utter unintelligible sounds, run around in circles, or cry out without apparent reason. It is also common to experience an aura before this type of seizure begins. Although there is usually not a total loss of consciousness during the seizure, children may appear drowsy or confused for a few minutes following the episode and should be encouraged to rest for a short time.

Most seizures can be controlled with medication. It is vital that children take their medications every day, even after seizures are under control. Initially, children may experience undesirable side effects to these drugs, such as drowsiness, nausea, and dizziness. However, these problems usually disappear after a short time. Children should be monitored closely by their physician to ensure that prescribed medications and dosages continue to be effective in controlling seizure activity and do not interfere with learning.

Each time a child experiences a seizure, parents should be notified. Also, any time seizures change in character or begin to recur after having once been under control, parents should be informed and encouraged to contact the child's physician. Informing parents enables them to keep accurate records of seizure activity and to monitor medical treatment. Teachers and caregivers should also complete a brief, written report documenting their observations following each seizure. The report should include a description of:

- events preceding the seizure
- length of seizure
- type and location of convulsive movements
- additional observations, e.g., breathing difficulties, loss of bowel or bladder control, skin color
- condition of the child following the seizure, e.g., injuries, length of sleep, complaints of headache, speech, memory

Completed reports should be filed in the child's permanent health folder. This information can be very useful to the child's physician for diagnosing a seizure disorder and evaluating treatments.

Teachers and caregivers can play an important role in helping young children accept and cope with their seizure disorder. They can also help other children develop a positive attitude toward persons who experience seizures. The teacher's reactions and displays of genuine acceptance can teach respect and understanding for persons with special problems.

ALLERGIES

Allergies are the greatest single cause of chronic health problems among young children. It is believed that allergies affect as many as one in every four children. The severity of allergic conditions ranges from symptoms that are only mildly annoying to those that are disabling and severely restrict a child's activity.

A substance capable of triggering an allergic reaction in the body is called an allergen. Most children are not bothered by these substances. However, because the allergic child's immune system is more sensitive, an allergic reaction takes place whenever they come in contact with a particular allergen (Synoground, 1990; Baker, 1980).

Allergic reactions are generally classified according to the body site where symptoms most commonly occur:

- ingestants—cause digestive upsets and respiratory problems. Common examples include foods such as milk, citrus fruits, eggs, wheat, chocolate, and oral medications.

- inhalants—affect the respiratory system causing a runny nose, cough, wheezing, and watery eyes. Examples include pollens, molds, dust, and animal dander.
- contactants—frequently cause skin eruptions such as rashes, hives, and eczema. Common contactants include soaps, cosmetics, dyes, fibers, medications placed directly on the skin, and some plants, e.g., poison ivy and poison oak.
- injectables—result in respiratory, digestive, and skin disturbances. Examples of injectables include insect bites, especially those of bees, wasps, and hornets, and medications that are injected directly into the body.

In addition to the acute distress experienced during allergic reactions, these children often do not feel well much of the time (Voignier, 1980). To understand how allergies affect them, a simple comparison can be made with the generalized discomfort felt during a cold or case of intestinal flu. Certainly, no child can fully benefit from any learning experience under such conditions. For these reasons, allergies may be an important contributing factor in many behavior and learning problems, including disruptive behaviors, hyperactivity, chronic fatigue, disinterest, irritability, and poor concentration.

Teachers and caregivers can be instrumental in recognizing the early signs of allergic conditions in young children. Daily observations and anecdotal records can help detect patterns of repetitious symptoms that may otherwise be blamed on everyday childhood illnesses (Marks, 1983). Common signs and symptoms of allergic disorders include:

- frequent colds and ear infections
- chronic congestion, e.g., runny nose, cough, or throat clearing
- headaches
- frequent nosebleeds
- unexplained stomachaches
- hives, eczema, or other skin rashes
- wheezing or shortness of breath
- intermittent or permanent hearing losses
- reactions to foods or medications
- dark circles beneath the eyes
- mottled tongue
- frequent rubbing, twitching, or picking of the nose
- chronic redness of the throat
- swollen eyelids
- irritability

At present, there are no known cures for allergic conditions. Sensitivities are thought to be inherited and are seldom outgrown. However, the types and numbers of substances that a child is allergic to can change periodically. This may give the impression that an allergy has disappeared, only to resurface and become troublesome again at some later time.

Symptoms and complications of allergies are generally less severe and easier to control if they are identified early. Treatment is aimed primarily at limiting a child's exposure to annoying allergens. In some instances, steps can be taken to completely remove these substances from the child's environment. For example, milk and milk products can be totally eliminated from the child's diet, or a dog kept outdoors. In other cases, only the amount of exposure can be controlled, as in allergies to dust or pollens. Smoking should always be discouraged around children with respiratory allergies because it can aggravate and intensify their problems (Child Health Alert, 1991). Left untreated, allergies can lead to more serious chronic health problems, including chronic bronchitis, permanent hearing loss, asthma, or emphysema.

Antihistamines, decongestants, and bronchodilators are commonly used to treat the symptoms of respiratory allergies. However, a major drawback is that most medications provide only temporary relief. They also have a tendency to cause drowsiness and, therefore, may interfere with children's cognitive abilities and concentration. Children taking such medications should be closely supervised, especially during outdoor times and activities that involve risk. In some cases, allergy shots (desensitization therapy) are given when other forms of treatment have been unsuccessful.

Most allergic conditions are not life threatening. However, *bee stings, sensitivities to medications, and asthma attacks can lead to death.* In these emergency situations, a child can quickly go into shock and experience extreme difficulty breathing. Prompt medical treatment is necessary to save the child's life.

The emotional effects of allergies on children's lives are often overlooked. Frequently, these children are overly protected from many everyday experiences in order to avoid the risk of unpleasant reactions. They are continually reminded to be cautious so that exposure to offending allergens is limited. In some cases, severe allergies may actually place limits on a child's level of physical activity. Eventually, such feelings can lead to excessive fear, withdrawn behaviors, and other maladjustment problems.

It is also important that children not be allowed to use their allergies as a means of gaining attention or special privileges. Instead, they can learn to become independent and self-confident in coping with their problems. Caregivers can help children learn to make simple adjustments in their daily lifestyles. Also, parenting classes and individual counseling can teach parents the skills they need to help children achieve these goals.

ASTHMA

Asthma is a significant health problem affecting millions of children. For many young children, asthma is both a chronic and acute respiratory disorder affecting boys twice as often as girls (Mailick, 1994; Synoground, 1990). It is commonly associated with allergic reactions to airborne allergens (e.g., pollen, animal dander, dust), foods (e.g., wheat, eggs, milk), and respiratory infections. Symptoms of acute attacks include wheezing, coughing, and difficulty breathing, especially exhalation. These symptoms are caused by swelling and spasms of the respiratory tract (bronchial tubes). Asthma attacks are thought to be triggered by stress, exposure to offending allergens and second-hand smoke, vigorous exercise, changes in temperature, fatigue, and occasionally by emotional upsets (especially anger). Treatment for asthma consists of removing irritating allergens from the child's environment and taking medication to control the symptoms. In child care settings, asthmatic children should participate in regular activities as much as their condition allows.

ECZEMA

Eczema is an inflammatory skin condition commonly associated with allergies. Patches of red, irritated skin may appear on the cheeks of an infant. Older children may develop itchy, scaly areas, either dry or moist, on their knees, elbows, wrists, or back of hands. Eczema frequently worsens in the winter when weather turns cold and full-length clothing is worn. Irritated skin should be watched closely so infection does not develop. Older children may be sensitive about their appearance and refuse to wear lighter clothing when summer arrives. Hydrocortisone creams are often used to treat the irritated skin.

ATTENTION DEFICIT DISORDERS (with or without hyperactivity)

The term ***hyperactivity*** is often used inappropriately to label children who are actually behaving within normal limits (Holvoet, 1989). Young children are, by nature, exceedingly energetic, curious, impatient, and restless, Figure 5–4.

Attention deficit disorder (ADD) is a developmental disorder that includes a variety of learning and behavior problems. Children may also have attention deficit disorder with hyperactivity (ADDH). This condition is sometimes also referred to as attention deficit hyperactivity disorder or (ADHD). The American Psychiatric Association (1987) defines the disorder as "a ***syndrome*** of attention and behavior disturbances that may improve when stimulant-type drugs are administered."

Despite attempts to describe the condition more precisely, much controversy still remains about its causes, diagnosis, and effective management. However, it is known that boys are affected 4–5 times more often than girls. Some of the behaviors typically used to describe a child with attention deficit disorder include:

- explosive
- inattentive
- fidgety
- aggressive
- defiant
- forgetful
- easily frustrated
- clumsy

Figure 5–4 Children are naturally energetic and curious.

Unfortunately, there are no specific symptoms or medical tests available for accurately diagnosing this disorder. Often this decision is based on a combination of personal beliefs and observations. Recently, the American Psychiatric Association set forth guidelines to aid in the identification of children with attention deficit disorder with hyperactivity:

- excessive levels of motor activity based on the child's age
- limited attention span; easily distracted and forgetful
- repeated incidences of impulsive behavior; aggressive and easily frustrated
- poor motor coordination
- disturbances of sleep

There is no one simple method for treating hyperactivity (AAP, 1993; Anastopoulos, 1991; Coleman, 1988). Each child requires an individualized approach. Often a combination of methods is used, although some are considered to be controversial.

One common approach involves the use of stimulant or antidepressant-type medications, such as Ritalin and Cylert. These drugs have an opposite effect from what might be expected in children who actually have an attention deficit disorder with hyperactivity. Rather than increasing children's activity level, these drugs often have a calming effect.

The medical profession has been criticized for its overuse of medications to treat hyperactive children. Drugs are viewed an easy way out for parents, doctors, and teachers and are often prescribed before other forms of therapy are tried. Also, there are undesirable side effects associated with these medications, including depression of children's appetite and growth, sleeplessness, listlessness, and a stuporlike state. Furthermore, medication seldom cures the child's problem behaviors. Problem behaviors usually reappear when drug therapy is discontinued. However, medication can be beneficial for some children when it is used under medical supervision, over a short period of time, and in combination with behavior management therapy (Landau, 1993).

Behavioral management and special education practices have been used successfully to treat children with ADDH. Their effectiveness can be attributed to the fact that these methods deal directly with the child's problem behaviors. Through carefully planned and controlled experiences, children can learn behaviors that are acceptable and appropriate. Some basic principles include:

- Creating a structured environment. The degree of structure depends on the type and severity of the child's problems. For example, structure for one child may involve restricting the number of furnishings in a classroom to a single table and chair. For another child, structure may be achieved by limiting the number of choices, e.g., choosing between only two toys or activities.
- Establishing a daily routine that is consistent and predictable. Children with ADDH function best when things are familiar, including a routine that is the same from day to day.
- Giving directions that are clear and easy for the child to follow. Let the child know exactly what is expected. "Andy, I want you to put the toys in this basket." The use of repetition is also important.
- Offering praise and positive reinforcement. This is an effective means for gaining children's cooperation. It also encourages them to attempt and complete even simple tasks. "Good work, Nel. You have found three of the red beads."
- Providing experiences that are challenging, yet, within the skill and tolerance level of the hyperactive child. Thus, a child can experience frequent success and avoid repeated frustration and failure.
- Providing opportunities for developing new interests, especially physical activities where children can channel excess energy and learn to relax.

Using these techniques with young children may help lessen the development of serious emotional problems that often accompany attention deficit disorders. Children's self-confidence improves as they become more successful and no longer see themselves as "always bad" or "failures" at whatever they do.

Dietary management has also been suggested as a treatment (Child Health Alert, 1995). The controversial Feingold diet, introduced during the 1970s, linked sugar, artificial colors and flavorings, and foods containing an aspirin-related compound to the uncontrollable behaviors associated with hyperactivity. Feingold reported that when sugar and foods with these additives were omitted from the child's diet, behavior improved dramatically.

Many authorities continue to question Feingold's theories and results. However, like many other forms of therapy, what works for one child does not necessarily work for another. If parents recognize this fact beforehand, they are less likely to be frustrated if dietary changes do not produce the results they hoped for. However, there is certainly no harm in feeding children foods that are nutritious, lower in sugar, and additive-free.

LEAD POISONING

Lead poisoning has recently attracted renewed public attention as increasing numbers of young children with elevated levels of lead in their blood are being identified, Figure 5–5. It has been estimated that approximately 17 percent of the children under 6 years of age are affected by this preventable illness (AAP, 1994;

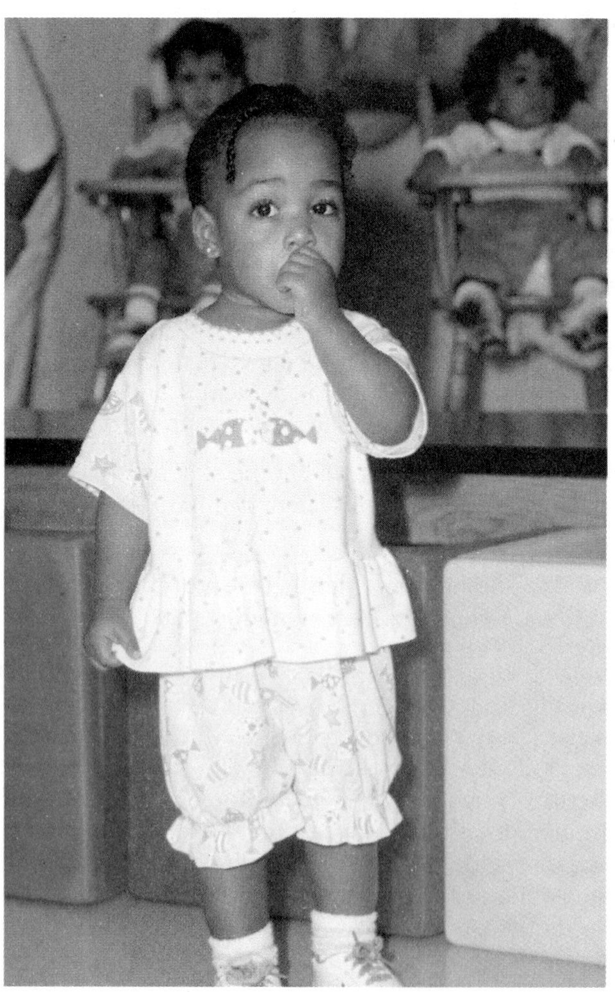

Figure 5–5 Lead poisoning is becoming an increasingly serious problem.

ATSDR, 1988). It should be noted that lead poisoning is not an exclusive problem associated with poverty and inner-city populations. Lead-containing sources are present in many environments.

Lead is most commonly found in old paint (prior to 1977), contaminated drinking water, polluted air, soil, some imported dishware and crystal, lead shot, and fishing weights. While legislation has been passed that will eventually eliminate leaded paints and fuels, many old sources still exist. Renovation of old houses, for example, often produces significant contamination in the form of paint dust and loose chips. Caution should also be exercised when purchasing toys and used furniture for children at garage sales or from second-hand stores.

The symptoms of lead poisoning develop slowly over a period of time and affect a child's central nervous system (Chisholm, 1992). Often these children appear irritable and may experience a loss of appetite, headaches, unexplained abdominal pain, constipation, nausea, listlessness, and learning disabilities.

Research has also demonstrated that elevated levels of lead can lower a child's IQ by as much as 4–5 percent (Needleman, 1991). Consequently, the Center for Disease Control (CDC) now recommends that all children, especially those at-risk, be screened for lead poisoning between 6 and 72 months (CDC, 1991). Children with elevated blood levels of lead may be treated with special medications. However, public awareness and community education are still the most effective preventive measures.

SICKLE CELL ANEMIA

Sickle cell anemia is an inherited disorder of the blood that is found primarily in the African-American population (Whaley, 1995; Richardson, 1983). It sometimes occurs in those of Mediterranean, Middle Eastern, Turkish, or Puerto Rican descent. Approximately 10 percent of African-Americans carry the trait for sickle cell anemia but do not necessarily experience symptoms of the disease themselves; these people are called carriers. When both parents have the sickle cell trait, some of their children may be born with the actual disease, while others may be carriers.

The abnormal formation of red blood cells in sickle cell anemia causes chronic health problems for the child. Red blood cells form in the shape of a comma or sickle, rather than their normal round shape. As a result, blood flow throughout the body is slowed and occasionally blocked. Symptoms of the disease do not usually appear until sometime after the child's first birthday.

Clumping of deformed blood cells results in periods of acute illness called crises. A crisis can be triggered by infection, injury, strenuous exercise, or dehydration. Symptoms of a sickle cell crisis include fever, severe abdominal and leg pain, vomiting, and ulcers (sores) on the arms and legs. Children must usually be hospitalized during a crisis. Between flare-ups, they may be free from any acute symptoms. However, because of chronic infection and anemia, these children are often small for their age, irritable, and tire easily.

At present there is no known cure for sickle cell anemia. However, genetic counseling offers prospective parents who are carriers the chance to decide whether or not they want to risk having children. Also, screening programs are now available to enable parents to obtain early diagnosis and medical care for infants with sickle cell disease.

Summary

Many young children are affected by a variety of chronic illnesses and long-term health problems. Teachers and caregivers play an invaluable role in recognizing the early signs and symptoms associated with these conditions. Some health problems (e.g., diabetes, allergies, lead poisoning) develop slowly and may be difficult, therefore, for parents to identify because of their closeness to their own child. Financial constraints, denial, and not knowing where to turn for help may also delay a parent's decision to seek treatment.

Diabetes is caused by a failure of the pancreas to produce adequate amounts of insulin. Early signs can include weight loss, frequent urination, fatigue, and excessive thirst. Treatment includes daily insulin injections and careful regulation of the child's diet. Many children also experience seizure disorders. It is important for teachers to observe all behaviors exhibited during a seizure, record their observations, and share this information with the child's parents. Allergies affect many children and are caused by an abnormal response to substances called allergens. Characteristic symptoms include congestion and runny nose, headaches, eczema, rashes, wheezing, asthma, stomachaches, and behavioral changes. Treatment for allergies is based on the type and location of allergic response. Teachers can help children adjust to limitations (e.g., diet, activity, environment) and improve coping skills.

ADD and ADDH are developmental disorders that include a variety of learning and behavioral problems. Causes, diagnosis, and treatments are not clear-cut and sometimes controversial. Often a combination of medication and behavior management helps children function more effectively in school.

Teachers and caregivers play an important role in helping children with chronic health problems adjust to new settings and routines. In turn, the inclusion of these children in day care and school programs also fosters understanding and acceptance among their peers. Teachers can also provide encouragement and support for parents who may be sensitive about their child's special needs.

Suggested Activities

1. Locate and read at least three children's books written about a chronic health disorder or disease. Prepare a bibliography card for each book and use the cards to begin a file of books for children on related topics.
2. Interview caregivers in three different settings. Find out what types of allergies they encounter most often and how they manage these problems in the

classroom. Develop a simple, five-day snack menu for a toddler who is allergic to milk and milk products, chocolate, and eggs.

3. Divide into several small groups. Practice good posture techniques for sitting, standing, walking, and lifting. Prepare a lesson plan for teaching two of these techniques to a group of preschool and school-aged children.

4. Invite a speaker from the nearest chapter of the Feingold Association. Read at least one of the following articles beforehand and be prepared to ask questions:

   Feingold, B. F. 1975. Hyperkinesis and Learning Disabilities Linked to Artificial Food Flavors and Colors. *American Journal of Nursing* 75: 797.

   Herbert W. January 23, 1982. Hyperactivity—Diet Link Questions. *Science News* 121: 53.

   Kaplan, B., McNicol, J., Conte, R., and Moghadam, H. 1989. Overall Nutrient Intake of Preschool Hyperactive and Normal Boys. *Journal of Abnormal Child Psychology*, 17(2): 127–132.

   Meister, K. A. 1981. Do Food Additives Cause Hyperactivity? *American Baby* 43: 10.

   Wolraich, M., Milich, R., Stumbo, P., and Schultz, F. 1985. The Effects of Sucrose Ingestion on the Behavior of Hyperactive Boys. *Pediatrics*, 106: 675–682.

   Robinson, L. A. 1980. Food Allergies, Food Additives and the Feingold Diet. *Pediatric Nurse* 6:38.

5. Obtain and view the film "Images of Epilepsy"; available from the Epilepsy Foundation of America, 4351 Garden City, Landover, MD (301) 459–3700.

Chapter Review

A. Define the following terms:

1. chronic
2. orthopedic problem
3. allergen
4. insulin
5. hyperglycemia
6. allergic reaction

B. Briefly answer the following questions:

1. List four possible causes of fatigue in young children.
2. Describe the proper way for children to sit on the floor and in a chair.

3. Why has the use of medication to treat hyperactive children stirred so much controversy?
4. List five common symptoms of early diabetes.
5. Distinguish between petit mal and grand mal seizures.
6. Why are many chronic health problems difficult to identify in the young child?

C. Read the case study and fill in the blanks with a word (or words) selected from the following list.

breathing	headache
sleep	anticonvulsants
seizure	affected
informed	consciousness
aura	written report
grand mal	time length
permanent health file	

While climbing up the playhouse ladder, Jamie let out a sudden shriek, released her grip and fell to the ground. Her teacher quickly ran to see what had happened. Jamie lay on the ground unconscious, her arms and legs jerking. The teacher realized that Jamie was having a ________________, and that it was probably a ________________ type. A warning or ________________ precedes this kind of seizure.

Jamie's teacher stood back and watched until the muscular contractions ended. In addition to the loss of consciousness, the teacher also carefully noted the exact ________________ of the seizure, the parts of the body ________________, and whether Jamie had any difficulty ________________. Later, this information would be included in a ________________, which would be placed in the child's ________________.

When Jamie regained ________________ she complained of a ________________. The teacher encouraged her to ________________ for a short while. Meanwhile, Jamie's parents were ________________ of her seizure. Her mother explained that the doctor had recently prescribed a new medication and was trying to regulate the dosage. The most common group of medications used to treat seizure disorders are ________________.

References

Agency for Toxic Substances and Disease Registry (ATSDR). July 1988. The Nature and Extent of Lead Poisoning in Children in the United States: A Report to Congress. Atlanta.

American Academy of Pediatrics (AAP) 1994. *School Health: Policy and Practice.* Committee on School Health, AAP, Elk Grove Village, IL.

American Psychiatric Association: Diagnostic and Statistical Manual for Mental Disorders III-R. 1987. Washington, DC: American Psychiatric Association.

Anastopoulos, A., DuPaul, G., and Barkley, R. 1991. Stimulant Medications and Parent Training Therapies for Attention Deficit —Hyperactivity Disorders. *Journal of Learning Disabilities,* 24(4): 210–218.

Baker, B., and Baker, C. 1980. Difficulties Generated by Allergies. *Journal of School Health,* 50(10): 583.

Balik, B., Haig, B., and Moynihan, P. 1986. Diabetes and the School-Aged Child. *Maternal/Child Nursing,* 11(5): 324–330.

Camfield, C., and Camfield, P. 1993. Febrile Seizures: What Are They and What To Do If They Occur. *Contemporary Pediatrics,* 26–44.

Center for Disease Control (CDC). 1991. *Preventing Lead Poisoning in Young Children.* Atlanta, GA: Department of Health and Human Services.

Child Health Alert. 1991. More Evidence that Air Pollution Affects Human Health: Air Pollution and Respiratory Infections in Children. *Child Health Alert;* 1–2.

Child Health Alert. 1995. Synthetic Food Colorings: Do They Affect Children's Behavior? *Child Health Alert,* 13: 1.

Chisholm, J. 1992. Increased Lead Absorption and Lead Poisoning. In R. Behrman's, *Nelson Textbook of Pediatrics.* Philadelphia, PA: W. B. Saunders Co.

Coleman, W. 1988. *Attention Deficit Disorders, Hyperactivity, and Associated Disorders: A Handbook for Professionals.* Madison, WI: Calliope Books (2115 Chadbourne Ave., Madison, WI 53705).

Holvoet, J., and Helmstetter, E. 1989. *Medical Problems of Students with Special Needs: A Guide for Educators.* Boston, MA: Little, Brown, and Co.

Landau, S., and McAninch, A. 1993. Young Children with Attention Deficits. *Young Children,* 48(4): 49–58.

Mailick, M., Holden, G., and Walther, V. 1994. Coping with Childhood Asthma: Caretaker's View. *Health & Social Work,* 19(2): 103–108.

Marks, M. 1983. Recognition of the Allergic Child at School: Visual and Auditory Signs. *Journal of School Health,* 44(5): 227–35.

Needleman, H., and Bellinger, D. 1991. The Health Effects of Low Level Exposure to Lead. *Annual Review of Public Health,* 12: 111–140.

Pica, R. 1995. *Experiences in Movement with Music, Activities, and Theory.* Albany, NY: Delmar Publishers Inc.

Richardson, E., and Milne, L. 1983. Sickle Cell Disease and the Childbearing Family: An Update. *Journal of Maternal/Child Nursing,* 8: 117–22.

Synoground, S. G., and Kelsey, M. 1990. *Health Care Problems in the Classroom.* Springfield, IL: Charles C. Thomas.

Voignier, R., and Bridgewater, S. 1980. Allergies in Young Children. *Young Children,* 35(4): 67–70.

Whaley, L., and Wong, D. 1995. *Essentials of Pediatric Nursing.* St. Louis, MO: C. V. Mosby Co.

Additional Reading

Child Health Alert. 1992. Lead in Our Environment: More Evidence of Harm at Low Levels. *Child Health Alert*, 10: 1–3.

Fauvre, M. 1988. Including Young Children with "New" Chronic Illnesses in an Early Childhood Setting. *Young Children*, 43(6): 71–77.

Franklin, D. 1991. Lead: Still a Poison After all These Years. *In Health*, 5(5): 39–48.

Goldberg, E. 1994. Including Children with Chronic Health Conditions: Nebulizers in the Classroom. *Young Children*, 49(2): 34–37.

Haslam, R., and Valletutti, P. 1985. *Medical Problems in the Classroom.* Austin, TX: ProEd Press.

MacDonald, A. 1993. Lead-Poisoning. *Parents*, 68(5): 66–70.

Rose, M., and Thomas, R. 1987. *Children with Chronic Conditions.* NY: Harcourt Brace Jovanovich Publishers.

Segal, M. 1989. New Hope for Children with Sickle Cell Disease. *FDA Consumer*, 23: 14.

Striph, K. 1995. Prevalence of Lead Poisoning in a Suburban Practice. *Journal of Family Practice*, 41(1): 65–70.

Waldman, S. July 15, 1991. Lead and Your Kids. *Newsweek*, pp. 42–48.

White, J., and Owsley, V. 1982. Helping Families Cope with Milk, Wheat, and Soy Allergies. *Maternal/Child Nursing*, 8: 423–28.

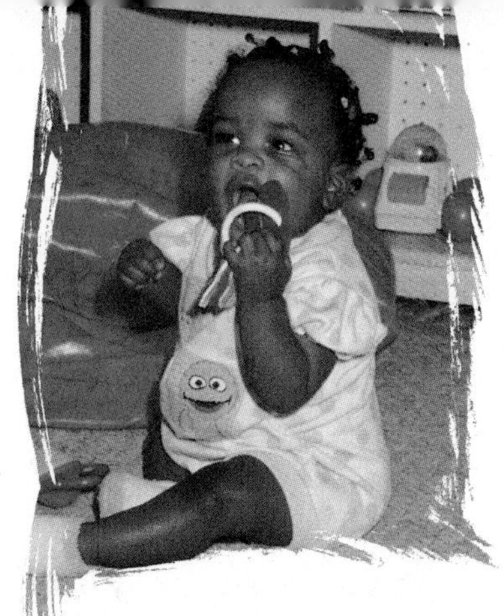

Chapter 6

The Infectious Process and Effective Control

Terms to Know

antibodies
communicable
pathogen
susceptible host
respiratory tract
immunized
airborne transmission
fecal-oral transmission
incubation
contagious
prodromal
acute
convalescent
universal infection control precautions
lymph glands

Objectives

After studying this chapter, you should be able to:

- Define communicable illness.
- List the three factors that are essential for an infection to be communicable.
- Name four control measures that child care facilities can use to reduce communicable illnesses.
- Identify signs and symptoms of common communicable diseases.

Young children, especially those under 3 years of age, are very susceptible to communicable and acute illness and infection. Repeated illnesses are not uncommon during their first experiences in group care settings. Several factors may contribute to this increased risk. First, children with limited exposure to groups of children have had fewer opportunities to encounter illness and, thus, to build up *antibodies* for protection. This lack of immunity makes young children more vulnerable to germs that cause communicable and acute illnesses. Chronic illness and handicapping conditions also increase children's susceptibility to infections.

Second, immature development of body structures contributes to a higher rate of illness. For example, shorter distances between an infant's or toddler's ears, nose, and throat are more favorable to infection of the respiratory tract.

Third, group care settings, such as preschool, day care centers and homes, and elementary schools are conducive to the transfer of illness among children and adults. Many of children's habits, such as sucking on fingers, mouthing toys, carelessness with bodily secretions (runny noses, drool, urine, stool), and lots of physical contact also encourage the rapid spread of communicable illness, Figure 6–1. For this reason, every attempt must be made to establish and implement policies, practices, and educational programs that will protect young children from unnecessary exposure.

COMMUNICABLE ILLNESS

A *communicable* illness is an illness that can be transmitted or spread from one person or animal to another. Three factors are necessary for this process to occur:

- a pathogen
- a susceptible host
- a method of transmission

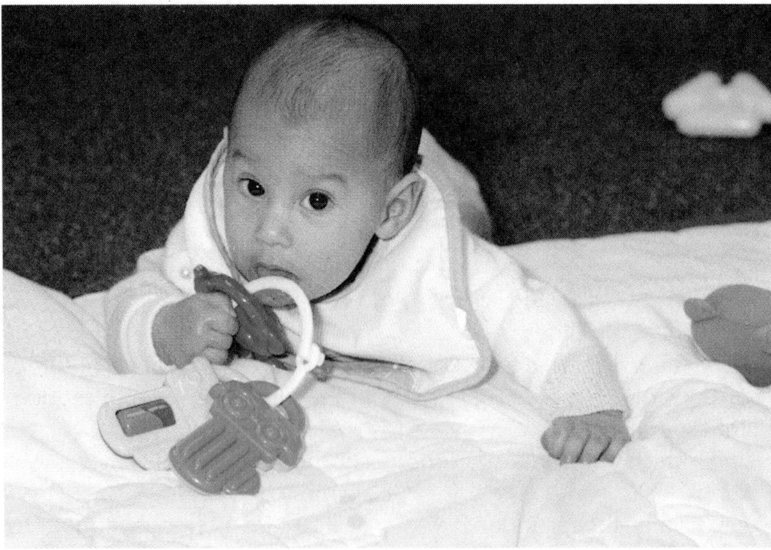

Figure 6–1 Mouthing of toys contributes to the spread of communicable illness.

First, a *pathogen* or disease-causing agent, such as a bacteria, virus, or parasite, must be present and available for transmission. These invisible germs are specific for each illness and are most commonly located in discharges from the respiratory (nose, throat, lungs) and intestinal tracts of infected persons. They can also be found in the blood, urine, and discharges from the eyes and skin. Most pathogens require a living host for their survival. One exception, however, is the organism that causes tetanus; it can survive in soil and dust for several years.

Second, there must be a *susceptible host* or person who can become infected with the pathogen. The types of communicable illnesses experienced most often by young children generally enter their new host through either a break in the skin, the *respiratory tract*, or digestive tract. The route of entry depends on the specific illness or disease involved.

Not every child who is exposed to a particular virus or bacteria will become infected by it. Conditions must be favorable to allow an infectious organism to successfully avoid the body's defense systems, multiply, and establish itself. Children who are well rested, adequately nourished, *immunized*, and in a good state of health are generally less susceptible to communicable illnesses. Also, in many instances, a previous case of the same illness affords protection against repeated infections. However, the length of this protection varies with the illness and may range from several days to a lifetime. Children who experience a very mild or subclinical case of an illness or who are carriers of an infection are often resistant to the illness without realizing that they have experienced it.

Third, a method for transmitting the infectious agent from the original source to a new host is necessary to complete the communicable process. One of the most common modes of transmitting infectious agents in child care settings involves *airborne transmission*. Disease-causing pathogens are carried on tiny droplets of moisture that are expelled during coughs, sneezes, or while talking, Figure 6–2. Influenza, colds, meningitis, tuberculosis, and chickenpox are examples of infectious illnesses spread in this manner.

Fecal-oral transmission is the second most common way infectious illnesses are spread in child care settings, particularly when there are infants and toddlers in diapers. Caregivers who fail to wash their hands properly after changing diapers or helping children with toileting needs are often responsible for spreading disease-causing germs, especially if they also handle food. For this reason it is advisable to assign diaper changing and food preparation responsibilities to different caregivers. It is also critical to wash children's hands after diaper changes or using the bathroom because their hands often end up in their mouths. Pinworms, hepatitis A, salmonella, and giardiasis are examples of illnesses transmitted by fecal-oral contamination.

A third common method of transmission involves direct contact with an infected area on another individual. The infectious organisms are transferred directly from a source of infection to a new host. Ringworm, athlete's foot, impetigo, and conjunctivitis are some of the conditions spread in this manner.

Communicable illnesses can also be transmitted through indirect contact. This method involves the transfer of infectious organisms from an infected host to an intermediate object, such as water, milk, dust, food, toys, towels, eating utensils,

Figure 6–2 Close contact facilitates the spread of infectious illnesses.

animals, or insects, and finally to the new susceptible host. Recent studies suggest that it may be possible to infect oneself with certain viruses, such as those causing colds and influenza, by touching the moist linings of the eyes and nose with contaminated hands.

The absence of any one of these factors (pathogen, host, or method of transmission) will prevent the spread of communicable illness. This is an important fact for teachers and caregivers to remember in their attempts to control outbreaks of communicable illness in group settings. It also lessens the risk of carrying such illnesses home to their families.

STAGES OF ILLNESS

Communicable illnesses follow a fairly predictable progression of stages: incubation, prodromal, acute, convalescence. Since many of these stages overlap, it is often difficult to identify when each one begins and ends.

The *incubation* stage includes the time between exposure to a pathogen and the appearance of the first signs or symptoms of illness. During this period, the infectious organisms enter the body and multiply rapidly in an attempt to overpower the body's defense systems and establish themselves. The length of the incubation stage is described in terms of hours or days and varies for each communicable disease. For example, the incubation period for chickenpox ranges from two to three weeks following exposure, while for the common cold it is thought to be only 12 to 72 hours. Many infectious illnesses are already communicable near the end of this stage. The fact that children are often *contagious* before any symptoms are apparent makes the control of infectious illness in the classroom more difficult, despite teachers' careful observations.

The *prodromal* stage begins when an infant or young child experiences the first nonspecific signs of infection and ends with the appearance of symptoms characteristic of a particular communicable illness. This stage may last from several hours to several days. However, not all communicable diseases have a prodromal stage. Early symptoms commonly associated with the prodromal stage may include headache, low-grade fever, a slight sore throat, a general feeling of restlessness or irritability. Many of these complaints are so vague that they often go unnoticed. However, because children are highly contagious during this stage, caregivers and parents must learn to recognize that these subtle changes may signal impending illness.

During the *acute* stage an infant or child is definitely sick. This stage is marked by the onset of symptoms that are typical of the specific communicable illness. Some of these symptoms such as fever, sore throat, cough, runny nose, rashes, or enlarged lymph glands are common to many infectious diseases. However, there are usually characteristic patterns and variations of these symptoms that can be used to identify a particular communicable illness. An infant or child continues to be highly contagious throughout this stage.

The *convalescent* or recovery stage generally follows automatically unless complications develop. During this stage, symptoms gradually disappear, the child begins to feel better, and usually is no longer contagious.

CONTROL MEASURES

Teachers and caregivers have an obligation and responsibility to help protect young children from communicable illnesses. Classrooms, day care centers, and homes are ideal settings for the rapid spread of many infectious conditions. However, there are a variety of practical control measures that can be implemented in these settings to reduce the incidence of illness.

Observations

One effective control measure available to teachers and caregivers is to identify and remove sick children from a group setting. This eliminates the immediate source of infection. However, because many communicable illnesses are infectious before symptoms appear, additional cases may still develop. Early recognition of sick children requires that adults develop a sensitivity to changes in children's normal appearance and behavior patterns (Kendrick, 1995). This process is facilitated by the fact that young children generally look and behave differently when they are not feeling well. Their actions, facial expressions, skin color, sleep habits, appetite, and comments can present valuable warnings of impending illness and may include:

- unusually pale or flushed skin
- red or sore throat
- enlarged *lymph glands*

- nausea, vomiting, or diarrhea
- rash, spots, or open lesions
- watery or red eyes
- headache or dizziness
- chills, fever, or achiness
- fatigue or loss of appetite

It is also important to be alert to signs of illness during seasons of the year when certain diseases are more prevalent or whenever there is known outbreak in the community.

However, these same signs and symptoms may not always warrant concern in all children. For example, a teacher who knows that Tony's allergies often cause a red throat and cough in the fall, or that Shadra's recent irritability is probably related to her mother's hospitalization would not be alarmed by these observations. Teachers and caregivers must be able to distinguish between children with potentially infectious illnesses and those with health problems that are explainable and not necessarily contagious.

Policies

Written policies offer another important method for controlling infectious illnesses. For example, exclusion policies can serve as important guidelines for parents and caregivers by specifying when children are to be kept home because of illness and when they are well enough to return, Figure 6–3. Other policies should define acceptable levels of immunization for children and actions for dealing with those who do not comply.

Opinions differ on how restrictive exclusion policies should be (Shapiro, 1986). Some experts believe that children with mild illnesses can remain in child care, while others feel that children exhibiting symptoms should not attend. Because many early signs of communicable illnesses are similar, it is often difficult for caregivers to distinguish between conditions that warrant exclusion and medical attention and those that involve only mild infections. Consequently, child care programs may decide to set exclusion policies that are fairly conservative unless they are equipped to care for sick children.

It is also important for programs to adopt policies for notifying parents when children are exposed to communicable illnesses. This measure enables parents to watch for early symptoms and to keep sick children home, Figure 6–4. Local public health authorities can offer much useful information and assistance to centers when they are formulating new policies or are confronted with a communicable health problem.

Ideally, such policies are established before a center begins accepting children for care. These policies should comply with any state regulations where they exist. Periodic reviews of policies with all staff members improves the likelihood that they will be enforced consistently. Parents should also receive copies of all policies at the time of enrollment. Parents are more likely to cooperate when they know in advance what to expect if their child becomes ill.

EXCLUSION POLICY

Control of communicable illness among the children is a prime concern. Policies and guidelines related to outbreaks of communicable illness in this center have been developed with the help of the health department and local pediatricians. In order to protect the entire group of children, as well as your own child, we ask that parents assist us by keeping sick children at home if they have experienced any of the following symptoms *within the past 24 hours*:

- a fever over 100°F (37.8°C) orally or 99°F (37.2°C) axillary (under the arm)
- signs of a newly developing cold or severe coughing
- diarrhea, vomiting, or an upset stomach
- unusual or unexplained loss of appetite, fatigue, irritability, or headache
- any discharge or drainage from eyes, nose, ears, or open sores

Children who become ill with any of these symptoms will be returned home. We appreciate your cooperation with this policy. If you have any questions about whether or not your child should attend school or group care that day, please call the center *before* bringing your child.

Figure 6–3 Sample exclusion policy.

Date____________________

Dear Parent:

There is a possibility that your child has been exposed to chickenpox. If your child has not had chickenpox, observe carefully from __________ to ________ (more likely the first part of this period), for signs of a slight cold, runny nose, loss of appetite, fever, listlessness, and/or irritability. Within a day or two, watch for a spot (or spots) resembling mosquito bites on which a small blister soon forms. Chickenpox is contagious 24–48 hours *before* the rash appears. Children who develop chickenpox may return when all pox are covered by a dry scab (about 5 or 6 days).

If you have any questions, please call the Center before bringing your child. We appreciate your cooperation in helping us keep incidences of illness to a minimum.

Figure 6–4 Sample letter to parents indicating their child has possibly been exposed to a communicable disease.

Guidelines for Sick Caregivers. Teachers and caregivers are exposed to many infectious illnesses while working with young children. Often, they experience an increased incidence of illness, especially during the initial months of employment, that is similar to when young children are in care for the first time. However, one's resistance generally improves over time. Pregnant employees may want to reconsider their position, since some infectious illnesses can affect the fetus. Completing a pre-employment health assessment, tuberculin test, and updating immunizations are some of the precautionary measures caregivers can take to minimize the risk of illness. However, practicing good handwashing technique always offers the most effective protection.

When teachers or caregivers do become ill, it is important for them to follow the same exclusion guidelines, established by the center with regard to sick children, when deciding whether or not to come to work. Caregivers who do not feel well will find it difficult to meet the rigorous demands of caring for children and will run an increased risk of sustaining injury. Consequently, centers should have substitute caregivers available so that adults will not feel pressured to work when they are sick.

Administration of Medication. The administration of medicine to young children is a responsibility that should always be taken seriously. Explicit policies and procedures pertaining to the administration of both prescription and nonprescription medication, including ointments and creams, eye, ear and nose drops, cough syrups, baby aspirin, vitamins, or other tablets should be carefully developed for the protection of staff members and to safeguard the children. Descriptions of these policies and procedures should be in writing, familiar to all staff members, filed in an accessible location, and distributed to every parent.

Part-day care arrangements allow greater flexibility for parents to adjust medication schedules and administer prescribed medications at times when the child is at home. However, this option is not feasible for children enrolled in full-day care settings. In these instances parents will need to make prior arrangements with caregivers to administer prescribed medication in their absence.

Medication should never be administered by a teacher or caregiver without the written consent of the child's parent and written direction of a licensed physician. The label on a prescription drug is considered an acceptable directive from the physician. In the case of nonprescription medicines, the parent should obtain written instructions from the physician stating the child's name, the medication to be given, the dose, frequency it is to be administered, and any special precautions that may be necessary. There are risks associated with giving children over-the-counter medications that have not been authorized by a physician. Thus, to protect themselves from possible liability, caregivers should not assume these risks. It is the professional and legal responsibility of the physician to determine the type and exact dosage that is appropriate for an individual child.

Some additional points to remember include:

1. Be honest when giving young children medication! Do not use force or attempt to trick children into believing that medicines are candy. Instead, use the opportunity to help children understand the relationship between taking

a medication and recovering from an illness or infection. Also, acknowledge the fact that the taste of medicine may be disagreeable or a treatment may be somewhat unpleasant; offer a small sip of juice or cracker to eliminate an unpleasant taste or to read a favorite story as a reward for cooperating.

2. In care centers, designate one individual to be personally responsible for accepting medication from parents and administering it to children; this could be the director or the head teacher. This step will help minimize the opportunity for errors, such as omitting a dose or giving a dose twice.
3. When medication is accepted from a parent, it should be in the original container, labelled with the child's name, name of the drug, and include directions for the exact amount and frequency the medication is to be given. NEVER give medicine from a container that has been prescribed for another individual.
4. Store all medicines in a locked cabinet. If it is necessary to refrigerate a medication, place it in a locked box and store on a shelf in the refrigerator.
5. Be cautious during the process of administering medications to children. Concentrate on what you are doing and do not talk with anyone until you are finished.
   a. Read the label on the bottle or container three times:
      - when removing it from the locked cabinet
      - before pouring it from the container
      - after pouring it from the container
   b. Give only the *exact* amount of medication that is ordered and on time.
   c. Be sure you have the correct child! If the child is old enough to talk, ask "What is your name?" and let the child state his/her name.
6. Record and maintain a permanent record of each dose of medicine that is administered, Figure 6–5. Include the:
   - date and time the medicine was given
   - name of the caregiver administering the medication
   - dose of medication given
   - any unusual physical changes or behaviors observed after the medicine was administered.
7. Inform parents of the dosage(s) and time medication was given, as well as any unusual reactions that may have occurred.
8. Adults should never take any medication in front of children.

Immunization

Immunization offers permanent protection against all preventable childhood diseases, including diphtheria, tetanus, whooping cough, polio, measles, mumps, and rubella. However, not all children are completely immunized. Current figures estimate

ADMINISTRATION OF MEDICATION FORM

Child's name ____________________
Prescription number ____________________
Date of prescription ____________________
Doctor prescribing medicine ____________________
Medication being given for ____________________
Time medication is to be given by staff ____________________
Time medication last given by parent ____________________
Amount to be given at each time (dosage) ____________________

....

I, ____________________ give my permission for the staff to administer the above prescription medication (according to the above guidelines) to ____________________ (child's name). I understand that the staff cannot be held responsible for allergic reactions or other complications resulting from administration of the above medication given according to the directions.

Signed ____________________
(parent or guardian)

Date ____________________

....

Staff Record

Staff accepting medication and form ____________________
Is drug in original bottle, or in other container? ____________________
Is original label intact? ____________________
Is there written permission from the doctor attached (or the original prescription)? ______

Signature of accepting staff ____________________

....

Administration Record

DATE	TIME	AMOUNT GIVEN	STAFF ADMINISTERING	INITIAL

Figure 6–5 Sample medication record.

that only 70 to 80 percent of preschool children are immunized against all preventable childhood diseases (U. S. Department of Health and Human Services, 1993).

Why are some parents so seemingly unconcerned about obtaining immunizations for their children? Perhaps they do not realize how life threatening some communicable illnesses still are. Others may believe these diseases have been eliminated and are no longer necessary to worry about. Also, the convenience of modern medicines has led to a more relaxed attitude toward serious infections and diseases in general.

Current immunizations are required of all children entering child care programs in 46 states. In states where no immunization laws exist, individual teachers and caregivers should insist on complete immunization of every child according to the recommended standards. This rule should be followed unless parents are opposed on religious or medical grounds. At the same time, caregivers must continue, as a group, to support legislation establishing minimal immunization requirements at the state level.

Vaccines cause children to become immune (no longer susceptible) to invasion by a specific infectious organism. Protective substances called antibodies are formed by the body in response to the introduction of a specific infectious organism either in a vaccine or during an episode of the actual illness.

Babies are born with limited immunity, transferred from their mothers, to many communicable diseases. However, the temporary nature of this immunity makes it critical to begin the immunization process early in a baby's life. Table 6–1 shows the immunization schedule recommended by the American Academy of Pediatrics and Center for Disease Control (CDC).

Vaccines are currently available to protect infants and young children, particularly those in day care settings, against Haemophilus influenza Type b (Hib), a common

TABLE 6–1 Recommended Immunization Schedule

CHILD'S AGE	DPT	TOPV	MMR	Hib	DT
2 months	x	x		x	
4 months	x	x		x	
6 months	x	(optional)		x	
15 months	x	x	x	x	
4–6 years	x	x			
11–12 years			x		
Every 8–10 years					x

DPT — diphtheria, pertussis, and tetanus
TOPV — trivalent oral polio vaccine
MMR — measles, mumps, and rubella
Hib — Haemophilus influenza conjugate
DT — diphtheria and tetanus

cause of meningitis. Parents are also being advised to have children who attend group child care programs immunized against hepatitis B, a viral infection spread through contact with body secretions and feces (Phillips, 1991). Child care programs that employ one or more caregivers (including aides and substitutes) are also required to offer free hepatitis B immunizations to employees either during the first 10 days of employment or 24 hours following exposure to blood or body fluids containing blood (Child Care Law Center, 1994).

Immunizations can be obtained from the child's health care provider, neighborhood immunization clinics, or a local public health department where the cost may be reduced or free.

Environmental Control

Regulations passed by the U. S. Department of Labor's Occupational Safety and Health Administration (OSHA, 1992) now make it mandatory for all child care programs (except those that do not have any paid employees) to develop and practice *universal infection control precautions*. These measures include:

- handwashing (both proper technique and appropriate times)
- wearing disposable latex gloves whenever contact with blood or other body fluids (e.g., vomitus, urine, feces, saliva) is likely
- cleaning all surfaces with a disinfectant
- disposing of infectious materials (e.g., broken glass, contaminated clothing, diapers) in the proper manner
- subsidizing the cost of hepatitis B immunizations for all employees

In addition, programs must also prepare a written plan that addresses accidental exposure to potentially infectious secretions, provide annual training for employees in the handling of bloodborne pathogens and contaminated materials, and maintain records of any exposure (Child Care Law Center, 1994). As the incident of illnesses due to bloodborne pathogens, such as hepatitis and HIV, continue to increase, every program serving groups of young children should adapt these universal precautions.

Handwashing is perhaps the single most effective control measure against the spread of communicable and infectious illness in child care environments, Table 6–2. Therefore, it is of critical importance that teachers and caregivers use good technique and wash their hands often:

- upon arrival or return to the care setting
- before handling food or food utensils
- before feeding children
- after changing diapers or assisting a child in the bathroom
- after feeding a child or giving medication
- after handling items contaminated with mucus, urine, feces, vomitus, or blood
- after personally using the restroom

TABLE 6–2 Handwashing Technique
Correct handwashing procedures require only a very short time to be carried out by staff and children. ■ Rinse hands under warm, running water. ■ Lather hands with soap to loosen and suspend dirt and bacteria. ■ Rub hands together vigorously. Friction helps to remove microorganisms and dirt. (Young children may need help with this step.) ■ Pay special attention to rubbing soap and water on the backs of hands, between fingers, and around nails. ■ Rinse hands thoroughly under running water to remove dirt and soap. Keep hands lower than wrists to prevent recontaminating cleaned areas of hands. ■ Dry hands well with paper towel. ■ Use the same paper towel to turn off water faucets. (This prevents hands from becoming recontaminated.) ■ Dispose of paper towel in an appropriate receptacle. ■ Use hand cream to avoid dry, cracked skin (optional).

Particular attention should also be given to infants and toddlers who are crawling and eating with their hands. Individual washcloths moistened with soap and water or washing children's hands under running water are the methods of choice, Figure 6–6.

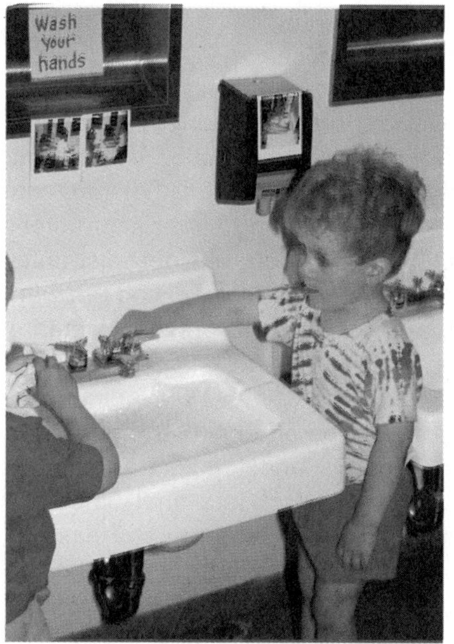

Figure 6–6 Infants and toddlers should have their hands washed under running water.

Strict sanitary procedures must be followed by all personnel. Play equipment, cribs, mats, and strollers should be wiped off routinely with a solution of 1/4 cup chlorine bleach to 1 gallon of water (or, 1 T./1 qt). **Note:** *A new bleach solution must be prepared daily to maintain its disinfecting strength.* Changing tables, mats, and potty chairs should be constructed of nonporous materials and free of any tears or cracks for ease of cleaning. They should be disinfected thoroughly after each use with a bleach solution that can be sprayed on and wiped off with paper towels. A stronger bleach solution (1 part chlorine bleach to 10 parts water) should be used to disinfect surfaces contaminated with blood or large amounts of urine, stool, or vomitus.

Toys that infants place in their mouths should be removed for cleaning before they are used by another child. Items should be washed with soap and water, rinsed in a diluted bleach solution, and allowed to air-dry. A dishwasher can also be used to sanitize some toys. Washable cloth and stuffed objects should be laundered between use by children. Other surfaces, such as tables, gate tops, car seats, and crib rails that children mouth or drool on, should be scrubbed daily with soap and water and disinfected.

Modifications in child care environments can also have a positive influence on the control of communicable illnesses. Room temperatures, for example, can be adjusted to 68°–72°F. This range of temperatures is less favorable for the spread of contagious illnesses and is often more comfortable for young children. Children's smaller body surfaces make them less sensitive than adults to cooler temperatures.

Rooms should be well ventilated. Circulating fresh air helps to reduce the concentration of infectious organisms within a given area. Large child care facilities should be equipped with a mechanical ventilating system that is in good operating condition. Fresh air can also be let in by opening doors and windows, even for brief times on cold days. However, doors and windows should have screens to prevent disease-carrying flies and insects from entering. Encouraging children to play outdoors, even in winter, can also improve their resistance to illness.

The humidity level in rooms should also be checked periodically, especially in winter when rooms are heated and there are fewer opportunities to let in fresh air. Extremely warm, dry air increases the chances of respiratory infection by causing the mucous lining of the mouth and nose to become dry and cracked. Moisture can be added by means of a humidifier built into the central heating system. An alternative method is to run a cool-mist vaporizer in individual rooms. (Cool-mist units eliminate the possibility of burns.) These units should be emptied, washed out with soap and water and refilled with fresh distilled water each day to prevent bacterial growth. Plants or small dishes of water placed around a room will also provide increased humidity.

The physical arrangement of a classroom can also be an effective method for controlling communicable and infectious illness. Infants and toddlers should be separated from toilet-trained children to limit the spread of intestinal illnesses. Surfaces, e.g., floors, walls, counter tops, furniture should be smooth and easy to clean. Laundry and food preparation areas should be separated from each other as well as from the classrooms. Pedal-operated sinks or infrared-triggered faucets are ideal for encouraging frequent handwashing and avoiding recontamination.

Measures to group children and limit the amount of close contact are also desirable. Crowding at tables or in play areas can be avoided by dividing children into smaller groups. During naptimes, children's rugs, cots, or cribs can be arranged in alternating directions, head to foot, to decrease talking, coughing, and breathing in each other faces. Provisions should also be made for children to have individual lockers or storage space for personal items, such as blankets, coats, hats, toys, toothbrushes, and combs to reduce the transfer of communicable illnesses.

Several additional areas in children's environments deserve special attention. Sandboxes should be covered to prevent contamination from animal feces. Water tables and wading pools need to be emptied and washed out daily to prevent the spread of communicable illness; a water pH of 7.2–8.2 and chlorine level of 0.4–3.0 parts per million should be maintained in swimming pools at all times (as specified in commercial test kits). Hats, wigs, and beauty parlor items can also contribute to the spread of head lice, and therefore, may not be appropriate in group settings. Play clothes should be washable and laundered often.

Education

Teachers and caregivers make a valuable contribution to the control of communicable illness through education. Continuous instruction on subjects such as personal health habits, exercise, and nutrition can be a key factor in improving children's resistance to infectious organisms and shortening the length of convalescence. Topics of special value for young children include:

- appropriate technique and times for handwashing
- proper method for covering coughs and blowing noses
- sanitary use of drinking fountains
- not sharing personal items, e.g., drinking cups, toothbrushes, shoes, hats, towels, eating utensils
- dressing appropriately for the weather
- good nutrition
- the need for rest and exercise

Outbreaks of contagious illness provide excellent opportunities for teachers and caregivers to review preventive health concepts and practices with children. Learning is more meaningful for young children when a friend or classmate has, for example, chickenpox or pink eye. Teachers can also reinforce learning by modelling good health practices; children frequently imitate adult behaviors.

Parents must be included in any educational program that hopes to reduce the incidence of communicable illness. Families should be kept informed of special health practices and information being taught to the children. Teachers and caregivers can also reinforce the importance of (1) serving nutritious meals and snacks, (2) making sure that children get sufficient rest and exercise, (3) obtaining immunizations for infants and young children, and (4) routine medical and dental supervision. Caregivers and parents must work together to control the spread of communicable illness and promote children's health.

Summary

Outbreaks of communicable illness are not uncommon in child care settings. Close contact, immature physiological development, habits typical of young children, and poor hygienic practices of children and staff members encourage the rapid spread of infectious disease.

A communicable illness is one that is spread or transmitted from one person or animal to another. The infectious process requires the availability of a pathogen, a susceptible host, and a method for transmission. The absence of any one factor will interrupt this process and prevent infection from occurring. Most contagious illnesses progress through an incubation, prodromal, acute, and convalescence stage.

Control and management of communicable and acute illness in group settings requires that teachers and caregivers possess some knowledge and understanding of these conditions. Control measures that can be implemented in child care settings include observations, establishing policies and guidelines, requiring immunizations, regulating the environment, education, and cooperating with parents.

Suggested Activities

1. Obtain several agar growth medium plates. With sterile cotton applicators, culture one toy and the top of one table in a preschool classroom or child care center. Observe the "growth" after 24 hours and again after 48 hours. Wash the same item with a mild chlorine solution and repeat the experiment. Compare the results.

2. Write to the Office of Public Health in your state (province/territory). Request information on the immunization requirements for preschool children attending child care programs. If possible, obtain data on the percentage of children under 6 years of age who are immunized in your state.

3. Obtain a copy of the OSHA pamphlet on regulations and instructions for implementing a bloodborne pathogen policy (CFR 1910.1030) from your nearest regional office. Prepare a written compliance plan for a child care center.

4. Discuss how you would handle the following situations:
   a. The father of one of the toddlers in your center is upset because of his child's frequent colds.
   b. You observe your teacher covering a cough and then continuing to prepare snacks for the children.
   c. Your toddler group has experienced frequent outbreaks of strep throat in the past 6 months.
   d. While reviewing immunization records, you discover that one of the children in your group has received only one dose of DPT and TOPV.

e. During health checks, Gabriel announces that he threw up all night. You notice that his eyes appear watery and his cheeks are flushed.

f. You find that one of your aides has stored all of the children's toothbrushes together in a sealed, plastic container.

Chapter Review

A. Define the following terms:

1. pathogen
2. contagious
3. universal precautions
4. incubation period
5. immunity
6. convalescence
7. antibodies
8. communicable illness

B. Briefly answer the following questions:

1. Describe how an illness can be spread by:
   a. airborne transmission
   b. indirect contact
2. What immunizations and how many of each should a 30-month-old child have?
3. Where can parents obtain immunizations for their children?
4. Children are contagious during what stages of most communicable diseases?
5. What three factors must be present for an infection to be communicable?
6. Name three early signs of communicable illness that can be observed in young children.
7. Describe specific practices that caregivers can use to limit the spread of illnesses transmitted via:
   a. the respiratory tract
   b. the fecal-oral route
   c. skin conditions
   d. contaminated objects, e.g., toys, towels, changing mats

C. Case Study

Laura arrived at the day care center with a runny nose and cough. Her mother informed the teachers that it was probably just allergies and left before Laura could be checked in. In addition to having a part-time job, Laura's mother is a single parent and student at the local community college. Shortly after Laura's mother left, the teachers discovered that Laura had a fever, red throat, and swollen glands.

1. How should the teachers handle Laura's immediate situation? Should she be allowed to stay or should an attempt be made to contact Laura's mother?
2. If Laura is allowed to stay at the center, what measures can be taken to limit the risk of spreading illness to other children?
3. If this is a repeated occurrence, what steps can be taken to make sure Laura's mother complies with the center's policies?
4. How can the center help Laura's mother avoid similar situations in the future?

References

Bloodborne Pathogens. 1992. Occupational Safety and Health Administration (OSHA). U. S. Department of Labor, Occupational Safety and Health Administration. Washington, DC

Child Care Law Center. October 1994. *Revised Description of OSHA Regulations on Bloodborne Pathogens.* San Francisco, CA.

Kendrick, A. S., Kaufman, R., and Messenger, K. 1995. *Healthy Young Children: A Manual for Programs.* Washington, DC: NAEYC.

Phillips, C. F. 1991. Keeping Up with the Changing Immunization Schedule. *Contemporary Pediatrics,* 20–46.

Shapiro, E., Kuritsky, J., and Potter, J. 1986. Policies for the Exclusion of Sick Children from Group Day Care: An Unresolved Dilemma. *Review of Infectious Diseases,* 8(4): 622–625.

U. S. Department of Health and Human Services, Public Health Service, Centers for Disease Control and Prevention, National Vaccine Advisory Committee. 1993. *Standards for Pediatric Immunization Practices.* Washington, DC.

Additional Reading

American Academy of Pediatrics. 1991. *Report of the Committee on Infectious Diseases.* Elk Grove, IL.

Bacterial Contamination in Child Care Centers and Diaper Types. May 1995. *Child Health Alert,* p. 1.

Building Quality Child Care: Health and Safety. Washington, DC: NAEYC. (This video addresses handwashing, diapering, and food service practices for caregivers.)

Child Care Issues: More on Fecal Contamination, Diapers, and Child Care. July/August 1995. *Child Health Alert,* p. 2.

Daum, R., Granoff, D., Gilsdorf, J., Murphy, T., and Osterholm, M. 1986. Haemophilus Influenza Type B Infections in Day Care Attendees: Implications for Management. *Reviews of Infectious Diseases,* 8(4): 558–567.

Having a Cold Doesn't Affect MMR Vaccine. October 1995. *Child Health Alert,* p. 3.

Moukaddem, V. 1990. Preventing Infectious Diseases in Your Child Care Setting. *Young Children,* 45(2): 28–29.

OSHA Requires Employers to Give Hepatitis B Immunization and Protection to First Aiders. *Young Children,* 48(1): 43.

Rivest, P. 1995. Risk Factors for Measles and Vaccine Efficacy During an Epidemic in Montreal. *Canadian Journal of Public Health,* 86(2): 86–88.

Sharts-Hopko, N. 1994. Current Immunization Guidelines. *Maternal-Child Nursing,* 19(2): 82–84.

Tamblyn, S. E. 1995. Measles Elimination—Time to Move Forward. *Canadian Journal of Public Health,* 86(2): 83–85

U.S. Department of Health and Human Services. 1989. *People 2000: National Health Promotion and Disease Prevention Objectives.* Public Health Service. Washington, DC DHHS Publication No. PHS91-50212.

Chapter 7

Communicable and Acute Illness: Identification and Management

Terms to Know

symptom
asymptomatic
apnea
infection
dehydration
listlessness
abdomen
hyperventilation
temperature
fever
disorientation
Lyme disease
Reye's syndrome
intestinal
urinate
salmonellosis

Objectives

After studying this chapter, you should be able to:

- Identify the signs and symptoms of four common illnesses.
- Check axillary and oral temperatures with a thermometer.
- Describe actions to be taken when a child in a group setting shows signs of illness.

Children, especially those under three years of age, have an increased susceptibility to illness and infection. Group settings such as preschools, child care centers, and day care homes encourage the rapid transfer of illness among children and adults. Therefore, every attempt must be made to establish policies and practices that will protect young children from unnecessary exposure.

Figure 7–1 Every caregiver should know how to identify sick children.

IDENTIFYING SICK CHILDREN

Every caregiver should know how to identify sick children, Figure 7–1. By learning to recognize the early signs and *symptoms* of common illnesses, teachers, parents, and child caregivers can exclude sick children from group settings when necessary. They can also take advantage of these opportunities to promote children's wellness by including educational experiences that teach and strengthen principles of good health.

COMMON COMMUNICABLE ILLNESSES

Effective control and protection of other children in group care settings requires teachers and caregivers to have a general knowledge and understanding of communicable illnesses. Table 7–1 presents brief descriptions of communicable illnesses common among young children.

SPECIAL CONCERNS

Acquired Immunodeficiency Syndrome (AIDS)

One of the most controversial and emotionally-laden communicable illnesses to appear in recent years is AIDS (acquired immunodeficiency syndrome). AIDS is rapidly becoming a major public health concern. For this reason, the implications for children and caregivers in group care settings is given special attention.

TABLE 7–1 Common Communicable Illnesses

COMMUNICABLE ILLNESS	SIGNS AND SYMPTOMS	INFECTIOUS AGENT	METHODS OF TRANSMISSION	INCUBATION PERIOD	LENGTH OF COMMUNICABILITY	CONTROL MEASURES
Acquired Immunodeficiency Syndrome (AIDS)	Flu-like symptoms, including fatigue, weight loss, enlarged lymph glands, persistent cough, fever, and diarrhea.	Virus	Children acquire virus when born to infected mothers, from breast milk of infected mothers, and from contaminated blood transfusions. Adults acquire the virus via sexual transmission, contaminated drug needles, and blood transfusions.	6 weeks to 8 years	Lifetime	Exclude children 0-5 yr. if they have open lesions, uncontrollable nosebleeds, bloody diarrhea, or are at high risk for exposing others to blood-contaminated body fluids. Wear disposable gloves to clean up body fluids; use good handwashing techniques. Seal contaminated items, e.g., diapers, paper towels in plastic bags. Disinfect surfaces with chlorine solution (1:10) or other disinfectant.
Chickenpox	Slight fever, irritability, cold-like symptoms. Red rash that develops blister-like head, scabs later. Most abundant on covered parts of body, e.g., chest, back, neck, forearm.	Virus	Airborne: through contact with secretions from the respiratory tract. Transmission from contact with blisters not common.	2–3 weeks after exposure	2–3 days prior to the onset of symptoms until 5–6 days after first eruptions. Scabs are not contagious.	Specific control measures: (1) Exclusion of sick children (2) Practice good personal hygiene, especially careful handwashing. Children can return to group care when all blisters have formed a dry scab (approximately 1 week).

Table 7–1 Continued

Cold Sores (Fever blisters)	Clear blisters usually on face and lips that crust and heal within a few days.	Virus	Direct contact with saliva of infected persons.	Up to 2 weeks	Virus remains in saliva for as long as 7 weeks following recovery.	No specific control. Good personal hygiene. Child does not have to be excluded from school.
Conjunctivitis (Pinkeye)	Redness of the white portion (conjunctiva) of the eye, and inner aspects of the lids, swelling of the lids, and a yellow discharge from eyes.	Bacteria or virus	Direct contact with discharge from eyes or upper respiratory tract of an infected person; through contaminated fingers and objects, e.g., tissues, washcloths, towels.	1–3 days	Throughout active infection; several days up to 2–3 weeks.	Antibiotic treatment. Exclude child from care until eyes have been treated and there is no discharge or physician provides a note. Strict personal hygiene and careful handwashing.
Common Cold	Highly contagious infection of the upper respiratory tract accompanied by slight fever, chills, runny nose, fatigue, and muscle aches. Onset may be sudden.	Virus	Airborne: through contact with secretions from the respiratory tract, e.g., coughs, sneezes, eating utensils, etc.	12–72 hours	About 1 day before onset of symptoms to 2–3 days after acute illness.	Prevention through education and good personal hygiene. Avoid exposure. Exclude first day or two. Antibiotics not effective against viruses. Avoid aspirin products (possible link to Reye's Syndrome). Watch for complications, e.g., earaches, bronchitis, croup, pneumonia.

TABLE 7–1 Common Communicable Illnesses (Continued)

COMMUNICABLE ILLNESS	SIGNS AND SYMPTOMS	INFECTIOUS AGENT	METHODS OF TRANSMISSION	INCUBATION PERIOD	LENGTH OF COMMUNICABILITY	CONTROL MEASURES
Dysentery (Shigella)	Sudden onset of vomiting; diarrhea, may be accompanied by high fever, headache, abdominal pain, Stools may contain blood, pus, or mucus. Can be fatal in young children.	Bacteria	Fecal-oral transmission via contaminated objects or indirectly through ingestion of contaminated food or water.	1–7 days	Variable; may last up to 4 weeks or longer in the carrier state.	Careful handwashing after bowel movements. Proper disposal of human feces; control of flies. Strict adherence to sanitary procedures for food preparation.
Encephalitis	Sudden onset of headache, high fever, convulsions, vomiting, confusion, neck and back stiffness, tremors, and coma.	Virus	Indirect spread by bites from disease-carrying mosquitoes; in some areas transmitted by tick bites.	5–15 days	Man is not contagious.	Spraying of mosquito breeding areas and use of insect repellents; public education.
Giardiasis	An intestinal parasite infection of the small bowel. Many persons are *asymptomatic*. Typical symptoms include chronic diarrhea, abdominal cramping, bloating, pale and foul-smelling stools, weight loss, and fatigue.	Parasite (protozoa)	Fecal-oral transmission; through contact with infected stool (e.g., diaper changes, helping child with soiled underwear), poor handwashing, passed from hands to mouth (toys, food). Also transmitted through contaminated water sources.	1–4 days	As long as parasite is present in the stool.	Infected persons must be treated with medication. Scrupulous handwashing before eating, preparing food, and after using the bathroom. Good sanitary conditions maintained in bathroom areas.

Table 7–1 Continued

Haemophilus influenza Type b	An acute respiratory infection; frequently causes meningitis. Other complications include pneumonia, epiglottitis, arthritis, infections of the bloodstream and conjunctivitis.	Bacteria	Airborne: via secretions of the respiratory tract (nose, throat). Persons can also be carriers with or without symptoms.	2–4 days	Throughout acute phase; as long as organism is present. Noncommunicable 36–48 hours after treatment with antibiotics.	Identify and remove sick children. Treat with medication 3–4 days before returning to group care. Notify parents of exposed children to contact their physician. Immunize children. Practice good hand-washing techniques; sanitize contaminated objects.
Hepatitis (Infectious; Type A)	Fever, fatigue, loss of appetite, nausea abdominal pain (in region of liver). Illness may be accompanied by yellowing of the skin and eyeballs (jaundice) in adults, but not always in children.	Virus	Fecal-oral route. Also spread via contaminated food, water, milk, and objects.	10–50 days (average range 30–35 days)	7–10 days prior to onset of symptoms to not more than 7 days after onset of jaundice.	Exclude from group settings a minimum of 2 weeks following onset. Special attention to careful handwashing after going to the bathroom and before eating is critical following an outbreak. Report disease incidences to public health authorities. Exclude persons exposed to the virus for 6 weeks unless they obtain gamma globulin injection.
Impetigo	Infection of the skin forming crusty, moist lesions usually on the face, ears, and around the nose. Highly contagious. Common among children.	Bacterial	Direct contact with discharge from sores; indirect contact with contaminated articles of clothing, tissues, etc.	2–5 days; may be as long as 10 days	Until lesions are healed.	Exclusions from group settings until lesions have been treated with antibiotics for 24–48 hours.

TABLE 7–1 Common Communicable Illnesses (Continued)

COMMUNICABLE ILLNESS	SIGNS AND SYMPTOMS	INFECTIOUS AGENT	METHODS OF TRANSMISSION	INCUBATION PERIOD	LENGTH OF COMMUNICABILITY	CONTROL MEASURES
Lice (head)	Lice are seldom visible to the naked eye. White nits (eggs) may be apparent on hair shafts. The most obvious symptom is itching of the scalp, especially behind the ears and at the base of the neck.	Head louse	Direct contact with infected persons or with their personal articles, e.g., hats, hair brushes, combs, or clothing. Lice can survive for 2–3 weeks on bedding, carpet, furniture, car seats, clothing, etc.	Nits hatch in 1 week and reach maturity within 2 weeks	While lice remain alive on infested persons or clothing; until nits have been destroyed.	Infested children should be excluded from group settings until treated. Hair should be washed with a special medicated shampoo and rinsed with a vinegar/water solution (any concentration will work) to ease removal of all nits (using a fine-toothed comb). Heat from a hair dryer also helps destroy the eggs. All friends and family should be carefully checked. Thoroughly clean child's environment; vacuum carpets/upholstery, wash/dry or dry clean bedding, clothing, hairbrushes. Seal non-washable items in plastic bag for one month.
Measles (Rubeola)	Fever, cough, runny nose, eyes sensitive to light. Dark red blotchy rash that often begins on the face and neck, then spreads over the entire body. Highly communicable.	Virus	Airborne: through coughs, sneezes, and contact with contaminated articles.	8–13 days; rash develops approximately 14 days after exposure	From beginning of symptoms until 4 days after rash appears.	Most effective control method is immunization. Good personal hygiene, especially handwashing, and covering coughs. Exclude child for at least 4 days after rash appears.

Table 7–1 Continued

Mononucleosis	Characteristic symptoms include sore throat, intermittent fever, fatigue, and enlarged lymph glands in the neck. May also be accompanied by headache and enlarged liver or spleen.	Virus	Airborne: also direct contact with the mouth of an infected person.	10–14 days for children; 30–50 days for adults	Unknown. Organisms may be present in oral secretions for as long as one year following illness.	None known. Child should be kept home until over the acute phase (6–10 days).
Mumps	Sudden onset of fever with swelling of the salivary glands.	Virus	Airborne: through coughs and sneezes; direct contact with oral secretions of infected persons.	12–26 days	4–6 days prior to the onset of symptoms until swelling in the salivary glands is gone (7–9 days).	Immunization provides permanent protection. Peak incidence is in winter and spring. Exclude children from school or group settings until all symptoms have disappeared.
Pinworms	Irritability, and itching of the rectal area. Common among young children.	Parasite; not contagious from animals.	Infectious eggs are transferred from person to person by contaminated hands (oral-fecal route). Indirectly spread by contaminated bedding, food, clothing, swimming pool.	Life cycle of the worm is 3–6 weeks; persons can also reinfect themselves.	2–8 weeks or as long as a source of infection remains present.	Infected children must be excluded from school until treated with medication; may return after initial dose. All infected and noninfected members of a family must be treated at one time. Frequent handwashing is essential; discourage nail biting or sucking on fingers. Daily baths and change of linen are necessary.

TABLE 7–1 Common Communicable Illnesses (Continued)

COMMUNICABLE ILLNESS	SIGNS AND SYMPTOMS	INFECTIOUS AGENT	METHODS OF TRANSMISSION	INCUBATION PERIOD	LENGTH OF COMMUNICABILITY	CONTROL MEASURES
Pinworms (continued)		seats at least			Disinfect school toilet	once a day. Vacuum carpeted areas daily. Eggs are also destroyed when exposed to temperatures over 132°F. Education and good personal hygiene are vital to control.
Ringworm	An infection of the scalp, skin, or nails. Causes flat, spreading, oval-shaped lesions that may become dry and scaly or moist and crusted. When it is present on the feet it is commonly called athlete's foot. Infected nails may become discolored, brittle, or chalky or they may disintegrate.	Fungus	Direct or indirect contact with infected persons, their personal items, showers, swimming pools, theater seats, etc. Dogs and cats may also be infected and transmit it to children or adults.	1–4 days, (unknown for athlete's foot)	As long as lesions are present.	Exclude children from gyms, pools, or activities where they are likely to expose others. May return to group care following medical treatment with a fungicidal ointment. All shared areas, such as pools and showers should be thoroughly cleansed with a fungicide.

Table 7–1 Continued

Rocky Mountain Spotted Fever	Onset usually abrupt; fever (101°–104°F); joint and muscle pain, severe nausea and vomiting, and white coating on tongue. Rash appears on 2nd to 5th day over forehead, wrist, and ankles; later covers entire body. Can be fatal if untreated.	Bacteria	Indirect transmission: tick bite.	2–14 days; average 7 days	Not contagious from person to person.	Prompt removal of ticks; not all ticks cause illness. Administration of antibiotics. Use insect repellent on clothes when outdoors.
Roseola Infantum (6 mo. to 3 yr.)	Most common in the spring and fall. Fever rises abruptly (102°–105°F) and lasts 3–4 days; loss of appetite, listlessness, development of rash on trunk, arms, and neck lasting 1–2 days.	Virus	Unknown	10–15 days	1–2 days before onset to several days following fading of the rash.	Exclude from school or group care during the acute phase.
Rubella (German Measles)	Mild fever; rash begins on face and neck and rarely lasts more than 3 days. May have arthritislike discomfort and swelling in joints.	Virus	Airborne: through contact with respiratory secretions, e.g., coughs, sneezes.	14–21 days	From one week prior to 5 days following onset of the rash.	Immunization offers permanent protection. Children must be excluded from school for at least 5 days.

TABLE 7–1 Common Communicable Illnesses (Continued)

COMMUNICABLE ILLNESS	SIGNS AND SYMPTOMS	INFECTIOUS AGENT	METHODS OF TRANSMISSION	INCUBATION PERIOD	LENGTH OF COMMUNICABILITY	CONTROL MEASURES
Salmonellosis	Abdominal pain and cramping, sudden fever, severe diarrhea (may contain blood), nausea and vomiting lasts 5–7 days.	Bacteria	Fecal-oral transmission: via dirty hands. Also contaminated food (especially improperly cooked poultry, milk, eggs) water supplies, and infected animals.	6–48 hours	Throughout acute illness; may remain a carrier for months.	Attempt to identify source. Exclude children/adults with diarrhea; may return when symptoms end. Carriers should not handle or prepare food until stool cultures are negative. Practice good handwashing and sanitizing procedures.
Scabies	Characteristic burrows or linear tunnels under the skin, especially between the fingers and around the wrists, elbows, waist, thighs, and buttocks. Causes intense itching.	Parasite	Direct contact with an infected person.	Several days to 2–4 weeks	Until all mites and eggs are destroyed.	Children should be excluded from school or group care until treated. Affected persons should bathe with prescribed soap and carefully launder all bedding and clothing. All contacts of the infected person should be notified.
Streptococcal Infections (strep throat, scarlatina, rheumatic fever)	Sudden onset. High fever accompanied by sore, red throat; may also have nausea, vomiting, headache, white patches on	Bacteria	Airborne: via droplets from coughs or sneezes. May also be transmitted by food and raw milk.	1–4 days	Throughout the illness and for approximately 10 days afterward, unless treated with antibiotics. Medical	Exclude child with symptoms. Antibiotic treatment is essential. Avoid crowding in classrooms. Practice frequent handwashing,

Table 7–1 Continued

	tonsils, and enlarged glands. Development of a rash depends on the infectious organism.				treatment eliminates communicability within 36 hours. Can develop rheumatic fever or become a carrier if not treated.	educating children, and careful supervision of food handlers.
Tetanus	Muscular spasms and stiffness, especially in the muscles around the neck and mouth. Can lead to convulsions, inability to breathe, and death.	Bacteria	Indirect: organisms live in soil and dust; enter body through wounds, especially puncture-type injuries, burns, and unnoticed cuts.	4 days to 2 weeks	Not contagious.	Immunization every 8–10 years affords complete protection.

Approximately 3,000 cases of children with AIDS have been identified in the United States. The majority of these are infants who have acquired the human immunodeficiency virus (HIV) from their mother during gestation or the birth process. They are usually quite ill, seldom live longer than 3 years and, therefore, are unlikely to be placed in traditional child care settings. A small percentage of children have been infected with the HIV virus through blood transfusion (Rudigier, 1990).

HIV, which causes AIDS, is not transmitted through casual contact, such as hugging, touching, kissing, sitting next to an infected person, or even sharing their bathroom or eating utensils (Quackenbush, 1988). It is, however, transmitted through sexual contact with an infected individual and by receiving blood or blood products contaminated with the HIV virus (U. S. Department of Health and Human Services, 1988). Because these circumstances are not likely to occur in child care settings, the risk of AIDS being spread to caregivers or other children is extremely low. To this date there are no known cases of AIDS in the United States that have been transmitted among children in group care settings (Trowbridge, 1991). The risk may actually be greater of an unidentified, infected adult caregiver transmitting the virus to uninfected children, especially while caring for bleeding injuries. For this reason, disposable latex gloves should be worn by all caregivers whenever administering first aid, and careful handwashing should follow.

The Center for Disease Control (CDC) recommends that children infected with AIDS *only* be excluded from group child care programs if they have open sores, uncontrollable nosebleeds, bloody diarrhea, or are at high risk for exposing others to blood-contaminated body fluids. However, children with AIDS run a more serious risk of contracting illnesses and infections from the other children because their immune systems are not functioning properly. These infections pose a serious threat to the child's life.

Despite the relatively low incidence of AIDS among young children, caregivers should always follow universal precautions for the safe handling of items contaminated with blood or other body fluids, including vomit, urine, saliva, and feces. Disposable latex gloves should always be worn whenever administering first aid and changing diapers. Contaminated surfaces should be disinfected promptly. A 1:10 solution of household bleach to water is effective and inexpensive. Changing tables can be covered with disposable paper; tissues and towels should also be disposable if possible. Soiled items should be sealed in plastic bags for disposal. Sponges and mops should be soaked for 20–30 minutes in disinfectant at least once a week. However, *handwashing is always the most effective control measure available to caregivers.*

Caregivers who test positive for HIV may not always choose to reveal this information because they are wary of its negative consequences. However, if strict sanitary procedures are followed and care is exercised in the handling of bleeding injuries, there should be no reason why an infected caregiver cannot continue working with children.

Every day more is understood about HIV and AIDS. Local health departments and medical centers can provide valuable information concerning this disease and can assist centers in establishing apppropriate guidelines and safety procedures.

Sudden Infant Death Syndrome (SIDS)

Sudden infant death syndrome is a leading cause of death among seemingly healthy infants under one year of age. Approximately 6000–8000 infants die each year. No single cause for this condition has yet been identified. However, certain abnormalities and immature development of the respiratory system have been suggested as possible factors (Barness, 1992).

Many infants who die from SIDS, especially those born prematurely or who had a low birth weight, experience repeated interruptions of breathing called *apnea*. Some children have colds or mild upper respiratory infections. Male and minority infants seem to be at greater risk than other groups, especially those 6 weeks to 6 months old. More deaths occur during the winter months and at night. Other risk factors that have been studied include poverty, teenage or substance-abusing mothers, mothers who smoke, a family history of SIDS (Haglund, 1990), and sleep position. Infants who sleep on their stomachs appear to be at a higher risk (Wong, 1993). Many infants appear to be in good health at the time of death. While there is no specific treatment for SIDS, electronic home monitors are sometimes used to detect breathing irregularities in infants suspected to be at-risk: however, their use remains controversial.

Since there is often no identifiable cause, parents may blame themselves for being negligent or having used poor judgment. They believe that somehow they could have prevented this tragedy. Consequently, parents who have experienced the unexpected death of an infant from SIDS require special emotional support and counselling. Local chapters of the National Sudden Infant Death Foundation provide support to help parents cope with their grief. The SIDS Alliance and the National SIDS Clearinghouse also provide information and support to families. (See Appendix C.)

COMMON ACUTE ILLNESSES

Children experience many forms of acute illness; however, not all of these are contagious. Caregivers must be able to distinguish conditions that are contagious from those that are limited to an individual child. However, teachers and caregivers must never attempt to diagnose children's health problems. Their primary responsibilities include identifying children who are ill, making them comfortable until parents arrive, and advising the family to contact their health care provider. The remainder of this unit is devoted to several acute illnesses and health complaints commonly experienced by young children.

Colds

Colds are a common ailment of young children; they may experience as many as seven to eight colds during a year, Figure 7–2. Colds are caused by a viral *infection* of the nose and throat. Antibiotics are not effective against most viruses and are, therefore, of limited value for treating simple colds. However, antibiotics may be prescribed to treat complications, or secondary infections, that develop.

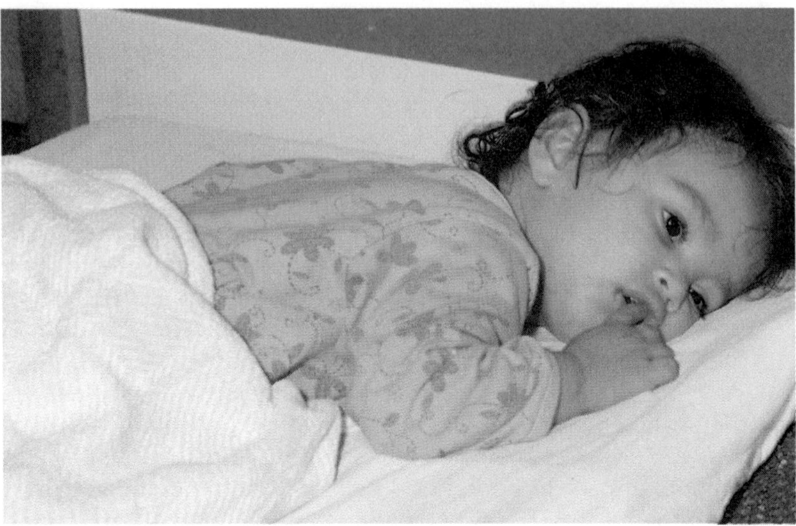

Figure 7–2 Listlessness may be an early indication of an oncoming cold.

Because colds are highly contagious during the first two or three days, children should be kept home and away from group care settings. Treatment, including rest, increased intake of liquids (water, fruit juices, soups), and nonaspirin fever-reducing medication can be provided by the child's parents and is usually adequate for most colds.

Although colds themselves are not serious, complications can sometimes develop. Toddlers and preschool-aged children are often more susceptible to complications such as earaches, bronchitis, croup, and pneumonia. Parents should watch children closely and contact their physician if any complications develop or the child does not improve within four to five days. Parents should also be advised to seek immediate medical attention for children who develop white spots in their throats or on tonsils in order to rule out the possibility of strep throat.

Diaper Rash

Diaper rash is an irritation of the skin in and around the buttocks and genital area. It is caused by prolonged contact with ammonia in urine and organic acids in diarrheal stools. Severe burning causes affected patches of the skin to appear reddened and covered with tiny pimples. Diaper rash occurs more often in formula-fed infants than in breast-fed infants (Pringle, 1982). Reactions to fabric softeners, soaps, lotions, powders, and disposable diapers can also cause diaper rash in infants with sensitive skin.

Prompt changing of wet and soiled diapers followed by a thorough cleansing of the skin is often sufficient prevention and treatment of diaper rash. Avoid using baby powders and talcs because babies are apt to inhale the fine powder (Child Health Alert, 1991). Also, when combined with urine, powders become good media for bacterial growth. A thin layer of zinc oxide ointment can be applied to help protect irritated areas. Allowing the infant to go without diapers (when at home) and exposing irritated skin to the air also speeds the healing process. Plastic pants and disposable diapers with a plastic outer layer should be avoided because they tend to hold in moisture.

Diarrhea

The term diarrhea refers to frequent watery or very soft bowel movements. They may be foul-smelling and also contain particles of blood or mucus. Some causes of diarrhea in children include:

- viral, bacterial, or parasite infections, such as giardia or hepatitis A
- antibiotic therapy
- recent dietary changes
- food allergies
- food poisoning
- illnesses, such as earaches, colds, strep throat, or cystic fibrosis

Frequent or prolonged diarrhea can result in *dehydration*, especially in infants and toddlers. Dehydration involves a loss of body water and can occur quickly in young children because of their small body size. Excessive dehydration can be fatal (Wong, 1993). For this reason, it is critical that caregivers observe carefully for signs of dehydration:

- dryness of the mouth
- *listlessness*
- sunken eyes
- absence of tears
- decreased urinary output
- rapid, weak pulse
- skin loses elasticity; doughlike

It is also important to keep track of the number and size or amount of bowel movements and to observe them for color, consistency, and the presence of blood, mucus, or pus. Medical advice should be sought immediately if diarrhea is severe or the child becomes lethargic or drowsy.

Children who have experienced diarrhea within the past 24 hours should be excluded from group care settings. Exceptions to this policy would include children whose diarrhea resulted from noncontagious conditions such as food allergies, changes in diet, or recent treatment with antibiotics. However, even these children may not feel well enough to attend school or group care and participate in activities. The problem and inconvenience of frequent accidental soiling may also be too time-consuming for caregivers to manage.

Most cases of acute diarrhea can be treated simply by placing the child on a clear liquid diet for a period of 24 hours. Clear broths or soups, flavored gelatin, noncitrus juices, ginger ale, 7-UP®, or water can be offered in small amounts. Other liquids and soft foods can gradually be added to the diet. Any complaint of pain that is continuous or located in the lower right side of the *abdomen* should be reported promptly to the child's parents and checked by a physician.

Diarrhea that lasts longer than several days should be cause for concern, especially if it is accompanied by bloating, change of appetite, or weight loss. The child should be excluded from group care settings until a cause is determined, and conditions such as giardia, dysentery, or hepatitis A have been ruled out.

Dizziness

Occasionally, young children will complain of feeling dizzy, usually after vigorous activity or play. The sensation of spinning or unsteadiness usually lasts only a few seconds. However, repeated complaints of dizziness should be noted and reported to the child's parents. They should be advised to contact their physician. Dizziness can be a symptom of other health conditions including:

- ear infections
- fever
- headaches
- head injuries
- anemia
- nasal congestion and sinus infections
- brain tumor (rare)

Temporary episodes of dizziness usually respond to simple first aid measures. Have the child lie down quietly or rest with head on or between the knees until the sensation has passed. Quiet play can be resumed when the child no longer feels dizzy. Alert parents of this experience so they can continue to observe the child at home.

If dizziness is accompanied by any loss of balance or coordination, the child's parents should contact a physician at once for advice. Dizziness that results from an underlying health problem will usually not respond to first aid measures.

Earache

Earaches and ear infections occur more frequently during the toddler and preschool years, especially in boys. As children grow older, structures in the nose, ear, and throat mature and resistance to infection (antibody formation) increases. As a result, fewer ear infections are likely to occur.

Earaches frequently accompany colds and the congestion of allergies. Passageways located between the ear and nose swell and can lead to a buildup of fluid in the middle ear. This condition is known as otitis media. If is often accompanied by pain, fever, and temporary or chronic hearing loss (Froom, 1991). Other possible causes of earache can include dental cavities, excessive wax, or foreign objects such as stones, pieces of a toy, or food that have been pushed into the ear canal. Feeding infants in a reclining position also increases the likelihood of developing ear infections (Child Health Alert, 1990).

Not all children recognize or complain of discomfort due to earaches. This is especially true of children who are too young to talk. Teachers and caregivers should observe children for signs that may indicate an ear infection, including:

- tugging or rubbing of the affected ear
- refusal to eat or swallow
- redness of the outer ear
- fever
- dizziness
- irritability
- discharge from the ear canal
- difficulty hearing

Any complaint of ear pain or earache should be checked by the child's physician. Persistent otitis media can interfere with the child's speech and language development. Ear infections must be treated with antibiotics to prevent further complications from developing. It is important that children take all of the prescribed medication, and then be rechecked by their physician to be sure the infection is gone. Additional medication may be necessary to completely clear up some ear infections. Decongestants and antihistamines may also be prescribed to help dry up fluid accumulation.

Surgical insertion of tubes into the eardrum is sometimes recommended for children with repeated infections and chronic fluid build-up to lessen the risk of permanent hearing loss. Caregivers should be alert to any children with tubes in their ears. Special precautions must be taken to avoid getting water in the outer ear canal during activities that involve water play, such as swimming, bathing, or playing in pools or sprinklers. Ear plugs or special plastic putty are commonly used for this purpose.

Caregivers can provide temporary relief from the pain of an earache by having the child lie down and rest the affected ear on a warm water bottle or blanket. However, care must be used so that the child is not accidentally burned. A small, dry cotton ball, placed in the outer ear, will sometimes also help lessen the pain of an earache by blocking contact with the air. Excess wax and foreign objects should only be removed by a physician.

Fainting

Fainting, a momentary loss of consciousness, occurs when blood supply to the brain is temporarily reduced. Possible causes for this condition in young children include:

- anemia
- breathholding
- *hyperventilation*
- extreme excitement or hysteria

- drug reactions
- illness or infection
- poisoning

Initially, children may complain of feeling dizzy or weak. Very quickly the skin becomes pale, cool, and moist, and the child may collapse. Injuries can be avoided by gently lowering the child to the floor.

Immediate care of a child who faints involves lying the child down and elevating the legs 8 to 10 inches on a pillow. A light blanket can be placed over the child for extra warmth. Breathing is made easier if clothing is loosened from around the neck and waist. No attempt should be made to give the child anything to eat or drink until consciousness is regained. Parents should be notified and encouraged to consult the child's physician.

Fever

Activity, age, eating, sleeping, and the time of day can cause normal fluctuations in children's temperatures. However, an elevated ***temperature*** is usually an indication of illness or infection, especially if the child complains of other discomforts such as headache, coughing, nausea, or sore throat. Teachers and child caregivers may first notice a child's ***fever*** by observing:

- flushed or reddened face
- listlessness or desire to sleep
- skin that is warm to the touch
- "glassy" eyes
- loss of appetite
- complaints of not feeling well
- increased perspiration

A child's temperature should be checked if there is any reason to believe that a fever might be present, Table 7–2. Only the oral and axillary methods are recommended; only the axillary method should be used with infants. A number of studies have examined the reliability and accuracy of thermometers currently on the market. Readings from plastic strip and aural (ear) infrared thermometers were found to be inconsistent when compared to glass thermometers. While these newer thermometers may be more convenient and user-friendly, their routine use is being discouraged (*Child Health Alert*, September 1994). Children with an oral temperature over 100°F (37.8°C) or axillary temperature over 99°F (37.2°C) should be sent home where they can be monitored by parents (unless the center has a policy of caring for sick children). Glass thermometers should be cleaned carefully after each use, Table 7–3.

Work schedules or prior commitments may make it difficult for parents to respond promptly and take a sick child home. When these situations arise, there are measures teachers or caregivers can take to make a feverish child more comfortable. The child should be moved to a separate room or to a cot or crib in a quiet

TABLE 7-2 How to Take a Child's Temperature

Oral Method

1. Rinse the thermometer under running water if it has been stored in a chemical solution.
2. Carefully inspect the thermometer for any broken edges, especially around the mercury bulb.
3. Shake the mercury down to the lowest point.
4. Place the thermometer (mercury bulb end) in the child's mouth and under the tongue. Caution children not to bite down on the thermometer, but only to close their lips tightly around it. Continue to hold onto the thermometer as long as it is in the child's mouth. Leave in place 3 minutes.
5. Remove the thermometer. Wipe with a clean tissue. Hold it at eye level and rotate it gently until the mercury level can be read. Normal oral temperature is 98°F–99.4°F (36.7°C–37.4°C).
6. Clean the thermometer thoroughly after each use.

Axillary Method

1. Rinse the thermometer under running water if it has been stored in a chemical solution.
2. Carefully inspect the thermometer for any broken or sharp edges, especially around the bulb.
3. Shake the thermometer down until the mercury is at the lowest point.
4. Place the thermometer against the child's skin under the armpit. Bring the child's arm down and press it gently against the side of the body.
5. Hold the thermometer in place for 3 minutes.
6. Remove and read. Normal axillary temperature is 97°F–98°F (36.1°C–36.7°C).
7. Clean the thermometer thoroughly after each use.

TABLE 7-3 How to Clean a Thermometer

1. Wash the thermometer with a soapy cotton ball.
2. Rinse under cool, running water. (Hot water may cause the thermometer to break.)
3. Dry thoroughly.
4. Soak thermometer in an antiseptic solution (isopropyl or rubbing alcohol) for at least 20 minutes.
5. Rinse under running water and store in a clean container.

corner of the room to rest. Cool room temperatures, removing warm clothing, and giving extra fluids to drink will help make the child feel more comfortable. Sponging the child with cool water will also help lower a high temperature. No medications should be given unless ordered by a physician.

Headaches

Headaches are not a common complaint of young children. When they do occur, it is usually as a symptom of some other condition, such as:

- bacterial or viral infections
- allergies
- head injuries
- emotional tension or stress
- reaction to medication
- lead poisoning
- hunger
- eye strain
- nasal congestion
- brain tumor (rare)
- constipation
- carbon monoxide poisoning

In the absence of any fever, rash, vomiting, or *disorientation*, children can remain in the child care setting and continue to be observed. Frequently, their headaches will disappear with rest and interest in a new activity. Patterns of repeated or intense headaches should be noted and parents encouraged to discuss the problem with the child's physician.

Heat Rash

Heat rash is characterized by fine, red, raised bumps. Generally, it is located around the neck, chest, waistline, cheeks, and inner areas of the forearm. Heat rash is caused by a blockage of sweat glands and usually develops suddenly during hot weather or when children are dressed too warmly.

Heat rash is not contagious. However, there are several measures that can be taken to make a child more comfortable. Affected areas can be washed with cool water, dried thoroughly, and dusted sparingly with cornstarch. Overdressing should be avoided, both during summer and winter months. Parents should be encouraged to help children dress in clothing that is lightweight and made of nonsynthetic fabrics.

Lyme Disease

Lyme disease is a bacterial illness caused by the bite of infected deer ticks commonly found in grassy and wooded areas during the summer and fall months.

Because these ticks are only about the size of a large pinhead, they can easily go unnoticed.

Early symptoms of Lyme disease are often vague and difficult to diagnose. Within the first few weeks of a bite, a small red, flat, or raised area may develop at the site, followed by a localized rash that gradually disappears. Flulike symptoms, including fever, chills, fatigue, headache, and joint pain may also be experienced during this stage. If the bacterial infection is not diagnosed early and treated with antibiotics, complications, including arthritis, heart, and/or neurological problems can develop within two years of the initial bite. A new blood test is now available for early detection.

Not everyone who is bitten by a deer tick will develop Lyme disease. While the infection is more common along the East coast, it has been identified in nearly every U.S. state and many provinces of Canada. Because the bite and early stages of the illness may not be recognized, prevention is the most desirable approach, especially with young children. Insect/tick repellents containing DEET (avoid aerosol sprays) should be applied whenever children play outdoors in affected areas (Child Health Alert, June 1994). Children's hair, bodies (especially around the waist and underarms), and the inside seams of clothing and socks should be inspected carefully. If a tick is discovered on the skin, it should be removed immediately (see Chapter 10) and the area cleansed thoroughly. The development of any unusual symptoms or rash should be reported to a physician at once.

Reye's Syndrome

Reye's syndrome is an acute childhood illness that can develop within 3–5 days following viral infections, particularly chickenpox, influenza, and upper respiratory illnesses. While aspirin does not cause Reye's syndrome, its use has been linked to the onset of this disease in over 90 percent of the cases (Margolis, 1995). Consequently, parents are now warned not to administer aspirin to children who have chickenpox or flulike symptoms. Aspirin bottles also carry this mandatory warning on the label. Many cold medications contain aspirin or aspirinlike compounds and should be used only on the advice of a physician.

Reye's syndrome equally affects boys and girls under sixteen. The onset of symptoms appears just as the child seems to be recovering from a viral illness. Frequent vomiting, sudden fever, mental confusion, drowsiness, irritability, body rigidity, and coma are characteristic indicators. However, the incidence of Reye's syndrome continues to decrease as a result of greater awareness and improved diagnostic techniques.

Sore Throat

Sore throats are a fairly common complaint among young children, especially during the fall and winter seasons. Most sore throats are caused by viral infections that are relatively harmless. Antibiotics are not effective against most viral infections and so are not usually prescribed.

It is extremely important, however, not to ignore a child's complaint of sore throat. A small percentage of sore throats are caused by a highly contagious streptococcal infection, Table 7–1. Although most children are quite ill with these infections, some may experience only mild symptoms or none at all. They can unknowingly become carriers of the infection and capable of spreading it to others. Strep throat must be identified and treated with antibiotics. A routine throat culture can safely determine whether or not a strep infection is present. Left untreated, strep throat can lead to serious complications, including rheumatic fever and rheumatic heart disease (Margolis, 1995).

Stomachaches

Most children experience stomachaches at one time or another. There are many causes for stomachaches in children:

- food allergies or intolerance
- appendicitis
- *intestinal* infections, e.g., parasites, Salmonella
- urinary tract infections
- gas or constipation
- side effect to medication, especially antibiotics
- change in diet
- emotional stress
- need for attention
- hunger
- diarrhea
- vomiting
- strep throat

There are a number of things teachers and caregivers can check to determine whether or not a child's stomach pain is serious. First, check to see if the pain is continuous or a cramping-type pain that comes and goes. Second, check for a fever. If no fever is present, the stomachache is probably not serious. Encourage the child to go to the bathroom and see if *urination* or having a bowel movement relieves the pain. Have the child rest quietly to see if the discomfort goes away. Check with parents to see if the child is taking any medication. Stomach pain or stomachaches should be considered serious if they:

- disrupt a child's activity, e.g., running, playing, eating, sleeping
- cause tenderness of the abdomen
- are accompanied by diarrhea, vomiting, or severe cramping
- last longer than 3 to 4 hours
- result in stools that are bloody or contain mucus

If any of these conditions occur while the child is attending school or group care, parents should be notified and advised to seek prompt medical attention for the child.

Teething

While each child responds differently to the teething process, most do not experience significant discomfort or changes in behavior. An increase in drooling and chewing activity for several days may be all that is noticeable. Fever, diarrhea, and vomiting are not caused by teething, but may be an indication of illness. Chilled teething rings and firm objects that can be chewed on can provide some relief to swollen gums.

Toothache

Tooth decay is the most common cause of toothache. Children may complain of a throbbing pain that sometimes radiates into the ear. Redness and swelling can often be observed around the gumline of the affected tooth. Foods that are hot or very sweet may intensify pain. Similar tooth discomfort may be experienced by older children during the process of losing baby teeth and eruption of permanent teeth.

Toothaches should be checked promptly by the child's dentist. In the meantime, an icepack applied to the cheek on the affected side may make the child more comfortable. Aspirin-free products can also be administered by the child's parents for pain relief. Proper brushing after eating will help to eliminate a significant amount of tooth decay, Figure 7–3.

Figure 7–3 Brushing teeth after eating helps to reduce tooth decay.

Vomiting

Vomiting is usually a symptom of an acute illness or some other health problem, such as:

- emotional upset
- viral or bacterial infection, e.g., stomach flu, strep throat
- Reye's syndrome
- ear infections
- meningitis
- *salmonellosis*
- indigestion
- severe coughing
- drug reactions
- head injury
- poisoning

The exact number of times, amount, and composition of vomited material is very important to record. Dehydration and disturbance of the body's chemical balance can occur with prolonged or excessive vomiting, especially in infants and toddlers. Children should be observed carefully for:

- high fever
- abdominal pain
- signs of dehydration
- headache
- excessive drowsiness
- difficulty breathing
- sore throat
- exhaustion

Any child who continues to vomit and shows signs of a sore throat, fever, or stomach pains should be sent home as soon as possible. The teacher or child caregiver should also advise the child's parents to contact their physician for further advice.

In the absence of any other symptoms, a single episode of vomiting may simply be the result of emotional upset, dislike of a particular food, excess mucus, or a reaction to medication. Usually the child feels better immediately after vomiting. These children can remain at the school or child care center and be encouraged to rest until they feel better.

In addition to not feeling well, the act of vomiting itself may be very upsetting and frightening to the young child. Extra reassurance and comforting from teachers and child caregivers can make the experience less traumatic. Infants should be positioned on their stomachs with their hips and legs raised. This position allows vomited material to flow out of the mouth and prevent choking. Older children should also be watched very closely so they don't choke or inhale vomitus.

Summary

Illness is a common occurrence whenever groups of children spend time together. Teachers and child caregivers must learn to recognize the early signs of illness and exclude sick children in order to protect the entire group.

Exclusion policies serve as guidelines for deciding when a child is too ill to be admitted to preschool or child care programs. Early recognition of noncontagious illnesses can help to avoid serious complications from developing later. Teachers and child caregivers can carry out temporary measures to make sick children more comfortable until parents arrive to take them home.

Suggested Activities

1. With a partner, practice taking each other's axillary and oral temperatures. Follow steps for cleaning the thermometer between each use.
2. Divide the class into groups of five to six students. Discuss how each of you feels about caring for children who are ill. Could you hold or cuddle a child with a high fever or diarrhea? What are your feelings about being exposed to children's contagious illnesses? How might you react if an infant just vomited on your new sweater? If you feel uncomfortable around sick children, what steps can you take to better cope with the situation?
3. Select another student as a partner and observe that person carefully for 20 seconds. Now look away. Write down everything you can remember about this person, such as eye color, hair color, scars or moles, approximate weight, height, color of skin, shape of teeth, clothing, etc. What can you do to improve your observational skills?

Chapter Review

A. Match the signs/symptoms in Column I with the correct communicable illness in Column II.

Column I	Column II
1. swelling and redness of white portion of the eye	a. chickenpox
2. frequent itching of the scalp	b. strep throat
3. flat, oval-shaped lesions on the scalp, skin; infected nails become discolored, brittle, chalky, or they may disintegrate	c. lice
4. high fever; red, sore throat	d. dysentery
5. mild fever and rash that lasts approximately three days	e. conjunctivitis
6. irritability and itching of the rectal area	f. ringworm
7. red rash with blisterlike heads; coldlike symptoms	g. German measles
8. sudden onset of fever; swelling of salivary glands	h. scabies
9. burrows or linear tunnels under the skin; intense itching	i. pinworms
10. vomiting, abdominal pain, diarrhea that may be bloody	j. mumps

B. Case Study

The teacher has noticed that Kati seems quite restless today and is having difficulty concentrating on any task she starts. She is continuously squirming whether in a chair or sitting on the floor. On a number of occasions throughout the morning, the teacher has observed Kati scratching her bottom.

1. What type of problem might the teacher suspect Kati is having?
2. What control measures should be taken?
3. When can she return to school?
4. For what length of time after an outbreak must the teacher watch for the development of similar problems in other children?
5. What special personal health measures should be emphasized to the other children?

C. Describe what you would do in each of the following situations:

1. You have just finished serving lunch to the children, when Mara begins to vomit.
2. The class is involved in a game of Keep-Away. Ted suddenly complains of feeling dizzy.
3. During check in, a parent mentions that his son has been experiencing stomachaches every morning before coming to school.
4. Leandra wakes up from her afternoon nap, crying because her ear hurts.
5. You have just changed a toddler's diaper for the third time in the last hour because of diarrhea.
6. Sami enters the classroom, sneezing and blowing his nose.
7. While you are helping Erin put on her coat to go outdoors, you notice that her skin feels very warm.
8. Richard refuses to eat his lunch because it makes his teeth hurt.
9. While you are cleaning up the blocks, Tommy tells you that his throat is sore and it hurts to swallow.
10. You have just taken Juanita's temperature (orally) and it is 101°F.

References

An Infant's Feeding Position May Increase the Likelihood of Ear Infections. *Child Health Alert*, February 1990. p. 6.

Aural Infrared Thermometers—Are They Accurate. *Child Health Alert*, September 1994. 12: 2.

Barness, L. A., and Gilbert-Barness, E. 1992. Cause of Death: SIDS or Something Else? *Contemporary Pediatrics*, 9: 13-31.

Froom, J., and Culpepper, L. 1991. Otitis Media in Day-Care Children: A Report from the International Care Network. *Journal of Family Practice*, 32(3): 289–294.

Haglund, B., and Cnattinguis, S. 1990. Cigarette Smoking as a Risk Factor for Sudden Infant Death Syndrome. *American Journal of Public Health* 80(1): 29–32.

Margolis, J. (Ed.) 1995. *Johns Hopkins: Symptoms and Remedies*. New York: Rebus.

Mosquitos, Ticks, and Insect Repellents. *Child Health Alert*. June 1994. p. 1.

Persistent Hazards to Young Children: Inhalation of Baby Powder. June 1991. *Child Health Alert*, pp. 4–5.

Pringle, S., and Ramsey, B. 1982. *Promoting the Health of Children*. St. Louis, MO: C. V. Mosby Co.

Quakenbush, M., and Villarreal, S. 1988. *Does AIDS Hurt: Educating Young Children (Ages 1–12)*. Santa Cruz, CA: Network Publications.

Rudigier, A. 1990. The Dilemmas of Childhood HIV Infection. *Children Today* 19(4): 26–29.

Surgeon General's Report on Acquired Immune Deficiency Syndrome. 1988. Washington, DC: U. S. Department of Health and Human Services.

Trowbridge, G., Marshall, G., Fahner, J., and Barbour, S. 1991. HIV: Recognizing and Managing the Infant At Risk. *Contemporary Pediatrics*. 10: 118–134.

Wong, D. 1993. *Essentials of Pediatric Nursing*. St. Louis, MO: C. V. Mosby.

Additional Reading

Aspirin As a Cause of Reye's Syndrome—Is the Question At Last Resolved?" April 1987. *Child Health Alert*, pp. 1–3.

Can We Predict When Children Have Ear Infections? *Child Health Alert*. May 1995. 13: 1.

Child Care and Ill Children and Healthy Child Care Practices. 1994. Washington, DC: NAEYC.

Friedman, M. and Weiss, E. 1992. All About Ear Infections. *Parents*, 67(3): 172–182.

Improper Use of Acetaminophen by Parents. January, 1988. *Child Health Alert*, pp. 1–2.

Kerr, D. L. 1988. AIDS Update: Pediatric Guidelines for Infection Control of HIV (AIDS Virus) in Schools and Day Care Settings. *Journal of School Health* 58(10): 419–420.

Lyme Disease: Hard to Catch. *UC Berkeley Wellness Letter*. August 1995. p. 4.

Long-Term Complications of Bacterial Meningitis in Children. January 1991. *Child Health Alert*, pp. 1–2.

Merrifield, M. 1990. *Come Sit By Me*. Toronto, Ontario, Canada: Women's Press.

Moser, P. W. September 1991. Danger in Diaperland (Giardia). *In Health*. pp. 77–80.

Pomeranz, V. "Your Child Has Been Exposed (Head Lice, Scabies, Pinworms)." *Parents* 58(3): 94.

Reye's Syndrome—Continuing the Decline. June 1989. *Child Health Alert* pp. 3–4.

Skeen, P., and Hodson, D. "AIDS: What Adults Should Know About AIDS." May 1987. *Young Children* 42(4): 65–71.

UNIT

3

Safety for the Young Child

Chapter 8

Creating a Safe Environment

Terms to Know

environment
cognitive
accreditation
licensing
regulation
compliance
registration
notarized

Objectives

After studying this chapter, you should be able to:

- State the relationship between environment and a child's growth and development.
- State the purpose of licensing requirements.
- List the necessary steps for securing a license to operate a child care program.
- Describe ways of making a child's environment safe.

Children's growth and development are continually influenced by their *environment* Growth is enhanced by love, good nutrition, shelter, medical care, and protection from harm. New experiences and planned challenges foster intellectual development, while social interaction and communication skills promote psychological development.

Figure 8–1 Environments can have a positive effect on children's growth and development.

Teachers, caregivers, and parents must continuously be aware of the significant role played by environment. They must make every attempt to create physical, *cognitive*, and psychological environments that have positive effects on children's growth and development, Figure 8–1.

QUALITY SETTINGS

Demands for child care have increased dramatically in recent years for several reasons. First, more than 50 percent of children under 5 years of age have mothers who are employed outside of the home. Second, the number of single parent families with young children is increasing. Locating quality child care is often a difficult task for these families. Although many new centers, programs, and forms of child care services have emerged, quality has not always accompanied this rapid expansion.

Research has demonstrated that a positive relationship exists between quality child care and optimum child development (Howes, 1992; Jacobs, 1992; Kontos, 1991). Although parents may desire quality child care arrangements for their children, the necessity and, at times, the desperation of securing care may force parents to overlook this important issue.

Evaluating the quality of child care settings and educational programs is also difficult for many parents. They may feel uncomfortable questioning caregivers and unsure of what features to look for. They may have few other alternatives to choose from even if they are dissatisfied. Consequently, attempts are being made, both within and outside of the child care profession, to assist parents with this formidable task and assure that child care settings and programs are safe and healthful for young children.

Parent Education

Considerable efforts are being made to increase parents' awareness of criteria that can be useful for evaluating the quality of child care programs. Areas of particular importance include:

- physical facilities, e.g., clean, safe, licensed
- program philosophy, e.g., developmental and educational objectives
- group size
- staff/child ratios
- nutritious meals
- parent involvement
- toys and activities, e.g., variety, age appropriate, stimulating
- health related services
- caregiver's qualifications

Professional organizations and advocacy groups are actively involved in getting this information out to parents. The obvious benefit of their efforts will enable parents to make informed decisions about child care arrangements. And, as competition for quality care increases, more programs will be forced to improve their services.

Resource and Referral Services

Resource and referral agencies are a fairly new development on the child care scene. Their main purpose is to help parents locate child care arrangements that meet their particular needs in terms of hours, child's age, cost, philosophy, location, and type of care.

These agencies maintain listings of programs and current openings for a wide range of child care options, from center-based to in-home care. However, agencies do not always restrict their listings to high quality programs. Some agencies will include any program with available openings, while others screen programs carefully to ensure quality care.

Professional Accreditation

A national system of voluntary *accreditation* for early childhood programs was established in 1985 by the National Association for the Education of Young Children (NAEYC). Its primary goal is both to promote excellence and foster improvement in quality child care through a process of self-study. The accreditation process identifies and recognizes outstanding child care programs and offers centers an added credential signifying their commitment to providing quality care. Programs are accredited for three years, at which time they must reapply.

Specialized accreditation is offered through some private organizations, such as Montessori (a school of educational theory and practice).

Figure 8–2 Licensing standards help to protect children's well-being.

LICENSING

Licensing standards, established by individual states, represent an attempt to encourage and ensure child care environments that are safe and healthful for young children (Morgan, 1987), Figure 8–2. However, these standards usually reflect only minimal requirements and also vary considerably from one state to another. They do not necessarily imply quality care.

Licensing requirements serve a twofold purpose. First, they protect children's physical and psychological well-being by regulating the quality of child care environments and educational programs. Second, licensing *regulations* offer minimal protection to child care personnel and established programs. Centers are often less vulnerable to charges of negligence if they adhere to basic licensing standards.

Early attempts to regulate child care facilities dealt primarily with the sanitary and safety conditions of large institutions. However, current licensing regulations go beyond strict concern only for the safety of physical settings. Today, the qualifications of caregivers and the quality of educational programs planned for young children are also recognized as important. Programs are expected to meet certain predetermined standards.

At present, all states have established some method for licensing child care programs. One agency in each state is invested with the legal authority to conduct inspections and issue licenses to child care and preschool programs. This agency is also responsible for developing licensing standards and methods for enforcing *compliance*. As a result, there are many differences in licensing standards and degree of enforcement. This fragmented approach also lacks any method for making certain that individual states are indeed carrying out their responsibilities.

In some areas, day care homes have the option of either being licensed or registered. Those choosing to be licensed are usually inspected by a member of the licensing agency and expected to meet certain standards. ***Registration***, on the other hand, varies from participants merely placing their names on a list maintained by the licensing agency, to requiring attendance at inservice programs on various child care topics. On-site inspection of these homes is seldom conducted unless a complaint is registered.

Determining licensing requirements that will adequately protect young children's health and safety, yet are realistic enough for caregivers and centers to achieve, is a challenging task. Some people believe that too much control or standards that are set too high will reduce the number of available child care facilities. The licensing process is also costly to administer and often difficult to enforce. Lowering standards may be a tempting option. On the other hand, many parents and caregivers favor stricter regulations to ensure high-quality child care facilities and programs and improved respect for the profession.

Despite the controversy, licensing of child care programs is necessary. Ideally, licensing standards should adequately safeguard children, but not be so overly restrictive that qualified individuals and centers who are interested in providing a much needed service are eliminated. The development of separate licensing requirements for home child care services and center-based programs has been suggested as one logical solution to this dilemma (Kendall, 1989).

Obtaining a License

A license permits a caregiver to conduct a child care program on a regular basis. As mentioned earlier, the process for obtaining a license differs from one state to another. However, the steps described here are representative of the procedure that is generally involved. In some cases, the process may require considerable time and effort, especially if major renovations must be made in the proposed facility.

Persons interested in operating a child care program should first contact their state or local licensing agency. Questions can also be answered at this time regarding the applicant's eligibility and specific requirements that must be met.

In addition to complying with state licensing regulations, child care facilities must also be in accordance with local laws and ordinances. Zoning codes must be checked carefully to determine whether or not the location of a child care center is permissible in a particular neighborhood. Often this requires meeting with local planning authorities and reviewing proposed floor plans.

Buildings that house child care programs must also pass a variety of inspections to be sure they meet fire, safety, and sanitation codes. These inspections are usually conducted by personnel from the local fire and public health departments. From these inspections, it is possible to determine what, if any, renovations are necessary in order to comply with licensing regulations. In most cases, these are relatively simple; in other cases, it may not be feasible or economical to complete all of the required changes.

After these steps have been completed, the licensing office should again be contacted. Formal applications can be made at this time for a permanent license. Copies of the program's plans and policies are then submitted to the licensing authorities for review. Final approval usually includes an on-site inspection of the facilities to see that all requirements and recommendations have been satisfied.

Federal Regulations

In addition to meeting state licensing regulations, child care programs receiving federal funds must also conform to special supplemental guidelines (U. S. DHEW, 1981). Governmental requirements adopted in the spring of 1981 apply to all child care centers funded through Title XX of the Social Security Act. Additional regulations also exist for all Head Start programs.

ENVIRONMENTAL STANDARDS

Each child care program is unique. This uniqueness is both important and desirable as it fulfills many different types of needs for parents and young children. However, a system of standards for routine monitoring of facilities is essential to protect children's health and safety in such a diverse range of settings.

Building Facilities

In a time of increasing demand for child care and shrinking budgets, the selection of a building appropriate for child care programs often requires a creative approach. It would be ideal to plan and design a facility specifically for this purpose. However, few programs have sufficient funds to accomplish such a project. Instead, it is frequently necessary to locate child care services in existing buildings. Unused classrooms in public schools, older houses, unoccupied stores, church basements, or places of business such as factories or hospitals can usually be modified or remodeled to make them suitable for infant and child care. This type of work can be expensive and may actually be impractical in certain instances. However, it is sometimes possible to use the talents of willing parents to help complete at least a small portion of the work.

How much space a school or center needs depends to some extent on the type of child care program and services that will be offered. Thirty-five square feet of usable floor space per child is considered an absolute minimum for adequate child care. Teachers and caregivers often find even this amount of space crowded and difficult to work in. Quality environments may provide 45–50 square feet of space per child. This amount seems to be more workable for both children and caregivers. Additional space may be needed to accommodate large indoor play structures, special equipment for children with physical disabilities, or cribs for infants. However, it should be kept in mind that spaces that are too large may be difficult to supervise. Ground floor levels are always preferable for infants and preschool-aged children, although basement areas can be used for several hours at a time provided there are at least two exits.

Location is also an important factor to consider when selecting a site. Buildings chosen for child care programs must first meet local zoning requirements. These ordinances often make it difficult to locate preschools and child care centers in residential neighborhoods where often they are most needed. Child care facilities

Figure 8–3 Infants need open space where they can move about and explore.

should preferably be located away from sources of excessive noise, heavy traffic, and other safety hazards, such as railroad tracks, airports, and busy streets.

Local fire safety codes will also affect building selection. Although these codes may take extra effort to satisfy, they are critical in terms of children's safety. Older buildings and those not originally designed for infants and young children may require extensive changes before they pass inspection. Rooms that children occupy must have a minimum of two exits, one of which leads directly outdoors. All doors leading out of a classroom should be hinged so they swing out of the room. Programs located above ground level should also have an enclosed stairwell.

The arrangement of space, or basic floor plan, should be examined carefully to determine the ease of conducting specific activities (Greenman, 1988). For example, the traffic flow should allow ample room for children to arrive and depart without disturbing others who are playing. Small rooms that lack storage space, good lighting, accessible bathrooms, or adequate outdoor play areas are inconvenient and frustrating for both the staff and children.

Play spaces for infants and toddlers should be separated from those of older children to avoid injuries and confrontations. Large, open space, free of obstacles, also encourages very young children to move about and explore without hesitation, Figure 8–3.

Smoke and carbon monoxide detectors are invaluable in any child care setting, but are especially important where infants and young children will be sleeping. Additional fire safety precautions include installing flame-retardant floor coverings and draperies and having at least one multipurpose fire extinguisher available. Staff should also be familiar with the location of building exits and emergency procedures, and trained to conduct monthly fire drills, Table 8–1.

TABLE 8–1 How to Conduct a Fire Drill

Develop an Evacuation Plan

- Plan at least one alternate escape route from every room.
- Post a written copy of the plan by the door of each room.
- Inform new personnel.

Assign Specific Responsibilities

- Designate someone to call the fire department, preferably from a telephone outside of the building. Be sure to give the fire department complete information: name, address, approximate location of the fire inside the building, whether or not anyone is inside; *do not* hang up until the fire department hangs up first.
- Designate several adults to assemble children and lead them out of the building; assign extra adults, e.g., cooks, secretaries, to assist with evacuation of younger children.
- Designate one adult to take a flashlight and the notarized emergency cards or class list.
- Designate someone to turn off the lights and close the doors to all rooms.

Establish a Meeting Place

- Once outside, meet at a designated location so that everyone can be accounted for.
- DO NOT GO BACK INTO THE BUILDING!

Practice Fire Evacuation Drills

- Conduct drills at least once a month; have some of these be unannounced.
- Practice alternate routes of escape.
- Practice fire evacuation safety, e.g., feel closed doors before opening them, select an alternate route if hallway or stairwells are filled with smoke, stay close to the floor (crawl) to avoid heat and poisonous gases, learn the stop-drop-roll technique.
- Use a stopwatch to time each drill and record the results; work for improvement.

Heating and cooling systems should be in good operating condition and able to maintain room temperatures between 68°F (20°C) and 85°F (29.4°C) year round. Rooms occupied by young children should not have hot radiators, pipes, furnaces, or fireplaces exposed where children can come in contact with them; wire screen can be wrapped around freestanding heaters and fans to prevent injury.

Adequate bathroom facilities are also essential. They should be accessible to both indoor and outdoor play areas. Installation of child-sized fixtures, including

Figure 8–4 Child-sized fixtures encourage independence.

sinks, toilets, and towel racks, allow children to care for their own needs, Figure 8–4. If only adult-sized fixtures are available, foot stools, large wooden blocks, or platforms, securely anchored to the floor, will facilitate children's independence. One toilet and sink should be available for every 10 to 12 children. In centers that serve children with physical disabilities, bathrooms and equipment should be designed to accommodate their special needs. A separate bathroom area should also be available for adults and staff members.

Handwashing facilities located near toilets and sleeping areas encourage good handwashing habits. Hot water temperatures should be maintained between 105°F (40.5°C) and 120°F (48.8°C) to prevent children from accidental burns. The use of individual paper towels and cups also improves sanitation and limits the spread of communicable illness among young children. Smooth surfaces on walls and floors facilitate cleaning. Light colors, especially in bathrooms, make dirt more easily visible and, therefore, able to be cleaned promptly. Fixtures such as mirrors, light switches, and towel dispensers placed within children's reach, good lighting, and bright paint create a functional and pleasant atmosphere in which young children can learn to help care for themselves.

Low windows and glass doors should be constructed of safety glass or plastic to prevent serious injuries if they are broken. Colorful pictures or decals placed at children's eye level also help to discourage children from accidentally walking into the glass. Doors and windows should be covered with screens that can be locked.

Good lighting is essential in classrooms and hallways. Rooms that are sunny and bright are inviting and attractive to both caregivers and children. Natural light from windows and glass doors is one of the most desirable ways to supply rooms with light. Sunlight costs nothing to use and has a positive psychological effect.

Proper arrangement of artificial lighting is equally as important as the amount of brightness it produces. Areas of a room that are used for close activities, such as reading centers or art tables, require more lighting. Fluorescent lights are ideal for this purpose because they give off greater amounts of soft light than incandescent bulbs. Although fluorescent lighting is more costly to install, it uses less electricity to operate.

Furniture and equipment should be selected carefully. Children are less likely to be injured if chairs and tables are appropriately proportioned. Quality is also an important feature to consider. Furniture should be sturdy so that it can withstand hard use by groups of children and meet federal safety standards (see Chapter 9). Items with sharp corners or edges should be avoided. Bookcases, lockers, pianos, and other heavy objects should be anchored securely to the wall or floor to prevent children from pulling them over. Tall bookshelves should be replaced or cut in half to make them more child accessible.

Materials used for wall and floor coverings should be easy to clean. Vinyl floor coverings are popular choices for use in child care centers for this reason. However, they do become very slippery when wet. Care must be taken to wipe up spills immediately or to place rugs or newspapers in areas where floors are likely to get wet. Often a combination of carpeted and tiled areas is most satisfactory because it provides soft, warm surfaces where children can sit as well as surfaces that can easily be cleaned.

Each child should have an individual storage space, cubby, or locker where personal belongings and outdoor clothing can be stored, Figure 8–5. A child's private space is particularly important in group settings. It has the psychological benefit of belonging to only that child, whereas most other objects in the classroom are expected to be shared. Individual lockers help minimize the loss of prized possessions; they also help to control the spread of some communicable illnesses.

Other standards aimed at improving the quality and safety of child care facilities include having locked cabinets available for storing medicines and other potentially poisonous substances, e.g., cleaning products, paints, gasoline, Figure 8–6.

Figure 8–5 Each child should have a personal space or cubby to store belongings.

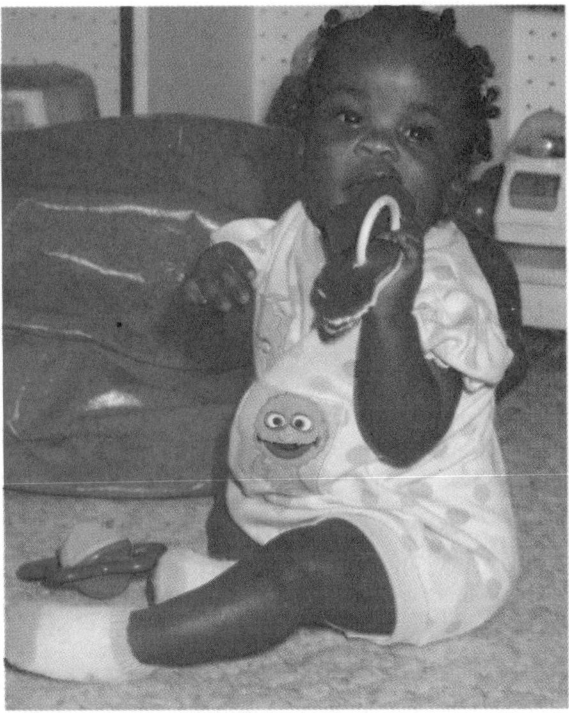

Figure 8–6 Only toys made of non-toxic substances should be placed in children's play area.

A sample safety checklist is shown in Table 8–2. Extension cords should not be used. All electrical outlets should be covered with safety caps, which can be purchased in most grocery or hardware stores. However, caps are only a temporary solution because they are frequently removed and lost. Conventional outlets can be replaced by an electrician with hinged caps or specially designed receptacles to make them permanently childproof.

For emergency use, a telephone should be located conveniently in the building. A list of emergency phone numbers, including the fire department, police, hospital, ambulance, and poison control center should be placed nearby.

Indoor Air Quality. Every day, children are exposed to a variety of indoor air pollutants, including formaldehyde (in carpet and building materials), carbon monoxide, radon, asbestos, cigarette smoke, paint fumes, lead, and numerous household chemicals and pesticides. More studies are demonstrating a close relationship between these pollutants and an increased rate of respiratory illnesses among children (Child Health Alert, 1991). The toxic properties of these substances may pose an even greater health risk for young children because of their immature body systems and rapid growth, Table 8–3. However, little is known about the long-term effects of air pollution on children's health.

TABLE 8–2 Safety Checklist

	DATE CHECKED	PASS/ FAIL	COMMENTS
Indoor Areas			
1. A minimum of 35 square feet of *usable* space is available per child			
2. Room temperature is between 68°–85°F (20°–29.4°C)			
3. Rooms have good ventilation			
a. windows and doors have screens			
b. mechanical ventilation systems in working order			
4. There are two exits in all rooms occupied by children			
5. Carpets and draperies are fire-retardant			
6. Rooms are well lighted			
7. Glass doors and low windows are constructed of safety glass			
8. Walls and floors of classrooms, bathrooms, and kitchen appear clean; floors are swept daily, bathroom fixtures are scrubbed at least every other day			
9. Tables and chairs are child sized			
10. Electrical outlets are covered with safety caps			
11. Smoke detectors are located in appropriate places and in working order			
12. Furniture, activities and equipment are set up so that doorways and pathways are kept clear			
13. Play equipment and materials are stored in designated areas; they are inspected frequently and are safe for children's use			
14. Large pieces of equipment, e.g., lockers, piano, bookshelves, are firmly anchored to the floor or wall			
15. Cleaners, chemicals and other poisonous substances are locked up			
16. If stairways are used:			
a. a handrail is placed at children's height			
b. stairs are free of toys and clutter			
c. stairs are well lighted			
d. stairs are covered with a nonslip surface			
17. Bathroom areas:			
a. toilets and washbasins are in working order			
b. one toilet and washbasin available for every 10–12 children; potty chairs provided for children in toilet training			
c. water temperature is no higher than 120°F (48.8°C)			
d. powdered or liquid soap is used for handwashing			
e. individual or paper towels are used for each child			
f. diapering tables or mats are cleaned after each use			

TABLE 8–2 Safety Checklist (Continued)

	DATE CHECKED	PASS/ FAIL	COMMENTS
18. At least one fire extinguisher is available and located in a convenient place; extinguisher is checked annually by fire-testing specialists			
19. Premises are free from rodents and/or undesirable insects			
20. Food preparation areas are maintained according to strict sanitary standards			
21. At least one individual on the premises is trained in emergency first aid and CPR; first aid supplies are readily available			
22. All medications are stored in a locked cabinet or box			
23. Fire and storm/disaster drills are conducted on a monthly basis			
Outdoor Areas			
1. Play areas are located away from heavy traffic, loud noises and sources of chemical contamination			
2. Play areas are located adjacent to premises or within safe walking distance			
3. Play areas are well drained			
4. Bathroom facilities and drinking fountain easily accessible			
5. A variety of play surfaces, e.g., grass, concrete, sand are available; there is a balance of sunny areas and shady areas			
6. Play equipment is in good condition, e.g., no broken or rusty parts, missing pieces, splinters, sharp edges, frayed rope			
7. Selection of play equipment is appropriate for children's ages			
8. Soft ground covers present in sufficient amounts under large, climbing equipment; area is free of sharp debris			
9. Large pieces of equipment are stable and anchored in the ground			
10. Equipment is placed sufficiently far apart to allow a smooth flow of traffic and adequate supervision			
11. Play areas are enclosed with a fence at least four feet high, with a gate and a workable lock			
12. There are no poisonous plants, shrubs, or trees in the area			
13. Chemicals, insecticides, paints and gasoline products are stored in a locked cabinet			
14. Grounds are maintained on a regular basis and are free of debris; grass is mowed; broken equipment is removed			
15. Wading or swimming pools are always supervised; water is drained when not in use			

TABLE 8–3 Some Common Air Pollutants and Their Health Effects

SOURCES	
organic particles (e.g., dust mites)	formaldehyde
molds	insulation (e.g., asbestos, fiberglass)
pollen	ozone
carbon monoxide	

COMMON HEALTH EFFECTS		
chronic cough	fatigue	skin irritation
headache	eye irritation	shortness of breath
dizziness	sinus congestion	nausea

While it is impossible to avoid exposure to all toxic chemicals in an environment, increased awareness and understanding of control measures can effectively reduce the risks to young children (Noyes, 1987). Indoor air quality can be improved significantly by simply increasing ventilation (opening doors and windows daily) and substituting alternative products for toxic chemicals. Only toys and art materials made of nontoxic substances should be purchased. Also, the safety of all building materials and heating and ventilating systems should be checked regularly.

Outdoor Play Areas

The outdoors presents an exciting environment for an endless array of imaginative activities and opportunities (Frost, 1992; Rivkin, 1995). For quality and maximum use, play areas should include a variety of surfaces. Large, open areas encourage active play such as running or tossing balls, while protected, hard surfaces allow children to ride bikes and play outside despite inclement weather. Trees add a natural touch and provide shade from hot summer sun. Play yards should also include separate areas for quiet and active play.

Safety must be a prime consideration in the design of outdoor play areas. Minimum space requirements for outdoor play yards range from 75–100 square feet per child. Ideally, play areas should be located adjacent to the child care facility and bathrooms are within a very short walking distance. Traveling even short distances to playgrounds with young children requires considerable time and effort and often discourages spontaneous outdoor play.

A fence, at least four feet high with a latched gate, should surround the play yard to prevent children from wandering away. However, sharp wire or picket-type fences are inappropriate choices.

Safety must also be a major consideration when outdoor equipment is selected and placed in play yards (see Chapter 9). Choices should be based on:

- amount of available play area
- ages and developmental levels of children
- variety of learning experiences provided
- quality and safety of construction

Large pieces of equipment and portable climbing structures should be firmly anchored in the ground with metal pins or cement. Play equipment should be no taller than 6 feet, be spaced a minimum of 8 feet apart, and arranged so that all pieces can be seen and easily supervised. Swings and climbing structures should be located away from other equipment and hard surfaces such as asphalt and concrete to prevent children from being seriously injured if they should fall, Figure 8–7. Avoid equipment that has angles or openings that could entrap a child's head or extremity. Surface materials placed under play equipment should be relatively soft and resilient. Sand, pea gravel, finely chopped rubber, and specially designed safety mats are good choices for fall zones,

Some of the safest and most inviting pieces of outdoor play equipment are not necessarily the modern, high-tech structures designed by manufacturers. Few structures are more attractive and safe for young children than a simple sandbox, bucket of water, collection of old boxes, and crates, tires or boards, a tent fashioned from an old sheet, a wagon, or a set of large wooden building blocks that can challenge their imagination for hours. The play yard itself provides endless opportunities for a wide variety of activities, including a small garden, a marching band, "camping trips," leaves for art projects, or just watching the clouds change shape. These alternatives are especially valuable if resources and storage space are limited.

Wading or swimming pools can also be an interesting addition to outdoor play yards. However, they do require extra supervision, safety, and sanitation precautions. Whenever children are in the water, there should be extra adults in attendance; at least one adult should be knowledgeable about water safety procedures

Figure 8–7 Climbing structures should be located away from hard surfaces.

and lifesaving techniques (CPR). Children's swimming activities are safer and easier to monitor if the numbers of children are also limited. Safety rules should be carefully explained to the children and strictly enforced. Pool water should be disinfected prior to each use. Inexpensive water-quality test kits are available from stores where pool supplies are sold. Permanent pools or natural bodies of water should be fenced in or drained to prevent accidental drownings.

Inspecting outdoor play areas on a daily basis helps to identify hazardous conditions before a child is hurt. Equipment with broken parts, jagged or sharp edges, loose screws or bolts, or missing pieces should be removed. Surface materials under equipment should be checked periodically to be sure that amounts are adequate. Sharp sticks, broken glass, or other debris that might harm young children should be removed. Great care should also be exercised to identify and eliminate poisonous vegetation, including shrubs, trees, and flowers, see Table 8–4 for a partial listing.

Staff Qualifications

Perhaps one of the weakest areas in many state licensing regulations pertains to staff qualifications (*Young Children*, July 1983). Emphasis is commonly focused on the safety of physical settings, while staff requirements such as years of experience, educational preparation, and personal qualities are often lacking or poorly defined. Where requirements for caregivers and teachers do exist, they tend to differ a great deal from state to state. Often the nature of the child care program itself determines the qualifications of the staff.

Staff qualifications are critical to quality child care programs (NAEYC, 1994). Unfortunately, an individual 18 years of age or older with a high school diploma satisfies the educational requirement in many states. However, the range of training and educational opportunities in early childhood education is diverse, and includes:

- personal experiences (child rearing)
- on-the-job training
- CDA (Child Development Associates credential)
- one-year vocational training
- two-year associate degree (community college)
- four-year bachelor degree
- advanced graduate training (M.A. and Ph.D.)

Ideally, all directors and head teachers should have a minimum of a CDA (Child Development Associate) credential or a two-year associate arts degree with specialized training in early childhood (Phillips, 1990). However, in many areas of the country, teachers and caregivers with such preparation are in short supply.

Paraprofessionals can be a valuable source of additional staff to help relieve shortages of child care personnel. They may be aides who work for wages or unpaid volunteers. Paraprofessionals should receive a brief, but intensive, orientation and training period before they begin to work in the classroom. Preparing staff members in this manner enables them to be more productive and successful when they start working with children.

TABLE 8–4 Common Poisonous Vegetation

VEGETATION	POISONOUS PART	COMPLICATIONS
Bittersweet	Berries	Causes a burning sensation in the mouth. Nausea, vomiting, dizziness, and convulsions.
Buttercup	All parts	Irritating to the digestive tract. Causes nausea and vomiting.
Castor Bean	Beanlike pod	Extremely toxic. May be fatal to both children and adults.
Daffodil, hyacinth, narcissus, jonquil	Bulbs	Nausea, vomiting, and diarrhea. Can be fatal.
Iris	Underground roots	Digestive upset causing nausea, vomiting, and diarrhea.
Lily-of-the-Valley	Leaves and flowers	Nausea, vomiting, dizziness, and mental confusion.
Mistletoe	Berries	Extremely toxic. Diarrhea and irregular pulse.
Poinsettia	Leaves	Very irritating to throat, mouth, and stomach.
Rhubarb	Raw leaves	Can cause convulsions, coma, and rapid death.
Sweet Pea	All parts, especially the seeds	Shallow respirations, possible convulsions, paralysis, and slow pulse.
Black Locust Tree	Bark, leaves, pods and seeds	Causes nausea and weakness, especially in children.
Cherry Tree	Leaves and twigs	Can be fatal. Causes shortness of breath, general weakness, and restlessness.
Golden Chain Tree	Beanlike seed pods	Can cause convulsions and coma.
Oak Tree	Acorns and leaves	Eating large quantities may cause poisoning. Gradually causes kidney failure.
Rhododendron	All parts	Causes vomiting, convulsions, and paralysis.
Wisteria	Seed pods	Causes severe diarrhea and collapse.
Yews	Berries and foliage	Foliage is very poisonous and can be fatal. Causes nausea, diarrhea, and difficult breathing.

Staff/child ratios are determined by individual states and frequently reflect only the minimal number of adults considered necessary to protect children's well-being (Whitebrook, 1990). However, quality learning experiences, personalized child care, and conditions that favor children's health and safety require more adult caregivers than is typically recommended (Canadian Child Day Care Federation,

1993). Programs based on these objectives will often have more adults to work with smaller groups of children.

Ideally, staff ratios for high-quality child care should include one full-time adult caregiver for every 8–10 children three to six years of age. Programs serving children with disabilities should have one teacher or adult caregiver for every 4–6 children, depending on the age group and severity of children's limitations. If children younger than two years are included in preschool or child care programs, the staff/child ratio should be lowered to one full-time staff member per 3–4 children. In the event of illness or sudden resignations, centers can avoid being caught short of staff by maintaining a list of substitute caregivers.

Recent research data suggests that small group size and low staff/child ratios improve the quality of child care programs. However, low ratios do not always guarantee that children will be safer (Howes, 1992). Much depends on the knowledge and supervisory skills of individual caregivers.

Teachers and caregivers who are part of quality programs attend a variety of professional meetings, training sessions, and workshops throughout the year. Exposure to new concepts, ideas, and approaches promotes continued professional growth and competence. Contact with other members of the profession also provides teachers and caregivers with opportunities for discussing common problems and sharing ideas and unique solutions.

The ability to relate well to children as well as other adults, including parents, staff members, and professional personnel, is important for teachers. Warmth, patience, sensitivity to children's needs, a positive attitude, and respect for individual differences are important characteristics of quality caregivers. The ability to plan, organize, and make decisions is also essential for success. Teachers and caregivers who enjoy good health are better able to cope with the physical and emotional demands of long, action-packed days. These qualities are important not only because they make an individual a better teacher or caregiver but also because they can have a positive effect on children's growth and development.

Group Size and Composition

When a license is issued to a child care center, family day-care home, or preschool, it defines specific conditions or limits under which the program is allowed to operate. These conditions usually identify the:

- ages of children that can be enrolled
- total group size
- maximum enrollment limits
- special populations of children to be served, e.g., children with behavior problems; children with developmental disabilities.

For example, a preschool program may be licensed to provide two half-day sessions for children 3–5 years of age, with a maximum enrollment of 18 children per session. A home day-care program might be licensed to accept only six children, ages birth to two years.

Group size is recognized as one of the most important factors affecting quality child care (Howes, 1992; *Young Children*, 1983). For this reason, restrictions are often placed on the number of children a program can enroll. This figure is determined by the amount of available space, ages and special populations of children served, as well as the number of adult caregivers. However, it should be remembered that licensed group size is often larger than ideal.

A description of group composition should be included in a center's admission policies. The ages, special populations, and total numbers of children that a program will accept must be clearly stated to inform potential consumers and avoid misunderstandings.

Program Content

The value of early stimulation and learning experiences is well documented. Because many children spend the majority of their waking hours in various child care arrangements, it is important that opportunities for learning be included. Educational and recreational activities should be planned to meet children's developmental needs in the areas of:

- fine and large motor skills, Figure 8–8
- language acquisition
- social skills
- problem solving
- self-care skills
- emotional development

Figure 8–8 Carefully planned activities foster children's development.

In addition to providing developmentally appropriate learning experiences for young children, the arrangement of their daily schedules and routines is also important to plan carefully. The organization of various activities can affect children's physical stamina as well as their attitudes. Fatigue and lack of interest can often be avoided by planning activities that provide alternating periods of rest and activity. For example, a long walk outdoors might be followed by a teacher-produced flannel board story or puppet show. A copy of daily schedules and curriculum plans should be posted where they can easily be read by parents.

Health Services

Concern for children's health and well-being is a fundamental part of any child care program (Kendrick, 1995). Only when children are healthy can they fully benefit from learning experiences and opportunities. Therefore, basic health services provided by child care programs should reflect their commitment to the philosophy of health promotion for young children and address:

- written policies
- children's medical records
- provisions for first aid and emergency care
- preparations for emergencies and disasters
- plans for health and safety education

There are many differences in the types of policies and records that each state's licensing agency requires programs to maintain. However, certain health and safety records are essential for any center to keep on file, including:

- children's health assessments
- attendance
- emergency contact information
- developmental profiles
- adult health assessments
- fire and storm drills
- accidents and injuries
- health observations

Licensing authorities will carefully review these records for completeness.

Personnel in quality child care programs are trained to handle emergencies and provide first aid and emergency care to ill or injured children. Ideally, they have also completed training in cardiopulmonary resuscitation (CPR). Programs meeting minimal standards should have at least one staff member who is trained in these techniques and can respond immediately to emergencies.

Notarized permission forms, similar to the one shown in Figure 8–9, listing the name, address, and telephone number of the child's physician should be completed by parents when the child is first enrolled. This measure grants caregivers the authority to administer emergency care or secure emergency medical treatment. A

EMERGENCY CONTACT INFORMATION

Child's Name ______________________ Date of Birth __________

Address ______________________ Home Phone __________

Mother's Name ______________________ Business Phone __________

Father's Name ______________________ Business Phone __________

Name of other person to be contacted in case of an emergency:

1. ______________________ Address __________

   Relationship (sitter, relative, friend, etc.) __________ Phone __________

2. ______________________ Address __________

   Relationship (sitter, relative, friend, etc.) __________ Phone __________

Authorization is hereby given for the Child Development Center Staff to release the above name child to the following persons, provided proper identification is first established (list *all* names of authorized persons, including immediate family):

1. ______________________ Relation: __________
2. ______________________ Relation: __________
3. ______________________ Relation: __________

Physician to be called in an emergency:

1. ______________________ Phone __________ or __________
2. ______________________ Phone __________ or __________

I, the undersigned, authorize the staff of the Child Development Center to take what emergency medical measures are deemed necessary for the care and protection of my child enrolled in the Child Development Center program.

______________________ (Signature of Parent or Guardian)

______________________ Signature witnessed by: (Notary)

______________________ (Signature of Parent or Guardian)

The above statement sworn before me on:

____

____

Figure 8–9 An emergency contact information form.

list of emergency telephone numbers, e.g., ambulance, fire department, poison control, should also be placed in a convenient location for quick reference.

Ideally, a special room is available for times when children become ill. However, a quiet area away from other children can also provide privacy for a child who is sick or injured and protect other children from illnesses that may be contagious.

TABLE 8–5 Principles of Emergency Preparedness

- Don't panic—stay calm!
- Be informed. Tune in a local station on your battery-powered radio.
- Get to a safe place. Develop and practice an appropriate disaster plan.
- Keep a first aid kit and flashlight handy.
- Learn basic emergency first aid.

Medical supplies and equipment can be stored in or near this area so they are readily available.

Child care programs are also expected to develop a set of plans and guidelines for emergency preparedness, Table 8–5. These plans should describe actions that will be taken to protect children's safety in the event of fire, severe storms, or major disasters. Persons from local fire and police departments, Red Cross, and Civil Defense are usually quite willing to assist with this planning. Parents should be encouraged to read through these guidelines so they will be reassured and use the information to develop similar plans in their own homes.

Transportation

Some child care centers and day care homes provide transportation for children to and from their homes, or occasionally for field trips. Whenever motor vehicles are used to transport young children, special safety precautions are necessary.

First, the driver of any vehicle must be a responsible individual and possess a current license appropriate for the number of passengers that will be transported. Parents whose children will ride on a regular basis should become familiar with the driver so they feel more confident. Written permission should be obtained from each parent before allowing children to be transported.

Second, vehicles should be equipped with appropriate safety restraints:

- an infant carrier for infants weighing up to 20 pounds (9.1 kg) (installed facing the rear of the car)
- a child safety seat for children weighing 20–40 pounds (9.1–18.2 kg) and able to sit up by themselves (installed facing the front of the car)
- a booster seat used in combination with a lap belt and shoulder harness for children who have outgrown child seats and are under 54 inches (135 cm) in height
- a vehicle lap belt and shoulder harness for children who are at least 55–58 inches (137.5–145 cm) in height

Safety seats and restraints must not only be appropriate but also used correctly to protect young children:

- they must be correctly installed (facing the front or back as is appropriate) and anchored in the vehicle
- they must meet federal standards for manufacturing
- children must be buckled into the seat

Children and adults must be buckled in for every trip even though it may be a time-consuming process.

Motor vehicles used to transport children must be in good repair. Copies of children's health forms and emergency cards should also be kept in the vehicle. Periodic inspections of all safety and mechanical features ensure the vehicle's safe performance. An ABC-type fire extinguisher should be fastened in the front of the vehicle where it is readily available for emergencies. Liability insurance should be purchased to cover the vehicle, driver, and maximum number of passengers it will be carrying.

Whether parents or child care programs are responsible for transporting children, additional precautions can be taken to improve children's safety. Special off-street areas can be designated for the purpose of loading and unloading young children. If conditions do not allow programs to make this safety measure available, greater emphasis must be placed on safety education. Parents should be reminded from time to time to have children get into and out of the car door closest to the curb rather than directly out into the street. Also, having an adequate number of parking spaces available helps to reduce traffic hazards around school areas.

It is not an uncommon practice for child care programs to occasionally ask parents to provide transportation for off-site field trips. However, this practice is risky and has the potential for creating many serious legal problems in the event of an accident. Centers have no guarantee that privately owned vehicles or individual drivers meet the standards and qualifications previously discussed. As a result, centers may be vulnerable to unnecessary lawsuits and charges of negligence. To avoid these problems, various forms of public transportation can be safely substituted. These systems have taken the necessary precautions to ensure passengers' safety.

Summary

The quality of children's environments can influence their physical growth as well as their intellectual and psychological development. Consequently, care must be given to planning and providing settings that are both enriching and safe for young children.

Careful regulation of child care facilities and programs is necessary. Individual states are responsible for developing specific licensing standards, and methods for enforcing these standards. Unfortunately, the standards are only minimal, vary considerably from state to state and seldom encourage optimal conditions.

Licensing regulations help to ensure safe facilities and learning programs that are planned for young children. They also extend protection to parents, young children, and child caregivers who adhere to them. Controversy continues over how much control is necessary.

Although procedures for securing a license differ in each state, many of the basic steps are similar. Buildings selected for child care programs must meet local zoning regulations in addition to fire, safety, and sanitation codes. A review of staff qualifications, program content and policies is also conducted before final approval is granted. Additional areas of concern in the licensing process include a center's provisions for health services, transportation guidelines, and sanitary food service.

Parents can be effective advocates for improving the overall quality of child care programs by being informed, selecting quality programs for their children and supporting quality licensing standards (for facilities, personnel and educational programs) that are feasible for caregivers.

Suggested Activities

1. Develop a safety checklist that can be used by child caregivers or parents to inspect outdoor play areas for hazardous conditions. Using your list, conduct an inspection of two different play yards, or the same play area on two separate occasions.
2. Contact the local licensing agency for your area. Make arrangements to accompany licensing personnel on an on-site visit of a child care facility. Be sure to review licensing regulations beforehand. Observe to see how a licensing inspection is conducted. In several short paragraphs, describe your reactions to this experience.
3. Often licensing personnel are viewed as unfriendly or threatening authority figures. However, their major role is to offer guidance and help caregivers create safe environments for children. Role play how the following situations might be handled during a licensing visit. Keep in mind the positive role of licensing personnel, e.g., offering explanations, providing suggestions, planning acceptable solutions and alternatives.
   - electrical outlets not covered
   - all children's toothbrushes found stored together in a large plastic bin
   - open boxes of dry cereals and crackers in kitchen cabinets
   - an adult-sized toilet and wash basin in the bathroom
   - a swing set located next to a cement patio
   - incomplete information on children's immunization records
   - a caregiver who prepares snacks without first washing his or her hands
4. Obtain and read a copy of your state's licensing regulations. Organize a class debate on the topic of minimal vs. quality standards for child care facilities.
5. Prepare a brochure or simple checklist for parents on how to select quality child care.
6. Send for information about the Child Development Associate program (available from the Child Development Consortium, 1341 G. Street, NW, Suite 802, Washington, DC 20005; phone 1-800-424-4310). After reading the materials, write a brief summary describing the program.

7. Contact the U.S. Consumer Product Safety Commission (Washington, DC 20207) and check the product safety of at least eight playground items.

Chapter Review

A. Multiple Choice. Select the best answer.

1. The minimum educational requirement for preschool teachers in many states is
   a. special training in early childhood education
   b. a high school diploma
   c. graduate work in child development
   d. accreditation from CDA
2. Bathroom facilities for preschool children should include
   a. one toilet and one wash basin for every five to seven children
   b. child-sized fixtures
   c. carpeted floors
   d. hot water temperatures no higher than 135°F
3. Potentially poisonous substances should be
   a. labeled "Poison"
   b. stored in locked cabinets
   c. stored on a high shelf out of children's reach
   d. none of the above
4. Minimum space required per child for an outdoor play area is
   a. 35 square feet
   b. 50 square feet
   c. 75–100 square feet
   d. over 100 square feet
5. Health services are an essential part of any early childhood program because they
   a. protect and promote children's health
   b. provide for emergency and first aid care
   c. include health and safety education as part of health promotion
   d. all of the above
6. Schools can help to reduce traffic accidents by
   a. having parents transport the children
   b. eliminating field trips
   c. prohibiting parking in front of the building
   d. including traffic safety education for children
7. To be suitable for child care programs, buildings should
   a. have a cooling system
   b. be located away from excessive noise and traffic
   c. have a minimum of 50 square feet of space per child
   d. have safety glass in all windows

8. Staff ratio for high-quality child care for children ages 3 to 6 is one-full time adult caregiver for every
   a. 3 to 5 children
   b. 4 to 7 children
   c. 9 to 10 children
   d. 12 children

B. Briefly answer the following questions:

1. How does environment affect a child's growth and development?
2. What steps are generally involved in obtaining a license to operate a child care program?
3. Why is it important for each child to have a personal locker or cubby?
4. Name three features that help to make an outdoor play yard safe for young children.
5. List four conditions that identify group composition.
6. Describe eight features of a quality child care program.

C. Match the definition in column I with the term in column II.

Column I	Column II
1. local ordinance that indicates what type of facility shall be in an area	a. regulation
2. rule dealing with procedures	b. minimal standards
3. method of action that determines present and future decisions	c. staff qualification
4. witnessed form that indicates the signature that appears on the form is really that of the person signing the form	d. notarized permissions
5. skills possessed by the people responsible for the operation of a business	e. policy
6. meeting the least possible requirements	f. zoning code

References

Canadian Child Day Care Federation. 1993. *National Statement on Quality Child Care.* Ottawa, Ontario: Canadian Child Day Care Federation.

Collins, Raymond C. More Evidence that Air Pollution Affects Human Health: Air Pollution and Respiratory Infections in Children. August 1991. *Child Health Alert,* pp. 1–2.

Frost, J. 1992. *Play and Playscapes.* Albany, NY: Delmar Publishers Inc.

Greenman, J. 1988. *Caring Spaces, Learning Places: Children's Environments That Work.* Redmond, VA: Exchange Press Inc.

Howes, C., Phillips, D., and Whitebrook, M. 1992. Thresholds of Quality: Implications for the Social Development of Children in Center-Based Care. *Child Development,* 63(4): 449–460.

Jacobs, E., Selig, G., and White, D. 1992. Classroom Behavior in Grade One: Does Quality of Preschool Experience Make a Difference? *Canadian Journal of Research in Early Childhood Education*, 3(2): 89–100.

Kendall, E. D. 1989. Enforcement of Child Care Regulations. In J. Lande, S. Scarr, and Gunzenhauser (eds.), *Caring for Children*. Hillsdale, NJ: Lawrence Earlbaum Associates.

Kendrick, A. S., Kaufman, R., and Messenger, K. P. 1995. *Healthy Young Children: A Manual for Programs*. Washington, DC: NAEYC.

Kontos, S. 1991. Child Care Quality, Family Background, and Children's Development. *Early Childhood Research Quarterly*, 6(2): 249–262.

Morgan, G. 1987. *The National State of Child Care Regulation*. Watertown, MA: Work/Family Directions.

NAEYC. 1994. NAEYC Position Statement: A Conceptual Framework for Early Childhood Professional Development. *Young Children*, 49(3): 68–77.

Noyes, D. 1987. Indoor Pollutants; Environmental Hazards to Young Children. *Young Children*, 42(6): 57–65.

Phillips, C. B. 1990. The Child Development Associate Program: Entering a New Era. *Young Children* 45(3): 24–27.

Rivkin, M. 1995. *The Great Outdoors: Restoring Children's Right to Play Outside*. Washington, DC: NAEYC.

"Three Components of High-Quality Early Childhood Programs: Administration, Staff Qualifications and Development, and Staff-Parent Interaction." July 1983. *Young Children* 38(5): 53–58.

"Three Components of High-Quality Early Childhood Programs: Physical Environment, Health and Safety, and Nutrition." May 1983. *Young Children* 38(4): 51–56.

U.S. Department of Health, Education and Welfare. 1981. *Summary Report of the Assessment of Current State Practices in Title XX Funded Day Care Programs: Report to Congress*. Washington, DC: Day Care Division Administration for Children, Youth and Families, Office of Human Development Services.

Whitebrook, M., Howes, C., and Phillips, D. 1990. *Who Cares? Child Care Teachers and the Quality of Care in America. Final Report of the National Child Care Staffing Study*. Oakland, CA: Child Care Employee Project.

Additional Reading

Caldwell, B. 1984, January. "NAEYC Adopts Child Care Licensing Position." *Young Children* 39(2): 49–51.

Elicker, J. and Fortner-Wood, C. 1995. Adult-Child Relationships in Early Childhood Programs. *Young Children*, 51(1): 69–78.

Finn-Stevenson, M. and Stevenson, J. 1990, March–April. "Safe Care/Safe Play." *Children Today*.

Galinsky, E., Howes, C., Kontos, S., and Shinn, M. 1994. The Study of Children in Family Child Care and Relative Care—Key Findings and Policy Recommendations. *Young Children*, 50(1): 58–61.

Harms, T. and Clifford, R. 1980. *Early Childhood Environmental Rating Scale*. New York: Teachers College Press.

Harms. T., Cryer, D., and Clifford, R. 1990. *Infant/Toddler Environment Rating Scale (ITERS)*. NY: Teachers College Press.

Harms, T., Jacobs, E., and White, D. 1996. *School-Age Care Environment Rating Scale (SACERS)*. NY: Teachers College Press.

Heiligman, D. 1992, January. Choosing a Great Preschool. *Parents*, 67(1): 66–71.

Honig, A. S. 1989. Quality Infant/Toddler Caregiving: Are There Magic Recipes? *Young Children*, 44(4): 4–9.

Lande, J. S., Scarr, S., and Gunzenhauser, N. (eds). 1989. *Caring for Children: Challenge to America*. Hillsdale, NJ: Lawrence Earlbaum Associates.

Lovell, P. and Harms, T. 1985, March. How Can Playgrounds Be Improved? *Young Children* 40(3): 3–5.

Miller, J. and Weissman, S. 1986. *The Parent's Guide to Daycare*. New York: Bantam Books.

NAEYC. 1995. NAEYC Position Statement on Quality, Compensation, and Affordability. *Young Children*, 51(1): 39–41.

Phillips, D., McCartney, K., and Scarr, S. 1987. Child Care Quality and Children's Social Development. *Developmental Psychology*, 23: 537–543.

Safe Daycare. Massachusetts Department of Public Health, 150 Tremont Street, Boston, MA 02111.

Pamphlets

Home/Environmental Safety

Baby-Safe Houseplants and Cut Flowers: A Guide to Keeping Children and Plants Safe Under the Same Roof. Storey Communications Inc., Schoolhouse Road, Pownal, VT 05261.

Handbook for Public Playground Safety. U. S. Consumer Product Safety Commission, Washington, DC 20207.

Home Safe: A Child's Eye View, P.O. Box 1114, Carrollton, TX 75006.

Home Safety, KinderGard Corporation, Dallas, TX 75234.

How To Choose A Good Early Childhood Program. NAEYC, 1834 Connecticut Avenue, N. W., Washington, DC 20009.

Open The Door To Safety, National Safety Council, 444 North Michigan Ave., Chicago, IL 60611.

Playground Safe & Sound. NAEYC, 1834 Connecticut Ave., NW, Washington, DC.

Poison Perils In the Home, National Safety Council, 444 North Michigan Ave., Chicago, IL 60611.

Safety Education Data Sheets, National Safety Council, 444 North Michigan Ave., Chicago, IL 60611.

Tips on Selecting the Right Day Care Facility. American Academy of Pediatrics, 141 Northwest Point Road, P. O. 927, Elk Grove, IL 60009.

Toxic Plant List. The Children's Hospital of Eastern Ontario, Ottawa, Ontario.

Disaster Preparedness

Coping with Children's Reaction to Earthquakes and Other Disasters, Family Earthquake Drills, Earthquake Safety Checklist, Federal Emergency Management Agency, Washington, DC 20472.

Farish, J. *When Disaster Strikes: Helping Young Children*. Washington, DC: NAEYC.

Learn Not to Burn Curriculum, National Fire Protection Association, Batterymarch Park, Quincy, MA 02269.

Teaching Poison Prevention in Kindergarten and Primary Grades, Public Health Services, U. S. Department of Health and Human Services, Division of Accident Prevention, Washington, DC 20201.

Tornado, Superintendent of Documents, U. S. Government Printing Office, Washington, DC 20402.

Chapter 9

Safety Management

Terms to Know

accident
prevention
supervision
incidental learning
liability
negligence

Objectives

After studying this chapter, you should be able to:

- List the most frequent causes of accidental death among young children.
- Describe several reasons why preschool children are more likely victims of accidents.
- Describe the four basic principles of accident prevention.
- State two types of negligence.

Accidents are the leading cause of death and permanent disabilities among young children. They are also responsible for thousands of nonfatal injuries that are costly in terms of time, energy, anxiety, and medical costs. Curiosity and impulsive behaviors often lead young children into new and unexpected dangers. At the same time, children are not always able to anticipate the possible consequences of their actions because they lack an adult's maturity, experience and intellectual sophistication. Parents, teachers, and caregivers must, therefore, take extra precautionary measures to provide environments and activities that are safe for infants and young children, Figure 9–1.

Providing for the protection and safety of children placed in their care is a primary concern that administrators, caregivers, and teachers in the field of early childhood education face. This task is especially challenging and demanding because of the ages of children involved. Their normal developmental characteristics and limited past experiences make it necessary for adults to establish and practice high standards of safety.

WHAT IS AN ACCIDENT?

The term *accident* refers to an unplanned or unexpected event. For example, children do not plan on pinching a finger in a door or being hit by a car. Likewise, an infant is not likely to intentionally roll off of a changing table. Accidents are often caused by carelessness that results in harm or injury to the person(s) involved.

Young children are involved in many different kinds of accidents. The most common causes of death, in order of rank from most to least common, are:

- motor vehicles—as pedestrians and passengers
- burns—from fireplaces, appliances, stoves, chemicals, electrical outlets
- drownings—in swimming pools, bathtubs, sinks, ponds, toilets
- falls—from stairs, play equipment, furniture, windows
- poisoning—from aspirin and other medicines, cleaning products, insecticides, and cosmetics

Figure 9–1 Parents expect child care facilities to be safe.

There are also a number of interesting facts concerning accidents that can be useful in planning for children's safety. First, boys are more likely to be involved in accidents than girls (Scheidt, 1995; Chang, 1989). This may be due in part to their behavior, which is generally more active, aggressive, and risk-oriented. Second, their play frequently involves greater physical contact and roughhousing. Fatigue also seems to be an important contributing factor. Accidents are more likely to occur toward the end of the day when children and caregivers are tired.

Certain conditions have also been identified as increasing the likelihood of accidents in child care settings. Staff members should take extra precautions whenever:

- they are not feeling well
- there are new staff members or visitors who are unfamiliar with the children
- they are upset or faced with a difficult experience, e.g., an uncooperative child, an unpleasant conversation with a parent, a strained relationship with another staff member, or a personal problem
- there is a shortage of staff members
- children are not able to play outdoors due to bad weather, e.g., rain, snow, extreme cold
- conditions are rushed
- there are new children in the group
- rules have not been explained carefully

Also, in group care settings, children are more likely to be injured on playground equipment, especially swings, climbing apparatus, and slides. At home, the majority of accidents take place indoors (Child Health Alert, 1989).

ACCIDENT PREVENTION

Accident *prevention* is based on the ability of parents, teachers, and caregivers to accurately assess children's developmental skills and to be able to anticipate their actions, Table 9–1. This information can be used for planning and organizing children's environments and activities, selecting appropriate play equipment, establishing rules, supervising their work and play, and developing safety education programs (Canadian Institute of Child Health).

Accident prevention requires continuous awareness and implementation of safe practices. Teachers, caregivers, and parents must always consider the element of safety in everything they do with young children. This includes the environments they create, the selection of equipment, and individual activities. To new or busy teachers or parents this may seem overly time-consuming and unnecessary. However, if the teacher or parent is new or busy, it is even more important to focus attention on children's safety. Any amount of effort is worthwhile even if it spares only one child from injury!

In many communities, local building codes and licensing regulations provide standards that influence the quality and safety of child care centers and homes.

TABLE 9–1 Developmental Characteristics and Accident Prevention

AGE	DEVELOPMENTAL CHARACTERISTICS	HAZARDS	PREVENTIVE MEASURES
Birth to 4 months	Eats, sleeps, cries	Burns	Check bath water with elbow. Always keep a hand on baby.
	Rolls off flat surfaces Wriggles	Falls	Never turn back on or walk away from baby who is on table or bed.
		Toys/Choking	Select toys that are too large to swallow, too tough to break with no sharp points or edges and have nontoxic finishes.
		Sharp objects	Keep pins and other sharp objects out of baby's reach.
		Smothering	Filmy plastics, harnesses, zippered bag, and pillows can smother or strangle. A firm mattress and loose covering for baby are safest. Babies of this age need complete protection.
4–12 months	Grasps and moves about Puts objects in mouth	Play areas	Keep baby in a safe place near attendant. The floor, full-sized bed, and yard are unsafe without supervision.
		Bath	Check temperature of bath water with elbow. Keep baby out of reach of faucets. Don't leave baby alone in bath for any reason.
		Toys	Large beads on strong cord and unbreakable, rounded toys or smooth wood or plastic are safe.
		Small objects	Keep buttons, beads, coins, and other small objects from baby's reach.
		Poisoning	Children of this age still need full-time protection.
		Falls	Don't turn your back or walk away when baby is on an elevated surface. Place gates in doorways and on stairways.
		Burns	Place guards around registers and floor furnaces. Keep hot liquids, hot foods, and electric cords on irons, toasters, and coffee pots out of baby's reach. Use sturdy and round-edged furniture. Avoid hot steam vaporizers.

TABLE 9–1 Developmental Characteristics and Accident Prevention (Continued)

AGE	DEVELOPMENTAL CHARACTERISTICS	HAZARDS	PREVENTIVE MEASURES
1–2 years	Investigates, climbs, opens doors and drawers; takes things apart; likes to play	Gates, windows, doors	Securely fasten doors leading to stairways, driveways, and storage. Put gates on stairways and porches. Keep screens locked or nailed.
		Play areas	Fence the play yard. Provide sturdy toys with no small removable parts or with unbreakable materials. Keep electric cords to coffee pots, toasters, irons, and radios out of reach.
		Water	*Never* leave child alone in tub, wading pool, or around open or frozen water.
		Poisons	Store all medicines and poisons in locked cabinets. Store cosmetics and household products, especially caustics, out of child's reach. Store kerosene and gasoline in metal cans and out of children's reach.
		Burns	Provide guards for wall heaters, registers, and floor furnaces. Never leave children alone in the house. Close supervision is needed to protect child from accidents.
2–3 years	Fascinated by fire. Moves about constantly. Tries to	Traffic	Keep child away from street and driveway with strong fence and firm discipline.
	do things alone. Imitates and explores.	Water	Even shallow wading pools are unsafe unless carefully supervised.
	Runs and is lightning fast. Is impatient with restraint.	Toys	Large sturdy toys without sharp edges or small removable parts are safest.
		Burns	Keep matches and cigarette lighters out of child's reach. Teach them about the danger of fire. Never leave children alone in the house.
		Dangerous objects	Lock up medicine, household and garden poisons, dangerous tools, firearms, and garden equipment. Teach safe ways of handling appropriate tools and kitchen equipment.
		Playmates	Accidents are more frequent when playmates are older—the two-year-old may be easily hurt by bats, hard balls, bicycles, rough play.

(Continued)

TABLE 9–1 Developmental Characteristics and Accident Prevention (Continued)

AGE	DEVELOPMENTAL CHARACTERISTICS	HAZARDS	PREVENTIVE MEASURES
3–6 years	Explores the neighborhood, climbs, rides tricycles. Likes and plays rough games. Frequently out of sight of adults. Likes to imitate adult actions.	Tools and equipment	Store in a safe place, out of reach, and locked. Teach safe use of tools and kitchen equipment.
		Poisons and burns	Keep medicines, household cleaning products, and matches locked up. Provide nontoxic art materials.
		Falls and injuries	Check play areas for attractive hazards such as old refrigerators, deep holes, trash heaps, construction, and old buildings.
		Drowning	Teach the danger of water and begin swimming instruction.
		Traffic	Help children learn rules and dangers of traffic, insist on obedience where traffic is concerned.
6–12 years	Away from home many hours a week. Participates in active sports, is part of a group and will "try anything once" in traffic on foot or bicycle. Teaching must gradually replace supervision.	Traffic	Drive safely as an example. Use safety belts. Teach pedestrian and bicycle safety rules. Don't allow play in the streets or alleys.
		Firearms	Store safely, handle carefully, teach proper use.
		Sports	Provide instruction, safe area, and equipment, and supervise any competition.
		Drowning	Teach swimming and boating safety.

Adapted from *Health Services: A Guide for Project Directors and Health Personnel*, U.S. Department of Health, Education, and Welfare, Washington, DC, 1971.

In addition to these requirements, the following four basic safety principles can be used by teachers, caregivers, and parents as guidelines for setting up environments that are safe for young children:

- advanced planning
- establishing rules
- careful supervision
- safety education

It is not possible to prevent all accidents. Regardless of how much care is exercised, there will always be some circumstances that are beyond a teacher's or caregiver's control. No amount of planning can prevent a child from suddenly releasing a grip on climbing equipment or a foot from slipping on dry pavement. However, adults who conscientiously implement safety principles can significantly reduce the number and seriousness of such accidents.

Advanced Planning

Considerable thought and careful planning should go into the selection of equipment and activities that are appropriate for young children (Bredekamp, 1987; Jones, 1994). Choices must take into account the children's skill levels and developmental abilities. Activities should be planned and equipment selected that stimulate children's curiosity, exploration, and sense of independence without endangering their safety (Abrams, 1990). Advanced planning allows teachers and caregivers to provide children with opportunities to practice their current level of skills and safely acquire new ones.

Planning for children's safety requires that caregivers recognize the risks or hazards that are involved in each activity. Many problems can easily be avoided if time is taken to examine materials, methods, and equipment before they are presented to children. This process also includes thinking through each step of an activity before allowing children to begin. Advanced planning means being prepared for the unexpected. This includes anticipating children's often unpredictable behaviors and developing specific safety rules for each activity, Figure 9–2.

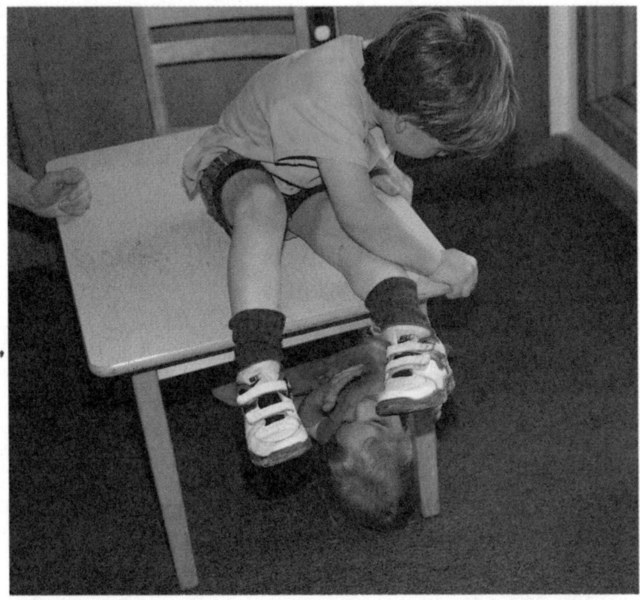

Figure 9–2 Caregivers should anticipate children's often unpredictable behaviors.

Organization is also a basic ingredient of advanced planning. Teachers and caregivers must be knowledgeable about an activity or experience before they actually begin the project with children. Anytime a teacher forgets supplies or is unsure of how to proceed, the chances of an accident occurring greatly increase. Foresight also enables teachers to substitute safe alternatives for those of questionable risk.

Examination of accident records can be very useful during the planning stage (Kinne, 1982). For example, if teachers begin to recognize a pattern in the type of injuries children receive, steps can be taken to alter the way an activity is conducted. If children are repeatedly injured on a particular piece of outdoor play equipment, a cause should immediately be sought. Plans should be made to modify either the rules, amount of supervision, or the equipment itself so that it will be safe for children to use.

Establishing Rules

Rules are statements of what is considered to be acceptable behavior as it relates to the welfare of an individual child, concern for group safety, and respect for shared property, Table 9–2. Too often, rules only inform children about what they should not do. They leave unclear what behaviors are acceptable or correct. However, rules can help children learn appropriate ways to use play equipment and interact with each other by defining the limits of safe behavior.

Teachers and caregivers can use rules to encourage children's appropriate behavior by stating them in positive terms, e.g., "Slide down the slide on your bottom, feet first, so you can see where you are going." To be most effective, rules should be stated clearly and in terms that are simple enough for even very young children to understand. Children are generally more willing to accept rules if they are given a clear explanation of the reasons why such rules are necessary.

There are no universal safety rules that teachers and caregivers can adopt. Each classroom or child care program must develop their own safety guidelines and rules based on the:

- population of children being served
- individual facilities and equipment (indoor and outdoor)
- number of adults available for supervision
- type of activity involved

It is often necessary to establish more precise rules and limits with young or difficult to manage children. Different pieces of equipment and whether they are being used in classroom, outdoor or home settings also affect the types of rules that are essential for safety.

When parents or teachers establish rules, they must also be sure that they are enforced. Unless children are consistently expected to obey rules, they quickly learn that rules have no meaning. However, a teacher must never threaten children or make them afraid in order to gain compliance. Rather, children should be praised whenever they demonstrate appropriate safety behaviors. For example, a teacher might recognize a child's efforts by saying, "Carlos, I liked the way you rode your

TABLE 9–2 Rules for Safe Use of Play Equipment

CLIMBING APPARATUS

Rules for Children

- Always hold on with both hands.
- No pushing or shoving.
- Look carefully before jumping off equipment; be sure the area below is clear of objects and other children.
- Be extra careful if equipment or shoes are wet from snow or rain.

Rules for Caregiver

- Inspect equipment before children begin to play on it. Check for broken or worn parts and sharp edges; be sure the equipment is firmly anchored in the ground.
- Be sure surface material under equipment is adequate and free of sharp stones, sticks, and toys.
- Limit the number of children on climber at any one time.
- Always have an adult in direct attendance when children are on the equipment.
- Supervise children carefully if they are wearing slippery-soled shoes, sandals, long dresses or skirts, mittens, bulky coats, or long scarves.

SWINGS

Rules for Children

- Wait until the swing comes to a full stop before getting on or off.
- Always sit on the swing seat.
- Only one child per swing at any time.
- Only adults should push children.
- Stay away from moving swings.
- Hold on with both hands.

Rules for Caregivers

- Check equipment for safety, e.g., condition of chain/rope and seat, security of bolts or S-rings; also check ground beneath swings for adequate cushioning material and sharp debris.
- Designate a "safe" area where children can wait their turn.
- An adult should be in attendance at all times.

bike carefully around the other children who were playing," or "Tricia, you remembered to lay your scissors on the table before getting up to leave." Through repeated positive verbal encouragement, children soon learn that these behaviors are both acceptable and desirable.

Occasionally, a child will misuse play equipment or not follow directions. A gentle reminder concerning rules is usually sufficient. If this approach fails and the child continues to behave inappropriately, the teacher or caregiver must remove the child from the activity or area. A simple statement such as, "I cannot allow you to hit the other children," lets the child know that this is not acceptable behavior.

Figure 9–3 Rules never replace adult supervision.

Permitting the child to return later to the same activity conveys confidence in the child's ability to learn the proper way.

Rules never replace the need for careful adult *supervision*, Figure 9–3. Young children tend to quickly forget rules, especially when they are busy playing or excited about what they are doing.

Rules should be realistic for young children. They should allow enough freedom so that children can work and play, yet remain within the boundaries of safety. Rules should not be so overly restrictive that children are discouraged or afraid to explore and experiment with their environment. Gradually, as children learn to recognize danger and establish their own standards for protecting themselves, the need for extensive rules is lessened.

Careful Supervision

Parents and teachers of young children are faced with many responsibilities. Their supervisory role is, perhaps, one of the most important of these duties. Children depend on the guidance of responsible adults to help them learn appropriate safety behaviors. The younger the children, the more protective this supervision must be. As children gain additional coordination, skill, and experience in handling potentially dangerous situations, adult supervision can become less restrictive.

The amount of adult supervision necessary is also directly related to the type of activity involved, Figure 9–4. For example, a cooking project that requires the use of a hot appliance must be more carefully supervised than a "dress-up" center

Figure 9–4 The amount of adult supervision depends on the activity.

containing play clothes. Certain pieces of play equipment are also more hazardous than others and teachers must station themselves near these structures so children can be watched more closely.

The number of children a teacher can safely manage is also affected by the nature of the activity. One adult may be able to oversee a game of Farmer-in-the-Dell, while a field trip to the fire station requires several adults. **Caution:** *Never leave children unattended.* If a teacher must leave an area, it should be supervised by another adult.

Occasionally, there are children in a classroom or group setting who are known to be physically aggressive or who engage in behaviors that could possibly bring harm to themselves or other children. Caregivers and centers can be held liable by the courts if an accident or injury is caused by the actions of a child known to have such a reputation. Teachers are obligated to supervise these children more closely. Their responsibility goes beyond merely issuing a warning to the child to stop—they must intervene and actually stop the child from continuing the dangerous activity even if it means physically removing the child from the area.

For safety purposes, the minimal adult/child ratios for both indoor and outdoor settings are generally defined by state regulations. NAEYC has also recommended that there never be fewer than two adults with any group of children. However, it must also be recognized that there are considerable differences in each caregiver's ability to supervise and manage children's activities and behavior. Some teachers are less effective at controlling unruly or disruptive children. In these situations, it may be necessary to have more than the required number of adults available to safely monitor children's play.

Safety Education

One of the prime methods for avoiding accidents and injuries is through safety education (Chang, 1989). It is most desirable to begin informal safety training with children as soon as they understand the meanings of words. The earlier children learn about safety, the more naturally they will develop the attitudes and respect that lead to lifelong patterns of safe behavior.

Much safety education takes place through *incidental learning* experiences and imitation of adult behaviors. Young children who already show many safe attitudes and practices can also serve as valuable role models. For example, several children may be jumping from the top of a platform rather than climbing down the ladder. Suddenly, one child yells, "You shouldn't be doing that. You could get hurt!" As a result, the children stop and begin to use the ladder instead. Taking advantage of teachable moments can also prove to be an effective educational tool. For example, when children stand up on a swing or run with sharp objects in their hand, teachers should use these opportunities to explain why such actions are not appropriate. Suggestions can also be made for safer alternatives. Often learning of this type is more meaningful to the young child.

Safety education should also prepare young children to cope with emergencies. Personal safety awareness and self-protection skills enable even young children to avoid many potentially harmful situations. Children must know what to do in an emergency and how to get help. They should learn their home address and phone number as well as how to use the telephone. Older children can also begin to learn basic first aid skills.

Teachers and caregivers should not overlook their own safety in their concern for children. It is easy for adults to be careless when they are under stress or have worked long, hard hours. Sometimes, in their zealous attempts to help children, teachers take extraordinary risks; it is at such times that even greater caution must be exercised.

IMPLEMENTING SAFETY PRACTICES

Much of the responsibility for maintaining a safe environment belongs to teachers and caregivers. Their knowledge of child development and daily contact with children gives them an advantageous position for identifying many problem areas. However, safety must be a concern of all school personnel, including support staff such as aides, cooks, janitors, secretaries, and bus drivers. One person may spot a safety hazard that had previously gone unnoticed by others.

Safety must be a continual concern. Each time teachers or caregivers arrange a classroom, add new play equipment, plan an activity, or take children on a field trip or walk they must first stop to assess whether or not there is any risk involved for the children. Even differences among groups of children can affect the types of safety problems that occur and the kinds of rules that are necessary. For example, extra precautions may be needed when children with special needs, chronic health problems, or behavior problems are present.

Toys and Equipment

The majority of accidents involving toys and equipment result from their improper use. Many of these injuries can be prevented by carefully selecting toys and equipment that are appropriate for young children (Abrams, 1990). The ages, interests, behavioral characteristics, and level of motor skills of the children serve as useful guidelines when choosing toys and equipment, Tables 9–3 and 9–4. Accidents are more likely to occur when children try to use educational materials and play equipment that are intended for older children:

- toys that are too heavy for small children to lift
- rings that are too large for small hands to grip
- steps that are too far apart
- climbing equipment that is too tall
- balloons that can be choked on

The opposite may also occur. When play equipment is limited or intended for younger children, older children may misuse it in attempts to create their own challenges.

The amount of available classroom or play yard space will also influence choices. Large pieces of equipment or toys that require spacious room for their use will be a constant source of accidents if they are set up in areas that are too small.

Quality is also very important to consider. The construction of toys or equipment should be examined carefully and not purchased if they have:

- sharp wires, pins, or staples
- small pieces that might come loose, e.g., buttons, "eyes," screws
- moving parts that can pinch fingers
- inappropriate size
- unstable bases or frames
- toxic paints and materials
- sharp edges
- defective parts
- construction that will not hold up under hard use
- possibility of causing electrical shock
- parts made of brittle plastic or glass that could break

Extreme care should be taken to thoroughly examine any equipment that is purchased secondhand.

Toys and play equipment should be inspected on a daily basis, especially if they are used frequently by children or are located outdoors and exposed to variable weather conditions. They should be in good repair and free of splinters, rough edges, protruding bolts or nails, and broken or missing parts. Ropes on swings or ladders should be checked routinely and replaced if they begin to fray. Large equipment should be checked often to be sure that it remains firmly anchored in the ground and that surface materials are adequate and free of debris (see Chapter 8).

TABLE 9–3 Guidelines for Selecting Toys and Play Equipment

1. Carefully consider children's ages, interests, and developmental abilities; check manufacturer's label for recommendations.
2. Choose fabric items that are washable and labeled flame-retardant or nonflammable.
3. Look for quality construction; check durability, good design, stability, absence of sharp corners or wires.
4. Select toys that are made from nontoxic materials.
5. Avoid toys and play materials with small pieces that a child could accidentally choke on.
6. Select toys and equipment that are appropriate for the amount of available play and storage space.
7. Avoid toys with electrical parts or those that are propelled through the air.
8. Choose play materials that children can use with minimal adult supervision.

TABLE 9–4 Appropriate Toy Choices for Infants, Toddlers, and Preschoolers

INFANTS	TODDLERS	PRESCHOOLERS
nonbreakable mirrors	peg bench	puppets
cloth books	balls	dolls and doll houses
wooden cars	records	dress-up clothes
rattles	simple puzzles	simple art materials, e.g., crayons, markers, watercolors, playdough, blunt scissors
mobiles	large building blocks	books and puzzles
music boxes	wooden cars and trucks	simple musical instruments
plastic telephone	dress-up clothes	cars, trucks, fire engines
balls	bristle blocks	tricycle
toys that squeak	large wooden beads to string	simple construction sets, e.g., Legos®, bristle blocks
blocks	cloth picture books	play dishes, empty food containers
nesting toys	nesting cups	
teething ring	pull and riding toys	
washable, stuffed animals	plastic dishes, pots and pans	
	fat crayons and paper	

Regularly scheduled maintenance of toys and play equipment ensures their safety and helps them to last longer. Play equipment that is defective or otherwise unsafe for children to use should be removed promptly until it can be repaired. Items that cannot be repaired should be discarded.

Special precautions are necessary whenever large equipment or climbing structures are set up indoors. This type of equipment should be placed in an open area away from furniture or objects that could injure the children. Mats, foam pads, or large cushions placed around and under structures that are any distance above the floor will protect children from getting hurt if they accidentally fall. Rules for the safe use of such equipment should be clearly explained to the children before they use it. At least one adult should be in a position of direct attendance whenever children are using this equipment, Figure 9–5.

Safety is a prime concern whenever new equipment, toys, or educational materials are introduced into a classroom or outdoor setting. Initially, rules are developed and should be limited to those that protect children's well-being. Too many rules may dampen children's enthusiasm for using new equipment and restrict their inventiveness. Also, if more than one new item is to be introduced, it is best to do this over a period of time so that children are not overwhelmed by multiple sets of rules.

Selection of equipment, e.g., beds, cribs, playpens, strollers, carriers, and toys for infants and toddlers must be made with great care. The designs of many of these products have contributed to a significant number of deaths. Consequently, strict criteria have been established by the U. S. Consumer Safety Product Commission and Canadian Consumer Corporate Affairs for the manufacturing of children's furniture since 1977, Table 9–5. However, toys and furniture purchased at second-hand shops or garage sales may have been manufactured before these standards went into effect. They should, therefore, be examined carefully. Also, new toys and products that do not always meet these standards are continually being introduced. Therefore, consumers must be knowledgeable about quality and safety features when purchasing toys and furniture for young children (Jones, 1994; Gillis, 1986).

Figure 9–5 An adult should always be in direct attendance when children are using playground structures.

TABLE 9–5 Infant Equipment Checklist

	YES	NO
Back Carriers		
1. Carrier has restraining strap to secure child.		
2. Leg openings are small enough to prevent child from slipping out.		
3. Leg openings are large enough to prevent chafing.		
4. Frames have no pinch points in the folding mechanism.		
5. Carrier has padded covering over metal frame near baby's face.		
Bassinets and Cradles		
1. Bassinet/cradle has a sturdy bottom and a wide base for stability.		
2. Bassinet/cradle has smooth surfaces—no protruding staples or other hardware that could injure the baby.		
3. Legs have strong, effective locks to prevent folding while in use.		
Carrier Seats		
1. Carrier seat has a wide, sturdy base for stability.		
2. Carrier has nonskid feet to prevent slipping.		
3. Supporting devices lock securely.		
4. Carrier seat has crotch and waist strap.		
5. Buckle or strap is easy to use.		
Changing Tables		
1. Table has safety straps to prevent falls.		
2. Table has drawers or shelves that are easily accessible without leaving the baby unattended.		
Cribs		
1. Slats are spaced no more than 2 3/8 inches (6 cm) apart.		
2. No slats are missing or cracked.		
3. Mattress fits snugly—less than two fingers width between edge of mattress and crib side.		
4. Mattress support is securely attached to the head and footboards.		
5. Corner posts are no higher than 5/8 inch (1.6 cm) to prevent entanglement.		
6. There are no cutouts in head and footboards to allow head entrapment.		
7. Drop-side latches cannot be easily released by a baby.		
8. Drop-side latches securely hold sides in raised position.		
9. All screws or bolts which secure components of crib together are present and tight.		
Crib Toys		
1. Crib toys have no strings longer than 12 inches (30 cm) to prevent entanglement.		
2. Crib gym or other crib toy suspended over the crib must have devices that securely fasten to the crib to prevent it from being pulled into the crib.		
3. Components of toys are not small enough to be a choking hazard.		
Gates and Enclosures		
1. Gate or enclosure has a straight top edge.		
2. Openings in gate are too small to entrap a child's head.		
3. Gate has a pressure bar or other fastener so it will resist forces exerted by a child.		

TABLE 9–5 Infant Equipment Checklist (Continued)

	YES	NO
High Chairs		
1. High chair has restraining straps that are independent of the tray.		
2. Tray locks securely.		
3. Buckle on waist strap is easy to fasten and unfasten.		
4. High chair has a wide base for stability.		
5. High chair has caps or plugs on tubing that are firmly attached and cannot be pulled off and choke a child.		
6. If it is a folding high chair, it has an effective locking device.		
Hook-On Chairs		
1. Hook-on chair has a restraining strap to secure the child.		
2. Hook-on chair has a clamp that locks onto the table for added security.		
3. Hook-on chair has caps or plugs on tubing that are firmly attached and cannot be pulled off and choke a child.		
4. Hook-on chair has a warning never to place chair where child can push off with feet.		
Pacifiers		
1. Pacifier has no ribbons, string, cord, or yarn attached.		
2. Shield is large enough and firm enough so it cannot fit in child's mouth.		
3. Guard or shield has ventilation holes so baby can breathe if shield does get into mouth.		
4. Pacifier nipple has no holes or tears that might cause it to break off in baby's mouth.		
Playpens		
1. Drop-side mesh playpen or mesh crib has warning label about never leaving a side in the down position.		
2. Playpen mesh has small weave (less than 1/4-inch openings).		
3. Mesh has no tears or loose threads.		
4. Mesh is securely attached to top rail and floorplate.		
5. Top rail has no tears or holes.		
6. Wooden playpen has slats spaced no more than 2 3/8 inches apart.		
7. If staples are used in construction, they are firmly installed—none missing, or loose.		
Rattles/Squeeze Toys/Teethers		
1. Rattles and teethers have handles too large to lodge in baby's throat.		
2. Rattles have sturdy construction that will not cause them to break apart in use.		
3. Squeeze toys do not contain a squeaker that could detach and choke a baby.		
Strollers		
1. Stroller has a wide base to prevent tipping.		
2. Seat belt and crotch strap are securely attached to frame.		
3. Seat belt buckle is easy to fasten and unfasten.		
4. Brakes securely lock the wheel(s).		
5. Shopping basket low on the back and located directly over or in front of rear wheels.		
Toy Chests		
1. Toy chest has no latch to entrap child within the chest.		
2. Toy chest has a spring-loaded lid support that will not require periodic adjustment and will support the lid in any position to prevent lid slam.		
3. Chest has ventilation holes or spaces in front or sides, or under lid.		

Adapted from *The Safe Nursery*, U.S. Consumer Product Safety Commission, Washington, DC, 1986.

Classroom Activities

Safety must also be a major concern when teachers or caregivers select and plan activities for young children. Many teachers and caregivers are sensitive to the need for safety awareness in outdoor settings, but they often have a more relaxed attitude and effort where indoor activities are concerned. This false sense of security may result from the belief that fewer accidents take place when children are indoors. While this may be the case in large group settings, it is no excuse for overlooking strict safety precautions. Also, accidents are more likely to occur indoors in day care home settings, where nearly one-third of the children currently receive care. Therefore, safety must always be a priority. The potential for accidental injury is present in most activities. Even wooden building blocks can be dangerous if children use them incorrectly.

It is difficult to provide a precise checklist for evaluating the safety of classroom activities. However, there are several guidelines that teachers and caregivers can follow when they select and conduct learning activities.

Teachers should ask themselves the following questions:

- Is the activity age-appropriate?
- What are the possible risks involved?
- What special precautions are needed to make an activity safe?

After these questions have been answered, the next step involves applying the basic principles of safety, e.g., advanced planning, formulating rules, deciding on the type of supervision that is necessary, and instituting an educational program.

Extra safety precautions and more precise planning are necessary for some types of activities. This is especially true for activities that involve:

- pointed or sharp objects such as scissors, knives, and woodworking tools, e.g., hammers, nails, saws
- pipes, boards, blocks, or objects made of glass
- electrical appliances, e.g., hot plates, radio, mixers
- hot liquids, e.g., wax, syrup, oil, water
- cosmetics or cleaning supplies

For added safety, a separate area can be set aside for any activity that involves harmful materials. Boundaries can be established with portable room dividers or a row of chairs.

The number of children participating in an activity at any one time can also be restricted. Some activities may need to be limited to even one child. Limiting the number of children improves a teacher's ability to effectively supervise a given space. Color-coded necklaces can be used to control the number of children in an area at any one time. This system also makes it easy for children to determine if there is space available for them.

The condition of all electrical appliances should be checked very carefully before they are used. Be sure that the plugs are intact and cords are not frayed. Avoid the use of extension cords that children could trip over. Always place electrical appliances on a table nearest the outlet and against the wall for safety. Never use appliances near a source of water, including sinks, wet floors, or large pans of water.

When children will actually be operating an electrical appliance, it should be set on a low table or the floor so that it is easy for them to reach. Equipment that is placed any higher than children's waist level is dangerous. Teachers should continuously remind children to stand back away from machinery with moving parts to prevent their hair, fingers, or clothing from getting caught or burned. Special precautions such as turning the handles of pots and pans toward the back of the stove or hot plate should be taken whenever hot liquids or foods are involved. Always detach cords from the electrical outlet, never the appliance. Safety caps should be promptly replaced in all electrical outlets when the project is completed.

Safety must also be a concern in the selection of art media and activities. Art materials such as paints, glue, crayons, and clay must always be nontoxic when they are used by young children, Figure 9–6. Avoid using dried beans, peas, toothpicks, berries, or beads that are very small in size for art activities. Children can stuff these objects into their ears or nose, or swallow them in an instant. Fabric pieces, dried leaves or grasses, styrofoam, packing materials, yarn, or ribbon are safer alternatives for children's art creations. Some safe substitutions for hazardous art materials are provided in Table 9–6. Proper storage of liquid paints and glue is also an important consideration. Plastic containers should always be used in place of glass bottles, jars, or dishes that could break.

Special precautions should be taken in classrooms with hard-surfaced or highly polished floors. Spilled water, paint, or other liquids and dry materials such as beans, rice, sawdust, flour, or cornmeal cause these floors to be very slippery. Spills should be cleaned up promptly. Newspapers or rugs spread out on the floor help prevent children from slipping and falling.

Figure 9–6 Nontoxic art materials must be used by young children.

TABLE 9–6 Safe Substitutes for Hazardous Art Materials

UNSAFE SUBSTANCES	SUBSTITUTES
Clay in dry form. Dry powder contains silica which is easily inhaled and may damage the lungs.	Clay in wet form only. Wet clay cannot be inhaled.
Glazes that contain lead.	Poster paints or water-based paints.
Solvents such as turpentine, benzene, toluene, rubber cement and its thinner.	Use water-based paints and glues.
Cold water or commercial fabric dyes.	Food coloring or natural vegetable dyes made from onion skins, parsley, nuts, cranberries, etc.
Permanent markers which may contain toluene or other toxic solvents.	Water-based markers.
Instant papier maches that may contain asbestos fibers or lead pigments.	Use black and white newspaper and white paste or flour and water.
Aerosol sprays such as paints and lacquers.	Water-based paints and brushes for splatter techniques.
Powdered tempera paints. Their dusts may contain toxic pigments.	Use only nontoxic paints. Purchase liquid paint or mix powders in a well-ventilated area, preferably wearing a dust mask.
Pastels or chalk that create dust.	Crayons or oil-based cra-pas.
All photographic chemicals.	Use blueprint paper and sun to make prints.
Epoxy or other solvent-based glues.	Water-based white glue or library paste.
Solvent-based silk screen and other printing inks.	Paper stencils and water-based inks.

Adapted with permission from the Art Hazards Information Center, 5 Beckman Street, New York, NY 10038.

Environments and activities that are safe for young children are also less stressful for the adults. When classrooms and play yards are free of potential hazards, teachers and caregivers can concentrate on selecting safe activities and providing quality supervision.

Field Trips

Excursions away from a center's facilities can be an exciting part of children's educational experiences. They present added risks and liability concerns for child care programs, however, and require special precautions to be taken.

Most importantly, centers should have a written policy describing procedures for conducting field trips. Parents should be informed in advance of an outing and their written permission should be obtained for each excursion. On the day of the trip, a notice should be posted reminding parents and staff of the trip, where the children will be going, and when they will leave and return to the center. At least one adult accompanying the group should have first aid and CPR training. A first aid kit should be taken along and include quarters to use for emergency telephone calls. Tags can be pinned on children with the center's name and phone number. However, *do not* include children's names: this enables strangers to call children by name, making it easier to lure them away from a group. A list with children's emergency information, e.g., parents' telephone numbers, name of physician, and number of various emergency services should also be taken along. Prior to the outing, procedures and safety rules should be carefully reviewed with the children.

Transporting children for field trips poses a serious liability concern for centers, especially when parents, staff, or volunteers drive their own cars. Centers are liable for children's safety while they are travelling in private vehicles, and it is difficult for centers to control the safeness of these cars and the driver's skill. Vehicles must also be equipped with appropriate safety restraints for each child. Therefore, it may be in the center's best interest not to use private vehicles to transport children on field trips. Vehicles owned and operated by a center are generally included in their liability insurance and are therefore, preferable. Neighborhood walks and public bus rides are always safe alternatives.

Pets

Pets can be a special addition to child care settings, but care must be taken so they are a safe experience for both children and animals. Children's allergies should be considered before pets visit or become permanent residents of a classroom. Also, make sure animals are free of disease and current on immunizations (if appropriate). Some animals, such as turtles and birds, are known carriers of illnesses that are communicable to humans and are not good choices for young children. Instructions for the animal's care should be posted to serve as both a guideline and reminder to staff. Precautions must also be taken to protect pets from curious and exuberant children who may unknowingly cause harm or injury to the animal.

LEGAL IMPLICATIONS

Safety generates more concern than any other aspect of early childhood education. Recent lawsuits, legal decisions, and increased public awareness have added to a feeling of uneasiness. As demand for child care services continues to grow, interest in regulating programs and facilities has also increased. Parents want, and have a right, to be assured that facilities are safe. Parents expect schools and child care centers to be responsible for the safety of their children.

Persons who teach and care for young children should be aware of the legal issues and responsibilities that affect their positions. There are several reasons why this is essential. First, caregivers are expected, by law, to provide for children's safety. Second, the incidence of injury and accident is known to be high among this age group. Third, it helps teachers, administrators, and caregivers to protect themselves against possible legal action. The combination of immaturity and the unpredictable behavior of young children necessitates careful safety management.

The most important legal concerns for teachers and caregivers center around the issue of liability (Scott, 1983; Treadwell, 1980). The term *liability* refers to the legal obligations and responsibilities, especially those related to safety, that are accepted by administrators, teachers, and caregivers when they agree to care for children. Failure to carry out these duties in an acceptable manner is considered *negligence*.

Negligence often results from questionable safety practices and management. For legal purposes, negligent acts are generally divided into two catagories according to the circumstances and the resulting damages or injuries. The first category includes situations in which a teacher or caregiver fails to take precautionary measures necessary to protect children from danger. Standards for determining what is necessary are based on what precautionary measures most people with comparable training would take in a similar situation (Sheldon, 1983). A person who fails to take the proper precautions could be considered negligent. A lack of adequate supervision, play equipment that is defective or in need of repair, and allowing children to engage in harmful activities such as throwing rocks or standing on swings are some examples of this form of negligence.

The second category of negligent acts includes situations in which the actions or decisions of a teacher or caregiver involve a risk to the children. An example of this type of negligence might include a teacher making arrangements to have children transported in private vehicles that are not insured, or planning classroom activities that allow children to use poisonous chemicals or sophisticated electrical equipment without careful supervision.

Prevention is always the best method for ensuring the safety of young children and avoiding difficult legal problems and lawsuits. However, there are several measures that provide additional protection to child care programs and their staff.

Teachers and caregivers are legally responsible for their actions (Sheldon, 1983). Despite careful attempts at providing safe conditions for children, staff members may, at some time, be accused of negligence or wrong-doing. For this reason, it is wise for every administrator, teacher, and caregiver to obtain personal liability insurance. Such policies can be purchased from most private insurance companies and through the National Association for the Education of Young Children (NAEYC). Accident insurance, purchased on individual children who are enrolled, also affords child care programs extra protection.

Administrators and staff should not hesitate to seek legal assistance on issues related to child care and education. Legal advice can be a valuable source of protection. Preschool and day-care programs might also want to consider selecting a member of the legal profession to fill a position on their board of directors or advisory council.

Careful examination of job descriptions before accepting employment offers teachers and caregivers an additional measure of protection against future legal problems. Potential employees should be sure they have the appropriate training and skills to perform required duties. For example, if teachers are expected to administer first aid to injured children, then they should complete first aid and CPR training before they begin to work.

Accurately maintained records, particularly accident reports, are also an added source of legal protection, Figure 9–7. Information contained in these reports can be used in court as evidence to prove a teacher's or school's innocence against charges of negligence. A thorough report should be completed for each accident that occurs, regardless of how minor or unimportant it may seem to be at the time. This is very important because the results of some injuries are not always immediately apparent. There is also the possibility that complications may develop at a later date. A special form such as the one shown in Figure 9–8 can be used for this purpose. These forms should be filled out by the person who saw the accident and administered first

ACCIDENT REPORT FORM

Child's Name ______________________ Date of Accident __________

Parent ____________________________ Time ______ AM ___ PM ___

Address ___________________________ Parent notified ______ AM ___ PM ___

Description of injuries____

____

Action taken at home or center (first aid) ______________________________

____

Doctor consulted __________________ Address __________________

Doctor's diagnosis____

____

Number of days missed from the child care facility as a result of the accident _____

Adult in charge when accident occurred ________________________________

Description of activity, location in facility and circumstances, immediately before and at the time of the accident

____

____

____

____

____

____

What corrective measures could be taken to eliminate such accidents in the future?

____

____

____

Report prepared by ____________________________ Date ___________

Figure 9–7 Accident form for recording serious injuries courtesy of the Kansas Department of Health and Environment, Bureau of Adult and Child Care Facilities.

SUNNY DAYS CHILD CARE CENTER
Record of Children's Accidents

Date and Time	Child's Name	Nature of Child's Injuries	How the Accident Occurred	Observed By	Type of First Aid Treatment Administered	By Whom

Figure 9–8 A sample accident record form.

aid treatment. The information should be clear, precise, and objective. Such forms provide a composite picture of the accident and are also useful for detecting patterns of injury. Accident records are considered legal documents and should be kept on file at the child care center for a period of at least five years.

Summary

The normal characteristics and nature of infants and young children demand that safety be a major concern of all teachers, caregivers, and parents. Because accidents are the leading cause of death for young children, every effort must be taken to prevent them. This obligation requires much time, deliberate effort, and careful planning.

Aside from the moral obligations caregivers have to protect children's safety, parents also expect this type of treatment from professional child care personnel. Liability is the term used to describe the legal aspect of this responsibility. Two types of negligence may be proven by the courts: failure to take adequate precautionary safety measures, and intentional acts or decisions that involve elements of risk.

In addition to practicing principles of safety, child care personnel can provide some protection for themselves by purchasing personal liability insurance, reading job descriptions carefully before accepting a new job, filling out accident reports when children are injured, and seeking professional legal assistance when necessary. Prevention is always the preferred method for ensuring the safety of young children.

Accident prevention is based on four basic principles: advanced planning, establishing rules, careful supervision, safety education. One of the teacher's and caregiver's most important functions is implementing these principles in classrooms and outdoor play areas. Specific guidelines should be followed carefully for the selection and presentation of toys, equipment, and various activities.

Suggested Activities

1. Visit a preschool play yard or public playground. Select one piece of play equipment and observe children playing on or with it for at least 15 minutes. Make a list of actual or potential dangers that could result from improper use. Develop a set of workable safety rules for children to follow.
2. Role play how a teacher might handle a child who is not riding a tricycle in a safe manner.
3. Imagine that you have been asked to purchase outdoor play equipment for a new child development center. Make a list of safety features you would look for when you make your selections. Write to several companies for equipment catalogues. Using the catalogues, select basic outdoor equipment to furnish the play yard of a small child care center that has two classes of 20 children each and a budget of $6000.
4. Prepare room-by-room home safety checklists for parents of infants, toddlers, and preschoolers (one for each).

Chapter Review

A. Match the item in Column I with those in Column II.

Column I	Column II
1. basic element of advanced planning	a. foresight
2. legal responsibility for children's safety	b. supervision
3. the ability to anticipate	c. education
4. limits that define safe behavior	d. planning
5. failure to protect children's safety	e. rules
6. watching over children's behavior	f. safe
7. environments free of hazards	g. negligence
8. the process of learning safe behavior	h. prevention
9. a key factor in accident prevention	i. liability
10. measures taken to insure children's safety	j. organization

B. Fill in the blanks with one of the words listed below:

removed	accidents	anticipate
legal	responsible	safety principles
supervision	safety education	safety
inspected		

1. Broken play equipment must be ____________ immediately from a classroom or play yard.
2. The leading cause of death for young children is ____________ .
3. Adults must be able to ____________ children's actions as part of advanced planning.
4. Parents expect teachers and caregivers to be ____________ for their child's safety.
5. Basic ____________ ____________ include advanced planning, establishing rules, careful supervision, and safety education.
6. Accident records are ____________ records.
7. A continuous concern of teachers and caregivers is ____________ .
8. Rules never replace the need for adult ____________ .
9. Toys and play equipment should be ____________ daily.
10. A prime method for avoiding accidents is through ____________ ____________ .

References

Abrams, B. W. and Kauffman, N. A. 1990. *Toys for Early Childhood Development.* West Nyack, NY: Center for Applied Research in Education.

Bredekamp, S. (Ed.). 1987. *Developmentally Appropriate Practice in Early Childhood Programs Serving Children From Birth Through Age 8.* Washington, DC: NAEYC.

Chang, A., Lugg, M., and Nebedum, A. 1989. Injuries Among Preschool Children Enrolled in Day-Care Centers. *Pediatrics,* 83(2): 272–277.

Gillis, J. and Fise, M. 1986. *The Childwise Catalog: A Consumer's Guide to Buying the Safest and Best Products for Your Children (newborn through age five).* NY: Pocket Books.

Injury Hazards in Home Day-Care. May, 1989. *Child Health Alert.*

Jones, S. and Freitag, W. 1994. *Guide to Baby Products* (4th ed.). New York: Consumer Reports Books.

Kinne, Marilyn. 1982, November. "Accidents." *Journal of School Health* 52(9): 564–65.

Safe Not Sorry. Canadian Institute of Child Health. (pamphlet)

Scheidt, P., Harel, Y., Trumble, A., Jones, D., Overpeck, M., and Bijur, P. 1995. The Epidemiology of Nonfatal Injuries Among U. S. Children and Youth. *American Journal of Public Health,* 85(7): 932–938.

Scott, Carol L. 1983, September. "Injury in the Classroom: Are Teachers Liable?" *Young Children,* 38(6): 10–18.

Sheldon, J. 1983. "Protecting the Preschooler and the Practitioner: Legal Issues in Early Childhood." In *Early Childhood Education: Special Environmental, Policy and Legal Considerations.* E. Goetz and K. E. Allen (eds). Rockville, MA: Aspen.

The Safe Nursery. 1986. U. S. Consumer Product Safety Commission, Washington, DC.

Treadwell, L. W. 1980. *The Family Day Care Provider's Legal Handbook.* Oakland, CA: Bananas.

When Child's Play is Adult Business. Canadian Institute of Child Health.(pamphlet)

Which Toy for Which Child. 1986. U. S. Consumer Product Safety Commission, Washington, DC.

Additional Reading

Adams. P. K., and Taylor, M. K. 1980, Spring. "Liability: How Much Do You Really Know?" *Day Care and Early Education.*

Caruso, D. 1984, November. "Infants' Exploratory Play: Implications for Child Care." *Young Children* 40(1): 27–30.

Child Care Law Publications, 625 Market St., Suite 915, San Francisco, CA 94105.

Comer, D. 1987. *Developing Safety Skills With The Young Child.* Albany, NY: Delmar Publishers Inc.

Injury Control for Children and Youth; 1987. American Academy of Pediatrics, P. O. Box 927, 141 Northwest Point Blvd., Elk Grove, IL 60009–0927.

Kendrick, A., Kaufmann, R., and Messenger, K. (Eds.). 1995. *Healthy Young Children.* Washington, DC: NAEYC.

MeKenzie, J. F., and Williams, I. C. 1982, May. "Are Your Students Learning In A Safe Environment?" *Journal of School Health* 52(5): 284–85.

National Safe Kids Campaign. *Safe Kids Are No Accident.* Washington, DC: Children's Hospital National Medical Center.

Safe Day Care: A Teacher's Guide to Creating Environments For Preschool Children. Massachusetts Department of Public Health, 150 Tremont Street, Boston, MA 02111.

Pamphlets

Equipment Safety

A Parent's Safety Guide to Kid Stuff, National Safety Council, 444 North Michigan Ave., Chicago, IL 60611.

Backyard Play Equipment Accidents, National Safety Council, 444 North Michigan Ave., Chicago, IL 60611.

Care and Safety of Young Children, Council on Family Health, Department F., 633 Third Ave., New York, NY 10017.

Choosing Toys for Children, Toy Manufacturers of America, Inc., 200 Fifth Avenue, New York, NY 10010.

Is Your Child Safe? Consumer and Corporate Affairs, Canada, Hull. Quebec K1A0C9.

Let's Learn About Safety, Public Relations Services Department, Eli Lily and Company, Box 618, Indianapolis, IN 46206.

Playgrounds Safe and Sound. Washington, DC: NAEYC.

Safety Sampler—Hazards of Children's Products, U. S. Consumer Products Safety Commission, Washington, DC 20207.

The Swing That Swung Back, U. S. Consumer Products Safety Commission, Washington, DC 20207.

Think Play Safety. U. S. Consumer Product Safety Commission, Washington, DC 20207.

Toys and Playground Equipment, National Safety Council, 444 North Michigan Ave., Chicago, IL 60611.

Toys: Tools for Learning. National Association for the Education of Young Children, 1834 Connecticut Avenue, NW, Washington, DC 20009.

Your Child's Safety, Metropolitan Life Insurance Company, 1 Madison Avenue, New York, NY 10010.

Chapter 10

Management of Accidents and Injuries

Terms to Know

negligent
aspiration
sterile
elevate
resuscitation
paralysis
ingested
alkalis
submerge
reimplant

Objectives

After studying this chapter, you should be able to:

- State the difference between emergency care and first aid.
- Identify the ABCs for assessing emergencies.
- Name eight life-threatening conditions and state the emergency treatment for each.
- Name ten conditions that are not life-threatening and state the first aid treatment for each.
- Describe the teacher's or caregiver's role and responsibilities as they relate to management of accidental injuries and illness.

Accident prevention is a major responsibility of preschools and child care centers. This goal is best achieved by providing safe environments, presenting health/safety education, and establishing proper procedures for handling emergencies.

Serious Injury and Illness Plan

1. *Remain with the child at all times.* Keep calm and reassure the child that you are there to help. Your presence can be a comfort to the child, especially when faced with unfamiliar surroundings and discomfort. You can also provide valuable information about events preceding and following the injury/illness, symptoms the child exhibited, etc.
2. **Do not** move the child unless there is danger of additional harm (such as fire, electrical shock, etc.).
3. Immediately begin appropriate emergency care procedures. Meanwhile, send for help. Have another adult or child alert the person designated to handle such emergencies in your center.
4. **Do not** give food, fluids, or medications unless specifically ordered by the child's physician or Poison Control Center.
5. Call for emergency medical assistance if in doubt about the severity of the situation. Don't attempt to handle difficult situations by yourself. A delay in contacting emergency authorities could make the difference in saving a child's life. If you are alone, have a child dial the emergency number in your community (commonly 911).
6. If the child is transported to a medical facility before parents arrive, a teacher or caregiver should accompany, and remain with, the child until parents arrive.
7. Contact the child's parents. Inform them of the nature of the illness/injury and the child's general condition. If the child's condition is not life-threatening, discuss plans for follow-up care, e.g., contacting the child's physician, transporting the child to a medical facility. If parents cannot be reached, call the child's emergency contact person or physician.
8. Record all information concerning serious injury/illness on appropriate forms within 24 hours; place in the child's folder and provide parents with a copy. If required, notify local licensing authorities.

Figure 10–1 Sample emergency plan for centers: management of serious illness and injury.

Unfortunately, many programs overlook the necessity for developing emergency policies and plans until something unexpected happens. To avoid confusion and unfortunate experiences, every early childhood program should establish plans for emergency care, Figure 10–1. Such plans should include:

- personnel trained in lifesaving and first aid techniques, Figure 10–2.
- staff member(s) assigned to coordinate and direct emergency care
- notarized parental permission forms for each child authorizing emergency medical treatment
- a listing of emergency telephone numbers, including those of parents, emergency contact person, hospital, fire department, ambulance, police, poison control
- the availability of a telephone
- arrangements for emergency transportation
- completely equipped first aid kit, Table 10–1

Figure 10–2 Every caregiver should know the fundamentals of emergency and first aid care.

These plans should be made available to parents and staff members and reviewed on a regular basis.

Concerns regarding AIDS and other transmissible infections must also be taken into consideration when formulating plans for emergency care. Universal precautions, including the use of latex gloves, must always be followed when caring for children's injuries, especially when there is contact with blood or other body fluids. It is also essential to practice good handwashing techniques at all times.

TABLE 10–1 Basic First Aid Supplies	
activated charcoal	safety pins
adhesive tape—1/2 and 1 inch widths	scissors—blunt tipped
alcohol	soap—preferably liquid
bandages—assorted sizes	spirits of ammonia
blanket	splints
cotton balls	syrup of ipecac
flashlight	thermometers—2
gauze pads—sterile, 2x2s, 4x4s	tongue blades
hot water bottle	towel—large and small
instant ice pack or plastic bags	triangular bandages for slings
needle—sewing	tweezers
roller gauze—1- and 2-inch widths	Vaseline
latex gloves	first aid book, e.g., *Sigh of Relief* by M. I. Green

TABLE 10–2 The ABCs for Assessing Emergencies

A—Airway	Make sure the air passageway is open and clear. Roll the infant or child onto its back. Tilt the head back by placing your hand on the child's forehead and gently push downward (unless back or neck injuries are suspected). At the same time, place your other hand under the child's chin and lift it upward.
B—Breathing	Watch for the child's chest to move up and down. Feel and listen for air to escape from the lungs.
C—Circulation	Check for a pulse. In an infant, feel on the inside of the upper arm, Figure 10–3. For an older child, the pulse can be felt along the large artery on the side of the neck, Figure 10–4.

Despite careful planning and supervision, accidents, injuries, and illness will still occur. For this reason, it is very important that teachers and caregivers learn the fundamentals of emergency care and first aid, Table 10–2. Prior training and preparation allow personnel to handle emergencies with skill and confidence (American Academy of Pediatrics, 1993).

Teachers and caregivers are primarily responsible for providing initial and urgent care to young children who are seriously injured or ill. These measures are considered to be temporary and aimed at saving lives, reducing pain and discomfort, and preventing complications and additional injury. Responsibility for obtaining additional treatment or care is then transferred to the child's parents (Sheldon, 1983).

EMERGENCY CARE VS. FIRST AID

Emergency care refers to immediate treatment administered for life-threatening conditions. It includes a quick assessment of the emergency ABCs, Table 10–2. The victim is also checked and treated for severe bleeding, shock, and signs of poisoning.

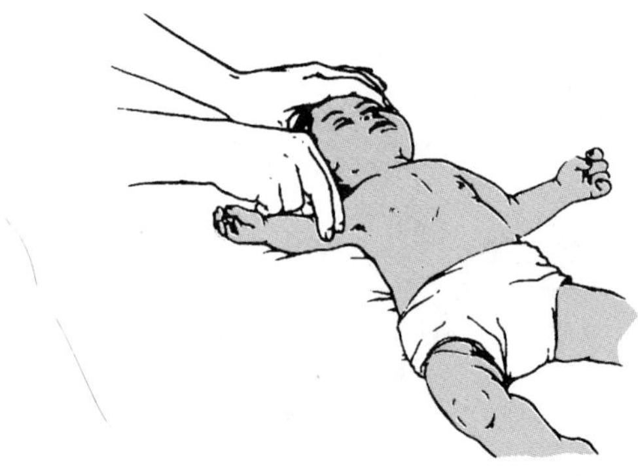

Figure 10–3 How to locate an infant's pulse.

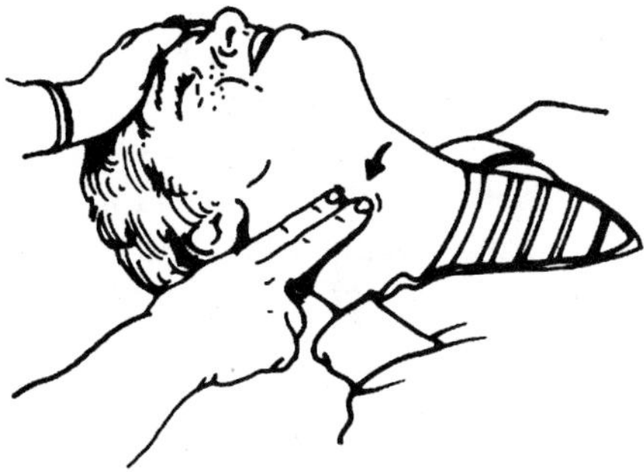

Figure 10–4 How to locate a child's pulse.

First aid refers to treatment administered for injuries and illnesses that are not considered life-threatening. Emergency care and first aid are based on principles that should be familiar to everyone involved in child care:

1. Summon emergency medical assistance (911 in many areas) for any injury or illness that requires more than simple first aid.
2. Stay calm and in control of the situation.
3. Always remain with the child. If necessary, send another adult or child for help.
4. Don't move the child until the extent of injuries or illness can be determined. If in doubt, have the child stay in the same position and await emergency medical help.
5. Quickly evaluate the child's condition, paying special attention to an open airway, breathing, and circulation.
6. Carefully plan and administer appropriate emergency care. Improper treatment can lead to other injuries.
7. Don't give any medications unless they are prescribed for certain lifesaving conditions.
8. Don't offer diagnoses or medial advice. Refer the child's parents to health professionals.
9. Always inform the child's parents of the injury and first aid care that has been administered.
10. Record all the facts concerning the accident and treatment administered; file in the child's permanent folder.

In most states, legal protection is granted to individuals who administer emergency care, unless their actions are judged grossly ***negligent*** or harmful. This protection is commonly known as the Good Samaritan Law.

LIFE-THREATENING CONDITIONS

Situations that require emergency care to prevent death or serious disability are discussed in this section. The emergency techniques and suggestions included here are not intended as substitutes for certified first aid and cardiopulmonary resuscitation (CPR) training. Rather, they are included as a review of basic instruction and to enhance the caregiver's ability to care for children's emergencies. A course involving actual practice is necessary to master these skills. It is also important to take a refresher course from time to time.

Absence of Breathing

Breathing emergencies accompany many life-threatening conditions, e.g., asthma, drowning, electrical shock, convulsions, poisoning, severe injuries, suffocating, choking, Sudden Infant Death Syndrome. Any adult who is responsible for the care of young children should complete certified training in basic first aid and cardiopulmonary resuscitation (CPR). This training is available from most chapters of the American Red Cross and the American Heart Association or from a local ambulance service, rescue squad, fire department, or high school.

It is important to remain calm and perform emergency lifesaving procedures quickly and with confidence. Have someone call for an ambulance or emergency medical assistance while you begin mouth-to-mouth breathing. The procedure for mouth-to-mouth breathing follows and is also illustrated in Figure 10–5.

1. Gently shake the child or infant to determine if conscious or asleep. Call out the child's name in a loud voice. If there is no response, quickly assess the child's condition and immediately begin emergency breathing procedures.
2. Position the infant or child on its back on a hard surface. Using extreme care, roll an injured child as a unit, keeping the spine straight.
3. Remove any vomitus, excess mucus or foreign objects (only if they can be seen) by quickly sweeping a finger around the inside of the child's mouth.
4. To open the airway, gently tilt the child's head up and back by placing one hand on the forehead and the fingers (not thumb) of the other hand under the chin; push downward on the forehead and lift the chin upward. **Caution:** Do not tip the head back too far. Tipping the head too far can cause obstruction of the airway in an infant or small child. Keep your fingers on the jawbone, not on the tissue under the chin.
5. Carefully listen for any spontaneous breathing by placing your ear next to the child's nose and mouth; also watch for a rise and fall of the chest and abdomen.
6. **For an infant**, place your mouth over the infant's nose and mouth to create a tight seal. Gently give 2 small puffs of air (1–1 1/2 seconds per breath with a short pause in between) into the infant's nose and mouth. **Caution:** Too much air forced into an infant's lungs may cause the stomach to fill with air (may cause vomiting and increased risk of *aspiration*). Always remember to use small, gentle puffs of air from your cheeks.

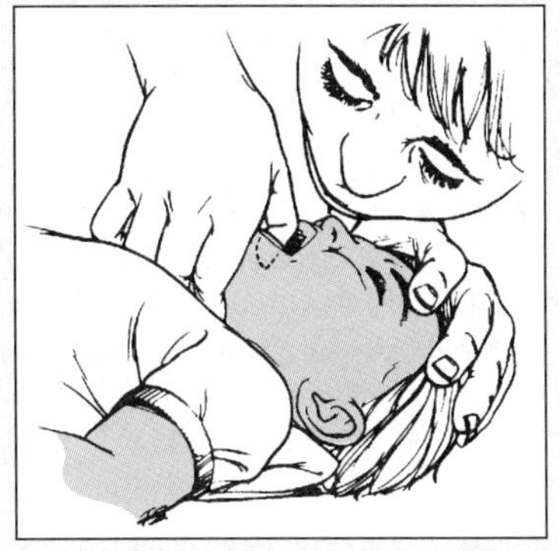

IF VOMITUS OR FOREIGN OBJECTS ARE VISIBLE, USE THE TONGUE-JAW LIFT TO OPEN THE MOUTH. THEN USE A FINGER TO QUICKLY CHECK FOR THE OBJECT. REMOVE IF VISIBLE.

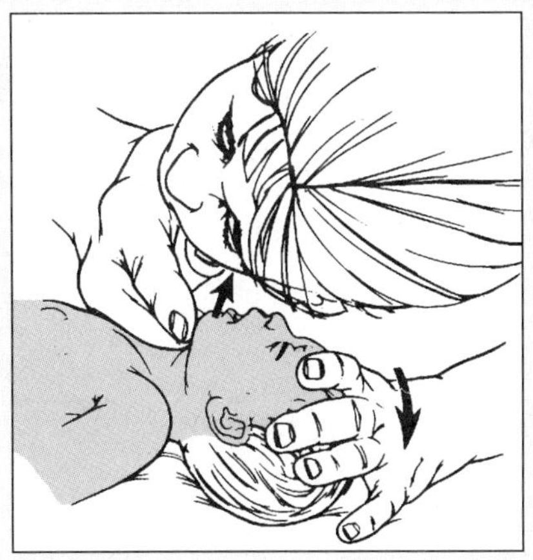

POSITION CHILD ON ITS BACK. GENTLY TILT THE HEAD UP AND BACK BY PLACING ONE HAND ON CHILD'S FOREHEAD AND FINGERS OF THE OTHER HAND UNDER THE JAWBONE. LIFT UPWARDS (HEAD TILT/CHIN LIFT).

FOR AN INFANT, PLACE YOUR MOUTH OVER THE INFANT'S NOSE AND MOUTH CREATING A TIGHT SEAL. SLOWLY AND GENTLY, GIVE 2 SMALL PUFFS OF AIR (1–1 1/2 SECONDS), PAUSING BETWEEN BREATHS. CHECK (LOOK/LISTEN) FOR BREATHING. CONTINUE THESE STEPS, BREATHING AT THE RATE OF 1 BREATH EVERY 3 SECONDS. IF AIR DOES NOT GO IN, REPOSITION AND TRY TO BREATHE AGAIN.

(Continued)

Figure 10–5 Emergency breathing techniques for the infant and child.

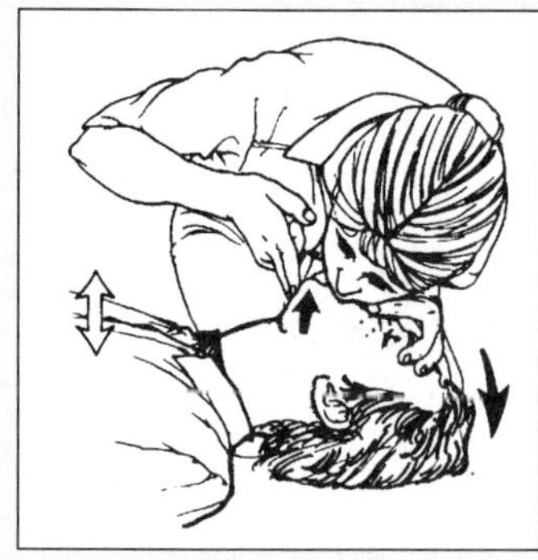

FOR AN OLDER CHILD, PLACE YOUR MOUTH OVER THE CHILD'S MOUTH FORMING A TIGHT SEAL. GENTLY PINCH THE CHILD'S NOSTRILS CLOSED. QUICKLY GIVE 2 SMALL BREATHS OF AIR. CHECK (LOOK/LISTEN) FOR BREATHING. CONTINUE BREATHING FOR THE CHILD AT A RATE OF ONE BREATH EVERY 4 SECONDS. IF AIR DOES NOT GO IN, REPOSITION AND TRY TO BREATHE AGAIN.

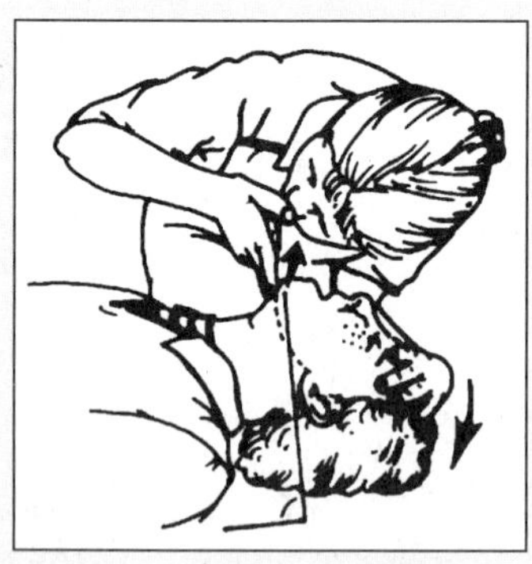

LIFT YOUR HEAD AND TURN IT TO THE SIDE AFTER EACH BREATH. THIS ALLOWS TIME FOR AIR TO ESCAPE FROM THE CHILD'S LUNGS AND ALSO GIVES YOU TIME TO TAKE A BREATH AND TO OBSERVE IF THE CHILD IS BREATHING.

Figure 10–5 Emergency breathing techniques for the infant and child.

7. **For the child 1–8 years old**, gently pinch the nostrils closed, place your open mouth over the child's open mouth forming a tight seal. Give 2 small breaths of air in quick succession, pausing between breaths.
8. Observe the child's chest and abdomen for movement (rising and falling) to be sure air is entering the lungs.
9. Continue breathing at the rate of one breath every 3 seconds for infants and children 1–8 years; or one breath every 5 seconds for children 8 years and older.
10. Pull your mouth away and turn it to the side after blowing each breath. This allows time for air to escape from the child's lungs and also gives you time to take a breath and see if the child is breathing on his own.
11. DO NOT GIVE UP! Continue breathing procedures until the child breathes alone or emergency medical assistance arrives. Failure to continue mouth-to-mouth breathing can lead to cardiac arrest in children.

If the entry of air seems blocked or the chest does not rise while administering mouth-to-mouth breathing, check for foreign objects in the mouth and airway and remove only if they are visible (refer to Airway Obstruction). Continue mouth-to-mouth breathing until the child breathes alone or medical help arrives.

If the child resumes breathing, keep the child lying down with feet slightly elevated. Turn the child's head and body to one side if vomiting begins. (Roll child as a unit.) Maintain body temperature by covering with a light blanket. Closely observe the child's breathing until medical help arrives.

Airway Obstruction

Children under five years of age account for nearly 90 percent of deaths due to airway obstruction. More than 65 percent of the deaths occur in infants (Chandra, 1994). Toys, small objects, balloons, and certain foods (Table 10–3) are common causes of aspiration and choking, and should not be accessible to children under five. In most instances, these objects can be successfully coughed out (Harris, 1984). However, emergency lifesaving measures must be started immediately if:

- breathing is labored or absent
- lips and nailbeds turn blue
- cough is weak or ineffective
- the child is unconscious
- there is a high-pitched sound when the child inhales

Respiratory infections in children can sometimes lead to swelling and obstruction of their airway. If this should occur, call immediately for emergency medical assistance. Time should not be wasted on attempting techniques for clearing airway obstruction (foreign body). They are not effective and may actually cause more harm to the child. Emergency techniques to relieve an airway obstruction should only be attempted if a child has been observed choking on an object or is unconscious and not breathing after attempts have been made to open the airway and breathe for the child.

Different emergency techniques are used to treat infants, toddlers, and older children who are choking (American Heart Association, 1994). Regardless of the child's age, attempt to remove the object if it can be seen. Extreme care must be

TABLE 10–3 Foods Commonly Linked to Childhood Choking

raw carrots	peanuts and other nuts
hot dogs	cookies and crackers
pieces of raw apple	cough drops
grapes	potato chips
fruit seeds and pits	pretzels
round and ring-shaped hard candies	popcorn
peanut butter sandwich	gum

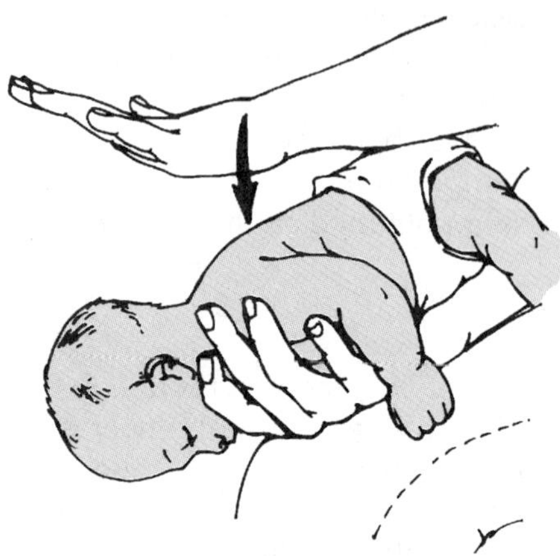

Figure 10–6 Position the infant with the head lower than the chest.

taken not to push the object further back into the airway. If the object cannot be removed easily and the infant is conscious, do the following:

- Have someone summon emergency medical assistance.
- Position the infant face down over the length of your arm, with the child's head lower than its chest and the head and neck supported in your hand, Figure 10–6. The infant can also be placed in your lap with its head lower than its chest.
- Use the heel of your hand to give 5 quick back blows between the infant's shoulder blades. **Caution:** Do not use excessive force as this could injure the infant.
- Support and turn the infant over, face up, with the head held lower than the chest.
- Give 5 chest thrusts, using the hand not supporting the infant's head. Place 2–3 fingers over the breastbone and approximately the width of one finger below the infant's nipples, Figure 10–7. Rapidly compress the infant's chest

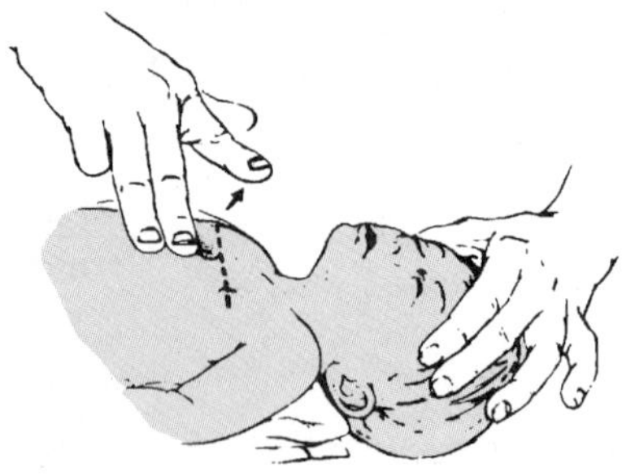

Figure 10–7 Location of fingers for chest thrusts on an infant.

approximately 1/2–1 inch (1.3–2.5 cm); release pressure between thrusts, allowing the chest to return to its normal position.

- Repeat the steps (5 back blows, 5 chest thrusts) until the object is dislodged or the infant loses consciousness.

If the infant **LOSES CONSCIOUSNESS AND IS NOT BREATHING**:

- Have someone call for an ambulance or emergency medical assistance if this has not already been done.
- Place the infant on its back. Perform jaw lift and look inside of the infant's mouth to see any object; carefully remove it only if the object can be seen.
- Begin lifesaving breathing procedures. Open the airway using head tilt/chin lift.
- Give the infant 2 small breaths of air, 1–1 1/2 seconds per breath. Watch for the chest to rise and fall.
- If the infant's lungs inflate, continue breathing assistance, giving one breath every 3 seconds. If the lungs cannot be inflated, give one breath of air, 5 back blows, 5 chest thrusts, check in mouth for the object, reposition the airway, and give one breath of air. Repeat these steps until help arrives or the object is dislodged: **open airway, breath, 5 back blows, 5 chest thrusts, reposition the airway, breath.**

To give emergency aid to the child 1–8 years who is choking, first attempt to remove the object from the blocked airway only if it can be seen. Use care not to push the object further back into the throat. If the object cannot be dislodged and the child **IS CONSCIOUS**.

- Summon emergency medical assistance.
- Stand or kneel behind the child with your arms around the child's waist, Figure 10–8.
- Make a fist with one hand, thumbs tucked in.
- Place the fisted hand (thumb-side) against the child's abdomen, midway between the base of the rib cage (xiphoid process) and the navel.
- Press your fisted hand into the child's abdomen with a quick, inward and upward thrust.
- Continue repeating abdominal thrusts until the object is dislodged or the child becomes unconscious.

If the child **IS UNCONSCIOUS AND NOT BREATHING**:

- Immediately summon emergency medical assistance.
- Place the child flat on the floor (on back, face up).
- Straddle the child's hips and kneel at the foot of a small child, Figure 10–9.
- Perform the jaw lift and look inside of the child's mouth; carefully remove any object that can be seen.

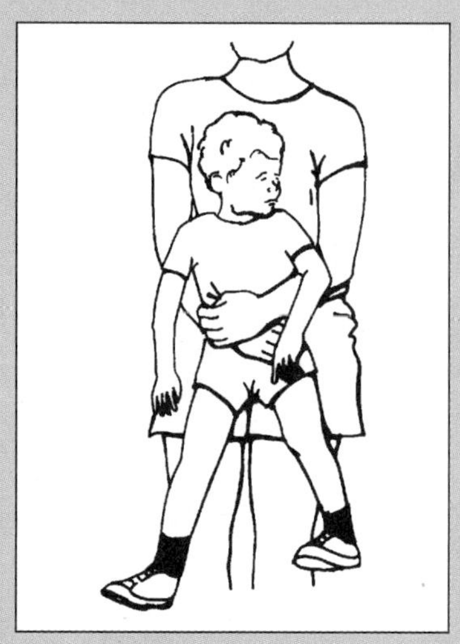

STAND OR KNEEL BEHIND THE CHILD WITH YOUR ARMS AROUND THE CHILD'S WAIST.

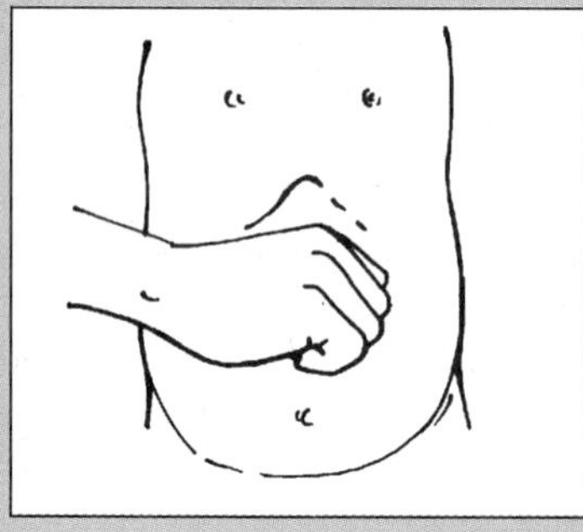

MAKE A FIST WITH ONE HAND. PLACE THE FISTED HAND AGAINST THE CHILD'S ABDOMEN BELOW THE TIP OF THE RIB CAGE, SLIGHTLY ABOVE THE NAVEL.

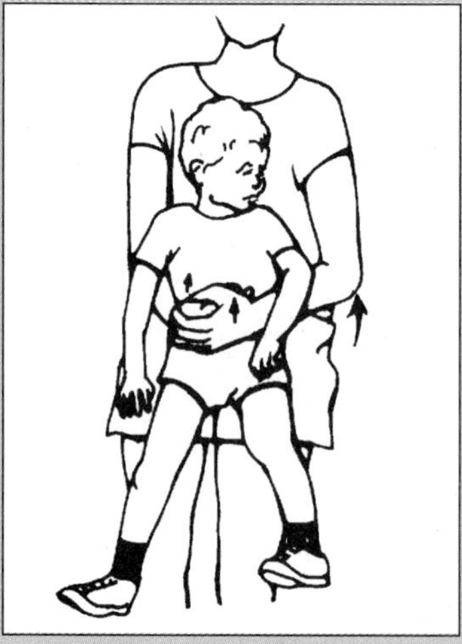

GRASP THE FISTED HAND WITH YOUR OTHER HAND. PRESS YOUR FISTS INTO THE CHILD'S ABDOMEN WITH A QUICK UPWARD THRUST.

Figure 10–8 The Heimlich maneuver.

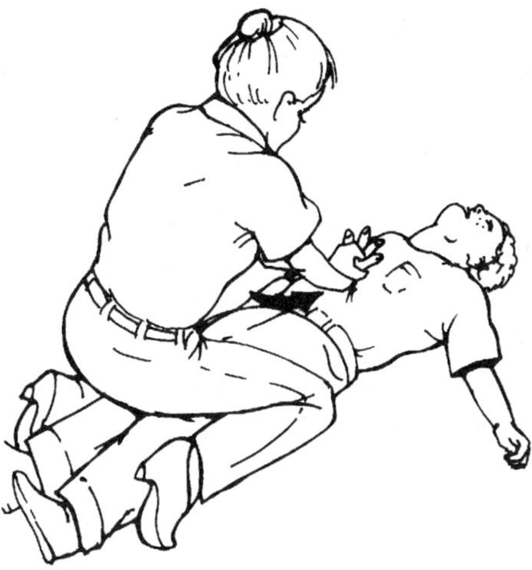

Figure 10–9 Heimlich maneuver with child lying down.

- Begin lifesaving breathing procedures. Open the airway using head tilt/jaw lift technique. Give 2 small breaths of air, 1–1 1/2 seconds each. Stop if the child begins breathing.
- If the child does not begin to breathe, place the heel of one hand on the child's abdomen, slightly above the navel and well below the base of the breastbone. Position the other hand on top of the first hand.
- Press hands into the child's abdomen with a quick upward thrust. Always keep hands positioned in the middle of the abdomen to avoid injuring nearby organs.
- Repeat abdominal thrusts 5 times. Repeat the sequence: **perform head tilt/chin lift technique, visually inspect the mouth for the object, attempt mouth-to-mouth breathing, give 5 abdominal thrusts and repeat the sequence. Do not give up!** Continue this sequence until the object is dislodged and you can get air in and out of the child's lungs or emergency medical help arrives.
- If the child begins to breathe on his own, stop mouth-to-mouth breathing, and continue to observe closely until medical help arrives.

After the object is dislodged and breathing is restored, always be sure the child receives medical attention.

Shock

Shock frequently accompanies many injuries, especially those that are severe and should, therefore, be anticipated. Shock can also result from extreme emotional upset, bleeding, pain, heat exhaustion, poisoning, burns and fractures. It is a serious emergency that requires immediate first aid treatment to prevent death.

Early indicators of shock include:

- skin that is pale, cool, and clammy
- confusion, anxiety, restlessness
- increased perspiration
- weakness
- rapid, shallow breathing

Later, and more serious, signs of shock may include:

- rapid, weak pulse
- bluish discoloration around lips, nails, and ear lobes
- dilated pupils
- extreme thirst
- nausea and vomiting

Teachers and caregivers can carry out the following emergency first aid measures to treat the child in shock:

1. Have someone call for emergency medical assistance.
2. Quickly try to identify the main cause of shock and treat the cause first, e.g., bleeding, poisoning.
3. Keep the child lying down.
4. Elevate the child's feet 8 to 10 inches, if there is no indication of fractures to the legs, or head or back injuries.
5. Maintain body heat by covering the child lightly with a blanket.
6. If the child complains of thirst, moisten a clean cloth and use it to wet the child's lips, tongue, and inside of mouth. *Do not* give the child food, fluids, or medication.
7. Stay calm and reassure the child until medical help arrives.
8. Observe the child's breathing closely; give mouth-to-mouth resuscitation if necessary.

Asthma

Asthma is a disorder of the respiratory system characterized by periods of wheezing, gasping, and labored breathing. Acute asthma attacks are thought to be triggered by allergic reactions, infections, emotional stress, or physical activity. Occasionally, an infant's or child's life may be placed in danger during an attack because of the intense struggle to breathe (Sander, 1991).

Remaining calm and confident during a child's asthmatic attack is one of the most important first aid measures. At the same time, teachers and caregivers can also:

1. Summon emergency medical help immediately if the child shows signs of fatigue, anxiety, wheezing, restlessness, loss of consciousness, or blue discoloration of the nailbeds or lips.
2. Reassure the child.

3. If the child has medication at the center that is to be given in the event of an acute asthmatic attack, administer it immediately.
4. Encourage the child to relax and breathe slowly and deeply (anxiety makes breathing more difficult).
5. Have the child assume a position that is most comfortable. (Breathing is usually easier when sitting or standing up.)
6. Contact the child's parents.

Bleeding

Occasionally, young children receive injuries such as a deep gash or head laceration that may bleed profusely. Severe bleeding requires prompt emergency first aid treatment. Again, it is extremely important that the teacher or caregiver act quickly, yet remain calm. To stop bleeding:

1. Summon emergency medical assistance immediately if bleeding comes in spurts or is profuse and cannot be stopped.
2. Follow universal precautions, including the use of latex gloves.
3. Place a pad of *sterile* gauze or clean material over the wound.
4. Apply firm pressure directly over the site of bleeding, using the flat parts of the fingers.
5. Maintain pressure for approximately 5–10 minutes before letting up.
6. *Elevate* the bleeding part if there is no sign of a fracture.
7. An ice pack, wrapped in a cloth or towel, can be applied to the site to help slow bleeding and decrease swelling.
8. If blood soaks through the bandage, place another pad over the original bandage; bleeding may restart if the pad next to the skin is disturbed.
9. When bleeding is stopped, secure the pad in place.
10. If bleeding cannot be stopped by direct pressure and elevation, locate the nearest pressure point above the injury and apply pressure, Figure 10–10.

    WARNING: Tourniquets should only be used as a last resort and with the understanding that the extremity will probably have to be amputated.

Save all blood-soaked dressings. Doctors will need them to estimate the amount of blood loss. Contact the child's parents when bleeding is under control and advise them to seek medical attention for the child.

Diabetes

Two major medical emergencies associated with diabetes are hypoglycemia and hyperglycemia. Emergency first aid treatment requires that the teacher or caregiver quickly distinguish between the two conditions. The causes and symptoms of these complications are, in many respects, opposites of each other, Table 10–4.

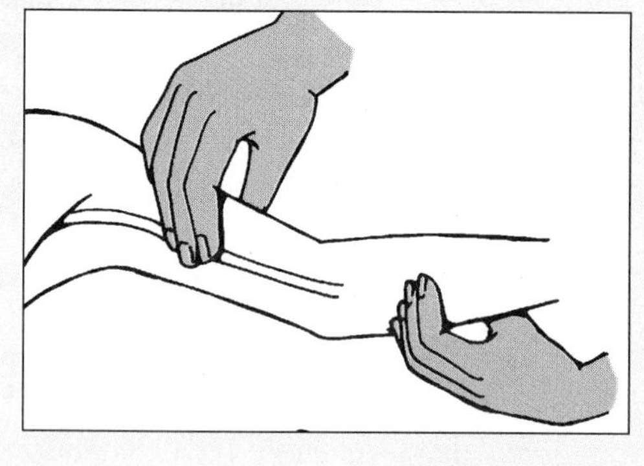

PLACE FINGERS ON THE INNER ARM AT THE EDGE OF THE BICEP MUSCLE HALFWAY DOWN THE ARM. KEEP THUMB ON OUTER ARM AND PRESS TOWARD THE BONE.

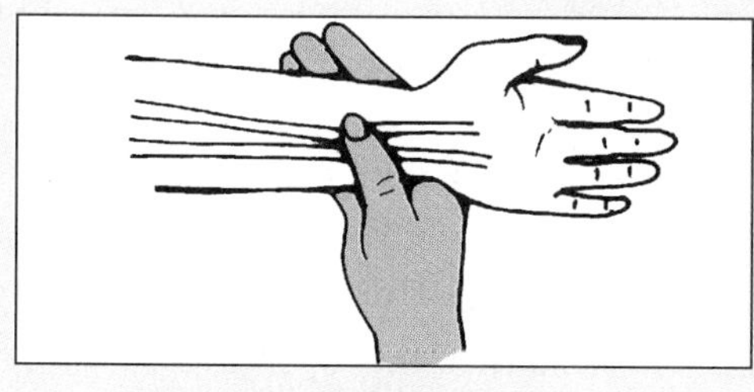

PLACE THUMB ON INNER WRIST AND PRESS TOWARD THE BONE.

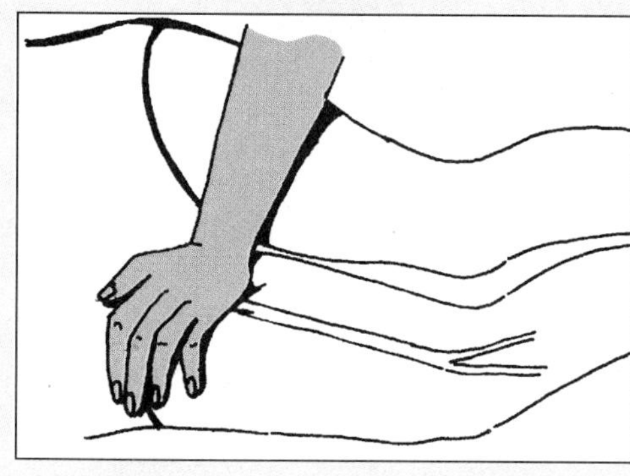

PLACE HEEL OF HAND ON INNER THIGH AT THE CREASE OF THE GROIN AND PRESS AGAINST THE BONE.

Figure 10–10 Important pressure points used to control bleeding.

Hypoglycemia, or insulin shock, is caused by low levels of sugar in the blood. It can occur whenever a diabetic child receives either an excessive dose of insulin or an insufficient amount of food. Other causes may include illness, delayed eating times, or increased activity. Similar symptoms are experienced by nondiabetic children when they become overly hungry. Hypoglycemia can be reversed very quickly by administering a sugar substance. Orange juice is ideal for this purpose because it is absorbed rapidly by the body. A concentrated glucose gel, such as Glutose™, can also be purchased and kept on hand for emergencies. Hard candies, such as Life Savers™ or lollipops, should not be given because a child could easily choke on them.

TABLE 10–4 Signs and Symptoms of Hyperglycemia and Hypoglycemia

HYPERGLYCEMIA (diabetic coma)	HYPOGLYCEMIA (insulin shock)
Causes	**Causes**
High blood sugar caused by too little available insulin, improper diet, illness, stress, or omitted dose of insulin.	Low blood sugar caused by too much insulin, insufficient amounts of carbohydrates, increased activity, decreased food intake, and illness.
Symptoms	**Symptoms**
■ Slow, gradual onset	■ Sudden onset
■ Slow, deep breathing	■ Skin cool and clammy
■ Increased thirst	■ Faintness
■ Skin flushed and dry	■ Shakiness
■ Confusion	■ Nausea
■ Staggering; appears as if drunk	■ Headache
■ Drowsiness	■ Hunger
■ Sweet smelling, winelike breath odor	■ Rapid, shallow breathing
■ Nausea, vomiting	■ Convulsions
■ Excessive urination	■ Unconsciousness
Treatment	**Treatment**
Summon emergency medical assistance. Keep the child quiet and warm.	Summon emergency medical assistance if the child's state of consciousness is altered. If *conscious*, quickly administer orange juice or a concentrated glucose source, such as Glutose™. If *unconscious*, summon emergency medical assistance or rush the child to the nearest hospital.

Hyperglycemia, or diabetic coma, results when there is too much sugar circulating in the blood stream. This condition is a potential problem for every diabetic child. Illness, infection, emotional stress, poor dietary control, fever, or a dose of insulin that is forgotten or too small can lead to hyperglycemia. Anytime a teacher or caregiver observes the symptoms of hyperglycemia in a diabetic child, parents should be notified immediately so they can consult with the child's physician. Emergency treatment usually requires the administration of insulin by medical personnel.

Drowning

Drowning is the second leading cause of accidental death among young children (MMWR, 1992). Even small amounts of water, such as toilet bowls, buckets, wading pools, and bathtubs pose a serious danger. Poor muscle coordination and large upper body proportion make it difficult for young children to escape from water hazards.

Cardiopulmonary *resuscitation* must be started immediately upon rescuing a child from a drowning emergency. For this reason, every parent and adult caregiver should complete CPR training. A child who has been rescued from drowning is likely to vomit during resuscitation attempts because large amounts of water are often swallowed. Therefore, the child's head should be turned to one side to decrease the possibility of choking. Also, observe closely for signs of shock. Even if a child appears to have fully recovered from a near drowning incident, medical care should be obtained immediately. Complications, such as pneumonia, can develop from water, chemicals, or debris remaining in the lungs.

Electric Shock

Although it is a natural response, never touch a child until the source of electricity has been turned off or disconnected. Quickly unplug the cord, remove the appropriate fuse from the fusebox, or turn off the main breaker switch. A dry, nonconductive object such as a piece of wood, folded newspaper or magazine, or rope can be used to push or pull the child away from the source of current. Be sure to stand on something dry such as a board or cardboard while you attempt to rescue the child.

Severe electric shock can cause breathing to stop, severe burns, symptoms of shock, and the heart to stop beating. To treat the infant or young child who has received an electrical shock, do the following:

1. Have someone call for emergency medical assistance while you remove the child from the source of electric current.
2. Begin cardiopulmonary resuscitation (CPR) if the child is pulseless and breathless.
3. Observe for and treat signs of shock and burns.
4. Have the child transported to a medical facility as quickly as possible.

Head Injuries

The greatest danger of severe head injuries is internal bleeding and swelling (Synoground, 1990). Signs of bleeding and internal swelling may develop within minutes or hours following the injury, or perhaps not until several days later.

Early signs of head injury may include:

- repeated or forceful vomiting
- bleeding or clear fluid coming from nose or ears

- disorientation, aggressive behavior, apathy, or loss of consciousness
- drowsiness
- severe headache

Symptoms that may develop later can include:

- weakness or *paralysis*
- poor coordination or gait
- unequal size of the pupils of the eye
- speech disturbances
- double vision
- seizures
- an area of increasing swelling beneath the scalp

If any of these signs develop, call the child's parents and have them contact the child's physician immediately.

Children who receive even a minor blow or bump to the head should not be moved until it can be determined that there are no fractures or additional injuries. If the injury does not appear to be serious, the child should be encouraged to rest or play quietly for the next few hours. Always report to parents any blow or injury to a child's head regardless of how insignificant it may seem at the time. It is also important to observe these children carefully during the next 24–36 hours for any changes in behavior or appearance.

Scalp wounds have a tendency to bleed profusely, causing even minor injuries to appear more serious than they actually are. Therefore, when a child receives an injury to the scalp, it is important not to become overly alarmed at the sign of profuse bleeding. Pressure applied directly over the wound with a clean cloth or gauze dressing is usually sufficient to stop most bleeding. An ice pack can also be applied to the area to decrease swelling and pain. Parents should be advised of the injury so they can continue to monitor the child's condition.

Poisoning

Accidental poisonings can result from the ingestion of a variety of substances, including plants and berries, cleaning products, chemicals, and insecticides. The possibility of a child ingesting medication from a purse, or pods from a plant on the way to school, must not be overlooked. Signs of poisoning may appear quickly or be delayed, and can include:

- nausea or vomiting
- abdominal cramps or diarrhea
- unusual odor to breath
- skin that feels cold and clammy
- burns or visible stains around the mouth, lips, and tongue
- restlessness

- convulsions
- confusion, disorientation, apathy, or listlessness
- loss of consciousness
- seizures

Emergency treatment of accidental poisoning is determined by the type of poison the young child has *ingested* (Committee on Injury & Poison Prevention, 1994). Poisons are categorized into three basic types: strong acids and *alkalis*, petroleum products, all others. Some examples of each type are shown in Table 10–5.

If a child is suspected of swallowing a poisonous substance:

- Quickly check for redness or burns around the child's lips, mouth and tongue. These are indications of a chemical burn, usually caused by strong acids or alkalis. **Do not make the child vomit.**
- Smell the child's breath. If the poison is a petroleum product the odor of gasoline or kerosene will be present. **Do not make the child vomit.**

If the child is **conscious**:

- Give 1/2–1 cup of water or milk to drink.
- Quickly try to locate a container that may provide clues about what the child ingested.
- Call the nearest Poison Control Center, hospital emergency room or your city's emergency number (911 in many areas). If you cannot find a container, do not delay calling.
- Observe the child closely for signs of shock or difficulty breathing.

If the child is **unconscious**:

- Summon emergency medical assistance immediately.
- **Do not give any fluids to drink.**

TABLE 10–5 Poisonous Substances

Strong Acid and Alkalis	Petroleum Products	All Others
bathroom, drain, and oven cleaners,	charcoal lighter	medicines
battery acid	cigarette lighter fluid	plants
dishwasher soaps	furniture polish and wax	berries
lye	gasoline	cosmetics
wart and corn remover	kerosene	nail polish remover
	naphtha	insecticides
	turpentine	mothballs
		weed killers

- Position the child on one side to prevent choking on vomited material.
- Observe the child closely for signs of difficulty breathing.

If the ingested poison is not an acid, alkali or petroleum product, you may be instructed to make the child vomit. This can be achieved by giving syrup of ipecac (check with Poison Control before giving) or by causing the child to gag by touching the back of the throat with a finger, spoon handle, or other blunt object (Child Health Alert, 1991). Be sure to keep the child's head lower than the stomach to prevent aspiration. Contact the child's parents as soon as possible.

CONDITIONS THAT ARE NOT LIFE-THREATENING

Most of children's injuries and illnesses are not life-threatening but they do require first aid. Teachers and caregivers are not qualified nor expected to provide comprehensive medical treatment. However, they can perform temporary first aid to limit complications and make children more comfortable until parents arrive and assume responsibility for the child's care. The remainder of this unit describes conditions typically encountered with young children that require first aid care.

Abrasions, Cuts, and Other Minor Skin Wounds

Simple cuts, scrapes, and abrasions are among the most common types of injury young children experience. First aid care is concerned primarily with the control of bleeding and the prevention of infection. To care for the child who has received a simple skin wound, do the following:

1. Follow universal precautions (Chapter 6), including the use of latex gloves.
2. If the wound is bleeding, apply direct pressure over the wound with a clean or sterile pad.
3. An ice pack, wrapped in cloth or a towel, can be applied to the site to slow bleeding and reduce swelling.
4. When bleeding has been stopped, clean the wound carefully with soap and water or hydrogen peroxide. Begin at the center of the wound and cleanse in a circular motion toward the outer edges. This method reduces the amount of bacteria and foreign matter that is carried across the wound.
5. Cover the wound with a sterile bandage, Figure 10–11.
6. Inform parents of the injury. Have them check the child's tetanus immunization to be sure it is current.

Bites

Human and animal bites are painful and can lead to serious infection. The possibility of rabies should be considered with any animal bite that is unprovoked, unless the animal is known to be free of the rabies virus. A suspected animal should be confined and observed by a veterinarian for a period of ten days. In cases where

Figure 10–11 A bandage helps to protect cuts and skin abrasions against infection.

the bite was provoked, the animal is not as likely to be rabid. First aid care for human and animal bites includes the following:

1. If possible, let the wound bleed for a short time to help remove the animal's saliva.
2. Cleanse the wound thoroughly with soap and water or hydrogen peroxide.
3. Cover the wound with a dressing.
4. Notify the child's parents and advise them to have the wound checked by the child's physician.
5. Immediately notify local law enforcement authorities and provide a description of the animal and its location.

Most insect bites cause little more than local skin irritations. However, some children are extremely sensitive to certain insects, especially bees, hornets, wasps, and spiders. When stung or bitten, these children may experience severe allergic reactions, including:

- difficulty breathing
- joint pain
- abdominal cramps
- vomiting
- fever
- red, swollen eyes
- hives or generalized itching
- shock
- death

Allergic reactions to insect bites can be life-threatening. If a child experiences any of these reactions, immediately do the following:

1. Call for emergency medical assistance, especially if the child has never experienced this type of reaction before.
2. Keep the child quiet. Let the child assume a position that is most comfortable for breathing.
3. If the child has medication for this type of allergic reaction at school, administer it immediately.

Most first aid measures for insect bites are temporary and aimed at relieving discomfort and preventing infection. If a stinger remains in the skin after a bee bite, it can be carefully removed with a tweezers or by scraping the skin with a dull knife. A paste or baking soda and water applied to the area relieves some discomfort. An ice pack can also be used to decrease swelling and pain.

Blisters

A blister is a collection of fluid that builds up beneath the outer layer of skin. Blisters most commonly develop from rubbing or friction, burns, or allergic reactions.

First aid care of blisters is aimed at protecting the irritated skin from infection. If at all possible, blisters should not be broken. However, if they do break, wash the area with soap and water and cover with a bandage.

Bruises

Bruises result from the rupture of small blood vessels beneath the skin. They are often caused by falls, bumps, and blows. Fair-skinned children tend to bruise more easily. First aid care is aimed at controlling subsurface bleeding and swelling. Apply ice or cold packs to the bruised area for 15 to 30 minutes and repeat 3 to 4 times during the next 24 hours. Later, warm moist packs can be applied to improve healing. Alert parents to watch for signs of infection and unusual bleeding if the bruising is extensive or severe.

Burns

Burns that involve children are more serious because of their smaller body surface. Burns are classified according to how deeply the skin is burned:

- first degree—surface skin is red
- second degree—surface skin is red and blistered
- third degree—burn is deep; skin and underlying tissues are brown, white and/or charred.

Immediate first aid care of burns includes the following:

1. Quickly *submerge* the burned part in cool water, or hold under running water, for 15 to 20 minutes. Cool water temperatures lessen the depth of burn as well as decrease swelling and pain, Figure 10–12.

Figure 10–12 Burns can be cooled under running water.

2. Elevate the burned part to relieve discomfort.
3. Cover the burn with a sterile gauze dressing and tape in place. *Do not* use greasy ointments or creams. Dirt and bacteria can collect in the ointments and creams increasing the risk of infection. Burns that involve feet, face, hands, or genitals, cover a large area or cause moderate blistering are critical and require immediate medical attention. Parents should be advised to contact the child's health care provider.

Chemical burns should be rinsed for 10–15 minutes under cool running water. Remove any clothing that might have some of the chemical on it. Call the nearest Poison Control Center for further instructions. The child's parents should also be contacted and advised to check with their physician.

Eye Injuries

Children's curiosity and active play can lead to a variety of eye injuries. Most injuries are simple and can be treated by the teacher or caregiver (Green, 1995). It is very important to inform parents of any eye injury so they can continue to observe the child and consult the child's physician if necessary.

A sudden blow to the eye from a snowball, wooden block, or other hard object is usually quite painful. First aid treatment includes the following:

1. Keep the child quiet.
2. Apply an ice pack to the eye for 15 minutes if there is no bleeding.
3. Use direct pressure to control any bleeding around the eye. *Do not* apply pressure to the eyeball itself. Cleanse and cover wounds with a sterile gauze pad.
4. Emergency medical assistance should be summoned at once if the child complains of inability to see, seeing spots or flashes of light.
5. Report any blow to the eye to parents so they can continue to monitor the child's condition.

Foreign particles such as sand, cornmeal, or specks of dust frequently find their way into children's eyes. Although it is very natural for children to want to rub their eyes, this must be discouraged to prevent further injury to the eyeball. Often spontaneous tearing will be sufficient to wash the object out of the eye. If the particle is visible, it can also be removed with the corner of a clean cloth or flushed out using an eye syringe and warm water. If the particle cannot be removed easily, the eye should be covered and medical attention sought.

An object that penetrates the eyeball must not be removed. Place a paper cup, funnel or small cardboard box over *both* the object and the eye. Place a gauze pad over the unaffected eye and secure both dressings in place by wrapping a bandage around the head. Movement of the injured eyeball should be kept to a minimum and can be achieved by covering both eyes. Seek immediate medical treatment.

A thin cut on the eye's surface can result from a piece of paper, toy, or child's fingernail. Injuries of this type cause severe pain and tearing. The teacher should cover *both* of the child's eyes with a gauze dressing. Notify the parents and advise them to take the child for *immediate* medical care.

Chemical burns to a child's eye are very serious. Another staff member should call immediately for emergency medical assistance so that the child can be transported to the nearest medical facility. Quickly tip the child's head toward the affected eye. Gently pour large amounts of warm water over the eyeball for at least 15 minutes. Meanwhile, contact the child's parents.

Fractures

A fracture is a break or crack in a bone. A teacher or caregiver can check for possible fractures by observing the child for:

- particular areas of extreme pain or tenderness
- an unusual shape or deformity of a bone
- a break in the skin with visible bone edges protruding
- swelling
- a change in skin color around the injury site

A child who complains of pain after falling should not be moved, especially if a back or neck injury is suspected. Have someone call immediately for an ambulance or emergency medical assistance. Keep the child warm and observe carefully for signs of shock. Avoid giving the child anything to eat or drink in the event that surgery is necessary.

If no emergency medical help is available, only persons with prior first aid training should attempt to splint a fracture. Splinting should be completed before the child is moved. Splints can be purchased from medical supply stores or improvised from items such as a rolled-up magazine or blanket, a ruler, a piece of board or a tissue box. Never try to straighten a fractured bone. Cover open wounds with a sterile pad but do not attempt to clean the wound. Elevate the splinted part on a pillow and apply an ice pack to reduce swelling and pain. Watch the child closely for signs of shock. Contact the child's parents immediately and have them contact the child's physician.

Frostbite

Infants and young children should be watched very closely during extremely cold weather so they don't remove hats, boots, or mittens. Large amounts of body heat are lost through the head. Frostbite occurs within minutes and most commonly affects the nose, ears, cheeks, fingers, and toes. Frostbite results when body tissue is frozen. The skin takes on a waxy, white appearance and may be blistered. The child with frostbite often suffers from extreme pain or feels none at all. First aid treatment for frostbite consists of the following:

- Rewarm the affected part by immersing it in lukewarm, then warm, water (104°F, 40°C). **Caution:** Never use hot water.
- Handle the frostbitten part with care; avoid rubbing or massaging the part as this could further damage frozen tissue.
- Cover the frostbitten area with sterile gauze.
- Wrap the child in a blanket for extra warmth.
- Contact the parents so they can take the child for medical treatment.

Heat Exhaustion and Heat Stroke

First aid treatment of heat related illness depends on distinguishing heat exhaustion from heat stroke. The following symptoms can be observed in a child who is suffering from heat exhaustion:

- skin is pale, cool, and moist with perspiration
- weakness or fainting
- sweating
- thirst
- nausea
- abdominal cramps
- headache
- normal or below normal body temperature

Heat exhaustion is not a life-threatening condition. It usually occurs when a child has been playing vigorously in extreme heat or humidity. First aid treatment for heat exhaustion is similar to that of shock:

1. Have the child lie down in a cool place.
2. Elevate the child's feet 8–10 inches (20–25 cm).
3. Loosen or remove the child's clothing.
4. Sponge the child's face and body with cool water.
5. Offer frequent sips of cool water.

Heat stroke is a life-threatening condition that requires immediate treatment. Failure of the body's temperature-regulating mechanism during extremely hot weather allows a child's temperature to rise rapidly and dangerously. Symptoms of heat stroke include:

- high body temperature (102°–106°F; 38.8°–41.1°C)
- dry, flushed skin
- headache
- convulsions
- diarrhea, abdominal cramps
- loss of consciousness
- shock

Emergency treatment for heat stroke is aimed at cooling the child as quickly as possible:

1. Summon emergency medical assistance at once.
2. Move the child to a cool place and remove outer clothing.
3. Sponge the child's body with cool water. The child can also be placed in a cool tub of water or gently sprayed with a garden hose.
4. Elevate the child's legs to decrease the possibility of shock.
5. If the child is conscious, offer sips of cool water.
6. Notify the child's parents.

Nosebleeds

Accidental bumps, allergies, nose picking, or sinus congestion can all cause a child's nose to bleed. Most nosebleeds are not serious and can be stopped quickly. If a nosebleed continues more than 30 minutes, get medical help. To stop a nosebleed, do the following:

1. Place the child in a sitting position; do not tilt head back.
2. Firmly grasp the child's nostrils and squeeze together for at least five minutes before releasing the pressure, Figure 10–13.

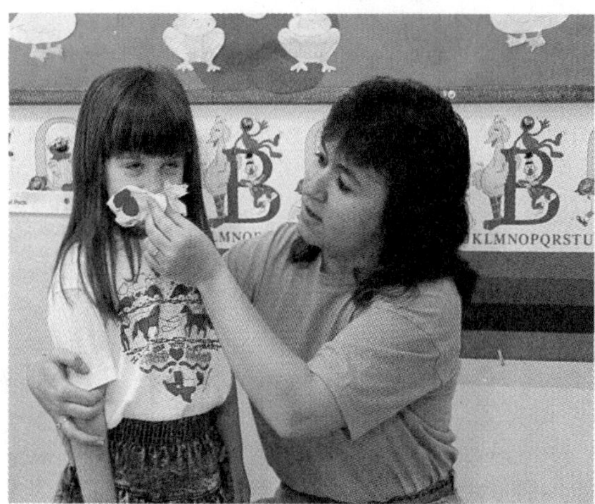

Figure 10–13 Firmly grasp and squeeze the child's nostril to stop nosebleeds.

3. If bleeding continues pinch the nostrils together for another 10 minutes.
4. Apply an ice pack to the bridge of the nose, if desired, to slow down bleeding.
5. Caution children not to run or blow their nose vigorously for several hours.
6. Encourage parents to discuss the problem with the child's physician if nosebleeds occur repeatedly.

Seizures

Seizures occur in infants and young children for a variety of reasons. Simple precautionary measures can be taken during and immediately after a seizure to protect a child from additional injury, and include the following:

1. Call for emergency medical assistance if this is the first time a child has experienced a seizure. If the child has a known seizure disorder, call for emergency help if the seizure lasts longer than 3–5 minutes or the child stops breathing.
2. Encourage everyone to remain calm.
3. Carefully lower the child to the floor.
4. Move furniture and other objects out of the way.
5. Do not hold the child down.
6. Do not attempt to force any protective device into the child's mouth.
7. Loosen tight clothing around the child's neck and waist to make breathing easier.
8. Watch carefully to make sure the child is breathing.
9. Turn the child to one side after the seizure. This prevents choking by allowing oral secretions to drain out of the mouth.

Following the seizure, the child can be moved to a quiet area and encouraged to rest or sleep. Always be sure to notify the child's parents of any seizure.

Splinters

Most splinters under the skin's surface can be easily removed with a sterilized needle and tweezers. Clean the skin around the splinter with soap and water or alcohol before starting and after it is removed. Cover the area with a bandage. If the splinter is very deep, do not attempt to remove it. Inform the child's parents to seek medical attention.

Sprains

A sprain is caused by an injury to the tissues around a joint. In most cases, only an X ray can confirm whether an injury is a sprain or fracture. If there is any doubt, it is always best to splint the injury and treat it as if it were broken. Elevate the injured part and apply ice packs for several hours. Notify the child's parents and encourage them to have the child checked by a physician.

Tick Bites

Ticks are small, oval-shaped insects that generally live in wooded areas and on dogs. On humans, ticks frequently attach themselves to the scalp or base of the neck. The child is seldom aware of the tick's presence. Rocky Mountain Spotted Fever and Lyme disease are rare complications of the tick bite. If a child develops chills, fever, or rash following a known tick bite, medical treatment should be sought at once.

Ticks should be removed carefully. Grasp the tick closely to the skin with tweezers, pulling steadily and straight out to remove all body parts; do not squeeze or twist. Wash the area thoroughly with soap and water and apply a disinfectant such as alcohol. Watch the site carefully for any signs of infection and/or rash.

Tooth Emergencies

The most common injuries to children's teeth involve chipping or loosening of a tooth. A tooth that has been knocked loose by a blow or fall will often retighten itself within several days. Care should be taken to keep the tooth clean and avoid chewing on hard foods.

If a tooth is completely dislodged, the child should be seen by a dentist. If the lost tooth is a deciduous or baby tooth, the dentist will usually not attempt to replace it. If the tooth is a permanent tooth, it should be kept wet by immediately wrapping it in a damp cloth or placing it in a small cup of water or milk. Often, the tooth can be *reimplanted* if it is done within an hour of the injury (Child Health Alert, 1990).

Summary

Emergency care is the immediate care given for life-threatening conditions. First aid is treatment given for conditions that do not endanger life.

Plans and procedures established ahead of time allow teachers and caregivers to respond efficiently and effectively during times of emergency. These plans include having trained personnel on hand, a coordinator of emergency care, notarized permissions for treatment, a telephone and listings of emergency telephone numbers, transportation, and adequate first aid supplies.

Training in lifesaving and first aid techniques is essential. These skills allow teachers and caregivers to fulfill their responsibility to save lives, relieve pain, and prevent complications. However, teachers do not diagnose or offer medical advice; they are only required to provide temporary care. Any additional treatment that is necessary is the responsibility of the child's parents.

Suggested Activities

1. Complete CPR and first aid courses.
2. Design a poster or bulletin board illustrating emergency first aid for a young child who is choking. Offer your project to a local preschool or child care center where it can be displayed for parents to see.
3. Divide the class into small groups of students. Discuss and demonstrate the emergency first aid care for each of the following situations. A child:
   - burned several fingers on a hot plate
   - ate de-icing pellets
   - splashed turpentine in the eyes
   - fell from a climbing gym
   - is choking on popcorn
   - slammed fingers in a door
   - is found chewing on an extension cord
4. As a class project, prepare listings of emergency services and telephone numbers in your community. Distribute them to local early childhood centers/or day care homes.

Chapter Review

A. Complete each of the given statements with a word selected from the following list. Take the first letter of each answer and place it in the appropriate space following question 10 to spell out one of the basic principles of first aid.

airway	evaluate
breathing	plans
diagnose	pressure
elevating	responsible
emergency	resuscitation

1. Always check to be sure the child is _______________.
2. The immediate care given for life-threatening conditions is _______________ care.
3. Early childhood programs should develop _______________ for handling emergencies.
4. If an infant is found unconscious and not breathing, begin mouth-to-nose/mouth _______________ immediately.
5. The first step in providing emergency care is to quickly _______________ the child's condition.
6. Bleeding can be stopped by applying direct _______________.

7. When evaluating a child for life-threatening injuries, be sure to check for a clear ______________, breathing and circulation.
8. Parents are ______________ for any additional medical treatment of a child's injuries.
9. Treatment of shock includes ______________ the child's legs 8 to 10 inches.
10. Teachers never ______________ or give medical advice.

A basic principle of first aid is _ _   _ _ _ _ _ _ _ _

B. Select the best answer from the choices offered to complete each statement:

1. In a case of heat stroke, you would expect the child's temperature to be
   a. normal
   b. elevated
   c. below normal
   d. unstable
2. Emergency treatment of accidental poisoning
   a. includes making the child vomit
   b. is always the same
   c. depends on the type of poison ingested
   d. is based on the child's age and body weight
3. Signs of head injuries
   a. may not show up for several days
   b. appear immediately
   c. are nothing to worry about if the child can get up and walk away
4. Bleeding can be stopped by
   a. elevating the injured part
   b. applying direct pressure
   c. placing an ice pack on the site
   d. all of these
5. A chemical burn to the eye should be treated *immediately* by
   a. bandaging the eye and rushing the child to a medical facility
   b. flushing the eye with warm water for 15 minutes
   c. calling the child's parents
   d. left alone so that the child's excess tears can wash the chemical out
6. Immediate treatment of burns includes
   a. submerging the burned part in cool water
   b. applying warm packs to the burned area to aid healing
   c. covering the burned area with an ointment
   d. all of these
7. A conscious diabetic child with symptoms of hypoglycemia should be given
   a. insulin
   b. dry toast
   c. nothing to eat or drink
   d. a glass of orange juice
8. In mouth-to-mouth resuscitation, the rate of breathing for a 7-year-old child is
   a. once every 3 seconds
   b. 30 times per minute
   c. once every 4 seconds
   d. 4 times per minute

9. The Heimlich maneuver is used to treat a child who is
   a. overweight
   b. in shock
   c. asthmatic
   d. choking

10. Frostbitten fingers should be
    a. massaged briskly to increase circulation
    b. quickly placed in water as hot as the child can tolerate
    c. rewarmed quickly in lukewarm water
    d. elevated to reduce pain and swelling

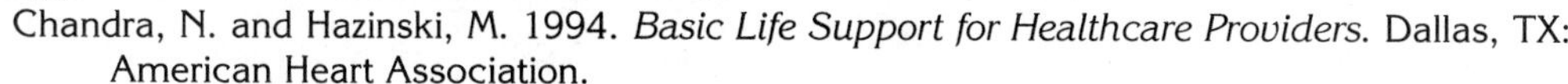

References

Chandra, N. and Hazinski, M. 1994. *Basic Life Support for Healthcare Providers.* Dallas, TX: American Heart Association.

Committee on School Health. 1993. *School Health Policy and Practice.* Elk Grove Village, IL: American Academy of Pediatrics.

Committee on Injury and Poison Prevention. 1994. *Handbook of Common Poisonings in Children.* Elk Grove Village, IL: American Academy of Pediatrics.

____. 1992. Drowning Risks. *Morbidity & Mortality Weekly Report (MMWR),* May 15, 1992: 320–333.

Green, M. 1995. *A Sigh of Relief.* New York: Bantam Books.

Harris, C., Baker, S., Smith G., and Harris, R. 1984, May. Childhood Asphyxiation by Food. *Journal of the American Medical Association,* 251(7): 2231–2235.

____.1991 (March). Poison Prevention Week: Some Timely Advice. *Child Health Alert,* pp. 1–2.

Sander, N. 1991. *So You Have Asthma Too.* Research Triangle Park, NC: Allen & Hanburys.

Sheldon, J. 1983. Protecting the Preschooler and the Practitioner: Legal Issues in Early Childhood Programs. In *Early Childhood Education: Special Environmental, Policy, and Legal Considerations.* E. Goetz and K. E. Allen (eds.) Rockville, MD: Aspen Publications.

Synoground, G. and Kelsey, M. C. 1990. *Health Care Problems in the Classroom.* Springfield, IL: Charles C. Thomas Publisher.

____. 1990, September. Teeth That Get Knocked Out: A Dental Emergency. *Child Health Alert,* pp. 2–3.

Additional Reading

First Things First. Upjohn Laboratories, 99 Park Avenue, 3rd Floor, New York, New York 10016. (A Children's first aid booklet)

Hunt, W. T. 1973. *Elements of Emergency Health Care and Principles of Tort Liability for Educators.* Dubuque, IA: Kendall/Hunt Publishing Co.

Keim, K. 1983, July/August. Preventing and Treating Plant Poisonings in Young Children. *Journal of Maternal Child Health,* 8(4): 287–289.

Loomis, C. 1987, May. "Childhood Asthma: What You Should Know." *Parents* 62(5): 227–8,232,234.

Marchand, N., and McDermott, R. 1986, December. "Mouse Calls: A Storytelling Approach to Teaching First Aid Skills to Young Children." *Journal of School Health* 56(10): 453–454.

Radican, K., Olsen, L., and Baff, C. 1993. *Organization of School Health Programs.* New York: MacMillan.

Richards, W. 1986, April. "Allergy, Asthma, and School Problems." *Journal of School Health* 56(4): 151–2.

Chapter 11

Child Abuse and Neglect

Terms to Know

abuse	intentionally	failure to thrive
neglect	innocent	mandatory
discipline	verbal assault	expectations
punishment	latch-key	precipitating
reprimand		

Objectives

After studying this chapter, you should be able to:

- Distinguish between abuse and neglect.
- Identify three types of abuse and two types of neglect.
- State four ways that teachers can help abused or neglected children.
- Describe characteristics of abusive adults and abused children.
- Identify six sources of support and assistance for abusive and neglectful parents.
- Describe actions the teacher should take in a case of suspected child abuse.

It is difficult to determine the actual incidence of *abuse* and *neglect* with any accuracy. However, it is estimated that one to two million cases occur in the United States and Canada each year (American Humane Association, 1991). Many times that number probably go unreported. In addition, two to four thousand children die every year as a result of inhumane treatment. Many more are severely injured, suffer permanent physical and mental damage, or develop serious emotional problems.

Although child abuse and neglect have occurred throughout history, it is only in the last thirty years that public attention has been drawn to the problem. And, only now are professionals and lay persons realizing the extent of child abuse and neglect as they exist in our society.

Accounts of child abuse date from ancient times to the present. Throughout history children have been abused in every imaginable way, including physical, emotional, verbal, and sexual abuse. Understandably, the most likely victims of abusive practices have always been young children, especially those with developmental disabilities. In many societies, children had no rights or privileges whatsoever including the right to live.

One of the first child abuse cases in this country to attract widespread public attention involved a young girl named Mary Ellen. Friends and neighbors were concerned about the regular beatings Mary Ellen received from her adoptive parents. However, in 1874 there were no organizations responsible for dealing with the problems of child abuse and neglect. Consequently, Mary Ellen's friends contacted the New York Society for the Prevention of Cruelty to Animals on the basis that she was a human being and, therefore, also a member of the animal kingdom. Her parents were found guilty of cruelty to animals and eventually Mary Ellen was removed from their home. This incident brought gradual recognition to the fact that some form of care and protection was needed for the many maltreated, abandoned, and developmentally delayed children in this country.

Although child abuse continued to be a major problem, it wasn't until 1961 that the subject once again received national attention. For a period of years, Dr. C. Henry Kempe studied various aspects of child abuse. He was greatly concerned about children whose lives were endangered. He first introduced the phrase "battered child syndrome" in 1961 during a national conference that he organized to discuss the problems related to harsh treatment of children (Kempe, 1982).

Nearly twelve years later, on January 31, 1974, the Child Abuse Prevention and Treatment Act (Public Law 93–247) was signed into law creating the National Center on Child Abuse and Neglect. The law also required states, for the first time, to establish definitions, policies, procedures, and laws regarding child abuse and neglect. As a result, there are many variations in definitions and reporting procedures.

The passage of Public Law 93–247 marked a turning point in the history of child abuse and neglect. It required each state to appoint an agency, and grant it legal authority to investigate and prosecute incidences of maltreatment.

DISCIPLINE VS. PUNISHMENT

The term *discipline* is derived from the word disciple and means to teach or guide. The appropriate use of discipline can be effective for teaching children socially acceptable ways of behaving. However, when it is used improperly or involves threats, fear, or harsh physical *punishment* it only teaches children anger and violence.

Concern about the maltreatment of children has increased because of major changes in public attitude toward the rights of families to discipline their children and the invasion of family privacy. For decades, the right to punish or discipline children as families saw fit was considered a parental privilege. Consequently, outsiders often overlooked or ignored incidences of cruelty to children so as not to interfere in a family's personal affairs. Eventually, however, educators, professionals, neighbors, and concerned friends realized that maltreatment of young children could no longer be tolerated. It became apparent that someone had to speak out against brutality and represent the innocent children who were being victimized by their families and caretakers.

One of the most difficult aspects of this problem is deciding at what point discipline or punishment becomes abuse or neglect. For example, when does a spanking or verbal *reprimand* constitute abuse? In an attempt to establish some guidelines, the federal government passed legislation forcing states to define abuse and neglect and to establish policies and procedures for handling individual cases.

Figure 11–1 The legal definition of a child is an individual under 18 years of age.

ABUSE AND NEGLECT

Abuse and neglect are generally defined as any situation or environment in which a child is not considered safe because of inadequate protection that may expose the child to hazardous conditions, or because of caretakers who mistreat or *intentionally* inflict injury on the child. For legal purposes, a child is defined as an individual under 18 years of age, Figure 11–1. As further insight is gained into the problem, specific categories of abuse and neglect have been identified:

- physical abuse
- emotional or verbal abuse
- sexual abuse
- physical neglect
- emotional or psychological neglect

Of all the types, physical abuse is the easiest to recognize because the signs are usually quite visible. Physical injuries may include cuts, burns, bruises, bites, welts, fractures, and missing teeth or hair; often there is a combination of fresh and old untreated injuries present. Observable changes in children's behavior, such as increased aggressiveness, shyness, fearfulness, passiveness, or apprehension are also likely to appear.

Physical abuse frequently begins as an *innocent* means of punishment; in other words, most parents do not set out to intentionally harm their child. However, during the process of disciplining the child, quick tempers and uncontrollable anger lead to punishment that is severe and sufficiently violent to cause injuries and sometimes death (see Table 11–2). Explanations may not be consistent or reasonable given the nature of the child's injuries. Also, it is often difficult to predict when and if incidences of physical abuse will be repeated, as it is more likely to occur during times when the abuser has lost control. Consequently, days, weeks, and even months may pass between attacks.

The shaken baby syndrome is a pattern of physical abuse that is most commonly seen among infants. It is caused by the vigorous shaking or tossing of an infant into the air and results in bleeding or bruising of the brain, blindness, seizures, retardation, fractures, and even death.

Emotional or **verbal abuse** is sometimes very difficult to detect and prove. Adult demands and expectations that are unrealistic and not based on a child's age and developmental abilities are a common cause of this form of abuse. Frequent put-downs are another example. ("Why can't you ever do things right?," or "I knew you were too stupid.") However, careful observation and documentation of interactions between child and adult can be very helpful in identifying emotional or verbal abuse. Children subjected to this type of abuse live in an environment that is often unpredictable. Consequently, they are *verbally assaulted* and repeatedly criticized, harassed, and belittled for both their behavior and achievements. Understandably, toddlers, preschool, and school-aged children are the most likely victims of emotional abuse. One of the first indications that a child has suffered from verbal abuse is changed or disturbed behavior. Unfortunately, the effects of verbal abuse often do not show up until later in life. This fact makes it difficult to identify and correct the situation before it leaves permanent scars on a child's personality or development. Over time, verbal assaults frequently turn into attacks of physical abuse.

Sexual abuse includes any sexual involvement between an adult and a child, such as fondling, exhibitionism, rape, incest, child pornography, and prostitution. Such acts are considered abuse regardless of whether or not the child agreed to participate (Bowman, 1992; Plummer, 1986). It is felt that children are not capable of making rational decisions in these situations or that often they are not free of adult pressure to make the decision they would like to make. Each year there are an estimated 200,000 cases of sexual abuse in the United States (NCCAN, 1990). Far more cases go unreported than with other forms of abuse. Girls are victims of sexual abuse more than twice as often as boys. Usually, the abuser is not a stranger. Rather, it is someone the child knows and trusts, e.g., babysitter, relative, caregiver, stepparent, teacher. Consequently, many times sexual abuse is discovered indirectly or not until years later.

Failure of a parent or legal guardian to provide for a child's basic needs and care is considered **physical neglect**. Children may be denied adequate or appropriate food, shelter, clothing, personal cleanliness, or medical and dental care. In many states, parents who fail to send their children to school or to encourage regular attendance are also considered guilty of neglect.

Leaving young children unsupervised can also result in charges of physical neglect. The term *latch-key* was originally coined to describe school-aged children who were responsible for letting themselves in and out of a house either before and/or after school. This term is now being replaced in the literature with the label self-care children to more accurately reflect their dilemma. The shortage of adequate school-aged child care for children of working parents is a major cause of this problem. Many unanswered questions have been raised about whether these children are at greater risk for accidental injury and/or feelings of loneliness and fear of being left alone (Lovko, 1989; Gray, 1987).

Emotional or **psychological neglect** is perhaps the most difficult of all types to identify and document. For this reason, many states do not include it in their reporting laws. Emotional neglect reflects a basic lack of parental interest or responsiveness to a child's psychological needs and development. Parents fail to see the need, or do not know how, to show affection or converse with their infant or child. The absence of emotional stimulation, such as hugging, kissing, touching, conversation, or indications of pleasure or displeasure, can lead to developmental delays and stunted physical growth. The term *failure to thrive* is used to describe this condition when it occurs in infants and young children. Absence of measurable gains in either weight or height is often one of the first indicators of psychological neglect.

REPORTING LAWS

Reporting laws support the philosophy that parenthood carries with it certain obligations and responsibilities toward children, Figure 11–2. Punishment of abusive adults is not the primary concern. Instead, the purpose of these laws is to protect children who are not of legal age from maltreatment and exploitation. Every attempt is made to maintain family unity by helping families find solutions to problems that may contribute to child abuse or neglect. Contrary to common belief, removing children from their homes is not always the best solution. Criminal action against parents is reserved for only those cases where the parents are not willing or able to cooperate with treatment programs.

Each case of child abuse and/or neglect involves a unique and complex set of conditions, including home environments, economic pressures, individual temperaments, cultural differences, along with many other factors. For this reason, most child abuse laws and definitions are purposely written in general terms. This practice allows the legal system and social agencies greater flexibility in determining whether or not a parent has acted irresponsibly.

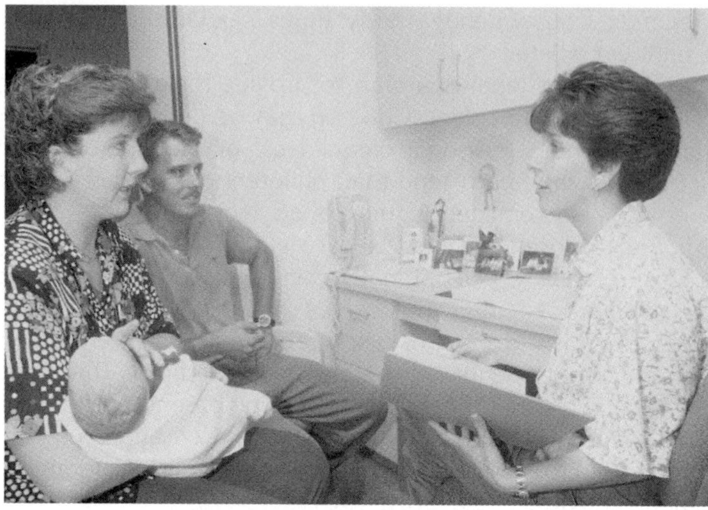

Figure 11–2 Parenthood involves the acceptance of certain obligations and responsibilities toward children.

In every state it is mandatory for certain groups or professionals to report any suspected incidences of abuse or neglect, including:

- teachers and caregivers
- center directors or principals
- health care providers, e.g., doctors, nurses, dentists, pharmacists, psychologists
- law enforcement personnel
- social workers
- clergy

Every center should establish a written plan for handling suspected incidences of abuse and neglect (Maddin, 1986). In large centers, responsibility for contacting appropriate local authorities and filing a report may be delegated to the director or health consultant. However, if at any time a staff member is not satisfied that their concerns have been reported, they must personally carry out this obligation. In day care homes or small centers, an individual staff member may be responsible for initiating a report. Failure to do so only prolongs a potentially harmful situation for the child, and can result in criminal prosecution and fines for the teacher or caregiver. These policies and procedures should be reviewed with staff to ensure understanding and compliance.

Initial reports are usually made by telephone, and a written report is completed within several days, Table 11–1. All information is kept strictly confidential, including the identity of the person making the report. Protection against liability and criminal charges is afforded by most reporting laws to anyone who reports abuse or neglect without intent to harm another person.

TABLE 11–1 Items to Include in a Written Child Abuse/Neglect Report

1. The name and address of the child and the parents or caretakers (if known).
2. The child's age.
3. The nature and extent of the child's injuries or description of neglect including any evidence of previous injuries or deprivation.
4. The identity of the offending adult (if known).
5. Other information that the reporting person believes may be helpful in establishing the cause of injuries or neglect.
6. The name, address, telephone number, and professional title of the individual making the report.

Suspicions of abuse and neglect do not have to be proven before they are reported. If there is reason to believe that a child is being mistreated or inadequately cared for, child protective services should be contacted immediately. As long as a report is made in good faith, the teacher or caregiver is merely indicating that a family may be in need of help. The law does not require that the family or adult be notified when a report is filed. In some cases, doing so could place the child in additional danger, especially if sexual or harsh physical abuse is involved. Other families may experience relief when their problems are finally recognized. Therefore, the decision of whether or not to inform the family or adult may depend on the particular circumstances.

Reporting a parent, colleague, or acquaintance is seldom an easy task. However, as advocates for children's rights, caregivers and teachers must always be concerned about children's well-being. Trained personnel will meet with the family, evaluate circumstances surrounding the reported incidence, and work with them to improve conditions.

Steps should also be taken by centers to protect themselves against employing staff members with prior child abuse/neglect or felony convictions. Most states currently require employers to submit names of new child care volunteers and employees to a central registry for the purpose of identifying individuals with prior records (Moriarty, 1990). Additional protective measures that can be taken by a center include:

- hiring individuals with educational training in early childhood
- requesting and contacting an applicant's references (nonrelative)
- reviewing the employee's past employment record, including reasons for leaving previous jobs
- establishing a code of conduct regarding appropriate child-teacher behavior
- providing continued inservice training, especially on topics related to identification of abuse/neglect, teaching children self-protection skills
- informing new employees that abuse, including sexual abuse, will not be tolerated and any signs of such will be closely monitored.

FACTORS CONTRIBUTING TO ABUSE AND NEGLECT

Abusive adults come from all levels of social, economic, educational, racial, religious, and occupational backgrounds (Kempe, 1982). They live in rural areas, as well as small towns and large cities. It is a common misconception that child abuse and neglect are committed by people who are uneducated, alcoholics, or have low income. While it is true that the incidence of abuse and neglect is higher among this group, like most assumptions about complex social and economic issues, such generalizations often are too simplistic.

Perhaps one explanation for why a larger percentage of individuals are identified from disadvantaged families is because of their greater use of, and dependency on, public and social services. Furthermore, daily living is often more stressful for low income families. Simply finding adequate food, clothing, housing, and transportation can be an overwhelming task.

On the other hand, persons from upper socioeconomic levels generally can afford private medical care and the services of multiple doctors in nearby cities. These factors may make it easier to cover up abuse or neglect and avoid being caught.

To help understand the complex nature of child abuse and neglect, three risk factors have been identified:

- characteristics of adults with potential for abuse/neglect
- presence of a "special" child
- family and environmental stresses

It is usually thought that for abuse and neglect to take place, all three risk factors must be present at the same time.

Characteristics of Abusive/Neglectful Adults

More is known about the personalities and traits of the abusive adult than perhaps any other aspect of child abuse and neglect. Certain behaviors and predispositions are known to be consistent from one case to another. Although not every abusive or neglectful adult fits the description, likewise not all persons who fit the pattern are necessarily abusive or neglectful.

Many abusive adults were themselves abused as children (Egeland, 1990). Consequently, they believe that harsh punishment is the only way to discipline children because this is the method with which they are most familiar. Repeated anger, rejection, and fear have filled their lives. They often turn to early marriage and children to satisfy the need to be wanted and loved. A large percentage of abusive parents also have drug- or alcohol-related problems.

Feelings of inadequacy and poor self-image are also common. As if to reinforce these feelings, abusive adults often seek jobs that they see as having little importance and status, such as factory work, waitressing, and cleaning. Their relationships with others, including spouses, are often unstable. A lack of trust makes it difficult for them to get along with anyone. The inability to form supportive friendships gradually leads to social isolation and feelings of helplessness.

An absence of good parenting skills is also common among many abusive and neglectful adults. Inadequate knowledge often contributes to the impression that a parent or caregiver does not care about the child. However, in many instances, it is simply that these adults do not know how to provide proper care and protection for children. Consequently, their expectations are often unrealistic and developmentally inappropriate based on the child's age. For example, a parent may become angry and abusive because a 15-month-old child wets the bed, a toddler spills milk, or a 7-year-old loses a mitten.

Many abusive and neglectful adults also have a low tolerance for stress or have a great deal of stress in their lives. They are easily frustrated, impulsive, and impatient with children. Eventually, anger provokes abuse.

Presence of a "Special" Child

Often an abusive or neglectful parent or adult singles out one child whom they consider to be different in some way from their *expectations*. These differences may be real or only imagined, but the adult is convinced that they actually exist. Qualities that are frequently cited by abusive adults include a child who is:

- developmentally delayed
- disobedient or uncooperative
- physically unattractive
- unintelligent
- hyperactive
- fussy
- clumsy
- frequently ill
- very timid or weak
- resembles someone the adult dislikes

Children under three years of age and developmentally delayed children are the most frequent victims of abuse. However, abuse incidents are also very high among children born out of wedlock, from unwanted or unplanned pregnancies, and stepchildren. Neglect is more commonly reported among infants and children over six years of age. Both sexes are abused and neglected almost equally.

Family and Environmental Stresses

All individuals and families face conflict and crises from time to time. However, some are able to cope with stressful events better than others. In many cases of abuse or neglect, stress is the *precipitating* factor. That is, conflict is sufficient to push them to action (abuse) or withdrawal (neglect) as a caretaker.

The abusive or neglectful adult often reacts to stressful events without distinguishing the true magnitude of the conflict. Instead, they find all crises overwhelming and difficult to deal with. The following examples illustrate the wide range of family and environmental stresses that can lead to loss of control when they occur in combination with other factors:

- flat tire
- clogged sink
- broken window
- lost keys
- job loss
- illness, injury, or death
- financial pressures
- divorce or other marital problems
- moving
- birth of another child

Some of these events may seem trivial in comparison to others. Yet, they may become the "straw that breaks the camel's back" and may be responsible for triggering abusive behavior when they occur in conjunction with other stressful events. A parent or caretaker frequently responds by losing control and reacting inappropriately regardless of the seriousness of the actual event. In turn, anger and frustration are taken out on the child.

THE ROLE OF THE TEACHER

Teachers and caregivers are in an ideal position to help identify children who are abused and neglected. Daily health inspections and close contact with children makes it possible to observe changes in behaviors and physical appearance, Table 11–2. Also, a teacher may be the only person whom a child trusts enough to reveal abusive or neglectful treatment.

Child abuse and neglect is often exhibited as a pattern of behavior. Therefore, careful written documentation of each incident is important (Tower, 1993). Written reports should be precise and include the following information:

- the type, location, size, and severity of any injury
- the child's explanation of how the injury occurred
- any explanation provided by the parents or caretakers of how the injury happened
- obvious signs of neglect, e.g., malnutrition, uncleanliness, inappropriate dress, excessive fatigue, lack of medical or dental care
- recent or drastic changes in the child's behavior
- quality of parent/child interactions.

Such information is useful for deciding on appropriate services and rehabilitative treatment programs for children and their families. A teacher's written observations can also be extremely valuable to child protective agencies as evidence should the need arise.

Helping Abused or Neglected Children

As educators, teachers and caregivers also play an important role in helping maltreated children deal with the effects of abuse and neglect. As a positive role model, the teacher can accept children for what they are, listen to their problems,

TABLE 11–2 Observation List for Recognizing Abused and Neglected Children

Physical Abuse

- repeated or unexplained injuries, e.g., burns, fractures, bruises, bites, eye or head injuries
- frequently complains of pain
- wears clothing to hide injuries; may be inappropriate for weather conditions
- reports harsh treatment
- frequently late or absent; arrives too early or stays after dismissal from school
- unusually fearful of adults, especially parents
- appears malnourished or dehydrated
- avoids logical explanations for injuries
- withdrawn, anxious or uncommunicative or may be outspoken and disruptive
- lacks affection, both giving and seeking
- may be given inappropriate food, beverage, or drugs

Emotional Abuse

- generally unhappy; seldom smiles or laughs
- aggressive and disruptive or unusually shy and withdrawn
- reacts without emotion to unpleasant statements and actions
- displays behaviors that are unusually adultlike or childlike
- delayed growth and/or emotional and intellectual development

Sexual Abuse

- underclothing torn, stained, or bloody
- complains of pain or itching in the genital area
- has venereal disease
- has difficulty getting along with other children, e.g., withdrawn, babylike, anxious
- rapid weight loss or gain
- sudden failure in school performance
- involved in delinquency, including prostitution, running away, alcoholism, or drug abuse
- fascination with body parts, talks about sexual activities

Physical Neglect

- repeatedly arrives unclean; may have a bad odor from dirty clothing or hair
- is in need of medical or dental care; may have untreated injuries or illness
- frequently hungry; begs or steals food while at school
- dresses inappropriately for weather conditions; shoes and clothing often sized too small or too large
- is chronically tired; falls asleep at school, lacks the energy to play with other children
- has difficulty getting along with other children; spends much time alone

Emotional Neglect

- poor academic performance
- appears apathetic, withdrawn and inattentive
- frequently absent or late to school
- uses any means to gain teacher's attention and approval
- seldom participates in extracurricular activities
- engages in delinquent behaviors, e.g., stealing, vandalism, sexual misconduct, abuse of drugs or alcohol

Adapted from *New Light on an Old Problem*. U.S. Department of Health, Education, and Welfare (DHEW Publication No. 70-31108), Washington, DC, 1978.

encourage their efforts and praise their successes (Caughey, 1991). For many children it may be the first time any adult has shown a sincere interest in them as a person without threatening or causing them harm.

As a trusting relationship is established, children can gradually be encouraged to verbalize their feelings. Play therapy is especially useful with young children. It can help them act out anger, fears, and anxieties related to abusive incidents. Housekeeping activities and doll play are ideal activities for this purpose. Talking about how the doll (child) feels when it is mistreated can help to bring out a child's real feelings about their own treatment. At the same time, teachers can demonstrate good parenting skills, such as appropriate ways to talk with, treat, and care for the dolls.

Artwork can also be an effective means for helping young children express their feelings and concerns. For example, self-portraits may reveal an exaggeration of certain body parts or how children actually feel about themselves. Pictures may also depict unusual practices that children have been subjected to, such as being tied up or locked in a closet or dark room.

Extreme caution must be exercised in any attempt to interpret children's artwork. A child's immature drawing skills and lack of special training can easily lead an inexperienced observer to misinterpretation and false conclusions. Therefore, it is best to view unusual items in children's drawings as additional clues, rather than absolute indications of abuse or neglect.

Annoying or irritating behaviors used by some children to gain attention can sometimes trigger an adult's abusive actions. Teachers can help children who display such behaviors by teaching them how to express their feelings in ways that are both appropriate and socially acceptable. For example, a teacher might say, "Rosa, if you want another cracker, you need to use your words to ask for it. No one can understand you when you whine or cry." They can also do much to build and strengthen trusting relationships with these children. Gradually, the abused or neglected child's self-concept will also improve as teachers or caregivers:

- respond to children in a loving and accepting manner
- set aside a private space that children can call their own
- establish gradual limits for acceptable behavior; set routines and schedules that provide order in children's lives that often have been dominated by turmoil
- let children know they are available whenever they need someone, whether it be for companionship, extra attention, or reassurance, Figure 11–3
- take time to prepare children for new experiences; knowing what is expected enhances the "safeness" of the child's environment
- encourage children to talk about their feelings, fears and concerns

Increasing numbers of new and innovative materials and programs have been developed to help educate children, Table 11–3. Many of these resources are available through local public libraries. Materials should be selected carefully so that they are instructive and not frightening to young children (Kendrick, 1995). Social workers, nurses, doctors, mental health specialists, and public service groups can also be called upon to present special programs for children and parents.

Figure 11–3 Caring adults can provide extra companionship, reassurance, and individualized attention.

TABLE 11–3 Sexual Abuse Resources for Children

"It's My Body: A Book to Teach Young Children How to Resist Uncomfortable Touch." (Also available in Spanish) Send $3.00 to:
Book Order
2730 Hoyt
Everett, WA 98201
(206) 259-0096

A resource book is also available for parents and teachers to use in conjunction with the above booklet. To order, send $5.00 ($1.25 postage and handling) to the same address and request "A Parent's Resource Booklet."

"Private Zone" by Francis S. Dayee. To order, send $2.00 ($.75 postage and handling) to:
The Charles Franklin Press
Department FW, 18409
90th Avenue W.
Edmonds, WA 98020

"Red Flag, Green Flag People" by Joy Williams. Send $4.00 to:
Rape and Abuse Crisis Center of Fargo-Moorhead
317 8th Street North
Fargo, ND 58102
(701) 293-7273

"No More Secrets" by Caren Adams and Jennifer Fay. Order from:
Impact Publishers
P. O. Box 1094
San Luis Obispo, CA 93406

"He Told Me Not to Tell." To order, send $2.95 to:
Network Publications
ETR Associates
1700 Mission St., Suite 203
P. O. Box 8506
Santa Cruz, CA 95061-8506

"The Secret of the Silver Horse"
Communication and Public Affairs
Department of Justice Canada
Ottawa, Ontario
K1A 0H8
(613) 957-4222

It is important that all children learn self-protection skills. Even when they do not fully understand the complexity of abuse or neglect, these skills enable children to recognize "uncomfortable" situations, how and when to tell a trusted adult, and how to assert themselves by saying no when someone attempts to do something that is inappropriate. Informed children can be the first line of defense against abuse and neglect if they are aware that being beaten, forced to engage in sexual activity, or left alone for long periods is not normal or the type of treatment they deserve.

Helping Parents

Parenting is a demanding task. Many parents today have not had the same opportunities to learn parenting skills that past generations once had. Without sound knowledge and adequate resources, everyday stresses can lead to abusive and neglectful treatment of children.

There are many ways teachers can help parents. Contacts with parents provide opportunities for recognizing families in crises and helping them find solutions to their problems. Teachers can share valuable skills and a wealth of knowledge with parents to improve their child-rearing practices and strengthen family unity. Supportive relationships can also be established through parent-teacher interactions. These are important as early intervention and prevention measures.

On a more structured basis, teachers can get involved in presenting discussions and workshops for parents. These could be sponsored by a school, child development center or in cooperation with other community agencies. Topics most parents will find of interest include:

- information on child growth and development
- identification and management of behavior problems
- principles of good nutrition; feeding problems
- how to meet children's social and emotional needs at different stages
- preventive health care for children at various ages
- locating and utilizing community resources
- stress and tension relievers for parents
- financial planning
- organizing a parent self-help group

Participation in community organizations and public awareness programs is another valuable contribution teachers and caregivers can make. With knowledge of community resources and services available to children and parents, teachers and caregivers can direct families to appropriate sources of help. This can be one of the most important steps in avoiding abusive and neglectful situations. A wide range of services is offered in most communities, including:

- protective services
- day care and "crisis" nurseries

- family counselling
- help or "hot lines"
- temporary foster homes
- homemaker services
- transportation
- financial assistance
- parenting classes
- employment assistance
- home visitors
- self-help or support groups

Inservice Training

Teachers and child caregivers are morally and legally responsible for recognizing the early signs of child abuse and neglect. However, to be effective, they need to be well informed. Through inservice training sessions, teachers can gain the basic knowledge and understanding necessary to carry out this function. Suggested topics for inservice programs might include:

- an explanation of relevant state laws
- teachers' rights and responsibilities
- how to identify child abuse and neglect
- development of a school policy and procedures for handling suspected cases
- exploration of teachers' and staff reactions to abuse and neglect
- identifying community resources and services
- ways to help abused and neglected children in the classroom

Summary

Child abuse and neglect are not new problems. However, passage of the Child Abuse Prevention and Treatment Act (Public Law 93–247) has gradually brought about increased public awareness of the problem, along with legal protection for the children involved.

Each state has had to develop its own legal definition of what constitutes abuse and neglect. In general, resulting laws are designed to encompass any situation in which a child is not likely to be safe from abuse and neglect. For legal purposes, five categories of abuse and neglect have been identified: physical abuse, emotional or verbal abuse, sexual abuse, physical neglect, emotional or psychological neglect.

The major purpose of child abuse laws is to protect children and strengthen the family as a unit. Most states require teachers and child care personnel to report suspected incidences of child abuse or neglect to a designated agency.

The probability for abuse and neglect is thought to be greatest when a combination of three factors occur simultaneously: characteristics of abusing and neglectful adults, the presence of a "special" child, family and environmental stresses.

Frequently, abusive adults were themselves abused or neglected as children. As a group, abusive adults tend to exhibit feelings of inadequacy, poor self-image, isolation, loneliness, and difficulty handling stressful situations. They often lack good parenting skills and proper knowledge of child growth and development. In addition, they commonly believe that harsh forms of punishment are necessary to discipline children.

The risk and incidence of abuse and neglect are known to be greater for certain groups of children. Those who are developmentally delayed, under three years of age, viewed as being different by parents, born out of wedlock, or are stepchildren run the highest risk for being abused and neglected.

A crisis or series of crises is often the factor that triggers explosive or inattentive behaviors on the part of the adult caretaker. Low tolerances for stress and limited ability to deal with it make every crisis seem overwhelming.

Teachers perform many valuable roles in the prevention and treatment of child abuse and neglect through:

- identification and documentation of suspected cases
- emotional support for abused or neglected children
- helping children learn socially acceptable behaviors
- alerting children to situations involving maltreatment in the home and community
- parent education
- participation in community programs
- inservice training

These contributions are essential to lowering the incidence of child abuse and neglect.

Suggested Activities

1. Gather statistics on the incidence of child abuse and neglect for your city, county, and state. Compare them to the national rates.
2. Write a two-minute public service announcement for radio and television alerting the community to the problems of child abuse and neglect.
3. Locate at least five agencies or services in your community that provide assistance to abusive or neglectful families. Collect materials from these agencies describing their services.
4. Prepare a pamphlet to help young children develop self-protection skills and awareness.

5. See what organizations are available in your community to help parents whose children have been sexually abused. Do they also offer programs for children?
6. Develop a bibliography of resources on parenting issues.

Chapter Review

A. Briefly define each of the following terms:

1. child
2. abuse
3. neglect
4. reporting laws
5. environmental stresses

B. Complete the given statements by selecting a correct answer from the following list.

teacherstrust
physical
psychological
neglect
confidential
sexual
childhood
definition
expectations
identify
reported

1. A child's fascination with body parts and talk about sexual activities may be an indication of ____________ abuse.
2. Public Law 93–247 requires states to write a legal ____________ of child abuse and neglect.
3. Injury that is intentionally inflicted on a child is called ____________ abuse.
4. Malnutrition, lack of proper clothing, or inadequate adult supervision are examples of physical ____________ .
5. Verbal abuse sometimes results because of unrealistic parent demands and ____________ .
6. Emotional or ____________ neglect is one of the most difficult forms of neglect to identify.
7. Reporting laws usually require ____________ to report suspected cases of child abuse and neglect.
8. Information contained in reports of child abuse or neglect is kept ____________ .
9. Many abusive adults were abused during their own ____________ .
10. Lack of ____________ makes it difficult for many abusive and neglectful adults to form friendships.
11. Daily contact with children helps teachers to ____________ children who are abused or neglected.
12. Abuse or neglect does not have to be proven before it should be ____________ .

C. Briefly answer each of the following questions:

1. List five clues that would help caregivers recognize a child who is being physically abused.
2. What should teachers do if they suspect that a child is being abused or neglected?
3. What information should be included in both an oral and written report?
4. Discuss four ways that teachers and caregivers can help abused and neglected children in the classroom.
5. List six types of services that are available in many communities to help abusive or neglectful families.
6. Why does the incidence of child abuse and neglect appear to be higher among disadvantaged families?

C. Case Study

When it was time for snacks, four-year-old Jimmy said he wasn't hungry and refused to come over and sit down. At the teacher's gentle insistence, Jimmy reluctantly joined the other children at the table. Tears began to roll down his cheeks as he tried to sit in his chair. Jimmy's teacher watched for a few moments and then walked over to talk with him. Initially, he denied that anything was wrong, but later told the teacher that he "had fallen the night before and hurt his leg."

The teacher took Jimmy aside and comforted him. She asked Jimmy if he would show her where he had been hurt. When Jimmy loosened his jeans, the teacher observed what appeared to be a large burn with some blistering approximately two inches in length by one inch in width on his left buttock. Several small bruises were also evident along one side of the burn. Again, the teacher asked Jimmy how he had been hurt and again he replied that "he had fallen."

1. What actions should Jimmy's teacher take? Should she tell anyone else?
2. Would you recommend that Jimmy's teacher report the incident right away or wait until she has gathered more evidence? Why?
3. To whom should the teacher report what she observed?
4. Using the information provided, write up a complete description of Jimmy's injury.
5. If you were Jimmy's teacher, would your feelings and responses be any different if this was a first-time versus a repeated occurrence?
6. Is it necessary for the teacher to notify Jimmy's parents before making a report?
7. In what ways can the teacher be of immediate help to Jimmy?
8. What should the teacher do if this happens again?

References

American Humane Association. 1991. *National Analysis of Official Child Neglect and Abuse Reporting*. Denver, CO: American Humane Association.

Bowman, B. 1992. Who Is At Risk for What and Why? *Journal of Early Intervention*, 16(2): 101–108.

Caughey, C. 1991. Becoming a Child's Ally: Observations in a Classroom for Children Who Have Been Abused. *Young Children*, 46(4): 22–28.

Egeland, B. and Erickson, M. F. 1990. Rising Above the Past: Strategies for Helping New Mothers Break the Cycle of Abuse and Neglect. *Zero to Three*, 11(2): 29–35.

Gray, E., and Coolsen, P. 1987. How Do Kids Really Feel About Being Home Alone? *Children Today*, (16)4: 30–32.

Kempe, C. H., and Helfer, R. (Eds.) 1982. *The Battered Child*. Chicago: University of Chicago Press.

Kendrick, A., Kaufmann, R., and Messenger, K. 1995. *Healthy Young Children*. Washington, DC: NAEYC.

Lovko, A. M., and Ullman, D. 1989. Research on the Adjustment of Latchkey Children: Role of Background/Demographic and Latchkey Situation Variables. *Journal of Clinical Child Psychology*, (18)1: 16–24.

Maddin, B. J., and Rosen, A. L. 1986. Child Abuse and Neglect: Prevention and Reporting. *Young Children*, 41(4): 26–30.

Moriarty, A. 1990. Deterring the Molester and Abuser: Pre-Employment Testing for Child and Youth Care Workers. *Child and Youth Quarterly*, 19(1): 59–66.

National Center on Child Abuse and Neglect. 1990. *Current Trends in Child Abuse Reporting and Fatalities: 1989 Survey*. Washington, DC: NCCNA.

Plummer, C. Winter, 1986. "Preventing Sexual Abuse." *Day Care and Early Education*, pp. 6–13.

Tower, C. 1993. *Understanding Child Abuse and Neglect*. Boston, MA: Allyn and Bacon.

Additional Reading

Child Abuse: A Handbook for Early Childhood Educators. 1990. The Association for Early Childhood Education, Ontario, Canada.

Furman, E. 1987. More Protections, Fewer Directions. *Young Children*, 42(5): 5–7.

Gargarino, J., and Kostelny, K. 1992. Child Maltreatment as a Community Problem. *Child Abuse and Neglect*, 16(4): 455–464.

Helberg, J. L. 1983, February. "Documentation in Child Abuse." *American Journal of Nursing*, 83(2): 234–39.

McNulty, C. 1994. Adult Disclosure of Sexual Abuse: A Primary Cause of Psychological Distress? *Child Abuse and Neglect*, 18(7): 549–555.

O'Brien, S. 1980. *A Crying Shame*. Provo, UT: Brigham Young University Press.

Pelton, L. H. 1978, October. "Child Abuse and Neglect: The Myths of Classlessness." *American Journal of Orthopsychiatry*, 48: 608–16.

Rose, B. 1980. Child Abuse and the Educator. *Focus on Exceptional Children*, 16(9): 1–13.

Strickland, J., and Reynolds, S. 1989. *The New Untouchables: Risk Management of Child Abuse in Child Care*. Redmond, WA: Exchange Press.

Tourigny, M., and Bouchard, C. 1994. Incidence et Characteristiques des Signalements D'enfants Maltraite's Comparaison Interculturelle. *Child Abuse and Neglect*, 18(10): 797–808.

U.S. Advisory Board on Child Abuse and Neglect. September 1991. *Creating Caring Communities: Blueprint for an Effective Federal Policy on Child Abuse and Neglect.* Washington, DC: U. S. Department of Health and Human Services.

Wodarski, J., Kurtz, P., Gaudin, J., and Howing, P. 1990. Maltreatment and the School-age Child: Major Academic, Socioemotional, and Adaptive Outcomes. *Social Work*, 35: 506–513.

Filmstrip

"Child Abuse and Neglect." Parents Magazine, Inc., distributed by PMF Films, Inc., Mount Kisco, NY 10549.

Chapter 12

Educational Experiences for Young Children

Terms to Know

attitudes
values
inservice
spina bifida
criteria
concept
objective
retention
evaluation

Objectives

After studying this chapter, you should be able to:

- Explain the four principles of instruction.
- Develop a lesson plan for teaching health and safety concepts.
- Explain the importance of including parents in children's learning experiences.
- List five health/safety topics that are appropriate for toddlers, and five that are appropriate for preschool-aged children.

Many of today's health problems result from a combination of environmental and self-imposed factors. Communicable illnesses no longer threaten lives as they once did. Instead, poor eating habits, lack of exercise, pollution, increased stress, poverty, and substance abuse (alcohol, drugs, and tobacco) are lessening the quality of children's health (American Association of School Administrators, 1990; U. S. Department of Health and Human Services, 1989).

The early years are formative years. Children spend much of their time gathering information and imitating the practices of others. It is also a time when children are more receptive to new ideas, changes, and suggestions. Many health/safety attitudes and habits established during this period will be carried over into adulthood. Consequently, early childhood is an ideal time to help children acquire the basic health/safety information, skills, and attitudes necessary both now and in future years. The key to improvement lies with education (Redican, 1993; Kolbe, 1992). Education involves a sharing of information, ideas, *attitudes*, *values*, and skills. The desired outcomes of this learning process are positive changes in behavior.

One of the major goals of health/safety education is to encourage the use of newly acquired knowledge and skills in daily living situations. For children, this means making them more aware of things that influence their health and safety, to assume greater responsibility for making positive decisions, and to become more involved in their own health care and safety.

THE ROLE OF PARENTS IN HEALTH AND SAFETY EDUCATION

Seldom is anyone more influential to children than their families (Jaffe, 1991). Many of children's health/safety habits and beliefs are acquired from their parents. The number of hours children spend in their home environments during the first few years of life often encourages health/safety behaviors patterned after those of family members.

Teachers and caregivers can significantly enrich the health/safety knowledge, values, and practices of young children. Much of what children learn at home takes place through incidental learning. That is, teaching is usually spontaneous and occurs in conjunction with daily routines and activities. Understanding the rationale for desired behaviors is not always a prime consideration.

In contrast, teachers know that it is important for children to understand the principles behind their actions. Instruction and learning experiences are, therefore, planned to provide young children with a component of understanding. It is also important to work together with parents and encourage them to include explanations when teaching new skills or reinforcing values and habits. For children to attain the ultimate goal of health/safety education programs, that is, to make choices and decisions that will maintain or improve the quality of their lives, they must understand the reasons and purposes for their behavior.

One way to increase understanding is to include parents in children's educational programs. Information about the health/safety concepts children receive in school can be shared with parents and actually enhance what the child learns at home. Most parents welcome additional information and ideas for expanding children's knowledge and learning experiences.

Successful parent education is built on involvement, Figure 12–1. There are many resourceful ways teachers and caregivers can involve parents in children's health/safety instructional programs, including:

- newsletters
- parent meetings

Figure 12–1 Successful parent education is built on involvement.

- observations
- participation in class projects, demonstrations, films, lectures
- assisting with field trips, health assessments, or making special arrangements
- preparing and presenting short programs on special topics

Parent involvement and cooperation encourage greater uniformity of health/safety information and practices between the child's home and school. Frustration that often stems from a child being told to do things differently at school and home can be minimized. Other advantages of sharing health/safety instruction with parents include:

- better understanding of children's needs and development
- improved parental esteem
- expanded parental knowledge and outlook
- reinforcement of children's learning
- strengthening good parenting skills
- improved communication between home and school

The resources and efforts of parents, children, and teachers can be united to bring about long-term improvements in health and safety for everyone.

THE ROLE OF TEACHER INSERVICE PROGRAMS IN HEALTH AND SAFETY EDUCATION

Teachers and caregivers are expected to conduct educational programs in health and safety as part of children's early learning experiences. Yet, few teachers are prepared to take on such responsibilities. Most teachers have only limited formal training in health and safety instruction. Consequently, *inservice* education for early childhood educators can improve their teaching skills, especially as they relate to matters of health and safety.

Inservice education should be an ongoing process of expanding and updating teachers' information and skills. Many professionals in the community can be called upon to present informative inservice programs on topics, such as:

- caregivers and the law
- emergency preparedness
- identifying child abuse
- advances in health screening
- review of sanitary procedures
- relaxation techniques
- working with parents
- disease updates
- information on specific health problems, e.g., epilepsy, *spina bifida*, AIDS, allergies
- review of first aid techniques
- health promotion
- nutrition education

It is important that all levels of personnel, aides, volunteers, support staff, teachers, and caregivers, among others, be included in these educational opportunities. However, the different roles and educational backgrounds of these people require that information and materials be presented in a manner that is meaningful to everyone involved.

PRINCIPLES OF INSTRUCTION

Opportunities to help children develop health awareness and bring about desired changes in their behavior present exciting challenges for early childhood teachers and caregivers. Carefully planned educational experiences prepare children to be responsible, healthy adults. The challenge becomes one of developing long-range goals and plans that will systematically teach children basic health concepts and skills.

Topic Selection

Long-range planning is essential in any educational program, including health/safety education. However, too often health/safety instruction is approached in a haphazard fashion. Topics are selected by individual teachers, rather than developed according to long-range goals for the children's benefit.

There are several *criteria* teachers and caregivers can use to aid in the selection of appropriate health/safety topics for young children. Once such a list is compiled, long-range instructional programs can then be developed. *Concepts* that have been left out can easily be identified and included in a revised plan. This process ensures that children will receive instruction in all essential areas.

Most importantly, topics should be selected to meet children's immediate needs and interests (Kendrick, 1995). These will vary with different backgrounds and special abilities of children in each group. Ideally, key issues should be addressed before problems arise. Isolated facts and concepts are meaningless to young children and quickly forgotten. However, helping children to understand the value and usefulness of information increases their motivation to make changes in their present behavior.

The age-group of children also requires special consideration when topics are selected. Practices and concepts should be matched not only to children's ages, but also to their particular stage of development, Figure 12–2. The principle that children learn when they are ready certainly is critical to the success of health/safety education. For example, teaching three and four year olds how to brush teeth and wash hands correctly can contribute to their sense of independence. However, health issues such as drug and alcohol abuse do not meet any of a young child's immediate needs.

Figure 12–2 Blowing away bubbles can demonstrate, in a manner meaningful to a child, how germs travel through the air.

Learning experiences should also be selected for their ability to improve the quality of children's lives. Children need to understand the value of making healthful decisions and following good health and safety practices. They must be able to see the ultimate rewards and benefits for behaving in a safe and healthy manner. A simple explanation is all that is often needed, e.g., "Washing your hands gets rid of germs that can make you sick. When you aren't sick, you can come to school and be part of the fun things we do."

There are many appropriate health/safety concepts that can be introduced throughout the early childhood curriculum. Toddlers enjoy learning about:

- body parts
- growth and development
- nutritious food
- social skills/positive interaction, e.g., getting along with others
- the five senses
- personal care skills, e.g., brushing teeth, handwashing, bathing, toilet routines, dressing
- friendship
- developing self-esteem and positive self-concepts
- cooperation
- exercise/movement routines
- safe behaviors

Topics of interest to preschool children include:

- growth and development
- dental health
- safety and accident prevention, e.g., home, playground, traffic, poison, fire
- community helpers
- poison prevention
- mental health, e.g., fostering positive self-image, feelings, responsibility, respecting authority, dealing with stress
- cleanliness and good grooming
- good posture
- food and good nutrition
- the values of sleep and relaxation techniques
- families
- exercise/movement activities
- control and prevention of illness
- manners
- environmental health and safety
- personal protection skills

School-aged children are eager to explore topics in greater detail, including:

- personal appearance
- dental health
- food and nutrition
- consumer health, e.g., taking medicines, understanding advertisements, reading labels, quackery
- factors affecting growth
- mental health, e.g., personal feelings, making friends, family interactions, getting along with others
- roles of health professionals
- communicable illnesses
- safety and accident prevention, e.g., bicycle, pedestrian, playground and home safety, first aid techniques
- coping with stress
- physical fitness

Objectives

The ultimate goal of health and safety education is the development of positive knowledge, behavior, and attitudes. Learning is demonstrated by children's ability to make good decisions and carry out health and safety practices that maintain or improve their present state of health. ***Objectives*** describe the exact quality of change in knowledge, behavior, attitude, or value that can be expected from the learner upon completion of the learning experiences (Redican, 1993).

Objectives serve several purposes:

- as a guide in the selection of content material
- to identify desirable changes in the learner
- as an aid in the selection of appropriate learning experiences
- as an evaluation or measurement tool

To be useful, objectives must be written in clear and meaningful terms; for example, "The child will be able to identify appropriate clothing to wear for three different types of weather conditions." The key word in this objective is "identify." It is a specific behavioral change that can be evaluated and measured. In contrast, the statement, "The child will know how to dress for the weather," is too vague and difficult to accurately measure. Additional examples of precise and measurable terms include:

- draw
- list
- discuss
- explain
- select
- write
- recognize
- describe
- identify
- answer
- demonstrate
- match
- compare

Specific and measurable objectives are a bit more difficult to develop for learning experiences that involve values, feelings, and/or attitudes. Results may not be immediately apparent. Instead, it must be assumed that children's actions and behavior will at some point reflect what they have actually learned.

Curriculum Presentation

Teachers serve as facilitators in the educational process, selecting strategies that are appropriate for children and support the stated objectives. How a teacher or health caregiver conveys health and safety information, skills, and values to children depends on the instructional method that is selected. This component is one of the most challenging and creative in the educational process (Ames, 1995). When deciding on a method, teachers should consider:

- presenting only a few, simple concepts or ideas during each session
- limiting presentations to a maximum of 7–10 minutes for toddlers and 10–15 minutes for preschool and school-aged children
- class size, age group, type of materials being presented and available resources
- emphasizing the positive aspects of concepts; avoid confusing combinations of do's and don'ts, good and bad
- ways to involve children as participants
- opportunities for repetition (to improve learning)
- ways to use encouragement and positive reinforcement to acknowledge children's accomplishments

There are a variety of methods that can be used to present health/safety instruction, including:

- adult-directed vs. group discussions
- audiovisuals, e.g., filmstrips, records, models, specimens, cassettes
- demonstrations and experiments
- teacher-made displays, e.g., posters, bulletin boards, booklets
- printed resource material, e.g., pamphlets, posters, charts (See Table 12–1 for ways to evaluate printed resource material.)
- guest speakers
- personal example

Methods that actively involve young children in learning experiences are the most desirable. It is easier to attract and hold the attention of the children if they participate in an activity. Such methods are also more appealing to young children and increase learning and *retention* of ideas. Examples of some methods that actively involve children in learning include:

- dramatic play, e.g., dressing up, hospital, dentist office, restaurant, traffic safety, supermarket

TABLE 12–1 How to Evaluate Printed Resource Material

Look for materials that:

- are prepared by authorities or a reliable source
- contain unbiased information; avoid promotion or advertisement of products
- present accurate, up-to-date facts and information
- involve the learner, e.g., suggested projects, additional reading
- are thought provoking, or raise questions and answers
- are attractive
- add to the quality of the learning experience
- are worth the costs involved
- support your program's philosophy

- field trips, e.g., visits to a hospital, dental office, exercise class, supermarket, farm
- art activities, including posters, bulletin boards, displays, pictures or flannelboards created by children
- actual experiences, e.g., handwashing, brushing teeth, grocery shopping, cooking projects, growing seeds, animal care
- puppet shows, e.g., care when you are sick, protection from strangers, health checkups, good grooming practices
- games and songs
- guest speakers, e.g., firefighters, dental hygienists, nurses, aerobics or dance instructor, nutritionist, poison control staff, mental health professionals

Combinations of these approaches may also be very useful for maintaining interest among children, especially when several sessions will be presented on a similar topic or theme. Health and safety concepts should be embedded in children's play activities to provide a totally integrated approach, Figure 12–3.

Evaluation

Ongoing *evaluation* is an integral part of the educational process. It is also an important step during all stages of health/safety instruction. Evaluation provides feedback concerning the effectiveness of instruction. It reveals whether or not students have learned what a teacher set out to teach. Evaluation procedures also help teachers and caregivers determine the strengths, weaknesses, and areas of instruction that need improvement (Ames, 1995).

Evaluation is accomplished by measuring positive changes in children's behavior. The goals and objectives established at the onset of curriculum development are used to determine whether or not the desired behavioral changes have been achieved. Do children remember to wash their hands after using the bathroom without having to be reminded? Do children check for traffic before dashing out into the street after a runaway ball? Do children brush their teeth at least once daily? Are

Figure 12–3 Health and safety concepts can be incorporated into play activities.

established rules followed by children when they are alone on the playground? In other words, evaluation is based on demonstrations of change in children's behaviors. Many of these changes can simply be observed. However, written tests may also be an appropriate method for evaluating learning in older children.

Evaluation must not be looked upon as a final step. Rather, it should add a dimension of quality throughout the entire instructional program. The following criteria may be used for the evaluation process:

- Do the objectives identify areas where learning should take place?
- Are the objectives clearly stated and realistic?
- Were children able to achieve the objectives?
- Was the instructional method effective? Were children involved in learning experiences?
- How can the lesson be improved?

Evaluation should be a nonthreatening process. Results of an evaluation can be used to make significant improvements in the way future health/safety programs are presented to children. It then becomes a tool that teachers, caregivers, and other professionals can use to improve the communication of health/safety knowledge, and skills to young children.

ACTIVITY PLANS

A teacher's day can be filled with many unexpected events. Activity plans encourage advanced planning and organization. They can also improve the efficiency of classroom experiences because teachers and caregivers are better prepared and more likely to have instructional materials ready.

A written format for activity plans is often as individualized as are teachers. However, activity plans for health/safety instruction should include several basic features:

- subject title or concept to be presented
- specific objectives
- materials list
- step-by-step learning activities
- evaluation and suggestions for improvement

Activity plans should contain enough information so they can be used by another person, such as a substitute teacher, caregiver, classroom aide, or volunteer. The objectives should clearly indicate what children are expected to learn. Activities can then be modified to meet the needs of a particular age group. A description of materials, how they are to be used, and safety precautions required for an activity are also necessary information to include. Following are examples of several activity plans.

Sample Activity Plan #1: Germs and Prevention of Illness

CONCEPT: Sneezing and coughing release germs that can cause illness.

OBJECTIVES:

- Children will be able to identify the mouth and nose as major sources of germs.
- Children will cover their coughs and sneezes without being reminded.
- Children will be able to discuss why it is important to cover coughs and sneezes.

MATERIALS LIST: Two large balloons and a small amount of confetti.

LEARNING ACTIVITIES:

A. Fill both balloons with a small amount of confetti. When the activity is ready to be presented to children, carefully inflate one of the balloons by only blowing into the balloon. **Caution:** Remove your mouth from the balloon each time before inhaling. When it is inflated, quickly release pressure on the neck of the balloon, but do not let go of the balloon itself. Confetti will escape as air leaves the balloon, imitating germs as they leave the nose and mouth during coughs and sneezes. Repeat the procedure. This time, place your hand over the mouth of the balloon as the air escapes (as if to cover a cough or sneeze). Your hand will prevent most of the confetti from escaping into the air.

B. Discuss the differences in the two demonstrations with the children:
"What happens when someone doesn't cover their mouth when they cough?"
"How does covering your mouth help when you cough or sneeze?"

C. Include a discussion of why it is important to stay home when you are sick or have a cold.

D. Have several books available for children to look at and discuss:
Clean Enough by Kevin Hankes. New York: Greenwillow Books, 1982.

Figure 12–4 Children learn to cover their coughs and sneezes.

Germs Make Me Sick by M . Berger. New York: Harper & Row, 1983.
Phoebe Dexter Has Harriet Peterson's Sniffles by Laura J. Numeroff. New York: Greenwillow Books, 1977.
Morris Has A Cold by Bernard Wiseman. New York: Dodd, Mead & Co., 1978.

EVALUATION:

- Children can describe the relationship between germs and illness.
- Children can identify coughs and sneezes as a major source of germs.
- Children voluntarily cover their own coughs and sneezes, Figure 12–4.

Sample Activity Plan #2: Handwashing

CONCEPT: Germs on our hands can make us sick and/or spread illness to others.

OBJECTIVES:

- Children can describe when it is important to wash their hands.
- Children can demonstrate the handwashing procedure without assistance, Figure 12–5.
- Children will value the concept of cleanliness as demonstrated by voluntarily washing their hands at appropriate times.

MATERIALS LIST: Liquid or bar soap, paper towel, sink with running water.

LEARNING ACTIVITIES:

A. Present the fingerplay, "Bobby Bear and Leo Lion." Have children gather around a sink to observe the handwashing procedures as it is demonstrated.

"One bright, sunny morning, Bobby Bear and Leo Lion (make a fist with each hand, thumbs up straight), who were very good friends, decided to go

Figure 12–5 Good handwashing technique is important for children to learn.

for a long walk in the woods (move fists in walking motion). They walked and walked, over hills (imitate walking motion raising fists) and under trees (imitate walking motion lowering fists) until they came to a stream where they decided to cool off.

Bobby Bear sat down on a log (press palm of hand on faucet with adequate pressure to release water) and poured water on Leo Lion and Leo Lion danced and danced under the water (move hand and fingers all around underneath the water) until he was all wet. Then it was Bobby Bear's turn to get wet, so Leo Lion (hold up other fist with thumb up) sat down on a log (press palm of hand on faucet with adequate pressure to release water) and Bobby Bear danced and danced under the water until he was all wet (move other hand under water).

This was so much fun that they decided to take a bath together. They found some soap, picked it up (pick up bar of soap), put a little on their hands (rub a little soap on hands), then laid it back down on the bank (place soap in dish on side of sink). Then they rubbed the soap on their fronts and backs (rub hands together four or more times) until they were all soapy.

After that, Bobby Bear jumped back on his log (press faucet) and poured water on Leo Lion until all his soap was gone (move hand under water). Then Leo Lion jumped back on his log (press other faucet) and poured water on Bobby Bear and rinsed him until all his soap was gone (move other hand under water).

Soon the wind began to blow and Bobby Bear and Leo Lion were getting very cold. They reached up and picked a leaf from the tree above (reach up and take a paper towel from the dispenser) and used it to dry themselves off (use paper towel to dry both hands). When they were all dry, Bobby Bear and Leo Lion carefully dropped their leaves into the trash can (drop paper towel into wastebasket). They joined hands (use fists, thumbs up and joined; walking motion, rapidly) and ran merrily back through the woods."[1]

B. Review the handwashing procedure with small groups of children at a time. Ask simple questions and encourage all children to contribute to the discussion.
"When is it important to wash our hands?"
"What do we do first? Let's list the steps together."
"Why do we use soap?"
"Why is it important to dry our hands carefully after washing them?"

C. Help children understand why it is important to wash their hands, especially after blowing their noses, playing outdoors, using the bathroom, and before eating. (Teachers and caregivers must set a good example by *always* remembering to wash their hands before handling food). Set up a messy art activity, e.g., fingerpaint, clay, glue. Have children look at their hands before and after washing them. Point out the value of washing hands carefully.

D. Obtain and use the materials: *T. Bear Handwashing Prevents Infection*, U. S. Department of Health and Human Services, 200 Independence Avenue, SW, #633F, Washington, DC 20201 (posters, stickers, buttons).

E. Read and discuss with the children several of the following books:
Clean As a Whistle by Aileen Fisher. New York: Cromwell, 1969.
Dirty Feet by Steven Kroll. New York: Parents Magazine Press, 1980.
Harry The Dirty Dog by Gene Zion. New York: Harper and Row, 1956.
I Hate To Take A Bath by Judith Barrett. New York: Four Winds Press, 1975.
Messy by Barbara Bottner. New York: Delacorte Press, 1979.
No More Baths by Brock Cole. New York: Doubleday, 1980.
Swampy Alligator by Jack Gantos. New York: Windmill/Wanderer Books, 1980.
The Messy Rabbit by Ruth Nivola. New York: Pantheon Books, 1978.
The Sticky Child by Malcolm Bird. New York: Harcourt Brace Jovanovich, 1981.

F. Observe children washing their hands from time to time to make sure they continue to follow good procedures.

EVALUATION:

- Was the fingerplay effective for demonstrating the handwashing technique?
- Can children wash their hands correctly and alone?
- Do children wash their hands at the appropriate times, without being prompted?

[1]The authors would like to acknowledge Rhonda McMullen, a former student and graduate of the Early Childhood Program, University of Kansas, for sharing her delightful story and creative ways with young children.

Sample Activity Plan #3: Dressing Appropriately for the Weather

CONCEPT: Clothing helps to protect our bodies.

OBJECTIVES:

- When given a choice, children will be able to match appropriate items of clothing with different kinds of weather, e.g., rainy, sunny, snowy, hot, cold.
- Children will be able to perform two of the following dressing skills: button a button, snap a snap, or zip up a zipper.
- Children will demonstrate proper care and storage of clothing by hanging up their coats, sweaters, hats, etc., at least two out of three days.

MATERIALS LIST: Items for a clothing store, such as clothing, cash register, play money, mirror; old magazines and catalogues containing pictures of children's clothing, paste, and paper or newspaper; buttons, snaps and zippers sewn on pieces of cloth; dolls and doll clothes; books and pictures.

LEARNING ACTIVITIES:

A. Read and discuss with the children several of the following books:
   The Cat's Pajamas by Ida Chittum. New York: Parents Magazine Press, 1980.
   What Will I Wear? by Helen Olds. New York: Knopf, 1961.
   What Should I Wear? by Pamela Rowland. Chicago: Children's Press, 1975.
   The Emperor's New Clothes by Hans Christian Andersen. New York: Four Winds Press, 1977.
   How Do I Put It On? by Shigeo Watanabe. New York: Collins, 1979.

B. Help children set up a clothing store. Provide clothing for both boys and girls. Include items that could be worn for different types of weather conditions. Talk about the purpose of clothing and how it helps to protect our bodies. Help children identify qualities in clothing that differ with weather conditions, e.g., short sleeves vs. long sleeves, light colors vs. dark colors, lightweight fabrics vs. heavyweight fabrics, etc.

C. Have children select two different seasons or weather conditions. Give children old magazines or catalogues from which they can choose pictures of appropriate clothing. Display completed pictures where parents can see them.

D. Provide children with pieces of cloth on which a button, zipper, and snap have been sewn. Working with a few children at a time, help each child master these items. Have several items of real clothing available for children to practice putting on and taking off.

EVALUATION:

- Children can select at least two appropriate items of clothing for three different types of weather.
- Children can complete two of the following skills—buttoning a button, snapping a snap, zipping a zipper.
- Children hang up their personal clothing, e.g., hats, coats, sweaters, raincoats, at least three out of four days.

Sample Activity Plan #4: Dental Health

CONCEPT: Good dental care helps to keep teeth healthy.

OBJECTIVES:

- Children will be able to identify at least two functions that teeth serve.
- Children can name at least three foods that are good for healthy teeth.
- Children can describe three ways to promote good dental health.

MATERIALS LIST: Order pamphlets on dental health and proper dental care from:

American Dental Association
Bureau of Dental Health, Education and Audio-Visual Services
211 Chicago Avenue
Chicago, IL 60611-2616 (Preschool to sixth grade)

Colgate-Palmolive Company
300 Park Avenue
New York, NY 10022

Lever Brothers Company
390 Park Avenue
New York, NY 10022 (Kindergarten to sixth grade)

Public Health Service
U. S. Department of Health and Human Services
Washington, DC 20201
(Order PHS Publication #1483, "Research Explores Dental Decay")

Old magazines, paper, glue, and string; selected snack food items.

LEARNING ACTIVITIES:

A. Distribute pamphlets. Discuss the information with children. Talk about the purposes teeth serve, e.g., chewing, formation of word sounds, spacing for new teeth, shaping of the jaw and face, a pretty smile.
B. Discuss ways children can help to keep their teeth healthy, e.g., daily brushing with a fluoride toothpaste; regular dental checkups; eating nutritious foods/snacks (especially raw fruits, vegetables); avoiding chewing on non-food items, e.g., pencils, spoons, keys; limiting sweets.
C. Help children construct "good food" mobiles. Use old magazines to cut out pictures of foods that are good for healthy teeth. Paste pictures on paper, attach with string or yarn and tie to a piece of cardboard cut in the shape of a smile.
D. Have children help plan snacks for several days; include foods that are both nutritious and good for the teeth.

EVALUATION:

- Children can identify at least two functions that teeth serve.
- Children can name at least three foods that are good for healthy teeth.
- Children can describe three good dental health practices that help to keep teeth healthy.

Sample Activity Plan #5: Toothbrushing

CONCEPT: Teeth should be brushed after meals and snacks to stay white and healthy.

OBJECTIVES:

- Children can state appropriate times when teeth should be brushed.
- Children can demonstrate good toothbrushing technique.
- Children can describe one alternate method for cleaning teeth after eating.

MATERIALS LIST: 1 white egg carton per child, cardboard, pink construction paper; several old toothbrushes, cloth, and grease pencil.

LEARNING ACTIVITIES:

A. Invite a dentist or dental hygienist to demonstrate toothbrushing to the children. Ask the speaker to talk about how often to brush, when to brush, how to brush, alternate ways of cleaning teeth after eating, what type of toothpaste to use, and care of toothbrushes. This may also be a good opportunity to invite parents to visit so they can reinforce toothbrushing skills at home.

B. Help children construct a set of model teeth from egg cartons, Figure 12–6. Cut an oval approximately 14 inches in length from lightweight cardboard; crease oval gently along the center. Cut the bottom portion of an egg carton lengthwise into two strips. Stable egg carton "teeth" along the small ends of the oval. Glue pink construction paper along the edges where "teeth" are fastened to form "gums." Also cover the backside of the oval with pink construction paper. Use a grease pencil to mark areas of plaque on the teeth. Cover the head of an old toothbrush with cloth and fasten. With the toothbrush, have children demonstrate correct toothbrushing technique to remove areas of plaque (grease pencil markings).

C. Send a note home to parents and request that children bring a clean toothbrush to school. Practice toothbrushing, step-by-step with small groups of children.

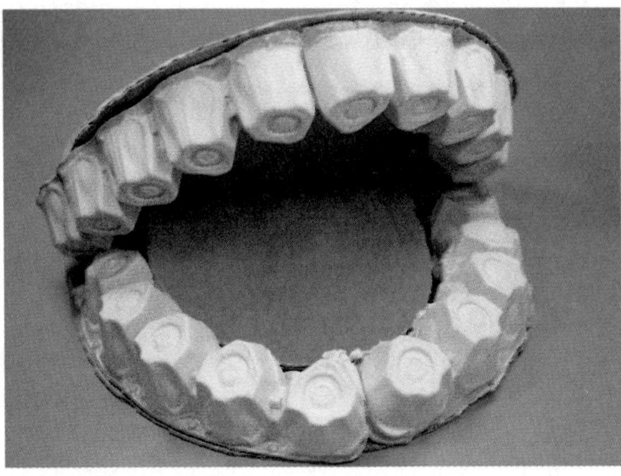

Figure 12–6 A set of "egg carton" teeth.

D. Older children will enjoy designing posters or bulletin board displays that reinforce good dental hygiene.

EVALUATION:

- Children can identify times when teeth should be brushed.
- Children can demonstrate good toothbrushing technique.
- Children can correctly identify at least one alternate method for cleaning their teeth after eating.

Sample Activity Plan #6: Understanding Feelings (Mental Health)

CONCEPT: Feelings affect the state of one's mental as well as physical well-being.

OBJECTIVES:

- Children will be able to name at least four feelings or emotions.
- Children can express their feelings in words.

MATERIALS LIST: Old magazines, glue, paper; large, unbreakable mirror; shoe boxes.

LEARNING ACTIVITIES:

A. Read and discuss with the children several of the following books:

Feelings by Richard Allington and Kathleen Cowles. Milwaukee: Raintree Children's Books, 1980.

How I Feel by June Behrens. Chicago: Children's Press, 1973.

Robbers, Bones and Mean Dogs by Barry and Velma Berkey. Reading, MA: Addison-Wesley Publishers, 1978.

The Me I See by Barbara Hazen. Abingdon: Nashville, 1978.

I Hate It by Miriam Schlein. Chicago: Albert Whitman and Co., 1978.

Why Am I Different? by Norma Simon. Chicago: Albert Whitman and Co., 1976.

Sometimes I Like to Cry by Elizabeth Stanton. Chicago: Albert Whitman and Co., 1978.

Feeling Angry by Sylvia Root Teater. Elgin, IL: Children's World, 1976.

Sometimes I Hate School by Carol Barkin and Elizabeth James. Milwaukee: Raintree Publishing, Ltd., 1975.

B. Have children sit in a circle on the floor. Discuss the fact that children and adults have many different kinds of feelings. Stress that many of these feelings are normal and that it is important to learn acceptable and healthy ways of expressing them. Ask children, one at a time, to name a feeling, e.g., happy, sad, tired, bored, special, excitement, surprise, fear, lonely, embarrassed, proud, angry. Have children act out the feeling. Encourage children to observe the expressions of one another. Help children learn to recognize these feelings. "Have you ever seen someone look like this?" "Have you ever felt like this?" "What made you feel like this?" Role play healthy and acceptable ways of coping with these feelings.

C. Place an unbreakable mirror where children can see themselves. Encourage them to imitate some of the feelings they have identified and observe their own facial expressions.

D. Make a collage of feelings using pictures of people from old magazines. Help children identify the feelings portrayed in each picture.
E. Construct "I Am Special" boxes. Have children decorate old shoe boxes with pictures of things that reflect their individuality, such as favorite foods, activities, toys, etc. Have children fill their boxes with items that tell something special about themselves; for example, a hobby, favorite toy, photograph, souvenirs from a trip, pet, picture of their family. Children can share their boxes and tell something special about themselves during "Show and Tell" or large group time.
F. Older children can be involved in role play. Write out problem situations on small cards; for example, "you and another child want the same toy," "someone knocks down the block structure you just built," "another child pushes you," "a friend says they don't like you anymore." Have pairs of children select a card and act out acceptable ways of handling their feelings in each situation. Discuss their solutions.

EVALUATION:
- Children can name at least four different feelings or emotions.
- Children begin using words rather than physical aggression to handle difficult or emotional situations.

Sample Activity Plan #7: Safety in Cars

CONCEPT: Good safety rules are important to follow in and around vehicles.
OBJECTIVES:
- Children will wear an appropriate seat belt restraint or use an appropriate safety car seat for children, Figures 12–7 and 12–8.
- Children can name at least one important safety rule to follow in and around cars.

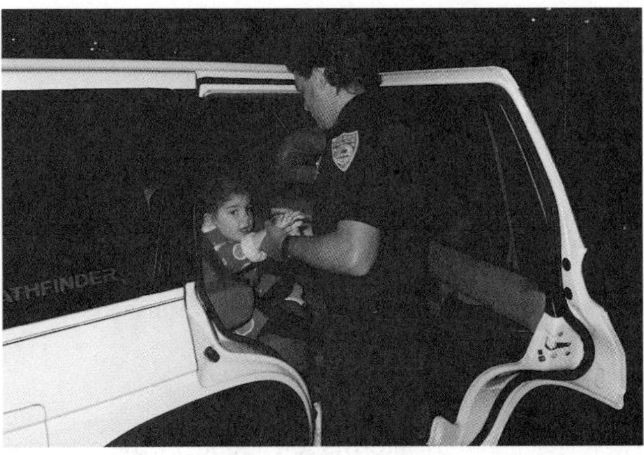

Figure 12–7 Seat belts should be worn by children who are at least 55–58 inches (139.7–147.32 cm) in height.

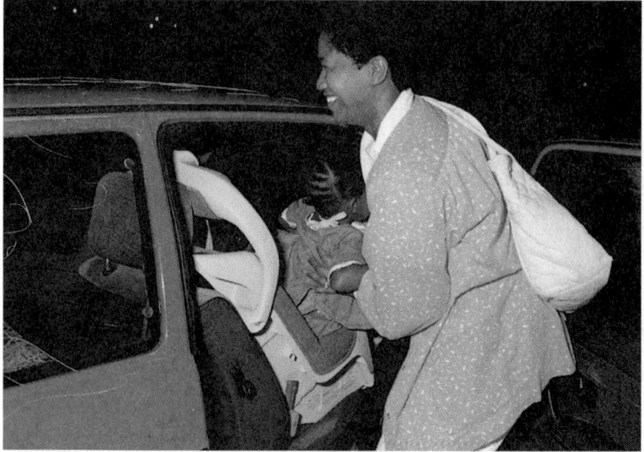

Figure 12–8 Safety car seats provide protection for infants and toddlers.

MATERIALS LIST: Order pamphlets about seat belt restraints and car safety from:

National Passenger Safety Association
1050 17th Street, N.W., Suite 770
Washington, DC 20036

OR

National Highway Traffic Safety Administration
U. S. Department of Transportation
400 Seventh Street, S. W.
Washington, DC 20590
(*Child Safety Seats for Your Automobile*, #DOT HS 805 174, 1982).

- Prepare photographs of children demonstrating the following safety rules:
  a. Always hold an adult's hand when going to and from the car; never dash ahead.
  b. Always get in and out of a car on the curbside.
  c. Open and close car doors properly. Place both hands on the door handle to reduce the possibility of getting fingers caught in the door.
  d. Sit in the car seat; never ride standing.
  e. Put on seat belt or use safety car seat.
  f. Lock all car doors before starting out.
  g. Ride with arms, legs, head, and other body parts inside the car.
  h. Don't play with controls inside of the car.
  i. Ride quietly so as not to disturb the driver.

LEARNING ACTIVITIES:

A. Discuss with the children information found in the pamphlets. Stress the importance of wearing seat belts or riding in an appropriate car seat restraint. Later, have children take the pamphlets home to share with parents.

B. Mount photographs of safety rules on posterboard or display on a table. Encourage children to identify the safe behavior demonstrated in each picture.
C. Use large group time to discuss with the children the importance of each safety rule pictured in the photographs.
D. For dramatic play, use large wooden blocks, cardboard boxes or chairs, and a "steering wheel" to build a pretend car. Have children demonstrate the car safety rules as they play.
E. Prepare a chart with all of the children's names. Each day, have children place a checkmark next to their name if they wore their seat belt on the way to school.
F. Establish a parent committee to plan a "Safe Riding" campaign. On randomly-selected days, observe parents and children as they arrive and depart from the center; record whether or not they were wearing seat belt restraints. Enlist children's artistic abilities to design and make awards to be given to families who ride safely. Repeat the campaign again in several months.

EVALUATION:

- Children can be observed wearing seat belts or sitting in a proper safety car seat.
- Children can name one safety rule to observe when riding in a car.

TEACHER RESOURCES:

"Seat Belts Activity Book" (Teacher's Guide), U. S. Department of Transportation, National Highway Traffic Safety Administration, Washington, DC 20590.

"We Love You, Buckle Up!" (Preschool curriculum kit on use of seat belt restraints). Order from: NAEYC, 1834 Connecticut Avenue, NW, Washington, DC 20009.

Sample Activity Plan #8: Pedestrian Safety

CONCEPT: Young children can begin to learn safe behaviors in and around traffic and a respect for moving vehicles.

OBJECTIVES:

- Children will be able to identify the stop, go, and walk signals.
- Children can describe two rules for safely crossing streets.
- Children will begin to develop respect for moving vehicles.

MATERIALS LIST: Flannelboard and characters; cardboard pieces, poster paint, wooden stakes; masking tape, yarn or string; 6-inch paper plates; red, green, and yellow poster paint; black marker.

LEARNING ACTIVITIES:

A. Obtain the booklets (5): "Preschool Children in Traffic" from the American Automobile Association, 1000 AAA Drive, Heathrow, FL 32746. Also read *Play It Safe* by Joan Webb, Golden Books, 1986.
B. Discuss rules for safe crossing of streets:
   a. always have an adult cross streets with you (this is a must for preschool children)

b. only cross streets at intersections
c. always look both ways before stepping out into the street
d. use your ears to listen for oncoming cars
e. don't walk out into the street from between parked cars or in the middle of a block
f. ask an adult to retrieve balls and toys from streets
g. always obey traffic signs

C. Introduce basic traffic signs (only those that have meaning to young pedestrians), e.g., stop, go, walk, pedestrian crossing, one-way traffic, bike path, railroad crossing. Help children learn to recognize each sign by identifying certain features, such as color, shape, location.
D. Help children to construct the basic traffic signs using cardboard and poster paint. Attach signs to wooden stakes. Set up a series of "streets" in the outdoor play yard using string, yarn or pieces of cardboard to mark paths; place traffic signs in appropriate places. Select children to ride tricycles along designated "streets" while other children practice pedestrian safety.
E. Prepare a flannelboard story and characters to help children visualize pedestrian safety rules.
F. Help children construct a set of stop-go-walk signs. Have each child paint three paper plates—one red, one green, one yellow. On a plain white plate write the word WALK. Fasten all four plates together with tape or glue to form a traffic signal.

EVALUATION:

- Children respond correctly to the signals stop, go, walk.
- Children can state two rules for safely crossing streets. (Puppets can be used to ask children questions.)
- Children demonstrate increased caution in the play yard while riding tricycles and other wheeled toys and also as pedestrians.

Sample Activity Plan #9: Poisonous Substances—Poison Prevention

CONCEPT: Identification and avoidance of known and potentially poisonous substances.

OBJECTIVES:

- Children will be able to name at least three poisonous substances.
- Children will be able to describe what the "Mr. Yuk" symbol represents.
- Children can identify at least one safety rule that can help prevent accidental poisoning.

MATERIALS LIST: old magazines, large sheet of paper, glue; small squares of paper or self-adhesive labels, marking pens.

LEARNING ACTIVITIES:

A. Invite someone from the hospital emergency room or Public Health Department to talk with the children about poison prevention.
B. Show children pictures and/or real labels of poisonous substances. Include samples of cleaning items, grooming supplies, medicines, perfumes, plants,

and berries. Show the children a "Mr. Yuk" symbol. Emphasize that children should stay away from any product displaying this label. ("Mr. Yuk" labels can be obtained for $1.00 from the National Poison Center Network, 125 DeSoto Street, Pittsburgh, PA 15213). Also caution children that not all poisonous substances are identified in this manner.

C. Discuss rules of poison prevention:
   a. Only food should be put into the mouth, Figure 12–9.
   b. Medicine is not candy and should only be given by an adult.
   c. An adult should always inform a child that they are taking medicine, not candy.
   d. Never eat berries, flowers, leaves, or mushrooms before checking with an adult.

D. Have children make their own "Mr. Yuk" labels by drawing a sad face on small pieces of paper or self-adhesive labels. Encourage parents to place the labels on products that are poisonous.

E. Make a wall mural for the classroom displaying pictures of poisonous substances. Be sure to include a sampling of cleaning products, personal grooming supplies, medicines, plants, products commonly found in garages, such as insecticides, fertilizers, gasoline, and automotive fluids. Glue pictures of these products on a large sheet of paper. Display the mural where parents and children can look at it.

EVALUATION:

- Children can identify the "Mr. Yuk" label as a symbol of poisonous substances.
- Children can name at least three poisonous substances.
- Children can name at least one safety rule that can help prevent accidental poisoning.

Figure 12–9 Only food belongs in children's mouths.

TEACHER RESOURCES:

A Guide to Teaching Poison Prevention in Kindergarten and Primary Grades. Public Health Service, U. S. Department of Health, Education and Welfare, Division of Accident Prevention, Washington, DC 20013.

Common Poisonous and Injurious Plants by Kenneth F. Lampe, U. S. Government Printing Office, Washington, DC [HHS Publication No. (FDA)81-7006].

Poisonous Plants by Laurence Gadd. New York: Macmillan Publishing Co., 1980.

Your Child and Household Safety. American Academy of Pediatrics, 141 Northwest Point Blvd., Elk Grove, IN 60009-0927.

Summary

Poor health practices and habits are responsible for many of today's health problems. However, education can significantly improve the overall quality of children's health. Education creates an awareness of health and provides the necessary information to make wise decisions. Health and safety education encourages individuals to assume responsibility for, and become actively involved in, their own health care. Education promotes good health/safety behaviors that can improve the quality of one's life.

The development of long-range plans for health and safety educational programs ensures that young children will receive comprehensive instruction. Topic selection should be based on children's immediate health needs and interests, age, and the ability to improve the quality of their lives. Objectives identify the changes in children's behavior that can be expected following instruction. They can also be useful for selecting content material, child learning experiences, and serve as an evaluation tool. Instructional methods should include opportunities for children to participate in learning activities. Involvement increases what young children learn and remember. Evaluation determines whether or not desired behavior changes have been achieved.

Including parents in children's education programs encourages consistency between school and home. Parents can reinforce information, skills, and values when they are aware of what children have learned. Continuous inservice education also helps teachers and caregivers expand and update their information and skills.

Suggested Activities

1. Interview a teacher of toddler or preschool children and a first or second grade teacher. Ask them to describe the kinds of health and safety concepts that are stressed with each group. Arrange to observe one of the teachers or

caregivers conducting a health/safety session with children. What were the teacher's objectives? Was the instructional method effective? Did the teacher involve children in learning activities? Were the children attentive? Were the objectives met?

2. Write to several organizations for materials on seat belt restraints and car safety seats. Read and compare the information. Do all statements agree? Do the statements disagree? For whom is the material written, e.g., parents, children, professionals?
3. Develop a lesson plan for a unit to be taught on "What Makes Us Grow?" Include objectives, time length, materials, learning activities, measures for evaluation and any teacher resource information. Exchange lesson plans with another student; critique each other's lesson plan for clarity of ideas, thoroughness and creativity.
4. Select, read, and evaluate three children's books from the reference lists provided in this unit.

Chapter Review

A. Select the best answer in each of the following statements:

1. Objectives
   a. measure a teacher's expertise
   b. define instructional methods
   c. describe an open-minded attitude
   d. identify desired behavior changes
2. The early years of a child's life are
   a. unimportant
   b. unproductive
   c. formative
   d. incidental
3. Health and safety learning experiences should
   a. involve children
   b. encourage children to be passive
   c. be spontaneous
   d. be difficult so as to challenge children
4. Evaluation
   a. measures positive changes in behavior
   b. should be a final step in the teaching process
   c. is generally a threatening experience
   d. only determines the quality of instructional methods

5. Inservice educational programs should
   a. be conducted three to four times each year
   b. be developed specifically for classroom teachers
   c. include only new personnel
   d. expand and update information and skills
6. Involving parents in children's health/safety education programs
   a. is frustrating to parents
   b. encourages consistency of information and practices
   c. disrupts teacher/child relationships
   d. all of these
7. Long-range planning for health/safety education
   a. is very difficult
   b. should only take advantage of spontaneous learning opportunities
   c. ensures systematic teaching of basic concepts
   d. is not essential
8. Many of today's health problems are
   a. not preventable
   b. the result of poor habits and practices
   c. caused by life-threatening communicable illnesses
   d. unpredictable

B. Matching. Match the definition in Column I with the correct term in Column II.

Column I	Column II
1. to assess the effectiveness of instruction	a. education
2. favorable changes in attitudes, knowledge and/or practices	b. outcome
3. a sharing of knowledge or skills	c. positive behavior changes
4. ideas and values meaningful to a child	d. attitude
5. subject or theme	e. relevance
6. feeling or strong belief	f. topic
7. occurs in conjunction with daily activities and routines	g. incidental learning
8. the end product of learning	h. evaluation

C. Following is a list of suggested health/safety topics. Place an *A* (appropriate) or *NA* (not appropriate) next to each of the statements. Base your decision on whether or not the topic is suitable for preschool-aged children.

_________ dental health

_________ feelings and how to get along with others

_________ primary causes of suicide

_________ consumer health, e.g., understanding advertisements, choosing a doctor, medical quackery

_________ eye safety

_________ the hazards of smoking

_________ how to safely light matches

_________ physical fitness for health

_________ cardiopulmonary resuscitation

_________ the values of rest and sleep

_________ safety at home

_________ animal families

References

American Association of School Administrators. 1990. *Healthy Kids for the Year 2000: An Action Plan for Schools.* Arlington, VA.

Ames, E., Trucano, L., Wan, J., and Harris, M. 1995. *Designing School Health Curricula.* Dubuque, IA: Brown & Benchmark.

Jaffe, M. 1991. *Understanding Parenting.* Dubuque, IA: Wm. C. Brown Publishers.

Kendrick, A., Kaufman, R., and Messenger, K. 1995. *Healthy Young Children.* Washington, DC: NAEYC.

Kolbe, L., Tolsma, D., Dhillon, D., O'Bryne, P., and Jones, J. 1992. School Health Education: Challenge for National and International Agencies. *Hygiene,* 11: 72–76.

Redican, K., Olsen, L., and Baffi, C. 1993. *Organization of School Health Programs.* Dubuque, IA: Brown & Benchmark.

U. S. Department of Health and Human Services.1989. *Better Health for Our Children: A National Strategy.* Washington, DC: U. S. Department of Health, Education and Welfare.

Additional Reading

Adams, L., and Garlick, B., eds. 1987. *Ideas That Work with Children.* Vol. II. Washington, DC: National Association for the Education of Young Children.

Associate for the Advancement of Health Education. 1994. *Cultural Awareness and Sensitivity: Guidelines for Health Educators.* Reston, VA.

Brown, J. 1985, May. "Annotated Bibliography on Preschool Transportation Safety." *Young Children* 4(4): 16–17.

Comer, D. 1987. *Developing Safety Skills With The Young Child.* Albany, NY: Delmar Publishers Inc.

Davis, A. P. 1983. Project HITE (Health Individualization and Teacher Education): A Health Curriculum for 3-, 4-, and 5-Year-Olds. *Journal of School Health*, 53(7): 433–434.

Fetter, M. 1983, September. "Nonverbal Teaching Behavior and the Health Educator." *Journal of School Health* 53(7): 431–32.

Glanz, K., Lewis, F., and Rimer, B. (Eds.) 1990. *Health Behavior and Health Education.* San Francisco: Jossey-Bass Publishers.

Hendricks, C., Peterson, F., Windsor, R., Poehler, D., and Young, M. 1988. Reliability of Health Knowledge and Measurement in Very Young Children. *Journal of School Health*, 58(10): 21–25.

Machado, J. M., and Meyer, H. C. 1984. *Early Childhood Practicum Guide.* Albany, NY: Delmar Publishers Inc.

Mahoney, B., and Olsen, L. 1993. *Health Education: Teacher Resource Handbook.* Millwood, NY: Kraus International Publications.

Matiella, A. (Ed.) 1994. *The Multicultural Challenge in Health Education.* Santa Cruz, CA: ETR Associates.

Mayesky, M. 1995. *Creative Activities for Young Children.* Albany, NY: Delmar Publishers Inc.

McKenzie, J. F. 1987. A Checklist for Evaluating Health Information. *Journal of School Health*, 57(1): 31–32.

National Center for Health Education. 1989. *Growing Health: Health Education Curricular Progression Chart.* New York.

Nelson, G. D., and Hendricks, C. 1988. Health Education Needs in Child Care Programs. *Journal of School Health*, 58(9): 360–364.

Scott, D. 1985, May. "Child Safety Seats—They Work." *Young Children*, 4(4): 13–15.

U. S. Department of Health and Human Services, Public Health Service. 1991. *Healthy People 2000: National Health Promotion and Disease Prevention Objectives.* Washington, DC: U. S. Government Printing Office.

Walk in Traffic Safely (WITS): A Traffic Safety Kit. Washington, DC, NAEYC.

We Love You—Buckle Up! Curriculum packet. Washington, DC, NAEYC.

Wisconsin Department of Public Instruction. 1992. *Healthy Kids: A Team Approach to Integrating Developmental Guidance and Health Education K–6.* Madison, WI.

UNIT

4

Foods and Nutrients: Basic Concepts

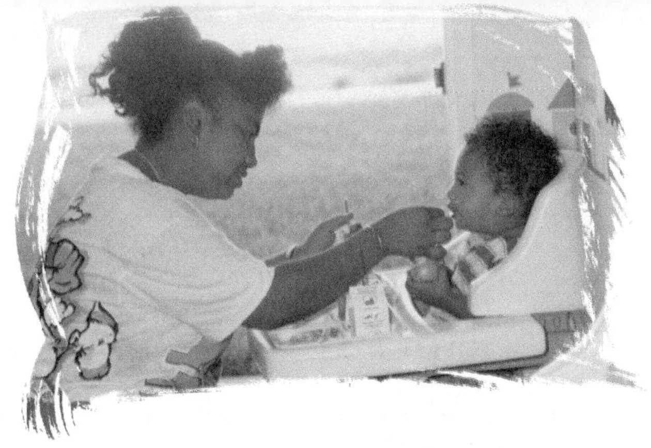

Chapter 13

Nutritional Guidelines

Terms to Know

nutrition
nutrients
malnutrition
undernutrition
essential nutrients
calcium
protein
Percent Daily Values
nutrition claims

Objectives

After studying this chapter, you should be able to:

- Outline the steps required to evaluate the nutrient content of a meal or meals.
- Apply the Dietary Guidelines for Americans to your personal nutritional goals.
- Classify foods according to the Food Guide Pyramid.
- Identify nutrient strengths and weaknesses for each major food group in the Food Guide Pyramid.
- Evaluate the nutritional quality of a food from its package label.

Good nutrition affects the health and well-being of individuals of all ages. It is important to note that all persons throughout life need the same nutrients, but in varying amounts. Small children need nutrients for growth and energy; adults need nutrients to maintain or repair body tissue and to provide energy.

To teach good food habits, the care provider or parent must first set a good example. Children frequently model behaviors they see in people they love and admire, such as parents and teachers. To set a good example, the care provider must possess the knowledge to maintain good personal nutrition. A good basic understanding of one's own nutrient needs is essential for good personal dietary practices. The ability to apply nutrition knowledge to the care of children will hopefully follow.

Nutrition is the study of food and how it is used by the body. Nutritionists study foods because foods contain *nutrients*, which are chemical substances with specific uses in the body. The body has three main uses for nutrients:

- sources of energy
- materials for growth and maintenance of body tissue
- regulation of body processes

Table 13–1 shows the relationship between nutrients and their functions.

Nutrients are needed in adequate amounts for normal body function to take place. An inadequate supply of nutrients or poor utilization of nutrients may result in *malnutrition* (*undernutrition*) resulting in abnormal body function and general poor health. Malnutrition may result from excessive intake of one or more nutrients and this, too, may interfere with normal body functions and be health-threatening.

TABLE 13–1 Nutrients: Their Functions

	Calories per Gram	Energy	Build Body Tissues	Regulators
Carbohydrates	4	X		
Fats	9	X		
Proteins (needed for every function)	4	X	X	X
Minerals			X	X
Water			X	X
Vitamins				X*

*are required in a regulatory role only.

Currently there is much concern about excessive consumption of fats and cholesterol in the diet and of minerals and vitamins from self-supplementation.

Approximately fifty nutrients are known to be essential for humans. An *essential nutrient* is one that must be provided by food substances as the body is unable to manufacture it in adequate amounts. Scientists have been able to determine the approximate amounts of many nutrients needed by the body. Information is also available listing the amounts of many nutrients found in specific foods.

Good nutrition is dependent upon combinations of foods that provide nutritious meals on a daily basis. In the interest of simplifying this process, a number of meal plans or guidelines have been developed. Any of the guidelines discussed will promote healthful eating habits; the choice lies with the individual and may depend on time available, ease of use, and interest.

Regardless of the guideline selected, the common factor necessary for good nutrition is the inclusion of a wide variety of foods. A variety of foods is most likely to supply the greatest number of nutrients. Some foods contain many nutrients while others contain only a few nutrients. No single food contains enough of all nutrients to support life. The only exception is breast milk, which contains all the nutrients known to be needed by an infant until about six months of age.

RECOMMENDED DAILY DIETARY ALLOWANCES

Recommended Daily Dietary Allowances (RDA) are guidelines published in the U. S. by the Food and Nutrition Board of the National Academy of Sciences for the amounts of nutrients needed by most healthy people, categorized according to age and sex. See Table 13–2 for the 1989 Recommended Dietary Allowances (RDA) and read footnote (a) to understand the basis for these values. These guidelines are updated frequently in an effort to reflect the most up-to-date knowledge about nutrient needs.

For the Recommended Daily Dietary Allowances guidelines to be meaningful, nutrient content of foods must be known. (Check the references at the end of this chapter.) Evaluation of a diet by means of the Recommended Daily Dietary Allowances guidelines requires the following steps:

1. List the amounts of all foods and beverages consumed during one 24-hour period.

2. Use nutrient value tables or a computer program to determine the nutrient content of each food and beverage consumed (See Table 13–3).

3. Total the amount of each nutrient consumed during the day.

4. Determine if nutrients consumed are in sufficient amounts by comparing the total amount of each nutrient consumed with the Recommended Daily Dietary Allowances for the appropriate age and sex group, Tables 13–2 and 13–3.

TABLE 13–2 Recommended Dietary Allowances[a], Revised 1989
Designed for the maintenance of good nutrition of practically all healthy people in the United States

							Fat-Soluble Vitamins			
		Weight[b]		Height[b]			Vitamin A	Vitamin D	Vitamin E	Vitamin K
Category	Age (years) or Condition	(kg)	(lb)	(cm)	(in)	Protein (g)	(μg RE)[c]	(μg)[d]	(mg α-TE)[e]	(μg)
Infants	0.0–0.5	6	13	60	24	13	375	7.5	3	5
	0.5–1.0	9	20	71	28	14	375	10	4	10
Children	1–3	13	29	90	35	16	400	10	6	15
	4–6	20	44	112	44	24	500	10	7	20
	7–10	28	62	132	52	28	700	10	7	30
Males	11–14	45	99	157	62	45	1,000	10	10	45
	15–18	66	145	176	69	59	1,000	10	10	65
	19–24	72	160	177	70	58	1,000	10	10	70
	25–50	79	174	176	70	63	1,000	5	10	80
	51+	77	170	173	68	63	1,000	5	10	80
Females	11–14	46	101	157	62	46	800	10	8	45
	15–18	55	120	163	64	44	800	10	8	55
	19–24	58	128	164	65	46	800	10	8	60
	25–50	63	138	163	64	50	800	5	8	65
	51+	65	143	160	63	50	800	5	8	65
Pregnant						60	800	10	10	65
Lactating	1st 6 months					65	1,300	10	12	65
	2nd 6 months					62	1,200	10	11	65

[a] The allowances, expressed as average daily intakes over time, are intended to provide for individual variations among most normal persons as they live in the United States under usual environmental stresses. Diets should be based on a variety of common foods in order to provide other nutrients for which human requirements have been less well defined. See text for detailed discussion of allowances and of nutrients not tabulated.

[b] Weights and heights of Reference Adults are actual medians for the U. S. population of the designated age, as reported by NHANES II. The median weights and heights of those under 19 years of age were taken from Hamill et al. (1979) (see pages 16–17). The use of these figures does not imply that the height-to-weight ratios are ideal.

[c] Retinol equivalents. 1 retinol equivalent = 1 μg retinol or 6 μg β-carotene. See text for calculation of vitamin A activity of diets as retinol equivalents.

[d] As cholecalciferol. 10 μg cholecalciferol = 400 IU of vitamin D.

[e] α–Tocopherol equivalents. 1 mg d-α tocopherol = 1 α-TE. See text for variation in allowances and calculation of vitamin E activity of the diet as α-tocopherol equivalents.

[f] 1 NE (niacin equivalent) is equal to 1 mg of niacin or 60 mg of dietary tryptophan.

TABLE 13–2 (Continued)

Water-Soluble Vitamins							Minerals						
Vitamin C (mg)	Thiamin (mg)	Riboflavin (mg)	Niacin (mg NE)[f]	Vitamin B_6 (mg)	Folate (μg)	Vitamin B_{12} (μg)	Calcium (mg)	Phosphorus (mg)	Magnesium (mg)	Iron (mg)	Zinc (mg)	Iodine (μg)	Selenium (μg)
30	0.3	0.4	5	0.3	25	0.3	400	300	40	6	5	40	10
35	0.4	0.5	6	0.6	35	0.5	600	500	60	10	5	50	15
40	0.7	0.8	9	1.0	50	0.7	800	800	80	10	10	70	20
45	0.9	1.1	12	1.1	75	1.0	800	800	120	10	10	90	20
45	1.0	1.2	13	1.4	100	1.4	800	800	170	10	10	120	30
50	1.3	1.5	17	1.7	150	2.0	1,200	1,200	270	12	15	150	40
60	1.5	1.8	20	2.0	200	2.0	1,200	1,200	400	12	15	150	50
60	1.5	1.7	19	2.0	200	2.0	1,200	1,200	350	10	15	150	70
60	1.5	1.7	19	2.0	200	2.0	800	800	350	10	15	150	70
60	1.2	1.4	15	2.0	200	2.0	800	800	350	10	15	150	70
50	1.1	1.3	15	1.4	150	2.0	1,200	1,200	280	15	12	150	45
60	1.1	1.3	15	1.5	180	2.0	1,200	1,200	300	15	12	150	50
60	1.1	1.3	15	1.6	180	2.0	1,200	1,200	280	15	12	150	55
60	1.1	1.3	15	1.6	180	2.0	800	800	280	15	12	150	55
60	1.0	1.2	13	1.6	180	2.0	800	800	280	10	12	150	55
70	1.5	1.6	17	2.2	400	2.2	1,200	1,200	300	30	15	175	65
95	1.6	1.8	20	2.1	280	2.6	1,200	1,200	355	15	19	200	75
90	1.6	1.7	20	2.1	260	2.6	1,200	1,200	340	15	16	200	75

Reproduced from "Recommended Dietary Allowances", 10th ed., 1989, with the permission of the National Academy of Sciences, Washington, DC

TABLE 13–3 Nutrient Value Tables

(A)		(B)		(C)	(D)	(E)	(F)	(G)	(H)	(I)	(J)	(K)	(L)	(M)	(N)	(O)	(P)	(Q)	(R)	(S)
83	Soft serve (about 2.6% fat)	1 cup	175	70	225	8	5	2.9	1.2	0.1	38	274	202	0.3	412	180	0.12	0.54	0.2	1
84	Sherbet (about 2% fat)	1/2 gal	1,542	66	2,160	17	31	19.0	7.7	.7	469	827	594	2.5	1,585	1,480	.26	.71	1.0	31
85		1 cup	193	66	270	2	4	2.4	1.0	.1	59	103	74	.3	198	190	.03	.09	.1	4
	Milk desserts, other:																			
86	Custard, baked	1 cup	265	77	305	14	15	6.8	5.4	.7	29	297	310	1.1	387	930	.11	.50	.3	1
	Puddings:																			
	From home recipe:																			
	Starch base:																			
87	Chocolate	1 cup	260	66	385	8	12	7.6	3.3	.3	67	250	255	1.3	445	390	.05	.36	.3	1
88	Vanilla (blancmange)	1 cup	255	76	285	9	10	6.2	2.5	.2	41	298	232	Trace	352	410	.08	.41	.3	2
89	Tapioca cream	1 cup	165	72	220	8	8	4.1	2.5	.5	28	173	180	.7	223	480	.07	.30	.2	2
	From mix (chocolate) and milk:																			
90	Regular (cooked)	1 cup	260	70	320	9	8	4.3	2.6	.2	59	265	247	.8	354	340	.05	.39	.3	2
91	Instant	1 cup	260	69	325	8	7	3.6	2.2	.3	63	374	237	1.3	335	340	.08	.39	.3	2
	Yogurt:																			
	With added milk solids:																			
	Made with lowfat milk:																			
92	Fruit flavored[9]	1 container, net wt., 8 oz	227	75	230	10	3	1.8	.6	.1	42	343	269	.2	439	[10]120	.08	.40	.2	1
93	Plain	1 container, net wt., 8 oz	227	85	145	12	4	2.3	.8	.1	16	415	326	.2	531	[10]150	.10	.49	.3	2
94	Made with nonfat milk	1 container, net wt., 8 oz	227	85	125	13	Trace	.3	.1	Trace	17	452	355	.2	579	[10]20	.11	.53	.3	2
	Without added milk solids:																			
95	Made with whole milk	1 container, net wt., 8 oz	227	88	140	8	7	4.8	1.7	.1	11	274	215	.1	351	280	.07	.32	.2	1
		EGGS																		
	Eggs, large (24 oz per dozen):																			
	Raw:																			
96	Whole, without shell	1 egg	50	75	80	6	6	1.7	2.0	.6	1	28	90	1.0	65	260	.04	.15	Trace	0
97	White	1 white	33	88	15	3	Trace	0	0	0	Trace	4	4	Trace	45	0	Trace	.09	Trace	0
98	Yolk	1 yolk	17	49	65	3	6	1.7	2.1	.6	Trace	26	86	.9	15	310	.04	.07	Trace	0
	Cooked:																			
99	Fried in butter	1 egg	46	72	85	5	6	2.4	2.2	.6	1	26	80	.9	58	290	.03	.13	Trace	0
100	Hard-cooked, shell removed	1 egg	50	75	80	6	6	1.7	2.0	.6	1	28	90	1.0	65	260	.04	.14	Trace	0
101	Poached	1 egg	50	74	80	6	6	1.7	2.0	.6	1	28	90	1.0	65	260	.04	.13	Trace	0
102	Scrambled (milk added) in butter. Also omelet.	1 egg	64	76	95	6	7	2.8	2.3	.6	1	47	97	.9	85	310	.04	.16	Trace	0
		FATS, OILS; RELATED PRODUCTS																		
	Butter:																			
	Regular (1 brick or 4 sticks per lb):																			
103	Stick (1/2 cup)	1 stick	113	16	815	1	92	57.3	23.1	2.1	Trace	27	26	.2	29	[11]3,470	.01	.04	Trace	0
104	Tablespoon (about 1/8 stick)	1 tbsp	14	16	100	Trace	12	7.2	2.9	.3	Trace	3	3	Trace	4	[11]430	Trace	Trace	Trace	0
105	Pat (1 in square, 1/3 in high; 90 per lb).	1 pat	5	16	35	Trace	4	2.5	1.0	.1	Trace	1	1	Trace	1	[11]150	Trace	Trace	Trace	0
	Whipped (6 sticks or two 8-oz containers per lb).																			
106	Stick (1/2 cup)	1 stick	76	16	540	1	61	38.2	15.4	1.4	Trace	18	17	.1	20	[11]2,310	Trace	.03	Trace	0
107	Tablespoon (about 1/8 stick)	1 tbsp	9	16	65	Trace	8	4.7	1.9	.2	Trace	2	2	Trace	2	[11]290	Trace	Trace	Trace	0
108	Pat (1 1/4 in square, 1/3 in high; 120 per lb).	1 pat	4	16	25	Trace	3	1.9	.8	.1	Trace	1	1	Trace	1	[11]120	0	Trace	Trace	0

[3] Applies to product without vitamin A added.
[4] Applies to product with added vitamin A. Without added vitamin A, value is 20 International Units (1.1.).
[5] Yields 1 qt of fluid milk when reconstituted according to package directions.
[6] Applies to product with added vitamin A.
[7] Weight applies to product with label claim of 1 1/3 cups equal 3.2 oz.
[8] Applies to products made from thick shake mixes and that do not contain added ice cream. Products made from milk shake mixes are higher in fat and usually contain added ice cream.
[9] Content of fat, vitamin A, and carbohydrate varies. Consult the label when precise values are needed for special diets.
[10] Applies to product made with milk containing no added vitamin A.
[11] Based on year-round average.

Courtesy of *Nutritive Values of Food*, U. S. Department of Agriculture, Home and Garden Bulletin No. 72.

DIETARY GUIDELINES FOR AMERICANS

The National Nutrition Monitoring and Related Research Act of 1990 requires that the Secretaries of Health and Human Services (HHS) and the U. S. Department of Agriculture (USDA) jointly issue a report, *Dietary Guidelines for Americans*, at least every five years.

At this time, the *Dietary Guidelines* has come to serve as the basis for nearly all nutrition information in the United States. While the Recommended Daily Dietary Allowances (RDA) address nutrients only, the *Dietary Guidelines* relates to food and behaviors and their impact on health.

The recommendations contained in the *Dietary Guidelines* are based on current scientific knowledge about the role of nutrition in maintaining health and minimizing disease risks. Periodical updates allow incorporation of new findings about the relationship between food and health.

The *Dietary Guidelines for Americans* are as follows in order of importance:

- Eat a variety of foods. Note that the emphasis in this guideline is on foods since they contain nutrients and other substances that promote health.
- Balance the food you eat with physical activity. Maintain or improve your weight.
- Choose a diet with plenty of grain products, vegetables, and fruits.
- Choose a diet low in fat, saturated fat, and cholesterol.
- Choose a diet moderate in sugars.
- Choose a diet moderate in salt and sodium.
- If you drink alcoholic beverages, do so in moderation. This guideline includes a list of persons who should not drink: (1) children or teens, (2) persons who cannot restrict their drinking to moderate levels, and (3) women who are pregnant or trying to become pregnant.

THE FOOD GUIDE PYRAMID

The graphic illustration of the *Dietary Guidelines for Americans* is the Food Guide Pyramid (Figure 13–1). If the age-related recommended number and size of servings of foods from the Food Guide Pyramid are consumed, the nutrient needs of children and adults should be met. A pattern of consuming the same foods over time provides the same nutrient strengths but also the same nutrient weaknesses.

The food groups that constitute the Food Guide Pyramid are:

- the Bread, Cereal, Rice, and Pasta Group
- the Vegetable Group
- the Fruit Group
- the Milk, Yogurt, and Cheese Group
- the Meat, Poultry, Fish, Dry Beans, Eggs, and Nuts Group
- the Fats, Oils, and Sweets Group

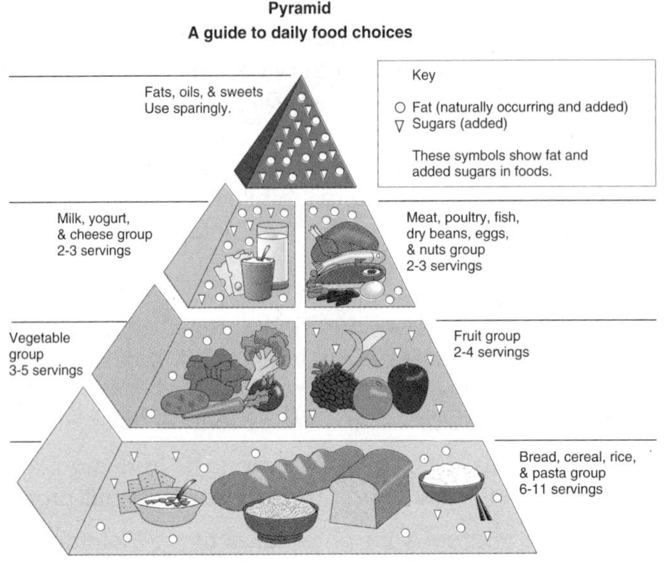

Figure 13–1 The USDA Food Guide Pyramid was designed to illustrate what Americans should eat each day. Courtesy of the U.S. Department of Agriculture.

The Bread, Cereal, Rice, and Pasta Group

Such foods as breads, breakfast cereals, pastas, and flour make up the Bread and Cereal Group. Food choices from this group should be whole grain or enriched products. Whole grain products retain all of the grain. Enriched breads and cereals are products that have been processed and specified amounts of nutrients have been added. The nutrients that are added are iron, thiamin, riboflavin, and niacin. The amounts of these added nutrients are equal to those found in the whole grain. Whole grain bread and cereals are better choices for children and adults. Some minerals and vitamins are removed in the processing of cereals that are not put back into enriched cereals. Whole grain products also provide needed fiber.

A serving from this group consists of one slice of bread, one cup of dry, ready-to-eat cereal, or 1/2 cup of cooked cereal or pasta. As with the other groups, the child's serving is one-half the adult serving. Four or more servings daily are recommended. The U. S. plan recommends 6 or more servings of bread and cereal.

Nutrient Summary: Bread, Cereal, Rice, and Pasta Group

Nutrient Strengths	*Nutrient Weaknesses*
Iron	Calcium
Thiamin	Vitamin A
Niacin	Vitamin C
Riboflavin	
Complex Carbohydrates	

Figure 13–2 Carrots, grapes, and crackers are popular choices from the food pyramid.

The Vegetable Group and the Fruit Group

The Vegetable Group and the Fruit Group indicate a separation of the "Fruits and Vegetable Group" of the Basic Four Food Groups. Careful study of the Pyramid reveals that more servings of vegetables (3–5) are recommended than of fruit (2–4). Vegetables are emphasized on the Food Guide Pyramid because they contribute notable amounts of minerals and vitamins, whereas fruits contribute mainly vitamins (Journal of American Dietetic Association, September, 1994) (Figure 13–2).

One example of the effort to promote increased consumption of vegetables and fruits is the "5 a Day for Better Health" campaign. The key points are:

- Eat five servings of vegetables and fruits a day.
- Eat at least one Vitamin C-rich selection every day, Table 13–4.

TABLE 13–4 Good to Excellent Sources of Vitamin C

Orange*	Tomatoes*
Orange Juice*	Grapefruit*
Strawberries*	Mustard greens
Cauliflower	Spinach
Broccoli	Cabbage
Sweet Peppers, red or green	Tangerine*

*May cause allergic reactions

TABLE 13–5 Good to Excellent Sources of Vitamin A

Cantaloupe	Winter Squash
Carrots	Greens
Pumpkin	Apricots
Sweet Potatoes	Watermelon*
Spinach	Broccoli

*May cause allergic reactions

- Eat at least one Vitamin A-rich selection every day, Table 13–5.
- Eat at least one high-fiber selection every day.
- Eat cabbage-family vegetables several times a week (i.e., cabbage, broccoli, cauliflower, brussels sprouts).

Fiber in the diet has received increasing attention. Very high fiber intake in childhood could have adverse effects. A practical recommendation for fiber intake for children over two years of age is the "Age + 5" rule. See Table 13–6 for food sources and amounts of fiber.

TABLE 13–6 Dietary Fiber Content of Some Commonly Eaten Foods

Food	Amount	Fiber (gm)
Cornflakes	1/2 cup	0.5
Oatmeal	1/4 cup	1.4
Wheat flakes	1/2 cup	1.5
Macaroni	1/2 cup	1.1
Bread, whole wheat	1/2 slice	0.8
Bread, white	1/2 slice	0.5
Graham crackers	1 square	0.7
Apple with skin	1/2	1.5
Banana	1/2	0.9
Raisins	1 Tbsp.	0.5
Potato, baked with skin	1/2	1.1
Green beans	1/4 cup	0.5
Pinto beans	1/2 cup	3.4

Courtesy of Pennington, J. A. T., *Bowes and Church's Food Values of Portions Commonly Used*. 1994. 16th ed. Philadelphia, PA. J. B. Lippincott Co.

Milk, Yogurt, and Cheese Group

This group includes milk and dairy products. Children should have a total of three cups of milk or the equivalent from this group daily. The servings may be divided into one-half cup portions in consideration of children's smaller appetites and capacity. Adults need two cups of milk or the equivalent daily. Equivalent foods include cheese, yogurt, ice cream, custards, and puddings. Equivalent amounts of foods may vary due to the addition of other ingredients such as fruit or sugar. Foods that provide *calcium* equal to that in one cup of milk are:

1 1/2 ounces cheddar cheese
1 cup pudding
1 3/4 cup ice cream
1 cup plain yogurt

Nutrient Summary: Milk, Yogurt, and Cheese Group

Nutrient Strengths	*Nutrient Weaknesses*
Calcium	Vitamin C
Protein	Iron
Riboflavin	

Meat, Poultry, Fish, Dry Beans, Eggs, and Nuts Group

The recommended daily amount from the Meat, Poultry, Fish, Dry Beans, Eggs, and Nuts Group is two or more servings. The amount of food in a serving varies with the age of the individual. Small children need and often will eat only 1 to 1 1/2 ounces in a serving, while the adult serving consists of 2 to 3 ounces of meat or equivalent. Beef, veal, pork, lamb, fish, and poultry are included in the Meat, Poultry, Fish, Dry Beans, Eggs, and Nuts Group. Other foods included in this group are eggs, legumes such as dry peas and beans, nuts, and nut butters. Cheese may also be substituted for meats; however, it should be remembered that cheeses do not contain iron, which is a nutrient strength of this group. The following foods contain *protein* equal to that in one ounce of meat:

1 egg
1 ounce of cheese
1/4 cup cottage cheese
1/2 cup dried peas or beans
2 tablespoons peanut butter

Nutrient Summary: Meat, Poultry, Fish, Dry Beans, Eggs, and Nuts Group

Nutrient Strengths	*Nutrient Weaknesses*
Protein	Calcium
Thiamin	Vitamin C
Riboflavin	Vitamin A
Niacin	
Iron	

TABLE 13–7 Comparison of Caloric Increase and Nutrient Decrease When Sugar and Fats Are Added to the Diet

	CALORIES	VITAMIN C
Apple, raw 3/#	80	6 mg
Applesauce, sweetened, 1 cup	230	3 mg
Apple pie, 1/7 pie	342	2 mg
Pie a la Mode, 1/7 plus 1/2 cup ice cream	480	2 mg

Courtesy of Home and Garden Bulletin No. 72.

Fats, Oils, and Sweets Group

The tip of the Pyramid is called the Fats, Oils, and Sweets Group. Most items in the tip are condiments or contribute no important nutrients. Examples of items in the tip of the Pyramid are butter or margarine, jelly, and honey. **Note:** Symbols for fat and sugar have been added. Circles on the Pyramid signify added or naturally occurring fat; inverted triangles signify added but not naturally occurring, sugar. The purpose of the symbols is to teach that fat and sugar are found in all food groups.

In general, the nutrient content of this group is low and the calorie content is high. The addition to the diet of large amounts of foods from the Fats, Oils, and Sweets Group can dilute the nutrient content of foods from the Pyramid. Table 13–7 illustrates the dilution of the Vitamin C in an apple by the addition of sugar and fat. Calorie content increases with the addition of sugar. Further increases in calories occur with the addition of fat and flour in making apple pie. At the same time the calories are increasing, the amount of Vitamin C present decreases.

NUTRITIONAL LABELING

The Nutritional Labeling and Education Act, passed in 1990, resulted in many changes in the labeling of food products. The food label was revised in 1994 and is regulated by the Food and Drug Administration (FDA) and the U. S. Department of Agriculture (USDA), Figure 13–3. This resulted in a label that provides:

- Easy-to-read nutrition information on packaged foods.
- Food labels must report serving sizes in commonly consumed amounts. This prevents using small serving sizes to make food products that are high in fat, cholesterol, sodium, or calories look better than they are.
- All foods must list all ingredients (in decreasing order relative to amount) on their label.
- *Percent Daily Values (%DV)* that show how a serving of food fits into a total day's diet. (This replaces the previously used USRDA.)
- *Nutrition claims* that mean the same on every product (see Figure 13–4).
- Voluntary information for the most commonly eaten fresh fruits and vegetables, and raw fish and cuts of meat. This information may appear on posters or in brochures in the same area as the food.

Nutrition Facts

Serving Size 3/4 cup (30g)
Servings Per Container about 15

Amount Per Serving	Cereal	Cereal with 1/2 cup Skim Milk
Calories	100	140
Calories from Fat	5	5
	% Daily Value**	
Total Fat 0.5g*	1%	1%
Saturated Fat 0g	0%	0%
Polyunsaturated Fat 0g		
Monounsaturated Fat 0g		
Cholesterol 0mg	0%	0%
Sodium 220mg	9%	12%
Potassium 190mg	5%	11%
Total Carbohydrate 24g	8%	10%
Dietary Fiber 5g	21%	21%
Soluble Fiber 1g		
Insoluble Fiber 4g		
Sugars 6g		
Other Carbohydrate 13g		
Protein 3g		
Vitamin A	15%	20%
Vitamin C	0%	2%
Calcium	0%	15%
Iron	45%	45%
Vitamin D	10%	25%
Thiamin	25%	30%
Riboflavin	25%	35%
Niacin	25%	25%
Vitamin B_6	25%	25%
Folate	25%	25%
Vitamin B_{12}	25%	35%
Phosphorus	15%	25%
Magnesium	15%	20%
Zinc	10%	15%
Copper	10%	10%

*Amount in Cereal. One half cup skim milk contributes an additional 40 calories. 65mg sodium. 200mg potassium. 6g total carbohydrate (6g sugars). and 4g protein.

**Percent Daily Values are based on a 2.000 calorie diet. Your daily values may be higher or lower depending on your calorie needs:

	Calories:	2.000	2.500
Total Fat	Less than	65g	80g
Saturated Fat	Less than	20g	25g
Cholesterol	Less than	300mg	300mg
Sodium	Less than	2.400mg	2.400mg
Potassium		3,500mg	3.500mg
Total Carbohydrate		300g	375g
Dietary Fiber		25g	30g

Figure 13–3 Food label.

WHAT SOME CLAIMS MEAN

high-protein: at least 10 grams (g) high-quality protein per serving

good source of calcium: at least 100 milligrams (mg) calcium per serving

more iron: at least 1.8 mg more iron per serving than reference food. (Label will say 10 percent more of the Daily Value for iron.)

fat-free: less than 0.5 g fat per serving

low-fat: 3 g or less fat per serving. (If the serving size is 30 g or less or 2 tablespoons or less, 3 g or less fat per 50 g of the food.)

reduced or fewer calories: at least 25 percent fewer calories per serving than the reference food

sugar-free: less than 0.5 g sugar per serving

light (two meanings):

- one-third fewer calories or half the fat of the reference food. (If 50 percent or more of the food's calories are from fat, the fat must be reduced by 50 percent.)
- a "low-calorie," "low-fat" food whose sodium content has been reduced by 50 percent of the reference food.

Figure 13–4 Definitions of commonly used food labeling terms. Courtesy of FDA Consumer, September 1995.

CALORIES FROM FAT

Labels now provide both the amount of fat and the amount of saturated fat. Also provided are calories from fat. With the amount of fat and calories from fat given on the label, determining the percent of calories from fat is simple.

$$\text{Percent of calories from fat} = \frac{\text{fat calories/serving}}{\text{total calories/serving}} \times 100$$

To calculate the number of calories from fat, use this formula:

$$\text{calories from fat} = \text{grams (g) of fat/serving} \times 9 \text{ (cal/g)}$$

The following calculations of percent of calories from fat in some selected foods will show how fat content reports on labels may be misleading:

Cheddar cheese—1 ounce = 115 calories and 9 g of fat:
Calories from fat = 9 × 9 = 81
Percent calories from fat = 81/115 × 100 = 70%

Eggs—one egg = 75 calories and 6 g of fat:
Calories from fat = 6 × 9 = 54
Percent calories from fat = 54/75 × 100 = 72%

90% fat-free ground beef—3 ounces = 185 calories and 10 g fat:
Calories from fat = 10 × 9 = 90
Percent calories from fat = 90/185 × 100 = 49%

For all of these examples, the grams of fat (9, 6, and 10) are low, yet they all presented more than 30 percent of calories from fat.

The recommendation that only 30 percent of calories should come from fat does not mean that all healthy food choices must derive less than 30 percent of their calories from fat. This would virtually eliminate all red meat and most dairy products. However, it does mean that if you eat a lean hamburger with 49 percent fat-calories it might be better to skip the french fries at 47 percent fat-calories and substitute an apple, banana, or orange with less than 10 percent of calories from fat.

The calculations for percent of fat-calories, seem tedious at first, but after a few calculations you will find that you can skim a label and judge its nutrient density or fat-calorie level. You will not need to take a calculator with you when you go grocery shopping.

Summary

Nutrition is the study of nutrients and how the human body uses them. Foods serve as sources of nutrients; the body uses the nutrients from foods.

Various food guidelines ease the problem of knowing which foods and how much of them to select to provide adequate amounts of essential nutrients.

The Food Guide Pyramid divides foods into groups that contain similar kinds and amounts of nutrients.

Recommended Daily Dietary Allowances are guidelines for the amounts of nutrients needed by most healthy persons, divided according to age and sex groups.

The *Dietary Guidelines for Americans* are suggestions to help people eat nutritiously and yet deal with the harmful effects of overnutrition.

The major factor to remember in the use of any guideline is the selection of as wide a variety of foods as possible.

Suggested Activities

1. Using the following format, summarize each of the food groups from the Food Guide Pyramid:
   a. Recommended number of servings
      - child
      - adult (where different)
   b. Recommended size of serving
      - child
      - adult
   c. Nutrient strengths
   d. Nutrient weaknesses
2. Plan a day's diet for a 4-year-old child. Include the recommended number of servings and the appropriate serving sizes from the Food Guide Pyramid.
3. Assume that a child is allergic to citrus fruit and strawberries (common food allergies). What fruit and/or vegetable choices could be substituted to provide adequate Vitamin C?
4. Visit a child care center. Analyze the posted menus according to the Food Guide Pyramid. Identify nutrient strengths of each food served.

Chapter Review

A. Multiple Choice. Select the best answer.

1. The Recommended Daily Dietary Allowances are:
   a. recommended amounts of food
   b. required amounts of food
   c. recommended amounts of nutrients
   d. minimum amounts of nutrients

2. The Recommended Daily Dietary Allowances are for
   a. children only
   b. adults only
   c. individuals four years of age or older
   d. nearly all healthy people
3. *Dietary Guidelines for Americans*
   a. makes recommendations for nutrients for adults
   b. ensures an adequate food supply
   c. is based on current research relating food choices to health
   d. recommends the use of supplements
4. *Dietary Guidelines for Americans* includes all but
   a. eat a variety of foods
   b. take supplements to provide additional nutrients
   c. balance food intake with physical activity
   d. reduce fat intake to 30 percent or less or total calories
5. The Food Guide Pyramid is the graphic illustration of
   a. the Recommended Daily Dietary Allowances
   b. the Basic Four Food Groups
   c. the *Dietary Guidelines for Americans*
   d. Percent Daily Values
6. The nutrient strengths of the Vegetable Group and the Fruit Group are
   a. calcium and protein
   b. thiamin, niacin, and fiber
   c. Vitamin C, Vitamin A, and fiber
   d. Vitamin B_{12}
7. The food group that is the major contributor of calcium to the diet is the
   a. Vegetable Group and the Fruit Group
   b. Milk, Yogurt, and Cheese Group
   c. Meat, Poultry, Fish, Dry Beans, Eggs, and Nuts Group
   d. Bread, Cereal, Rice, and Pasta Group
8. *Dietary Guidelines for Americans* recommends no more than 30 percent of calories come from fat. The group or groups that provide the least fat are
   a. the Milk, Yogurt, and Cheese Group
   b. the Meat, Poultry, Fish, Dry Beans, Eggs, and Nuts Group
   c. the Vegetable Group and the Fruit Group
   d. the Fats, Oils, and Sweets Group
9. Percent Daily Values
   a. are the same for children as for adults
   b. aid in evaluating the nutrient content of foods
   c. are stated in the *Dietary Guidelines for Americans*
   d. are part of the ingredient label on food packages

10. Food X yields 180 calories per serving and has 90 calories from fat. The percent of calories from fat is
    a. 10 percent
    b. 18 percent
    c. 50 percent
    d. 90 percent

B. Briefly answer the following questions:

1. Betsy, age 3 1/2 years, drinks milk to the exclusion of adequate amounts of food from other food groups. What nutrient is Betsy receiving in excess? What two nutrients are most likely to be deficient?
2. Jason, age 4 years, refuses to eat vegetables. He will occasionally accept a small serving of applesauce but no other fruits. What two nutrients are probably deficient in Jason's diet?
3. Jeremy, age 3 years, is allergic to milk and dairy products. What nutrient is deficient in Jeremy's diet?

C. Match the foods in column I to the appropriate food group in column II. Some foods may include more than one food group.

Column I	Column II
1. navy beans	a. Milk, Cheese, and Yogurt Group
2. rice	b. Meat, Poultry, Fish, Dry Beans, Eggs, and Nuts Group
3. spaghetti	c. Bread, Cereal, Rice, and Pasta Group
4. hamburger pizza	d. Vegetable Group/Fruit Group
5. macaroni and cheese	e. Fats, Oils, and Sweets Group
6. peanut butter sandwich	
7. french fries	
8. ice cream	
9. popcorn	
10. carbonated beverages	

References

Nutritive Values of Foods. Home and Garden Bulletin No. 72. Washington, DC: U. S. Department of Agriculture.

Pennington, J. A. T. 1994. *Bowes and Church's Food Values of Portions Commonly Used.* 16th ed. Philadelphia, PA: J. B. Lippincott Co.

Position of the American Dietetic Association: Vegetarian Diets. 1993. Journal of the American Dietetic Association: 1317–1319.

Additional Reading

Christian, J. L. and Geigher, J. L. 1988. *Nutrition for Living.* 2nd ed. Menlo Park, CA: Benjamin Cummings Publishing Company.

Composition of Foods. Agriculture Handbook No. 8. Washington, DC: U. S. Department of Agriculture.

The Food Guide Pyramid. 1992. Washington, DC: U. S. Department of Agriculture.

Franz, M. J. *Fast Food Facts.* 1994. Minneapolis, MN: Chronimed Publishing.

Hamilton E. N., Whitney, E., and Sizer, F. S. *Nutrition: Concepts and Controversies.* 1991. St. Paul, MN: West Publishing Co.

Health and Diet Pro for Windows. 1992. Digital System Research Inc.

Home and Garden Bulletin No. 252. Washington, DC: U. S. Department of Agriculture.

Nutrition and Your Health: Dietary Guidelines for Americans. 1990. Washington, DC: U. S. Department of Agriculture.

Recommended Nutrient Intakes for Canadians. 1990. Bureau of Nutritional Services. Ottawa, Canada.

Chapter 14

Nutrients That Provide Energy

(carbohydrates, fats, and proteins)

Terms to Know

energy
calories
enzyme/coenzyme
gram
basal metabolic rate
thermic energy of food
digestion
absorption
metabolism
linoleic acid/linolenic acid
PUFA

Objectives

After studying this chapter, you should be able to:

- Identify the three classes of nutrients that supply energy.
- State the amount of energy supplied by each class of nutrients.
- List three factors that determine individual energy requirements.
- Identify foods containing good sources of energy-supplying nutrients.
- Calculate daily caloric requirements of a child based on the child's weight.
- Plan a day's diet eliminating refined sucrose.
- Plan a day's diet that meets the recommended 30 percent of calories from fat and is low in saturated fatty acids and cholesterol.

Energy is generally defined as the ability to do work. Examples of work done by the body are (1) moving the body, (2) building new tissues, (3) maintaining body temperature, and

(4) digesting, absorbing, and metabolizing food. Energy is required for all body functions. In terms of survival, the need for energy is second only to the need for oxygen and water.

The amount of potential energy in a food is expressed in *calories*, e.g., a one-cup serving of ice cream supplies 185 calories. The energy cost of a given activity is also measured and expressed in calories, e.g., swimming for 30 minutes expends about 150 calories.

Carbohydrates, fats, and proteins found in foods supply energy for the body's activities. Vitamins, minerals, and water do not supply calories but they are essential for the functioning of *enzymes*, *coenzymes*, and hormones. Enzymes and coenzymes are nutrient-containing substances that initiate and participate in the many metabolic reactions that are necessary for the release of energy from carbohydrates, fats, and proteins. Hormones, while not directly involved in energy-releasing reactions, do regulate many of these reactions. The caloric value of any given food is determined by its carbohydrate, fat, and protein content. The relative numbers of calories contained in carbohydrates, fats, and proteins are:

- carbohydrates—4 calories per gram
- fat—9 calories per gram
- proteins—4 calories per gram

A *gram* is a metric unit of measurement for weight. There are 28 grams in one ounce, and 454 grams in one pound. A metal paper clip weighs about one gram.

Every individual has different energy requirements; these requirements vary slightly on a day-to-day basis. Individual energy requirements are determined by:

- basal metabolic rate (BMR)
- physical activity
- energy spent to release energy from food (thermic energy of food)

The *basal metabolic rate* (BMR) is a term used to describe the energy needed just to carry on vital involuntary body processes. The BMR is a measure of the energy required for blood circulation, breathing, cell activity, body temperature maintenance, heartbeat, and other involuntary activities. It does not measure voluntary activity. For most children and adults, the energy required to meet basal metabolic needs is greater than energy expended for voluntary physical activity.

Physical activity is the aspect of energy need that is subject to the greatest conscious control. For instance, participation in tennis or swimming as a recreational activity requires far more energy than reading or watching television, Figure 14–1. Children should be encouraged to participate in physical activity. The benefits of physical activity include motor development, the opportunity for socialization, a sense of accomplishment, and increased fitness. The additional calories required by increased physical activity provide the opportunity to increase food intake and thus make it easier to meet other nutrient requirements.

Thermic energy of food refers to the energy required to *digest*, *absorb*, transport, and *metabolize* nutrients in food. This factor accounts for approximately 10 percent of the total energy requirement.

Figure 14–1 Quiet activities require lesser amounts of energy than more strenuous activities.

Growing children need more energy per unit of body weight than adults, Figure 14-2. Growth requires energy for division and/or enlargement of existing cells (Alford and Bogle, 1982). Rates of growth, physical activity, and body size cause variations in the amount of energy needed by individual children. The number of calories needed daily is calculated on the basis of normal body weight. A four-year-old child needs

Figure 14–2 The energy needs of active growing children are relatively greater than those of an adult.

approximately 40 calories per pound of body weight. (The energy needs of infants are detailed in Chapter 17.) For comparison, a moderately active adult female requires approximately 18 calories per pound; a moderately active adult male needs approximately 21 calories per pound. (Moderately active has been described as equal time "on the feet and on the seat.")

Balancing the number of calories eaten with the number of calories expended results in stable body weight (see *Dietary Guidelines for Americans).* Eating fewer calories than are needed leads to weight loss. The result of eating too few calories is more serious in growing children than in adults. Too few calories can result in slowed growth as a result of burning body tissue to provide needed energy for body function. Children need sufficient calories from carbohydrates and fat to spare protein that is needed for growth. For children as well as adults, it is better to get one half or more of their calories from carbohydrates; starch is the preferred carbohydrate because its food sources contribute needed vitamins, minerals, and fiber as well as energy.

Too many calories consumed over a period of time may lead to obesity. Obese children are often less active than their slimmer playmates, and may require fewer calories due to their lower activity level. The obese child's bulkier body can lead to less coordinated movements and greater danger of accidents. Obese children are often teased by their playmates and excluded from play activities. Exclusion from play groups often adds to problems encountered by the obese child, such as poor self-image, decreased fitness level, and fewer opportunities for socialization. The child with a weight problem should be encouraged to exercise and offered adequate amounts of nutrient-dense foods, Table 14–1. Calories should not be drastically reduced, as reduction of calories may result in reduction of essential nutrients (*Manual of Pediatric Nutrition*, 1990). One safe plan is to adjust calorie intake to keep body weight stable while the child grows linearly. Over time, this will bring the weight:height ratio back into a normal range.

According to the 1995 *Dietary Guidelines for Americans* children need enough food for proper growth. Physical activity, not food restriction, is recommended to encourage weight loss. Children on weight-reduction programs must be under the supervision of a physician to ensure that their nutritional needs are met.

TABLE 14–1 Tips for Managing an Overweight Child

- Increasing exercise often is the most effective way to help a child control weight.
- Slight changes in snacks can help a child control weight. For example, offer fat-free animal crackers rather than a chocolate cookie or chips.

Examples of pediatric weight control programs are:

- Weight Watchers®
- Shapedown

CARBOHYDRATES AS ENERGY SOURCES

Carbohydrates that yield four calories per gram should be primary sources of energy for children. At least half the energy required by a child should be derived from carbohydrates. A child requiring 1600 calories should derive at least 800 calories from carbohydrates; eight hundred calories are supplied by 200 grams of carbohydrates. Many experts recommend a minimum intake for adults of 125 grams (500 calories) of carbohydrates daily. Children need more, but the exact minimum amount needed is not known. The main portion of carbohydrates should be complex with no more than 10 percent of calories coming from refined sugar.

Foods that contain complex and unprocessed carbohydrates are wise choices for children's snacks. Fresh fruits and vegetables, fruit and vegetable juices, and whole grain products such as breads, cereals, and crackers are nutritious and readily accepted snack foods for growing children. Carbohydrates are present in foods in simple and complex forms.

Consumption of refined sugar has increased since 1900; the use of complex carbohydrates, such as starches, has dropped during that same period. Current nutrition recommendations suggest increased amounts of complex carbohydrates and decreased amounts of refined sugars. This simply means less sugar and more starch and fiber from the Bread, Cereal, Rice, and Pasta Group, the Vegetable Group, and the Fruit Group. Three general classes of carbohydrates are found in foods: simple sugars, compound sugars, and complex carbohydrates.

Simple Sugars

Simple sugars consist of one sugar unit that needs no further digestion prior to absorption. Most simple sugars result from the digestion of more complex carbohydrates. Examples of simple sugars are:

- glucose
- fructose
- galactose

Glucose is the form in which sugar is used by body cells. However, most glucose in the blood is a result of digestion of more complex carbohydrates.

Fructose is present in honey and high-fructose corn syrup; it is sweeter than all other sugars. In some cases, smaller amounts of fructose may be used to give a desired degree of sweetness.

Galactose is not found free in foods. It results from the digestion of "milk sugar."

Compound Sugars

Compound sugars are made up of two simple sugars joined together. Compound sugars must be digested to their component simple sugars before they can be absorbed and utilized by the body. Two important examples of compound sugars are:

- sucrose
- lactose

In its refined form, sucrose is commonly known at table sugar. Sucrose is found in sugar beets and sugar cane and in fruits, vegetables, and honey. When sucrose occurs in fruits and vegetables it is accompanied by other essential nutrients such as vitamins, minerals, and water, Figure 14–3. Refined sucrose, or table sugar, is the cause of concern in several aspects of health. Refined table sugar contributes no nutrients—only calories. For this reason, calories from table sugar are frequently called "empty calories." Eating too many empty calories can lead to obesity accompanied by a deficiency of some essential nutrients. Children who are allowed to eat too many foods containing refined sugar may not be hungry for more healthful foods containing the nutrients they need.

Refined sucrose has also been linked to tooth decay in children. Other important factors contributing to tooth decay are the stickiness of the food containing the sugar, the frequency of eating, the frequency of toothbrushing, whether the sugar is contained in a meal with other foods or in a snack, and whether the sugar-containing food is accompanied by a beverage.

Lactose is found in milk and is referred to as "milk sugar." it is the only carbohydrate found in an animal-source food. Lactose occurs in milk of mammals, including breast milk. It has advantages over other sugars in that lactose aids in

Figure 14–3 Sugar in fruits is accompanied by other essential nutrients.

establishing and maintaining beneficial intestinal bacteria. Calcium is more efficiently used by the body if lactose is also present. Fortunately, calcium and lactose occur in the same food—milk.

While usually a beneficial sugar, lactose can present problems to some individuals. Some persons do not produce the enzyme to break lactose down to its component simple sugars that can be absorbed. This lactose intolerance may cause intestinal discomfort, cramping, gas, and diarrhea. Often small amounts of milk (1–2 cups a day in small feedings) are tolerated. Dairy products such as yogurt and buttermilk are tolerated better than milk. Adults tend to display more severe lactose intolerance than do children.

Complex Carbohydrates

Complex carbohydrates are composed of many units of simple sugar joined together. Complex carbohydrates must be broken down to their component simple sugars before the body can absorb and use them. Digestion of only one complex carbohydrate can result in thousands of simple sugars. Complex carbohydrates that are important to human nutrition are:

- starch
- cellulose
- glycogen

Starches are the only digestible complex carbohydrates found in foods. They are found in large amounts in grains, legumes, and root vegetables such as potatoes and breads and cereals. When contained in these foods, starches are accompanied by vitamins and minerals that the body needs. Starches are desirable components of a healthful diet.

Cellulose is an indigestible complex carbohydrate. Humans cannot digest cellulose; therefore, it cannot be absorbed and used by body cells. Cellulose, because it cannot be absorbed, is a good source of insoluble fiber that increases the rate of transit of food through the intestinal tract and increases the frequency of elimination of intestinal waste material. Cellulose is found in whole grains, nuts, legumes, and fruits and vegetables. It is also thought to provide some detergent effect to teeth thus aiding good dental health.

Another complex carbohydrate of physiological importance is glycogen. Glycogen is often referred to as animal starch. It is the form in which carbohydrate is stored in the body for future conversion into sugar and subsequent use for performing body activity.

The use of artificial sweeteners to replace sugar as a means of reducing calorie intake has become a common practice. The three FDA-approved artificial sweeteners are saccharin, aspartame (Nutrasweet™) and acesulfame (approved in 1988). Used in moderation, these sweeteners are accepted as safe for adult consumption. However, their use in children's diets is questionable. Children with phenylketonuria (PKU), a genetic disease characterized by an inability to properly metabolize the essential amino acid phenylalanine, must not use aspartame. It contains phenylalanine. Accumulation of this toxic substance may cause severe and irreversible brain damage.

FATS AS ENERGY SOURCES

Fats are the richest food source of energy, supplying nine calories per gram consumed. Foods in which fats are readily identified are butter, margarine, shortening, oils, and salad dressings. Less obvious sources of fats are meats, whole milk, egg yolks, nuts, and nut butters. Fruits and vegetables contain little fat; with the exception of the avocado, which is quite rich in fat. Bread and cereal products are naturally low in fat. However, the many baked goods such as cakes, pies, doughnuts, and cookies that use grain products are high in added fat. Some dietary fat is required for good health. Recommendations have been made to reduce average fat intake to about 30 percent of total calories. The *Dietary Guidelines for Americans* (1995) advises that after age two, children "should gradually adopt a diet that, by about five years of age contains no more than 30% of calories from fat." For a child requiring 1600 calories, this means 480 calories or 50–55 grams of fat in the diet. This is equivalent to approximately four tablespoons of butter or oil.

Although they provide more than twice as much energy per gram as carbohydrates, fats are a less desirable energy source for children. Fats are harder to digest than carbohydrates and are accompanied by fewer essential nutrients. Fats should not be reduced below the level of providing 30 percent of calories because fats perform important functions for the child:

- allow normal growth and development of brain and nerve tissues.
- provide the essential fatty acids (**linoleic** and **linolenic**).
- are carriers of the required fat-soluble vitamins.
- allow infants and children with limited stomach capacity to meet their calorie needs.

The practice of lowering a very young child's fat intake through the use of skim milk is questionable. Most authorities believe that this practice may lead to insufficient calorie intake and essential fatty acid (EFA) deficiency. In addition, skim milk may provide excessive intakes of protein and minerals, resulting in difficulty in excreting minerals or urea (Williams and Caliendo, 1984). Children under two years of age should not be given skim milk in an effort to lower fat. Beyond 2 years of age, low fat (2%) milk may be given and might be advised for a child if there is a high incidence of cardiovascular disease (CVD) among adult relatives.

Before fats present in foods can provide energy they must undergo digestion and absorption into the body. Digestion of dietary fats produces:

- fatty acids
- glycerol

The resulting fatty acids and glycerol can be absorbed for use by the body. Fatty acids in foods are either saturated or unsaturated.

Fats found in animal-source foods such as meat, milk, and eggs contain fatty acids that are saturated. Fats containing predominantly saturated fatty acids are solid at room temperature, and are often accompanied by cholesterol. Cholesterol and saturated fats have been extensively investigated as undesirable dietary components. However, after years of study, few definite conclusions have been reached regarding the role of dietary cholesterol in cardiovascular disease or the advisability of lowering the saturated fatty acid and cholesterol intake of children. It is important to remember that cholesterol is found only in animal-source food fats. Do not equate high fat with high cholesterol. For example, coconut derives 83 percent of its calories from fat and 89 percent of its fatty acids are saturated, but it has no cholesterol.

Unsaturated fats are usually soft at room temperature or are in oil form. Monounsaturated fatty acids (MUFA), which have only one point of unsaturation, are currently being reported to be most effective in controlling the kind and amount of fat and cholesterol circulating in the blood. Thus olive oil and canola oil, high in MUFA, are recommended for use by CVD-prone persons.

Fats found in plant-source foods such as corn oil or sunflower oil contain mostly unsaturated fatty acids. Many plant oils are polyunsaturated, which means the fatty acids contain numerous unfilled attachment sites. Polyunsaturated fatty acids are often called *PUFAs*. Linoleic and linolenic acids are polyunsaturated fatty acids that are essential for all humans, but are needed in greater amounts for infants and children than for adults. These essential fatty acids cannot be produced by the body and so must be obtained from food sources. Plant-source foods are better sources of these essential fatty acids than animal-source foods and do not give cholesterol. Protein links with fat to produce lipoproteins, which are involved in the transport of fat and cholesterol in the blood. A high blood level of High Density Lipoproteins (HDLs), which have a high ratio of protein to fat, are currently considered to reduce the risk of cardiovascular disease.

PROTEINS AS ENERGY SOURCES

Proteins are the third class of nutrients that the body can use as an energy source. Proteins supply four calories per gram; the same amount of energy as that derived from carbohydrates. "Eating protein to meet energy needs... represents a waste like burning furniture for heat when firewood is available" (Longacre, 1976). Proteins must be digested to their component amino acids prior to absorption and utilization by the body.

Each protein is unique in the number, arrangement, and specific amino acids from which it is built. Since proteins (amino acids) function as materials to build body tissues and as regulators of body functions, they will be discussed in detail in subsequent chapters.

Summary

Energy is defined as the ability to do work. Carbohydrates, proteins, and fats in foods are sources of energy for the body, Table 14–2. Energy needs vary from individual to individual; children need more energy per pound of body weight than adults. Individual energy needs are based on (1) basal metabolic rate, (2) physical activity, and (3) energy spent to get energy from food (thermic energy of food).

TABLE 14–2 Summary of Energy-Supplying Nutrients

NUTRIENT	CALORIES PER GRAM	CONVERSION NEEDED FOR USE IN BODY	FOOD SOURCES
Carbohydrate	4		
Simple sugars		none needed	
glucose			honey, some fruits and vegetables, corn syrup
fructose			honey, fruits, and high fructose corn syrup
galactose			none
Compound sugars		simple sugars	
sucrose			sugar beets, sugar cane, honey, fruits, vegetables
lactose			milk
Complex carbohydrates		simple sugars	
starch			grains, legumes, root vegetables
cellulose	0	nondigestible	whole grains, nuts, legumes, fruits, vegetables
glycogen	0		none
Fat	9	fatty acids and glycerol	
saturated			meats, eggs, milk and dairy products
unsaturated			plant-source foods, corn oil, vegetable oils
Protein	4	amino acids	meats, eggs, legumes, dairy products

Carbohydrates supply four calories per gram. Carbohydrates occur in several forms: simple sugars, compound sugars, and complex carbohydrates. Sugars, starches, and cellulose are carbohydrates that are important in foods.

Fats supply nine calories per gram. Fatty acids are either saturated or unsaturated. Oils, dairy products, eggs, and meats are sources of fat. Unsaturated fatty acids are important to infants and children as a source of the two essential fatty acids.

Proteins supply four calories per gram. Proteins are composed of amino acids and are found in meats, eggs, legumes, and dairy products.

Suggested Activities

1. Using the cereal label given in Figure 14–4, determine the following:
   a. the number of calories derived from carbohydrate
   b. the approximate percentage of total calories derived from:
      (1) starches and related carbohydrates
      (2) sucrose and other sugars

Nutrition Facts

Serving Size 3/4 cup (30g)
Servings Per Container about 15

Amount Per Serving	Cereal	Cereal with 1/2 cup Skim Milk
Calories	100	140
Calories from Fat	5	5
	% Daily Value**	
Total Fat 0.5g*	**1%**	**1%**
Saturated Fat 0g	**0%**	**0%**
Polyunsaturated Fat 0g		
Monounsaturated Fat 0g		
Cholesterol 0mg	**0%**	**0%**
Sodium 220mg	**9%**	**12%**
Potassium 190mg	**5%**	**11%**
Total Carbohydrate 24g	**8%**	**10%**
Dietary Fiber 5g	**21%**	**21%**
Soluble Fiber 1g		
Insoluble Fiber 4g		
Sugars 6g		
Other Carbohydrate 13g		
Protein 3g		
Vitamin A	15%	20%
Vitamin C	0%	2%
Calcium	0%	15%
Iron	45%	45%
Vitamin D	10%	25%
Thiamin	25%	30%
Riboflavin	25%	35%
Niacin	25%	25%
Vitamin B_6	25%	25%
Folate	25%	25%
Vitamin B_{12}	25%	35%
Phosphorus	15%	25%
Magnesium	15%	20%
Zinc	10%	15%
Copper	10%	10%

*Amount in Cereal. One half cup skim milk contributes an additional 40 calories. 65mg sodium. 200mg potassium. 6g total carbohydrate (6g sugars). and 4g protein

**Percent Daily Values are based on a 2.000 calorie diet. Your daily values may be higher or lower depending on your calorie needs:

	Calories:	2.000	2.500
Total Fat	Less than	65g	80g
Saturated Fat	Less than	20g	25g
Cholesterol	Less than	300mg	300mg
Sodium	Less than	2.400mg	2.400mg
Potassium		3,500mg	3.500mg
Total Carbohydrate		300g	375g
Dietary Fiber		25g	30g

Figure 14–4 Cereal label

Is this cereal predominantly starch or sucrose? Why is the amount of total carbohydrate increased with the addition of milk? Do starches and complex carbohydrates increase with the addition of milk?

2. Using the cereal label given in Figure 14–4, determine those ingredients that contribute to total carbohydrates. Further classify those ingredients that contribute to sucrose or compound sugars. Hint: Dextrose, corn syrup, malt syrup, and corn sugar are all forms of simple or compound sugars.
3. Calculate the caloric requirement of a 4-year-old child who weighs 42 pounds.
4. Determine the number of calories in a serving of food that contributes the following:
   carbohydrate—12 grams
   protein—8 grams
   fat—10 grams

Chapter Review

A. Multiple Choice. Select the best answer.

1. Energy is defined as
   a. running and playing
   b. activity
   c. physical activity
   d. the ability to do work
2. Nutrients that supply energy are
   a. carbohydrates, proteins, and water
   b. carbohydrates, fats, and vitamins
   c. carbohydrates, fats, and proteins
   d. carbohydrates, proteins, and vitamins
3. A food that has 20 grams of carbohydrates and 2 grams of protein yields how many calories?
   a. 198 calories
   b. 188 calories
   c. 88 calories
   d. 98 calories
4. The factor affecting energy requirements that may be consciously controlled by the individual is
   a. basal metabolic rate
   b. physical activity
   c. energy spent to get energy from food
   d. none of the above

5. A four-year-old child weighing 40 pounds needs approximately
   a. 1200 calories daily
   b. 1900 calories daily
   c. 800 calories daily
   d. 1600 calories daily
6. Energy cannot be derived from energy-supplying nutrients without the help of
   a. vitamins
   b. minerals
   c. water
   d. all of these
7. The food combination that contains the most carbohydrates is
   a. butter, milk, corn oil
   b. bread, fruits, vegetables, meat
   c. bread, fruits, vegetables, milk
8. The food combination that contains the most protein is
   a. vegetables, milk, eggs
   b. meat, milk, eggs
   c. bread, fruits, vegetables, meat
   d. bread, fruits, vegetables, milk
9. The food combination that contains the most fat is
   a. butter, milk, corn oil
   b. meat, milk, eggs
   c. bread, fruits, vegetables, meat
   d. bread, fruits, vegetables, milk
10. At least half of the calories in a child's diet should be derived from
    a. protein
    b. carbohydrate
    c. fat
11. The nutrient that provides the greatest amount of energy per gram is
    a. protein
    b. carbohydrate
    c. fat
    d. vitamins
12. The nutrient that can perform functions other than supplying energy is
    a. protein
    b. carbohydrate
    c. fat
    d. none of these
13. Fats found in beef, lamb, and butter contain more
    a. polyunsaturated fatty acids
    b. cholesterol
    c. saturated fatty acids
    d. linoleic acid
    e. a and b
    f. b and c

14. Fatty acids found in vegetable oils, such as corn oil, are predominantly
    a. polyunsaturated
    b. saturated
    c. solid at room temperature
    d. none of these
15. Cholesterol is found in
    a. eggs
    b. butter
    c. foods of animal origin
    d. all of these
16. Proteins are composed of
    a. polyunsaturated fatty acids
    b. unsaturated fatty acids
    c. amino acids
    d. simple sugars
17. Proteins can be used to
    a. supply energy
    b. build body tissue
    c. regulate body functions
    d. all of these
18. Cellulose adds bulk to the diet because it
    a. is indigestible
    b. contains saturated fatty acids
    c. is composed of amino acids
    d. is easily digested

B. Match the terms in column II to the correct phrase in column I.

Column I	Column II
1. a simple sugar	a. amino acids
2. digestible complex carbohydrate	b. cellulose
3. found in meats, dairy products, legumes, and eggs	c. protein
4. building blocks of proteins	d. carbohydrate
5. found in grains, fruits, vegetables, and milk products	e. glucose
	f. fats
6. richest source of energy	g. starch
7. indigestible complex carbohydrate	h. sucrose
8. table sugar	

C. Case Study

Terry, age 5, has several decayed teeth. His dentist has suggested a program of good dental hygiene plus limiting his intake of refined sucrose.

Plan a day's diet for Terry that contains at least 200 grams of carbohydrates without any refined sucrose (table sugar). Use the following *average* amounts of carbohydrates:

bread, cereals, pastas	15 grams/slice or ounce
fruits and juices	10 grams/1/2 adult serving
starchy vegetables	10 grams/1/2 adult serving
milk	6 grams/1/2 cup

References

Alford, B., and Bogle, M.L. 1982. *Nutrition During the Life Cycle.* Englewood Cliffs, NJ: Prentice Hall, Inc.

Dietary Guidelines for Americans, 1995. Washington, DC: U. S. Department of Health and Human Services and U. S. Department of Agriculture.

Longacre, D. J. 1976. *More-with-Less Cookbook.* Scottsdale, PA: Herald Press.

Manual of Pediatric Nutrition. 1990. St. Paul, MN: Twin Cities District Dietetic Association.

Williams, E. R., and Caliendo, M. A. 1984. *Nutrition: Principles, Issues and Applications.* New York: McGraw Hill Book Company.

Additional Reading

Christian, J. L., and Geiger, J. L. 1988. *Nutrition for Living.* Menlo Park, CA: Benjamin/Cummings Publishing Co.

Hamilton, E. M. N., Whitney, E. N., and Sizer, F. S. 1991. *Nutrition: Concepts and Controversies.* St. Paul, MN: West Pub. Co.

Hegarty, V. 1988. *Decisions in Nutrition.* St. Louis, MO: C. V. Mosby Co.

Manhan, L. K. and Arlin, M. 1992. *Krause's Food, Nutrition, and Diet Therapy.* Philadelphia, PA: W. B. Saunders Co.

Satter, E. 1987. *How to Get Your Kid to Eat...But Not Too Much.* Palo Alto, CA: Bull Publishing Company.

Wardlow, G. W., and Insel, P. M. 1990. *Perspectives in Nutrition.* St. Louis, MO: C V. Mosby Co.

Chapter 15

Nutrients that Promote Growth of Body Tissues

(proteins, minerals, and water)

Terms to Know

amino acids
complete protein
incomplete protein
complementary proteins
minerals
collagen
hemoglobin
iron-deficiency anemia

Objectives

After studying this chapter, you should be able to:

- State how growth occurs.
- Name three classes of nutrients that promote growth of body tissue and list food sources for each.
- Describe the role that proteins, minerals, and water play in body growth.
- Differentiate between nonessential and essential amino acids.
- Identify food sources for complete protein and for incomplete protein.
- Identify examples of complementary incomplete protein combinations.

Growth may be defined as an increase in physical size of either the entire body or of any body part. Growth may occur by (1) an increase in the number of cells, or by (2) an increase in the size of individual cells. At various stages of the child's life, either or both types of growth may be occurring.

Infancy and early childhood are periods of rapid growth, Figure 15–1. During the first six months of life, infants can be expected to approximately double their birth weight. By the end of the first year, their birth length should have increased by 50 percent. Birth weight and length are the baselines for evaluating infant growth.

PROTEINS FOR GROWTH

Proteins play an important role in growth. Protein is the material from which all body cells are built. Approximately 15 percent of body weight is protein. Examples of types of body tissues that consist of large amounts of protein are muscles, glands, organs, bones, blood, and skin.

Proteins are composed of hundreds of individual units called *amino acids*. The human body is able to manufacture some of the amino acids it needs to build proteins; these amino acids are termed nonessential amino acids. Amino acids that the body cannot manufacture in needed amounts must be provided by proteins in foods; these amino acids are termed essential amino acids.

When all essential amino acids occur in adequate amounts in food protein, that protein is said to be a *complete protein*. Complete proteins occur in animal-source foods such as meats, milk, eggs, and cheese.

Incomplete proteins are those that lack adequate amounts of one or more essential amino acids. Proteins from plant sources such as grains, legumes, and

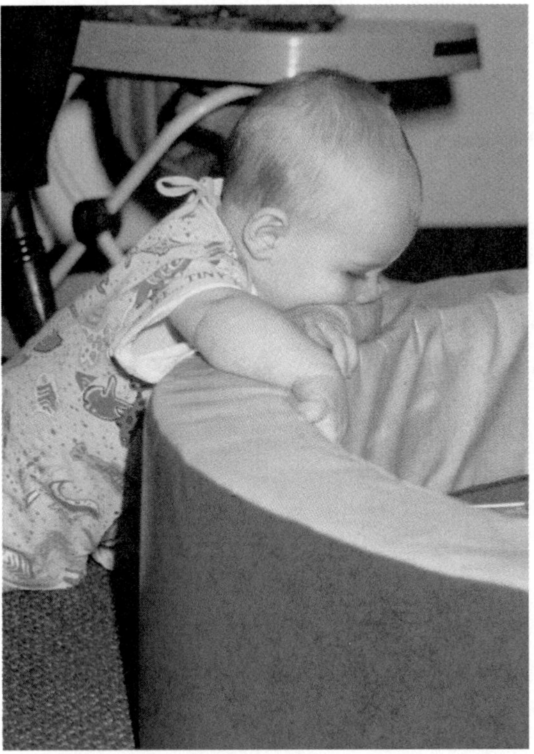

Figure 15–1 Infancy is a period of rapid growth.

vegetables are incomplete proteins. One exception is the soybean, which supplies adequate amino acids to support growth in young children. However, soybean consumption in large amounts can decrease iron absorption. Gelatin, an animal-source food, is also an incomplete protein.

Complete protein intake may also be achieved by combining two or more complementary incomplete proteins. A food that supplies an amino acid that is absent or in low quantities in another food is said to complement that food. For example, wheat, which is deficient in lysine, may be combined with peanuts, which contain adequate amounts of lysine but lack another essential amino acid provided by wheat (Vyhmeister, 1984). The resulting combination of wheat and peanuts contains all the essential amino acids and is equivalent to a complete protein. The wheat-peanut combination could be served as a peanut butter sandwich. Plant proteins tend to be less costly than complete animal proteins.

Rapidly growing children need some complete protein or equivalent combinations daily to support that growth. A greater amount of incomplete protein is needed to achieve the equivalent of a complete protein (Lappe, 1975). For instance, 1 cup of beans is required to complement 2 2/3 cups of rice (Longacre, 1976).

Small children may not have enough stomach capacity to hold the larger amounts of food they must eat to meet their protein needs solely from incomplete protein. Children on such diets grow and thrive, but are often small for their age (Mahan and Arlin, 1992). Free amino acids resulting from digestion of food protein must be used within a short time as they are not stored for future use. All essential amino acids must be provided several times each day. Therefore, the more efficient complete proteins are better able to support rapid growth.

Many favorite dishes are good examples of combinations of proteins that result in the equivalent of a complete protein. Foods may be combined in either of two ways to obtain adequate protein for less money than by using the more costly complete protein sources:

- *complementary proteins*—incomplete protein combined with another incomplete protein to equal complete protein.

  Examples: peanut butter sandwich, beans and rice, chili, peas and rice, macaroni salad with peas, lentil soup with crackers, navy beans with cornbread, baked beans and brown bread

- *supplementary proteins*—incomplete protein combined with a small amount of complete protein to equal complete protein.

  Examples: macaroni and cheese, rice pudding, cheese sandwich, cheese pizza, cereal and milk

Protein Requirements

The total amount of protein needed daily is based on desirable body weight. An infant's requirements for protein and other nutrients are shown in Tables 13–5 and 13–6. Due to the infant's extremely rapid rate of growth, nutrient needs are greater in relation to size during infancy than at any other period of life.

Growing children need more protein per pound than adults. A four- to six-year-old child needs approximately 2/3 of a gram of protein for each pound of body weight. Thus, a child weighing 45 pounds needs 30 grams of protein each day. To be meaningful, these figures must be considered in terms of amounts of food. The following selection of foods provides slightly more than the 30 grams of protein recommended for a 4-year-old child.

Food	*Protein*
2 cups of milk	16 grams
1 1/2 slices bread	3 grams
2 ounces meat or meat alternate	14 grams
	TOTAL 33 grams

Table 15–1 shows a menu for one day that would provide the daily recommended amount of protein for a 4- to 6-year-old child.

TABLE 15–1 Menu Supplying Recommended Daily Allowances of Protein for 4- to 6-Year-Olds

Breakfast	**Grams of Protein**
1/2 c fruit juice	trace
1/2 c dry oat cereal	1
1/3 c milk*	4
1/2 banana	trace
Midmorning Snack	
1/2 c milk*	4
1/2 slice buttered toast	1
Lunch	
1/2 peanut butter and jelly sandwich (1 slice bread, 1/2 tablespoon peanut butter, 1/2 tablespoon jelly)+	4
carrot sticks	1
1/2 apple	trace
1/2 c milk*	4
Midafternoon Snack	
1/2 c fruit juice	trace
2 rye crackers	1
Dinner	
1 chicken leg (1 oz)*	6
1/4 c rice	1
1/4 c broccoli	trace
1/4 c strawberries	trace
1/2 c milk*	4
TOTAL	31 grams of protein

*Complete protein

+ Complementary proteins

MINERALS FOR GROWTH

Minerals are inorganic elements that help to regulate body functions, and also help to build body tissue. This unit deals with minerals that help to build body tissue. The regulatory functions performed by minerals will be covered in the succeeding unit. (Check Table 16–4, the mineral summary, for more information on minerals.)

Minerals provide no energy. They are required in far smaller amounts than are energy-producing nutrients. For example, RDA for protein is 30 grams for a 4-year-old child; this amount is slightly more than one ounce. In contrast, the RDA for calcium for that same child is 0.8 gram. Other minerals are required in even smaller amounts.

Growth involves creating increased amounts of body tissue, which requires attention to receiving adequate amounts of specific minerals. Two types of body tissues most dependent on minerals for growth are bones and teeth, and blood.

Building Bones and Teeth

Calcium and phosphorus are the major minerals found in bones and teeth, Figure 15–2. Bones are formed by the deposition of phosphorus and calcium crystals on *collagen*, a flexible protein base composed of amino acids. Young children's bones are soft and pliable; as growth occurs, the amount of calcium and phosphorus deposited in their bones increases, resulting in larger, harder bones. While bones appear to be solid and unchanging, calcium, phosphorus, and other minerals are replaced on a regular basis. The calcium content of bone is thought to be

Figure 15–2 Calcium and phosphorus are needed for strong teeth and bones.

replaced every five years. Children need calcium not only for bone growth, but also for replacement of existing bone. Adults need calcium only for replacement. Other minerals are also needed for normal bone and tooth formation, but they are rarely limiting factors in the development of these tissues.

Sources of Calcium. Milk and milk products are the major food source of calcium. With the exception of the vegetables broccoli, collard greens, kale, and Chinese cabbage or the soy products tofu and miso there are no good food sources of calcium other than milk and products made from it. A one-cup serving of the above vegetables and soy products will only provide about one-half the amount of calcium that is available in one cup of milk. Milk, cheese, and yogurt are excellent sources of calcium. Custards, pudding, and ice cream provide calcium, but they also contain varying amounts of added sugar and fat, which reduce their nutrient density relative to calcium.

The calcium content of many dishes may be increased by the addition of nonfat dry milk. The addition of nonfat dry milk to casseroles, cooked cereals, breads, and ground meat dishes not only increases the amount of calcium and protein in those dishes, but also improves the quality of the incomplete proteins in pastas, cereals, or flours.

Sources of Phosphorus. Phosphorus is also found in milk and milk-containing foods as well as other high protein and whole grain foods. Good sources of phosphorus are milk, meats, fish, eggs, and grain products. Calcium and phosphorus occur in approximately equal amounts in milk. Ideally, calcium and phosphorus should be obtained in about equal amounts; the recommended daily amount for both minerals is 0.8 gram for children. Relative to body size this represents a greater need by children. It is easier to obtain phosphorus than calcium since it occurs in more kinds of foods. The balance between calcium and phosphorus may be upset if a child is permitted to drink large amounts of carbonated beverages that contain phosphorus. If the child drinks more carbonated beverages than milk, phosphorus in the diet outweighs calcium and calcium absorption may be impaired. This could result in reduced deposition of calcium in the bones and, in extreme cases, withdrawal of calcium from the bones. When carbonated beverages are substituted for milk as a child's beverage, the potential calcium available for consumption is further reduced.

The Role of Fluoride. Fluoride should be considered in connection with bone and tooth formation. Many communities add fluoride to the community water supply in an effort to reduce tooth decay in children. Fluoride-containing toothpastes are also recommended for use by children. Fluoride incorporated into a growing tooth from drinking water makes the tooth harder and more resistant to decay. Fluoride applied to the exterior surface of the tooth is less effective in hardening of the tooth, but it is also thought to reduce the incidence of decay. Excess amount of fluoride may cause mottling and brown-staining of the teeth. Children who are drinking fluoridated water should be taught not to swallow toothpaste after brushing in order to prevent possible excess consumption.

The most consistent source of fluoride is the local water supply; either as naturally occurring fluorine or as fluoride added to a level of 1 p.p.m. (1 part fluoride per million parts of water). Food sources of fluoride are variable and depend on the fluorine content of the soil where grown.

Building Blood

Iron is a mineral that is essential to the formation of hemoglobin. *Hemoglobin* is the iron-containing protein in red blood cells that carries oxygen to the cells and removes waste (carbon dioxide) from the cells. Normal growth depends on a healthy blood supply to nourish an increasing number of cells. Iron plays an important role in the formation of healthy blood.

Iron-deficiency anemia is often found in children 2 to 3 years of age. Iron-deficiency anemia is characterized by low levels of hemoglobin in red blood cells, which results in the cells' reduced ability to carry oxygen to tissues. The end result is reduced growth rate, fatigue, lack of energy, possible reduction in learning ability, and reduced resistance to infections.

Sources of Iron. The Meat, Poultry, Fish, Dry Beans, Eggs, and Nuts Group and the Bread, Cereal, Rice, and Pasta Group are the best sources of iron. Liver is an especially rich source of iron. Milk, which is usually a major part of the diet of young children, contains very little iron. A child who drinks large amounts of milk to the exclusion of iron-containing foods may not receive enough iron to support a growing blood supply.

Studies of the nutritional status of preschool children have repeatedly indicated that neither calcium nor iron is received in adequate amounts. There may be several reasons for this. One reason may be that neither calcium nor iron are widely distributed in foods. Also, many factors affect the absorption of calcium and iron. Therefore, the presence of either mineral in foods does not always assure that the mineral will be absorbed for use by body cells. Another factor may be that many foods containing calcium or iron are expensive.

Factors That Affect Absorption of Calcium and Iron

Calcium	Factor	Iron
↑	Adequate Vitamin C	↑
↑	Increased Need	↑
↓	Large Dose	↓
↓	Fiber (bulk) in Diet	↓
↓	High Protein Level	↑

Factors that *increase* the absorption of calcium and iron:

- Vitamin C aids in keeping calcium and iron more soluble and, therefore, more readily absorbed by the body.
- Vitamin C maximizes the absorption of iron in foods in the same meal.

- In cases where need is increased, inadequate intake or rapid growth-absorption of calcium and iron is increased.

Factors that *decrease* the absorption of calcium and iron:

- Large single doses of calcium and iron are not as well-absorbed as several smaller doses.
- Large amounts of fiber in the diet speed intestinal movement, decreasing the time calcium and iron are in contact with absorption surfaces.

Proteins aid the overall absorption of iron; the iron in meats (known as heme iron) is more readily absorbed than the iron in grains and other nonmeat foods. Protein has the opposite effect on calcium in that high intakes of protein may increase the need for calcium.

THE ROLE OF WATER

Water is an important constituent of all body tissues. Approximately 60 percent of normal adult body weight is water; an infant's body weight is nearly 75 percent water. A gradual decline in water content occurs throughout the life cycle. Need for water is affected by body surface area, environmental temperature, and activity. Water is essential for survival; humans can survive much longer without food than they can without water. Water is supplied to the body through drinking water and other beverages, solid foods, and water that results from energy metabolism.

Vomiting and diarrhea cause excess loss of water that can very rapidly cause dehydration. This is especially threatening to infants, toddlers, and small children, since the amount of water loss necessary to produce dehydration is small in comparison to that of an adult.

Children experience more rapid loss of water through evaporation and dehydration than do adults. Since children are busily involved in other activities, they may need reminders to drink fluids, Figure 15–3. This is important at any time but especially in hot weather. Both children and adults should be encouraged to drink water rather than sugared beverages since the presence of sugar is known to slow the absorption of water (DeVries, 1980). Many children request fruit juice instead of water to drink. This practice should be discouraged. While nutritious juices can contribute to a healthy diet in children, excess intake of juices can lead to a number of problems:

- Stunted growth. Toddlers who fill up on fruit juice may not get the fuel they need to grow. They will have less room for milk and other foods that are richer in calories and other important nutrients, including protein and fat, which should not be restricted in very young children.
- Diarrhea. Too much fluid in itself can cause loose stools. Some juices, notably apple juice, also contain sorbitol, a natural sugar that can be difficult to digest in large quantities, compounding that effect. Most children who drink a lot of juice experience only loose stools; some develop diarrhea.

Figure 15–3 Young children absorbed in play may need to be reminded to drink fluids.

- Tooth decay. Toddlers sometimes use a bottle more for comfort than nourishment or refreshment. Overreliance on a bottle, especially as a way to fall asleep, can lead to nursing-bottle caries—dental decay resulting from prolonged exposure to sugars, in juice or in milk (*Consumer Reports on Health*, September 1995).

THE ROLE OF VITAMINS

Vitamins are not structural parts of growing tissue; however, some of them play critical roles in the use of minerals and proteins as building material for the body. For example, bones could not be properly formed or maintained without vitamins A, D, and C and blood components could not be produced without Vitamins C, B, B_{12}, and folic acid. (See Table 16–1.)

Summary

Growth is an increase in the physical size of either the entire body or any part of the body. Growth occurs both by increasing the number of cells and increasing the size of the cells.

Nutrients most necessary to build body tissue are proteins, minerals, and water. Proteins are components of every living cell and are composed of individual units called amino acids. Essential amino acids must be provided in food proteins since the body cannot manufacture them in needed amounts. Proteins that contain all the essential amino acids in adequate amounts for growth are said to be complete proteins. Meats, fish, poultry, soybeans, eggs, and dairy products contain complete proteins. Proteins that lack one or more essential amino acids in adequate amounts are said to be incomplete proteins; examples are grains, most legumes, and vegetables. Complementary incomplete proteins may be combined to make up the equivalent of a complete protein at a lower cost.

Calcium and phosphorus are the major constituents of bone and teeth. Crystals of calcium and phosphorus are deposited on a flexible protein base composed of collagen. As increasing amounts of calcium and phosphorus are deposited, bones become harder.

The major food source of calcium is the Milk, Yogurt, and Cheese Group. Milk, yogurt, and cheese are excellent sources of calcium. Phosphorus is more widely distributed in foods, since it is found in the Milk, Yogurt, and Cheese Group, the Meat, Poultry, Fish, Dry Beans, Eggs, and Nuts Group, and the Bread, Cereal, Rice, and Pasta Group.

Blood cell information depends on the presence of adequate amounts of iron. Iron is the mineral component of hemoglobin, a protein found in red blood cells. Food sources of iron are the Meat, Poultry, Fish, Dry Beans, Eggs, and Nuts Group and the Bread, Cereal, Rice, and Pasta Group. Liver is the richest food source of iron; some green vegetables such as spinach contain iron, but much of it is in an insoluble form.

Many factors can interfere with the absorption of both calcium and iron.

Water is a constituent of all body tissues, making up sixty to seventy-five percent of body weight. Sources of water are beverages, solid foods, and water derived from metabolism for release of energy.

Suggested Activities

1. Compare nutrition information labels from prepared cereals. Common iron content levels are 98 percent Daily Value, 45 percent Daily Value, and 25 percent Daily Value. After reviewing the "Factors that Affect Absorption of Calcium and Iron," discuss which cereal(s) would be the wisest choice in terms of iron absorption. What other step(s) could be taken to increase the absorption of the iron available in the cereal?

2. Explain why early childhood is a time of risk for iron-deficiency anemia. Consider factors such as food groups in which iron occurs, typical food preferences, and relative ease of eating various foods.

3. Determine the amount of protein recommended for a child who weighs 42 pounds.

Chapter Review

A. Match the terms in column II with the definition in column I. Use each term in column II only once.

Column I	Column II
1. an essential amino acid	a. calcium
2. a nutrient class that functions both to build tissues and provide energy	b. Milk, Yogurt, and Cheese Group
3. the mineral component of hemoglobin	c. iron
4. the mineral that is a major component of bones and teeth	d. Meat, Poultry, Fish, Dry Beans, Eggs, and Nuts Group
5. the food group that provides the greatest amounts of calcium	e. lysine
6. the food group that provides the greatest amounts of iron	f. minerals
7. a nutrient class that helps to regulate body processes and also helps to build body tissue	g. protein
8. comprises approximately 60 percent of normal adult body weight	h. water

B. Multiple Choice. Select the correct choice:

1. The two major *mineral* components of bones and teeth are
   a. protein and calcium
   b. phosphorus and iron
   c. calcium and phosphorus
   d. protein and water
2. Proteins are composed of
   a. amino acids
   b. fatty acids
   c. simple sugars
   d. none of the above
3. Collagen forms the flexible protein matrix upon which bone is built. Collagen is composed of
   a. fatty acids
   b. amino acids
   c. calcium
   d. phosphorus

4. Amino acids that cannot be manufactured within the body are termed
   a. nonessential
   b. essential
   c. complete
   d. incomplete
5. Essential amino acids must be derived from
   a. within the body
   b. food sources
   c. other amino acids
   d. all of these
6. Most proteins from animal sources are
   a. complete
   b. incomplete
   c. complementary
   d. saturated
7. Sources of complete protein are
   a. meat, eggs, milk
   b. cereals, pastas, legumes
   c. fruits, vegetables, grains
   d. butter, cream, salad dressings
8. Examples of incomplete complementary proteins are
   a. macaroni and cheese
   b. tuna and noodles
   c. cornflakes and milk
   d. rice and peas
9. A factor that increases iron and calcium absorption is
   a. adequate vitamin C
   b. a large amount of fiber
   c. a large single dose
   d. all of these
10. Milk and milk products are excellent sources of the *mineral*
    a. iron
    b. calcium
    c. protein
    d. none of these
11. The minerals that are usually consumed in less than adequate quantities by preschoolers are
    a. calcium and phosphorus
    b. iron and calcium
    c. calcium and fluoride
    d. none of these
12. The nutrient that makes up the greatest percentage of body weight is
    a. protein
    b. water
    c. calcium
    d. iron

13. The means by which growth occurs is
    a. increase in cell size
    b. increase in total body size
    c. increase in number of cells
    d. both a and c
14. Which of the following would provide water for the body?
    a. lettuce
    b. milk
    c. metabolism for release of energy
    d. all of these

C. Case Study

The following chart shows a fairly typical daily intake for Timothy, age 4 1/2. Consider this daily pattern in terms of balance between calcium and phosphorus.

Breakfast:
- 1 slice of toast
- 1 scrambled egg
- 1/2 cup orange juice

Midmorning Snack:
- 2 graham crackers (milk offered but refused)

Lunch:
- 2 fish sticks
- 1/4 cup peas
- 1/2 slice bread
- water (milk offered but refused)

Midafternoon Snack:
- 1 small soft drink

Dinner:
- hamburger
- french fries
- 1 small soft drink

1. What foods provide calcium?
2. What foods provide phosphorus?
3. Change the menu to eliminate the phosphorus/calcium imbalance.

References

Consumer Reports on Health, September 1995.

DeVries, H. A. 1980. *Physiology of Exercise for Education and Athletics.* 3rd ed. Dubuque, IA: William C. Brown Company Publisher.

Lappe, F. M. 1975. *Diet for a Small Planet.* rev. ed. New York: Ballantine.

Longacre, D. J. 1976. *More-with-Less Cookbook.* Scottsdale, PA: Herold Press.

Mahan, L. K. and Arlin, M. 1992. *Krause's Food Nutrition and Diet Therapy.* Philadelphia, PA: W. B. Saunders Co.

Vyhmeister, I. B. May, 1984. "Vegetarian Diets—Issues and Concerns." Nutrition and the M. D.

Additional Reading

"ADA's Child Nutrition and Health Campaign." 1995. *Journal of the American Dietetic Association.* 95: 1121–1149.

Barnes, L. A. (Ed.) *Pediatric Nutrition Handbook.* 1993. Committee on Nutrition, Academy of Pediatrics.

Williams, S. R., and Worthington-Roberts, B. S. 1988. *Nutrition Throughout the Life Cycle.* St. Louis, MO: Times Mirror/Mosby College Publishing.

Chapter 16

Nutrients That Regulate Body Functions

(proteins, minerals, water, and vitamins)

Terms to Know

microgram (mcg)
milligram (mg)
neuromuscular
megadose
toxicity
synthesis
DNA
RNA
catalyst
coenzyme
adenosine triphosphate (ATP)
hormones

Objectives

After studying this chapter, you should be able to:

- Name general types of body functions regulated by nutrients.
- Identify nutrients that perform regulatory functions in the body.
- List at least one specific function performed by each of the four nutrient classes identified as regulators.

Energy cannot be produced or released from carbohydrates, proteins, and fats without specific nutrients catalyzing sequential steps. New tissues such as bone, blood, or muscles cannot be formed unless specific vitamins, minerals, and proteins are available for their specific functions in each of these processes. Nerve impulses will not travel from one nerve cell to another, nor will muscles contract unless the required nutrients are available in adequate amounts at the appropriate times. Some body functions may be regulated by one or two nutrients in one or two reactions. Many other functions involve intricate sequences of reactions that require many nutrients. All body functions are subject to regulation by nutrients.

Regulation of body functions is an extremely complex process. While much has been learned about the role of nutrients in regulation, there is still much that is unknown. It is important to remember that nutrients and functions are intricately interrelated. No single nutrient can function alone; thus regulation of body functions depends on many nutrients. This unit briefly discusses four nutrient classes involved in regulating body functions.

- vitamins
- minerals
- proteins
- water

Protein has been discussed earlier in terms of both energy and growth. Minerals and water were introduced as tissue-building nutrients and will now be considered as regulatory nutrients. Vitamins are able to perform only regulatory functions. They do not yield energy directly, nor do they become part of body structure. However, no energy can be released or any tissue built without benefit of the specific regulatory activities performed by vitamins.

Vitamins and minerals are needed in extremely small amounts. In Tables 16–1 and 16–4 you will find that their RDAs are in *milligrams (mg)*, which are one-thousandth of a gram and in *micrograms (mcg)*, which are one-millionth of a gram. One standard size metal paperclip weighs approximately one gram.

The regulatory functions discussed in this unit are crucial to the normal growth and development of young children. Generally these functions are:

- energy metabolism
- cellular reproduction and growth
- bone growth
- *neuromuscular* development and function
- blood composition control

Other functions are also crucial to normal development. However, these functions were chosen because of their critical relationship to normal growth, learning, and general good health of infants, toddlers, and young children.

VITAMINS AS REGULATORS

Vitamins are needed in extremely small amounts, but they are essential for normal body function. Each vitamin plays a specific role in a variety of body activities, Table 16–1. Vitamins frequently depend upon one another to perform their functions. For example, the vitamins thiamin and niacin are both needed as crucial coenzymes for the release of energy, but thiamin cannot function in the place of niacin, nor can niacin function in the absence of thiamin's action in a prior step.

TABLE 16–1 Vitamin Summary

VITAMIN	FUNCTIONS	RDA	SOURCES	DEFICIENCY SYMPTOMS	TOXICITY SYMPTOMS
Fat-soluble Vitamins					
Vitamin A	Maintenance of: ■ remodeling of bones ■ all cell membranes ■ epithelial cells; skin ■ mucous membranes, glands Regulation of vision in dim light.	1–3 yrs-400RE/2000IU 4–6 yrs-500RE/2500IU	Liver, whole milk, butter, fortified margarine, orange and dark green vegetables, orange fruits (apricots, nectarines, peaches).	Depressed bone and tooth formation, lack of visual acuity, dry epithelial tissue, increased frequency of infections related to epithelial cell vulnerability.	Headaches, nausea, vomiting, fragile bones, loss of hair, dry skin. Infant: Hydrocephalus, hyperirritability.
Vitamin D	Regulates calcium/ phosphorus absorption Mineralization of bone.	1–3 yrs-10 mcg 4–6 yrs-10 mcg	Vitamin D fortified milk, exposure of skin to sunlight.	Rickets (soft, easily bent bones), bone deformities.	Elevated blood calcium; deposition of calcium in soft tissues resulting in cerebral, renal, and cardiovascular damage (Dubick Rucker, 1983).
Vitamin E	Antioxidant	1–3 yrs-6 mg 4–6 yrs-6 T.E. 7 mg	Vegetable oils, wheat germ, egg yolk, leafy vegetables, legumes, margarine.	Red blood cell destruction; creatinuria.	Fatigue, skin rash, abdominal discomfort.
Vitamin K	Normal blood coagulation	Estimated safe range: 1–3 yrs-15 mcg 4–6 yrs-20 mcg	Leafy vegetables, vegetable oils, liver, pork; synthesis by intestinal bacteria.	Hemorrhage	None reported for naturally occurring Vitamin K.

Table 16–1 (Continued)

Water-soluble Vitamins Vitamin C (Ascorbic acid)	Formation of collagen for: ■ bones/teeth ■ intercellular cement ■ wound healing Aid to calcium/iron absorption Conversion of folacin to active form Neurotransmitter synthesis.	1–3 yrs-40 mg 4–6 yrs-45 mg	Citrus fruits, strawberries, melons, cabbage, peppers, greens, tomatoes.	Poor wound healing, bleeding gums, pinpoint hemorrhages, sore joints, scurvy.	Nausea, abdominal cramps, diarrhea. Precipitation of kidney stones in susceptible person; "conditioned scurvy" (Dubick and Rucker, 1983).
Thiamin	Carbohydrate metabolism Energy metabolism Neurotransmitter synthesis.	1–3 yrs-0.7 mg 4–6 yrs-0.9 mg	Whole or enriched grain products, organ meats, pork.	Loss of appetite, depression, poor neuromuscular control, Beri-Beri.	None reported.
Riboflavin	Metabolism of carbohydrates, fats, and proteins. Energy metabolism.	1–3 yrs-0.8 mg 4–6 yrs-1.1 mg	Dairy foods, meat products, enriched or whole grains, green vegetables.	Sore tongue, cracks at the corners of the mouth (cheilosis).	None reported.
Niacin	Carbohydrate, protein, and fat metabolism; energy metabolism; conversion of folacin to its active form.	1–3 yrs-9 mg 4–6 yrs-12 mg	Meat products, whole or enriched grain products, legumes.	Dermatitis, diarrhea, depression, and paranoia.	Flushing, itching, nausea, vomiting, diarrhea, low blood pressure, rapid heart beat, low blood sugar, liver damage (Dubick and Rucker, 1983).
Pantothenic Acid	Energy metabolism; fatty acid metabolism; neurotransmitter synthesis.	Estimated safe range: 3-4 mg	Nearly all foods.	Uncommon in humans.	None reported.

TABLE 16–1 Vitamin Summary (Continued)

VITAMIN	FUNCTIONS	RDA	SOURCES	DEFICIENCY SYMPTOMS	TOXICITY SYMPTOMS
Vitamin B_6 (Pyridoxine)	Protein and fatty acid synthesis; neurotransmitter synthesis; hemoglobin synthesis.	1–3 yrs-1.0 mg 4–6 yrs-1.1 mg	Meats, organ meats, whole grains, legumes, bananas.	Nervous system: ■ irritability ■ tremors ■ convulsions } infants	Unstable gait, numbness, lack of coordination (Schaumberg, 1983).
Folacin	Synthesis of DNA and RNA: cell replication protein synthesis	1–3 yrs-50 mcg 4–6 yrs-75 mcg	Liver, other meats, green vegetables.	Macrocytic anemia characterized by unusually large red blood cells; sore tongue, diarrhea.	None reported. (Large amount may hide a B_{12} deficiency.)
Vitamin B_{12} (Cobalamin)	Synthesis of DNA and RNA: conversion of folacin to active form; synthesis of myelin (fatty covering of nerve cells); metabolism of carbohydrates for energy.	1–3 yrs-0.7 mcg 4–6 yrs-1.0 mcg	Animal foods, liver, other meats, dairy products, eggs.	Macrocytic anemia, nervous system damage, sore mouth and tongue, loss of appetite, nausea, vomiting. (Pernicious anemia results from faulty absorption of B_{12}).	None reported.
Biotin	Carbohydrate and fat metabolism; amino acid metabolism.	Estimated safe range: 1–3 yrs-20 mcg 4–6 yrs-25 mcg	Organ meats, milk, egg yolk, yeast; synthesis by intestinal bacteria.	Nervous disorders, skin disorders, anorexia, muscle pain.	None reported.

Vitamins are needed and used in specific amounts. Large excesses do not serve any useful function and in some instances are known to be harmful. Toxic effects have long been known for excesses of vitamin A and vitamin D. Recent research has described neurological damage resulting from large amounts of vitamin B_6 and kidney stone formation and destruction of vitamin B_{12} stores as a result of megadoses of vitamin C (ascorbic acid). Megadoses are usually defined as ten times the recommended daily amount for an adult. There is not enough information to define toxic doses of all vitamins for young children; it is certainly smaller than the amount required to produce toxicity symptoms in an adult. Therefore, extreme caution should be used if giving children vitamin supplements without the advice of a physician. "If a little bit is good, a lot is better" is a dangerous practice relative to vitamins.

Vitamins have been the subject of much attention in the press, having been promoted as "cures" for numerous conditions including cancer, common colds, and mental illness (*Consumer Reports*, 1980). Many people take vitamins and give them to their children as an "insurance policy." Vitamins can supplement a "hit-or-miss" diet, but should not be given as a replacement for an adequate diet. There are a number of reasons why supplements cannot add up to an adequate diet by themselves. Vitamin and/or mineral supplements do not provide all of the nutrients known to be needed by humans nor do they provide any calories, a primary need. Poor diets may lack fiber or essential amino acids or essential fatty acids, which will not be corrected by vitamin/mineral supplements. Also, there may be substances as yet unknown, but essential, which are derived from foods that are not included in vitamin/mineral preparations. The *Dietary Guidelines for Americans* (1995) states "because foods contain many nutrients and other substances that promote health, the use of supplements cannot substitute for proper food choices."

Vitamins are classified as fat-soluble (dissolved in or carried in fats) or water-soluble (dissolved in water). Fat-soluble vitamins differ from water-soluble vitamins both chemically and functionally. Table 16–2 provides a summary of the characteristics of these two classes of vitamins.

TABLE 16–2 Characteristics of Vitamins

	FAT-SOLUBLE VITAMINS	WATER-SOLUBLE VITAMINS
Examples	A, D, E, K	Vitamin C (Ascorbic Acid), Thiamin, Niacin, Riboflavin, Pantothenic Acid, B_6 (Pyridoxine), Biotin, Folacin, B_{12} (Cobalamin)
Stored in body	Yes	No (B_{12} is an exception)
Excreted in urine	No	Yes
Needed daily	No	Yes
Deficiency	Develop slowly (months, years)	Develop rapidly (days, weeks)

Vitamins in Energy Metabolism

A slow steady release of energy is important to body needs. If energy is released in a haphazard fashion, much of it is lost as heat. Since young children require greater amounts of energy per pound, they cannot afford to lose energy in such a fashion. The primary vitamins involved in the regulation of metabolism for release of energy are:

- thiamin
- riboflavin
- niacin
- pantothenic acid

These four vitamins are not the only nutrients involved in this process; all the other nutrients required must also be available in adequate amounts at the time needed.

Vitamins in Cellular Reproduction and Growth

Two vitamins that are absolutely essential for cell growth are folacin and cobalamin (B_{12}). Both vitamins participate in the *synthesis* of *DNA* and *RNA*, which are the chemicals that provide the pattern for cell division and growth. So crucial are these vitamins for cell division and growth that deficiencies of them are quickly noticeable in tissues that are frequently replaced, such as red blood cells or the cells lining the intestine.

Young children may be considered at risk for both folacin and B_{12} deficiency. Requirements for these nutrients are always increased during periods of rapid growth such as that typical of early childhood. Another factor that must be considered is the fact that B_{12} is found only in food from animal sources. Parents who are vegetarians will find that very careful planning is required in order to meet their child's needs for vitamin B_{12} and other nutrients, Table 16–3.

TABLE 16–3 Replacing Animal Sources of Nutrients

Vegetarians who eat no animal products need to be more aware of nutrient sources. Nutrients most likely to be lacking and some nonanimal sources are:

- **vitamin B_{12}**—fortified soy beverages and cereals
- **vitamin D**—fortified soy beverages and sunshine
- **calcium**—tofu processed with calcium, broccoli, seeds, nuts, kale, bok choy, legumes (peas and beans), greens, lime-processed tortillas, and soy beverages, grain products, and orange juice enriched with calcium
- **iron**—legumes, tofu, green leafy vegetables, dried fruit, whole grains, and iron-fortified cereals and breads, especially whole-wheat. (Absorption is improved by vitamin C, found in citrus fruits and juices, tomatoes, strawberries, broccoli, peppers, dark-green leafy vegetables, and potatoes with skins.)
- **zinc**—whole grains (especially the germ and bran), whole-wheat bread, legumes, nuts, and tofu
- **protein**—tofu and other soy-based products, legumes, seeds, nuts, grains, and vegetables

Courtesy of *FDA Consumer*. October 1995.

Vegetarian diets are classified by the extent to which the diet includes animal foods:

- lacto-ovo-vegetarian—diary foods and eggs included.
- lacto-vegetarian—dairy foods included, but no eggs.
- vegan—no animal source foods included.

It was formerly thought that vegan diets could not meet the needs of infants and children. In a 1993 position paper on vegetarianism, the American Dietetic Association stated "vegan diets tend to be high in bulk, care should be taken to ensure that calorie intakes are sufficient to meet every need." Infants and children who consume well-planned vegetarian diets can generally meet all of their nutritional requirements for growth. Table 16–3 lists those nutrients most likely to be deficient in the vegetarian diet and nonanimal sources of those nutrients.

Some general recommendations include:

- Minimize intake of less nutritious foods such as sweets and fatty foods.
- Choose whole or unrefined grain products instead of refined products.
- Choose a variety of nuts, seeds, legumes, fruits, and vegetables, including good sources of vitamin C to improve iron absorption.
- Choose low fat varieties of dairy products, if they are included in the diet.
- Vegans should use properly fortified sources of vitamin B_{12}, such as fortified soy beverages or cereals, or take a supplement (*FDA Consumer*, October 1995).

In addition to needs for folacin and B_{12}, cellular reproduction and increase in cell size are also dependent on proteins. One vitamin that is essential to the metabolism of proteins is pyridoxine (B_6). Pyridoxine *catalyzes* the chemical changes that permit the building of proteins from amino acids, or the breakdown of proteins to provide needed amino acids.

Vitamins That Regulate Bone Growth

The minerals calcium and phosphorus are the major structural components of bones and teeth. However, bone growth also depends on a number of other nutrients as regulators including vitamins A, C, and D, Figure 16–1.

Vitamin A regulates the destruction of old bone cells and their replacement by new ones. This process is known as "remodeling."

Vitamins C functions in two ways in the formation of bone tissue:

- maintains the solubility of calcium, making it more available for absorption
- aids in the formation of collagen, the flexible protein foundation upon which phosphorus and calcium are deposited

Vitamin D is necessary for the absorption of calcium and phosphorus, the major constituents of bones and teeth. It is also needed to assure blood levels of calcium and phosphorus that allow for deposition of these minerals in bones and teeth.

Figure 16–1 Body function is regulated by many nutrients.

Vitamins That Regulate Neuromuscular Function

Vitamins play a role in a neuromuscular function either through the synthesis of neurotransmitters (chemical messengers) or through growth or maintenance of nerve cells.

Vitamin B_6 and vitamin C, thiamin, and niacin catalyze the synthesis of neurotransmitter. Deficiencies of these vitamins result in neurological abnormalities.

Vitamins B_6 and B_{12} are necessary for the formation and maintenance of the myelin sheath, the insulative layer surrounding nerve cells. Faulty myelin sheath formation and maintenance results in abnormal passage of nerve impulses, which may result in numbness, tremors, or loss of coordination.

Recent research has indicated that maternal deficiency of folacin may result in neural tube defects in infants. Prenatal vitamins contain folacin; however, neural tube defects occur before the mother is aware that she is pregnant. A recent attempt to remedy this situation has been the fortification of most grain products with folacin.

Vitamins That Regulate Blood Formation

Some vitamins play an important role in the formation of blood cells and hemoglobin. Hemoglobin, the red pigment of the red blood cells, carries oxygen to all cells of the body and carries the waste product, carbon dioxide, away from the cells to the lungs. Vitamins needed for the production of red blood cells and hemoglobin are:

- Vitamin E
- pantothenic acid

- Vitamin B_6 (pyridoxine)
- folacin
- Vitamin B_{12} (cobalamin)

MINERALS AS REGULATORS

Many body functions require the presence of specific minerals, Table 16–4. The amounts of minerals required for regulatory purposes are smaller than those required directly to build or repair body tissue. Minerals used by the body for regulatory purposes are usually parts of enzymes or coenzymes or catalyze their action.

Minerals in Energy Metabolism

Minerals also play an important role in the steady, efficient release of energy. This process of energy metabolism (production, storage, and release) depends on adequate amounts of:

- phosphorus
- magnesium
- iodine
- iron

Phosphorus is necessary for the production of enzymes and *coenzymes* required for energy-releasing metabolism and also for the formation of *adenosine triphosphate (ATP)*, the chemical substance in which potential energy is stored in body cells. Another mineral, magnesium, is necessary for both the storage and the release of the energy trapped in ATP. Iron functions as part of one of the key enzyme systems in the final stages of energy metabolism. Iodine is a component of the hormone, thyroxin. As such, iodine aids in the control of the rate at which the body uses energy (the basal metabolic rate) for involuntary activities.

Minerals in Cellular Reproduction and Growth

Minerals required for cellular reproduction and growth include:

- phosphorus
- magnesium
- zinc

Phosphorus is a structural component of both DNA and RNA. Magnesium is required both for the synthesis of DNA and for synthesis of proteins from the pattern provided by DNA. Zinc functions as part of an enzyme system that must be active during DNA and RNA synthesis. DNA allows cells to reproduce and to synthesize proteins needed for growth.

The effect of an inadequate zinc supply is reflected by signs and symptoms such as stunted growth, decreased acuity of taste and smell that may further decrease food intake, and delayed sexual maturity. Zinc is chemically related to

TABLE 16–4 Mineral Summary

MINERAL	FUNCTIONS	RDA	SOURCES	DEFICIENCY SYMPTOMS	TOXICITY SYMPTOMS
Calcium	Major component of bones and teeth; collagen formation; muscle contraction; secretion/release of insulin; neurotransmitters; blood clotting.	1–3 yrs-800 mg 4–6 yrs-800 mg	Dairy products, turnip or collard greens, canned salmon or sardines, soybeans or soybean curd (tofu).	Poor growth, small adult size, fragile and deformed bones, some form of rickets.	Unlikely. Absorption is controlled; symptoms usually result from excess vitamin D or hormonal imbalance.
Phosphorus	Major component of bones and teeth; energy metabolism; component of DNA and RNA.	1–3 yrs-800 mg 4–6 yrs-800 mg	Dairy products, meats, legumes, grains, additive in soft drinks.	Rare with normal diet.	Large amounts may depress calcium absorption.
Magnesium	Major components of bones and teeth; activator of enzymes for ATP use; required for synthesis of DNA and RNA and for synthesis of proteins by RNA.	1–3 yrs-150 mg 4–6 yrs-200 mg	Nuts, seeds, green vegetables, legumes, whole grains.	Poor neuromuscular coordination, tremors, convulsions.	Unlikely.
Sodium	Nerve impulse transmission; fluid balance; acid-base balance.	Estimated safe range: 1–3 yrs-225 mg 4–6 yrs-300 mg	Meats, fish, poultry, eggs, milk, (naturally-occurring sodium); many processed and cured foods (added sodium), salt, MSG.	Rare. (Losses from sweat may cause dizziness, nausea, muscle cramps.)	Linked to high blood pressure in some persons; confusion; coma.

Table 16–4 (Continued)

MINERAL	FUNCTIONS	RDA	SOURCES	DEFICIENCY SYMPTOMS	TOXICITY SYMPTOMS
Potassium	Nerve impulse transmission; fluid balance; acid-base balance.	1–3 yrs-1000 mg 4–6 yrs-1400 mg	Fruits (bananas, orange juice), vegetables, whole grains, fresh meats, fish.	Weakness, irregular heartbeat.	Unlikely from food sources.
Iron	Component of hemoglobin; enzymes involved in oxygen utilization.	1–3 yrs-10 mg 4–6 yrs-10 mg	Liver and other meats, enriched and whole grains, leafy green vegetables.	*Microcytic* anemia (characterized by small, pale red blood cells), fatigue, pallor, shortness of breath.	Unlikely. (May be due to genetic defect.)
Zinc	Component of many enzymes involved in: protein metabolism, DNA/RNA synthesis collagen formation wound healing.	1–3 yrs-10 mg 4–6 yrs-10 mg	Liver, oysters, meats, eggs, whole grains, legumes.	Retarded growth, loss of senses of taste and smell, delayed wound healing.	Excess supplementation may interfere with iron/copper metabolism. Nausea, vomiting, diarrhea, gastric ulcers.
Iodine	Component of thyroxin, which regulates basal metabolic rate. Regulates physical and mental growth.	1–3 yrs-70 mcg 4–6 yrs-90 mcg	Iodized salt, seafoods, many processed foods.	Goiter, physical dwarfing, cretinism if deficiency occurs during fetal life.	Iodism; rashes; bronchitis.

iron; its absorption is affected by many of the same factors. Zinc availability may be seriously reduced by excessive supplements with calcium and/or iron.

Minerals That Regulate Neuromuscular Function

Passage of nerve impulses from nerve cell to nerve cell or from nerve cell to muscle is dependent on the presence of:

- sodium
- potassium
- calcium
- magnesium

Sodium and potassium act to change the electrical charge on the surface of the nerve cell, allowing the passage of the nerve impulse. Calcium is required for the release of many neurotransmitters from nerve cells. The passage of a nerve impulse to a muscle cell causes the contraction of muscles. Calcium is required for the actual contraction of a muscle, while ATP, which contains phosphorus as a structural component, provides the energy for the contraction to take place.

PROTEINS AS REGULATORS

Proteins are the only class of nutrients that can perform all three general functions of nutrients. They build and repair body tissue, regulate body functions, and provide energy.

Proteins in Energy Metabolism and Growth Regulation

Proteins (amino acids) are important components of enzymes and some hormones and thus play a major role in regulation of energy metabolism. The body must have an adequate supply of protein in order to produce these important enzymes and hormones.

All body functions are dependent on the presence and activity of enzymes. Enzymes are defined as protein catalysts. A catalyst is a substance that regulates a chemical reaction without becoming part of that reaction. The sequential metabolism for release of energy requires many steps; each step requires at least one enzyme specific for the particular reaction. Many enzymes require vitamin-containing coenzymes to enable them to catalyze their specific chemical reactions.

Hormones are substances that are secreted by glands for action on tissue elsewhere in the body. As such, they regulate many body functions. While not all hormones are composed of amino acids, two amino-acid dependent hormones are required in energy metabolism. These hormones are thyroxin and insulin.

Thyroxin regulates the rate at which energy is used for involuntary activities. It is secreted by the thyroid gland. Insulin is secreted by the pancreas. Its presence is necessary for glucose to be absorbed by the body cells so that it may be used as an energy source for cellular activity. Insulin and adrenalin, another amino acid-dependent hormone, act together to maintain normal blood glucose levels.

WATER AS A REGULATOR

The initial step of processing food for use by the body is digestion. Digestion is the process by which food is broken down mechanically and chemically into nutrients that can be used by the body. Food composition is changed during chemical digestion through the breaking down of nutrient molecules by the addition of water. Water is added at appropriate places in the molecule of protein, fats, and carbohydrates to break them into units small enough to be absorbed and used by the cells. Water is essential for many processes as the medium in which chemical reactions take place, Figure 16–2.

After food is digested and the nutrients absorbed, the nutrients are carried in solution by the blood and lymph to the cells of the body. Water again is necessary as it is the main transporting agent of the body comprising all body fluids including blood, lymph, and tissue fluid. Water also is the major component of body secretions such as salivary juice, gastric juice, bile, perspiration, and expirations from the lungs. Urine is comprised of approximately 95 percent water. Water regulates body temperature during changes in environmental temperature and activity-related heat production.

Figure 16–2 Water is essential for regulation of body function.

SUMMARY FOR CHAPTERS 14, 15, AND 16

There are approximately 40 nutrients that are recognized as essential for providing energy, allowing normal growth for the child and maintenance for the adult. Each nutrient has its special function(s). Some nutrients share functions and in many cases the function of any given nutrient is dependent upon one or more other nutrients being present. The purpose of the following summary chart is to help you understand some of these functional interrelationships and reduce some confusion about what nutrients really do in the body. You might make this a personal study by associating each functional unit with the part of your own body. For example, when listing nutrient needs for bones and teeth, envision your own bones and teeth and what these nutrients are doing for them.

Summary of Biological Functions of Nutrients

FUNCTIONAL UNIT	NUTRIENTS INVOLVED	
Blood Formation and Maintenance	Calcium Vitamin K Protein	blood clotting
	Iron Vitamin B_6 Folacin	hemoglobin production
	Folacin Vitamin B_{12}	production of red blood cells
Bone and Teeth Development	Calcium Phosphorus Magnesium	components of bones and teeth
	Vitamin C Vitamin A Vitamin D	building and remodeling of bones
Nerve-Muscle Development and Activity	Vitamin C Thiamin Niacin Vitamin B_6 Pantothenic acid Calcium Potassium	transmission of nerve impulses
	Calcium Potassium Sodium Thiamin Pantothenic acid	regulates muscle contraction and relaxation

FUNCTIONAL UNIT	NUTRIENTS INVOLVED	
Growth and Maintenance of Body Parts	Protein Phosphorus Zinc Vitamin B_6 Folacin	regulates cell division and synthesis of needed cell proteins
	Iodine	regulates physical and mental growth
Availability of Energy for Cellular Activity	Carbohydrates Fats Proteins	may be "burned" to release energy
	Phosphorus Magnesium Thiamin Riboflavin Niacin Pantothenic acid Biotin	roles in enzyme and coenzyme production to release energy
	Iodine	regulates basal metabolic energy needs

Summary

Nutrient classes that regulate body functions are vitamins, minerals, proteins, and water. Vitamins can perform only regulatory functions. Some functions regulated by vitamins are energy metabolism, cellular reproduction and growth, bone growth, neuromuscular activities, and blood formation.

Minerals are also required for the regulation of energy metabolism, cellular reproduction and growth, and normal nerve and muscle function.

Proteins (amino acids) function as regulatory substances in the form of enzymes and some hormones. Most body reactions depend on the activity of specific enzymes at specific steps of the process. Hormones, in turn, may regulate the rate of many of these reactions. Thyroxin, insulin, and adrenalin are examples of hormones that are synthesized from amino acids.

Water is required as the medium in which most nutrients' functions take place. Water is also the prime regulator of body temperature.

Suggested Activities

1. Using the summary Tables 16–1 and 16–4 for vitamins and minerals, list two specific foods or types of foods that are rich sources of each of the following nutrients:

magnesium	thiamin
calcium	riboflavin

   a. What foods are good sources of more than one of these nutrients?
   b. Which nutrients occur in the same types of foods?
   c. Which nutrients do not occur in the same types of foods?

Chapter Review

A. Multiple Choice. Select the best answer:

1. Vitamins that regulate energy metabolism are
   a. magnesium, iron, and iodine
   b. thiamin, niacin, and riboflavin
   c. folacin, cobalamin, and pyridoxine
   d. calcium, phosphorus, and iron
2. Vitamins that regulate cell division and growth and metabolize protein are
   a. cobalamin, folacin, and pyridoxine
   b. magnesium, phosphorus, and zinc
   c. vitamin A, vitamin C, and vitamin D
   d. thiamin, niacin, and riboflavin
3. Vitamins that regulate normal bone growth are
   a. calcium, phosphorus, and fluoride
   b. vitamin A, vitamin C, and vitamin D
   c. pyridoxine, iron, and thiamin
   d. magnesium, niacin, and riboflavin
4. Which of the following foods are considered the best contributors of vitamin A?
   a. sweet potatoes, liver, broccoli
   b. peas, bananas, apples
   c. cherries, turnips, potatoes
   d. rice, beans, corn

5. Which of the following foods are considered the best contributors of vitamin C?
   a. milk, liver, whole wheat bread
   b. oranges, strawberries, tomatoes
   c. peas, bananas, apples
   d. cabbage, peanuts, grapes

6. Muscle contraction is regulated by the mineral
   a. calcium
   b. phosphorus
   c. fluoride
   d. zinc

7. Milk and dairy foods are good sources of
   a. calcium, riboflavin, protein
   b. vitamin C, zinc, copper
   c. niacin, iron, magnesium
   d. pyridoxine, folacin, thiamin

8. Breads and cereals are good sources of
   a. thiamin, phosphorus
   b. calcium, vitamin C
   c. vitamin A, calcium
   d. cobalamin

9. Nutrients that regulate blood formation are
   a. vitamin A, thiamin, and folacin
   b. thiamin, niacin, and pantothenic acid
   c. folacin, vitamin B_{12}, and vitamin B_6 (pyridoxine)
   d. vitamin B_{12}, niacin, and vitamin C

10. Vitamins that are essential for cellular division and growth and are provided by liver and other meats are
    a. folacin and vitamin B_{12}
    b. iron and copper
    c. vitamin C and vitamin D
    d. pantothenic acid and iodine

B. Briefly answer the following questions.

1. What two minerals are required for energy metabolism?
2. What two minerals are required for cellular division and growth?
3. What is the medium in which nutrient-related chemical reactions take place in the body?
4. Name an important nutrient component of enzymes and some hormones.
5. Which nutrient is the prime regulator of body temperature?

C. Case Study

Tony, age 4 1/2, is allergic to citrus fruits. Even a few drops of juice cause him to break out in hives.

1. For what nutrient should Tony's diet be closely monitored?
2. a. If Tony's diet is actually deficient in this nutrient, would symptoms appear rapidly or slowly?
   b. Why?
3. Suggest foods other than citrus fruits that could also provide this nutrient.
4. List two symptoms that Tony might display.
5. a. Should Tony be given large doses of this nutrient to offset possible deficiencies?
   b. Why or why not?

References

Dubick, M. A., and Rucker, R. B. February 1983. "Dietary Supplements and Health Aids—A Critical Evaluation. Part I Vitamins and Minerals." *Journal of Nutrition Education* 15: 47–51.

"More People Trying Vegetarian Diets." October 1995. *FDA Consumer.*

Schaumberg, H. A., et al. 1983, August 25. "Sensory Neuropathy from Pyridoxine Abuse." *New England Journal of Medicine* 309: 445–48.

Additional Reading

Christian, J. L., and Gregor, J. L. 1990. *Nutrition for Living.* Menlo Park, CA: Benjamin/Cummings Publishing Co.

Dietary Guidelines for Americans. 1995. Washington, DC: U. S. Department of Health and Human Services and U. S. Department of Agriculture.

Hegarty, V. 1988. *Decisions in Nutrition.* St. Louis, MO: C. V. Mosby Co.

Kreutler, P. A. 1990. *Nutrition in Perspective.* Englewood Cliffs, NJ: Prentice Hall, Inc.

Mahan, L. K. and Arlin, M. 1992. *Krause's Food, Nutrition, and Diet Therapy.* Philadelphia, PA: W. B. Saunders Company.

Pipes, P. 1981. *Nutrition in Infancy and Childhood.* St. Louis: The C. V. Mosby Company.

Position of the American Dietetic Association: Vegetarian Diets. *Journal of the American Dietetic Association*, November 1993.

Reed, P. B. 1980. *Nutrition: An Applied Science.* St. Paul: West Publishing Company.

Satter, E. 1991. *Child of Mine.* Palo Alto, CA: Bull Publishing Company.

Whitney, E. N., and Hamilton, E. M. N. 1988. *Understanding Nutrition.* 3rd ed. St. Louis: West Publishing Company.

Williams, E. R., and Calienda, M. A. 1984. *Nutrition: Principles, Issues, and Applications.* New York: McGraw-Hill Book Company.

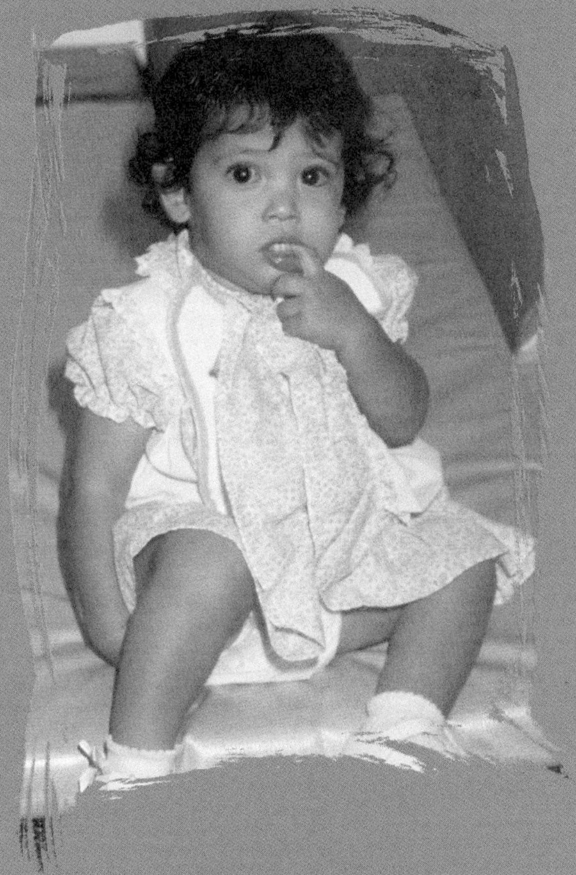

UNIT 5

Nutrition and the Young Child

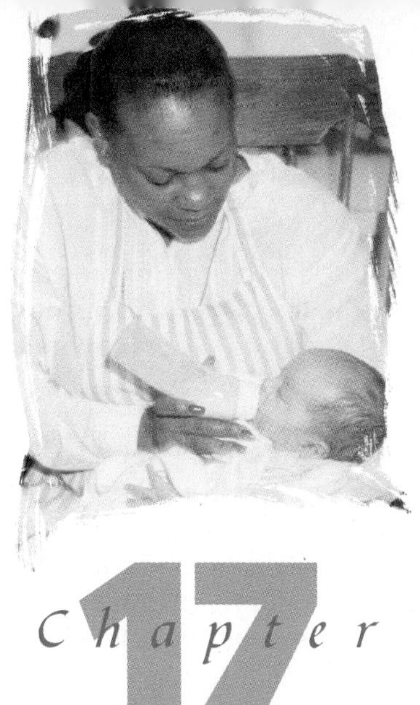

Chapter 17

Infant Feeding

Terms to Know

prenatal
low-birthweight infant
antibodies
aseptic procedures
distention
regurgitation
bottle-mouth syndrome
developmental readiness
physiological readiness
electrolyte

Objectives

After studying this chapter, you should be able to:

- Describe the proper way to bottle-feed an infant.
- Describe ways to feed the breast-fed infant in a child care setting.
- Identify the appropriate ages at which to introduce semi-solid foods to infants.
- Name recommended safe foods to use as first semi-solid foods.
- Give criteria for selecting nutritious solid food for the baby and evaluate benefits of commercial versus home-prepared semi-solid food.
- Evaluate nutrient contributions of different types of commercial baby food and make appropriate choices.

PROFILE OF AN INFANT

During the first year of a child's life, the rate of growth and development is more rapid than at any other period in the life cycle. The infant will double its birth weight during the first four to five months and will approximately triple its birth weight by the end of the first year. Birth length may be expected to increase by 50 percent by the child's first birthday.

Infants are totally dependent upon parents and/or caregivers to protect them from environmental hazards, such as temperature change and pathogenic organisms, and to provide the necessary nutrients in a safe and useable form. The giving of food must be coupled with socializing and much Tender Loving Care (TLC). Without TLC, infants' growth and development can be seriously delayed even when they are receiving all of the nutrients they need. Infants need much stimulation to help them learn and food can serve as an important medium for stimulating the infant—tastes, colors, temperatures, textures, etc. Within these first 12 months, infants will progress from a solely liquid diet of milk or milk plus semi-solid foods and finally to a modified adult diet that includes them in the family group at meal time, Table 17–1.

MEETING NUTRITIONAL NEEDS OF THE INFANT

The nutritional needs of the infant may be conditioned by the nutritional status of the mother during pregnancy. A common consequence of poor *prenatal* (conception to birth) nutrition is a *low-birthweight (LBW) infant*. The incidence of serious illness and death is very high for low-birthweight infants during their first year. A LBW infant presents serious problems such as:

- poor regulation of body temperature.
- increased susceptibility to infection.
- difficulty in metabolizing carbohydrates, fats, and proteins.
- delayed development of kidneys and digestive organs.
- poorly calcified bones—reduced bone density.
- poor iron stores resulting in neonatal anemia.
- presentation of vitamin deficiencies during neonatal period (birth to 28 days): vitamin E, folacin, and pyridoxine deficiencies are most common.

The infants at high risk for these problems are those born of teen-age mothers who must meet their own high nutrient needs to complete their growth in addition to providing nutrients for the growth and development of the fetus.

Common prenatal nutritional deficiencies that produce low-birthweight babies are:

- protein
- energy
- folacin
- vitamin D
- pyridoxine

TABLE 17–1 Infant Food Guide

	BIRTH TO 5 MONTHS	5 TO 6 MONTHS	7 TO 9 MONTHS	10 TO 12 MONTHS	FOODS TO AVOID (Birth–12 Months)
MILK PRODUCTS	Breast Milk or Infant Formula*. Maximum intake 36 oz/24 hours	Same as before	Same as before	Same as before. May add soft cheese, pudding, custard, occasionally.	Whole, low-fat, skim evaporated cow's milk
CEREALS		Start with one high iron infant cereal: rice, barley, or oatmeal. Give 2 servings per day by spoon; start with 1 tsp. per feeding and gradually increase to 3 Tbsp. per feeding. Mix cereal with breast milk or formula.	Continue high iron cereals. May add Cream of Wheat or farina. Add dry toast and crackers (not cookies) to chew after other foods are eaten.	Continue high iron cereals and breads for chewing.	Cereal in the bottle. Cereal-Egg-Meat mixtures in jars. Cookies, cakes, sweet breads.
VEGETABLES			Give 2 servings per day; start with 1 tsp. per feeding and increase to 2–3 Tbsp. per feeding. Add one new food every 5–6 days. Use strained carrots, green beans, green peas, squash, sweet potatoes.	Continue vegetables, increase variety, Give coarser foods; mashed or whole pieces of soft, cooked vegetables by spoon and as finger foods.	Vegetables seasoned with fat, salt, sugar, or other seasonings. Strong-flavored vegetables, whole kernel corn.
FRUIT/ FRUIT JUICES			After vegetables, start fruits. Give 2 servings per day; use up to 2–3 Tbsp. per feeding of single strained fruits or mashed banana. Start unsweetened fruit juice in a cup, 1 serving per day, 4 ounces/serving.	Give 3 servings per day (limit fruit juice to 1 serving/day). Offer more variety of fruits, include some soft, ripened, or canned fruits.	Infant or homemade desserts, pies, cobblers, tapioca fruit mixtures, honey fruit mixtures. Fruits with seeds, pits, or thick skins.
MEAT/EGGS			After vegetables and fruits, start meats. Give 1–2 servings per day; use up to 2 Tbsp. per feeding of strained beef, liver, veal, turkey, chicken, lamb, pork.	Give 1-2 servings per day; add cooked egg yolk (no egg whites). Offer other meats: ground table meats, flaked fish.	Vegetable/meat or pasta/meat combinations. Do not use fatback, bacon, salt pork, sausage, broth, gravy.
OTHERS			Junior baby foods should be discouraged due to the poor variety of foods, extended expense, and the limited nutritive values of the combination foods.		Candy, nuts, popcorn, fried foods, highly seasoned foods. Carbonated beverages, tea, sweetened beverages.

Courtesy of the Georgia Department of Human Resources, 1990.

Prenatal nutrient deficiencies may be partially corrected, but rarely totally reversed, by the generous provision of the nutrient needs of the baby immediately after birth. The WIC (Women, Infants, and Children) program, which provides food supplements for pregnant women, infants, and children up to the age of five, has been very effective in reducing the incidence of prenatal, infant, and child malnutrition. WIC also provides nutrition and child care information in a number of languages, Figure 17–1.

COMO ATENDER A UN BEBE MOLESTO

Abrazar a su bebé es muy importante. Le dará la seguridad y el amor que necesita para crecer.

Si su bebé está molesto, o llora mucho, posiblemente . . .

tiene hambre.

Aliméntele **cada vez** que tenga hambre.

necesita atención.

Levántele y abrázele seguido.

. . . está muy excitado o muy cansado.
★ Cálmele con luz suave, música suave, caricias, banos, y meciéndole.

. . . está teniendo un crecimiento rápido.
★ A los 3, 6, y 12 semanas su bebé puede tener hambre mas seguido porque esta creciendo mas rápido.
Alimentele **cada vez** que tenga hambre.

. . . es alérgico a algo en la dieta.
★ Trate de disminuir la cafeína, alcohol, cigarros o drogas.

. . . esta enfermo.
★ Si tiene fiebre, llame al médico.

Las operaciones de estas instalaciones están en conformidad con la política del Departamento de Agricultura de los Estados Unidos que prohibe la discriminación en base de raza, color, sexo, edad, impedimento físico, religión u origen nacional.

Figure 17–1 WIC provides nutrition and child care information in several languages. Developed by WIC Program, Research & Education Institute, Harbor-UCLA Medical Center, 1990.

The rapid rate of growth and development that is characteristic of infancy must be supported by adequate nutrient intake. The nutrient needs during this first year are high while the volume capacity of the infant's stomach is small. This explains the infant's need for frequent feedings of nutrient-dense food.

The calorie needs during the first four months are particularly high relative to an infant's size because of the high energy requirements for the rapid growth taking place. A newborn needs 45–55 calories per pound daily. One-fourth to one-third of these calories are used for growth. As the infant progresses through the first year, fewer calories are needed for growth and more are needed for physical activity as the infant becomes more mobile, Figure 17–2. By six months of age the infant requires only 40–45 calories per pound. The infant's needs for all nutrients are very high in proportion to their body size. In addition, a child's social and emotional needs must also be met to ensure optimal growth and development.

The First Six Months

During the first six months, the infant's nutritional needs can be met solely with breast milk or formula. Both breast milk and formula can provide all nutrients needed by the infant for the first six months of life. The full-term infant is born with a store of iron and vitamin A to supply these nutrients for six months. A premature infant may require supplements of these nutrients during this period. No semi-solid foods are needed or advisable until the infant is at least five months of age. Younger infants are not developmentally or physiologically ready to ingest solid foods (discussed

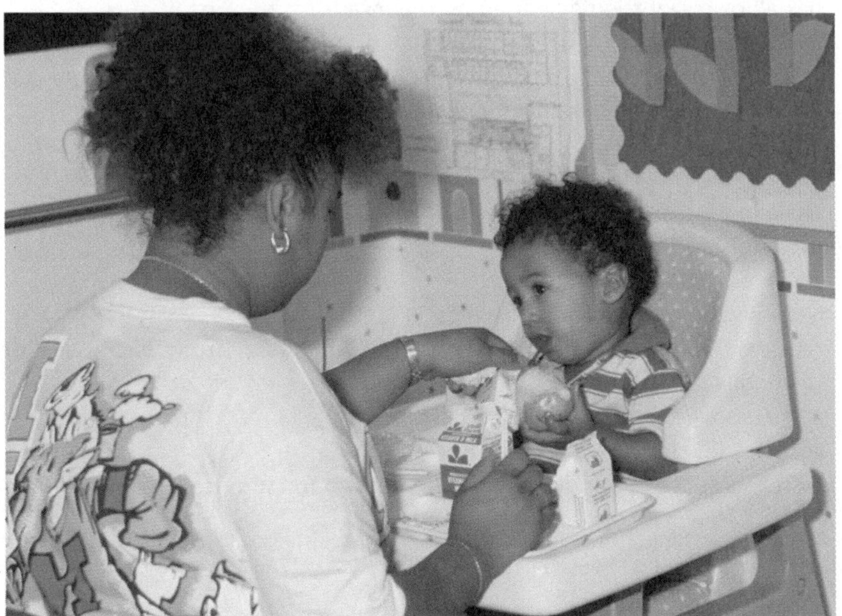

Figure 17–2 Older infants need fewer calories for growth and more calories for physical activity.

later in this chapter). Breast milk is the preferred food for an infant; Table 17–2 presents some advantages of breast milk over formula. However, after considering health factors and lifestyle, a mother may select formula feeding as the best approach for her and her infant. Some conditions that might cause a mother to choose formula feeding are:

- illness of the mother
- mother needs to take medications
- mother needs to be away from the child for long periods of time
- mother wishes not to nurse

The Caregiver and the Breast Feeding Mother

The mother who is employed outside the home may choose to continue to breast feed. She may use a breast pump or hand express her milk to be fed to her baby by the caregiver while she is at work. Breast milk may be refrigerated in a sterile container for up to 24 hours or may be frozen in a plastic bag for up to two weeks. The caregiver should be flexible and willing to assist the mother who wants to breast feed her infant.

TABLE 17–2 Advantages of Breast Feeding

Breast Milk:

- has all of the nutrients needed by the infant for the first 6 months
- contains proteins that are more digestible than cow's milk protein
- contains lactose, the carbohydrate present, which aids in calcium absorption and in establishing beneficial intestinal flora
- provides *antibodies* (immunoglobulins) that protect the infant from some infectious illnesses
- has a higher content of the essential fatty acids
- provides taurine*
- provides dietary nucleotides**
- is less likely to cause food allergies
- reduces the risk of bacteria entering the baby's body from unsanitary formula preparation
- is inexpensive, convenient and is always at the correct temperature
- contains less sodium (salt) than formulas
- fosters emotional bonding between mother and infant

* Taurine is a free amino acid (not found in proteins), which is particularly important for the normal growth and development of the central nervous system. It is now added to some formulas, especially those for premature infants.

** Dietary Nucleotides play a role in the infant's ability to produce antibodies in response to infectious organisms they may be exposed to. The American Academy of Pediatricians currently recommends that these be added to all prepared formulas.

The Caregiver and the Formula Fed Infant

Most infants in child care centers are formula fed. The type of formula to be fed will have been determined by the infant's parents and health care provider. Formula for infants is prepared to closely resemble breast milk in composition relative to the amount of protein, carbohydrate, and fat. Infant formula may be made from cow's milk, soy, or meat products. The formula may be purchased in powder or liquid concentrates or as ready-to-feed liquids. Unmodified cow's milk should not be given to infants prior to one year of age because it often causes digestive disorders and may cause intestinal bleeding.

Preparation of Formula

Safe preparation of formula is primarily dependent on two factors:

1. Sanitation—Sanitary formula preparation using **aseptic procedures** prevents serious illness that might result from bacteria introduced into the formula. This requires careful sanitizing of all utensils used in preparing formula and thorough handwashing prior to mixing the formula. When preparing formula from a powdered concentrate, the water to be used for dilution must be sterilized before it is used. Honey should never be added to a formula for an infant less than one year of age. Honey contains Clostridium botulinum spores, which in an infant's intestine, can produce a dangerous toxin that can be life-threatening.
2. Accuracy—Accurate measuring and mixing of formula (according to directions) assures the provision of needed calories and nutrients to allow for optimal growth and development. Adding too much water results in diluted formula that cannot provide adequate daily nutrients within the volume of formula that an infant will consume. Adding too little water results in an "over-rich" formula that may cause digestive problems. If given over a long period of time this rich formula results in excessive caloric intake and obesity. Skim milk or low-fat milk should not be used in formula preparation because infants need the fat to meet their calorie needs within the volume of feedings that can be comfortably taken in each day. Adequate fat in the diet is also a critical need relative to normal nerve development; fat is needed for myelin, the insulation on new nerve fibers. It is recommended that 30–50 percent of the infant's calories come from fat. The fat in the formula also must provide the essential fatty acids (linolenic and linoleic) that are required for cell growth. The equivalent of one tablespoon of a polyunsaturated fat, such as corn oil or safflower oil, will meet the infant's need for essential fatty acids.

FEEDING TIME FOR THE INFANT

How frequently a baby is fed is also determined by the parents and health care provider. For the first four months it is generally considered best to feed an infant on demand. Infants vary greatly as to how much food they can comfortably handle at one time and in how often they require food. The individual infant is the best source of information on when to feed. There is much variation in the frequency and amount of feeding. Some common guidelines suggest:

0–1 months	6 feedings of	3–4 oz./feeding
1–2 months	6 feedings of	3–5 oz./feeding
2–3 months	5 feedings of	4–6 oz./feeding
4–5 months	5 feedings of	5–7 oz./feeding
6–7 months*	5 feedings of	6–8 oz./feeding
8–12 months*	3 feedings of	8 oz./feeding

*Also taking solid foods

How to feed a baby involves much more than getting the nipple into the mouth. Cleanliness is of first importance at feeding time. The caregiver's hands must be soap-washed prior to feeding. The formula should not be too warm or too cold. If it feels slightly warm when tested against the inside of the wrist, it is the right temperature. **Caution:** Infant formula in the bottle should not be heated in the microwave. The fluid formula may become dangerously hot while the outside of the bottle feels cool. This method of heating has severely burned some infants.

Feeding time should be relaxed with actual feeding preceded by a few minutes of talking and playing with the infant. The infant should be held in a sitting position with its head against the caregiver's upper arm. The infant should be cuddled and talked to with eye-to-eye contact while being fed. This makes feeding time a pleasant social time for the infant. It also gives needed close human contact (bonding), Figure 17–3. The nipple of the bottle should be kept full of formula so that the baby does not swallow air, which can cause gas and *distention* of digestive organs. The infant should not be hurried; infants require at least 20 minutes per feeding.

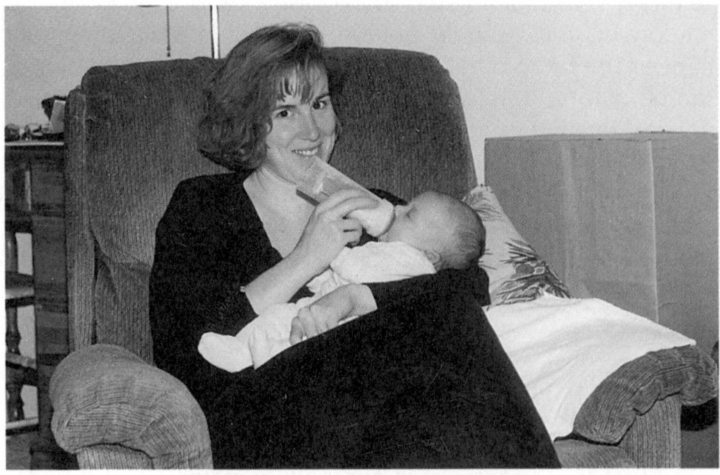

Figure 17–3 Feeding time is a time for infant and parent bonding.

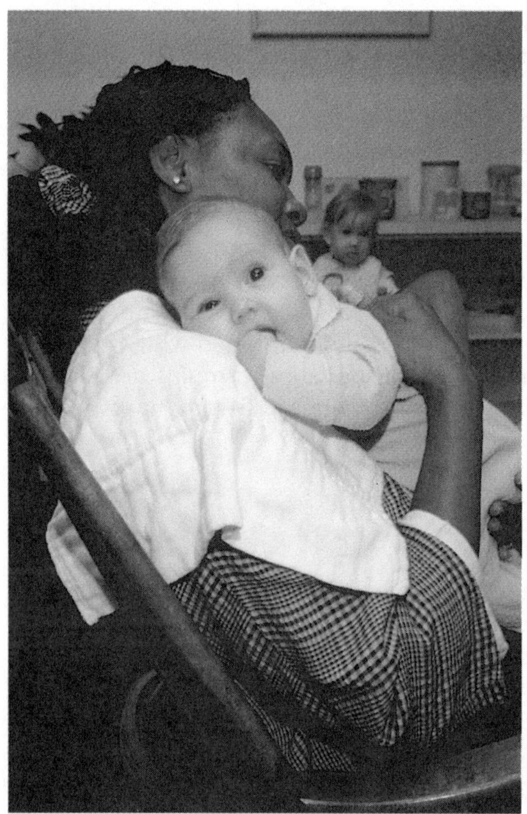

Figure 17–4 The caregiver should stop during and after feeding to burp the baby.

The caregiver should stop two or three times during each feeding and after the feeding to burp the baby, Figure 17–4. This may be done by placing the infant over the shoulder or face down across the lap and gently patting or rubbing the back. After feeding, the infant should be placed on its right side to aid passage of feeding into the stomach. This also prevents distention of the stomach and ***regurgitation***. Infants should not be placed on their stomachs for sleeping. This position may put a child at a higher risk for sudden infant death syndrome (Wong, 1993). **Caution:** The bottle should never be propped and the baby left unattended while feeding. Infants do not have the motor control to remove the bottle from their mouth and may aspirate the formula after they fall asleep. This practice also increases the risk of ***bottle-mouth syndrome*** and ear infections.

Until solid foods are added, breast milk or formula should meet the water needs of the baby. However, since the infant has a great need for water, it is not safe to assume that the formula has supplied all that is necessary. A thirsty baby acts much like a hungry baby. So, if the baby appears hungry after only a short interval after feeding, water can be offered. Also, if the temperature of the environment is high, water should be offered to the infant with increased frequency.

Vitamin and/or mineral supplements are sometimes recommended for the infant. Breast milk or formula is adequate to meet the nutritional needs of the infant except perhaps for vitamin D and the mineral fluoride. The breast-fed infant may benefit from a vitamin D supplement but the formula-fed infant is getting adequate amounts of vitamin D and should not be supplemented with this vitamin. Fluoride is not found in effective amounts in breast milk even though the mother may be drinking fluoridated water, and this mineral is not generally added to infant formulas. The infant who has no fluoride in his diet and consumes little water would also benefit from a fluoride supplement. Fluoride supplements started at birth may reduce tooth decay in a child's permanent teeth by 50–60 percent. The recommended level of supplementation is 0.25 mg fluoride per day. **Caution:** Be sure to monitor an infant's fluoride intake; fluoride in excess is toxic and at 0.5 mg/day levels may cause tooth discoloration. Fluoride supplements combined with vitamin D are not safe to use with the formula-fed infant. That is because formulas are already supplemented with vitamin D and excessive intake of vitamin D may have serious consequences for the infant.

INTRODUCING SEMI-SOLID (PUREED) FOODS

The caregiver, parent, and health care professional must cooperate closely in introducing semi-solid foods to the infant. Finely cut, pureed foods high in fluid content, such as cereals, pureed fruits, and vegetables, are introduced between four and six months of age. Introducing semi-solid foods prior to four months of age is inappropriate because the infant does not demonstrate *developmental* or *physiological* readiness.

Developmental Readiness

At approximately five months of age, the baby changes from only being able to suck to being able to move food to the back of the mouth and to swallow without initial sucking action. At this point, the baby is able to chew, to sit with some comfort and to lean forward toward the spoon. At four to five months, the infant shows interest in touching, holding, and tasting objects—food and otherwise, Figure 17–5. It is important to note that at this age the baby can turn his head away from food when satisfied, signalling a desire to stop eating. This signal should be watched for, respected, and the offering of food should be stopped.

Physiological Readiness

At four to six months the infant begins to produce enzymes capable of digesting complex carbohydrates, and proteins other than milk protein. This signals a readiness for semi-solid foods such as cereals and pureed fruits and vegetables. Pureed meat products may be offered at six months. By six to seven months of age the infant's kidneys are sufficiently developed to handle the nitrogen-containing wastes resulting from the addition of high protein meat products to the diet. Between four and six months of age, the infant's iron stores that were present at birth become exhausted. Consequently semi-solid foods need to be introduced in order to supply iron.

Figure 17–5 Infants sometimes find more pleasure in touching their food while tasting it.

Table 17–3 describes age-related, developmental factors that may influence feeding behavior. It is important to remember that infants vary greatly in rate of development. That is why there is no need for concern if a baby presents some of these behaviors ahead of or behind schedule.

New foods should be introduced slowly with a few baby spoonfuls offered one or two times daily. The food may be thinned with formula or water to make it more acceptable to the infant. Iron-fortified infant cereal is usually the first addition. Rice or barley cereals are less likely to cause allergic reactions and are therefore wise choices for the first solid food offered.

A suggested sequence for introducing solid foods is:

5–6 months	iron-enriched cereals
7–9 months	fruits and vegetables
7–9 months	meat or meat substitutes

Initially, it is better to offer individual foods rather than mixtures. If an allergy or sensitivity develops, the offending food can be identified more readily. Neither sugar nor salt should be added to an infant's food. When an infant begins to eat semi-solid food, parents may prepare the pureed food at home or use commercially prepared food. Either is acceptable as long as the types of food are chosen carefully. Food prepared for the family may be pureed in a blender using foods from the table before they have been seasoned. Doing this allows more control over what food shall be offered and usually presents a greater variety of food to the infant. Initially, it may be wise to offer only those family foods that are not too high in fiber. If the

TABLE 17–3 Age-Related Infant Behaviors

AGE	COMMON INFANT BEHAVIORS
4–6 months	■ Assumes more symmetrical sitting position ■ Grasps for objects ■ Puts objects in mouth ■ May close hands around bottle ■ Turns head away from food when no longer hungry ■ Leans toward food-containing spoon
6–7 months	■ Teeth erupt ■ Shows up and down chewing motions ■ Grasps finger foods and gets them to mouth ■ Drinks small amounts of liquid from a cup ■ Holds bottle with both hands
7–8 months	■ Sits alone with little support ■ Can manipulate food in the mouth better ■ More successful when drinking from a cup ■ Begins self-feeding with help
9–12 months	■ Can more precisely grasp and release objects ■ Reaches for the spoon ■ Feeds self with some help ■ Drinks successfully from a cup ■ More aware of environment ■ Mimics motions and activities observed

family is having baked chicken, peas, and rice an appropriate serving for the infant might be 2T chicken, 2T peas, and 1/4 c rice pureed in a blender. Home-prepared pureed food may be frozen in ice cube trays; when frozen the cubes may be removed, stored in the freezer in a tightly sealed container and removed, thawed, and used as needed. If the decision is to use commercially prepared baby food it is better to use plain fruits, vegetables, and meats rather than "dinners," which are often extended with starches and other additives. The labels on commercially prepared foods for infants and young children are helpful in making wise selections, Figure 17–6. Ingredients on food labels are listed in descending order according to amount present. The first ingredient in an acceptable infant food should be fruit, vegetable, or meat, not water or starch. When feeding a child prepared baby food, it is better to remove the small portion that you will use, put it in a small bowl and put the rest of the jar's contents into the refrigerator. This will reduce the chance of bacterial contamination of the remaining food. This practice will also save money.

Nutrition Facts	
Serving Size 1 jar (140g)	
Amount Per Serving	
Calories 110	
Total Fat	0g
Sodium	10mg
Total Carbohydrate	27g
Dietary Fiber	4g
Sugars	18g
Protein	0g
% Daily Value	
Protein 0% •	Vitamin A 6%
Vitamin C 45% •	Calcium 2%
Iron 2%	

Nutrition Label for Foods for Children Under 4

Nutrition Facts	
Serving Size 1 jar (140g)	
Amount Per Serving	
Calories 110	Calories from Fat 0
Total Fat	0g
Saturated Fat	0g
Cholesterol	0mg
Sodium	10mg
Total Carbohydrate	27g
Dietary Fiber	4g
Sugars	18g
Protein	0g
% Daily Value	
Protein 0% •	Vitamin A 6%
Vitamin C 45% •	Calcium 2%
Iron 2%	

Nutrition Label for Foods for Children 2 to 4

Figure 17–6 Special labeling rules apply to foods for infants and young children. Courtesy of Kurtzweil, P. (May 1995). Labeling Rules for Young Children's Food. *FDA Consumer*.

Infants may begin to drink small amounts of liquid from a cup around six to seven months of age. At six to seven months they may grasp finger foods and chew on them, Figure 17–7. At this age, teeth are beginning to erupt and the provision of "chew foods" such as dry toast or baby biscuits helps the teething process. (Refer to Table 17–1.)

Figure 17–7 The 6- to 8-month-old infant really enjoys finger food.

SOME COMMON FEEDING CONCERNS

Allergies. The most common chronic condition affecting infants is allergies. Allergic responses to food may result in a variety of symptoms such as runny nose, diarrhea, vomiting, abdominal pain, hives, and eczema. These symptoms are not specific for any given food or for allergies in general. Occurrence of any of these symptoms should be discussed with the infant's physician.

If there is a history of family members with allergies it is recommended that the introduction of semi-solid foods be delayed as long as possible. Certain foods such as orange juice, egg, and cereal products other than rice, are common allergens. Their addition to the baby's diet should be delayed until late infancy.

If allergic reactions seem to be linked with a specific food, the food should be eliminated from the diet and reintroduced at a later time. If a milk-based formula seems to be the offending food, it may be necessary to replace it with one formulated from soybeans or meat derivatives.

Vomiting and Diarrhea. There are many different causes for vomiting or diarrhea in the infant. Some common causes include:

- food allergies or food sensitivities
- overfeeding
- infections: systemic or food-borne
- feeding food that the baby is not yet ready for

When vomiting and diarrhea occur, the primary concern is to replace fluid and *electrolytes* that have been lost. The child with diarrhea should receive a liquid intake of approximately three ounces of fluid per pound of body weight. Good fluid choices include water and fruit juices because juices also replace electrolytes (minerals) as well as fluid.

Acute diarrhea due to an infection, and characterized by accompanying fever, must be attended to immediately. The infant's physician should be contacted and immediate and consistent attention should be given to replacing the fluid and electrolytes lost.

Anemia. Inadequate iron intake can result in low-hemoglobin type anemia that may delay the growth process and cause the infant to be lethargic. The iron stores present at birth are usually exhausted by six months of age unless the infant is on an iron-fortified formula. The addition of iron-fortified cereals at this age will provide iron needed to prevent anemia. Some infants show intestinal problems if on iron-fortified formula. These infants are given plain formula and should receive iron supplements by six months of age.

Bottle-Mouth Syndrome. Babies who are allowed to go to sleep with a bottle in their mouth may develop bottle-mouth syndrome. This condition is characterized by a high rate of tooth decay caused by the pooling of sugar-containing formula or juices in the baby's mouth.

Ear Infection. Propping the bottle so the infant may lie down and feed without being held may lead to ear infections. A child should be held in a semi-seated position during feedings to prevent milk from traveling into the eustachian tubes and into the ears.

Obesity. Obesity results when energy intake exceeds an infant's need for energy for growth, maintenance, and activity. Some infant feeding practices that are thought to play a role in obesity are overeating during bottle feeding and too early introduction of semi-solid foods.

It is important to be alert to signs that a baby is satisfied. Stopping periodically during the feeding gives infants a chance to assess their own hunger and respond appropriately when the bottle is again offered. It is important to respect an infant's judgment of the amount of food needed at a given time.

Since the parent or caregiver receives visual indicators of how much the child has drunk from a bottle, the bottle-fed infant is frequently urged to finish the feeding. In so doing, the parent or caregiver may ignore the infant's signs of fullness. Some authorities believe that continuously ignoring these signs may cause the infant to stop such signaling, thus ending a means of regulating food intake. This could have serious consequences later for the toddler, the preschooler, and the adult who does not know when to stop eating. To establish the point at which the infant is satisfied, the caregiver might stop after a few minutes of solid-food feeding and play with the child before offering food again. This helps determine whether the infant is eating because of hunger or to get attention.

Introducing semi-solid foods to the infant before they are needed or giving foods that are too high in sugar or fat may lead to babies taking more calories than they need with the consequence of obesity. Continuing to offer solid food after the baby seems satisfied also contributes to obesity and may set the stage for overeating later in life.

Choking. This can be avoided during breast or bottle feeding by holding the child properly with head elevated as previously described. Allowing the infant to lie down with the bottle propped up greatly increases the danger of choking. The six- to seventh-month-old infant wants and should be given finger foods such as dry bread, crackers, or dry cereal. However, these foods may cause choking. This danger can be minimized by having the child sit in an upright position and offering only foods that do not break into large pieces of food that are difficult for the infant to swallow. Offering semi-solid food that is finely ground and somewhat diluted will also minimize choking. Due to the high incidence of choking among infants, CPR training is vitally important.

Teething. Teeth begin to erupt around six months of age. This can be a stressful period for some infants. Teething may temporarily disrupt an infant's feeding pattern. As a result, some infants may begin to wean themselves from breast or bottle feedings. They may prefer foods that can be chewed such as dry toast or teething biscuits. Diarrhea accompanying teething is usually due to infectious organisms and it not caused by the teething process. Appropriate toys and food items should be made available for chewing to discourage infants from picking up inappropriate or unsafe objects to chew on.

Constipation. Infants who have difficulty with infrequent, hard bowel movements may be helped by increasing their intake of water and fibrous foods such as whole grain cereals, fruits, and vegetables. If the infant is still primarily on bottle feeding, the health care provider should be consulted about possible formula changes.

Summary

The first year of an infant's life is one of very rapid growth and change. At the end of the first year the baby will have tripled its birth weight and its length will have increased by fifty percent. Good nutrition is a major factor contributing to these gains in physical growth.

For the first six months of life either breast milk or formula will provide adequate nutrition for the infant. While breast milk is the preferred feeding method, modified cow's milk, soybean, or meat-based formulas may be used to provide adequate nutrients for the infant. Unmodified cow's milk should not be given during the first year of life. Regardless of what is fed, it is vitally important that infants be held, cuddled, and talked to while they are being fed.

At four to six months of age, the infant is developmentally and physiologically ready for semi-solid foods. Semi-solid foods should be introduced one at a time in small quantities as directed by a health care provider.

Feeding problems that may occur during the first year of life include allergies, anemia, obesity, vomiting, diarrhea, bottle-mouth syndrome, and ear infections.

Suggested Activities

1. Mrs. Jones, mother of two-month-old Kelly, has been on maternity leave from her job. At present, she is breast feeding Kelly. She is preparing to return to work and place Kelly with a caregiver.

   She is concerned that she must switch Kelly to formula, although she has found breast feeding quite rewarding. What feeding options can her caregiver offer her?

2. Visit the baby food section of the local grocery store and read the ingredients that are listed on the labels. Based on the ingredients listed, select several kinds of foods that are good choices to feed to a young infant.

3. Plan an instructional package with which to instruct a new employee in an infant care facility. What social aspects of infant feeding should be included in addition to nutritional and infant-handling factors?

4. If applicable, review state regulations for child caregivers relating to infant feeding.
5. Review the common problems associated with low-birthweight infants and report the prenatal nutrient deficiencies that most frequently result in the birth of low-birthweight infants.

Chapter Review

A. Multiple Choice. Select the best answer:

1. Infant formula is modified to most closely resemble
   a. cow's milk
   b. soybean milk
   c. breast milk
   d. evaporated milk
2. Semi-solid foods may be added to an infant's diet
   a. when the infant is developmentally ready
   b. so the infant will sleep through the night
   c. when nutritional need exists
   d. both a and c
3. Propping the bottle to feed an infant can result in
   a. choking
   b. bottle-mouth syndrome
   c. ear infections
   d. all of these
4. The first semi-solid food that should be added to an infant's diet is
   a. strained vegetables
   b. iron-fortified cereal
   c. pureed meats
   d. mashed egg yolks
5. The introduction of semi-solid foods before six months of age may result in all but
   a. the infant sleeping through the night at an earlier age
   b. development of food allergies
   c. obesity
   d. digestive upsets
6. To meet fluid needs beyond that provided by formula/breast milk, an infant should be given
   a. nothing
   b. honey water
   c. sugar water
   d. water

B. Briefly answer each of the following questions.

1. List three reasons for not propping the infant's bottle when the infant is feeding.
2. a) In what order should the following foods be introduced?
   pureed peas
   crisp toast
   iron-fortified cereal
   pureed meat products
   cereals

   b) At approximately what ages should each of the above foods be introduced?
3. Describe three social factors that make feeding time more enjoyable for an infant.
4. Why should unmodified cow's milk not be given to an infant before one year of age?
5. Why should reduced fat milk or skim milk not be used for preparing an infant's formula feeding?
6. Describe several feeding practices that are considered to contribute to infant obesity.

References

Wong, D. L. 1993. *Essentials of Pediatric Nursing.* St. Louis, MO: Mosby–Year Book.

Additional Reading

Carver, J. D., B. Pimenthal, Cox, W. J., and Marness, L. A. 1991. "Dietary Nucleotide Effects upon Immune Function in Infants." *Pediatrics* 88: 2, 359–363.

Committee on Nutrition, "Fluoride Supplementation: Revised Dosage Schedule." *Pediatrics* 63: 150, 1979.

Committee on Nutrition, American Academy of Pediatrics. 1981. "Nutritional Aspects of Obesity: Infancy and Childhood." *Pediatrics* 68: 880.

Gershoff, S. 1991. *Total Nutrition.* New York, NY: Harper and Row.

Guthrie, H. *Introductory Nutrition.* St. Louis, MO: Times Mirror/Mosby, 1986.

Hegarty, V. *Decisions in Nutrition.* St. Louis, MO: Times Mirror/Mosby, 1988.

"Labeling Rules for Young Children's Food." March 1995. *FDA Consumer.*

Liebman, B. 1990. "Baby Formula: Missing Key Fats." *Nutrition Action Health Letter* 17: 8, 8–9.

Pipes, P. L. 1989. *Nutrition in Infancy and Childhood.* St. Louis, MO: Times Mirror/Mosby.

Roberts, S. B. 1988. "Energy Expenditure and Intake in Infants Born to Lean or Overweight Mothers." *New England Journal of Medicine* 318: 461.

Satter, E. *Child of Mine; Feeding With Love and Good Sense* Palo Alto, CA: Bull Publishing Co., 1986.

Satter, E. 1991. *How to Get Your Child to Eat; But Not Too Much.* Palo Alto, CA: Bull Publishing Co.

Satter, E. 1980. "The Feeding Relationship," *Journal of the American Dietetic Association* 86: 352–356.

Williams, S. R., Worthington-Roberts, B. S., Schlenker, E. D., Pipes, P., Ries, J., and Mahan, L. K. 1988. *Nutrition Throughout the Life Cycle.* St. Louis, MO: Times Mirror/Mosby.

Chapter 18

Feeding the Toddler and Preschool Child

Terms to Know

neophobic
autonomy
reward
dental caries
hypertension
refusal

Objectives

After studying this chapter, you should be able to:

- Outline three major responsibilities of the caregiver in feeding the toddler.
- Estimate appropriate serving sizes of food for toddlers and preschoolers.
- Describe the possible consequences of overreliance on milk as a food for toddlers.
- List two strategies that will enable the caregiver to promote good eating habits.
- Name three health problems that are thought to be related to unhealthy eating habits acquired at an early age.

PROFILE OF TODDLERS AND PRESCHOOLERS

Toddlers (1 to 2 1/2 year olds) are a challenge! They are struggling for their autonomy. They want to assert their independence but need and want limits. As they become increasingly mobile and active they need to be protected from and taught about environmental hazards. Their insatiable curiosity can get them into trouble. Their daily routine, including food experiences, is affected by societal and cultural factors that affect the family they are a part of. Children of working mothers may spend considerable time each day outside of their home with caregivers and other children. This will give the child social experiences that differ from those in their home. The child thus learns that different people do things in different ways.

Toddlers begin to be avid television watchers and what they see will affect their behavior including their reactions to food, Figure 18–1. The hours spent sitting in front of the TV reduce valuable time that should be spent in physical activity, Figure 18–2. This in turn reduces the child's caloric needs and could contribute to child obesity problems. There is also cause for concern about the foods advertised during children's prime TV time. Many of these foods create a desire for foods that are both high in sugar and highly refined.

The toddler grows less rapidly than the infant, but still has a high nutrient need and limited stomach capacity. The infant was best fed on demand, but the toddler needs a consistent schedule for eating. In their struggle for independence, toddlers may resist this schedule and frequently reject the food served. They have learned the power of the word "no" and use it constantly. They quickly learn to shape parents' behavior by refusing to eat or, at other times, by eating to gain adult favor.

The toddler is described as being *neophobic*—having a fear of anything new (Satter, 1988). This may interfere with getting the child to eat an increasing variety of foods. However, recognizing this quality in the toddler may help caregivers be a bit more patient and ingenious as they introduce new foods.

Preschool-aged children (2 1/2–5 years) are easier to manage. They still assert their independence but they want to please and learn to express their *autonomy* in ways that are more appropriate. They are very sociable and want to be liked by peers,

Figure 18–1 Some young children spend too many hours sitting and watching television.

Figure 18–2 It is better for toddlers and preschoolers to be physically active than to sit and watch television.

as well as by parents and caregivers. The preschool-aged child wants structure and respects it more than the toddler did. However, they do not suddenly become overly compliant persons and are still somewhat hesitant to accept new things.

Preschoolers are involved with discovering ways to become individuals, while also being extremely social and making new friends. Many of these changes will be reflected in their reactions to food and eating.

THE CHALLENGE OF FEEDING A TODDLER

Toddlers, in asserting their independence, begin to make their preferences known. This includes their firm announcement of what foods they will or will not eat. Fortunately, their "will" and "will not" foods change almost daily. Great care must be taken so that the parent or caregiver does not become involved in a battle of wills over what the toddler will eat and when it will be eaten.

Basic to minimizing this friction is a clear understanding of the primary responsibilities of parent/caregiver and child in the feeding relationship. The caregiver is responsible for

- serving a variety of nutritious foods
- deciding when food is offered
- setting a good example by eating a variety of foods

The child is responsible for

- choosing what foods will be eaten from those that have been offered
- deciding how much of the offered food to eat

What Foods Should Be Served and How Much

Parents and caregivers have a responsibility to provide a variety of nutritious foods each day. As discussed in Chapter 13, the Food Guide Pyramid guidelines are easy to follow and ensure meeting daily nutritional needs. To review, the Food Guide Pyramid Groups and recommended daily servings are:

- Bread, Cereal, Rice, and Pasta Group (6 servings)
- Vegetable Group and Fruit Group (3–5 servings)
- Milk, Yogurt, and Cheese Group (2–3 servings)
- Meat, Poultry, Fish, Dry Beans, and Eggs Group (2–3 servings)
- Fats, Oils, and Sweets Group (use sparingly)

Foods from all food groups should be offered at each meal. They may be offered individually:

- ground beef patty
- whole grain bread
- sliced peaches
- milk

or be combined in one main dish:

- tuna noodle casserole with peas
- milk

Toddlers usually prefer foods presented individually. Toddler serving sizes are approximately one-fourth that of an adult serving for each food group with the exception of the milk group.

- milk and milk products—1/2 to 3/4 cup
- meat and meat alternates—1/2–1 ounce
- fruits and vegetables—2 Tbs.
- breads and cereals—2 Tbs. rice, cereal, or pasta.

When feeding a toddler, it is preferable to serve slightly less than what the caregiver thinks the child will eat and let the child ask for more. In this way toddlers are not overwhelmed by the serving size and are allowed to assert their independence by asking for more. The toddler's decreased rate of growth typically causes a decrease in appetite and lack of interest in food. This often causes parents and caregivers great concern. However, it is important that this concern does not lead to begging or forcing the child to eat more food than the child wants or needs.

Table 18–1 presents some age-related eating behaviors that may help understand a child's changing responses to food. This table also gives adults who are

TABLE 18–1 Expected Eating Behaviors According to Age

Age	Behavior
12–24 months	Has a decreased appetite Sometimes described as a finicky or fussy eater; may go on food jags Uses spoon with some degree of skill Helps feed self
2 year old	Appetite is fair Often has strong likes and dislikes; may go on food jags Likes simple food, dislikes mixtures, wants food served in familiar ways Learns table manners by imitating adults and older children
3 year old	Appetite is fairly good; prefers small servings, likes only a few cooked vegetables Feeds self independently, if hungry Uses spoon in semi-adult fashion; may even spear with fork Dawdles over food when not hungry
4 year old	Appetite fluctuates from very good to fair May develop dislikes of certain foods and refuse them to the point of tears if pushed Likes to help with meal preparation Uses all eating utensils; becomes skilled at spreading jelly or peanut butter or cutting soft foods such as bread
5 year old	Eats well, but not at every meal Likes familiar foods Often adopts food dislikes of family members and caregivers Makes breakfast (pours cereal, gets out milk and juice) and lunch (spreads peanut butter and jam on bread)

Adapted from Allen, K. E., and Marotz, L. 1994. *Developmental Profiles: Pre-Birth through Eight*. Albany, NY: Delmar Publishers.

feeding the toddler some clues as to how to help maximize positive feeding experiences at different ages.

When to Serve Food

Timing of meals and snacks is important when feeding the toddler. Too much time between feedings will result in an over-hungry, cranky child who is less likely to accept the food presented. Meals and snacks spaced too closely will not allow ample time for a child to become hungry, again resulting in a poor eating response.

Most young children also eat better at meals if they are not too tired and if they have been given a little warning so that they can "wrap up" their current play activity. Allowing time for reading a quiet story just before a meal may set the stage for a pleasant and more satisfying meal-time experience for both child and caregiver.

Because of toddlers' great need for nutrients and small stomach capacity, they must eat more often than the three-meal family pattern. A good eating pattern is:

- breakfast
- midmorning snack
- lunch
- midafternoon snack
- dinner
- bedtime snack, if needed

Snacks should be chosen from the Food Guide Pyramid and be planned carefully as part of the day's total food intake. If a food is appropriate to be in a child's meal, it is a good snack choice. Snacks for the toddler cannot be those commonly promoted on TV as "snacks." Foods such as chips, snack cakes, rich cookies, candy bars, and soft drinks have no place in the toddler's daily food plan. Some appropriate food choices for snacks are:

- cheese cubes
- lightly sweetened puddings
- crackers with peanut butter
- fruit juice—orange or other juices fortified with vitamin C
- raw vegetables—broccoli flowerettes, cauliflower pieces, carrots (cut in small pieces to reduce risk of choking)
- lightly cooked vegetables—green beans, carrots, lima beans
- fruits—apple and orange wedges, bananas, applesauce, diced peaches
- wholegrain crackers or bread
- dry, nonsweetened cereal

How to Make Eating Time Comfortable, Pleasant, and Safe

Children are more likely to eat in comfortable surroundings. Furniture should be at an appropriate size; table height should be at a comfortable height for children to eat from and the chairs should allow their feet to rest flat on the floor. If a highchair or youth chair is used, it must allow support for the child's feet and have a comfortable eating tray. Eating utensils should be child-sized and nonbreakable. An upturned rim around plates provides a means of "trapping" elusive bits of food. Use of plates that are divided into two or three compartments may help reduce frustration for toddlers as they develop their feeding skills. Small (4–6 ounce) cups with broad bases are easy for children to hold and reduce spilling. Forks chosen for children should have short, blunt tines and broad, short easy-to-grasp handles. Spoons should also have short, blunt handles and shallow bowls for easy use. While most

Figure 18–3 Preschoolers develop fine motor skills enabling them to better use eating utensils.

toddlers and preschoolers will have difficulty using knives for cutting, they should be encouraged to use them occasionally for spreading in order to help them develop this skill.

During the toddler and preschool years, children are developing better fine motor skills and hand/eye coordination. This enables them to better handle utensils and feed themselves, Figure 18–3. They should be encouraged to use these skills but should not be given too many hard-to-manage foods at one time. Serving finger foods along with those foods that require using a fork or spoon reduces mealtime frustration.

Finger foods encourage self-feeding; they are well accepted and easy to handle. Meats and cheeses may be cut into cubes or strips, vegetables into sticks and fruits into slices. Toddlers enjoy turning some nonfinger foods into finger foods and often accept them better because it was their individual choice. A parent may not think peas, mashed potatoes and rice are finger foods, but some toddlers do. A little flexibility in the choice of eating methods often pays off in the toddler's increased willingness to try eating by conventional methods.

Sanitation is an important consideration in feeding the toddler. The aseptic environment with which we surround the infant is not necessary or possible with the toddler. However, cleanliness is of prime importance when preparing, serving and eating food. The caregiver and toddler must thoroughly wash their hands before handling or eating food and again after eating or before returning to work or play, Figure 18–4. Handwashing is mandatory since this age group does a lot of eating with their hands.

Figure 18–4 Toddlers and preschoolers learn the importance of washing hands before handling food.

AS THE TODDLER BECOMES A PRESCHOOLER

As children grow older they begin to eat more willingly. However, preschoolers will have even firmer ideas of what they will and will not eat. The preschooler grows in "spurts" that are followed by periods of little or no growth, only weight gain. During active growth periods the child's appetite and food acceptance is usually good. However, as growth slows, so does the child's appetite. It is during this latter stage that parents and caregivers often are unduly concerned. (This concern can have the consequence of establishing a food emotion link that can lead to long-lasting feeding problems.) There is no real cause for concern; a growing energetic child will never starve. Remember that during this age, food is offered frequently. If Johnny does not eat a good lunch, it will soon be snack time and he can get the needed nutrients then. The important thing is to be sure that the snack food presented is of the same nutritious quality as the lunch.

During the preschool years, attitudes about food and eating patterns are formed that will be carried throughout adult life. The caregiver and parents share responsibilities for forming positive feelings about food and promoting healthful eating practices in the young child. Preschoolers like rules even though they resist them. Rules about acceptable eating behavior should be consistent but with enough flexibility to allow a parent or child to escape from a high-stress feeding situation without a battle.

Guidelines for Feeding the Preschooler

As with toddlers, the Food Guide Pyramid provides a simple guideline for feeding preschoolers. The main difference is in amount of food served. Suggested serving sizes for the preschooler are:

Figure 18–5 Children enjoy preparing some of the food that they will eat.

1/2 to 3/4 cup milk
1/2 to 1 slice of bread
1 Tbs. for each year of age for:
- fruits
- vegetables
- meats and meat alternates

Serving the preschooler a little less than you expect them to eat does not overwhelm them, but rather gives them an opportunity to ask for more. Three- to five-year-old children are also very aware of the appearance of food. Attention should be given to presenting a variety of colors, shapes, and textures in a meal. Doing so makes the food more attractive and increases its acceptance. At this age the child prefers foods that are lukewarm. Hot or cold foods are often rejected or played with until they reach an acceptable temperature. Involving the children in the preparation of a food to be served may enhance their interest in eating that food and the entire meal, Figure 18–5.

The same rules for making mealtime comfortable for the toddler also apply for the preschooler. The three-to five-year-old child still has trouble managing eating utensils and is more cooperative if some finger foods are provided and if unintentional messes are ignored.

GOOD EATING HABITS

Life-long eating habits are formed between the ages of one to five years. This makes the feeding of toddlers and preschoolers a very important task. Parents and caregivers can promote good eating habits in two ways:

- serving and enjoying a variety of nutritious foods
- eating with the children and showing enjoyment of a variety of nutritious foods

One of the most important goals in developing good eating habits is to gain the toddler's and preschooler's acceptance of a variety of foods from each of the various food groups. It is especially important to cultivate an interest for the fruit and vegetable group because there is a great difference in nutrient contribution from individual foods within this group. Children should be encouraged to accept a variety of new foods and familiar foods should be prepared in different ways. Toddlers and preschoolers may learn to like things that are sweet and not to like most vegetables. This presents a real challenge to caregivers to downplay sweets and increase children's interest in vegetables. Caregivers should eat a variety of vegetables in front of the children, comment on how delicious they are and usually display pleasure (such as smiling). This should help to promote healthy life-long eating habits.

Children are often avid mimics of the adults in their lives and of peers in a child care setting. Consequently, it is particularly important that adults sit with the children at mealtime and show pleasure in eating all kinds of food, never showing dislike for a food. Children quickly pick up on negative reactions to food and imitate them. Table 18–2 gives some suggestions for introducing new foods that may increase their acceptance by the young child.

Rewards should not be offered for trying a new food. Also, foods should never be used as a reward for any type of behavior. Studies with preschool children have shown that rewards for trying new foods increased the frequency of tasting a new food, but did not increase the long-term acceptance of the new food. Adults are often tempted to use food (especially dessert or popular sweet snacks) as a reward for eating nutritious foods presented in the meal. This practice makes these foods assume undue importance for the child. Appropriate desserts should be nutritious

TABLE 18–2 Introducing New Food
1. Introduce only one new food at a time.
2. Serve new food with familiar foods.
3. Serve only small amounts of the new food—begin with one teaspoonful.
4. Introduce new food only when the child is hungry.
5. Talk about the new food—taste, color, texture, etc.
6. Let the child help prepare the new food.
7. Encourage the child to taste the new food. If rejected, accept the refusal and try again later. As foods become more familiar, they are more readily accepted.
8. Find out what is not liked about a rejected food. The food may be accepted if it is prepared in a different way.
9. Let the child see you eat the new food and enjoy it!

Adapted from: *Food for the Preschooler. Vol. 2.* Washington State Department of Social and Health Services.

and planned as an important part of the meal. If they are nutritious, they can be served to the child along with the main dish, bread and vegetables. Also, a child should never be asked to present a "clean plate" before receiving their dessert. This is one sure way to start the child on a road to obesity.

HEALTH PROBLEMS RELATING TO EATING HABITS

Teaching the child healthful eating practices can benefit the child on through adulthood. A number of health problems are now thought to be directly or indirectly related to foods eaten. Three such problems are:

- *dental caries* (tooth decay)
- obesity (excess body fat)
- *hypertension* (high blood pressure)
- Cardiovascular Disease (CVD)

The occurrence of dental caries may be affected by sugar in the diet. However, the kind of sugar (soluble or not), the form it is in (adheres to tooth surface or not), and the time it is eaten (meals vs snacks) determine the decay potential more than total sugar intake. Providing sugar in the form of fruits and vegetables may give protection from tooth decay. They also provide needed nutrients for the actively growing young child.

Prevention of obesity should start with infant feeding. Look for the infant's signals of satiety and then stop feeding when they occur. The toddler and preschooler will usually stop feeding when they have had enough food, unless eating or not eating is their best way to get attention. A genetic potential for obesity exists in some families; this does not mean that obesity is inevitable for all family members. Children, with one or two obese parents, should be helped during early childhood years to make wise choices of nutrient-dense foods. Involving children in more physical activity and less TV watching will also help the child maintain normal body weight.

For many years hypertension (high blood pressure) has been correlated with a high intake of salt (sodium). At-risk children are those from families where hypertension is common. They may benefit from reducing the intake of salt. Sodium is an essential nutrient for infants and young children, but this need can be met easily without the use of the salt shaker. The increased use of convenience foods in the home, plus an increased frequency of eating out in fast food restaurants, may increase the intake of salt by both adults and children.

Cardiovascular Disease (CVD) is most often associated with high levels of certain fatty substances in the blood. Cholesterol is most often associated with CVD disease, however, a high intake of saturated fatty acids, and/or total fat are equal contributors to CVD.

The possible health benefit of testing and monitoring blood cholesterol levels in young children is a controversial issue. The American Academy of Pediatricians recommends that no cholesterol testing be done before the child is two years old. The two- to eight-year-old child should be tested for cholesterol only if there is a family history of early (<55 yrs. of age) cardiovascular disease.

Fats, including cholesterol, should not be restricted in the diet of the infant or toddler; fats are a source of essential fatty acids and are required for normal nerve development.

The diet for a child with high blood cholesterol levels should be carefully monitored to not have more than 30 percent of calories from fat and 10 percent or less calories from saturated fat. If a child's diet must be adjusted for any reason, the first priority must be that it meets all of the nutrient requirements for normal growth and development. Involving the child in more physical activity may also lower blood cholesterol.

Some Common Feeding Concerns During Toddler and Preschool Years

Consuming Excessive Amounts of Milk. The child who drinks milk to the exclusion of other foods may be at risk for iron-deficiency anemia and vitamin C (ascorbic acid) deficiency. Milk is very deficient in iron and in vitamin C. The child who drinks more than 16–24 ounces of milk daily usually does not consume enough foods from the other three food groups to adequately meet nutrient needs. Offering the child water between meals to satisfy thirst may help in solving this problem. Including iron-rich foods in the child's daily meals will also protect against iron-deficiency anemia. Table 19–1 presents some good food sources of iron.

Child's Refusal to Eat. Toddlers and preschoolers may refuse food either because they are not hungry or because they are asserting their newly found independence. Whatever the cause, the best response is to ignore it. Remember that active growing children will not let themselves starve—they will get hungry and eat. If nutritious food is provided for meals and snacks and if parents and caregivers do not give in to substituting the less nutritious foods that the child requests, hunger will eventually win over the challenge of *refusal*. However, it is important that the caregiver does not "try too hard." This can lead to battles and emotion-packed feeding sessions.

Dawdling and Messiness. These are the trademarks of the toddler and preschooler and cannot be avoided; however, they can be controlled. Children dawdle for various reasons—they have eaten enough, they'd rather eat something else, or they have learned that it gets attention. Establishing mealtime rules and consistently enforcing them will usually end dawdling. The caregiver should decide upon an appropriate length of time for eating (approximately 20–25 minutes), warn the child when there is not much time left and then remove the child from the table. This may result in some unhappiness for a time, but the young child learns quickly. However, it is always important to avoid hurrying children at mealtime and to allow sufficient time for eating.

Children need to learn to feed themselves and manage proper eating utensils, even though some foods may present a real challenge. This results in understandable and forgivable messiness and should be ignored. Attention-getting messiness should be ignored also; otherwise, the behavior will be reinforced. However, the caregiver has some rights too and continuous, avoidable messiness may be handled by removing the child from the table.

Food Jags. This problem can best be solved by prevention. Foods served to young children should be chosen so that a specific food does not appear too frequently. This helps to avoid the child getting fixed on a given food. Food jags are when children consume a limited variety of foods and eventually results in a deficient intake of certain nutrients.

Inconsistencies in Adult Approaches to Feeding Problems. This concern relates to several problems already cited. It is very important that parents and caregivers communicate and agree on the manner that certain food-related problems are going to be handled. It doesn't matter if the problem is weaning from excessive milk intake, decreasing dawdling and messiness behaviors, refusal to eat, or dealing with food jags, it is essential that a procedure to handle the problem is established and carried out consistently. The child cannot be expected to learn acceptable behavior if the rules constantly change.

Food Additives and Hyperactivity. Since 1973, when the Feingold diet was published, there has been considerable interest in the possible link between food additives and behavior problems, particularly hyperactivity. Several carefully controlled double-blind studies have failed to show a link between additives and/or sugar and hyperactivity. No doubt some children may be affected by certain additives in an allergic type reaction. For these children, the offending agent should be eliminated from their diet. Sugar has also been thought to be a cause of hyperactivity, but this, too, has been unproven. Actually, a biochemical case can be made for sugar as a calming and sleep-inducing agent (Guthrie, 1986, p. 43).

Fast Food Consumption By Toddlers and Preschoolers. The current cultural pattern of increased numbers of two-working parent and single parent families has changed family eating practices. More meals are eaten outside of the home, especially in fast food restaurants. There is growing concern about the repeated and long-term consumption of fast foods and its effect on young children. One concern centers around the lack of suitable seating and utensils for the young child. However, of major nutritional concern is that fast foods are very high in calories, fat and salt. These may later contribute to health problems such as cardiovascular disease, hypertension, or obesity. Fast foods are also low in vitamins A and C and calcium, unless milk is the selected beverage. A too frequent scenario is a mother and preschooler at a fast food shop. The mother shares a few bites of her hamburger with the child whose meal is rounded out with french fries and a small cola. An occasional fast food meal for the preschool child is no problem if care is taken when selecting food and lacking nutrients are made up when selecting food for the other meals served that day.

Effect of Television on Food Preferences and Food Choices. Television advertising affects a child's attitudes toward food more than TV programs do. Preschoolers watch TV for many hours each day. It is estimated that a child is exposed to three hours of commercials per week and to 19,000–22,000 commercials each year. Over one-half of these commercials are for food. Cereals (mostly sweetened), candy, other "sweets," and fast food offerings are the most frequently advertised foods. Many of these foods are high in sugar or fat and are too calorie-dense to be healthful choices for the young child. An additional concern is the extent to which a caregiver's choice of food in the market is influenced by the child's food preferences that were learned from TV food commercials.

Summary

After the first birthday, the child's physical growth rate slows. Behavioral change is very rapid. Toddlers are busy exploring limits and asserting their independence. Food frequently serves as a source of friction between the toddler and adults. The toddler and preschooler learn how to shape adult behavior by saying no to food. Adults are responsible for presenting the toddler with a variety of nutritious foods, deciding when food is offered, and setting a good example. The toddler and preschooler will decide what and how much of the food to eat. Foods offered should represent foods from each group in the Food Guide Pyramid.

The preschooler begins to eat more willingly. Long-term food attitudes are formed at this time. When feeding preschool children, it is important to make self-feeding as successful as possible. Successful self-feeding helps to foster their confidence and self-esteem.

Health problems such as dental caries, obesity, and hypertension are thought to relate to unhealthful childhood eating habits. Iron-deficiency anemia is a common health problem for young children. Two major factors contributing to this anemia are overconsumption of milk and poor snack habits. A current cultural pattern in which children frequently eat at fast food restaurants that serve foods high in calories, fat, and salt may well contribute to these health problems.

Suggested Activities

1. Eighteen-month-old Jason has recently been enrolled in a child care center. His health assessment reveals that he is anemic. Observation of his eating habits reveals that he dislikes meat and vegetables, but eats large quantities of fruits and drinks at least 2 cups of milk at every meal and snack. What changes in eating habits should the caregiver try to foster to improve Jason's iron status?
2. Formulate plans for the dining area of a child care center that will help develop self-feeding skills. Include a discussion of appropriate furniture and eating utensils. Plan a menu for one day (1 meal and 2 snacks) that will further enhance the child's self-feeding skills.

3. Four-year-old Traci arrives at her caregiver's home every morning with a bag of doughnuts. Her mother has told her that her daughter does not need to eat the food served to her, but may eat her doughnuts instead. The other children have also begun to ask for doughnuts. How should the caregiver handle this situation? What factors must be considered?

Chapter Review

A. Multiple Choice. Select the best answer:

1. The caregiver must
   a. decide how much the child will eat
   b. provide food when the child requests it
   c. set a good example of eating behaviors
   d. all of these
2. An appropriate serving size for a two year old is
   a. 1 slice of bread
   b. 2 teaspoons applesauce
   c. 1 cup milk
   d. 2 Tbs. peas
3. If a child refuses to eat, the caregiver should
   a. remove the child from the table
   b. remain calm and offer nutritious food
   c. force the child to eat
   d. prepare something the child will eat
4. Foods that should be encouraged for the anemic child include
   a. meats
   b. milk
   c. whole grain breads and cereals
   d. a and c
   e. all of these
5. The caregiver may encourage healthy eating habits by
   a. serving a variety of nutritious foods and insisting the children eat them
   b. serving a variety of nutritious foods and eating them with the children
   c. serving a variety of the children's favorite foods
   d. all of these

B. Briefly answer the following questions.

1. Name three ways that mealtimes can be made pleasant for children.
2. Explain the caregiver's major responsibilities in toddler feeding situations.

3. Suggest serving sizes for a two year old and for a four year old for each of the following foods:

bread	peas
applesauce	orange juice
banana	cooked chicken
noodles	baked beans

C. Suggested Class Projects

1. Watch one hour of Saturday morning cartoons on television and answer the following:
   a. What foods were presented in the commercials?
   b. What adjectives were used in describing the foods that were advertised?
   c. Imagine you are a four year old. On your next trip to the grocery store with your mother, what products would you want her to buy?
2. Go to a fast food restaurant featuring hamburgers and observe the following:
   a. How many toddlers and preschoolers are there?
   b. What are the children eating and drinking?

References

Guthrie, H. A. 1986. *Introductory Nutrition*. St. Louis: Times Mirror/Mosby.

Satter, E. 1988. *How to Get Your Child to Eat; But Not Too Much*. Palo Alto, CA: Bull Publishing Co.

Additional Reading

Alford, B. B., and Bogle, M. L. 1982. *Nutrition During the Life Cycle*. Englewood Cliffs, NJ: Prentice-Hall.

Burt, J. V., and Hertzler, A. A., 1980. "Parental Influence on the Child's Food Preference." *Journal of Nutritional Education*. 12:200.

Christian, J. L., and Greger, J. L. 1985. *Nutrition for Living*. Menlo Park, CA: Benjamin/Cummings Publishing Inc.

Committee on Nutrition: American Academy of Pediatrics. 1986. "Prudent Life Styles for Children: Dietary Fats and Cholesterol." *Pediatrics* 78:521.

Dietz, W., and Gortmaker, S. L., 1985. "Do We Fatten Our Children at the Television Set? Obesity and Television Viewing in Children and Adolescents." *Pediatrics* 75:807.

Ephron, D. 1978. *How to Eat Like a Child and Other Lessons in Not Being Grown Up*. New York, NY: Viking Press.

Essa, E. 1995. *Practical Guide to Solving Preschool Behavior Problems,* 3e. Albany, NY: Delmar Publishers Inc.

Harris, C. S., Baker, S. P., Smith, G. A., and Harris, R. M. 1984. "Childhood Asphyxiation by Food: A National Analysis and Overlook." *Journal of the American Medical Association* 251:2231–35.

Hegarty, V. 1986. *Decisions in Nutrition.* St. Louis, MO: Times Mirror/Mosby.

Highlights of the Report of the Expert Committee on Blood Cholesterol Levels in Children and Adolescents. 1991. National Cholesterol Education Program Coordinating Committee. NHBLI Information Center, 4733 Bethesda Ave., Suite 530 Bethesda, MD 20814.

Pipes, P. L. 1984. *Nutrition in Infancy and Childhood.* St. Louis, MO: Times Mirror/Mosby.

Satter, E., 1991. *Child of Mine; Feeding with Love and Good Sense.* Palo Alto, CA: Bull Publishing Co.

Shapiro, L. R., Crawford, P. B., Clark, M. J., Pearson, D. J., Raz, J., and Huenemann, R. L. 1984. "Obesity Prognosis: A Longitudinal Study of Children From the Age of 6 Months to 9 Years." *American Journal of Public Health.* 74: 968–972.

Vanchieri, C. November 1985. "Weak Link Between Diet and Hyperactivity." *Environmental Nutrition Newsletter.* New York, NY.

Williams, S. R., Worthington-Roberts, B. S., Schlenker, E. D., Pipes, P., Ries, J., and Mahan, L. K. 1988. *Nutrition Throughout the Life Cycle.* St. Louis, MO: Times Mirror/Mosby.

Chapter 19

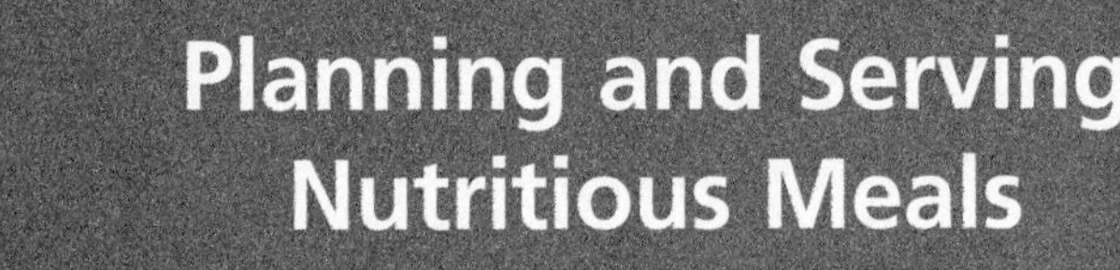

Planning and Serving Nutritious Meals

Terms to Know

- sensory qualities
- ethnic
- weekly menus
- cycle menus
- odd-day cycle menus
- whole grains
- enriched
- full-strength fruit drinks
- cost control

Objectives

After studying this chapter, you should be able to:

- Identify the criteria for adequate menus for young children.
- State where information can be obtained regarding licensing requirements for food and nutrition services.
- Plan meals and snacks that meet nutritional requirements for young children.

One of the basic human needs is nourishing the body. This is an activity that most people, including infants and young children, enjoy. Eating is a sensory, emotional, social, and learning experience. It is associated with the young child's feeling of well-being. As many infants and young children spend much of their early years in the care of caregivers other than parents, it is important that caregivers help the children establish proper attitudes toward meals. This can be accomplished by planning nourishing meals that are acceptable to children and serving these meals in a pleasant atmosphere that helps build the child both socially and emotionally.

MEAL PLANNING

A menu is a list of foods that are to be served; it is the basis of any food service. Menu planning requires thought and careful evaluation of the physical, developmental, and social needs of those for whom it is planned. Thought and planning are as necessary for a menu designed to feed a family of three as they are for an institution serving thousands of meals a day. The difference between the two situations is largely one of scale. The same careful planning must be applied to the development of menus suitable for young children. To be adequate, a menu planned for children must:

- meet the nutritional needs of children
- meet any existing funding or licensing requirements
- be appealing (have taste, texture, and eye appeal)
- make children comfortable by serving familiar foods
- encourage healthy food habits by introducing new foods
- provide safe food prepared and served in clean surroundings
- stay within budgetary limits
- provide alternatives for children with food allergies

A Good Menu Meets Nutritional Needs

The primary criterion for a good menu is nutritional adequacy. A menu must meet the nutritional needs of those for whom it is intended. When planning menus for young children in a care center, it is important to first determine what share of the day's total intake must be included in the menu. To determine the nutritional needs of young children, the Food Guide Pyramid and/or the *Dietary Guidelines for Americans* for that age group should be reviewed. Menus should be planned around servings from the Food Guide Pyramid.

Iron, calcium, and vitamin C are nutrients for which young children are most at risk; these nutrients should be provided daily. Tables 19–1 through 19–4 give sources for these nutrients and suggestions for preparation.

Federally funded food programs for children are required to provide one-third of the recommended daily requirements for calcium, iron, vitamin A, and vitamin C. However, it is recommended that nearly one-half the day's nutrients be included in the event that meals at home do not provide the other two-thirds of the needed nutrients.

TABLE 19–1 Sources of Iron and Suggested Preparation

Liver
- Strips, baked
- Loaf
- Braised, with tomato sauce
- Braised, with apple slices and onion

Beef
- Ground beef and macaroni casserole
- Ground beef patty
- Meat loaf
- Roast beef
- Hot beef sandwich with gravy
- Beef stew
- Meat balls and spaghetti
- Meat sauce and spaghetti
- Roast beef sandwich

Dried Peas, Beans, and Lentils
- With rice
- With small amounts of meat
- With vegetables
- In soup

Ham
- Creamed ham and peas
- Ham salad
- Ham and sweet potato casserole
- Scalloped ham and potatoes
- Sliced baked ham
- Ham sandwich

Prunes
- Stewed
- Whip
- Fruit soup

Chicken
- Chicken and rice
- Chicken and dumplings
- Chicken and noodles
- Creamed chicken
- Baked chicken
- Chicken salad

Grain Products (Whole or Enriched)
- Pasta with tomato or meat sauce
- Gingerbread
- Bran or cornmeal muffins
- Rice Pudding

Raisins
- In bread or rice pudding
- Plain
- Stewed
- In cereal

Spinach
- Raw
  - Salad with onions and bacon
- Cooked and Buttered
  - With hard cooked eggs
  - With cheese sauce
  - With onions and bacon

TABLE 19–2 Sources of Calcium and Suggested Preparation

Milk
- Plain
- In custards
- In puddings

Cheese
- In sandwiches
- In cream sauce
- Cubes
- In salads

Yogurt
- Plain
- With fruit
- As dip for fruits or vegetables

Salmon
- Patties
- Loaf

Vegetables
- Broccoli–stir fry with cheese sauce

TABLE 19–3 Sources of Vitamin C and Suggested Preparation

Rich Sources

- Oranges
  - Juice
  - Sections
  - Slices
  - Wedges
  - Juice in gelatin
- Strawberries
  - Plain
  - With milk
  - In fruit cup
- Cantaloupe
  - Cubed or balled
  - In fruit cup
- Cauliflower
  - Raw
    - Florets
    - With yogurt dip
  - Cooked
    - Buttered
    - With cheese sauce
    - With cream sauce
- Green Pepper
  - Strips
  - Rings
  - Seasoning in sauces, casseroles
- Broccoli
  - Raw
    - Strips
    - Chunks
    - Florets with yogurt dip
  - Cooked
    - Buttered
    - With cheese sauce
    - With lemon sauce
- Tomatoes
  - Raw
    - Slices
    - Wedges
    - Cherry
    - Juice
    - In tossed salad
  - Cooked
    - Baked
    - Broiled
    - Sauce
    - Scalloped
    - Stewed

Good Sources

- Cabbage
  - Raw
    - Coleslaw
    - Wedges
    - In tossed salad
  - Cooked
    - Buttered
    - In stew
- Spinach
  - Raw
    - Salad with onions and bacon
- Tangerine
  - Sections
  - Slices
  - In fruit cup

TABLE 19–4 Sources of Vitamin A and Suggested Preparation

Rich Sources

- Liver
  - Strips, baked
  - Loaf
  - Braised, with tomato sauce
- Carrots
  - Raw
  - Sticks, curls, coins
  - Salad, with raisins
  - Cooked
    - With celery
    - With peas
    - Creamed
- Pumpkin
  - Mashed
  - Bread
  - Custard
- Sweet Potatoes
  - Baked
  - Mashed
  - Bread
- Spinach
  - Raw
    - Salad with onions and bacon
  - Cooked
    - Buttered
      - With hard cooked eggs
      - With cheese sauce
      - With onions and bacon

Good Sources

- Apricots
  - Raw
  - Canned
    - Plain
    - In fruit cup
    - Whip
    - Nectar
- Cantaloupe
  - Balls
  - Cubes
  - In fruit cup
- Broccoli
  - Raw
    - Strips
    - Chunks
    - Florets with yogurt dip
  - Cooked
    - Buttered
    - With cheese sauce
    - With lemon sauce
    - Stir-fried with celery, onions

Federal guidelines for child care centers receiving federal reimbursement require the following menu pattern in order to ensure minimum nutritional adequacy:

1. Minimum Breakfast Requirement
   - whole grain or enriched bread or substitute
   - full-strength fruit or vegetable juice, or a fruit or vegetable
   - milk, fluid
2. Minimum Snack Requirement (choose two different components)
   - whole grain or enriched bread or substitute
   - milk, fluid
   - full-strength fruit or vegetable juice, or a fruit or vegetable
   - meat or alternate

3. Minimum Lunch or Supper Requirement
   - meat or substitute
   - fruits and/or vegetables, two or more
   - whole grain or enriched bread or substitute
   - milk, fluid

Minimum serving sizes are determined by the child's age in categories of 1 to 3 years and 3 to 6 years (USDA, 1984).

A Good Menu Meets Funding or Licensing Requirements

Many child care organizations depend on some form of government monies for their funding. Perhaps the best known of these government programs is the Child Care Food Program. This is a program that provides reimbursement for meals served to children in child care centers and home child care programs. This program provides support to child care centers for meal service. Meal service includes cost of food, labor, and administration. Funds are provided by the Food and Nutrition Service of the U. S. Department of Agriculture; the program is administered at the state level by the Department of Education. The meal plan cited in Table 19–5 is the minimum that must be served in order to qualify for reimbursement under this program. At this time, menus are planned using a food-based planning system. A computer-assisted nutrient-based plan will be a future option. Table 19–6 illustrates the proposed rules, which are slated to become effective for the 1996–1997 school year. The guidelines are quite specific as to the minimum amounts of food required to fulfill a serving. Guidelines are also available listing specific foods that are permitted as alternatives within each food group, Table 19–7. The menu planner working within these guidelines must take great care to keep up with the current information as this program undergoes frequent and sometimes sweeping changes. One change has been the addition of yogurt as an acceptable choice from the milk and milk products group. The National School Lunch Act requires that school meals comply with 1990 *Dietary Guidelines for Americans* by the 1996–1997 school year. These guidelines include: (1) eat a variety of foods; (2) limit total fat to 30 percent of calories; (3) limit saturated fat to less than 10 percent of calories; (4) choose a diet low in cholesterol; (5) choose a diet with plenty of vegetables, fruits, and grain products; and (6) use salt and sodium in moderation (*Federal Register*, June 13, 1995).

Licensing of child care facilities is administered by state agencies, usually the Department of Health. Each state has its own licensing requirements with regard to nutrition and food service. Caregivers who provide food for children should check the licensing requirements for their particular state. Aspects pertaining to nutrition often covered by licensing regulations include:

1. Administration and record keeping
   - sample menus
   - number of meals served daily

TABLE 19–5 Child Care Food Program Meal Pattern

	CHILDREN 1 UP TO 3 YEARS	CHILDREN 3 UP TO 6 YEARS
Breakfast		
Milk, fluid	1/2 cup	3/4 cup
Juice or fruit or vegetable	1/4 cup	1/2 cup
Bread and/or cereal, enriched or whole grain		
Bread or	1/2 slice	1/2 slice
Cereal: Cold dry or	1/4 cup[1]	1/3 cup[2]
Hot cooked	1/4 cup	1/4 cup
Midmorning or midafternoon snack (supplement) (Select 2 of these 4 components)		
Milk, fluid	1/2 cup	1/2 cup
Meat or meat alternate	1/2 ounce	1/2 ounce
Juice or fruit or vegetable	1/2 cup	1/2 cup
Bread and/or cereal, enriched or whole grain		
Bread or	1/2 slice	1/2 slice
Cereal: Cold dry or	1/4 cup[1]	1/3 cup[2]
Hot cooked	1/4 cup	1/4 cup
Lunch or Supper		
Milk, fluid	1/2 cup	3/4 cup
Meat or meat alternate		
Meat, poultry, or fish, cooked (lean meat without bone)	1 ounce	1 1/2 ounces
Cheese	1 ounce	1 1 /2 ounces
Egg	1	1
Cooked dry beans and peas	1/4 cup	3/8 cup
Peanut butter	2 tablespoons	3 tablespoons
Vegetable and/or fruit (two or more)[3]	1/4 cup	1/2 cup
Bread or bread alternate enriched or whole grain	1/2 slice	1/2 slice

[1]1/4 cup (volume) or 1/3 ounce (weight), whichever is less.

[2]1/3 cup (volume) or 1/2 ounce (weight), whichever is less.

[3]1/4 each to total 1/2 cup.

Courtesy of USDA, June 1984.

TABLE 19–6 Proposed Rules for School Lunch Program

Meal Component	Minimum quantities required for			
	Ages 1–2	Preschool	Grades K–6	Grades 7–12
Milk (as a beverage)	6 ounces	6 ounces	8 ounces	8 ounces
Meat or meat alternate (quantity of the edible portion as served):				
Lean meat, poultry or fish	1 oz.	1 1/2 oz.	2 oz.	2 oz.
Cheese	1 oz.	1 1/2 oz.	2 oz.	2 oz.
Large egg	1/2	3/4	1	1
Cooked dry beans or peas	1/4 cup	3/8 cup	1/2 cup	1/2 cup
Peanut butter or other nut or seed butters	2 Tbsp	3 Tbsp	4 Tbsp	4 Tbsp
The following may be used to meet no more than 50% of the requirement and must be used in combination with any of the above:				
Peanuts, soynuts, tree nuts, or seeds as listed in program guidance, or an equivalent quantity of any combination of the above meat/meat alternate (1 ounce of nuts/seeds = 1 ounce of cooked lean meat, poultry, or fish)	1/2 oz. = 50%	3/4 oz. = 50%	1 oz. = 50%	1 oz. = 50%
Vegetables/Fruits (2 or more servings of vegetables or fruits or both)	1/2 cup	1/2 cup	3/4 cup plus additional 1/2 cup over a week.[1]	1 cup
Grains/Breads Must be enriched or whole grain. A serving is a slice of bread or an equivalent serving of biscuits, rolls, etc., or 1/2 cup of cooked rice, macaroni, noodles, other pasta products, or cereal grains.	5 servings per week—minimum of of 1/2 per day.[1]	8 servings per week—minimum of 1 per day.[1]	12 servings per week—minimum of 1 per day.[2]	15 servings per week—minimum of 1 per day.[2]

[1]For the purposes of this chart, a week equals five days.

[2]Up to one grains/breads serving per day may be a dessert.

Courtesy of the Georgia Department of Education.

TABLE 19–7 Acceptable Bread and Bread Alternates

Important Notes:

- All products must be made of whole grain or enriched flour or meal.
- Serving sizes listed below are specified for children under 6 years of age.
- A "full" serving (defined below) is required for children 6 years of age and older.
- USDA recommends that cookies be served in a snack no more than twice a week.

They may be used for a snack only when:

- whole grain or enriched meal or flour is the predominant ingredient as specified on the label or according to the recipe; and
- the total weight of a serving for children under 6 years of age is a minimum of 18 grams (0.6 oz.) and for children over 6 years, a minimum of 35 grams (1.2 oz.).

- To determine serving sizes for products in Group I that are made at child care centers, refer to "Cereal products" in FNS-86, "Quantity Recipes for Child Care Centers."
- Doughnuts and sweet rolls are allowed as a bread item in breakfasts and snacks only.
- French, Vienna, Italian, and Syrian breads are commercially prepared products that often are made with unenriched flour. Check the label or manufacturer to be sure the product is made with enriched flour.
- The amount of bread in a serving of stuffing should weigh at least 13 grams (0.5 ounce).

Group I

When you obtain these items commercially, a *full* serving should have a minimum weight of 25 grams (0.9 ounce). The serving sizes specified below should have a minimum weight of 13 grams (0.5 ounce).

Item	Serving Size
Bagels	1/2 bagel
Biscuits	1 biscuit
Boston brown bread	1/2 serving
Buns (all types)	1/2 bun
Cornbread	1 serving
Doughnuts (all types)	1/2 doughnut
English muffins	1/2 muffin
French or Vienna Bread	1/2 serving
"Fry" bread	1/2 piece
Italian bread	1/2 serving
Muffins	1/2 muffin
Pretzels, Dutch (soft) twisted	1 pretzel
Pumpernickel	1/2 slice
Raisin bread	1/2 slice
Rolls (all types)	1 roll
Rye bread	1/2 slice
Salt sticks	1/2 stick
Stuffing (bread)	1/2 serving
Sweet rolls	1/2 roll
Syrian bread (flat)	1/2 section
White bread	1/2 slice
Whole wheat bread	1/2 slice

Group II

When you obtain these items commercially, a *full* serving should have a minimum weight of 20 grams (0.7 ounce). The serving sizes specified below should have a minimum weight of 10 grams (0.4 ounce).

Item	Serving Size
Bread sticks (dry)	2 sticks
Graham crackers	2 crackers
Melba toast	3 pieces
"Pilot" bread	1 piece
Rye wafers (whole-grain)	2 wafers
Saltine crackers	4 crackers
Soda crackers	2 crackers
Taco shells	1 shell
Zwieback	2 pieces

(Continued)

TABLE 19–7 Acceptable Bread and Bread Alternates (Continued)

Group III

When you obtain these items commercially, a *full* serving should have a minimum weight of 30 grams (1.1 ounces). The serving sizes specified below should have a minimum weight of 15 grams (0.6 ounce).

Item	Serving Size
Dumplings	1/2 dumpling
Hush puppies	1/2 serving
Meat or meat alternate pie crust	1/2 serving
Meat or meat alternate turnover crust	1/2 serving
Pancakes	1/2 pancake
Pizza crust	1/2 serving
Popovers	1/2 popover
Sopapillas	1/2 serving
Spoonbread	1/2 serving
Tortillas	1 tortilla
Waffles	1/2 serving

Group IV

When you serve these items, a *full* serving should have a minimum of 1/2 cup cooked product. The serving sizes specified below are the minimum *half* servings of cooked product.

Item	Serving Size
Bulgur	1/4 cup
Corn grits	1/4 cup
Macaroni or spaghetti	1/4 cup
Noodles	1/4 cup
Rice (white or brown)	1/4 cup

Courtesy of *A Planning Guide for Food Service in Child Care Centers*, USDA, FNS-64, January 1981.

2. Food service
   - specifications for kitchens and equipment
   - sanitation of dishes, utensils, and equipment
   - requirements for transport of food when kitchen facilities are not available
   - feeding equipment required for specific age groups
3. Staffing
   - requirements of person in charge of food service
4. Nutrition policies
   - number of meals to be served within given time spans
   - posting of menus and their availability to parents
   - seating of adults at the table with children
   - posting of food allergies in kitchen and eating area

A Good Menu Is Appealing

The French say, "We eat with our eyes." Menu planners who take into consideration how the food will look on the plate are likely to develop meals that are appealing and accepted by the children to whom they are served. Figure 19–1 shows an

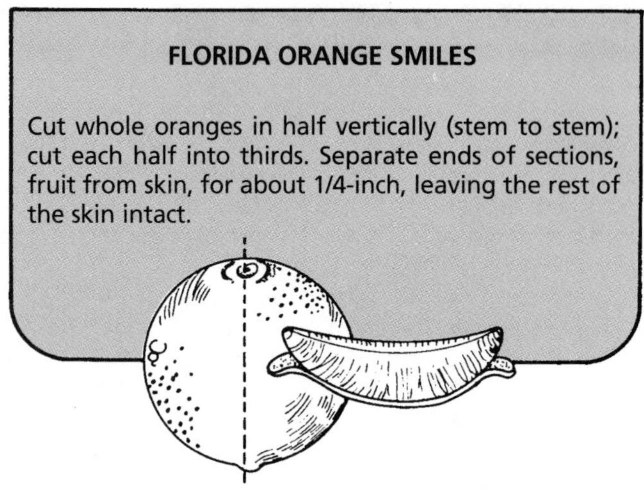

Figure 19–1 Orange "smiles" are a novel way to serve a familiar food in order to make it more appealing to children. Courtesy of *The Sunshine Cookbook*, © State of Florida, Department of Citrus, 1976.

interesting way to serve orange slices that will make them more appealing to children. Appeal can be increased by contrasting the following *sensory qualities*:

- color
- flavor (strong or mild; sweet or sour)
- texture (crisp or soft)
- shape (round, cubed, strings)
- temperature (cold or hot)

These sensory qualities of foods play an important part in a young child's choice of foods. Toddlers and young children think of foods in terms of color, flavor, texture, and shape rather than the nutrient content. Color plays a major role in children's knowledge of food (Rush, 1984; Contento, 1981). Using sensory qualities of food to appeal to young children takes advantage of their developmental level of interpreting their environment through the physical senses.

A comparison of the following two menus illustrates how menus can be made more appealing:

Menu #1
Grilled Cheese Sandwiches
Celery Sticks
Banana Chunks
Milk

Menu #2
Grilled Cheese Sandwiches
Buttered Broccoli
Red Apple Wedges
Milk

Menu #1 is essentially tones of yellow and light brown. Substituting broccoli for celery sticks adds color and increases the amount of vitamins A and C. Substituting red apples for bananas improves color contrast and adds a crunchier texture.

The sensory contrasts that contribute to the attractiveness of a meal also provide many opportunities for the caregiver or parent to expand the young child's language development. The child can be encouraged to identify foods and describe their qualities such as round, rectangular, red, yellow, hot, or cold.

While color is an important factor in food appeal, other aspects also contribute to acceptability. Young children often prefer mildly flavored, simple foods. Softer textured foods such as chicken or ground meats are often preferred because they are easy to chew. Many young children prefer plain foods that do not touch each other as opposed to mixed dishes. Sweet foods are frequently preferred. Since the basis for this preference may be biological, fruits and nutritious whole grain baked products could be offered if such a preference is shown.

A Good Menu Includes Familiar Foods and New Foods

While it is important to introduce nutritious new foods to children, it is also important to use many foods with which the children in the group are familiar. Familiarity plays a large part in young children's food choices. Familiarity of a food is a result of family food practices. Sharing of information, menu plans, recipes etc. with parents may be important in expanding family food choices that could give the child a better base of familiar foods.

Acceptance of a meal may depend on the number of familiar foods included. When introducing new foods, it is a good idea to include them along with familiar ones. It is a good idea to back up one unfamiliar new food with familiar foods; if the new food is not well-accepted, the children will not leave the table hungry. (See Table 18–2 for suggestions for introducing new foods to young children.) The menu planner might also consider introducing unfamiliar foods at snack time. Introducing unfamiliar foods at snack time prevents the new food from being labeled "breakfast food" or "lunch food."

When feeding young children, it is wise to include numerous finger foods, Table 19–8. Some children may not be skilled in the use of tableware and find finger foods to be reassuring. New foods should be introduced with little fanfare. Child involvement in preparation of an unfamiliar food may enhance its acceptance.

Most centers care for children from a variety of cultural and ethnic backgrounds. A good menu planner draws on this wealth of backgrounds and includes foods that are familiar to a number of cultures. The inclusion of *ethnic* foods serves several purposes:

- The children from the culture being featured are familiar with these foods. Since they accept them at meals or snacks, other children in the group are more willing to try them too.
- Foods of different cultural groups add variety to the meals and may serve as a basis for educational activities concerning various cultures.
- Serving ethnic food helps the caregiver establish rapport with the children and their families. This may foster increased parental participation in the center's activities.

TABLE 19–8 Suggested Finger Foods

Apple wedges	Grapefruit sections (seeded)
Banana slices	Green pepper sticks
Berries	Meat cubes
Cabbage wedges	Melon cubes
Carrot sticks	Orange sections
Cauliflowerets	Pitted plums
Celery sticks*	Pitted prunes
Cheese cubes	Raisins
Dried peaches	Tangerine sections
Dried pears	Tomato wedges
Fresh peach wedges	Turnip sticks
Fresh pear wedges	Zucchini sticks
Fresh pineapple sticks	

*May be stuffed with cheese or peanut butter
Courtesy of *A Planning Guide for Food Service in Child Care Centers.* USDA, FNS-64, 1981.

- Educating children about various cultures fosters greater respect for children who are from a culture different from theirs.
- The sharing of food is often an effective way of helping the ethnic child feel comfortable and accepted.

STEPS IN MENU PLANNING

Menu planning should be organized so that it may be done efficiently and effectively. Some of the materials that are helpful in menu planning are:

- menu forms
- a list of foods on hand that need to be used
- list of allergies
- recipe file
- old menus with notes and suggestions
- calendar
- grocery ads for short-term planning

The menu form shown in Figure 19–2 could be used for a child care center or home. The form may be adapted to provide only the meals that are served in the individual center. Components of each meal or snack are included in the form to serve as reminders of kinds of foods that should be included to provide a nutritious menu.

		Monday	Tuesday	Wednesday	Thursday	Friday
Breakfast	Fruit/Vegetable Bread Milk					
Snack	Bread Fruit/Vegetable or Milk					
Lunch	Protein Fruit/Vegetable Fruit/Vegetable Bread Milk					
Snack	Bread Fruit/Vegetable or Milk					
	# Served					
Notes						

Figure 19–2 A sample menu form.

Step 1. List the main dishes to be served for lunch during the week. These should include a meat or meat alternate. Include alternatives for children with food allergies. Appropriate combinations (see Chapter 13) of whole grain products, dried peas, beans, lentils, nuts, or nut butters may be acceptable protein-source substitutes for meat, eggs, or fish. However, many of these combinations do not contribute as much iron as meat would. To ensure that the iron needs are met attention should be given to including other iron-rich foods in the menu planned with a meat substitute.

Tuna noodle casserole with cheese	BBQ beef	Scrambled eggs	Chili	Macaroni and cheese	Protein

Step 2. List vegetables and fruits, including salads, for the main meal. Be sure to use fruits and vegetables in season. Fresh produce in season is less expensive and more nutritious than canned and some frozen foods. Fresh fruits and vegetables also offer excellent materials for learning activities. If planning seasonal menus months in advance, local County Extension Offices can provide information concerning produce in season and predicted supplies.

Peas Orange wedges	Broccoli Peach slices	Tomato juice 1/2 banana	Carrots and celery Canned pear slices	Green beans Apple wedges	Fruits and Vegetables

Step 3. Add enriched or whole grain breads and cereal products.

Enriched noodles (in casserole)	Enriched bun	Whole wheat toast	Corn muffin	Enriched macaroni (in casserole)	Bread

Step 4. Add beverage. Be sure to include the required amount of milk.

Milk	Milk	Milk	Milk	Milk	Milk

Step 5. Plan snacks to balance the main meal. Especially check for vitamin C, vitamin A, iron, and calcium.

A.M. Snack	Prepared oat cereal Milk	Bran muffin Apple juice	Pumpkin bread Milk	Raisin toast Orange juice	Rye crackers Milk
P.M. Snack	Carrot curls Wheat crackers Water	Cheese crackers Peanut butter Milk	Pizza biscuits Pineapple juice	Oatmeal cookies Milk	Brown-white sandwich Apricot-orange juice

Step 6. Review your menu. Be sure it includes the required amounts from the Food Guide Pyramid.

- Does it meet funding or licensing requirements?
- Does it include a variety of contrasting foods?
- Does it contain familiar foods?
- Does it contain new foods?

Step 7. Post the menu where it can be seen by staff and parents, Figure 19–3. Be sure to note any changes made and the likes and dislikes of the children. Communication between care center staff and parents is very important to ensure that each child's nutrient needs are met for the day and the week.

Step 8. Evaluate the menu. Did the children appear to like the foods that were served? Was there much plate waste? Keep a copy of the notes with menu planning materials. However, do not eliminate a food from the menu because it resulted in too much plate waste. A child's likes and dislikes are constantly changing and the rejected food of this week may become a favorite in a week or two.

WRITING MENUS

There are several methods of writing menus that the planner may wish to consider: weekly menus, cycle menus, and odd-day cycle menus. Among the factors that influence the method chosen are the child care center's schedule and hours,

WEEKLY MENUS
Week of ______________

Lunch and Snacks

	Monday	Tuesday	Wednesday	Thursday	Friday
Snack	Bagel with Cream Cheese Orange Juice	Blueberry Muffin Milk	Sausage Biscuit Milk	Waffles Applesauce Milk	Apple Butter Graham Crackers Orange Juice
Lunch	Turkey with Gravy Mashed Potatoes Peas Peaches Bread & Butter Milk	Macaroni & Cheese Bread & Butter Celery, Carrots Green Peppers Orange Slices Milk	Tomato Soup with Rice Bologna Sandwich Apple Slices Milk	Beef Barbecue Green Beans Bread Pears Milk	Spaghetti with Meatballs Tossed Salad Bread Sticks Fruit Cup Milk
Snack	Peanut Butter Celery Stick Milk	Yogurt Pineapple Tidbits Water	Granola Bar Pineapple/Orange Juice	Oatmeal Cookies Milk	Jello with Fruit Milk

Figure 19–3 Menus should be available to the parents.

and the personnel who will be preparing the foods on the menu. The means of buying food and sources of food supply also influence the chosen method of menu planning.

Weekly menus list the foods that are to be prepared and eaten for one week at a time. This is a very time-consuming method and should be extended to include a minimum of two or three weeks at a time. Planning more than one week allows utilization of larger, more economical amounts of food. It also permits an outline of all the foods to be served over a period of time, so that too frequent repetitions of foods may be avoided.

Cycle menus incorporate a series of weekly menus that are re-used or cycled over a period of two or three months. Frequently, cycle menus are written to parallel the seasons and reflect the fruit and vegetable offerings that are most available and affordable in a given season. A well-planned cycle menu is quite efficient since, after the initial expenditure of time in planning the cycle, little additional time is required for menu planning. Food ordering also becomes less time consuming and the use of food is more efficient. However, the planner should not hesitate to change parts of the cycle that prove difficult to produce or that are not well accepted by the children. Seasonal cycle menus may be used for a period of years with timely revisions.

Odd-day cycle menus involve planning menus for periods of days other than a week. Cycles of any number of days may be used. This type of cycling avoids the association of specific foods with certain days of the week. This type of menu requires very careful planning to avoid dishes or foods that require advance preparation in Monday to Friday child care centers.

NUTRITIOUS SNACKS

A snack is suitable if it is a nutrient-dense food and makes a serious contribution to meeting the nutrient needs of the child for that day. Calorie-dense snacks, high in sugar and fat, are not appropriate for the young child.

Snacks should contribute to the child's daily food needs and educational experiences. Snacks should contribute vitamins, minerals and other nutrients important in health, growth, and development, Figure 19–4. Snack foods should include nutrients that were not adequately provided by lunch and/or breakfast.

New or unusual foods can often be better introduced at snack time. This may often be accomplished in a party atmosphere such as a taste-testing party.

Snacks are a means of providing nutrients and energy between meals, since children have small stomach capacities and may not be able to eat enough at one meal to sustain them until the next meal. One and one-half or two hours between meals seems to be the best spacing for most children in order to prevent them from becoming too hungry or spoiling their appetite by inappropriate snacking.

Suitable Snack Foods

A variety of raw fruits and vegetables are ideal for snack foods. Raw fruits and vegetables are excellent sources of vitamin C and vitamin A, and should be included

Figure 19–4 Snacks should provide nutrients to balance the meals.

often. The caregiver must be sure the fruits and vegetables are sectioned or sliced so the children can chew them. The crispness of fruits and vegetables helps to remove food clinging to the teeth. The crispness and texture also stimulate the gums so they stay healthy. Fresh fruits and vegetables provide cellulose, which aids elimination. Another important factor not to be forgotten is exposure to the subtle flavors of fruits and vegetables.

Whole grains and cereal products or enriched breads and grain products are also good snack foods. The flavor of *whole grains* adds variety to the diet. Whole grain products also add fiber, which aids elimination. *Enriched* breads and cereals are refined products to which iron, thiamin, niacin, and riboflavin are added in amounts equal to the original whole grain product.

Unsweetened beverages such as *full-strength* fruit and vegetable juices are good choices for snacks. Juices made from oranges, grapefruits, tangerines, and tomatoes are rich in vitamin C. Vitamin C may also be added to apple, grape, and pineapple juices. Check the labels of these juices to determine if they are fortified with vitamin C. Carbonated beverages, *fruit drinks*, and some fruit ades are unacceptable for snacks. These beverages contain large amounts of sugar and no other nutrients, except perhaps some added vitamin C.

Careful attention to beverage labels enables one to avoid these expensive sugar-water offerings. Some guidelines are:

- Fruit juice must be 100 percent juice
- Juice drink may have as little as 39 percent fruit juice
- Fruit drink has from 0–10 percent real juice

Figure 19–5 Children should drink 6 to 8 small glasses of water daily.

Water is also essential for good health; children should drink 6 to 8 small glasses of water a day, Figure 19–5.

Water should be available to children at all times and may be served with their meals and snacks. Allowing children to pour the water from a pitcher, as they want it, may encourage them to drink more water. Special attention should be given to water intake after a period of physical activity and when the environmental temperature is high. A good plan might be to stop at the drinking fountain on the way in after a period of active outdoor play.

SERVING MEALS

A nutritious meal is of no value to a child if it is not eaten and enjoyed. The atmosphere in which meals are served can either forestall or further contribute to eating problems. All meals should be served in a relaxed, social atmosphere. The classroom should be tidied prior to mealtimes. This eliminates the distraction of scattered toys or unfinished games. The resulting uncluttered environment provides a more restful atmosphere in which to eat.

The table should be made as attractive as possible. Placemats made by the children add interest to the meal and give children the opportunity to contribute to the meal setting. Centerpieces may be constructed during art or assembled from objects gathered on field trips or nature hikes. Plates, cups, utensils, and napkins should be laid out neatly and appropriately. Table setting can be a learning experience for children and can provide positive experiences that enhance self-esteem. In addition, the food served should be made as attractive as possible to increase its appeal. Food can be more appealing by preparing it appropriately to retain its color and shape and neatly arranging it in serving dishes or on plates. (White or warm-hued plates enhance natural food colors; cool-hued plates tend to detract from most food colors.) Fresh, edible garnishes may be used if time and budget permit. Contrived or "cute" foods are time-consuming to prepare and may actually result in the children wanting to save them as "souvenirs" rather than eating them.

Food may be served in a variety of styles:

- plate service
- family-style service
- combination of the above

Plate service is when the food is placed on the plates in the kitchen. This style of service permits the greatest degree of portion control and leftover food. Thus, it permits the greatest degree of *cost control*.

In family-style service, the food is placed on the table in serving dishes. The children are then asked to help themselves and to pass the dish to the next child. Beverages are placed in small, easily managed pitchers and each child pours the amount desired before passing it to the next child. While this method does not permit the degree of portion control of plate service, it promotes decision making by the children. The child chooses how much food to serve and eat and thus enhances and acknowledges the very important aspect of self-regulation of food intake. The motor skills used to dip, serve, pass, and pour are practiced, as well as the social skills of cooperating and sharing. Many caregivers feel that the positive aspects of family-style service outweigh the benefits of lesser portions and cost control of plate service.

Positive aspects of both styles of service may lead the caregiver to choose a combination of the two. For example, the caregiver may place servings of the entree on the plates (the amount is determined by each child's request) while the children pass the bread, fruit, and vegetables. This style of service allows portion control, a very positive aspect since the entree is the most expensive item on the menu, and safety, since the entree is usually a hot food. If the vegetables are hot, they may also be served by the caregiver.

It is important that teachers and caregivers eat meals with the children as this offers the children role models for appropriate behavior and attitudes. Mealtime should be a time when teachers and caregivers sit and engage in pleasant conversions with the children about things that interest the children. Children should also be encouraged to talk with one another. Dwelling on table manners and behavior during meals should be avoided as much as possible. Only positive reinforcement of good behavior should be mentioned. Problem eaters need special positive reinforcement of good eating behavior; if possible, negative behavior should be ignored during mealtime. Table 19–9 gives some additional ideas on making mealtimes happy times.

TABLE 19–9 Make Mealtime a Happy Time

Feeding young children can be fun if you know:

- What foods children should have.
- How to bring children and foods together happily. Pleasant eating experiences are as important as nutritious foods. They provide pleasant associations with food and eating. Food habits and attitudes that form during the preschool years remain with most people throughout life.
- Try to understand each child's personality and reaction to foods.
- Children need to do as much for themselves as they are able to do. First efforts may be awkward, but encourage them. These efforts are a step toward growth.
- Children may be in no hurry to eat once the first edge is taken off their hunger. They do not have adults' sense of time. Urging them to hurry may spoil their pleasure in eating.
- Most 1-year- old children can handle bite-sized pieces of food with their fingers. Later they can handle a spoon by themselves. Since they are growing slower than infants, they may be less hungry. They may be choosy and refuse certain foods. Don't worry or force them to eat. Keep on offering different foods.
- Sometimes children 3 to 6 years old go on food "jags." They may want two or three servings of one food at one meal. Given time they will settle down and eat a normal meal. The overall pattern from week to week and month to month is more important.

Courtesy of *A Planning Guide for Food Service in Child Care Centers.* USDA, FNS-64, 1981.

Summary

The atmosphere in which meals are served is very important. Mealtimes should be happy, social times free from reprimands about table manners and behavior.

The menu is the basic tool of any food service. It is the plan for what is served when. The primary requirement for a good menu is that it meet the nutritional needs of those for whom it is intended. Other considerations when planning menus are: the satisfaction of funding and licensing requirements, providing for nutritious familiar foods, introduction of nutritious new foods, planning appealing foods, providing safe food cooked and served in clean surroundings, including alternatives for children with food allergies, and staying within budgetary limits. Menus that contrast sensory qualities of foods such as color, texture, flavor, and shape are more appealing than those that do not.

Menu planning should be made as efficient as possible through the use of a routine method and sequence of operations. The finished menu should be checked for nutritional adequacy, fulfillment of existing funding and/or licensing requirements, sensory contrasts, and inclusion of new foods, familiar foods, and foods rich in vitamin A, vitamin C, calcium, and iron.

Types of menus may vary from center to center. Some types that might be used are weekly menus, cycle menus, and odd-day menus. Foods from different cultures contribute further variety to the menu and also provide opportunities for extended learning experiences. Preparation of ethnic foods can promote increased parental participation.

Snacks should be planned as a nutritional contribution to the overall menu. Fresh fruits and vegetables, full-strength juices, and whole grain or enriched bread or cereal products are good snack foods.

Suggested Activities

1. Plan a five-day menu appropriate for 4-year-old children that includes morning snack, lunch, and afternoon snack. The menu should provide one-half of the foods needed according to the Food Guide Pyramid. Provide one good source each of vitamin C, calcium, and iron daily. Provide at least three good sources of vitamin A during the five-day period.

2. Four-year-old Jamie often comes to the child care center without having had breakfast at home. (Both his parents work and must leave early every day.) His mother often buys him a doughnut on the way to the center, explaining that she felt "he should have something to eat." During circle times, he's often inattentive and seems to be "in his own world" and somewhat lethargic. He rarely engages in large-motor activities voluntarily. At snack times and mealtimes, he tends to select only milk or juices and is resistant to eating vegetables and meats.
   a. What may be the cause of Jamie's behavior during circle times?
   b. How would you characterize Jamie's nutritional status?
   c. What eating patterns need to be corrected?
   d. What steps should be taken to improve Jamie's participation in activities, as well as his nutritional patterns and status?

3. Review the criteria given for menus. Rank the criteria as you perceive their degree of importance. Are there other factors that you feel should also be considered in planning adequate menus? Consider the needs of individual child care centers, child care homes, or family homes. Are the important factors the same or different for each situation?

4. Three-year-old Eiswari is allergic to eggs. Explain how this affects menu planning.

5. Using the listing of food sources of nutrients for which a vegan vegetarian child would be at risk, plan a menu that would enable the child to meet her needs for one day. Modify the menu for a lacto-ovo-vegetarian child. Include appropriate sizes of servings (refer to Chapter 16).

Chapter Review

A. Multiple Choice. Select the best answer:

1. The *primary* criterion for a good menu is
   a. sensory contrasts
   b. nutritional adequacy
   c. meeting funding requirements
   d. meeting licensing requirements
2. Nutrients for which young children's menus must be carefully monitored are
   a. vitamin A, vitamin C, thiamin, iron
   b. vitamin A, vitamin D, calcium, iron
   c. vitamin A, vitamin C, calcium, iron
   d. vitamin C, niacin, vitamin D, iron
3. The recommended daily allowance of nutrients that federally funded food programs for children are required to provide is a minimum of
   a. one-half
   b. one-third
   c. three-fourths
   d. one-fourth
4. Menu planning requires careful evaluation of
   a. physical needs
   b. developmental needs
   c. social needs
   d. all of these
5. Items appropriate for snacks include
   a. carbonated beverages
   b. fresh fruit slices
   c. fruit drinks
   d. potato chips
6. Food rich in vitamin A include
   a. tomatoes and cabbage
   b. apricots and carrots
   c. salmon and yogurt
   d. ham and raisins

B. Briefly answer the following questions.

1. State the serving size for a child 3 to 6 years old for each of the following foods:
   a. milk
   b. dry cereal
   c. fruit
   d. vegetable
   e. bread
2. Where can information relative to licensing requirements for nutrition and food services for young children be obtained?
3. Name four sensory qualities that can be contrasted to make food appealing.
4. What are two reasons for using fresh fruits and vegetables in season?
5. Name three methods of writing menus.

6. List the eight steps in preparing a menu.
7. Name three ways that mealtimes can be made pleasant for children.

References

"Child Nutrition Programs: School Meal Initiatives for Healthy Children; Final Rule." *Federal Register.* June 13, 1995.

Contento, I. 1981. "Children's Thinking About Food and Eating—A Piagetian-based Study." *Proceedings of the Workshop on Nutrition Education Research.*

A Planning Guide for Food Service in Child Care Centers, USDA, FNS-64, 1984. Food Nutrition Service, Washington, DC.

Additional Reading

Egan, M. C. 1981. "Federal Nutrition Support Programs for Children." In *Community Nutrition: People, Policies, and Programs.* Edited by H. S. Wright and L. S. Sims. Belmont, CA: Wadsworth, Inc.

Endres, J. B., and Rockwell, R. E. 1990. *Food, Nutrition and the Young Child.* Columbus, OH: Merrill Publishing Co.

Essa, E. 1996. *Introduction to Early Childhood Education*, 2E. Albany, NY: Delmar Publishers Inc.

Essa, E. 1995. *Practical Guide to Solving Preschool Behavior Problems*, 3E. Albany, NY: Delmar Publishers Inc.

Gordon, A., and Browne, K. 1996. *Beginnings and Beyond: Foundations in Early Childhood Education*, 4E. Albany, NY: Delmar Publishers Inc.

Rolfes, S. R., and DeBrugne, L. K. 1990. *Life Span Nutrition: Conception Through Life.* St. Paul, MN: West Publishing Co.

Rush, J. 1984. *Identification and Description of Some Dimensions of Young Children's Food Knowledge and Attributes.* Master's Thesis, University of Kansas.

Pamphlets

Conserving the Nutritive Value in Foods, USDA Home and Garden Bulletin No. 90. Superintendent of Documents, U. S. Government Printing Office, Washington, DC 20402.

Food is More than Just Something to Eat, Nutrition, Pueblo, CO 81009.

Growing Up with Breakfast, Kellogg Company, Department of Home Economics Services, 235 Porter Street, Battle Creek, MI 49016.

Buying Food, Superintendent of Documents, U.S. Government Printing Office, Washington, DC 20402.

Fun With Good Foods, USDA, PA-1204. Superintendent of Documents, U. S. Government Printing Office, Washington, DC 20402.

Chapter 20

Food Safety and Economy

Terms to Know

pasteurized
sanitized
food-borne illness
bacteria
viruses
parasites
irradiation
food infection
food intoxication

Objectives

After studying this chapter, you should be able to:

- State aspects of personal hygiene that relate to food safety.
- Describe proper ways to store food.
- Describe methods of sanitizing food preparation areas and equipment.
- Identify proper dishwashing practices.
- Explain how to prevent contamination of food.
- Cite examples of food-borne illnesses.
- Describe five ways to keep food costs within the budget.

This unit introduces factors other than the menu that contribute to effective food service in the child care setting. The success of a carefully planned menu depends upon the food being safe to eat. The menu must also stay within the allotted food budget.

FOOD SAFETY DEPENDS ON SANITATION

The safety of meals prepared for young children should be of great concern. Food-borne illnesses are unpleasant and may be very dangerous or even fatal to young children. Common illnesses such as colds and influenza can be better controlled by careful sanitary practices. Personal cleanliness, proper handling of food, and sanitation of food preparation and serving areas and equipment are essential for food safety.

Personal Cleanliness and Food Safety

Those who are involved in food preparation and service must take great care to maintain a high level of personal cleanliness. Food-borne illnesses can be transmitted by failure to wash one's hands carefully.

The food handler must meet health standards. Those working in licensed child care facilities are required to supply to the school or child care center written proof that they are currently free of tuberculosis. Sufficient evidence of their tuberculosis-free status is afforded by a negative skin test or a negative chest X ray. Food handlers should also undergo periodic physical examinations to document their state of general good health. Health standards for food service workers vary according to the regulations of individual states.

Everyone who is involved in food preparation and service should be free of communicable diseases. Those suffering from colds, respiratory or intestinal types of influenza, gastrointestinal upsets, or severe throat infections should not be involved in food handling. Even though persons suffering from mild forms of these diseases frequently feel that they are well enough to work, to do so may transmit their illness to others. Those suffering from any communicable disease should refrain from handling food. An emergency store of simply prepared foods can solve the problem of what to feed the children when the cook is ill. Foods that could be available for emergency use are:

- canned soups
- peanut butter
- canned fruits and vegetables
- tuna or chicken, canned

An adequate supply of these foods can provide meals that require a minimum of time or cooking skill to prepare.

Food handlers should wear clean, washable clothing and should change aprons frequently if they become soiled. Hair should be covered by a net, cap, or scarf while the worker is handling food. Head coverings should be put on and shoulders checked carefully for loose hair prior to entering the kitchen.

Food handlers should refrain from chewing gum or smoking while working with food. Both practices can introduce saliva to the food handling area.

Handwashing is of utmost important to personal cleanliness, Figure 20–1. Hands should be washed thoroughly:

- before work
- before touching food
- after handling nonfood items, such as cleaning or laundry supplies
- between handling different food items
- after using the bathroom
- after coughing, sneezing, or blowing the nose

Hands should be washed thoroughly for at least 20 seconds just before handling foods and after every interruption. When washing hands, use hot water with soap. Repeat the process of soaping and rinsing. Hands should be washed after handling raw foods, such as fish, shell fish, meat, and poultry, before handling other foods. If the food handler has cuts or abrasions on hands or arms, they should be bandaged and gloves should be worn. Gloved hands should be washed as often as bare hands because the gloves can also pick up bacteria.

Safe Food Handling

Food. All raw produce should be inspected for spoilage upon delivery and should be thoroughly washed before use. Careful washing and brushing removes sprays and other contaminants. All dairy products must be *pasteurized*. Tops of cans should be washed before opening; contaminants on cans can be passed to other cans or work surfaces by a dirty can opener. The can opener should also be washed daily.

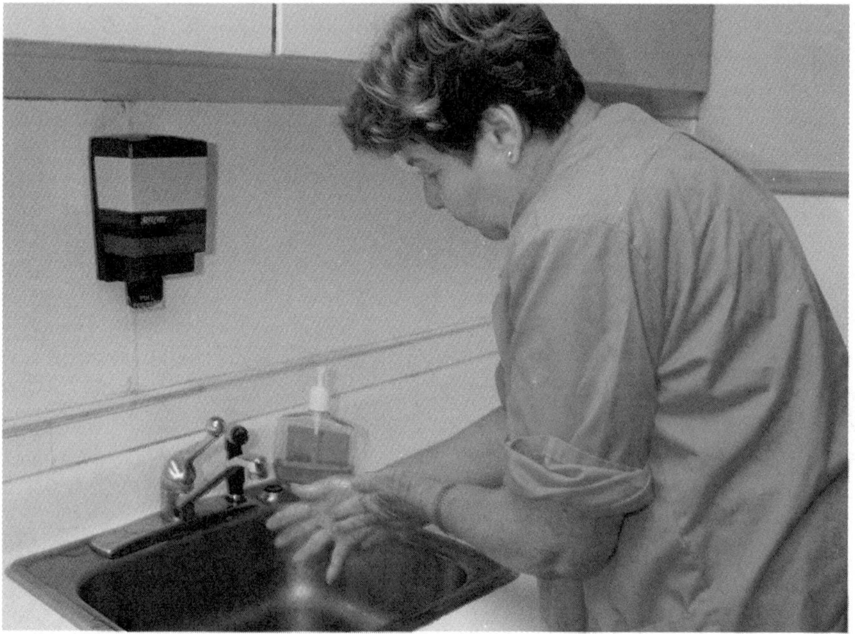

Figure 20–1 Hands should be washed thoroughly before handling food.

After washing raw meat, fish, or poultry, rinse the sink with hot, soapy water. The kitchen sink, drain, and faucet handles should also be sanitized periodically by pouring down the sink a solution of 1 teaspoon of chlorine bleach per 1 quart of water. Food particles trapped in the drain and disposal along with moisture in the drain provide an excellent environment for bacterial growth.

Food Storage. Careful storage and handling of food at appropriate temperatures are essential factors of food safety. Refrigerators should be maintained at 38°F to 40°F. A thermometer hung from a shelf in the warmest area of the refrigerator can be used to check whether appropriate temperatures are being maintained. Freezers should be maintained at 0°F or below. Frozen foods should be thawed:

- in the refrigerator
- in cold water (place food in watertight, plastic bag; change water every 30 minutes)
- in a microwave oven
- while cooking

Caution: Frozen food should never be thawed at room temperature!

Transport. Food should be covered or wrapped during transport. Covering provides additional temperature control and avoids the possibility of contamination during transport. When serving foods, each serving bowl, dish, or pan should have a spoon; spoons not be used to serve more than one food.

Food Service. Food that has been on the tables should not be saved. An exception to this rule is fresh fruits and vegetables that may be washed after removal from the table and served later. Food that has been held in the kitchen at safe temperatures (160°F for hot food or 40°F or below for cold foods) may be saved. Foods that are to be saved should be placed in shallow (3 inches or less) pans and refrigerated or frozen immediately. Spreading food in a thin layer in shallow pans allows it to cool more rapidly.

Foods such as creamed dishes, meat, poultry, or egg salads that are especially prone to spoilage should be prepared from chilled ingredients as quickly as possible and served or refrigerated in shallow containers immediately. All such foods should be maintained at temperatures below 40°F until cooked or served.

Sanitation of Food Preparation Areas and Equipment

The cleanliness of the kitchen and kitchen equipment is a vital factor of safe food service. These areas should be cleaned on a regular schedule. Minimizing traffic through the kitchen reduces the amount of dirt brought in. Schedules, such as that shown in Figure 20–2, should be maintained for the cleaning of floors, walls, ranges, ovens, and refrigerators. The equipment used in the direct handling of food must receive extra care. Surfaces on which food is prepared should be *sanitized* with chlorine bleach solution each time a different food is prepared on it. Cutting boards should be nonporous and should be washed with hot, soapy water and sanitized with

CLEANING SCHEDULE

Daily

- Cutting boards sanitized after each use
- Counter tops washed and sanitized between preparation of different foods
- Tables washed with sanitizing solution
- Can openers washed and sanitized
- Range tops cleaned
- Floors damp mopped

Weekly

- Ovens cleaned
- Refrigerator cleaned and rinsed with vinegar water

As Needed

- Refrigerator/freezer defrosted
- Walls washed
- Floors scrubbed

FIGURE 20–2 Kitchen sanitation depends on frequent, systematic cleaning.

bleach solution after cutting any meat. A separate cutting board should be used exclusively for poultry products. Sanitizing may be done with either a liquid chlorine bleach solution (1/4 cup bleach to each gallon of water, made up daily).

Dishwashing. Dishes may be washed by hand or with a mechanical dishwasher. If washing by hand:

- wash dishes with hot water and detergent
- rinse dishes in hot, clear water
- sanitize dishes with chlorine bleach solution or scald with boiling water

All dishes, utensils, and surfaces must be air dried (not dried with a towel), Figure 20–3.

If dishes are washed by a mechanical dishwasher, the machine must meet local health department standards. Some state licensing regulations provide guidelines as to the method of dishwashing to be used based on the number of persons served.

Sanitation of Food Service Areas

The eating area requires special attention. Cleanliness of the tables can be a problem, especially if they are also used as classroom tables. In order to maintain adequate sanitation, the tables should be washed with chlorine bleach solution:

- before each meal
- after each meal

Figure 20–3 Tables should be washed properly before and after meals.

- before each snack
- after each snack

The children should be taught to wash their hands carefully before eating. They should also be taught that serving spoons should be used to serve food and then replaced in the serving dishes. Children should never be allowed to eat from serving spoons.

The guidelines for sanitation evaluation shown in Figure 20–4 are a useful tool in assessing food service sanitation on a regular basis.

FOOD-BORNE ILLNESSES

Food poisoning refers to a variety of *food-borne illnesses* that may be caused by the presence of *bacteria*, *viruses*, *parasites*, or some kinds of molds growing on foods, Table 20–1. Foods that are visibly molded, soured, or beginning to liquify should not be used; nor should food from bulging cans or cans in which the liquid is foamy or smells strangely. Foods containing most food poisoning organisms carry few signs of spoilage. The food usually appears and smells safe, but still can cause severe illness. Proper sanitation procedures, preparation, and food handling should prevent most food-borne illnesses (Cody and Keith, 1991).

SANITATION EVALUATION

	EX	GOOD	FAIR	POOR
FOOD				
1. Supplies of food and beverages must meet local, state, and federal codes.				
2. Meats and poultry must be inspected and passed for wholesomeness by federal or state inspectors.				
3. Milk and milk products must be pasteurized.				
4. Home canned foods must not be used.				
FOOD STORAGE				
1. Perishable foods are stored at temperatures that will prevent spoilage: a. Refrigerator temperature: 40°F (4°C) or below				
b. Freezer temperature: 0°F (-18°C) or below				
2. Thermometers are located in the warmest part of each refrigerator and freezer and are checked daily.				
3. Refrigerator has enough shelves to allow space between foods for air circulation to maintain proper temperatures.				
4. Frozen foods are thawed in refrigerator or quick-thawed under cold water for immediate preparation, or thawed as part of the cooking process. (Never thawed at room temperature.)				
5. Food is examined when brought to center to make sure it is not spoiled, dirty, or infested with insects.				
6. Foods are stored in rodent-proof and insect-proof covered metal, glass, or hard plastic containers.				
7. Containers of food are stored above the floor (6 inches) on racks that permit moving for easy cleaning.				

FIGURE 20–4 Guidelines for sanitation evaluation.

	EX	GOOD	FAIR	POOR
8. Storerooms are dry and free from leaky plumbing or drainage problems. All holes and cracks in storeroom are repaired.				
9. Storerooms are kept cool: 60°F to 70°F (15°C–21°C).				
10. All food items are stored separately from nonfood items.				
11. Inventory system is used to be sure that stored food is rotated.				
FOOD PREPARATION AND HANDLING 1. All raw fruits and vegetables are washed before use. Tops of cans are washed before opening.				
2. Thermometers are used to check internal temperatures of: a. Poultry-minimum 165°F (74°C).				
b. Pork and pork products—minimum 150°F (66°C).				
3. Meat salads, poultry salads, potato salads, egg salad, cream-filled pastries and other potentially hazardous prepared foods are prepared from chilled products as quickly as possible and refrigerated in shallow containers or served immediately.				
4. All potentially hazardous foods are maintained below 40°F (4°C) or above 140°F (60°C) during transportation and holding until service.				
5. Foods are covered or completely wrapped during transportation.				
6. Two spoons are used for tasting foods.				
7. Each serving bowl has a serving spoon.				
8. Leftover food from serving bowls on the tables is not saved. An exception would be raw fruits and vegetables that could be washed. Food held in kitchen at safe temperatures is used for refilling bowls as needed.				

Figure 20–4 (Continued)

SANITATION EVALUATION

	EX	GOOD	FAIR	POOR
9. Food held in the kitchen at safe temperatures is re-used.				
10. Foods stored for re-use are placed in shallow pans and refrigerated or frozen immediately.				
11. Leftovers or prepared casseroles are held in refrigerator or frozen immediately.				
STORAGE OF NONFOOD SUPPLIES 1. All cleaning supplies (including dish sanitizers) and other poisonous materials are stored in locked compartments or in compartments well above the reach of children and separate from food, dishes, and utensils.				
2. Poisonous and toxic materials other than those needed for kitchen sanitation are stored in locked compartments outside the kitchen area.				
3. Insect and rodent poisons are stored in locked compartments in an area apart from other cleaning compounds to avoid contamination or mistaken usage.				
CLEANING AND CARE OF EQUIPMENT 1. A cleaning schedule is followed: a. Floors are wet mopped daily, scrubbed as needed.				
b. Food preparation surfaces are washed and sanitized between preparation of different food items (as between meat and salad preparation).				
c. Cutting boards are made of hard nontoxic material , and are smooth and free from cracks, crevices, and open seams.				

Figure 20–4 (Continued)

	EX	GOOD	FAIR	POOR
d. After cutting any single meat, fish, or poultry item, the cutting board is thoroughly washed and sanitized.				
e. Can openers are washed and sanitized daily.				
f. Utensils are cleaned and sanitized between uses on different food items.				
2. Dishwashing is done by an approved method: a. *Hand washed*—3-step operation including sanitizing rinse.				
b. *Mechanical*—by machine that meets local health department standards.				
3. Range tops are washed daily and as needed to keep them clean during preparation.				
4. Ovens are cleaned weekly or as needed.				
5. Refrigerator is washed once a week with vinegar.				
6. Refrigerator is defrosted when there is about 1/4" thickness of frost.				
7. Tables and other eating surfaces are washed with a mild disinfectant solution before and after each meal.				
8. All food contact surfaces are air-dried after cleaning and sanitizing.				
9. Cracked or chipped utensils or dishes are not used; they are disposed of.				
10. Garbage cans are leakproof and have tight-fitting lids.				
11. Garbage cans are lined with plastic liners and emptied and cleaned frequently.				
12. There is a sufficient number of garbage containers available.				

Figure 20–4 (Continued)

SANITATION EVALUATION

	EX	GOOD	FAIR	POOR
INSECT AND RODENT CONTROL				
1. Only an approved pyrithren base insecticide or fly swatter is used in the food preparation area.				
2. The insecticides do not come in contact with raw or cooked food, utensils, or equipment used in food preparation and serving, or with any other food contact surface.				
3. Doors and windows have screens in proper repair and are closed at all times. All openings to the outside are closed or properly screened to prevent entrance of rodents or insects.				
PERSONAL SANITATION				
1. Health of food service personnel meets standards: a. TB test is current.				
b. Physical examination is up to date.				
2. Everyone who works with or near food is free from communicable disease.				
3. Clean washable clothing is worn.				
4. Hairnets or hair caps are worn in the kitchen.				
5. There is no use of tobacco or chewing gum in the kitchen.				
6. Hands are washed thoroughly before touching food, before work, after handling nonfood items, between handling of different food items, after using bathroom, after coughing, sneezing, blowing nose.				

Figure 20–4 (Continued)

TABLE 20–1 Food-Borne Illnesses

DISEASE AND ORGANISM THAT CAUSES IT	SOURCE OF ILLNESS	SYMPTOMS	PREVENTION METHODS
salmonellosis *Salmonella* (bacteria; more than 1,700 kinds)	May be found in raw meats, poultry, eggs, fish, milk, and products made with them. Multiplies rapidly at room temperature.	Onset: 12–48 hours after eating. Nausea, fever, headache, abdominal cramps, diarrhea, and sometimes vomiting. Can be fatal in infants, the elderly, and the infirm.	■ Handling food in a sanitary manner ■ Thorough cooking of foods ■ Prompt and proper refrigeration of foods
E. coli *E. coli 0157:H7*	May occur in beef (primarily ground beef) unpasteurized apple cider, raw milk, raw potatoes, mayonnaise. Organism is naturally present in food animals.	Onset: 12–72 hours. Watery, profuse diarrhea, fever. Diarrhea may be bloody.	■ Cooking ground meats to 160°F. This temperature is high enough to inactivate *E. coli*. ■ Pasteurization
staphylococcal food poisoning staphylococcal enterotoxin (produced by *Staphylococcus aureus* bacteria)	The toxin is produced when food contaminated with the bacteria is left too long at room temperature. Meats, poultry, egg products; tuna, potato and macaroni salads; and cream-filled pastries are good environments for these bacteria to produce toxin.	Onset: 1–8 hours after eating. Diarrhea, vomiting, nausea, abdominal cramps, and prostration. Mimics flu. Lasts 24–48 hours. Rarely fatal.	■ Sanitary food handling practices ■ Prompt and proper refrigeration of foods
botulism botulinum toxin (produced by *Clostridium botulinum* bacteria)	Bacteria are widespread in the environment. However, bacteria produce toxin only in an anaerobic (oxygen-less) environment of little acidity. Types A, B, and F may result from inadequate processing of low-acid canned foods, such as green beans, mushrooms, spinach, olives, and beef. Type E normally occurs in fish.	Onset: 8–36 hours after eating. Neuro-toxic symptoms, including double vision, inability to swallow, speech difficulty, and progressive paralysis of the respiratory system. OBTAIN MEDICAL HELP IMMEDIATELY. BOTULISM CAN BE FATAL.	■ Using proper methods for canning low-acid foods ■ Avoidance of commercially canned low-acid foods with leaky seals or with bent, bulging, or broken cans ■ Toxin can be destroyed after a can is opened by boiling contents hard for 10 minutes—NOT RECOMMENDED

(Continued)

TABLE 20–1 Food-Borne Illnesses (Continued)

DISEASE AND ORGANISM THAT CAUSES IT	SOURCE OF ILLNESS	SYMPTOMS	PREVENTION METHODS
Listeriosis *Listeria monocytogenes*	Raw animal products and dairy foods, contaminated water.	Mild fever and diarrhea, severe sore throat, meningitis, encephalitis, still birth, or abortion.	■ Pasteurization ■ Sanitation ■ Hygiene
parahaemolyticus food poisoning *Vibrio parahaemolyticus* (bacteria)	Organism lives in salt water and can contaminate fish and shellfish. Thrives in warm water.	Onset: 15–24 hours after eating. Abdominal pain, nausea, vomiting, and diarrhea. Sometimes fever, headache, chills, and mucus and blood in the stools. Last 1–2 days. Rarely fatal.	■ Sanitary handling of foods ■ Thorough cooking of seafood
gastrointestinal disease enteroviruses, rotaviruses, parvoviruses	Viruses exist in the intestinal tract of humans and are expelled in feces. Contamination of foods can occur in three ways: (1) when sewage is used to enrich garden/farm soil, (2) by direct hand-to-food contact during the preparation of meals, and (3) when shellfish-growing waters are contaminated by sewage.	Onset: After 24 hours. Severe diarrhea, nausea, and vomiting. Respiratory symptoms Usually lasts 4–5 days but may last for weeks.	■ Sanitary handling of foods ■ Use of pure drinking water ■ Adequate sewage disposal ■ Adequate cooking of foods
hepatitis hepatitis A virus	Chief food sources: shellfish harvested from contaminated areas, and foods that are handled a lot during preparation and then eaten raw (such as vegetables).	Jaundice, fatigue. May cause liver damage and death.	■ Sanitary handling of foods ■ Use of pure drinking water ■ Adequate sewage disposal ■ Adequate cooking of foods
mycotoxicosis mycotoxins (from molds)	Produced in foods that are relatively high in moisture. Chief food sources: beans and grains that have been stored in a moist place.	May cause liver and/or kidney disease	■ Checking foods for visible mold and discarding those that are contaminated ■ Proper storage of susceptible foods

giardiasis *Giardia lamblia* (flagellated protozoa)	Protozoa exist in the intestinal tract of humans and are expelled in feces. Contamination of foods can occur in two ways: (1) when sewage is used to enrich garden/farm soil, and (2) by direct hand-to-food contact during the preparation of meals. Chief food sources: foods that are handled a lot during preparation.	Diarrhea, abdominal pain, flatulence, abdominal distention, nutritional disturbances, "nervous" symptoms, anorexia, nausea, and vomiting.	■ Sanitary handling of foods ■ Avoidance of raw fruits and vegetables in areas where the protozoa is endemic ■ Proper sewage disposal
amebiasis *Entamoeba histolytica* (amoebic protozoa)		Tenderness over the colon or liver, loose morning stools, recurrent diarrhea, change in bowel habits, "nervous" symptoms, loss of weight, and fatigue. Anemia may be present.	■ Sanitary handling of foods ■ Avoidance of raw fruits and vegetables in areas where the protozoa is endemic ■ Proper sewage disposal
perfringens food poisoning *Clostridium perfringens* (rod–shaped bacteria)	Bacteria are widespread in environment. Generally found in meat and poultry and dishes made with them. Multiply rapidly when foods are left at room temperature too long. Destroyed by cooking.	Onset: 8–22 hours after eating (usually 12). Abdominal pain and diarrhea. Sometimes nausea and vomiting. Symptoms last a day or less and are usually mild. Can be more serious in older or debilitated people.	■ Sanitary handling of foods especially meat and meat dishes and gravies ■ Thorough cooking of foods ■ Prompt and proper refrigeration
shigellosis (bacillary dysentery) *Shigella* (bacteria)	Food becomes contaminated when a human carrier with poor sanitary habits handles liquid or moist food that is then not cooked thoroughly. Organisms multiply in food stored above room temperature. Found in milk and dairy products, poultry, and potato salad.	Onset: 1–7 days after eating. Abdominal pain, cramps, diarrhea, fever, sometimes vomiting, and blood, pus, or mucus in stools. Can be serious in infants, the elderly, or debilitated people.	■ Handling food in a sanitary manner ■ Proper sewage disposal ■ Proper refrigeration of foods

(Continued)

TABLE 20–1 Food-Borne Illnesses (Continued)

DISEASE AND ORGANISM THAT CAUSES IT	SOURCE OF ILLNESS	SYMPTOMS	PREVENTION METHODS
campylobacterosis *Campylobacter jejuni* (rod-shaped bacteria)	Bacteria found on poultry, cattle, and sheep and can contaminate the meat and milk of these animals. Chief food sources: raw poultry and meat and unpasteurized milk.	Onset: 2–5 days after eating. Diarrhea, abdominal cramping, fever, and sometimes bloody stools. Lasts 2–7 days.	■ Thorough cooking of foods ■ Handling of food in a sanitary manner ■ Avoid unpasteurized milk
gastroenteritis *Yersinia enterocolitica* (non-spore-forming bacteria)	Ubiquitous in nature; carried in food and water. Bacteria multiply rapidly at room temperature, *as well as* at refrigerator temperatures of 39.2° to 48.2°F (4° to 9°C). Generally found in raw vegetables, meats, water, and unpasteurized milk.	Onset 2–5 days after eating. Fever, headache, nausea, diarrhea, and general malaise. Mimics flu. An important cause of gastroenteritis in children. Can also infect other age group, and, if not treated, can lead to other more serious diseases (such as lymphadenitis, arthritis, and Reiter's syndrome).	■ Thorough cooking of foods ■ Sanitizing cutting instruments and cutting boards before preparing foods that are eaten raw ■ Avoidance of unpasteurized milk and unchlorinated water
cerus food poisoning *Bacillus cereus* (bacteria and possibly their toxin)	Illness may be caused by the bacteria, which are widespread in the environment, or by an enterotoxin created by the bacteria. Found in raw foods. Bacteria multiply rapidly in foods stored at room temperature.	Onset: 1–18 hours after eating. Two types of illness: (1) abdominal pain and diarrhea, and (2) nausea and vomiting. Lasts less than a day.	■ Sanitary handling of foods ■ Thorough cooking of foods ■ Prompt and adequate refrigeration
cholera *Vibrio cholera* (bacteria)	Found in fish and shellfish harvested from waters contaminated by human sewage. (Bacteria may also occur naturally in Gulf Coast waters.) Chief food sources: seafood, especially types eaten raw (such as oysters).	Onset: 1–3 days. Can range from "subclinical" (a mild uncomplicated bout with diarrhea) to fatal (intense diarrhea with dehydration). Severe cases require hospitalization.	■ Sanitary handling of foods ■ Thorough cooking of seafood

Courtesy of "Who, Why, When, and Where of Food Poisons (And What to Do About Them)." *FDA Consumer*, July-August 1982.

The introduction of *irradiation* as a new food preservation technique may in time reduce the incidence of food-borne disease. Irradiation has recently been approved by the Food and Drug Administration as an "additive" for food to kill microorganisms that might cause illness. This procedure involves exposing food to low levels of gamma radiation with the amount of exposure and the kinds of food to be irradiated being controlled by the FDA. Irradiated foods must carry the symbol and message shown in Figure 20–5.

The use of irradiation as a preservative for food is still controversial and some people feel uncomfortable consuming food preserved in this manner. Irradiated foods are not radioactive. They have been changed chemically, so there may be considerable loss of some nutrients. Vitamins A, E, and C, beta carotene, and thiamin are particularly vulnerable to destruction by irradiation.

Irradiation is not as dangerous as its critics claim, but neither is it the solution to all food-borne illness problems as its promoters claim. Probably the most serious concerns should be that irradiation could be used to cover up unsanitary food processing procedures or that consumers will rely too much upon radiation protection and become careless in the handling of food. Until more is known about the safety of irradiation and the degree of protection that it affords, it is important that the prescribed procedures for sanitary handling of food be consistently and carefully practiced.

Food infections result from ingestion of large amounts of viable bacteria in foods that cause infectious disease. Symptoms usually develop relatively slowly (12–24 hours) since incubation of the bacteria takes time.

Food intoxications result from eating food containing toxins that are produced in the food by bacterial growth. Symptoms usually develop more rapidly (within 1–6 hours) than those associated with infections (Williams, 1981), except for botulinum toxins, which produce symptoms later (8–36 hours). The incidence of

Figure 20–5 Irradiated food must bear this radura symbol plus the message that it has been irradiated.

SAFE-HANDLING INSTRUCTIONS

THIS PRODUCT WAS PREPARED FROM INSPECTED AND PASSED MEAT AND/OR POULTRY. SOME FOOD PRODUCTS MAY CONTAIN BACTERIA THAT COULD CAUSE ILLNESS IF THE PRODUCT IS MISHANDLED OR COOKED IMPROPERLY. FOR YOUR PROTECTION, FOLLOW THESE SAFE-HANDLING INSTRUCTIONS.

KEEP REFRIGERATED OR FROZEN. THAW IN REFRIGERATOR OR MICROWAVE.

KEEP RAW MEAT AND POULTRY SEPARATE FROM OTHER FOODS. WASH WORKING SURFACES (INCLUDING CUTTING BOARDS), UTENSILS, AND HANDS AFTER TOUCHING RAW MEAT OR POULTRY.

COOK THOROUGHLY.

KEEP HOT FOODS HOT. REFRIGERATE LEFTOVERS IMMEDIATELY OR DISCARD.

Figure 20–6 Safe-handling instructions are given with packaged meats and poultry.

food-borne illnesses appear to be on the rise and are frequent causes of illness in infants and toddlers in daycare centers. The most common food carriers of infectious agents and/or toxins are milk, eggs, meat, fish, and poultry. Poultry products are one of the most frequent causes of food poisoning, which explains the recommendation that a separate cutting board be provided for poultry and raw meat products. An additional reason for concern is that the United States Department of Agriculture has relaxed its inspection rules, has no standards for bacterial contamination and allows federal inspectors of poultry products only two seconds to examine each bird. The consumer must assume full responsibility for choosing, storing, and preparing these products so that they do not cause illness. Safe-handling instructions attached to packaging aid the consumer in safely preparing these foods, Figure 20–6. Very thorough cooking of poultry, eggs, and other meat products will kill bacteria and destroy most toxins. It is NEVER safe to allow young children to eat raw or poorly cooked eggs, meat products, fish, or seafood. Their less-than fully developed immune systems leaves them more vulnerable to, and less able to cope with, a food-borne illness.

THE MENU MUST STAY WITHIN THE BUDGET

While the menu lists what foods are to be served, the budget defines the resources allotted for preparation of the menu. Items that must be included in the budget are food, personnel, and equipment. The food budget can be controlled through careful attention to:

- menu planning
- food purchasing
- food preparation
- food service
- record keeping

Cost control is essential if a food service is to stay within the budget. The goal is to feed the children appetizing, nutritious meals at a reasonably low cost. Cost control should never be attempted at the expense of good nutrition.

Menu Planning

Cost control begins at the menu-planning stage. To plan menus that stay within a budget, it is important to begin by including inexpensive foods. To do so, the planner must be aware of current prices and seasonal supplies.

To lower food costs, the menu planner should make careful use of leftovers and supplies on hand. To ensure that quality foods are selected from supplies on hand, a storage system should be devised that places newly purchased foods at the back of storage and older foods at the front so they can be used first. This method of rotating stocks of food can be facilitated by dating all supplies as they come into the storage area.

Food Purchasing

Food purchasing is a crucial step in cost control. Purchase of too much food or of inappropriate foods can transform a menu that is planned around inexpensive foods to an expensive menu at service. The key step is to determine as accurately as possible the amount of food that is needed to feed everyone an adequate amount. The use of standardized recipes can be a great help in determining how much and what kinds of food are needed. One such set of recipes is that developed by the U. S. Department of Agriculture for use in school lunches or Child Care Food Programs. These recipes provide the ingredients needed as well as the amounts required to produce the recipe for groups of various sizes.

Before purchasing food, a written food order should be prepared listing the following:

- market units—ounces, pounds, can size, cases, etc.
- quantity (number) of units needed
- style of food desired—pieces, slices, halves, chunks, etc.

For those who purchase food at local retail stores, a simple form that follows the floor plan of the store(s) where food is purchased may be helpful. When completing the market order, list the foods needed for the entire period of time for which food must be purchased in the following order:

- main dishes
- fruits and vegetables
- breads, cereals, pastas
- dairy products

Frozen foods should be selected last to minimize thawing between store freezer and food service freezer.

Food Preparation

Careful preparation methods that are appropriate for the specific food contribute both to the nutritional quality of the food and to cost control. Fruits and vegetables should be peeled only if necessary, as more nutrients are retained if the skin is left intact. If peeling is necessary, as it may be for very young children, only a thin layer of skin should be removed.

Correct heat and cooking time are important factors in cost control as well as nutrient retention. Foods cooked too long or at excessively high heat may undergo shrinkage or be burned. In either case, food costs increase because burned food is not usable and shrinkage results in fewer portions than originally planned. Nutrients, such as thiamin and vitamin C, are readily destroyed when exposed to heat.

Test standardized recipes, such as those available from the U. S. Department of Agriculture, help to ensure correct amounts of ingredients and to reduce leftovers. Leftover foods that have not been placed on the table may be promptly frozen and used when serving the same dish again. Leftovers should be reheated in a separate pan and not mixed with freshly-prepared portions. Leftovers should be reheated only once.

Food Service

If the recipe specifies a serving size, that amount should be served, for example, "one-half cup or 1 1/2" × 1 1/2" square." In child care centers using family-style service, the staff may serve standard portions to the children as a means of portion control. In centers where children are encouraged to serve themselves, each child should be asked to take only as much as can be eaten.

Serving utensils that are made to serve specific portions are an aid to portion and cost control. Examples of such utensils are soup ladles and ice cream scoops, which are available in a number of standardized sizes. These tools are available at restaurant supply companies.

Recordkeeping

Complete, accurate records should be kept of the amount of money spent for food, and the number of children and staff served daily. These records provide an idea of how much money is being spent for food and whether this amount is within the projected budget. Figure 20–7 shows an example of a form used to report the number of meals served.

A record of expenses for each month should be kept. For further accuracy, an inventory of foods on hand should be done and the cost of the inventory determined and deducted from the raw food cost for that month. (If inventories tend not to differ much from month to month, this last step may be omitted.) At the end of each month:

- calculate the total number of individuals served
- calculate the total food bills
- divide the total dollars spent by the total number served to determine monthly food costs per person

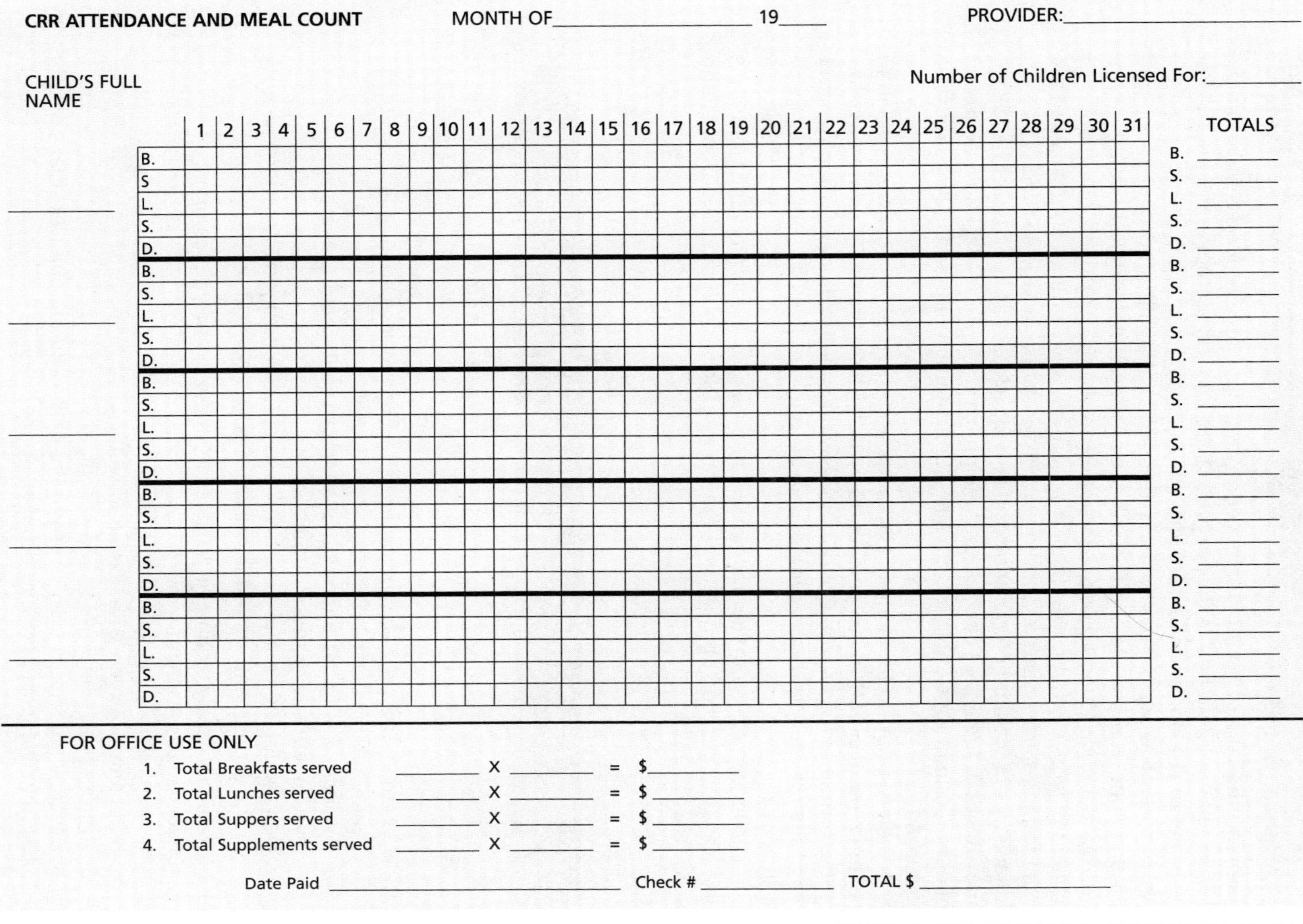

CRR ATTENDANCE AND MEAL COUNT MONTH OF__________ 19____ PROVIDER:__________

CHILD'S FULL NAME Number of Children Licensed For:________

		1	2	3	4	5	6	7	8	9	10	11	12	13	14	15	16	17	18	19	20	21	22	23	24	25	26	27	28	29	30	31	TOTALS
	B.																																B. ______
	S																																S. ______
______	L.																																L. ______
	S.																																S. ______
	D.																																D. ______
	B.																																B. ______
	S.																																S. ______
______	L.																																L. ______
	S.																																S. ______
	D.																																D. ______
	B.																																B. ______
	S.																																S. ______
______	L.																																L. ______
	S.																																S. ______
	D.																																D. ______
	B.																																B. ______
	S.																																S. ______
______	L.																																L. ______
	S.																																S. ______
	D.																																D. ______
	B.																																B. ______
	S.																																S. ______
______	L.																																L. ______
	S.																																S. ______
	D.																																D. ______

FOR OFFICE USE ONLY

1. Total Breakfasts served ________ X ________ = $________
2. Total Lunches served ________ X ________ = $________
3. Total Suppers served ________ X ________ = $________
4. Total Supplements served ________ X ________ = $________

Date Paid ______________ Check # __________ TOTAL $ __________

Figure 20–7 A sample attendance and meal count form. Courtesy of Douglas County Development Association.

Summary

Factors other than menu planning contribute to effective food service in the child care setting. Sanitation and cost control are integral factors in the success or failure of the total food service operation.

An important aspect of sanitation is the personal health and hygiene of personnel preparing and serving the food. A state of acceptable good health is confirmed by negative tuberculosis tests and periodic physical examinations. Cleanliness of work clothing, use of head coverings, and frequent handwashing are essential to the maintenance of good personal sanitation in food service.

Cleanliness of the food preparation and service areas requires frequent and systematic attention. Cleaning schedules are helpful in achieving a desirable degree of cleanliness. Counter tops, table tops, walls, floors, equipment, and utensils must all be kept clean.

Food safety refers to the handling of foods. Foods must be kept hot enough to kill bacteria (above 140°F) or cold enough to prevent bacterial growth (below 40°F). Bacteria that lead to food-borne illnesses include Salmonella, Staphylococcus, and Clostridium botulinum. Viruses, molds, and parasites can also cause food-borne illnesses.

Food costs can be controlled by careful attention to: menu planning, food purchasing and storage, food preparation and storage, serving standard portions, and accurate recordkeeping.

Suggested Activities

1. The following menu is planned for a child care center for one week in January.

Meat Loaf	Bread with margarine
Creamed new peas and potatoes	Fresh strawberry-banana fruit cup
Peach half in cherry gelatin	Milk

   a. Evaluate this menu and suggest changes that could make it less expensive but equally or more nutritious.
   b. How would the cost of this menu served in January compare to the cost of the same menu served in June?

2. Invite a laboratroy technician to class to make culture plates of a
   a. hand before washing
   b. hand after washing with water only
   c. hand after washing with soap and water
   d. strand of hair

   The technician should then return to the class with the cultures after the cultures have incubated for 2 to 3 days.

e. Is there bacterial growth on any of the culture plates?
f. Which cultures have the most bacterial growth?
g. Discuss how these results could be best utilized in terms of
   (1) food preparation and service
   (2) child care center meal and snack times

Chapter Review

A. Multiple Choice. Select the best answer:

1. Sanitation relative to food service refers to
   a. safe food handling
   b. personal cleanliness
   c. cleanliness of the service area
   d. all of these
2. Food-borne bacterial infections include
   a. salmonellosis
   b. botulism
   c. infectious hepatitis
   d. all of these
3. Refrigerator temperatures should be maintained at
   a. 28°F to 30°F
   b. 38°F to 40°F
   c. 45°F to 50°F
   d. 0°F
4. Bacterial growth requires the following condition(s)
   a. temperatures between 40°F and 140°F
   b. moisture
   c. darkness
   d. all of these
5. Milk served in child care centers must be
   a. homogenized
   b. skim
   c. pasteurized
   d. two percent
6. Hands should be carefully washed
   a. after using the bathroom
   b. before touching food
   c. between handling different foods
   d. all of these

7. Easily spoiled foods such as custards and creamed dishes should be
   a. placed in a shallow pan and cooled slowly to prevent curdling
   b. cooled on the counter to avoid warming the refrigerator
   c. placed in a shallow pan and refrigerated immediately
   d. both a and b
8. Frozen foods may be thawed safely
   a. in the refrigerator
   b. under hot running water
   c. at room temperature
   d. both a and b
9. Dishes or pots and pans that are washed by hand may be sanitized with
   a. hot tap water
   b. a chlorine bleach solution
   c. sudsy water
   d. all of these
10. Dishes and utensils that have been washed by hand must be
    a. air dried
    b. dried with a clean towel
    c. rinsed in cold water
    d. put in cupboards immediately

B. Briefly answer the following questions.

1. Name two ways the menu planner can control food costs.
2. What is the key step in cost control when purchasing food?
3. Name three ways to control food costs when preparing food.
4. How can food costs be controlled when serving food?
5. Of what value is keeping accurate food records?
6. List three means of keeping the food preparation area clean and germfree.

References

Cody, M. M. and Keith, M. 1991, *Food Safety for Professionals*, Chicago, IL: The American Dietetic Association.

Williams, S. R. 1981. *Nutrition and Diet Therapy*. 4th ed. St. Louis: The C. V. Mosby Company.

Additional Reading

"Can Your Kitchen Pass the Food Safety Test?" *FDA Consumer*, October, 1995.

Farber, J. M . and Huges, A., "General Guidelines for the Safe Handling of Foods." *Dairy, Food and Environmental Sanitation*. 18(2), 70-78 Des Moines, IA.

"Food Poisoning: Worse Than Ants At A Picnic." June 1984. *The Harvard Medical School Health Letter* 9: 5.

Jacobson, M., Lefferts, L. Y., and Garland, A. W. 1990. *Safe Food: Eating Wisely in a Risky World.* Center for Science in the Public Interest, Washington, DC.

Kroger, M. 1991. "Food Safety: What Are The Real Issues?" Annual Editions: Nutrition 91/92, Guilford, CT: Dushkin Publishing Group Inc.

Lefferts, L. Y., and Schmidt, S. July/August 1991. "Name Your (Food) Poison." *Nutrition Action Health Letter* 18(6), 3–11 Washington, DC.

"Who, Why, When, and Where of Food Poisons (And What To Do About Them)." *FDA Consumer* July–August, 1982.

Wardlow, G. M., and Insel, P. M. 1990. *Perspectives in Nutrition.* St. Louis, MO: Times Mirror/Mosby College Pub.

Williamson, C. C. 1992. "The Storm Seasons: Handling Food after Tornados, Hurricanes, Floods, and Fires." Food News for Consumers, 9:1, U.S.D.A., Washington, DC.

Pamphlets

Conserving the Nutritive Value in Foods USDA Home and Garden Bulletin No. 90. Superintendent of Documents, U. S. Government Printing Office, Washington, DC 20402.

Food is More Than Just Something to Eat Nutrition, Pueblo, CO 81009.

Growing Up with Breakfast Kellogg Company, Department of Home Economics Services, 235 Porter Street, Battle Creek, M I 49016.

Buying Food Superintendent of Documents, U. S. Government Printing Office, Washington, DC 20402.

Fun With Good Foods USDA, PA-1204. Superintendent of Documents, U. S. Government Printing Office, Washington, DC 20402.

A Planning Guide for Food Service in Child Care Centers USDA, FNS-64, Food Nutrition Service, Washington, DC.

Food and Nutrition in Day Care Centers, Agriculture Canada, Publication 1689.

Chapter 21

Nutrition Education Concepts and Activities

Terms to Know

nutrition education
concepts
sensorimotor
hands-on
serrated
preplan
evaluation
objectives
attitudes
peer

Objectives

After studying this chapter, you should be able to:

- Identify the primary goal of nutrition education for preschool children.
- List four basic concepts important to nutrition education.
- Explain the various roles child care personnel play in nutrition education.
- Describe four ways that nutrition education activities contribute to child development.
- Describe the general principles of safety that must be observed in planning nutrition education activities for children.

In the simplest of terms, *nutrition education* is any activity that tells a person something about food. These activities may be structured, planned activities or very brief, informal happenings. The primary goal of nutrition education at the preschool level is to introduce children to some simple, basic principles of nutrition and to encourage them to eat and enjoy a variety of nutritious foods.

BASIC CONCEPTS OF NUTRITION EDUCATION

Some basic concepts for teaching young children that nutrition is important for good health are:

1. Children must have food to grow and to have healthy bodies.
   - All animals and plants need food.
   - Eating food helps children grow, play, learn, and be happy.
   - Many foods are good for us.
   - Eating food makes us feel good.
2. Nutrients come from foods. It is these nutrients that allow children to grow and be healthy.
   - After food is eaten these nutrients are set free to work in our bodies.
   - Nutrients do different things in our bodies.
   - Many different nutrients are needed each day.
   - Foods are the sources of all of the nutrients that we know are needed.
3. A variety of foods need to be eaten each day. No one food gives all of the needed nutrients.
   - Different foods provide different nutrients so we need to eat many kinds of food.
   - Nutrients need to work together in our bodies; we need many different nutrients each day.
   - Children should be exposed to and encouraged to accept a variety of foods from each of the Food Guide Pyramid Groups.
   - Children should explore how foods differ relative to color, shape, taste, and texture. They can learn to group and to identify certain kinds of foods such as fruits, breads, and meats.
4. Foods must be carefully handled before they are eaten to ensure that they are healthful and safe.
   - Cleanliness of all materials and persons involved with food is most important.
   - Some foods need to be cooked and eaten hot.
   - Some foods must be kept refrigerated and may be served cold.
   - Involving children with food preparation helps them learn about the things that must be done to foods before they may be eaten.
   - Eating food that has not been handled properly can make children very ill.

These conceptual points require that the persons responsible for nutrition education have a basic knowledge of nutrition, in relation to both foods and nutrients.

Parents often ask the childcare staff questions about nutrition topics or about something they have read about nutrition. It is important that they get the correct information. If the staff person does not know the answer, they might provide a list of local allied health personnel (dietitians, health department officers, USDA extension service, etc.) that could answer their questions.

To evaluate resource material for parents or for use in planning a food experience for children certain questions should be asked:

1. Is its source known for its reliability in reporting?
2. What are the professional credentials of the author(s)?
3. Is it accurate and does it deal with known nutritional facts rather than theories?
4. Are unsubstantiated health claims presented?
5. Is it trying to sell something?
6. Is the material at the appropriate level or adaptable?
7. Are the suggested projects nutritious?
8. Are thc projects safe?

Nutrition knowledge should be combined with a knowledge of educational techniques appropriate for the age group. Food experiences should be planned with consideration for the developmental level of the age group and individual children in the group who will be participating in the activity. Food experiences should be fun and enhance a child's positive feelings about healthful food.

RESPONSIBILITY FOR NUTRITION EDUCATION

All personnel involved in the nutrition program are responsible for nutrition education. Effectiveness of the nutrition education program depends on cooperation between the director, teacher, and cook or food service personnel, Figure 21–1. While programs vary in their organization, these people generally have the responsibility for nutrition education.

The director's role is mainly supportive. The director should stress to the staff the importance of nutritious meals and snacks. The director should see that financial support is available for nutrition education in the curriculum.

The teacher is usually responsible for planning and executing the nutrition education program and for creating a pleasant atmosphere for meals and snacks. For this reason, the preschool teacher should be familiar with the conceptual framework behind nutrition education. The teacher should be aware of the nutritional value of foods and of educational methods and be able to clearly state objectives and realistically evaluate the results of nutrition activities.

The food service personnel are responsible for planning, preparing, and serving nutritious, attractive meals. Food service personnel can be a great asset to a nutrition education program by including foods in the menu that reinforce what the children have learned from nutrition activities. The cook is a valuable resource person

Figure 21–1 The effectiveness of the nutrition education program depends on cooperation between the director, teachers, and food service personnel.

for food preparation methods. Since the cook is also responsible for the kitchen equipment, the cook may determine what is available for use for food preparation experiences.

Underlying the effectiveness of the above child care personnel as nutrition educators is one very simple, basic concept: *Set a good example.* Children who observe a caregiver eating and enjoying a variety of nutritious foods will learn to eat more nutritiously than children who observe adults drinking soft drinks and eating other calorie-dense junk foods.

Parental Involvement in Nutrition Education

Parent involvement is vital to nutrition education in child care centers. Part of the nutrition program should involve helping parents understand their role in the provision of adequate nutrition for the child and the development of healthful eating habits. Communication between staff and parents is important so that parents may provide additional reinforcement for what has been learned at school.

To be effective, this communication should involve a real commitment of time and effort from both parents and caregivers. Some ways that childcare centers could encourage parental involvement with nutrition education are:

- Weekly posting of menus plus suggestions for foods that provide nutritional compliments to each menu.
- Provide parents with a report of, and recipes for, new foods that their children have recently been introduced to.
- Provide a report on nutrition education units (food experiences) to the parents and ask for parental feedback on the child's reaction to these experiences.

- Present some evening meetings or workshops for parents. These could include talks or questions/answer sessions with local health agency personnel, demonstrations of food preparation by a local chef, or presentations by a parent who may have some food or nutrition experience to share.

Other ways for parents to participate in nutrition education are:

- accompany children to food-related field trips
- occasionally eat lunch with their child at the daycare center
- help plan menus
- share special recipes that are nutritious and family favorites
- share ethnic or traditional foods with carecenter children and/or other parents
- assist and observe one food experience activity with their child
- help in developing guidelines for acceptable foods that parents could bring to the daycare center to celebrate a birthday or other holidays

Regardless of the degree of involvement chosen by the individual caregivers and parents, the overriding common goal is the optimal growth and development of the child. Such a goal can best be met when open, understanding, two-way communication exists between caregiver and parents.

RATIONALE FOR NUTRITION EDUCATION IN THE EARLY YEARS

There are several reasons for presenting information on nutrition to young children. Simple basic principles of good nutrition and how they relate to health can be effectively taught through nutrition education. Another advantage is that nutrition education activities foster child development in the following areas that relate directly to the preschool curriculum:

- *Promotion of language development*

  Children learn and use food names, food preparation terms, and names of utensils. Children also use language to communicate with their peers and caregivers throughout the nutrition activity. A variety of children's literature and music can also be introduced to reinforce both language skills and nutrition concepts.

- *Promotion of cognitive development*

  Children learn to follow step-by-step directions in recipes. Math concepts are learned through activities that involve measurement of food (cups, ounces, teaspoons), counting, and time periods. Science concepts, such as changes in form, are reinforced through activities that involve heating, mixing, cooking, or chilling foods.

- *Promotion of* sensorimotor *development*

  Hand and finger dexterity are developed through measuring, cutting, mixing, spreading, and serving food. Shapes, textures, and colors are learned through a variety of foods.

- *Promotion of social/emotional development*
  Through nutrition activities, children learn to work as part of a team in either large or small groups. Their knowledge and acceptance of cultural differences may also be enhanced through food activities that feature ethnic foods. In addition, children gain a more positive self-concept when they master such skills as pouring juice into a glass for themselves.

Figure 21–2 illustrates the potential contribution of food experiences to the early childhood curriculum.

PLANNING A NUTRITION EDUCATION PROGRAM

The nutrition education program should consist of well-planned activities that lead to specific outcomes. (A list of resources for children's activities involving nutrition education is given in Figure 21–3.) The desired outcome behaviors are the objectives of the program.

The overall program should be planned around some or all of the four basic nutrition education concepts. Concepts should be chosen that are appropriate for the children in the group according to their age and developmental level. Young children have the ability to comprehend that food is good. They can benefit from an introduction to a variety of nutritious foods. Older children can begin to understand the concept of food groups based on similar nutrient contributions.

The preschool nutrition program is the ideal place to increase familiarity with a variety of new foods. It is also an effective tool for showing children that common foods may be prepared in a number of ways. The 3 year old, for instance, may not yet realize that a head of lettuce, a leaf of lettuce on a sandwich, and torn lettuce in a salad are all the same food. Tasting parties are easy ways to introduce new foods, or different forms of the same food.

Nutrition education activities should be part of a coordinated program designed to explore each of the concepts chosen. They should be planned to meet specified goals rather than simply serving as a means of filling time or keeping the children busy.

The results of the program should be measurable in order to determine its effectiveness. Results may be evaluated by determining whether any of the desired behaviors outlined in the objectives are observed. Figures 21–4 and 21–5 give examples of how a nutrition concept can be outlined and incorporated into learning experiences for young children.

It should be remembered that setting goals does not imply that the activity should be rigidly imposed, or that the exact activities and discussion topics that are listed in the outline and lesson plans should be followed without deviation. Rather, as in any other curricular activity, the interests of the children and their optimal development, should be the governing factors for planning and extending learning activities.

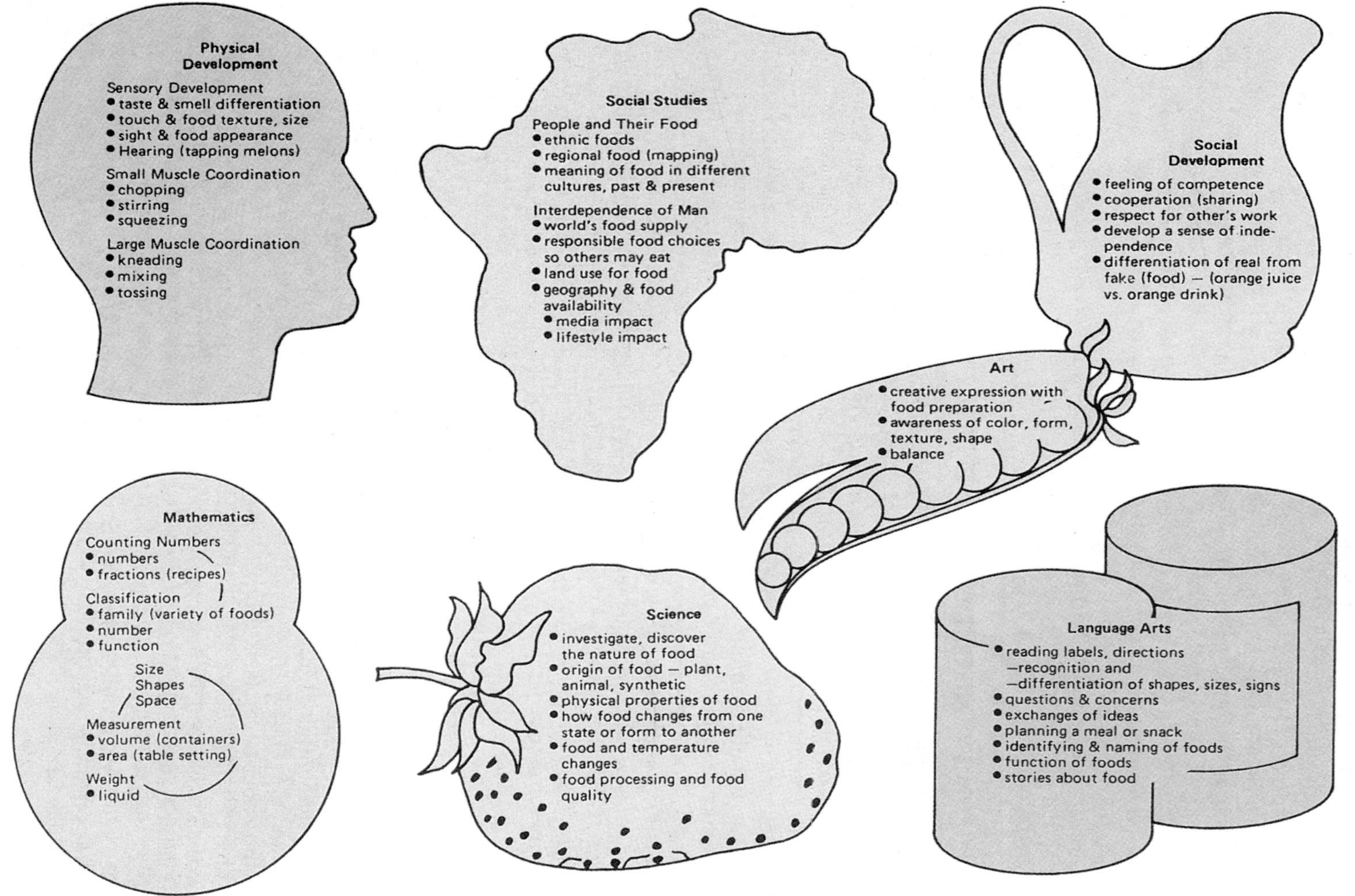

Figure 21–2 Potential contribution of food experiences to early childhood curriculum. Reprinted from "Creative Food Experiences for Children," which is available from the center for Science in the Public Interest, 1501 Sixteenth Street, NW, Washington, DC 20036.

Berman, C., Froman, J. 1991. *Meals Without Squeals*. Palo Alto, CA. Bull Publishing Co.

Berman, C., Froman, J. 1991. *Teaching Children About Food*. Palo Alto, CA. Bull Publishing Co.

Carl, E. *The Very Hungry Caterpillar*. Cleveland, OH: Williams Collins and World Publishing Company, Inc.

Children, Get a Headstart on the Road to Good Nutrition. 1987. A Nutrition Education Curriculum for Preschool Children Head Start. U. S. Department of Health and Human Services. Office of Human Development Services.

Food...Early Choices. 1980. Rosemont, IL: National Dairy Council.

Fraser, J., Farkas, J., and Stimmel, D. 1980. *Child Center Nutrition Handbook*. Cleveland, OH: Cleveland State University.

Food is Good, Books I–VI. 1973–1981. Yakima, WA: The Yakima Home Economics Association.

Galloway, J., Ivey, J. and Volster, G. 1990. *Daily Plans for Active Preschoolers*. West Nyack, NY. The Center for Applied Research in Education.

Goodwin, M. T. and Pollen, G. 1981. *Creative Food Experiences for Children*. Washington, DC: Center for Science in the Public Interest.

Mayesky, M., Newman, D. and Wlodkowsky, R. J. 1985. *Creative Activities for Young Children*. Albany, NY: Delmar Publishers Inc.

Palmer, M., and Edmonds, A. 1981. *Vegetable Magic: A Preschool and Nutrition Education Source Book*. Storrs, CT: CNETP Publications, Department of Nutritional Sciences, University of Connecticut.

Spencer, E., and Campbell, J. *Picture Recipes for Beginning Cooks*. Baltimore, MD: Preventive Medicine Administration, Department of Health and Mental Hygiene.

The Thing the Professor Forgot. Nutrition Department, General Mills, Inc.

Figure 21–3 Resources for children's activities involving food.

GUIDELINES FOR NUTRITION EDUCATION ACTIVITIES

1. Nutrition activities should be suitable for the developmental level of the participating children. **Caution:** Special consideration should be given to the chewing ability of the children involved, especially when raw fruits, nuts, popcorn, or vegetables are to be used in the food activity.
2. With consideration to food safety, funds, equipment available, and any known food allergies, actual foods should be used in nutrition projects as often as possible. These may be accompanied by pictures, games, and stories to reinforce what is learned in real food activities. **Caution:** The care provider should always check for allergies to any foods (or similar foods) introduced in the nutrition activity.

CONCEPT: CHILDREN NEED FOOD TO GROW AND HAVE HEALTHY BODIES

OBJECTIVES: The children should learn that

- all living things need food
- food is important for growth and for good health

SUGGESTED ACTIVITIES

- Caring for animals in the classroom with special attention to their diets.
- Taking field trips to the zoo or farm to learn what animals eat.
- Caring for plants in the classroom.
- Planting a vegetable garden in containers or a small plot of ground.
- Weighing and measuring the children periodically.
- Tracing outlines of each child on large sheets of paper.

QUESTIONS FOR EXTENDING LEARNING EXPERIENCES:

- What do animals eat?
- Do all animals eat the same foods?
- Do animals eat the same foods as people?
- Do animals grow faster or slower than people?
- What do plants eat?
- Can people see plants eating?
- Do plants eat the same foods as people?
- What does it mean to be healthy?
- Do people need food to be healthy?
- Do children need food to grow?

EVALUATION:

- Children can name what animals and plants eat.
- Children can describe some effects of not feeding plants and animals.

Figure 21–4 Sample outline for incorporating nutrition education concept #1 into learning experiences for the young child.

3. The foods used should be nutritious. Foods from the Food Guide Pyramid are nutritious. Foods from the Fats, Oils, and Sweets Group usually are not nutritious. Cakes, pies, and cookies, although made from grain products, are high in added sugars and fats and calories. Foods in this group should be included only if all nutrient needs are met and there is still need for more calories; this rarely happens with the young child.
4. The end products of a nutrition activity should be edible and should be eaten by the children. Pasta collages and chocolate pudding finger paintings are not suitable nutrition projects since it is not possible to eat the end product.

CONCEPT: FOODS MUST BE CAREFULLY HANDLED BEFORE THEY ARE EATEN

OBJECTIVES: Children should understand

- where foods come from
- how foods are handled

SUGGESTED ACTIVITIES:

- Grow, *harvest,* and prepare foods from a garden.
- Sprout alfalfa, radishes, or bean seeds.
- Discuss and illustrate the different parts of plants used as food (leaves, roots, fruits, seeds).
- Conduct simple experiments that show change in color or form of food.
- Play "store" or "farm".
- Take children on a field trip to a farm, dairy, bakery, or grocery store.

QUESTIONS FOR EXTENDING LEARNING EXPERIENCES:

- From where does food come?
- Where do grocery stores get food?
- Is food always eaten the way it is grown?
- Who prepares different foods?
- Does all food come from the store?

EVALUATION:

- Children can name sources of specific foods.
- Children can name who handles such foods as bread, milk, etc.

Figure 21–5 Sample outline for incorporating nutrition education concept #4 into learning experiences for the young child.

These activities say to the child that it is OK to play with food; this is not a desirable behavior to develop in a young child.

5. The children should be involved in the actual food preparation. *Hands-on* experiences such as cleaning vegetables, rolling dough, spreading butter, and cutting biscuits increase learning and help to develop a child's positive feelings about food, Figure 21–6. These activities not only enhance food experiences, but aid in the development of other skills such as manual dexterity, counting, or learning to follow directions. Children will often accept new, unfamiliar foods more readily if they have helped in its preparation.
6. Once the nutrition activity is completed, the food should be eaten within a short period of time, Figure 21–7. Delays between the completion of the activity and use of the food lessen the impact of the activity.

Figure 21–6 Hands-on experiences foster the development of positive feelings about food.

Figure 21–7 Foods prepared during nutrition activities should be eaten within a short period of time after the activity is completed.

SAFETY CONSIDERATIONS

Attention to the following points can contribute to the increased success and safety of all food experiences.

Basic Guidelines

- Be aware of all food allergies identified in children. Post a list of the names of these children, along with the foods they cannot eat. Some of the more common foods to which children may be allergic are: wheat; milk and milk products; juices such as orange or grapefruit juice that have a high acid content; chocolate; eggs; and nuts.
- Avoid serving foods such as nuts, raw vegetables and popcorn that could cause young children to choke.
- Children should always sit down to eat.
- Use low work tables and chairs.
- Use unbreakable equipment whenever possible.
- Supply enough tools and utensils for all of the children in the group.
- Use blunt knives or *serrated* plastic knives for cutting cooked eggs, potatoes, bananas, etc. Vegetable peelers should be used only under supervision and only after demonstrating their proper use to the children.
- Have only the necessary tools, utensils, and ingredients at the work table. All other materials should be removed as soon as they are no longer needed. Plan equipment needs carefully to avoid having to leave the work area during the activity. The teacher should never leave the activity area when utensils or foods are present that have the potential for causing injury.
- *Preplan* the steps of the cooking project; discuss these steps with the children before beginning. Children should understand what they are expected to do and what the adults will do before the cooking materials are made available to them.
- Long hair should be pulled back and fastened; floppy or cumbersome clothing should not be worn. Aprons are not essential, but may be helpful.
- Wash hands before beginning the activity.
- Begin with simple recipes that require little cooking. Once the children feel comfortable with those cooking projects, move on to slightly more complex ones.
- Allow plenty of time for touching, tasting, looking, and comparing, as well as for discussion. Use every step in the cooking project as an opportunity to expand the learning experience for the children.

Food Safety

- Wash hands before and after cooking project; this applies to caregivers as well as children.

- Children and adults with colds should not help with food preparation.
- Keep all cooking utensils clean. Have extra utensils available in case one is dropped or is put into a child's mouth.
- Teach children how to taste foods that are being prepared. Give each child a small plate and spoon to use. Never let the children taste foods directly from the bowl or pan in which the foods are being prepared.
- Avoid using foods that spoil rapidly. Keep sauces, meats, and dairy products refrigerated.

Cooking Safety

- Match the task to the children's developmental levels and attention spans.
- Instruct children carefully regarding the use of utensils.
- Emphasize that all cooking must be supervised by an adult.
- Adults should do the cooking over stove burners. Pot handles should always be turned away from the edge of the stove.
- Use wooden utensils or utensils with wooden handles for cooking. (Metal utensils conduct heat and can cause painful burns.)

DEVELOPING ACTIVITY PLANS FOR NUTRITION ACTIVITIES

The success of each classroom activity as it contributes to the total nutrition education program depends upon the careful development of a plan for each activity. The principles of instruction for general health education programs including topic selection, development of objectives, instructional procedures and *evaluation* are covered in depth in Chapter 8. Reviewing this material will be helpful in planning nutrition education activities.

Some special considerations when developing plans for an effective nutrition program are:

- The title (subject) and *objectives* chosen for each activity should contribute to the understanding of one or more of the four nutrition concepts considered appropriate for the young child.
- Classroom activities that involve hands-on experience with real food are most effective in teaching children about nutrition.
- Careful preplanning is essential for making each activity safe as well as a good learning experience. Most plans need a cautions list.
- Preplanning allows a sequencing of activities so that each new activity reinforces things that have been learned from prior lessons.
- Evaluation, in addition to giving feedback on the current activity, should be used in planning future activities.

Figure 21–8 presents a nutrition activity planning form to help in developing individual classroom activities.

FOOD ACTIVITY (TITLE): ______________________________

DATE: ______________ LENGTH OF TIME REQUIRED: ______________

TYPE OF GROUP: Individual ________ Small ________ Large ________

NUTRITIONAL CONCEPTS TO BE REINFORCED:

Children must have food to grow and have healthy bodies ________

Nutrients come from foods ________

A variety of foods must be eaten each day ________

Foods must be handled carefully before they are eaten ________

OBJECTIVES OF ACTIVITY (Reasons for choosing activity):

1.	3.
2.	4.

Motor Skills Involved:	mixing	dipping	pouring
	beating	peeling	spreading
	grinding	measuring	cutting
	grating	rolling	other ________
Sensory Experiences:	smelling	feeling	tasting
	seeing	hearing	

Related Concepts/Developmental Areas

MATERIALS/EQUIPMENT:

1.	5.
2.	6.
3.	7.
4.	8.

PRE-LESSON PREPARATION NEEDED: ________ yes ________ no

Describe.

PROCEDURE (step-by-step)/Discussion Questions:

1.	6.
2.	7.
3.	8.
4.	9.
5.	10.

CAUTIONS:

EVALUATION AND COMMENTS:

SUGGESTIONS FOR FOLLOW-UP ACTIVITIES:

Figure 21–8 Nutrition education lesson planning form.

Activity Plan #1 Weighing and Measuring Children

FOOD ACTIVITY (TITLE): Weighing and Measuring Children

DATE: ____________ LENGTH OF TIME REQUIRED: 10–15 minutes

TYPE OF GROUP: Individual ________ Small ___x___ Large________

NUTRITIONAL CONCEPTS TO BE REINFORCED:

Children must have food to grow and have healthy bodies ___x___

Nutrients come from foods ________

A variety of foods must be eaten each day ________

Foods must be handled carefully before they are eaten ________

OBJECTIVES OF ACTIVITY (Reasons for choosing activity):

1. Children learn that their growth is maximized by eating good food.
2. Children learn that growth may be measured by (1) height and (2) weight.

Motor Skills Involved:	mixing	dipping	pouring
	beating	peeling	spreading
	grinding	(measuring)	cutting
	grating	rolling	other _______
Sensory Experiences:	smelling	feeling	tasting
	(seeing)	hearing	

Related Concepts/Developmental Areas: Math: numbers on scale, units of measure (pounds, inches). Language: comparisons of size. Social skills: acceptance of individual differences.

MATERIALS/EQUIPMENT:

1. Balance-beam scale or bathroom scale
2. Yardstick
3. Sheets of paper

SETTING FOR ACTIVITY: Classroom or child care center

PRE-LESSON PREPARATION NEEDED: ______ yes ___x___ no

Describe.

PROCEDURE (step-by-step)/Discussion Questions

1. Help each child onto scale.
2. Help child read his/her weight.
3. Measure height.

4. Help child read his/her height.
5. Record height.
6. Record weight.

1. Does everybody weigh the same?
2. Is everyone the same height?
3. Do children stay the same size? Do adults?
4. What makes children grow?
5. Name some foods that help children grow.

CAUTIONS:

EVALUATION AND COMMENTS:

Each child can tell the care provider his/her height and weight.

Children can name foods that contribute to health and growth.

SUGGESTIONS FOR FOLLOW-UP ACTIVITIES:

Trace outline of each child on large sheets of paper.

Repeat this activity periodically to monitor each child's rate of growth.

Discuss individual differences between children, such as concepts of tall and short.

(The discussion should be positive—these differences are what make each child special.)

Activity Plan #2 Making Indian Fried Bread

FOOD ACTIVITY (TITLE): Indian Fried Bread

TYPE OF GROUP: Individual ______ Small __x__ Large ______

NUTRITIONAL CONCEPTS TO BE REINFORCED:

Children must have food to grow and have healthy bodies ______

Nutrients come from foods ______

A variety of foods must be eaten each day __x__

Foods must be handled carefully before they are eaten ______

OBJECTIVES OF ACTIVITY (Reasons for choosing activity):

1. To introduce foods from another culture.
2. To provide tactile sensations from kneading dough.

Motor Skills Involved: (mixing) dipping (pouring) beating peeling spreading grinding (measuring) cutting grating (rolling) other kneading

Sensory Experiences: (smelling) (feeling) (tasting) (seeing) (hearing)

Related Concepts/Developmental Areas: Science: melting butter, browning bread, addition of water to dough. Language: discussion of American Indian heritage. Social skills: learning safe cooking procedures.

MATERIALS/EQUIPMENT:

1. Electric skillet
2. Bowl
3. Spoon
4. Measuring cups
5. Measuring spoons
6. Recipe:
   2 c. whole wheat flour
   2 c. unbleached white flour
   1 tsp. salt
   3 Tbsp. corn oil
   Water to make soft dough
   (See Figure 21-9.)

SETTING FOR ACTIVITY:

Kitchen (or use electric skillet in the classroom)

PRE-LESSON PREPARATION NEEDED: __x__ yes ______ no

Describe. Gather equipment as listed.

PROCEDURE (step-by-step)/Discussion Questions

1. Wash hands.
2. Mix together and knead dough 5–10 minutes.
3. Put dough in bowl, cover with cloth.
4. Let dough stand for 1 hour.
5. Shape dough into balls the size of a marble and roll and pat them flat.
6. Melt butter in pan.
7. Fry 3–4 pieces of dough at one time.
8. Serve bread warm with butter, jelly, or honey.

1. Is this bread like the bread you have at home?
2. Can you describe the bread you usually eat?
3. How did Indians make their bread?

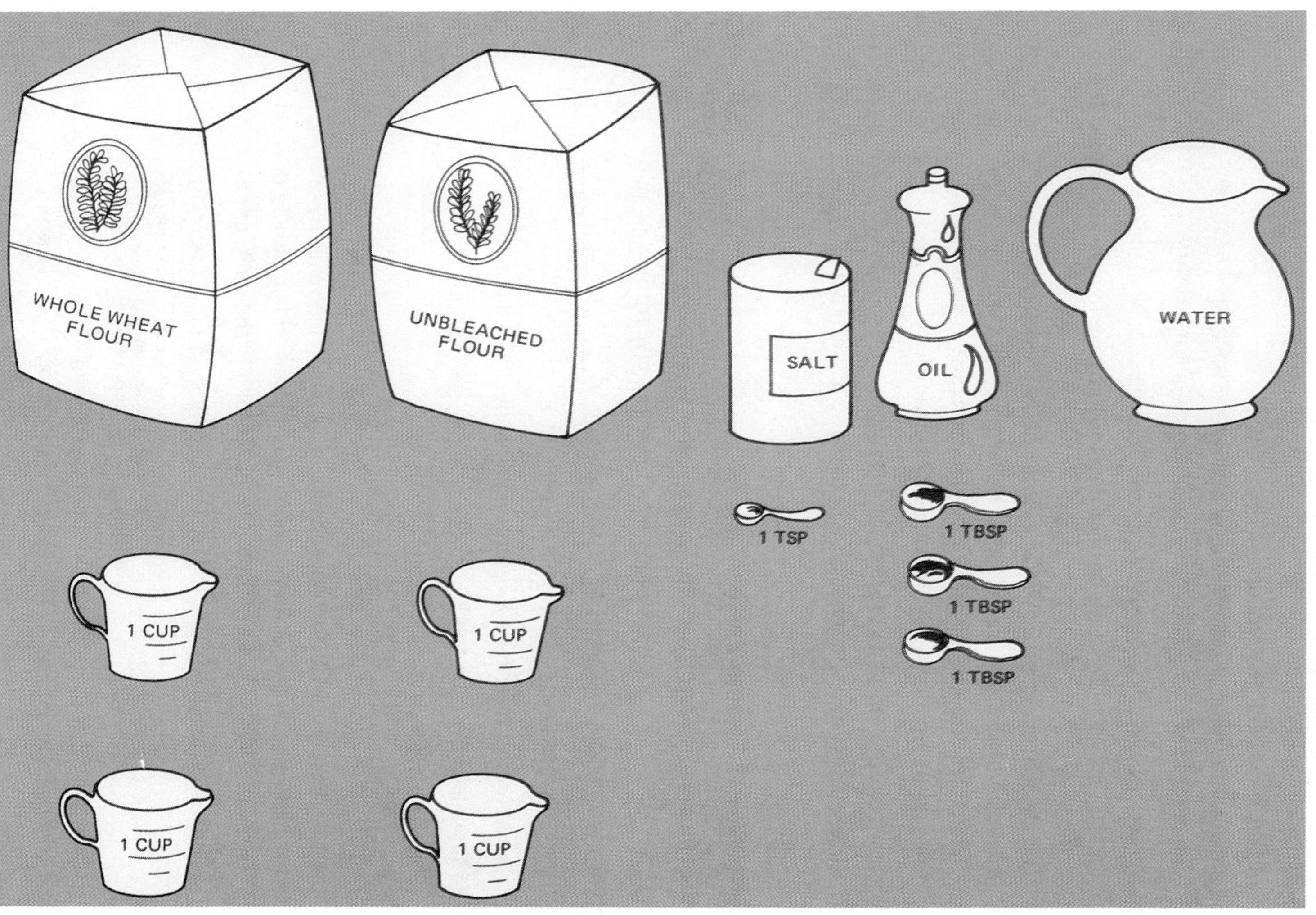

Figure 21–9 Picture recipe for Indian fried bread.

CAUTIONS:

Adults must cook the bread.

Table with electric skillet should be against the wall.

Check for food allergies; provide an alternative, if necessary.

EVALUATION AND COMMENTS:

Children's social skills were further developed by working together to make the bread.

The children experienced the feel of dough by kneading it.

Kneading helped to develop motor skills.

Children learned about American Indian food customs.

Children tasted a new food from another culture.

SUGGESTIONS FOR FOLLOW-UP ACTIVITIES:

Have children make another type of bread, e.g., corn pone.

Activity Plan #3 Tasting Party

FOOD ACTIVITY (TITLE): Tasting Party for Dairy Foods

DATE: ____________ LENGTH OF TIME REQUIRED: 10–15 minutes

TYPE OF GROUP: Individual ________ Small ________ Large ___x___

NUTRITIONAL CONCEPTS TO BE REINFORCED:

Children must have food to grow and have healthy bodies ___x___

Nutrients come from foods ___x___

A variety of foods must be eaten each day ___x___

Foods must be handled carefully before they are eaten ___x___

OBJECTIVES OF ACTIVITY (Reasons for choosing activity):

1. Children learn that common foods may be served in a variety of ways.
2. Children learn to recognize foods that belong to the dairy group.

Motor Skills Involved:	(mixing)	(dipping)	(pouring)
	beating	peeling	spreading
	grinding	(measuring)	(cutting)
	grating	rolling	other ________
Sensory Experiences:	(smelling)	feeling	(tasting)
	(seeing)	hearing	

Related Concepts/Developmental Areas: Social skills: task delegation, cooperation. Cognitive skills: classify foods as part of dairy group even though they look different than milk. Science: changes that took place to make cheese, yogurt, etc.

MATERIALS/EQUIPMENT:

1. Pitcher of milk
2. Yogurt, plain
3. Cottage cheese
4. Cheddar cheese
5. Bowl of apple chunks
6. Small bowl of granola
7. Orange juice concentrate
8. Cutting board
9. Bowls
10. Spoons
11. Cups
12. Blender

SETTING FOR ACTIVITY: Classroom or child care center

PRE-LESSON PREPARATION NEEDED: __x__ yes ______ no

Describe. Assemble necessary equipment and materials.

PROCEDURE (step-by-step)/Discussion Questions

1. Wash hands.
2. Blend part of cottage cheese with orange juice, using blender. Leave remainder as is.
3. Spoon yogurt into bowl.
4. Cut cheddar cheese into cubes.
5. Wash tables.
6. Wash hands.
7. Place all foods on table.
8. Taste small servings of each food.

1. Are all these foods made from milk?
2. Do they look alike?
3. Do they taste alike?
4. Is cottage cheese like cheddar cheese? How is it different?
5. Why were these foods chilled before preparation and why should they be eaten immediately?

CAUTIONS:

Instruct and demonstrate safe use of knife and blender.

Check for milk or dairy product allergies of any children in group; provide alternative, if necessary.

Stress that refrigeration and sanitation are very important when working with protein foods, such as milk and milk products.

EVALUATION AND COMMENTS:

Children can identify foods made from milk.
Children will taste each food served.
Children help with cleaning the tables.

SUGGESTIONS FOR FOLLOW-UP ACTIVITIES:

Make yogurt or cheese from milk.
Mix fruit with yogurt and discuss fruit and milk as "healthful" foods.

Activity Plan #4 Trip to the Grocery Store

FOOD ACTIVITY (TITLE): Trip to the Grocery Store

DATE: ________ LENGTH OF TIME REQUIRED: varies

TYPE OF GROUP: Individual x Small x Large________

NUTRITIONAL CONCEPTS TO BE REINFORCED:

Children must have food to grow and have healthy bodies x

Nutrients come from foods x

A variety of foods must be eaten each day x

Foods must be handled carefully before they are eaten x

OBJECTIVES OF ACTIVITY (Reasons for choosing activity):

1. Children are encouraged to make decisions about foods and to taste a variety of foods.
2. Children buy a food with which they are not familiar.

Motor Skills Involved:	mixing	dipping	pouring
	beating	peeling	spreading
	grinding	measuring	cutting
	grating	rolling	other ________
Sensory Experiences:	(smelling)	(feeling)	tasting
	(seeing)	hearing	

Related Concepts/Developmental Areas: Language: names of foods on list, color/shape/size concepts. Cognitive skills: classification (food sections in the store). Math: paying for food, number concepts (pick 2 red fruits). Social skills: working as a team to complete a task, interacting with grocers/clerks.

MATERIALS/EQUIPMENT:

1. Shopping list

SETTING FOR ACTIVITY: Grocery store, child care center

PRE-LESSON PREPARATION NEEDED: __x__ yes ______ no

Describe. Secure parental permission for field trip; make up grocery list.

PROCEDURE (step-by-step)/Discussion Questions

1. Select 1 to 3 children.
2. Travel to store.
3. Find produce section.
4. Find fruits.
5. Find red fruits.
6. Select 2 varieties of red fruit.
7. Count the number of each fruit needed.
8. Purchase fruit.
9. Return to child care center.
10. Ask cook to prepare fruit for snack or meal.

1. What will this fruit taste like?
2. What is the name of this food?
3. How does this fruit grow?
4. Is the skin peeled or eaten?
5. Will this fruit have seeds?
6. What ways can this fruit be prepared?

CAUTIONS:

Permission must be obtained from parents for field trip.

Fasten restraints if driving to store.

If walking to store, review safety rules for walking, crossing streets, etc.

Check for allergies; provide alternatives, if necessary.

EVALUATION AND COMMENTS:

Children are able to identify two varieties of red fruit.

Children eat and enjoy the prepared fruit.

SUGGESTIONS FOR FOLLOW-UP ACTIVITIES:

Children play "store" with some children acting as grocers, some acting as clerks, and some acting as shoppers. Have children select two types of green vegetables.

OTHER SOURCES OF INFORMATION ABOUT FOOD

Children learn about food from informal sources as well as from planned programs of instruction. The family, caregivers, other children, and television are additional sources of information about food and all have an effect on children's eating habits, Figure 21–10.

The Family

Food preferences and *attitudes* of the family unit are of primary importance in the formation of the young child's attitudes about and preferences for food. Family food choices are subject to cultural influences, money available for food, educational level, and specific preferences of family members. Since familiarity with a food is often a factor in choices, the child who comes from a family that eats a wide variety of foods is more willing to try new foods, because that is acceptable behavior in the home.

Figure 21–10 Additional sources of information about food have an effect on children's eating haabits. Source: Nutrition News for the 90's. 1994. Kansas Beef Council. Topeka, Kansas.

Caregivers

Caregivers exert considerable influence over children's attitudes about food. For this reason the caregiver should display positive attitudes about food and demonstrate both with actions and words enjoyment of food and enthusiasm for trying new foods.

Other Children

Young children's choices of food are frequently made on the basis of approval or disapproval of others within their group. A child with a strong personality who eats a variety of foods can be a positive influence on other children. On the other hand, children who are "picky eaters" can also spread their negative influence. A simple statement from the caregiver, such as, "You don't have to eat the broccoli, Jamie, but I can't allow you to spoil it for Tara and Pablo," should be effective in curbing this negative influence. Younger children may base their choices on familiarity of food and its taste. Older children (5–6) are more subject to *peer* influence when deciding whether or not to eat a food.

Television

Television is a major source of information about food for many children and their families. Unfortunately, nutrient-dense foods are rarely featured on television. Preferred foods for television advertising are those that taste good, are chocolaty, are really fun, or come with a prize. The role of television in determining food choices by the young child is discussed in Chapter 18. Both parents and caregivers can help counteract the influence of television by monitoring the programs that children view and by pointing out differences between programs and commercials. The child needs to learn that the purpose of a commercial is to sell a product.

Summary

Nutrition education is any activity that tells a person something about food. The basic concepts of nutrition education are (1) children must have food for growth and for healthy bodies, (2) nutrients come from foods, (3) a variety of foods must be eaten each day to have needed nutrients, and (4) foods must be handled carefully to assure that they are healthful and safe to eat.

The responsibility for teaching young children about nutrition rests with each member of the staff in an early childhood program, as well as with the parents of the children. Nutrition education in the early years should be based on some or all of the basic nutritional concepts and should promote children's skills in all developmental areas.

Nutrition education activities should be geared to the age and developmental level of the children within the group; nutrition activities should allow specific measurable goals to be attained. The primary goal of nutrition education in the early years is to teach children some simple basic principles of nutrition and to encourage them to eat and enjoy a variety of nutritious foods. The foods used in nutrition experiences should be nutritious, and the end product of a project should be edible. It is advisable to use actual foods whenever possible; however, books, games, and puppets are good reinforcing materials.

Hands-on food experiences can effectively teach children basic principles of good nutrition and how these principles relate to health. Food experiences also promote language, cognitive, sensorimotor, and social/emotional development.

In planning nutrition activities for young children, allergies and other safety factors must also be carefully considered. Activity plans may be helpful, especially to a beginning teacher. Careful planning involved in developing lesson plans contributes to the success of the activity.

Caregivers should also be aware of the other sources from which children receive information about nutrition—family members, peers, television. They should strive to reinforce the positive nutritional concepts presented by these sources and to counter any misinformation provided or implied by other sources.

Suggested Activities

1. Prepare lesson plans for a two-day nutrition education activity. Plans may be for two consecutive days or for any two days within one week. The lesson plan for each day should be in the format presented in this unit.
2. From the following list, choose three foods as the subjects of food experiences. Upon what criteria were the choices based? What was the primary basis for the decision to work with each food? What other considerations affected the choice of some foods and not others?
   a. raisin-oatmeal cookies
   b. granola
   c. brownies
   d. honey
   e. greens (lettuce, spinach) for salad
   f. pancakes
3. Outline an equipment list and safety plan for a food experience in which 4 and 5 year olds make pancakes in the classroom. Cooking will be done in an electric skillet on a table. What precautions should be taken? How should the room be safely arranged? What instructions should be given to the children?
4. Select 15–20 library books appropriate for young children. Note those instances where food is portrayed either in the story or pictures. What types of foods are shown? Chart these foods according to the Food Guide Pyramid. What percentage of foods were noted within each group? What was the general message about food presented in these books?
5. Watch one hour of children's television programs on Saturday morning.
   a. Determine the percent of observed advertisements that were for "sweets" (gum, candy, soft drinks, snack cakes, and pre-sweetened cereals).

b. Which food groups were least represented in these commercials?

6. Review an article about nutrition from a popular magazine. Apply the suggested criteria for a good nutrition resource. Is this a good article? Why or why not?

Chapter Review

A. Multiple Choice. Select the best answer:

1. The basic concept(s) upon which nutrition education for the young child is based is/are
   a. foods need special handling before they are eaten
   b. children need to eat a variety of different foods
   c. foods provide nutrients
   d. all of these
2. The *primary* goal of preschool nutrition education is that children learn
   a. the Food Guide Pyramid
   b. to eat and enjoy a variety of nutritious foods
   c. to identify nutrients in foods
   d. various ways that food is processed
3. Objectives are behaviors the children
   a. already know before the activity
   b. should learn from the activity
   c. both a and b
   d. none of the above
4. An activity that illustrates that all living things need food is
   a. growing plants in the classroom
   b. caring for animals
   c. weighing and measuring children
   d. all of these
5. Important safety concepts for children to learn include
   a. all cooking must be supervised by an adult
   b. hands must be washed before eating
   c. all cooking utensils must be kept clean
   d. all of these
6. Effectiveness of a nutrition education activity can be assessed by
   a. activity plans
   b. activities
   c. evaluation
   d. basic guidelines

7. Nutrition education activities can be a method of teaching
   a. math concepts
   b. team work
   c. basic nutrition
   d. all of these
8. Common sources of nutrition information for children are
   a. nutrition activities
   b. television
   c. parents and teachers
   d. all of these
9. Which of the following would be the best nutrition education project?
   a. Construction of a carrot puppet.
   b. A trip to the store on Monday to buy food for Thursday lunch.
   c. Stuffing celery with peanut butter for snacks served later that day.
   d. Necklaces made from macaroni.
10. Appropriate foods to use for a nutrition education activity include
    a. apples and oranges
    b. brownies
    c. frosted sugar cookies
    d. uncooked macaroni

B. Briefly answer the following questions.

1. What is the teacher's role in providing nutrition education activities for the young child?
2. List four ways that nutrition education activities aid child development.
3. What are the criteria used for choosing appropriate nutrition education concepts for young children?
4. Report four ways that parents may share in the nutrition education of their child.

References

American Dietetics Association, 1987. "Position Paper on Standards in Daycare for Children" *Journal of the American Dietetics Association*, 87: 502.

Cotterman, S. 1984. *You're In Charge: Nutrition for Preschool Children.* Society for Nutrition Education, Oakland, CA.

Gahagan, G. *East Central Kansas Community Action Program Head Start Comprehensive Nutrition Education Program.* Ottawa, KS: CCFP Nutrition Education and Training Project, not dated.

Jacobson, M. and Hill, L., 1991. *Kitchen Fun For Kids.* Washington, D.C. Center for Science in the Public Interest.

Kansas Beef Council. 1994. *Nutrition News for the 90s.* Topeka, KS: Kansas Beef Council.

Richard, K. A., et al. 1995. "The Play Approach to Learning in the Context of Families and Schools: An Alternative Paradigm for Nutrition and Fitness Education in the 21st Century." *Journal of the American Dietetic Association*, 95: 1121–1126.

Singleton, J. C., Achterberg, C. L., and Shannon, B. M. 1992. "Role of Food and Nutrition in the Health Perceptions of Young Children." *Journal of the American Dietetic Association.* 92: 67–70.

Williams, S. R. 1981. *Nutrition and Diet Therapy*. St. Louis: The C. V. Mosby Company.

Williams, S. R., and Worthington-Roberts, B. S. 1988. *Nutrition Throughout the Life Cycle*. St. Louis, MO: Times Mirror/Mosby.

Additional Reading

Baker, M. J. Winter 1972. "Influence of Nutrition Education on Fourth and Fifth Graders." *Journal of Nutrition Education.*

Holmes, C. L., and Bunda, M. A. May 1983. "Comparative Ratings of Printed Materials Developed by Industry and Governmental Producers." *Journal of School Health* 53: 320.

Whitney, E. M., and Hamilton, E. N. 1984. "Books Not Recommended." In *Understanding Nutrition*. 3rd ed. St. Paul: West Publishing Company.

Instructional Aids

ACE Child Care Food Program Correspondence Course. Littleton, CO: Arapahoe County Extension Service.

Endres, J., and Rockwell, R. 1980. *Food, Nutrition, and the Young Child.* St. Louis: C. V. Mosby Company.

Feeding Your Child (1–5). Oklahoma City, OK: Nutrition Division, Oklahoma State Department of Health.

Feeding Your Preschooler. 1981. Corvallis, OR: Nutrition Graphics. (poster)

Food Before Six. 1982. Rosemont, IL: National Dairy Council.

Food for the Preschooler; Volumes I, II, and III. 1981. Olympia, WA: Department of Social and Health Services.

Food for Your Child Ages 1–5: A Guide for Parents. 1980. Raleigh, NC: North Carolina Agricultural Extension Service and North Carolina Department of Human Resources.

Food Models and Food Models Guide for Teachers and Other Leaders. Rosemont, IL: National Dairy Council.

"Good-News-Letter. The Good News About Good Food." American Institute for Cancer Research. 1759 R Street NW, Washington, DC 20069.

Goodwin, M. T., and Pollen, G. 1981. *Creative Food Experiences for Children.* Washington, DC: Center for Science in the Public Interest.

Hinton, S., and Mann, B. 1981. *Foods for Toddlers and Preschoolers.* Raleigh, NC: North Carolina Agricultural Extension Service, A & T and North Carolina State Universities.

Ikeda, J. 1980. *To Mom and Dad—A Primer on Feeding the Preschooler.* Richmond, CA: Agricultural Sciences Publications.

Make Eating a Pleasure. Rochester, MN: Child Care Resource and Referral, Inc.

Making Mealtime a Happy Time for Preschoolers—A Guide for Teachers. 1982. Sacramento, CA: California State Department of Education.

Nasco Nutrition Teaching Aids (Catalog). 901 Janesville Ave., Fort Atkinson, WI 53538, or 4825 Stoddard Rd, Modesto, CA 95356.

Nutrition Counseling Education Services (Catalog). 1904 East 123rd Street, Olathe, KS 66061.

Pipes, P. 1985. *Nutrition in Infancy and Childhood.* St. Louis: C. V. Mosby Co.

Pugliese, M. *Nutrition and All That Jazz: A Nutrition Handbook for Preschool Teachers.* Boston, MA: Simmons College.

Snack Facts. 1981. NIH Publication No. 81-1680. Bethesda, MD: National Institute of Dental Research.

Appendices

APPENDIX A
NUTRITION ANALYSIS OF VARIOUS FAST FOODS

PRODUCTS	SERVING SIZE	CALORIES	CARBO-HYDRATE (gm)	PROTEIN (gm)	FAT (gm)	SAT. FAT (gm)	CHOLES-TEROL (mg)	SODIUM (mg)	EXCHANGES
BURGER KING									
Sandwiches									
Hamburger	1 (3.6 oz.)	260	28	14	10	4	30	500	2 starch, 2 med. fat meat
Whopper Sandwich	1 (9.5 oz.)	570	46	27	31	12	80	870	3 starch, 3 med. fat meat, 3 fat
Chicken Sandwich	1 (8 oz.)	620	57	26	32	7	45	1430	4 starch, 2 med. fat meat, 4 fat
French Fries (medium, salted)	1 (4 oz.)	372	43	5	20	5	0	238	3 starch, 3 fat
Breakfast Items									
Bacon, Egg, Cheese Croissanwich	1 (4 oz.)	353	19	16	23	8	230	780	1 starch, 2 med. fat meat, 3 fat
Hash Browns	1 (2.5 oz.)	213	25	2	12	3	0	318	1 1/2 starch, 2 fat
HARDEE'S									
Sandwiches/Subs									
Mushroom N Swiss Burger	1 (6.5 oz.)	490	33	30	27	13	70	940	2 starch, 3 1/2 med. fat meat, 2 fat
Frisco Burger	1 (8.5 oz.)	760	43	36	50	18	70	1280	3 starch, 4 med. fat meat, 5 fat
Hot Ham N Cheese	1 (5.25 oz.)	330	32	23	12	5	65	1420	2 starch, 2 1/2 med. fat meat
Grilled Chicken Breast Sandwich	1 (6.8 oz.)	310	34	24	9	1	60	890	2 starch, 2 1/2 lean meat
Side Orders									
Cole Slaw	4 oz.	240	13	2	20	3	10	340	2 vegetables, 4 fat
Breakfast Items									
Sausage & Egg Biscuit	1 (5.3 oz.)	490	35	18	31	8	170	1150	2 starch, 2 med. fat meat, 4 fat
Biscuit 'N Gravy	1 (8 oz.)	440	45	9	24	6	15	1250	3 starch, 5 fat
KFC									
Original Recipe Chicken									
Side Breast	1 (2.9 oz.)	245	9	18	15	4	78	604	1/2 starch, 2 1/2 med. fat meat, 1/2 fat
Drumstick	1 (2 oz.)	162	3	14	9	2	75	269	2 med. fat meat

PRODUCTS	SERVING SIZE	CALORIES	CARBO-HYDRATE (gm)	PROTEIN (gm)	FAT (gm)	SAT. FAT (gm)	CHOLES-TEROL (mg)	SODIUM (mg)	EXCHANGES
Extra Crispy Chicken									
Side Breast	1 (3.7 oz.)	379	16	19	27	7	77	646	1 starch, 2 med. fat meat, 3 1/2 fat
Drumstick	1 (2.4 oz.)	205	7	14	14	3	72	292	1/2 starch, 2 med. fat meat, 1/2 fat
Kentucky Nuggets and Sauces									
Kentucky Nuggets	6 (3.4 oz.)	284	15	16	18	4	66	865	1 starch, 2 med. fat meat, 1 fat
Side Orders									
Mashed Potatoes w/ Gravy	1 (3.5 oz.)	71	12	3	2	0	tr	339	1 starch
Potato Salad	1 (3 oz.)	141	13	2	9	NA	NA	396	1 starch, 2 fat
Baked Beans	1 (3 oz.)	105	18	5	1	NA	NA	387	1 starch
MCDONALD'S									
Sandwiches									
Quarter Pounder w/ Cheese	1 (6.8 oz.)	510	34	28	28	11	115	1110	2 starch, 3 1/2 med. fat meat, 2 fat
Big Mac	1 (7.6 oz.)	500	42	25	26	9	100	890	3 starch, 2 1/2 med. fat meat, 2 fat
McChicken	1 (6.5 oz.)	415	39	19	20	4	50	830	2 1/2 starch, 2 med. fat meat, 2 fat
Salads									
Garden Salad	1 (6.6 oz.)	50	6	4	2	tr	65	70	1 vegetable
Breakfast									
Egg McMuffin	1 (4.8 oz.)	280	28	18	11	4	235	710	2 starch, 2 med. fat meat
Fat-Free Apple Bran	1 (2.6 oz.)	180	40	5	0	0	0	200	2 1/2 starch
PIZZA HUT									
Thin 'N Crispy									
Cheese	1 slice of medium pizza	223	19	13	10	5	25	503	1 starch, 1 1/2 med. fat meat, 1 fat
Veggie Lovers	1 slice of medium pizza	192	20	11	8	3	17	551	1 starch, 1 1/2 med. fat meat
Supreme	1 slice of medium pizza	262	20	15	14	3	31	819	1 starch, 2 med. fat meat, 1 fat
Pan									
Pepperoni	1 slice of medium pizza	280	26	8	18	3	25	618	2 starch, 1 med. fat meat, 2 fat
Pepperoni Lovers	1 slice of medium pizza	362	27	14	25	5	34	861	2 starch, 1 1/2 med. fat meat, 3 fat
Personal Pan Pizza									
Supreme	1 whole	647	76	37	28	NA	53	1313	5 starch, 3 med. fat meat, 1 fat

PRODUCTS	SERVING SIZE	CALORIES	CARBO-HYDRATE (gm)	PROTEIN (gm)	FAT (gm)	SAT. FAT (gm)	CHOLES-TEROL (mg)	SODIUM (mg)	EXCHANGES
TACO BELL									
Specialties									
Beef Burrito	1 (6.7 oz.)	402	38	22	17	8	59	993	2 1/2 starch, 2 med. fat meat, 1 fat
Tostada	1 (5.5 oz.)	243	28	10	11	5	18	670	2 starch, 1 med. fat meat, 1 fat
Taco	1 (2.75 oz.)	184	11	10	11	4	32	274	1 starch, 2 lean meat
Pintos & Cheese	1 order (4.5 oz.)	194	19	9	10	5	19	733	1 starch, 1 med. fat meat, 1 fat
Soft Taco	1 (3.25 oz.)	228	18	12	12	5	32	516	1 starch, 1 1/2 med. fat meat, 1 fat
Condiments									
Taco Sauce	1 packet	2	tr	tr	tr	0	0	126	free
Guacamole	1 serving (.75 oz.)	34	3	tr	2	tr	0	113	1/2 fat
Salads									
Taco Salad with Ranch Dressing	1 (20 oz.)	1167	61	37	87	45	121	1959	4 starch, 3 1/2 med. fat meat, 13 fat
WENDY'S									
Sandwiches									
Single with Everything	1 (7.7 oz.)	440	36	26	23	7	75	850	2 starch, 1 vegetable, 3 med. fat meat, 1 fat
Grilled Chicken Sandwich	1 (6.25 oz.)	290	35	24	7	1	60	360	2 starch, 1 vegetable, 2 lean meat
Baked Potato									
Bacon & Cheese	1 (13.4 oz.)	510	75	17	17	4	15	1170	5 starch, 1 med. fat meat, 2 fat
French Fries, Nuggets, and Chili									
Chili	Small (8 oz.)	190	21	19	6	2	40	670	1 1/2 starch, 2 lean meat
Salads									
Grilled Chicken Salad	1 (12 oz.)	200	9	25	8	1	55	690	2 vegetable, 3 lean meat

Source: Reprinted with permission from Fast Food Facts, by Marion Franz, M.S., R.D., C.D.E.,

APPENDIX B
GROWTH CHARTS FOR BOYS AND GIRLS

Instructions For Using Charts:

1. Locate the child's age along the bottom of the chart.
2. Locate the child's height/weight along the right-hand side of the chart.
3. Place an *X* at the point where the two lines cross. This point represents a percentile (child's height/weight ranked in comparison to other children of the same age).

For example: A 5-year-old male who is 43.3 inches tall would be ranked at the fiftieth percentile. This means that approximately 50 percent of 5-year-old males are taller; 50 percent are shorter.

The following tables are courtesy of National Center for Health Statistics, U.S. Department of Health, Education, and Welfare.

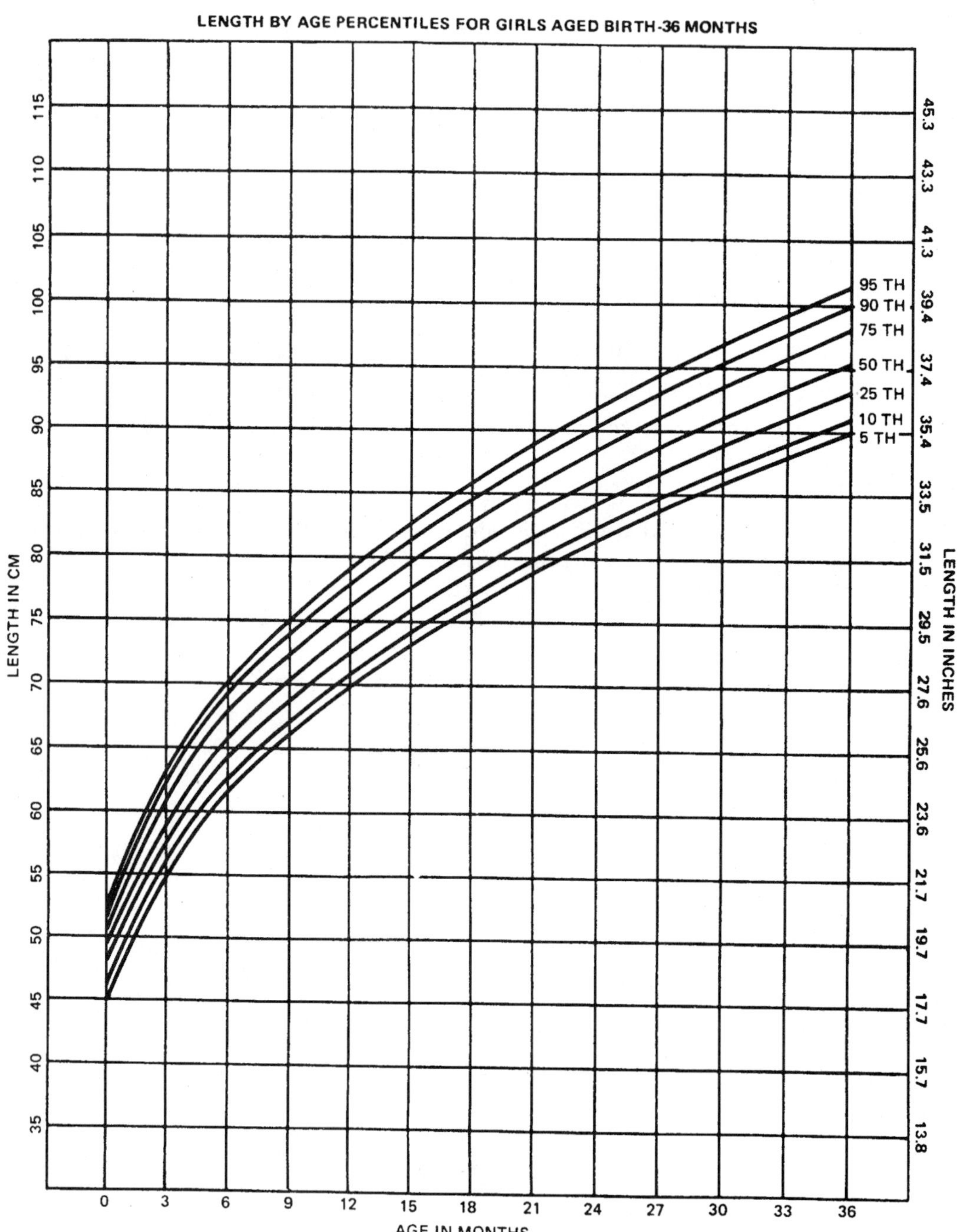
LENGTH BY AGE PERCENTILES FOR GIRLS AGED BIRTH-36 MONTHS
LENGTH IN CM
115
110
105
100
95
90
85
80
75
70
65
60
55
50
45
40
35
LENGTH IN INCHES
45.3
43.3
41.3
39.4
37.4
35.4
33.5
31.5
29.5
27.6
25.6
23.6
21.7
19.7
17.7
15.7
13.8
95 TH
90 TH
75 TH
50 TH
25 TH
10 TH
5 TH
0
3
6
9
12
15
18
21
24
27
30
33
36
AGE IN MONTHS

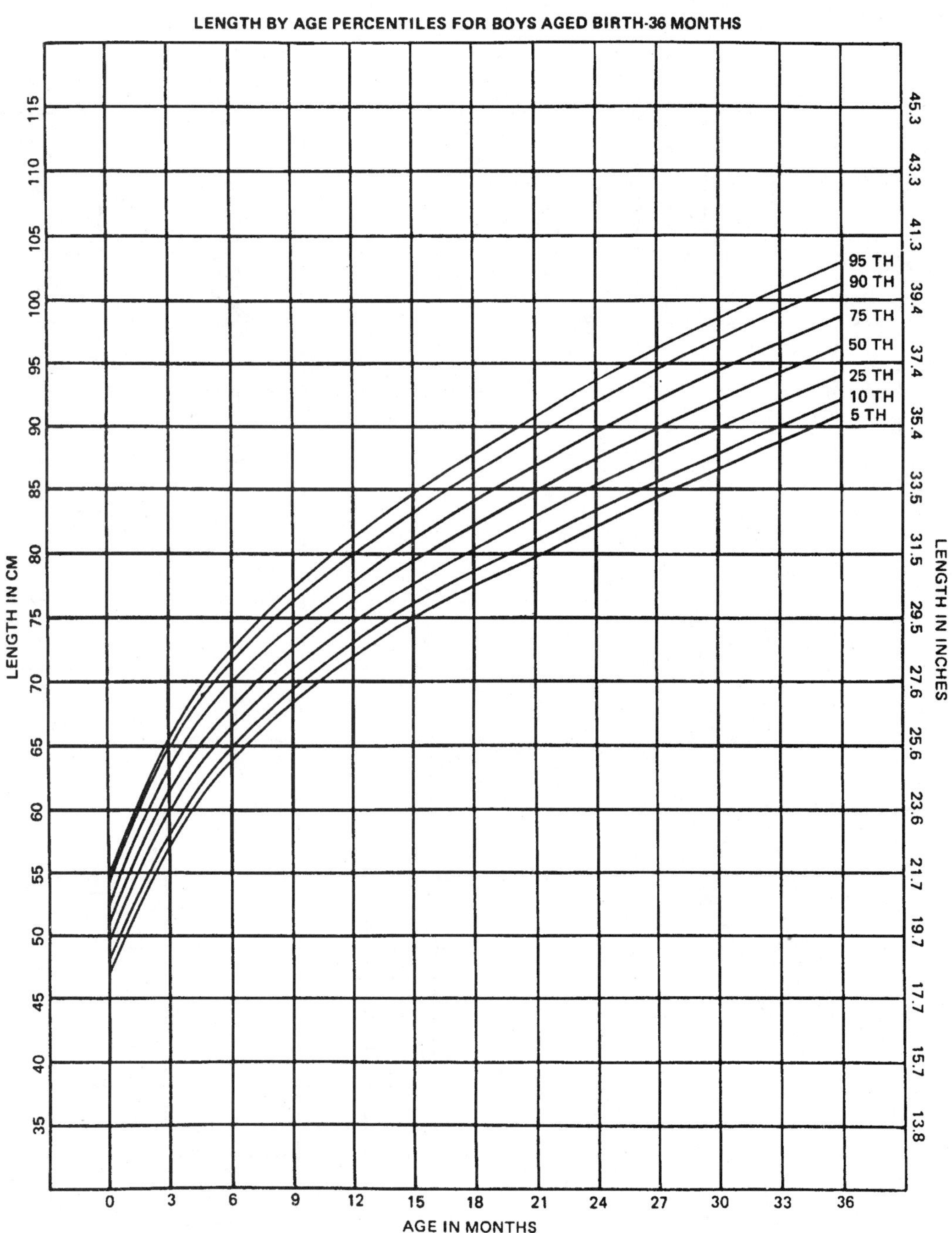
LENGTH BY AGE PERCENTILES FOR BOYS AGED BIRTH-36 MONTHS
LENGTH IN CM
115
110
105
100
95
90
85
80
75
70
65
60
55
50
45
40
35
LENGTH IN INCHES
45.3
43.3
41.3
39.4
37.4
35.4
33.5
31.5
29.5
27.6
25.6
23.6
21.7
19.7
17.7
15.7
13.8
95 TH
90 TH
75 TH
50 TH
25 TH
10 TH
5 TH
0
3
6
9
12
15
18
21
24
27
30
33
36
AGE IN MONTHS

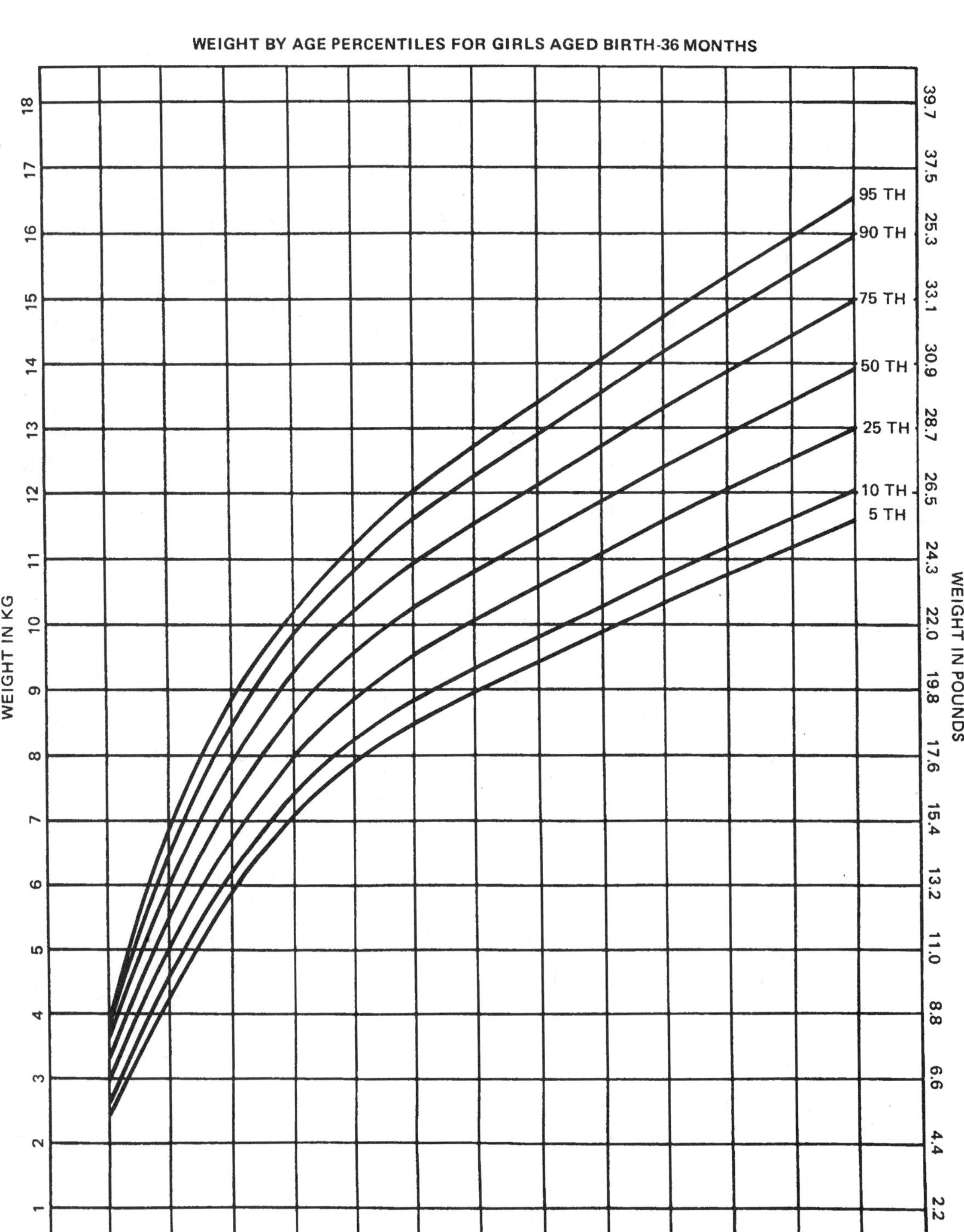
WEIGHT BY AGE PERCENTILES FOR GIRLS AGED BIRTH-36 MONTHS
WEIGHT IN KG
18
17
16
15
14
13
12
11
10
9
8
7
6
5
4
3
2
1
95 TH
90 TH
75 TH
50 TH
25 TH
10 TH
5 TH
WEIGHT IN POUNDS
39.7
37.5
25.3
33.1
30.9
28.7
26.5
24.3
22.0
19.8
17.6
15.4
13.2
11.0
8.8
6.6
4.4
2.2
0
3
6
9
12
15
18
21
24
27
30
33
36
AGE IN MONTHS

WEIGHT BY AGE PERCENTILES FOR BOYS AGED BIRTH-36 MONTHS

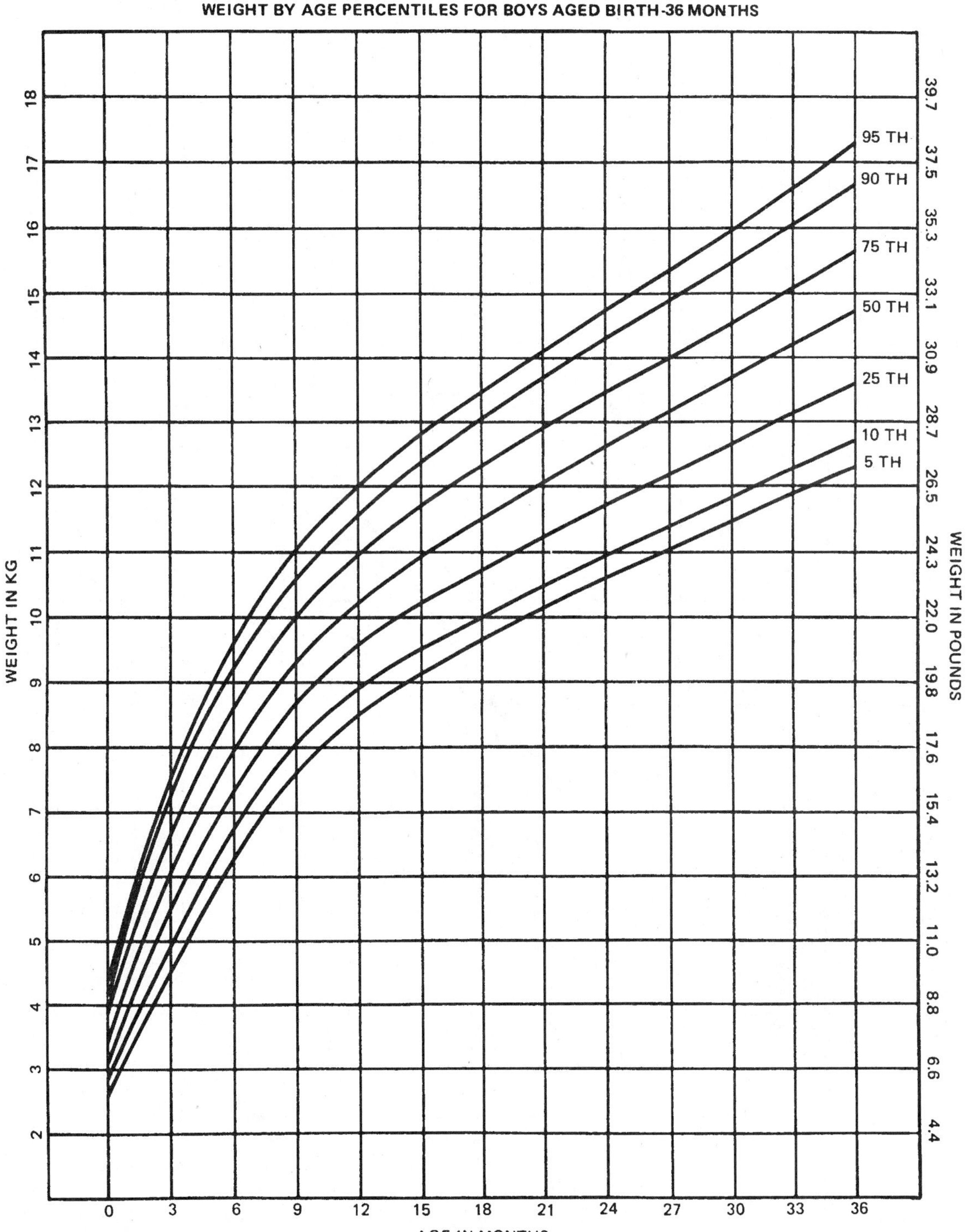

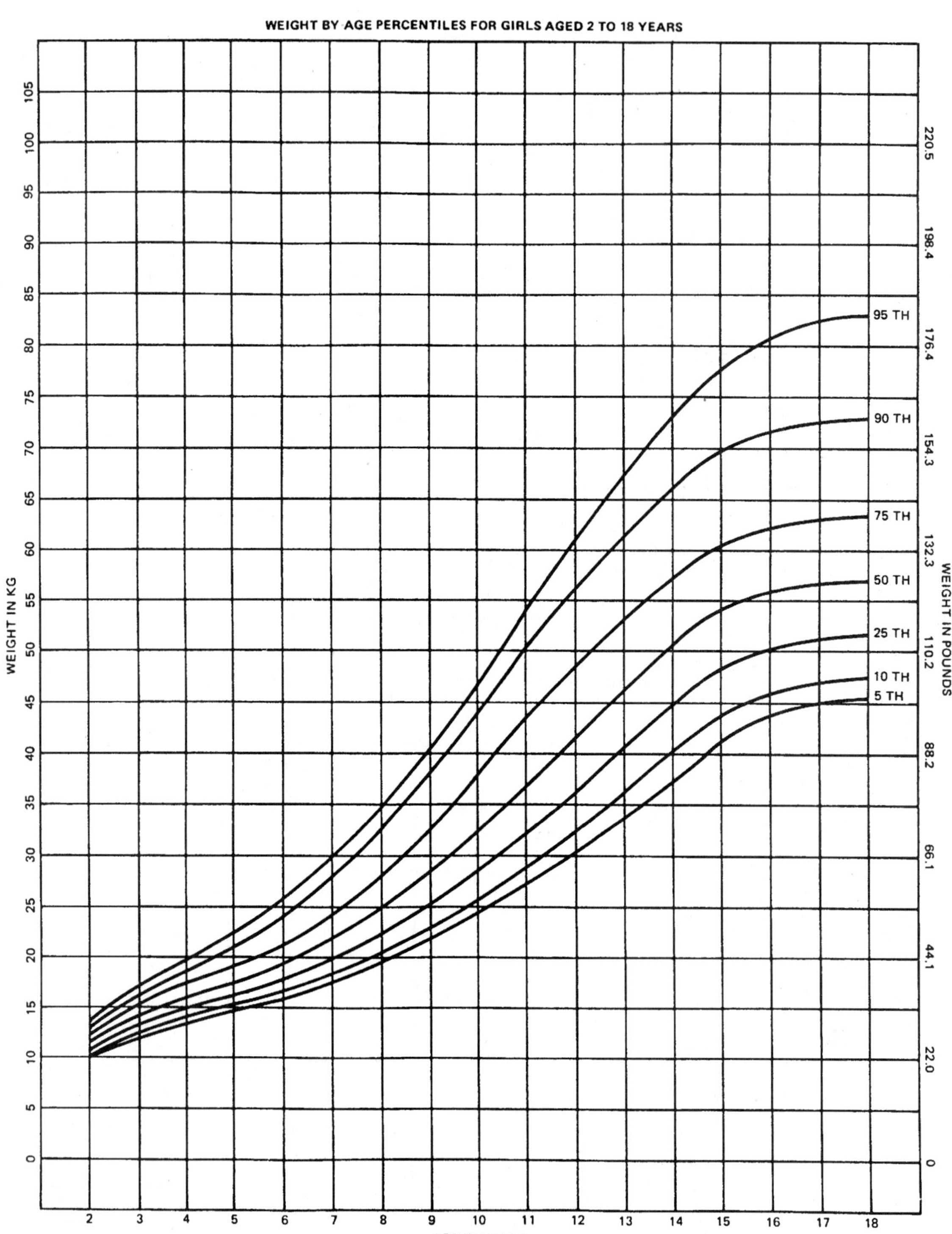
WEIGHT BY AGE PERCENTILES FOR GIRLS AGED 2 TO 18 YEARS
WEIGHT IN KG
105
100
95
90
85
80
75
70
65
60
55
50
45
40
35
30
25
20
15
10
5
0
WEIGHT IN POUNDS
220.5
198.4
176.4
154.3
132.3
110.2
88.2
66.1
44.1
22.0
0
95 TH
90 TH
75 TH
50 TH
25 TH
10 TH
5 TH
2
3
4
5
6
7
8
9
10
11
12
13
14
15
16
17
18
AGE IN YEARS

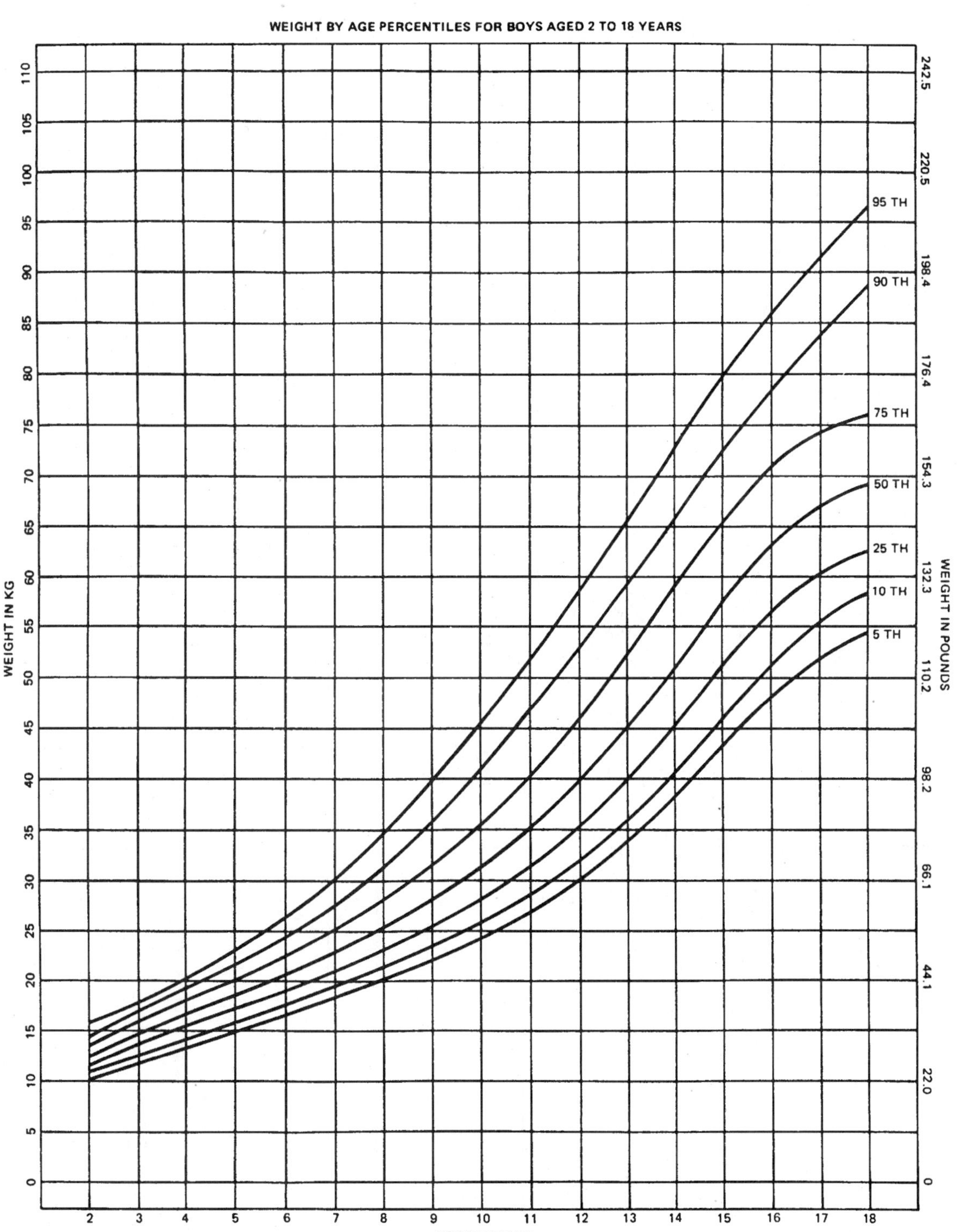
WEIGHT BY AGE PERCENTILES FOR BOYS AGED 2 TO 18 YEARS
WEIGHT IN KG
0
5
10
15
20
25
30
35
40
45
50
55
60
65
70
75
80
85
90
95
100
105
110
WEIGHT IN POUNDS
0
22.0
44.1
66.1
88.2
110.2
132.3
154.3
176.4
198.4
220.5
242.5
95 TH
90 TH
75 TH
50 TH
25 TH
10 TH
5 TH
2
3
4
5
6
7
8
9
10
11
12
13
14
15
16
17
18
AGE IN YEARS

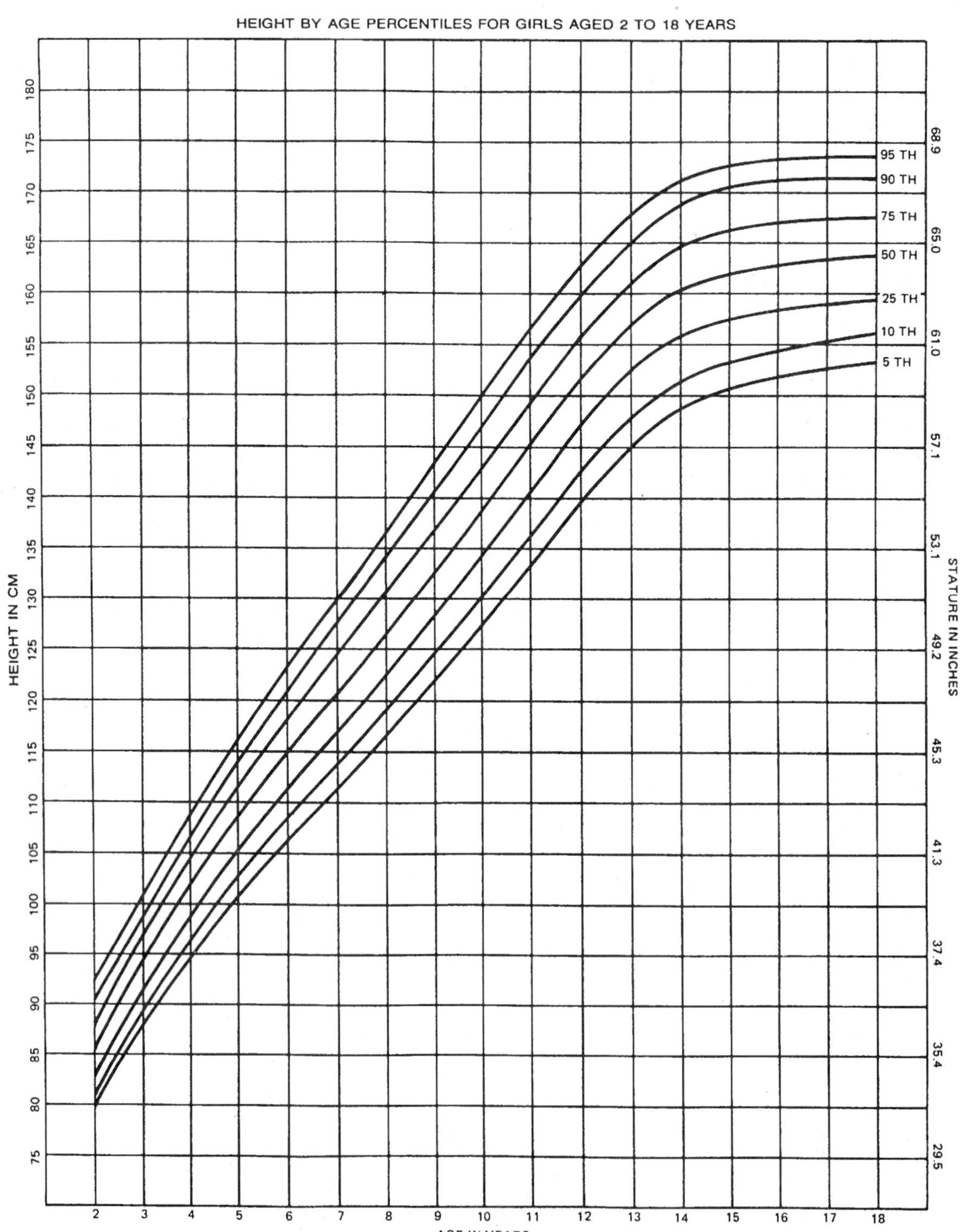

HEIGHT BY AGE PERCENTILES FOR GIRLS AGED 2 TO 18 YEARS
HEIGHT IN CM
75
80
85
90
95
100
105
110
115
120
125
130
135
140
145
150
155
160
165
170
175
180
STATURE IN INCHES
29.5
35.4
37.4
41.3
45.3
49.2
53.1
57.1
61.0
65.0
68.9
95 TH
90 TH
75 TH
50 TH
25 TH
10 TH
5 TH
AGE IN YEARS
2
3
4
5
6
7
8
9
10
11
12
13
14
15
16
17
18

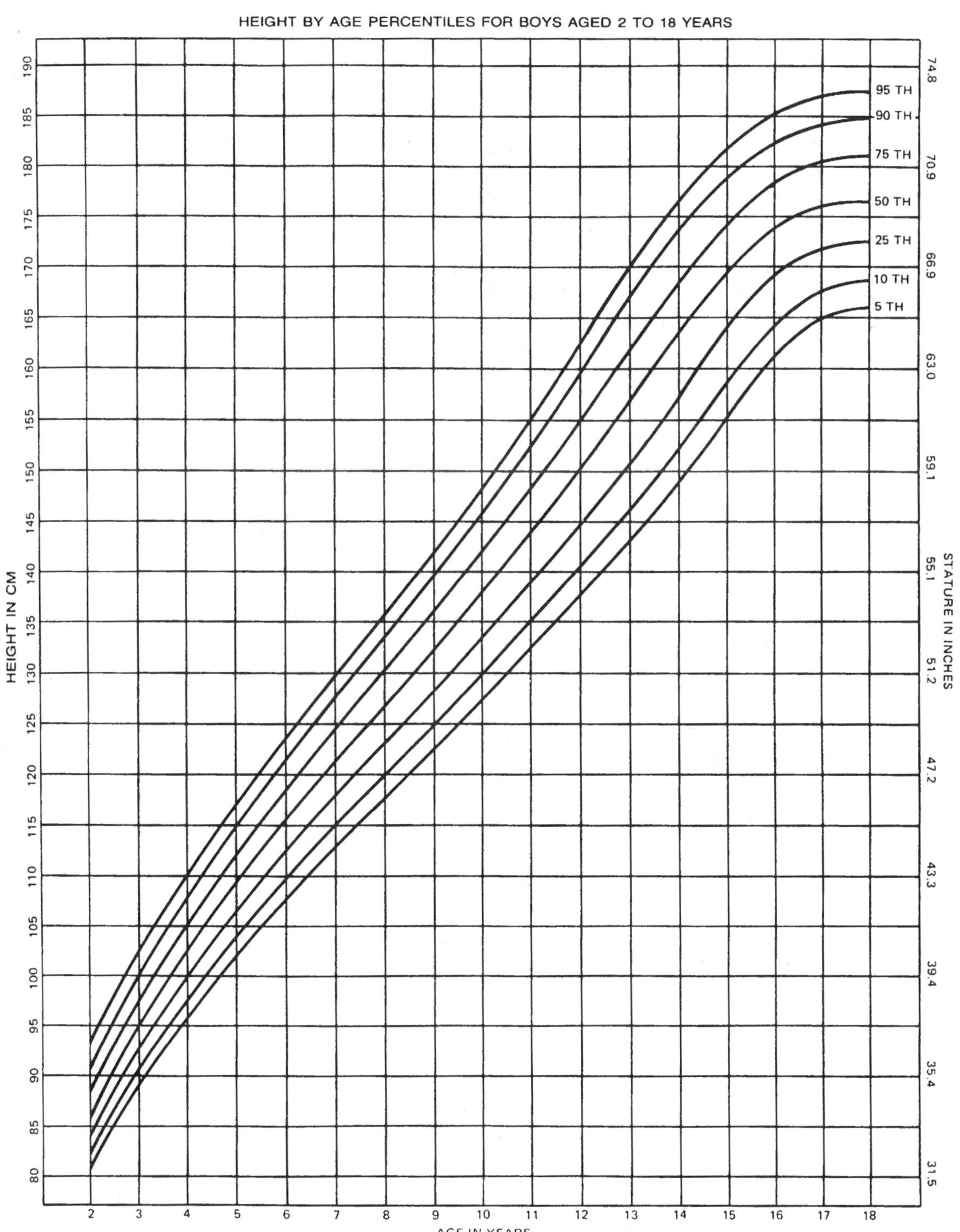
HEIGHT BY AGE PERCENTILES FOR BOYS AGED 2 TO 18 YEARS
HEIGHT IN CM
190
185
180
175
170
165
160
155
150
145
140
135
130
125
120
115
110
105
100
95
90
85
80
95 TH
90 TH
75 TH
50 TH
25 TH
10 TH
5 TH
STATURE IN INCHES
74.8
70.9
66.9
63.0
59.1
55.1
51.2
47.2
43.3
39.4
35.4
31.5
2
3
4
5
6
7
8
9
10
11
12
13
14
15
16
17
18
AGE IN YEARS

APPENDIX C
SOURCES OF FREE AND INEXPENSIVE MATERIALS RELATED TO HEALTH, SAFETY, AND NUTRITION

Abbott Laboratories
14th and Sheridan Road
North Chicago, IL 60064
(pharmacy, nutrition, drugs)

Aetna Life and Casualty Companies
Information and Public Relations Department
151 Farmington Avenue
Hartford, CT 06156
(health and safety)

Alexander Graham Bell Association for the Deaf, Inc.
The Volta Bureau for the Deaf
3417 Volta Place, NW
Washington, DC 20007

Alliance to End Lead Poisoning
600 Penn Avenue, SE
Suite 100
Washington, DC 20003

American Academy of Pediatrics
141 Northwest Point Boulevard
P. O. Box 927
Elk Grove, IL 60009-0927

American Allergy Association
P. O. Box 7273
Menlo Park, CA 94026

American Alliance for Health, Physical Education, Recreation and Dance
1900 Association Drive
Reston, VA 22091-1502

American Automobile Association
1000 AAA Drive
Heathrow, FL 32746

American Cancer Society
1599 Clifton Road, NE
Atlanta, GA 30329

American Dairy Association
O'Hare International Center, 10255 W. Higgins Rd, Suite 900
Rosemont, IL 60018-5616

American Dairy Products Institute
130 North Franklin Street
Chicago, IL 60606

American Dental Association
Bureau of Dental Health Education
211 East Chicago Avenue
Chicago, IL 60611-2616
(dental health)

American Diabetes Association, Inc.
National Service Center
P. O. Box 25757
1660 Duke Street
Alexandria, VA 22314-3427

American Dietetic Association
216 W. Jackson Blvd.
Suite 800
Chicago, IL 60606

American Foundation for the Blind
11 Pennsylvania Plaza, Suite 300
New York, NY 10001

American Heart Association
7272 Greenville Avenue
Dallas, TX 75231-4596

American Hospital Association
1 N. Franklin, Suite 27
Chicago, IL 60606

American Institute of Baking
Consumer Service Dept.
1213 Bakers Way
Manhattan, KS 66502
(nutrition education)

American Insurance Association
1130 Connecticut Avenue, NW
Suite 1000
Washington, DC 20036

American Lung Association
1740 Broadway
New York, NY 10019-4315

American Medical Association
515 N. State Street
Chicago, IL 60610
(health, safety, and poison prevention education)

American National Red Cross
431 18th Street, NW
Washington, DC 20006

American Optometric Association
Department of Public Information
243 North Lindbergh Boulevard
St. Louis, MO 63141-7851
(eye health)

American Printing House for the Blind
1839 Frankfort Avenue
Louisville, KY 40206-3148

American Public Health Association
1015 Fifteenth Street, NW
Suite 300
Washington, DC 20005-2605

American School Health Association
7263 State, Rt. 43
Kent, OH 44240

American Social Health Association
P. O. Box 13827
Research Triangle Park, NC 27709

American Speech, Language and Hearing Association
10801 Rockville Pike
Rockville, MD 20852-3226

The Arthritis Foundation
1314 Spring Street, NW
Atlanta, GA 30309

Association for the Care of Children's Health
7910 Woodmont Avenue, Suite 300
Bethesda, MD 20814

Association for Children and Adults with Learning Disabilities
4156 Library Road
Pittsburgh, PA 15234

Association for Children with Retarded Mental Development
345 Hudson Street
New York, NY 10014

Association for Retarded Citizens
500 E. Border Street, Suite 502
Arlington, TX 76010

Association of American Railroads
American Railroad Building
50 F Street, NW
Washington, DC 20001-1530

Asthma and Allergy Foundation of America
1125 15th St. NW, Suite 502
Washington, DC 20005

Better Vision Institute, Inc.
1800 N. Kent Street
Suite 1210
Rosslyn, VA 22209

Children's Defense Fund
25 E. Street, NW
Washington, DC 20001

Clearinghouse on Child Abuse and Neglect Information
P. O. Box 1182
Washington, DC 20013

Committee for Children
172 20th Avenue
Seattle, WA 98122
(sexual abuse)

Consumer Information Center
Pueblo, CO 81009
(an index of selected federal publications)

Consumer and Professional Relations
Division of HIAA
1025 Connecticut Avenue, NW
Washington, DC 20036
(health education)

Council for Exceptional Children
1920 Association Drive
Reston, VA 22091

Cystic Fibrosis Foundation
6931 Arlington Road, Suite #200
Bethesda, MD 20814-5231

Department of Community Health
1075 Ste-Foy Road, 7th Floor
Quebec, Quebec G1S 2M1, Canada

Department of Health and Human
Services
Public Health Services
Food and Drug Administration
Rockville, MD 20857

Eli Lily and Company
Public Relations Department
Box 618
Indianapolis, IN 46285

Environmental Protection Agency
401 M Street, SW
Washington, DC 20460

Epilepsy Foundation of America
4351 Garden City Drive
Landover, MD 20785

Feingold Association of the United States
P. O. Box 6550
Alexandria, VA 22306

Florida Department of Citrus Fruit
P. O. Box 148
Lakeland, FL 33802

Ford Motor Company
Research and Information Department
The American Road
Dearborn, MI 48127
(traffic safety, seat belts)

General Mills
Public Relations Department
Educational Services
P. O. Box 5588
Stacy, MN 55079
(nutrition)

Health Education Associates, Inc.
211 South Easton Road
Glenside, PA 19038-4497

Health Education Foundation
2600 Virginia Avenue, NW
Suite 502
Washington, DC 20037

Home Economics Directorate
880 Portage Avenue, 2nd Floor
Winnipeg, Manitoba R3G OP1,
Canada

Huntington's Disease Society of
America
140 W. 22nd Street, 6th Floor
New York, NY 10011-2420

International Life Sciences Institute
1126 16th Street, NW #300
Washington, DC 20036
(nutrition education)

Johnson and Johnson Health Care
Division
New Brunswick, NJ 08903
(first aid, dental health)

Joseph P. Kennedy Jr. Foundation
1350 New York Avenue, NW
Suite 500
Washington, DC 20005
(mental retardation)

Kellogg Company
Department of Consumer Education
Battle Creek, MI 49016

Lefthanders International
P. O. Box 8249
Topeka, KS 66608
(information and supplies)

Lever Brothers Company
390 Park Avenue
New York, NY 10022
(dental health)

March of Dimes Birth Defects Foundation
1275 Mamaroneck Avenue
White Plains, NY 10605

Mental Retardation Association of America
211 E. 300 South Street
Suite 212
Salt Lake City, UT 84111

Metropolitan Life Insurance Company
Health and Safety Division
1 Madison Avenue
New York, NY 10010
(health, safety, first aid)

Muscular Dystrophy Association
3300 E. Sunrise Drive
Tucson, AZ 85718

National Academy of Sciences
National Research Council, Office of Public Information
2101 Constitution Avenue, NW
Washington, DC 20418
(nutrition education)

National Association for Down's Syndrome
P. O. Box 4542
Oak Brook, IL 60522-4542

National Association for the Education of Young Children
1509 16th Street NW
Washington, DC 20036

National Association for Hearing and Speech
10801 Rockville Pike
Rockville, MD 20852

National Association for the Visually Handicapped
22 W. 21st
New York, NY 10010

National Center for Nutrition and Dietetics
216 West Jackson Boulevard
Suite 800
Chicago, IL 60606-6995

National Center for the Prevention of Sudden Infant Death Syndrome
10500 Little Patuxent Parkway, #420
Columbia, MD 21044

National Commission on Safety Education
National Education Association
1201 16th Street, NW
Washington, DC 20036
(safety education)

National Council on Family Relations
3989 Central Avenue NE
Suite 550
Minneapolis, MN 55421

National Dairy Council
Nutrition Education Division
6300 North River Road
Rosemont Road, IL 60019-9922

National Easter Seal Society
230 W. Monroe
Chicago, IL 60606

National Easter Seal Foundation
2023 West Ogden Avenue
Chicago, IL 60612

National Fire Protection Association
1 Batterymarch Park
P. O. Box 9101
Quincy, MA 02269-9101

National Foundation for Asthma
P. O. Box 30069
Tucson, AZ 85751

National Health Council
1730 M Street, NW, Suite 500
Washington, DC 20036
(health education)

National Health Information Center
Office of Disease Prevention and Health Promotion
P. O. Box 1133
Washington, DC 29913-1133

National Hemophilia Foundation
110 Green Street, Room 406
New York, NY 10012

National Homecaring Council
519 C Street, NE
Washington, DC 20002

National Information Center for Handicapped Children and Youth
P. O. Box 1492
Washington, DC 20013

National Institute of Allergy and Infectious Diseases
Office of Communications
Building 31, Room 7A-32
9000 Rockville Pike
Bethesda, MD 20892

National Institute of Health
U. S. Public Health Service
Bethesda, MD 20014

1. Allergy and Infectious Diseases
2. Arthritis and Metabolic Diseases
3. Cancer
4. Child Health and Human Development
5. Dental Research
6. General Medical Services
7. Heart
8. Neurological Diseases and Blindness
9. Microbiological data

National Kidney Foundation
30 E. 33rd Street
New York, NY 10016

National Livestock and Meat Board
Nutritional Department
444 N. Michigan Avenue
Chicago, IL 60611

National Lung Association
1740 Broadway
New York, NY 10019
(respiratory diseases)

National Maternal and Child Health Clearinghouse
38th and R Streets, NW
Washington, DC 20057

National Multiple Sclerosis
733 3rd. Avenue
New York, NY 10017

National Pediculosis Association
P. O. Box 149
Newton, MA 02161
(head lice)

National Reye's Syndrome Foundation
426 N. Lewis, P. O. Box 829
Bryan, OH 43506

National Safety Council
1121 Spring Lake Drive
Itasca, IL 60143-3201
(safety materials, films, posters)

National SIDS Clearinghouse
8201 Greensboro Drive
Suite 600
Alexandria, VA 82102

National Society for the Prevention of Blindness
500 E. Remington Road
Schaumberg, IL 60173

National Spinal Cord Injury Association
545 Concord Avenue, No 29
Cambridge, MA 02138-1122

National Wildlife Federation
Educational Services Section
1400 16th Street, NW
Washington, DC 20036-2266

Nutrition Information Service
234 Webb Building
Birmingham, AL 35294

Nutrition Programs
446 Jeanne Mance Building
Tunney's Pasture
Ottawa, Ontario K1A 1B4, Canada

Nutrition Services
P. O. Box 488
Halifax, Nova Scotia B3J 3R8, Canada

Nutrition Services
P. O. Box 6000
Fredericton, New Brunswick E3B 5H1, Canada

Office of Child Development
U. S. Department of Health and Human Services
P. O. Box 1182
Washington, DC 20013

Office of Civil Defense/Emergency Preparedness
Public Information
The Pentagon
Washington, DC 20310

Parents Anonymous
675 W. Foothill Blvd., Suite 220
Claremont, CA 91711-3416

Poison Prevention Week Council
P. O. Box 1543
Washington, DC 20013

Public Health Resource Service
15 Overlea Boulevard, 5th Floor
Toronto, Ontario M4H 1A9, Canada

Public Health Services
Public Inquiries Branch
U. S. Department of Health and Human Services
Washington, DC 20201
(health and poison prevention)

Ross Laboratories
Director of Professional Services
625 Cleveland Avenue
Columbus, OH 43216

Sex Information and Education Council of the United States
444 Lincoln Boulevard
Suite 107
Venice, CA 90291

State Farm Insurance Companies
Public Relations Department
One State Farm Plaza
Bloomington, IL 61701
(first aid, safety)

Sudden Infant Death Syndrome Clearinghouse
8201 Greensboro Drive, Suite 600
McLean, VA 22101

United Cerebral Palsy Association
7 Penn Plaza, Suite 804
New York, NY 10001

United States Department of Agriculture
Agriculture Research Associations
Bureau of Human Nutrition and Home Economics
Washington, DC 20402
(nutrition)

U. S. Government Printing Office
Superintendent of Documents
Washington, DC 20402

U. S. Office of Education
Department of Health and Human Services
P. O. Box 1182
Washington, DC 20013

Veterans of Safety
c/o Robert L. Baldwin Safety Center
Humphrey's Building
Central Missouri State University
Warrensburg, MO 64093
(accident prevention, traffic safety)

World Health Organization
Office of Public Information
525 23rd Street, NW
Washington, DC 20037
(international health)

APPENDIX D
FEDERAL FOOD PROGRAMS

Federal food programs are funded and regulated by the U. S. Department of Agriculture and administered at the state level by the Department of Education or the Public Health Department. Information about food programs available in a given locality may be obtained from City or County Health Departments, State Public Health Departments, or the State Department of Education.

CHILD NUTRITION PROGRAMS

Child nutrition programs provide cash and/or food assistance for children in public schools, nonprofit private schools, child care centers, home day care centers, and summer day camps.

National School Lunch Program (NSLP)

The National School Lunch Program is the oldest and largest federal child feeding program in existence, both in terms of number of children reached and dollars spent. The National School Lunch Program is administered at the national level by the United States Department of Agriculture and at the state level by the Department of Education. The U. S. Department of Agriculture reimburses the states for nutritionally adequate lunches served according to federal regulations. The amount of money received per meal depends upon whether the student must receive free meals or is able to pay either full or reduced price. The families of those students receiving free or *reduced price meals* must submit statements of income and meet family size and income guidelines to be eligible. These guidelines are adjusted periodically according to national *poverty guidelines*. Statements of family income must be submitted to the local school district at the beginning of each school year.

Meals funded by NSLP include five food components: meat or meat alternatives, such as peanut butter, eggs or beans, two or more servings of fruits and/or vegetables, bread and milk. The meals must provide at least one-third of the Recommended Daily Dietary Allowances for the age group served.

School Breakfast Program (SBP)

The School Breakfast Program was authorized by the Child Nutrition Act of 1966. This program also makes provision for free or reduced price meals along with full price meals. The same income eligible guidelines are used for the School Breakfast Program as for the School Lunch Program. The School Breakfast Program is available to schools and public or licensed nonprofit residential child care facilities.

Child and Adult Care Food Program (CACFP)

The Child Care Food Program that provides money for food and commodities for meals served to children in licensed child care centers and group child care homes (*Federal Register*, August 20, 1982) now includes funding for adults in adult care programs. The program includes children 12 years old and under, disabled persons in an institution serving a majority of persons 18 years old and under, migrant children 15 years old and younger, and adults with disabilities. Infant meal patterns are different, and include infant formula, milk, and other foods. The CACFP program is administered by the U. S. Department of Agriculture's Food and Nutrition Service (FNS). In most states it is administered by the Department of Education.

Reimbursement is for two meals and one snack or one meal and two snacks. Reimbursements are determined by income eligibility. The meal pattern is the same as that required in the National School Lunch Program, adjusted by age in categories of infants 1–3 years, 3–6 years, 6–12 years of age and adults.

FAMILY NUTRITION PROGRAMS

Two governmental programs that help to provide the family with adequate food are the Special Supplemental Program for Women, Infants and Children, better known as WIC, and the Food Stamp Program.

Special Supplemental Program for Women, Infants and Children (WIC)

The WIC program may be operated by either public or nonprofit health agencies. It provides nutrition counseling and supplemental foods rich in protein, iron, and vitamin C to pregnant or lactating women, infants, and children up to 5 years of age who are determined to be at risk by professional health assessment. Participants receive specified amounts of the following foods:

- iron-fortified infant formula
- iron-fortified cereal
- fruit/vegetable juices high in vitamin C
- fortified milk
- cheese
- eggs
- peanut butter
- dried beans and legumes

The Food Stamp Program

The Food Stamp Program may be administered by either state or local welfare agencies. It is the major form of food assistance in the United States. Its purpose is to increase the food purchasing power of low income persons. Those who meet eligibility standards may buy stamps that are worth more than the purchase price. The very poor receive stamps free. Stamps may be used to buy *allowed foods* or seeds from which to grow foods. Items not allowed include soap, cigarettes, paper goods, alcoholic beverages, pet foods, or deli foods that may be eaten on the premises.

Glossary*

abdomen – the portion of the body located between the diaphragm (located at the base of the lungs) and the pelvic or hip bones.

absorption – the process by which the products of digestion are transferred from the intestinal tract into the blood or lymph or by which substances are taken up by the cells.

abuse – to mistreat, attack, or cause harm to another individual.

accident – an unexpected or unplanned event that may result in physical harm or injury.

accreditation – the process of certifying an individual or program as having met certain specified requirements.

acuity – sharpness or clearness, as in vision.

acute – the stage of an illness or disease during which an individual is definitely sick and exhibits symptoms characteristic of the particular illness or disease involved.

adenosine triphosphate (ATP) – a compound with energy-storing phosphate bonds that is the main energy source for all cells.

AIDS – acquired immunodeficiency syndrome or acquired immune deficiency syndrome. A disease caused by the human immunodeficiency virus (HIV).

airborne transmission – when germs are expelled into the air through coughs/sneezes, and transmitted to another individual via tiny moisture drops.

alignment – the process of assuming correct posture or of placing various body parts in proper line with each other.

alkali – a group of bases or caustic substances that are capable of neutralizing acids to form salts.

allowed foods – foods that are eligible for reimbursement under School Lunch or Child Care Food Program Guidelines.

amblyopia – a condition of the eye commonly referred to as "lazy eye"; vision gradually becomes blurred or distorted due to unequal balance of the eye muscles. The eyes do not present any physical clues when a child has amblyopia.

amino acids – the organic building blocks from which proteins are made.

anecdotal – a brief note or description that contains useful and important information.

anemia – a disorder of the blood commonly caused by a lack of iron in the diet, resulting in the formation of fewer red blood cells and lessened ability of the cells to carry oxygen. Symptoms include fatigue, shortness of breath, and pallor.

anthropometric – pertains to measurement of the body or its parts.

antibodies – special substances produced by the body that help protect against disease.

apnea – absence of breathing for a period of time.

appraisal – the process of judging or evaluating; to determine the quality of one's state of health.

aseptic procedure – treatment to produce a product that is free of disease-producing bacteria.

*Definitions are based on usage within the text.

aspiration – accidental inhalation of food, fluid or an object into the respiratory tract.

assessment – appraisal or evaluation.

asymptomatic – having no symptoms.

attitude – a belief or feeling one has toward certain facts or situations.

atypical – unusual; different from what might commonly be expected.

autonomy – a state of personal or self-identity.

bacteria – one-celled microorganisms; some are beneficial for the body but pathogenic bacteria cause diseases.

basal metabolic rate – minimum amount of energy needed to carry on the body processes vital to life.

biochemical – pertains to chemical evaluation of body substances such as blood, urine, etc.

bonding – the process of establishing a positive and strong emotional relationship between an infant and its parent; sometimes referred to as attachment.

bottle-mouth syndrome – a pattern of tooth decay, predominantly of the upper teeth, that develops as the result of permitting a child to go to sleep with a bottle containing juice, milk, or any other caloric liquid that may pool in the mouth.

calories – units used to measure the energy value of foods.

calcium – mineral nutrient; a major component of bones and teeth.

catalyst – a substance that speeds up the rate of a chemical reaction but is not itself used up in the reaction.

catalyze – to accelerate a chemical reaction.

characteristics – qualities or traits that distinguish one person from another.

cholesterol – a fat-like substance found in animal-source foods, that is synthesized by humans and performs a variety of functions within the body.

chronic – frequent or repeated incidences of illness; can also be a lengthy or permanent status, as in chronic disease or dysfunction.

clinical – pertains to evaluation of health by means of observation.

coenzymes – a vitamin-containing substance required by certain enzymes before they can perform their prescribed function.

cognitive – the aspect of learning that refers to the development of skills and abilities based on knowledge and thought processes.

collagen – a protein that forms the major constituent of connective tissue, cartilage, bone, and skin.

communicable – a condition that can be spread or transmitted from one individual to another.

complementary proteins – proteins with offsetting missing amino acids; complementary proteins can be combined to provide complete protein.

complete proteins – proteins that contain all essential amino acids in amounts relative to the amounts needed to support growth.

compliance – the act of obeying or cooperating with specific requests or requirements.

concept – a combination of basic and related factual information that represents a more generalized statement or idea.

conductive hearing loss – affects the volume of word tones heard, so that loud sounds are more likely to be heard than soft sounds.

contagious – capable of being transmitted or passed from one person to another.

contrasting sensory qualities – differing qualities pertaining to taste, color, texture, temperature, and shape.

convalescent – the stage of recovery from an illness or disease.

cost control – reduction of expenses through portion control inventory and reduction of waste.

criteria – predetermined standards used to evaluate the worth or effectiveness of a learning experience.

cycle menus – menus that are written to repeat after a set interval, such as every 3-4 weeks.

Daily Value (DV) – a term the FDA has proposed to replace the USDA RDA values in the new nutrition food labels.

deciduous teeth – a child's initial set of teeth; this set is temporary and gradually begins to fall out around five years of age.

dehydration – a state in which there is an excessive loss of body fluids or extremely limited fluid intake. Symptoms may include loss of skin tone, sunken eyes, and mental confusion.

dermatitis – inflammation or irritation of the skin, such as in rashes and eczema.

development – commonly refers to the process of intellectual growth and change.

developmental norms – the mean or average age at which children demonstrate certain behaviors and abilities.

diagnosis – the process of identifying a disease, illness, or injury from its symptoms.

dietary nucleotides – amino acid combinations found to increase an infant's ability to produce antibodies in response to exposure to disease.

digestion – the process by which complex nutrients in foods are changed into smaller units that can be absorbed or used by the body.

digestive tract – pertains to, and includes, the mouth, throat, stomach, and intestines.

direct contact – the passage of infectious organisms from an infected individual directly to a susceptible host through methods such as coughing, sneezing, or touching.

discipline – training or enforced obedience that corrects, shapes, or develops acceptable patterns of behavior.

disorientation – lack of awareness or ability to recognize familiar persons or objects.

distention – stretched or enlarged.

DNA – deoxyribonucleic acid; the substance in the cell nucleus that codes for genetically transmitted traits.

elevate – to raise to a higher position.

endocrine – refers to glands within the body that produce and secrete substances called hormones directly into the blood stream.

energy – power to perform work.

enriched – adding nutrients to grain products to replace those lost during refinement; thiamin, niacin, riboflavin, and iron are nutrients most commonly added.

environment – the sum total of physical, cultural, and behavioral features that surround and affect an individual.

enzymes – proteins that catalyze body functions.

epithelial tissue – specialized cells that form the skin and mucus linings of all body cavities, such as the lungs, nose, and throat.

essential nutrient – nutrient that must be provided in food because it cannot by synthesized by the body at a rate sufficient to meet the body's needs.

ethnic – pertaining to races or groups of people who share common traits or customs.

evaluation – a measurement of effectiveness for determining whether or not educational objectives have been achieved.

expectations – behaviors or actions that are anticipated.

failure to thrive – a term used to describe an infant whose growth and mental development is severely slowed due to lack of mothering or mental stimulation.

family nutrition programs – nutrition programs that focus on the family unit. Examples are Food Stamps, WIC, and the Food Distribution Program.

fecal-oral transmission – when germs are transferred to the mouth via hands contaminated with fecal material.

fever – an elevation of body temperature above normal; a temperature over 99.4°F or 37.4°C orally is usually considered a fever.

food-borne illnesses – food infections due to ingestion of food contaminated with bacteria, viruses, some molds, or parasites.

food infection – illness resulting from ingestion of live bacteria in food.

food intoxication – illness resulting from ingestion of food containing residual bacterial toxins in the absence of viable bacteria.

food pyramid – a guide to daily food choices developed by the USDA.

fortified food – food with vitamins and/or minerals added that were not found in the food originally, or that are added in amounts greater than occur naturally in the food.

fruit drink – a product that contains 10 percent fruit juice, added water, and sugar.

full-strength juice – undiluted fruit or vegetable juice.

giardiasis – a parasitic infection of the intestinal tract that causes diarrhea, loss of appetite, abdominal bloating and gas, weight loss, and fatigue.

gram – a metric unit of weight; approximately 1/28 of an ounce.

growth – increase in size of any body part or of the entire body.

habit – the unconscious repetition of a particular behavior.

hands-on – active involvement in a project; actually doing something.

harvesting – picking or gathering fruit or grains.

head circumference – the distance around the head obtained by measuring over the forehead and bony protuberance on the back of the head; it is an indication of normal or abnormal growth and development of the brain and central nervous system.

health – a state of wellness. Complete physical, mental, social, and emotional well-being; the quality of one element affects the state of the others.

health promotion – engaging in behaviors, including concern for certain social issues affecting the diet and environment, that help to maintain and enhance one's health status.

hemoglobin – the iron-containing, oxygen-carrying pigment in red blood cells.

hepatitis – an inflammation of the liver.

heredity – the transmission of certain genetic material and characteristics from parent to child at the time of conception.

high-density lipoproteins (HDL) – a protein-fat combination with a high protein in fat ratio, which is formed in the blood to aid in fat transport; a high HDL blood value may decrease risk of cardiovascular disease.

high-fructose corn syrup – a frequently used sweetener produced by exposing corn starch to acid and enzyme action to increase the fructose content; it is much sweeter than sucrose.

HIV – human immunodeficiency virus; the virus that causes AIDS.

hormones – special chemical substances produced by endocrine glands that influence and regulate certain body functions.

hyperactivity – a condition characterized by attention and behavior disturbances, including restlessness, impulsive and disruptive behaviors. True cases of hyperactivity respond to the administration of stimulant-type medication.

hyperglycemia – a condition characterized by an abnormally high level of sugar in the blood.

hyperopia – farsightedness; a condition of the eyes in which an individual can see objects clearly in the distance but has poor close vision.

hypertension – elevation of blood pressure above the normally accepted values.

hyperventilation – rapid breathing often with forced inhalation; can lead to sensations of dizziness, lightheadedness, and weakness.

immunized – a state of becoming resistant to a specific disease through the introduction of living or dead microorganisms into the body, which then stimulates the production of antibodies.

impairment – a condition or malfunction of a body part that interferes with optimal functioning.

incidental learning – learning that occurs in addition to the primary intent or goals of instruction.

incomplete proteins – proteins that lack required amounts of one or more essential amino acids.

incubation – the interval of time between exposure to infection and the appearance of the first signs or symptoms of illness.

indirect contact – transfer of infectious organisms from an infected individual to a susceptible host via an intermediate source such as contaminated water, milk, toys, utensils, or soiled towels.

infection – a condition that results when a pathogen invades and establishes itself within a susceptible host.

ingested – the process of taking food or other substances into the body through the mouth.

innocent – not guilty; lacking knowledge.

inservice – educational training provided by an employer.

intentional – a plan of action that is carried out in a purposeful manner.

intervention – practices or procedures that are implemented to modify or change a specific behavior or condition.

intestinal – pertaining to the intestinal tract or bowel.

iron-deficiency anemia – a failure in the oxygen transport system caused by too little iron.

irradiation – food preservation by short-term exposure of the food to gamma ray radiation.

judicious – wise; directed by sound judgment.

lactating – producing and secreting milk.

language – form of communication that allows individuals to share feelings, ideas, and experiences with one another.

latch-key – a term that refers to school-age children who care for themselves without adult supervision before and after school hours.

lethargy – a state of inaction or indifference.

liability – legal responsibility or obligation for one's actions owed to another individual.

licensing – the act of granting formal permission to conduct a business or profession.

linoleic acid – a polyunsaturated fatty acid, which is essential (must be provided in food) for humans.

linolenic acid – one of the two polyunsaturated fatty acids that are recognized as essential for humans.

lipoprotein – protein linked with fat to aid in the transport of various types of fat in the blood.

listlessness – a state characterized by a lack of energy and/or interest in one's affairs.

low-birthweight infant (LBW) – an infant who weighs less than 5.5 pounds (2500 grams) at birth.

low-density lipoproteins (LDL) – a lipoprotein with a low protein to fat ratio that contains a high level of cholesterol; high blood levels of LDL may signal increased risk for heart disease.

Lyme disease – bacterial illness caused by the bite of infected deer ticks found in grassy or wooded areas.

lymph glands – specialized groupings of tissue that produce and store white blood cells for protection against infection and illness.

macrocytic anemia – a failure in the oxygen transport system characterized by abnormally large immature red blood cells.

malnutrition – prolonged inadequate or excessive intake of nutrients and/or calories required by the body.

mandatory – something that is required; no choices or alternatives available.

megadose – an amount of a vitamin or mineral at least ten times that of RDA.

meningitis – a disease, often caused by bacteria, that leads to inflammation of the brain and spinal cord.

metabolism – all chemical changes that occur from the time nutrients are absorbed until they are built into body tissue or are excreted.

microcytic anemia – a failure in the oxygen transport system characterized by abnormally small red blood cells.

microgram – a metric unit of measurement; one-millionth of a gram.

milligram – a metric unit of measurement; one-thousandth of a gram.

minerals – inorganic chemical elements that are required in the diet to support growth and repair tissue and to regulate body functions.

misarticulation – improper pronunciation of words and word sounds.

mold – a fuzzy growth produced by fungi.

monounsaturated fatty acid (MUFA) – a fatty acid that has only one bond in its structure, and that is not fully saturated with hydrogen.

mottling – marked with spots of dense white or brown coloring.

myopia – nearsightedness; an individual has good near vision, but poor distant vision.

neglect – failure of a parent or legal guardian to properly care for and meet the basic needs of a child under eighteen years of age.

negligence – failure to practice or perform one's duties according to certain standards; carelessness.

neophobic – fear of things that are new and unfamiliar.

neural tube deficit – a birth defect involving damage to the brain and spinal cord.

neurological – pertaining to the nervous system, which consists of the nerves, brain, and spinal column.

neuromuscular – pertaining to control of muscular function by the nervous system.

normal – average; a characteristic or quality that is common to most individuals in a defined group.

norms – an expression (e.g., weeks, months, years) of when a child is likely to demonstrate certain developmental skills.

notarized – official acknowledgment of the authenticity of a signature or document by a notary public.

nutrient – the components or substances that are found in food.

nutrient strengths – nutrients that occur in relatively large amounts in a food or food group.

nutrient weaknesses – nutrients that are absent or occur in very small amounts in a food or food group.

nutrition – the study of food and how it is used by the body.

nutrition claims – statements of reduced calories, fat, or salt on the food labels.

nutrition education – activities that impart information about food and its use in the body.

obese – a term used to describe an individual who has an excessive accumulation of fat.

obesity – excessive body fat, usually 15-20 percent above the individual's ideal weight based on height, age and gender.

objective – a clear and meaningful description of what an individual is expected to learn as a result of learning activities and experiences.

observations – to inspect and take note of the appearance and behavior of other individuals.

odd-day cycle menus – menus planned for a period of days other than a week that repeat after the planned period; cycles of any number of days may be used. These menus are a means of avoiding repetition of the same foods on the same day of the week.

overnutrition – the result of eating too much food, especially excess calories and excess fat. Overnutrition may or may not be accompanied by deficiencies of essential nutrients.

overweight – weight that exceeds (by 20 percent or less) the recommendations for "desirable" body weight.

pallor – paleness.

parallel play – a common form of play among young children in which two or more children, sitting side by side, are engaged in an activity but do not interact or work together to accomplish a task.

paralysis – temporary or permanent loss of sensation, function, or voluntary movement of a body part.

pasteurization – a process that destroys disease-producing bacteria by heating a food to a prescribed temperature for a specific time period.

pathogen – a microorganism capable of producing illness or infection.

peers – one of the same rank; equals.

Percent Daily Value – a measure of the nutritional value of food; used in nutrition labeling.

personal sanitation – personal habits, such as handwashing, care of illness, cleanliness of clothing.

poverty guidelines – family-size and income standards for determining eligibility for free or reduced-price meals under the National School Lunch Program.

precipitating – factors that trigger or initiate a reaction or response.

prenatal – the period from conception to birth of the baby.

preplanning – outlining a method of action prior to carrying it out.

prevention – measures taken to avoid an event such as an accident or illness from occurring; implies the ability to anticipate circumstances and behaviors.

preventive – the act of taking certain steps and measures so as to avoid or delay unfavorable outcomes, as in preventive health care.

primary goal – the aim that assumes first importance.

prodromal – the appearance of the first nonspecific signs of infection; this stage ends when the symptoms characteristic of a particular communicable illness begin to appear.

protein – class of nutrients used primarily for structural and regulatory functions.

PUFA – polyunsaturated fatty acids; fatty acids that contain more than one bond that is not fully saturated with hydrogen.

punishment – a negative response to what the observer considers to be wrong or inappropriate behavior; may involve physical or harsh treatment.

radura symbol – a required symbol placed on all food that has been treated with irradiation.

RDA – Recommended Daily Dietary Allowances; suggested amounts of nutrients for use in planning diets. RDAs are designed to maintain good nutrition in healthy persons. Allowances are higher than requirements in order to afford a margin of safety.

receptive hearing loss – affects the range of tones heard, so that high tones are more likely to be heard than low tones.

reduced-price meals – a meal served under the Child Care Food Program to a child from a family which meets income standards for reduced-price school meals.

referral – directing an individual to another source, usually for additional evaluation or treatment.

regulation – a standard or requirement that is set to ensure uniform and safe practice.

regurgitation – the return of partially digested food from stomach to mouth.

reimplant – to replace a part from where it was removed, such as a tooth.

reprimand – to scold or discipline for unacceptable behavior.

resistance – the ability to avoid infection or illness.

respiratory diseases – disease of the respiratory tract, such as colds, sore throats, flu.

respiratory tract – pertains to, and includes, the nose, throat, trachea, and lungs.

resuscitation – to revive from unconsciousness or death; to restore breathing and heartbeat.

retention – the ability to remember or recall previously learned material.

Reye's syndrome – an acute illness of young children that severely affects the central nervous system; symptoms include vomiting, coma, and seizures.

RNA – ribonucleic acid; the nucleic acid that serves as messenger between the nucleus and the ribosomes where proteins are synthesized.

Salmonella – a bacteria that can cause serious food-borne illness.

salmonellosis – a bacterial infection that is spread through contaminated drinking water, food or milk or contact with other infected persons. Symptoms include diarrhea, fever, nausea, and vomiting.

sanitizing solution – a solution of diluted chlorine bleach (1/4 cup chlorine to 1 gallon of water), used to sanitize utensils and work surfaces.

saturated fatty acid (SFA) – a fatty acid that has all carbon bonds satisfied by hydrogen.

scald – to rinse with boiling water.

sedentary – unusually slow or sluggish; a life-style that implies a general lack of physical activity.

seizures – a temporary interruption of consciousness sometimes accompanied by convulsive movements.

sensorimotor – Piaget's first stage of cognitive development, during which children learn and relate to their world primarily through motor and sensory activities.

sensorineural hearing loss – a type of loss that occurs when sound impulses cannot reach the brain due to damage of the auditory nerve, or cannot be interpreted because of prior brain damage.

serrated – saw-toothed or notched.

skeletal – pertaining to the bony framework that supports the body.

skinfold – a measurement of the amount of fat under the skin; also referred to as fat-fold measurements.

speech – the process of using words to express one's thoughts and ideas.

spina bifida – a birth defect in which incomplete formation of the body vertebrae allows a portion of the spinal cord to be exposed to the outside. Varying degrees of paralysis and lack of function are common in the portion of the body below the defect.

standardized recipe – a recipe that has been tested to produce consistent results.

Staphylococcus – a bacteria that can cause serious food-borne illnesses.

sterile – free from living microorganisms.

strabismus – a condition of the eyes in which one or both eyes appear to be turned inward (crossed) or outward (walleye).

submerge – to place in water.

supervision – watching carefully over the behaviors and actions of children and others.

susceptible host – an individual who is capable of being infected by a pathogen.

symptom – changes in the body or its functions that are experienced by the affected individual.

syndrome – a grouping of symptoms and signs that commonly occur together and are characteristic of a specific disease or illness.

synthesis – the process of making a compound by the union of simpler compounds or elements.

taurine – a free amino acid needed by infants for normal growth and development of the central nervous system.

tax exempt – excused from taxation, often on the basis of nonprofit status.

temperature – a measurement of body heat; varies with the time of day, activity, and method of measurement.

thermic energy of foods – energy required to digest, absorb, transport, and metabolize nutrients in food.

toxicity – a state of being poisonous.

tuberculosis – an infectious disease caused by the tubercle bacillus, characterized by the production of lesions.

undernutrition – an inadequate intake of one or more required or essential nutrients.

universal infection control precautions – special measures taken when handling bodily fluids, including careful hand-washing, wearing latex gloves, disinfecting surfaces, and proper disposal of contaminated objects.

urinate – the act of emptying the bladder of urine.

values – the beliefs, traditions, and customs an individual incorporates and utilizes to guide behavior and judgments.

verbal assault – to attack another individual with words.

viruses – any of a group of submicroscopic infective agents, many of which cause a number of diseases in animals and plants.

vitamins – organic substances needed in very small amounts to regulate many metabolic functions in the body.

weekly menus – menus that are written to be served on a weekly basis.

whole grains – grain products that have not been refined; they contain all parts of the kernel of grain.

WIC (Women, Infants, and Children) – a federal program that provides food supplements for pregnant women, infants, and children to age five.

Index

Note: Page numbers in **bold type** reference non-text material.